studysync

Reading & Writing Companion

GRADE 6

UNITS 1–6

Contents

Testing Our Limits

What do we do when life gets hard?

You and Me

How do relationships shape us?

In the Dark

How do we know what to do when there are no instructions?

Personal Best

Which qualities of character matter most?

Making Your Mark

What's your story?

True to Yourself

Who are you meant to be?

Reading & Writing Companion iii

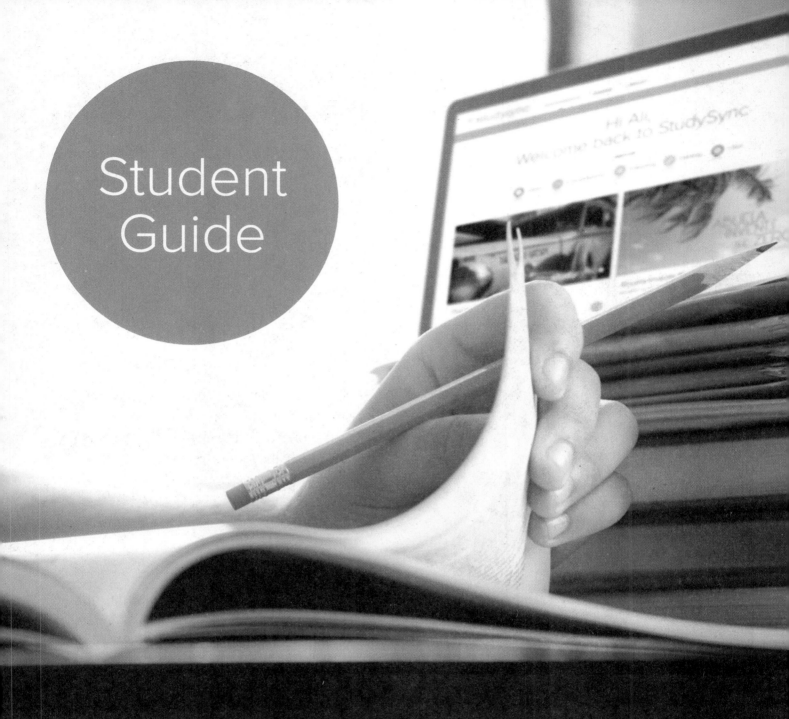

Student Guide

Getting Started

Welcome to the StudySync Reading & Writing Companion! In this book, you will find a collection of readings based on the theme of the unit you are studying. As you work through the readings, you will be asked to answer questions and perform a variety of tasks designed to help you closely analyze and understand each text selection. Read on for an explanation of each

In each unit, you will read texts that share a common theme, despite their different genres, time periods, and authors. Each reading encourages a closer look through questions and a short writing assignment.

Eleven

FICTION
Sandra Cisneros
1991

Introduction

studysync●

Sandra Cisneros (b. 1954) is a renowned Chicana writer whose poems, novels, and short stories explore the complicated struggle of finding one's own identity. Cisneros is best known for her novel *The House on Mango Street* and the collection *Woman Hollering Creek and Other Stories*. "Eleven" is from the latter, the story of a girl named Rachel who experiences growing pains on her eleventh birthday. When her teacher insists that an ugly red sweater belongs to Rachel, the eleven-year-old has exceptional thoughts but can't share them. Even so, it's evident that the protagonist of Sandra Cisneros's short story has insight beyond her years.

Eleven

"You open your eyes and everything's
just like yesterday, only it's today.
And you don't feel eleven at all."

What they don't understand about birthdays and what they never tell you is that when you're eleven, you're also ten, and nine, and eight, and seven, and six, and five, and four, and three, and two, and one. And when you wake up on your eleventh birthday you expect to feel eleven, but you don't. You open your eyes and everything's just like yesterday, only it's today. And you don't feel eleven at all. You feel like you're still ten. And you are—underneath the year that makes you eleven.

Like some days you might say something stupid, and that's the part of you that's still ten. Or maybe some days you might need to sit on your mama's lap because you're scared, and that's the part of you that's five. And maybe one day when you're all grown up maybe you will need to cry like if you're three, and that's okay. That's what I tell Mama when she's sad and needs to cry. Maybe she's feeling three.

Because the way you grow old is kind of like an onion or like the rings inside a tree trunk or like my little wooden dolls that fit one inside the other, each year inside the next one. That's how being eleven years old is.

You don't feel eleven. Not right away. It takes a few days, weeks even, sometimes even months before you say Eleven when they ask you. And you don't feel smart eleven, not until you're almost twelve. That's the way it is.

Only today I wish I didn't have only eleven years rattling inside me like pennies in a tin Band-Aid box. Today I wish I was one hundred and two instead of eleven because if I was one hundred and two I'd have known what to say when Mrs. Price put the red sweater on my desk. I would've known how to tell her it wasn't mine instead of just sitting there with that look on my face and nothing coming out of my mouth.

"Whose is this?" Mrs. Price says, and she holds the red sweater up in the air for all the class to see. "Whose? It's been sitting in the coatroom for a month."

Skill: Figurative Language

This narrator uses similes when she compares aging to everyday things. When I picture onions, tree trunks, and wooden dolls, I notice they all have layers. She must mean that when you get older, you keep getting more layers.

Introduction ①

An Introduction to each text provides historical context for your reading as well as information about the author. You will also learn about the genre of the text and the year in which it was written.

Notes ②

Many times, while working through the activities after each text, you will be asked to **annotate** or **make annotations** about what you are reading. This means that you should highlight or underline words in the text and use the "Notes" column to make comments or jot down any questions you have. You may also want to note any unfamiliar vocabulary words here.

You will also see sample student annotations to go along with the Skill lesson for that text.

First Read

During your first reading of each selection, you should just try to get a general idea of the content and message of the reading. Don't worry if there are parts you don't understand or words that are unfamiliar to you. You'll have an opportunity later to dive deeper into the text.

Think Questions

These questions will ask you to start thinking critically about the text, asking specific questions about its purpose, and making connections to your prior knowledge and reading experiences. To answer these questions, you should go back to the text and draw upon specific evidence to support your responses. You will also begin to explore some of the more challenging vocabulary words in the selection.

Skills

Each Skill includes two parts: Checklist and Your Turn. In the Checklist, you will learn the process for analyzing the text. The model student annotations in the text provide examples of how you might make your own notes following the instructions in the Checklist. In the Your Turn, you will use those same instructions to practice the skill.

First Read

Read "Eleven." After you read, complete the Think Questions below.

THINK QUESTIONS

1. How does Rachel feel about the red sweater that is placed on her desk? Respond with textual evidence from the story as well as ideas that you have inferred from clues in the text.

2. According to Rachel, why does Sylvia say the sweater belongs to Rachel? Support your answer with textual evidence.

3. Write two or three sentences exploring why Mrs. Price responds as she does when Phyllis claims the sweater. Support your answer with textual evidence.

4. Find the word **raggedy** in paragraph 9 of "Eleven." Use context clues in the surrounding sentences, as well as the sentence in which the word appears, to determine the word's meaning. Write your definition here and identify clues that helped you figure out its meaning.

5. Use context clues to determine the meaning of **nonsense** as it is used in paragraph 15 of "Eleven." Write your definition here and identify clues that helped you figure out its meaning. Then check the meaning in a dictionary.

Skill: Figurative Language

Use the Checklist to analyze Figurative Language in "Eleven." Refer to the sample student annotations about Figurative Language in the text.

CHECKLIST FOR FIGURATIVE LANGUAGE

To determine the meaning of figures of speech in a text, note the following:

- ✓ words that mean one thing literally and suggest something else
- ✓ similes, such as "strong as an ox"
- ✓ metaphors, such as "her eyes were stars"
- ✓ personification, such as "the daisies danced in the wind"

In order to interpret the meaning of a figure of speech in context, ask the following questions:

- ✓ Does any of the descriptive language in the text compare two seemingly unlike things?
- ✓ Do any descriptions include "like" or "as" that indicate a simile?
- ✓ Is there a direct comparison that suggests a metaphor?
- ✓ Is a human quality is being used to describe this animal, object, force of nature or idea that suggests personification?
- ✓ How does the use of this figure of speech change your understanding of the thing or person being described?

YOUR TURN

1. How does the figurative language in paragraph 18 help readers understand Rachel's reaction to the sweater?
   - A. The metaphors in the paragraph help readers understand how uncomfortable Rachel feels in the sweater.
   - B. The similes in the paragraph help readers understand how uncomfortable Rachel feels in the sweater.
   - C. The metaphors in the paragraph make it clear to readers that Rachel is overreacting about the sweater.
   - D. The similes in the paragraph make it clear to readers that Rachel is overreacting about the sweater.

2. How does the figurative language in paragraph 19 help readers visualize Rachel's behavior?
   - A. The mention of "little animal noises" tells readers that Rachel is acting more like an animal than a human.
   - B. The metaphor of "clown-sweater arms" shows that Rachel is able to see the humorous side in her experience.
   - C. The similes about her body shaking "like when you have the hiccups" and her head hurting "like when you drink milk too fast" connect to unpleasant experiences most readers have had.
   - D. The statement that "there aren't any more tears left in [her] eyes" suggests that Rachel is starting to calm down.

Close Read

Reread "Eleven." As you reread, complete the Skills Focus questions below. Then use your answers and annotations from the questions to help you complete the Write activity.

SKILLS FOCUS

1. Identify examples of figurative language and explain the purpose they achieve in the story.

2. Explain what you can infer about the narrator's feelings about the sweater based on her descriptions, actions, and reactions.

3. The narrator uses figurative language, including similes and metaphors, to describe aging. Identify these in the text. Explain what type of figurative language each one is an example of and what each piece of figurative language means.

4. Explain what the author implies about what the narrator really wants when she says, "today I wish I was one hundred and two."

5. Getting older can be tough. Identify and explain the textual evidence in the story that supports this statement.

WRITE

LITERARY ANALYSIS: How does the author's use of figurative language help readers understand the feelings that the narrator is expressing? Write a response of at least 200 words. Support your writing with evidence from the text.

Lost Island
FICTION

Introduction

Marina wakes up alone, thirsty, and hungry on a deserted island. How did she get here, and why is her head throbbing? As she slowly recalls a large wave smashing into Uncle Merlin's fishing boat, Marina takes her first steps towards survival.

VOCABULARY

damp
wet

capsized
tipped over in the water

intense
very strong

rescuer
someone who saves a person from harm or danger

Close Read & Skills Focus

After you have completed the First Read, you will be asked to go back and read the text more closely and critically. Before you begin your Close Read, you should read through the Skills Focus to get an idea of the concepts you will want to focus on during your second reading. You should work through the Skills Focus by making annotations, highlighting important concepts, and writing notes or questions in the "Notes" column. Depending on instructions from your teacher, you may need to respond online or use a separate piece of paper to start expanding on your thoughts and ideas.

Write

Your study of each selection will end with a writing assignment. For this assignment, you should use your notes, annotations, personal ideas, and answers to both the Think and Skills Focus questions. Be sure to read the prompt carefully and address each part of it in your writing.

English Language Learner

The English Language Learner texts focus on improving language proficiency. You will practice learning strategies and skills in individual and group activities to become better readers, writers, and speakers.

Extended Writing Project and Grammar

This is your opportunity to use genre characteristics and craft to compose meaningful, longer written works exploring the theme of each unit. You will draw information from your readings, research, and own life experiences to complete the assignment.

1 Writing Project

After you have read all of the unit text selections, you will move on to a writing project. Each project will guide you through the process of writing your essay. Student models will provide guidance and help you organize your thoughts. One unit ends with an **Extended Oral Project**, which will give you an opportunity to develop your oral language and communication skills.

2 Writing Process Steps

There are four steps in the writing process: Plan, Draft, Revise, and Edit and Publish. During each step, you will form and shape your writing project, and each lesson's peer review will give you the chance to receive feedback from your peers and teacher.

3 Writing Skills

Each Skill lesson focuses on a specific strategy or technique that you will use during your writing project. Each lesson presents a process for applying the skill to your own work and gives you the opportunity to practice it to improve your writing.

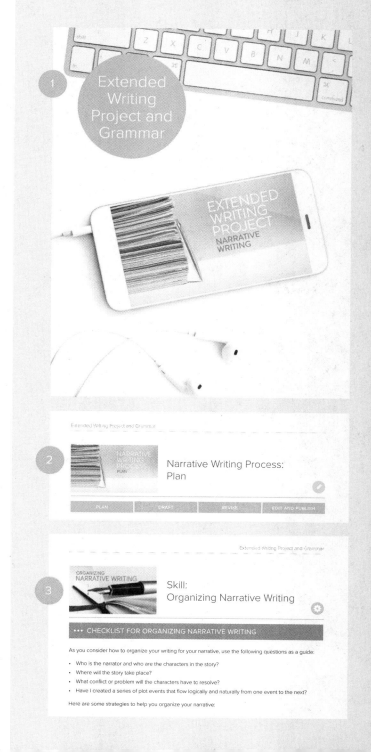

1 Extended Writing Project and Grammar

2 Narrative Writing Process: Plan

PLAN | DRAFT | REVISE | EDIT AND PUBLISH

3 Skill: Organizing Narrative Writing

••• CHECKLIST FOR ORGANIZING NARRATIVE WRITING

As you consider how to organize your writing for your narrative, use the following questions as a guide:

* Who is the narrator and who are the characters in the story?
* Where will the story take place?
* What conflict or problem will the characters have to resolve?
* Have I created a series of plot events that flow logically and naturally from one event to the next?

Here are some strategies to help you organize your narrative:

UNIT 1

Testing Our Limits

What do we do when life gets hard?

Genre Focus: FICTION

Texts

 Paired Readings

Extended Writing Project and Grammar

English Language Learner Resources

What do we do when life gets hard?

AVI

The name Avi (b. 1937) was given to American writer Edward Irving Wortis by his twin sister at an early age. Though he grew up in a highly literate and creative family of writers, artists, and musicians in Brooklyn, writing has never come easily to Avi, who suffers from dysgraphia. Now an author of over seventy-five books—everything from graphic novels to historical fiction and beyond—Avi enjoys showing error-addled drafts of his work to young writers as encouragement.

LEWIS CARROLL

Charles Lutwidge Dodgson, better known by his pen name Lewis Carroll (1832–1898), was a British writer of fiction for children. The author's best-known work, *Alice's Adventures in Wonderland* (1865), showcases his playful language and features "Jabberwocky," which is a nonsense poem about a make-believe creature called the Jabberwock. The poem has been so widely read and loved that some of the made-up words in the poem have entered the English dictionary—like the word "chortle."

SANDRA CISNEROS

A dual citizen of Mexico and the United States, Sandra Cisneros (b. 1954) is a writer of poetry, fiction, and essays. Her books have been translated into over twenty languages, and her novel *The House on Mango Street* is required reading in many schools. Cisneros is interested in how writing may serve as activism. In an *Electric Literature* interview, she argued that "the more you reach into the different things that make you who you are, the more you hold up a mirror to what makes you different from others."

CHRISTOPHER PAUL CURTIS

Christopher Paul Curtis (b. 1953) is an American writer of children's books, many of which are set in his hometown of Flint, Michigan. His award-winning book *Bud, Not Buddy* (1999) is based in part on the author's grandfather, who led the band Herman Curtis and the Dusky Devastators in the 1930s. For Curtis, placing characters against the historical backdrop of the Great Depression is an effective way to highlight the poverty and hunger that millions of people still face every day.

JI-LI JIANG

Ji-li Jiang (b. 1954) is a Chinese American author from Shanghai, who immigrated to Hawaii shortly after the Cultural Revolution. Her memoir *Red Scarf Girl* (1998) details her teenage years in China, where she found her position as Student Council President at odds with her family's political status. Today, Jiang lives in Seattle and promotes cultural exchange between Western countries and China through nonprofit work, and hopes that literature like her memoir can also nurture understanding and acceptance.

MADELEINE L'ENGLE

Madeleine L'Engle (1918–2007), the only child of a writer and a pianist in New York City, wrote her first story at the age of five. She continued writing as she grew up, and after college pursued a career in theater before publishing her first novel about an aspiring pianist. The author waded through an astounding twenty-six rejections before finding a publisher who championed her well-known novel *A Wrinkle in Time* (1962).

LOIS LOWRY

The author of forty-five children's books, Lois Lowry (b. 1937) is an American author who divides her time between Massachusetts and Maine. Her most famous novel, *The Giver* (1993) has three companion novels and takes place in a fictional future in which technology as we know it has been eliminated. Though Lowry has said she always wanted to be a writer and nothing else, she did not imagine writing books for a young audience until she was asked to do so by her publisher in 1977, with the book *A Summer to Die*.

GARY PAULSEN

Gary Paulsen (b. 1939) is a writer of young adult literature from Minnesota. At the age of seven, on a ship bound for the Philippines, Paulsen witnessed a plane crash and looked on as his mother tended to injured passengers. A plane crash figures prominently in his novel *Hatchet* (1987), which follows a young boy's survival after he is stranded in the wilderness. The author wrote a sequel, *Brian's Winter* (1996), after he received as many as two hundred letters a day from readers who wanted to know more of the story.

RENÉ SALDAÑA, JR.

René Saldaña, Jr. is an author and teacher who loosely bases many of his fictional works on his experiences growing up in southern Texas near the border of the United States and Mexico. His stories typically follow pre-teen and teenage characters as they address issues of love, danger, loyalty, and family. As an educator, Saldaña has written and stated the need to "simply validate who kids are" through diversity in literature for young readers.

Eleven

FICTION
Sandra Cisneros
1991

Introduction

Sandra Cisneros (b. 1954) is a renowned Chicana writer whose poems, novels, and short stories explore the complicated struggle of finding one's own identity. Cisneros is best known for her novel *The House on Mango Street* and the collection *Woman Hollering Creek and Other Stories.* "Eleven" is from the latter, the story of a girl named Rachel who experiences growing pains on her 11th birthday. When her teacher insists that an ugly red sweater belongs to Rachel, the 11-year-old has exceptional thoughts but can't share them. Even so, it's evident that the protagonist of Sandra Cisneros's short story has insight beyond her years.

"You open your eyes and everything's just like yesterday, only it's today. And you don't feel eleven at all."

1   What they don't understand about birthdays and what they never tell you is that when you're eleven, you're also ten, and nine, and eight, and seven, and six, and five, and four, and three, and two, and one. And when you wake up on your eleventh birthday you expect to feel eleven, but you don't. You open your eyes and everything's just like yesterday, only it's today. And you don't feel eleven at all. You feel like you're still ten. And you are—underneath the year that makes you eleven.

2   Like some days you might say something stupid, and that's the part of you that's still ten. Or maybe some days you might need to sit on your mama's lap because you're scared, and that's the part of you that's five. And maybe one day when you're all grown up maybe you will need to cry like if you're three, and that's okay. That's what I tell Mama when she's sad and needs to cry. Maybe she's feeling three.

3   Because the way you grow old is kind of like an onion or like the rings inside a tree trunk or like my little wooden dolls that fit one inside the other, each year inside the next one. That's how being eleven years old is.

4   You don't feel eleven. Not right away. It takes a few days, weeks even, sometimes even months before you say Eleven when they ask you. And you don't feel smart eleven, not until you're almost twelve. That's the way it is.

5   Only today I wish I didn't have only eleven years rattling inside me like pennies in a tin Band-Aid box. Today I wish I was one hundred and two instead of eleven because if I was one hundred and two I'd have known what to say when Mrs. Price put the red sweater on my desk. I would've known how to tell her it wasn't mine instead of just sitting there with that look on my face and nothing coming out of my mouth.

6   "Whose is this?" Mrs. Price says, and she holds the red sweater up in the air for all the class to see. "Whose? It's been sitting in the coatroom for a month."

7   "Not mine," says everybody, "Not me."

Skill: Figurative Language

The narrator uses similes when she compares aging to everyday things. When I picture onions, tree trunks, and nested wooden dolls, I notice they all have layers. She must mean that when you get older, you keep getting more layers.

Skill:
Text-Dependent
Responses

Rachel thinks the sweater is old, ugly, and "all stretched out." I don't think she likes it at all.

8   "It has to belong to somebody," Mrs. Price keeps saying, but nobody can remember. It's an ugly sweater with red plastic buttons and a collar and sleeves all stretched out like you could use it for a jump rope. It's maybe a thousand years old and even if it belonged to me I wouldn't say so.

9   Maybe because I'm skinny, maybe because she doesn't like me, that stupid Sylvia Saldivar says, "I think it belongs to Rachel." An ugly sweater like that all **raggedy** and old, but Mrs. Price believes her. Mrs. Price takes the sweater and puts it right on my desk, but when I open my mouth nothing comes out.

10   "That's not, I don't, you're not . . . Not mine." I finally say in a little voice that was maybe me when I was four.

11   "Of course it's yours," Mrs. Price says. "I remember you wearing it once." Because she's older and the teacher, she's right and I'm not.

12   Not mine, not mine, not mine, but Mrs. Price is already turning to page thirty-two, and math problem number four. I don't know why but all of a sudden I'm feeling sick inside, like the part of me that's three wants to come out of my eyes, only I squeeze them shut tight and bite down on my teeth real hard and try to remember today I am eleven, eleven. Mama is making a cake for me for tonight, and when Papa comes home everybody will sing Happy birthday, happy birthday to you.

13   But when the sick feeling goes away and I open my eyes, the red sweater's still sitting there like a big red mountain. I move the red sweater to the corner of my desk with my ruler. I move my pencil and books and eraser as far from it as possible. I even move my chair a little to the right. Not mine, not mine, not mine.

14   In my head I'm thinking how long till lunchtime, how long till I can take the red sweater and throw it over the schoolyard fence, or leave it hanging on a parking meter, or bunch it up into a little ball and toss it in the **alley.** Except when math period ends Mrs. Price says loud and in front of everybody, "Now, Rachel, that's enough," because she sees I've shoved the red sweater to the tippy-tip corner of my desk and it's hanging all over the edge like a waterfall, but I don't care.

15   "Rachel," Mrs. Price says. She says it like she's getting mad. "You put that sweater on right now and no more **nonsense.**"

16   "But it's not—"

17   "Now!" Mrs. Price says.

18   This is when I wish I wasn't eleven because all the years inside of me—ten, nine, eight, seven, six, five, four, three, two, and one—are pushing at the back of my eyes when I put one arm through one sleeve of the sweater that smells

like cottage cheese, and then the other arm through the other and stand there with my arms apart like if the sweater hurts me and it does, all itchy and full of **germs** that aren't even mine.

19 That's when everything I've been holding in since this morning, since when Mrs. Price put the sweater on my desk, finally lets go, and all of a sudden I'm crying in front of everybody. I wish I was **invisible** but I'm not. I'm eleven and it's my birthday today and I'm crying like I'm three in front of everybody. I put my head down on the desk and bury my face in my stupid clown-sweater arms. My face all hot and spit coming out of my mouth because I can't stop the little animal noises from coming out of me until there aren't any more tears left in my eyes, and it's just my body shaking like when you have the hiccups, and my whole head hurts like when you drink milk too fast.

20 But the worst part is right before the bell rings for lunch. That stupid Phyllis Lopez, who is even dumber than Sylvia Saldivar, says she remembers the red sweater is hers! I take it off right away and give it to her, only Mrs. Price pretends like everything's okay.

21 Today I'm eleven. There's a cake Mama's making for tonight and when Papa comes home from work we'll eat it. There'll be candles and presents and everybody will sing Happy birthday, happy birthday to you, Rachel, only it's too late.

22 I'm eleven today. I'm eleven, ten, nine, eight, seven, six, five, four, three, two, and one, but I wish I was one hundred and two. I wish I was anything but eleven, because I want today to be far away already, far away like a runaway balloon, like a tiny o in the sky, so tiny-tiny you have to close your eyes to see it.

From WOMAN HOLLERING CREEK. Copyright ©1991 by Sandra Cisneros. Published by Vintage Books, a division of Random House, Inc., New York and originally in hardcover by Random House, Inc. By permission of Susan Bergholz Literary Services, New York, NY and Lamy, NM. All rights reserved

 Skill: Textual Evidence

This is the second time Rachel has called one of her classmates stupid.

Rachel shows just how upset with Mrs. Price she really is by lashing out at her classmates. She is 11, but she is acting like a little kid because she doesn't know how else to act.

Please note that excerpts and passages in the StudySync® library and this workbook are intended as touchstones to generate interest in an author's work. The excerpts and passages do not substitute for the reading of entire texts, and StudySync® strongly recommends that students seek out and purchase the whole literary or informational work in order to experience it as the author intended. Links to online resellers are available in our digital library. In addition, complete works may be ordered through an authorized reseller by filling out and returning to StudySync® the order form enclosed in this workbook.

Reading & Writing Companion   3

Skill:
Text-Dependent Responses

Use the Checklist to analyze Text-Dependent Responses in "Eleven." Refer to the sample student annotations about Text-Dependent Responses in the text.

••• CHECKLIST FOR TEXT-DEPENDENT RESPONSES

In order to identify textual evidence to support an analysis of a text, consider the following:

✓ details from the text to make an inference or draw a conclusion. Inferences are logical deductions from information in a text that is not directly, or explicitly, stated by the author

   • read carefully and consider why an author gives particular details and information

   • think about what you already know and use your own knowledge and experiences to help you figure out what the author does not state directly

   • cite textual evidence, or the specific words, phrases, sentences, or paragraphs that led you to make an inference

✓ details that you can use to support your ideas and opinions about a text

✓ explicit evidence of a character's feelings or motivations, or the reasons behind an historical event in a nonfiction text

   • explicit evidence is stated directly in the text and must be cited accurately to support a text-dependent answer or analysis

To cite textual evidence to support an analysis, consider the following questions:

✓ What types of textual evidence can I use to support an analysis of a text?

✓ What explicit evidence can I use to support my analysis?

✓ If I infer things in the text that the author does not state directly, what evidence from the text, along with my own experiences and knowledge, can I use to support my analysis?

Skill:
Text-Dependent Responses

Read the second Think question from the First Read lesson for "Eleven." Then, using the Checklist on the previous page, complete the chart by deciding whether the evidence from the text can be used to form a response.

↻ YOUR TURN

	Evidence Options
A	"Maybe because I'm skinny. . ."
B	"That's not, I don't, you're not . . . Not mine."
C	"Of course it's yours," Mrs. Price says. "I remember you wearing it once."
D	"Maybe because she doesn't like me . . ."

Would Support a Response	Would Not Support a Response

First Read

Read "Eleven." After you read, complete the Think Questions below.

THINK QUESTIONS

1. How does Rachel feel about the red sweater that is placed on her desk? Respond with textual evidence from the story as well as ideas that you have inferred from clues in the text.

2. According to Rachel, why does Sylvia say the sweater belongs to Rachel? Support your answer with textual evidence.

3. Write two or three sentences exploring why Mrs. Price responds as she does when Phyllis claims the sweater. Support your answer with textual evidence.

4. Find the word **raggedy** in paragraph 9 of "Eleven." Use context clues in the surrounding sentences, as well as the sentence in which the word appears, to determine the word's meaning. Write your definition here and identify clues that helped you figure out its meaning.

5. Use context clues to determine the meaning of **nonsense** as it is used in paragraph 15 of "Eleven." Write your definition here and identify clues that helped you figure out its meaning. Then check the meaning in a dictionary.

Skill:
Textual Evidence

Use the Checklist to analyze Textual Evidence in "Eleven." Refer to the sample student annotations about Textual Evidence in the text.

••• CHECKLIST FOR TEXTUAL EVIDENCE

To support an analysis by citing textual evidence that is explicitly, or clearly, stated in the text, do the following:

- ✓ read the text closely and critically

- ✓ identify what the text says explicitly

- ✓ find the most relevant textual evidence that supports your analysis and ideas

- ✓ consider why an author explicitly states specific details and information

- ✓ cite the specific words, phrases, sentences, or paragraphs from the text that support your analysis and ideas

In order to interpret implicit meanings in a text by making inferences, do the following:

- ✓ combine information directly stated in the text with your own knowledge, experiences, and observations

- ✓ cite the specific words, phrases, sentences, or paragraphs from the text that led to and support this inference.

In order to cite textual evidence to support an analysis of what the text says explicitly as well as inferences drawn from the text, consider the following questions:

- ✓ Have I read the text closely and critically?

- ✓ What inferences am I making about the text? What textual evidence am I using to support these inferences?

- ✓ Am I quoting the evidence from the text correctly?

- ✓ Does my textual evidence logically relate to my analysis and ideas?

Skill:
Textual Evidence

Read the following excerpts from the story. Then, match the evidence found explicitly in the text and the inference drawn from the text for each excerpt. The first one is done for you.

⟳ YOUR TURN

	Evidence Options
A	The narrator dislikes the old sweater and wants to distance herself from it.
B	Because Mrs. Price is older and the teacher, her opinion about the sweater is correct.
C	Rachel is saying that Mrs. Price makes her feel powerless.
D	The narrator thinks the sweater is old, and she dislikes it.

Text	Evidence found explicitly in the text	Inference drawn from the text
Today I wish I was one hundred and two instead of eleven because if I was one hundred and two I'd have known what to say when Mrs. Price put the red sweater on my desk.	The narrator wishes she were 102 years old.	The narrator wishes she were older so she would know how to deal with difficult situations.
It's maybe a thousand years old and even if it belonged to me I wouldn't say so.		
"Of course it's yours," Mrs. Price says. "I remember you wearing it once." Because she's older and the teacher, she's right and I'm not.		

Reading & Writing Companion

Skill:
Figurative Language

Use the Checklist to analyze Figurative Language in "Eleven." Refer to the sample student annotations about Figurative Language in the text.

••• CHECKLIST FOR FIGURATIVE LANGUAGE

To determine the meaning of figures of speech in a text, note the following:

✓ words that mean one thing literally and suggest something else

✓ similes, such as "strong as an ox"

✓ metaphors, such as "her eyes were stars"

✓ personification, such as "the daisies danced in the wind"

In order to interpret the meaning of a figure of speech in context, ask the following questions:

✓ Does any of the descriptive language in the text compare two seemingly unlike things?

✓ Do any descriptions include "like" or "as" that indicate a simile?

✓ Is there a direct comparison that suggests a metaphor?

✓ Is a human quality is being used to describe this animal, object, force of nature or idea that suggests personification?

✓ How does the use of this figure of speech change your understanding of the thing or person being described?

In order to analyze the impact of figurative language on the meaning of a text, use the following questions as a guide:

✓ Where does figurative language appear in the text? What does it mean?

✓ Why does the author use figurative language rather than literal language?

Please note that excerpts and passages in the StudySync® library and this workbook are intended as touchstones to generate interest in an author's work. The excerpts and passages do not substitute for the reading of entire texts, and StudySync® strongly recommends that students seek out and purchase the whole literary or informational work in order to experience it as the author intended. Links to online resellers are available in our digital library. In addition, complete works may be ordered through an authorized reseller by filling out and returning to StudySync® the order form enclosed in this workbook.

Reading & Writing Companion   **9**

Skill:
Figurative Language

Reread paragraphs 14 and 19 of "Eleven." Then, using the Checklist on the previous page, answer the multiple-choice questions below.

⟳ YOUR TURN

1. How does the figurative language in paragraph 14 help readers understand Rachel's reaction to the sweater?

   ○ A. The metaphors in the paragraph help readers understand how Rachel feels about the sweater.

   ○ B. The simile in the paragraph helps readers understand how Rachel feels about the sweater.

   ○ C. The metaphors in the paragraph make it clear to readers that Rachel is overreacting about the sweater.

   ○ D. The simile in the paragraph makes it clear to readers that Rachel is overreacting about the sweater.

2. How does the figurative language in paragraph 19 help readers visualize Rachel's behavior?

   ○ A. The mention of "little animal noises" tells readers that Rachel is acting more like an animal than a human.

   ○ B. The metaphor of "clown-sweater arms" shows that Rachel is able to see the humorous side in her experience.

   ○ C. The similes about her body shaking "like when you have the hiccups" and her head hurting "like when you drink milk too fast" connect to unpleasant experiences most readers have had.

   ○ D. The statement that "there aren't any more tears left in [her] eyes" suggests that Rachel is starting to calm down.

Close Read

Reread "Eleven." As you reread, complete the Skills Focus questions below. Then use your answers and annotations from the questions to help you complete the Write activity.

SKILLS FOCUS

1. Identify examples of figurative language and explain the purpose they achieve in the story.

2. Explain what you can infer about the narrator's feelings about the sweater based on her descriptions, actions, and reactions.

3. The narrator uses figurative language, including similes and metaphors, to describe aging. Identify these in the text. Explain what type of figurative language each one is an example of and what each piece of figurative language means.

4. Explain what the author implies about what the narrator really wants when she says, "today I wish I was one hundred and two."

5. Getting older can be tough. Identify and explain the textual evidence in the story that supports this statement.

WRITE

LITERARY ANALYSIS: How does the author's use of figurative language help readers understand the feelings that the narrator is expressing? Support your writing with evidence from the text.

The Mighty Miss Malone

FICTION
Christopher Paul Curtis
2012

Introduction

The *Mighty Miss Malone* is author Christopher Paul Curtis's follow-up to 2000's Newbery Medal-winning *Bud, Not Buddy*. Both are stories of young African Americans set in Great Depression-era Flint, Michigan. This time, 12-year-old Deza Malone—new in Flint from Gary, Indiana, where she was at the top of her class—is the narrator. When her father doesn't return from a trip to find work, Deza, her brother Jimmie, and her mother go looking for him, journeying across the land by hopping aboard a boxcar. For a time, the Malones make their home outside of Flint, Michigan, in a "Hooverville," a town of small shelters built during the Great Depression. When Deza begins again at a new school, her teachers, unlike her beloved former teacher Mrs. Needham, treat her unfairly because of her race. As this excerpt begins, Deza has been busying herself helping Stew, the woman in charge

"You must be a genius to get a C plus!"

from Chapter Twenty-Two: Learning How to Settle in Flint

1   I'd been having such a good time being Little Stew and trying to fill in all the missing words from the *Reader's Digest* that time had completely run off and forgot all about me!

2   "But, Mother, Miss Stew needs me to—"

3   "You aren't suggesting you stay here and help Stew instead of going to school, are you?" When she said it like that, it did seem silly.

. . .

4   On the outside, schools in Flint seemed a lot like schools in Gary, but they weren't. Instead of having one teacher all day, in Flint we went from classroom to classroom and teacher to teacher for each subject. The teachers were different too. First, all of them were white, and second, they weren't anywhere as nice as the teachers in Gary. But one of Mrs. Needham's lessons stuck: I was learning how to toughen up.

5   I got my usual As on the tests in mathematics, geography, civics and history.

6   After my first mathematics test, when class was dismissed, Mrs. Scott called me to her desk.

7   "Deza, have you always done so well in math? You're the only student who got a perfect score."

8   I sounded very **humble,** but the truth's the truth. "Yes, ma'am. Mathematics is one of my favorite subjects."

9   It was great to be back in school!

10 "Could I ask you a favor?"

11 Maybe she wanted me to help some of my classmates. Even though they were white, some of them were the spittin' image of Dolly Peaches and Benny Cobb.

Please note that excerpts and passages in the StudySync® library and this workbook are intended as touchstones to generate interest in an author's work. The excerpts and passages do not substitute for the reading of entire texts, and StudySync® strongly recommends that students seek out and purchase the whole literary or informational work in order to experience it as the author intended. Links to online resellers are available in our digital library. In addition, complete works may be ordered through an authorized reseller by filling out and returning to StudySync® the order form enclosed in this workbook.

Reading & Writing Companion   13

12 She slid a paper toward me. It had five unsolved story problems on it.

13 "Could you sit right there, right now, and solve these for me?"

14 Maybe Mrs. Scott was seeing if I was ready for harder work. I finished in no time.

15 She looked them over. "Hmm, perfect again, but next time you *must* make sure to show all your work. You're dismissed."

16 I was surprised that was all she said.

17 In English class I *really* showed how much I'd toughened up.

18 Flint teachers don't have the imaginations that Gary teachers do, so instead of giving grades back so everyone knows what you got, they walk around the class and hand your test or paper back to you. Upside down.

19 Mr. Smith was passing out our first essay. I'd followed all of Mrs. Needham's advice. I'd written it at the Flint Public Library and was very careful not to use the dictionary or the thesaurus too much. And I didn't **digress** at all.

20 I made sure my posture was good, crossed my ankles and folded my hands on the desk when he got close to me.

**Skill:
Character**

Deza's reaction to her grade is to follow her brother's advice. When Deza turns the paper over, I notice she doesn't start crying or anything. She smiles. This reaction shows me that Deza knows her essay is good. She's changed—before she would have cried, but now she's strong.

21 He handed me my paper and smiled. "Very good job."

22 My heart flew! "Thank you, sir."

23 I turned my paper over.

24 He'd written, "Good for you!" and put a giant C+ with three exclamation points.

25 I turned the paper back over. Maybe I saw it wrong.

26 I looked again but it was the same.

27 One sign that I had toughened up was that instead of crying I thought of a little joke that Jimmie said he did whenever he didn't like his grade.

28 "I turn the paper over, then, the same way people bang on a machine it if ain't acting right, I smack my hand on the paper. Maybe if I bang it hard enough my grade will jump up a mark!"

29 It was nonsense, but I slapped my hand on Mr. Smith's essay.

30 I turned the paper back over and smiled.

31 I'd have to tell Jimmie that it still wasn't working.

32 Mrs. Needham would've been proud. Instead of bawling, I looked at Mr. Smith's back and said to myself, "OK, buster, I'm going to make sure my next essay is the best thing I've ever written. You won't have any choice but to give me my A plus."

33 When me and Loretta were walking back to camp I asked, "What grade did you get on your essay?"

34 "I don't know, the same old D. What'd you get?"

35 "C plus."

36 She stopped walking. "Uh-oh, no, you didn't!"

37 I showed her my grade.

38 "Ooh, girl, you must be *real* smart."

39 "For getting a C plus?"

40 "All these teachers up here at Whittier's prejudice. Katherine Williams was the smartest colored girl in the school and all she use to get was a C. You must be a genius to get a C plus!"

41 She laughed. "I'm gonna see if I can sit next to you when we take our next exam!"

• • •

42 Early every morning, Mother and I would leave the camp and walk for half a hour to downtown Flint. Jimmie would go his own way.

43 After school I'd go to the library and read until Mother picked me up. We didn't have a official address so I couldn't check out any books, but I still got to read.

44 It wasn't long before we stopped looking fresh and had **seniority** in camp. Stew said I had a **bubbly** personality so she had me help the new children get used to living here. Some of them didn't have any idea what to do, mostly the boys.

45 I pretended they were my students and was very patient.

46 Two little boys from Flint came in one day all by themselves. One of them reminded me of myself. He seemed scareder than his friend so I took him under my wing.

47 He was very nervous and shy, but you could see how sweet he was too.

**Skill:
Character**

Instead of complaining about her grade, Deza feels inspired to prove her teacher wrong. Instead of feeling sorry for herself, Deza is determined to impress her teacher and get a better grade.

48 His first evening in the camp, I didn't want him and his friend to think they were going to get a free ride so I had them help me with the dishes. I took the little boy and showed him the creek where we clean the camp's pots and dishes. We sat on a big rock and I washed and had him dry.

49 He said, "Are you leaving on the train tomorrow?"

50 "Uh-uh." I'd been lying so much about how we weren't alone that without thinking, I said, "My father's going out on it, he might leave for a day or two for work.'

51 "Where do you go to school?"

52 "Well, Mother says I might have to keep going here in Flint at Whittier."

53 The sad-eyed little boy said, "I'm hopping the freight to go west, me and Bugs are gonna pick fruit."

54 "I wish you two well."

55 I'd hand him the dish after I'd washed it and when my hand touched his he'd start blinking a lot and would get twitchity and **fumble** the cloth when he tried to dry the dish.

56 After a while I started touching his hand just to make him squirm. And squirm he did!

57 He counted softly, "One, two, three . . . ," then blurted out, "I'MNOTAFRAIDOFGIRLS!"

58 I laughed. "You aren't?"

59 "Uh-uh. I even kissed some in the home."

60 "Really?"

61 "Yup, I got three kisses."

62 He held up four fingers.

63 I looked up at the moon. It was huge and yellow and yolky. "Isn't the moon lovely?"

64 I looked back. The little boy had closed his eyes, puckered his lips and leaned in toward me!

65 I started to slug him, just a arm punch. But looking at how sad he was made my heart melt.

66 He was all alone except for a person named Bugs.

NOTES

67   What else could I do?

68   I kissed his forehead three times and said, "Kisses . . . kisses . . . kisses make you stronger."

69   He blinked six or seven times and when his eyes came open he looked lost and befumbled.

70   I put his hand in mine.

71   The harmonica man started playing "Shenandoah."

72   "Do you know that song?"

73   His head was wobbling back and forth and I wasn't sure if he was saying no or getting ready to swoon.

74   I said, "It's about a Indian princess who hasn't seen her husband for seven years."

75   I sang a little.

76   He said, "You sing beautiful."

77   Wow! He *was* befumbled!

78   "You should hear my brother, now that's a real singer."

79   I helped him up and we carried the dishes back to the camp.

80   As bad as things were for me, they were much worse for him. I still had my family, and like Mother always says, without a family you're nothing but dust on the wind.

81   I hoped he'd find kindness somewhere, but even with my exploding imagination, I couldn't figure out where that would be.

Excerpted from *The Mighty Miss Malone* by Christopher Paul Curtis, published by Wendy Lamb Books.

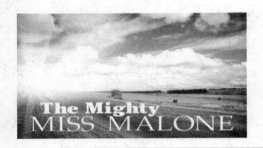

First Read

Read *The Mighty Miss Malone*. After you read, complete the Think Questions below.

☁ THINK QUESTIONS

1. What are the differences between Deza's old school in Gary, Indiana, and her new school in Flint, Michigan? Cite textual evidence to support your answer.

2. Write two or three sentences describing how Loretta reacts when she finds out what grade Deza received on her essay. Support your answer with evidence from the text.

3. What does Deza's attitude toward the boy she meets in the camp reveal about her character? Cite textual evidence from the selection to support your answer.

4. Find the word **seniority** in paragraph 44 of "The Mighty Miss Malone." Use context clues in the surrounding sentences, as well as the sentence in which the word appears, to determine the word's meaning. Write your definition here and identify clues that helped you figure out the meaning.

5. Use context clues to determine the meaning of **fumble** as it is used in paragraph 55 of "The Mighty Miss Malone." Write your definition here and identify clues that helped you figure out the meaning. Then check the meaning in the dictionary.

Skill: Character

Use the Checklist to analyze Character in *The Mighty Miss Malone*. Refer to the sample student annotations about Character in the text.

••• CHECKLIST FOR CHARACTER

In order to determine how the characters respond or change as the plot moves toward a resolution, note the following:

- ✓ the characters in the story, including the protagonist and antagonist

- ✓ key events or series of episodes in the plot, especially events that cause characters to react, respond, or change in some way

- ✓ characters' responses as the plot reaches a climax, and moves toward a resolution of the problem facing the protagonist

- ✓ the resolution of the conflict in the plot and the ways that it affects each character

To describe how a particular story's or drama's plot unfolds in a series of episodes as well as how the characters respond or change as the plot moves toward a resolution, consider the following questions:

- ✓ How do the characters' responses change or develop from the beginning to the end of the story?

- ✓ Do the characters in the story change? Which event or events in the story cause a character to change?

- ✓ Is there an event in the story that provokes, or causes, a character to make a decision?

- ✓ Do the characters' problems reach a resolution? How?

- ✓ How does the resolution affect the characters?

Skill:
Character

Reread paragraphs 6–16 from the text. Then, using the Checklist on the previous page, answer the multiple-choice questions below.

↻ YOUR TURN

1. Based on Mrs. Scott's actions in paragraphs 12 and 13, the reader can conclude that —

   ○ A. Mrs. Scott wanted Deza to solve more math problems for extra credit.
   ○ B. Mrs. Scott suspects that Deza may have cheated on her math test.
   ○ C. Deza did not finish the test.
   ○ D. Mrs. Scott wanted to see if Deza was good enough to be a tutor.

2. This question has two parts. First, answer Part A. Then, answer Part B.

   Part A: Deza's reaction to Mrs. Scott's request reveals that Deza —

   ○ A. is anxious about her performance in math.
   ○ B. is aware that Mrs. Scott thinks she might have cheated on her test.
   ○ C. is not aware that Mrs. Scott thinks she might have cheated on her test.
   ○ D. is aware that Mrs. Scott is prejudiced against African American students.

   Part B: Which paragraph best shows evidence for the answer to Part A?

   ○ A. 8
   ○ B. 9
   ○ C. 15
   ○ D. 16

Close Read

Reread *The Mighty Miss Malone*. As you reread, complete the Skills Focus questions below. Then use your answers and annotations from the questions to help you complete the Write activity.

◎ SKILLS FOCUS

1. Recall Deza's initial thoughts about what her Flint teachers say and do. Explain what these thoughts reveal about Deza's character.

2. Focus on Deza's words and actions as she interacts with the little boys who come to the camp. Identify what these indicate about her character.

3. Analyze how Deza's responses to change develop the plot by identifying evidence that shows how her relationship with the camp and Flint changes over time.

4. When life gets hard for Deza, what does she do? Identify evidence of her reactions to challenges and explain whether there are any differences between her thoughts and actions.

✏ WRITE

NARRATIVE: Consider how Deza responds to the C+ she received on her essay, both internally and externally. Then imagine how she will approach the next assignment she receives from Mr. Smith. Use the information you learned about both characters, as well as Deza's other interactions with characters in the text, to write a short scene that describes this event.

Please note that excerpts and passages in the StudySync® library and this workbook are intended as touchstones to generate interest in an author's work. The excerpts and passages do not substitute for the reading of entire texts, and StudySync® strongly recommends that students seek out and purchase the whole literary or informational work in order to experience it as the author intended. Links to online resellers are available in our digital library. In addition, complete works may be ordered through an authorized reseller by filling out and returning to StudySync® the order form enclosed in this workbook.

Reading & Writing Companion   21

Red Scarf Girl: A Memoir of the Cultural Revolution

INFORMATIONAL TEXT
Ji-li Jiang
1997

Introduction

Red Scarf Girl: A Memoir of the Cultural Revolution is an autobiography about the teenage life of Ji-li Jiang, who lived with her family in Shanghai during the 1960s when Communist Party leader Mao Zedong effectively declared war against capitalist and anti-establishment forces throughout China. As Zedong launched a series of purges aimed at purifying the Communist party, Ji-li and her family were dedicated Communists; she was initially embarrassed by her family's "landlord" background when the Cultural Revolution began in 1966. However, her feelings began to change when the government started attacking her family. In this excerpt, she has been pulled out of class and is being interrogated by people from her father's theater.

"I saw Dad looking at me hopelessly, tears on his face."

NOTES

1   "Sit down, sit down. Don't be afraid." Chairman Jin pointed to the empty chair. "These comrades from your father's work unit are just here to have a study session with you. It's nothing to worry about."

2   I sat down dumbly.

3   I had thought about their coming to my home but never imagined this. They were going to **expose** my family in front of my teachers and classmates. I would have no pride left. I would never be an educable child again.

4   Thin-Face sat opposite me, with a woman I had never seen before. Teacher Zhang was there too, his eyes encouraging me.

5   Thin-Face came straight to the point. "Your father's problems are very serious." His cold eyes nailed me to my seat. "You may have read the article in the *Workers' Revolt* that exposed your family's filthy past." I slumped down in my chair without taking my eyes off his face. "In addition to coming from a landlord family, your father committed some serious mistakes during the Antirightist Movement[1] several years ago, but he still obstinately refuses to confess." His cold manner became a little more animated. "Of course we won't tolerate this. We have decided to make an example of him. We are going to have a struggle meeting of the entire theater system to criticize him and force him to confess." He suddenly pounded the table with his fist. The cups on the table rattled.

6   I tore my eyes away from him and stared at a cup instead.

7   "As I told you before, you are your own person. If you want to make a clean break with your black family, then you can be an educable child and we will welcome you to our **revolutionary** ranks." He gave Chairman Jin a look, and Chairman Jin chimed in, "That's right, we welcome you."

8   "Jiang Ji-li has always done well at school. In addition to doing very well in her studies, she participates in educational reform," Teacher Zhang added.

---

1. **Antirightist Movement** a campaign, from roughly 1957 to 1959, to purge people in the Communist Party with alleged capitalist or anti-establishment sympathies

9   "That's very good. We knew that you had more sense than to follow your father," Thin-Face said with a brief, frozen smile. "Now you can show your revolutionary determination." He paused. "We want you to **testify** against your father at the struggle meeting."

10   I closed my eyes. I saw Dad standing on a stage, his head bowed, his name written in large black letters, and then crossed out in red ink, on a sign hanging from his neck. I saw myself standing in the middle of the stage, facing thousands of people, condemning Dad for his crimes, raising my fist to lead the chant, "Down with Jiang Xi-reng." I saw Dad looking at me hopelessly, tears on his face.

11   "I...I..." I looked at Teacher Zhang for help. He looked away.

12   The Woman from the theater spoke. "It's really not such a hard thing to do. The key is your class stance. The daughter of our former Party Secretary resolved to make a clean break with her mother. When she went onstage to condemn her mother, she actually slapped her face. Of course, we don't mean that you have to slap your father's face. The point is that as long as you have the correct class stance, it will be easy to testify." Her voice grated on my ears.

13   "There is something you can do to prove you are truly Chairman Mao's child." Thin-Face spoke again. "I am sure you can tell us some things your father said and did that show his landlord and rightist mentality." I stared at the table, but I could feel his eyes boring into me. "What can you tell us?"

14   "But I don't know anything," I whispered." I don't know—"

15   "I am sure you can remember something if you think about it," Thin-Face said. "A man like him could not hide his true beliefs from a child as smart as you. He must have made comments **critical** of Chairman Mao and the Cultural Revolution. I am sure you are loyal to Chairman Mao and the Communist Party[2]. Tell us!"

16   "But my father never said anything against Chairman Mao," I protested weakly. "I would tell you if he did." My voice grew stronger with conviction. "He never said anything against the Party."

---

2. **Communist Party** the ruling party of the People's Republic of China, established in 1949 and led by Chairman Mao Zedong

17 "Now, you have to choose between two roads." Thin-Face looked straight into my eyes. "You can break with your family and follow Chairman Mao, or you can follow your father and become an enemy of the people." His voice grew more **severe.** "In that case we would have many more study sessions, with your brother and sister too, and the Red Guard Committee[3] and the school leaders. Think about it. We will come back to talk to you again."

18 Thin-Face and the woman left, saying they would be back to get my statement. Without knowing how I got there, I found myself in a narrow passageway between the school building and the school-yard wall. The gray concrete walls closed around me and a slow drizzle dampened my cheeks. I could not go back to the classroom, and I could not go home. I felt like a small animal that had fallen into a trap, alone and helpless, and sure that the hunter was coming.

Excerpted from *Red Scarf Girl* by Ji-li Jiang, published by HarperCollins Publishers

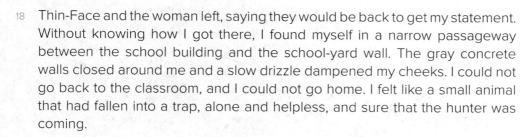

✎ WRITE

PERSONAL RESPONSE: Ji-li Jiang is facing a challenging decision—between defending her father and protecting herself. This decision was forced on her because of extraordinary political circumstances. Many people have to make difficult decisions, though often not at the same level of consequence. Think about a time you had to make a difficult decision. Explain the decision you had to make, why you had to make it, and who, if anyone, helped you. Does your experience help you empathize with Jiang? Use evidence from the text to support your response.

3. **Red Guard Committee** a student paramilitary organization that organized on behalf of Chairman Mao and the Communist Party, using violence as a means of coercion

Hatchet

FICTION
Gary Paulsen
1987

Introduction

*H*atchet is the first in a series of five novels by Gary Paulsen (b. 1939), who won a Newbery Honor in 1988 for this gripping tale of survival. The hero of *Hatchet* and its follow-ups is young Brian Robeson, who must rely on his wits and instincts alone to stay alive in the Canadian wilderness. Preceding this excerpt from Chapter 5, 13-year-old Brian is left stranded on his own after his pilot has a heart attack and their plane crashes in a lake. The excerpt describes the day

"Nothing.
It kept coming back to that.
He had nothing."

from Chapter 5

1 They would look for him, look for the plane. His father and mother would be frantic. They would tear the world apart to find him. Brian had seen searches on the news, seen movies about lost planes. When a plane went down they mounted **extensive** searches and almost always they found the plane within a day or two. Pilots all filed flight plans—a detailed plan for where and when they were going to fly, with all the courses explained. They would come, they would look for him. The searchers would get government planes and cover both sides of the flight plan filed by the pilot and search until they found him.

2 Maybe even today. They might come today. This was the second day after the crash. No. Brian frowned. Was it the first day or the second day? They had gone down in the afternoon and he had spent the whole night out cold. So this was the first real day. But they could still come today. They would have started the search immediately when Brian's plane did not arrive.

3 Yeah, they would probably come today.

4 Probably come in here with **amphibious** planes, small bushplanes with floats that could land right here on the lake and pick him up and take him home.

5 Which home? The father home or the mother home. He stopped the thinking. It didn't matter. Either on to his dad or back to his mother. Either way he would probably be home by late night or early morning, home where he could sit down and eat a large, cheesy, juicy burger with tomatoes and double fries with ketchup and a thick chocolate shake.

6 And there came hunger.

7 Brian rubbed his stomach. The hunger had been there but something else—fear, pain—had held it down. Now, with the thought of the burger, the emptiness roared at him. He could not believe the hunger, had never felt it this way. The lake water had filled his stomach but left it hungry, and now it demanded food, screamed for food.

8 And there was, he thought, absolutely nothing to eat.

Skill:
Setting

It's obvious that Brian is anxious to be rescued. He's alone and afraid in the wilderness. He's trying to calm himself down by guessing when his rescuers will come, but he has no idea if they ever will.

9   Nothing.

10 What did they do in the movies when they got stranded like this? Oh, yes, the hero usually found some kind of plant that he knew was good to eat and that took care of it. Just ate the plant until he was full or used some kind of cute trap to catch an animal and cook it over a slick little fire and pretty soon he had a full eight-course meal.

11 The trouble, Brian thought, looking around, was that all he could see was grass and brush. There was nothing **obvious** to eat and aside from about a million birds and the beaver he hadn't seen animals to trap and cook, and even if he got one somehow he didn't have any matches so he couldn't have a fire. . .

12 Nothing.

13 It kept coming back to that. He had nothing.

14 Well, almost nothing. As a matter of fact, he thought, I don't know what I've got or haven't got. Maybe I should try and figure out just how I stand. It will give me something to do—keep me from thinking of food. Until they come to find me.

15 Brian had once had an English teacher, a guy named Perpich, who was always talking about being positive, thinking positive, staying on top of things. That's how Perpich had put it—stay positive and stay on top of things. Brian thought of him now—wondered how to stay positive and stay on top of this. All Perpich would say is that I have to get **motivated.** He was always telling kids to get motivated.

16 Brian changed position so he was sitting on his knees. He reached into his pockets and took out everything he had and laid it on the grass in front of him.

17 It was pitiful enough. A quarter, three dimes, a nickel, and two pennies. A fingernail clipper. A billfold with a twenty dollar bill—"In case you get stranded at the airport in some small town and have to buy food," his mother had said—and some odd pieces of paper.

18 And on his belt, somehow still there, the hatchet his mother had given him. He had forgotten it and now reached around and took it out and put it in the grass. There was a touch of rust already forming on the cutting edge of the blade and he rubbed it off with his thumb.

19 That was it.

20 He frowned. No, wait—if he was going to play the game, might as well play it right. Perpich would tell him to quit messing around. Get motivated. Look at *all* of it, Robeson.

21   He had on a pair of good tennis shoes, now almost dry. And socks. And jeans and underwear and a thin leather belt and a T-shirt with a windbreaker so torn it hung on him in tatters.

22   And a watch. He had a digital watch still on his wrist but it was broken from the crash—the little screen blank—and he took it off and almost threw it away but stopped the hand motion and lay the watch on the grass with the rest of it.

23   There. That was it.

24   No, wait. One other thing. Those were all the things he had, but he also had himself. Perpich used to drum that into them—"You are your most valuable **asset.** Don't forget that. *You* are the best thing you have."

25   Brian looked around again. I wish you were here, Perpich. I'm hungry and I'd trade everything I have for a hamburger.

Excerpted from *Hatchet* by Gary Paulsen, published by Simon & Schuster.

First Read

Read *Hatchet*. After you read, complete the Think Questions below.

☁ THINK QUESTIONS

1. What happens to Brian? What problem does he have? Cite textual evidence from the selection to support your answer.

2. What is Brian's family situation? What makes you think so? State details from the text or ideas you have inferred from clues in the text.

3. Figurative language is language used for descriptive effect, often to illustrate or imply ideas indirectly. A type of figurative language is **personification**, in which an animal, object, force of nature, or an idea is given human form or qualities. Can you identify an example of personification from *Hatchet* that illustrates one of the problems Brian is facing? Cite textual evidence from the selection to support your answer.

4. Find the word **obvious** as used in paragraph 11 in *Hatchet*. Use context clues in the surrounding sentences, as well as the sentence in which the word appears, to determine the word's meaning. Write your definition here and identify clues that helped you figure out its meaning.

5. Use context clues to determine the meaning of **asset** as it is used in paragraph 24 of the excerpt. Write your definition here and identify clues that helped you figure out its meaning. Then check the meaning in a dictionary.

SETTING

Skill: Setting

Use the Checklist to analyze Setting in *Hatchet*. Refer to the sample student annotations about Setting in the text.

••• CHECKLIST FOR SETTING

In order to identify how a particular story's or drama's plot unfolds in a series of episodes, note the following:

- ✓ key elements in the plot
- ✓ the setting(s) in the story
- ✓ how the plot unfolds in a series of episodes
- ✓ how the setting shapes the plot

To describe how a particular story's or drama's plot unfolds in a series of episodes, consider the following questions:

- ✓ When and where does this story take place?
- ✓ How does the plot unfold in a series of episodes?
- ✓ How does the setting affect the plot? How does it affect the characters and their responses to events? How does the setting help move the plot to a resolution?

Please note that excerpts and passages in the StudySync® library and this workbook are intended as touchstones to generate interest in an author's work. The excerpts and passages do not substitute for the reading of entire texts, and StudySync® strongly recommends that students seek out and purchase the whole literary or informational work in order to experience it as the author intended. Links to online resellers are available in our digital library. In addition, complete works may be ordered through an authorized reseller by filling out and returning to StudySync® the order form enclosed in this workbook.

Reading & Writing Companion   31

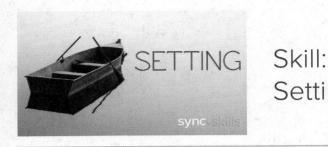

Skill:
Setting

Reread paragraphs 10–15 from the text. Then, using the Checklist on the previous page, answer the multiple-choice questions below.

⟳ YOUR TURN

1. Based on the description in paragraph 11, the reader can conclude that —

   ○ A. the story is set in a place far from water.
   ○ B. the story is set in a place that is heavily forested.
   ○ C. the story is set in a place with an obvious food source.
   ○ D. the story is set in a place covered with grass and brushland.

2. The description of Brian's thoughts in paragraphs 11–15 indicates that he feels —

   ○ A. unsure.
   ○ B. positive.
   ○ C. motivated.
   ○ D. resourceful.

3. Which paragraph best shows how the setting contributes to the conflict in the plot?

   ○ A. 10
   ○ B. 11
   ○ C. 14
   ○ D. 15

Skill:
Compare and Contrast

Use the Checklist to analyze Compare and Contrast in *Hatchet*.

••• CHECKLIST FOR COMPARE AND CONTRAST

In order to determine how to compare and contrast texts in different forms or genres, use the following steps:

- ✓ first, choose texts with similar subjects or topics

- ✓ next, identify the qualities or characteristics of each genre

- ✓ after, identify the theme in each work

- ✓ finally, analyze ways in which the texts are similar and different in the way they approach similar themes and topics

  - • think about what the characters or narrators do and say
  - • think about what happens as a result of the characters' or narrator's words and actions

To compare and contrast texts in different forms or genres in terms of their approaches to similar themes and topics, consider the following questions:

- ✓ How does each text approach the theme and topic? How does the form or genre of the text affect this approach?

- ✓ What are the similarities and differences in the subjects or topics of the texts I have chosen?

Please note that excerpts and passages in the StudySync® library and this workbook are intended as touchstones to generate interest in an author's work. The excerpts and passages do not substitute for the reading of entire texts, and StudySync® strongly recommends that students seek out and purchase the whole literary or informational work in order to experience it as the author intended. Links to online resellers are available in our digital library. In addition, complete works may be ordered through an authorized reseller by filling out and returning to StudySync® the order form enclosed in this workbook.

Reading & Writing Companion   33

Skill:
Compare and Contrast

Reread paragraphs 8–13 from *Hatchet* and paragraphs 17 and 18 from *Red Scarf Girl*. Then, using the Checklist on the previous page, complete the chart below to compare and contrast the passages.

↻ YOUR TURN

Inference Options	
A	Characters have to rely on their own good sense in order to solve a problem. The theme, or message, is that survival is possible if you can think clearly.
B	The main character is trapped into making a difficult decision. The genre is nonfiction.
C	The main character is alone in a strange, challenging setting. The genre is fiction.

Hatchet	Both	Red Scarf Girl

Close Read

Reread *Hatchet*. As you reread, complete the Skills Focus questions below. Then use your answers and annotations from the questions to help you complete the Write activity.

⊚ SKILLS FOCUS

1. Identify details that Brian shares about his surroundings and explain how the evidence helps you determine the setting.

2. Identify evidence of how Brian evaluates his surroundings and explain why the details are so important to him.

3. Identify details about the setting that contribute to the conflict in *Hatchet*, and explain how these details directly affect the plot.

4. In *Red Scarf Girl*, Ji-li Jiang is pulled out of class by Communist Party officials and questioned about her family's loyalty to the Cultural Revolution. Identify details in *Red Scarf Girl* that tell you about the setting, and explain how the details help you compare this setting to the setting in *Hatchet*.

5. Identify details that demonstrate how Brian deals with the challenges he faces.

✏ WRITE

COMPARE AND CONTRAST: *Red Scarf Girl* and *Hatchet* feature young people trapped in challenging situations. In both texts, the setting provides the context for the main conflict or problem. Compare and contrast the role that the setting plays in influencing the characters and events in the two texts.

The Magic Marker Mystery

DRAMA
René Saldaña, Jr.
2013

Introduction

Author René Saldaña, Jr. draws from both his Texas upbringing and his past as a middle-school teacher to create characters like the young sleuth Mickey Rangel. In this short play, Mickey is employed by his principal in order to find out who is behind some graffiti that has recently turned up at the school. Mickey is forced to use his detective skills, as well as a recent English class lesson on homophones, to figure out which of his classmates has been defacing

"I've got to do the job right, even if it means going against my gut instinct."

Characters

Mickey Rangel
Principal Abrego
Bucho
Joe
Belinda
Johnny

Setting

A middle school in a Midwestern suburb

1   **ACT ONE:** PRINCIPAL ABREGO's office. The principal is sitting at a large wooden desk. Sunlight streams in from two large windows to her right.

2   PRINCIPAL ABREGO (*buzzes phone*): Angie, can you please send Mickey in now?

3   (*door opens, MICKEY RANGEL reluctantly walks in*)

4   PRINCIPAL ABREGO (*shuffling papers, and without looking at MICKEY*): Won't you have a seat, Mr. Rangel? I'll be just a moment. (*continues shuffling papers for a couple more seconds, then sets them in order and places them on the desk*) So, (*looks up at MICKEY finally*) you must be wondering why I've called you to my office?

5   MICKEY (*leg shaking, swallows hard*): Sort of. I've been going over in my head what I could have possibly done to **merit** being summoned to the principal's office, and though there is that spitball **incident** from this morning on the bus, it was only this morning and mostly between my brother Ricky and me, so word couldn't have gotten to you this quickly, and even if it had, my actions weren't so bad that. . .(*MICKEY notices PRINCIPAL ABREGO has reached for a pen to begin taking notes, and that she also has the traces of a smile on her face.*) I mean, yes, ma'am, I am wondering why you would call me here.

NOTES

Skill: Dramatic Elements and Structure

I know that this is a drama about a student, and this scene shows me that the play takes place at school because he's talking to the principal.

Mickey seems nervous in this setting, but the principal is smiling. I wonder if Mickey is in trouble or not, and what will happen next...

6   PRINCIPAL ABREGO: Well. . .never mind about the, uh, spitball episode, at least for now. (*raises an eyebrow, then smiles*) As to why I've asked you to my office this morning, Mr Rangel—may I call you Mickey?

7   MICKEY: Certainly, ma'am.

8   PRINCIPAL ABREGO: I'm sure you've seen the graffiti marring our walls lately. The substance of the messages, mostly aimed at me, is fairly harmless. I'm a principal, so I've had to grow a thick skin over the years. What is bothersome beyond belief, though, is that someone thinks so very little of our school that they would show such disrespect. (*shakes her head*)

Graffiti

9   MICKEY: Mrs. Abrego, you don't think that I. . .?

Skill: Dramatic Elements and Structure

Principal Abrego didn't call Mickey to her office because he's in trouble. She's asking for his help! She must want him to use his detective skills to find the person responsible for the graffiti.

10 PRINCIPAL ABREGO: Oh, goodness, no, Mickey. I'm sorry I haven't made myself clear. No, I don't think for a second you have anything to do with this.

11 MICKEY (*sighs in relief*): So then why am I here, if you don't mind me asking?

12 PRINCIPAL ABREGO: Am I right in saying you're sort of a detective, young though you are?

13 MICKEY: Actually, Mrs. Abrego, I'm the real deal. I took the required online courses to earn my degree. I've got a framed diploma at home to prove it. (*pulls wallet from back pocket, rifles through it as though in search of something*) I also carry my official P.I. ID card. P.I.—that stands for *private investigator*. You want to see it? (*finds it and offers it to PRINCIPAL ABREGO*)

14 PRINCIPAL ABREGO (*takes it from MICKEY and studies it briefly, then returns it*): That's very impressive, Mickey.

15 MICKEY: Thank you, ma'am. But I still don't understand why I'm here.

16 PRINCIPAL ABREGO: Mickey, I'll be frank with you: I'm in a bit of a sticky situation. (*pushes aside a few papers on her desk, stands, and walks to the window overlooking the playground*) Take a look out the window with me and tell me what you see.

17 MICKEY: Yes, ma'am. (*rises, makes his way around the desk, and walks over to the window*)

18 PRINCIPAL ABREGO: Can you read it from here?

19   MICKEY (*reads aloud*): "Our Principle's no pal of nobodies!" Interesting spelling and punctuation choices this Magic Marker Mischief Maker has made.

20   PRINCIPAL ABREGO: You noticed? Good. Yes, it should read "principal," ending in "PAL," not "PLE." Major difference.

21   MICKEY: Yes, and "nobody" is spelled as though it were plural, ending in "-dies," though it should not be a plural. And is that a small letter "B" at the bottom right corner, like a signature?

22   PRINCIPAL ABREGO: You caught that too? Most impressive Mickey.

23   MICKEY (*smiles*): Thanks, ma'am.

24   PRINCIPAL ABREGO: I also got this anonymous email this morning right as I turned on my computer. The author claims to be an eye-witness to the wrongdoing. What do you make of it? (*hands MICKEY the sheet of paper*)

25   MICKEY (*reads the email*): Hmmmm. Incriminating, to say the least. So the letter "B" on the wall would make sense. Based on these two clues, all fingers point to Bucho being our mischief maker.

26   PRINCIPAL ABREGO: Yes, that's what I thought. But here's the thing, Mickey. I confronted him with this evidence, and he denies having anything to do with marking up our walls. Believe it or not, tough though he comes across, he was nearly in tears.

27   MICKEY: Ma'am, I'm not so sure you should be telling me this. Isn't there some kind of student-principal privilege?

28   PRINCIPAL ABREGO: Normally, yes, but he gave me permission to discuss this whole matter with you, every bit of it.

29   MICKEY: Wait—what? You mean he told you it was okay to talk to me about this? Why would he do that?

30   PRINCIPAL ABREGO: Mickey, Bucho was so **adamant** that he wasn't the **culprit** that he recommended I bring you in on the case. He's the one who told me you were a detective.

31   MICKEY: He said that?

32   PRINCIPAL ABREGO: Are you surprised?

33   MICKEY: Yes, ma'am. You might not know this about us, but he and I are not the best of friends. To be honest, Mrs. Abrego, he's a bit of a bully.

34   PRINCIPAL ABREGO: That he is. But he and I have been trying to work on that part of his life. In the last few months he's made some great strides, and so

when I got this email and put it together with the so-called signature, it was easy to jump to conclusions. And this is where you come in, Mickey. I was filled with indecision about what I should do about this, but now I think I've found an answer. I need you to find out who is to blame for the graffiti. Can you help me?

35 MICKEY: You can count on me. Mickey Rangel is on the case.

36 PRINCIPAL ABREGO: Good. Whatever you need, please don't hesitate to ask. In fact, think of me as your benefactor.

37 **ACT TWO, SCENE 1:** First lunch period. MICKEY is eating at a table in the school cafeteria; with him are his friends BELINDA and JOHNNY. JOE, another student, is sitting alone at a nearby table, eavesdropping on MICKEY and friends.

38 BELINDA: You know, Mickey, I'm not the only one who thinks this school would be a better place without that bully, Bucho. I can't even count the multitude of times he's knocked my book bag off my shoulder, as if that were some kind of big joke. (*BELINDA looks reflective for a moment.*) Come to think of it, though, he's walked past me a couple of times the past few weeks and nothing's happened.

39 JOHNNY: Well, all I can say is, I thought it was just a myth about the school bully taking your lunch, but it's true. He hasn't done it for a while, but I still bring rice cakes and celery sticks for lunch because it's the only stuff he won't try and steal from me.

40 MICKEY: Yeah, but what kind of a detective would I be if I'm **presuming** a kid is guilty instead of presuming he's innocent? Not a very good one. And Principal Abrego has been having talks with him, and she claims he's really trying hard to be less of a bully lately.

41 JOHNNY: You might be right about that, but I'd be able to bring a sandwich for lunch again if you did assume he's guilty and found the proof of it. I mean, it's Bucho we're talking about here.

42 *JOE looks over his shoulder at MICKEY and friends, smiles to himself and rubs his hands as if he's won a game of chess; he coughs into his fist: "Bucho's a loser!")*

43 MICKEY: (*turns to JOE*) I'm sorry; did you say something, Joe?

44 JOE: Who, me? Nope. You must be hearing things.

45 MICKEY: Maybe, Joe. But I thought I heard you say, "Bucho's a loser."

46 JOE: I said no such thing. Like I told you, Mickey, you must be hearing things. Get your ears checked.

Copyright © BookheadEd Learning, LLC

47 MICKEY: You're probably right. (*turns back to his friends, thinks for a split second, then turns back to JOE*) Say, Joe, why are you eating all alone? Don't you normally eat lunch with Bucho? He is your best friend, isn't he?

48 JOE: Yeah, well. . . (*JOE scans the room as if looking for somebody.*) Maybe he is and maybe he isn't. Anyway, I'll bet he's probably out marking up a wall somewhere. And I think your pals here are right: Bucho's your man. What is it they say about leopards and their dots?

49 MICKEY: Spots, Joe, you mean "spots."

50 JOE: Yeah, whatever. But like I'm saying, he's so dumb he's even signing his tags with a "B" right? (*JOE stands up and takes his tray off the table.*)

51 MICKEY: Funny way to talk about your best friend. (*JOE gives MICKEY a hard look and then departs without saying anything.*)

52 MICKEY (*turns back to his friends, thinks for a couple short beats*): Anyhow, I'd like to see Bucho gone, too, but I made a promise, Johnny. It's not so simple for me. I've got to do the job right, even if it means going against my gut instinct.

53 BELINDA: So what are you saying, Mickey? You think he's innocent? If you ask a hundred kids who they think is leaving those messages around the school, a hundred of them will say it's got to be Bucho. Who else would it be? He's probably not bullying people as much now because he has a new endeavor—writing graffiti.

54 MICKEY: But a survey isn't evidence.

55 JOHNNY: But you do have evidence, don't you? You said the principal showed you the email in which someone claimed to have seen Bucho in action, writing on the wall.

56 MICKEY: That's circumstantial. Not in the least incriminating without anything else of substance.

57 BELINDA: So, what about the letter "B" the culprit has left behind as a kind of signature—is Joe lying about that?

58 MICKEY: Also circumstantial. I mean, if a "B" is all we've got, who's to say it doesn't stand for "Belinda"? (*BELINDA looks as though she's been accused.*) Don't get me wrong—I'm not saying it's you, I'm saying a "B" is not enough to prove a guy's guilt.

59 BELINDA: Are you saying you're not willing to stand with me—(*looks at JOHNNY*) with us—and instead you're going to side with Bucho?

60   MICKEY: That's not it at all. What I'm saying is that I've got to do this the right way. I would think you'd understand that my work and doing it right are important to me.

61   BELINDA: No, Mickey. There's nothing "right" about Bucho's ugly behavior all these years. Do you really think a few weeks of acting nice can erase years of mean behavior? Whatever! It's up to you to do the right thing. (*BELINDA stands suddenly and walks away.*)

62   MICKEY: Belinda just doesn't get it, Johnny. I'm a detective; I took an oath to dig and dig until I find the truth, even if I don't like the outcome. I'm not saying it's not Bucho, it's just that I need extensive evidence to prove that it is him. (*he pauses, then looks at JOHNNY*) Besides, putting the blame on Bucho without evidence is just another form of bullying, isn't it? Only this time, we'd be the bullies. (*JOHNNY looks thoughtful and walks away.*)

63   **ACT TWO, SCENE 2:** Second lunch period. MICKEY is sitting alone, deep in thought, unaware that the bell has rung. Suddenly, BUCHO looms in front of MICKEY.

64   BUCHO: Hey, Mickey. . .I imagine Mrs. A told you the story. Somebody's trying to frame me for all this graffiti, and I bet you won't believe me, but it wasn't me. And you're the only one I trust to uncover the truth.

65   MICKEY: I told Mrs. A I would, so I'm going to help any way I can.

66   BUCHO: Ok, bro. Say, you going to eat that? (*Before MICKEY can answer, BUCHO reaches for MICKEY's brownie and swallows it in one bite; then he walks away from the table with his own tray in hand.*)

67   MICKEY: Hey, Bucho. (*BUCHO turns*) How do you spell "principal"? As in Mrs. Abrego, the school's big cheese?

68   BUCHO: First, are you kidding? What other kind of principal is there? Second, are you making fun of me? Because if you are. . .(*BUCHO shakes a fist at MICKEY, but then he thinks better of it and puts his hand down.*)

69   MICKEY: So spell it.

70   BUCHO (*scowling, exaggerating his pronunciation*): P-R-I-N-C-I-P-A-L. As in, Mrs. Abrego is our PAL. Satisfied?

71   MICKEY: Yup. (*BUCHO walks away, this time for good.*)

72   **ACT THREE:** Outside, the school playground, where PRINCIPAL ABREGO, BUCHO, and OTHERS have gathered in front of the site of the latest graffiti. BELINDA stands against a wall nearby. MICKEY enters from stage right.

73 PRINCIPAL ABREGO: There you are, Mickey. As you can see, I've asked Bucho to join us, as you requested. Can we get started now? (*Beyond PRINCIPAL ABREGO and BUCHO are a multitude of kids playing different games. Among them are JOE, who is noticeably nervous and keeping a careful eye on the developments from a safe distance, and BELINDA, who is standing against a wall nearby.*)

74 MICKEY: Sure thing. First of all, you were right. In the case of The Magic Marker Mischief Maker, someone other than Bucho is responsible for this graffiti. My first clue was the curious spelling. Only two weeks ago in English we were studying homophones. One set of words we were asked to learn included the "principal/principle" set.

75 BUCHO: Yeah, that's right. Miss Garza gave us a trick to remember how to spell it: "Mrs. Abrego, the principal, is our pal." (*BUCHO looks at MICKEY.*) Like I told you at lunch.

76 MICKEY: Exactly, but at lunch you also said, "What other kind of "principal" is there?" when in fact there are two. You had no clue about the other spelling; P-R-I-N-C-I-P-L-E, which means "a high standard that guides one's actions and reactions." You must've been looking at the insides of your eyelids when Miss Garza was going over that one.

77 BUCHO: Watch yourself.

78 PRINCIPAL ABREGO: No, watch yourself, Bernard. Mickey's trying to help, so help yourself by minding your temper.

79 BUCHO: Yes, ma'am.

80 MICKEY: *Bernard?* Really?

81 (*BUCHO scowls and tentatively takes a step in MICKEY's direction, but then he steps back.*)

82 MICKEY: Allow me to go on. If you don't know how to spell both words, much less that there are two variations, then you couldn't have written this graffiti. (*waves a hand at the wall*) This tells me that our culprit is also studying vocabulary in Miss Garza's class, though it's obvious he's not learning.

83 BUCHO: Well, spit it out: if it wasn't me, then who?

84 MICKEY: Hey, Joe, can you come here?

85 JOE (*walks over*): What's up, man? (*He refuses to acknowledge BUCHO.*)

86 MICKEY: Can you spell the word "principal" for us, as in Mrs. Abrego, our school's principal? You know, like we were supposed to have learned in Miss Garza's class.

Please note that excerpts and passages in the StudySync® library and this workbook are intended as touchstones to generate interest in an author's work. The excerpts and passages do not substitute for the reading of entire texts, and StudySync® strongly recommends that students seek out and purchase the whole literary or informational work in order to experience it as the author intended. Links to online resellers are available in our digital library. In addition, complete works may be ordered through an authorized reseller by filling out and returning to StudySync® the order form enclosed in this workbook.

Reading & Writing Companion   43

NOTES

87   JOE: Are you kidding me?

88   PRINCIPAL ABREGO: Mickey?

89   MICKEY: Ma'am? (*motions as though for support from MRS. ABREGO*)

90   PRINCIPAL ABREGO: Okay, then. Go on, Joe, do as he says.

91   JOE (*puffs his chest out proudly*): P-R-I-N-C-I-P-L-E, "principle," as in "The last thing I want is to be sent to the principle's office." Satisfied?

92   MICKEY: Quite.

93   PRINCIPAL ABREGO: Quite indeed. (*speaking to JOE*) Young man, though it's the last thing you want to do, you will follow me to my office. (*The two leave, though MRS. ABREGO does put an arm around JOE's shoulders indicating she will want to "work with" him in the same way she's been working with BUCHO.*)

94   BUCHO: Mickey, you did it! You proved my innocence!

95   MICKEY: I also proved you need to pay more attention in class.

96   BUCHO (*looks to make sure MRS. ABREGO is out of sight before taking a menacing step toward MICKEY*): Why, I oughta…

Used with permission of McGraw-Hill Education.

First Read

Read *The Magic Marker Mystery*. After you read, complete the Think Questions below.

☁ THINK QUESTIONS

1. How does Bucho's past behavior make him an easy target for the real graffiti artist? Cite textual evidence from the selection to support your answer.

2. Write two to three sentences describing how Bucho reacts to being the target of bullying. Cite textual evidence from the selection to support your answer.

3. The stage directions for Act Three say that Belinda stands "against a wall nearby." How would you explain Belinda's behavior during this scene? Cite textual evidence from the selection to support your answer.

4. Find the word **culprit** in paragraph 30 of *The Magic Marker Mystery*. Use context clues in the surrounding sentences, as well as the sentence in which the word appears, to determine the word's meaning. Write your definition here and identify clues that helped you figure out its meaning.

5. Use context clues to determine the meaning of **presuming** as it is used in paragraph 40 of *The Magic Marker Mystery*. Write your definition here and identify clues that helped you figure out its meaning. Then check the meaning in a dictionary.

Skill: Dramatic Elements and Structure

Use the Checklist to analyze Dramatic Elements and Structure in *The Magic Marker Mystery*. Refer to the sample student annotations about Dramatic Elements and Structure in the text.

••• CHECKLIST FOR DRAMATIC ELEMENTS AND STRUCTURE

In order to identify the dramatic elements and structure of a play, note the following:

- ✓ the order of acts and scenes in the play

- ✓ what happens in each act and scene

- ✓ how the acts and scenes work together to develop the plot

- ✓ the setting of the play and how it changes by act and scene

- ✓ the information in stage directions, including lighting, sound, and set, as well as details about characters, including exits and entrances

To analyze how a particular scene fits into the overall structure of a text and contributes to the development of the theme, setting, or plot, consider the following questions:

- ✓ When does this particular scene appear?

- ✓ How does this scene fit into the overall structure of the text?

- ✓ How do setting, characters, and other elements in the scene contribute to the development of the plot?

- ✓ What does the scene contribute to the theme or message of the drama?

Skill: Dramatic Elements and Structure

Reread paragraphs 75–92 from Act Three of *The Magic Marker Mystery*. Then, using the Checklist on the previous page, answer the multiple-choice questions below.

⟳ YOUR TURN

1. Why is mentioning the conversation in the lunchroom (paragraphs 75–76) important to the plot?

   ○ A. Mickey understands that Bucho never pays attention in class.
   ○ B. Mickey is able to grasp that Bucho is not the guilty party.
   ○ C. Bucho realizes that Mickey is attempting to make fun of him.
   ○ D. Bucho admires Mickey's thorough detective skills.

2. What does the dialogue exchanged between Mickey and Principal Abrego in paragraphs 88–90 reveal about the plot?

   ○ A. Principal Abrego is upset with Mickey for overstepping his authority in the situation.
   ○ B. Principal Abrego shows amazement at Mickey's detective skills.
   ○ C. Mickey checks in with Principal Abrego when he needs help solving the case.
   ○ D. Mickey is disappointed that Principal Abrego doesn't trust him to solve the case.

3. In the drama, Mickey asks Joe to spell the word "principal." What does the dialogue exchanged between Mickey and Joe in paragraphs 84–92 reveal about the plot?

   ○ A. Joe admires Miss Garza's clever vocabulary tricks.
   ○ B. Joe makes fun of Mickey for being called to the principal's office.
   ○ C. Joe is a top vocabulary student in Miss Garza's class.
   ○ D. Joe is the culprit because this spelling matches the graffiti.

Close Read

Reread *The Magic Marker Mystery*. As you reread, complete the Skills Focus questions below. Then use your answers and annotations from the questions to help you complete the Write activity.

◎ SKILLS FOCUS

1. Identify a scene or line of dialogue in Act 1 that helps to develop or move the plot forward.

2. Identify how the other characters feel about Bucho in Act Two, Scene 1.

3. Identify lines of dialogue or stage directions that show Bucho's attempt to change from being a bully.

4. Think about the challenges the characters face in *The Magic Marker Mystery*. Identify the challenges and what the characters choose to do about it.

✏ WRITE

LITERARY ANALYSIS: Think about how the playwright uses specific scenes to develop the plot. How would Act Three of *The Magic Marker Mystery* be different if it gave more insight into a particular character's perspective, perhaps through details or stage directions? In your response, indicate how this would affect the development of the play as a whole. Support your writing with specific evidence from the text.

Scout's Honor

FICTION
Avi
1996

Introduction

Avi is the pen name of Edward Irving Wortis (b. 1937), the Newbery Medal-winning author of more than 75 books for children and young adults. Avi was born and raised in New York City, and his childhood and adolescence were an inspiration for many of his stories and books. "Scout's Honor," presented here, is the humorous story of a nine-year-old boy and his Boy Scout friends who set out to the New Jersey "wilderness" to prove their toughness. Avi's body of work spans many genres, from historical fiction to graphic novels. Yet his stories and books are united by their relatable and evocative depictions of young people in challenging circumstances, struggling to learn and grow.

"The way they agreed made me nervous. Now I really was going to have to be tough."

NOTES

Skill: Story Structure

These sentences tell me that this story will be about an overnight camping adventure. It will be a new experience for the narrator since he will be leaving Brooklyn for the first time, without adult supervision.

This sentence in paragraph 2 tells me that the setting plays an important role in the story. It will probably have an effect on what happens to the boys because the narrator isn't used to the country.

1   Back in 1946, when I was nine, I worried that I wasn't tough enough. That's why I became a Boy Scout. Scouting, I thought, would make a man of me. It didn't take long to reach Tenderfoot rank. You got that for joining. To move up to Second Class, however, you had to meet three requirements. Scout Spirit and Scout Participation had been cinchy. The third requirement, Scout Craft, meant I had to go on an overnight hike in the *country*. In other words, I had to leave Brooklyn, on my own, for the first time in my life.

2   Since I grew up in Brooklyn in the 1940s, the only grass I knew was in Ebbets Field where the Dodgers played. Otherwise, my world was made of slate pavements, streets of asphalt (or cobblestone), and skies full of tall buildings. The only thing "country" was a puny pin oak tree at our curb, which was noticed, mostly, by dogs.

3   I asked Scoutmaster Brenkman where I could find some country. Now, whenever I saw Mr. Brenkman, who was a church pastor, he was dressed in either church black or Scout khaki. When he wore black, he'd warn us against hellfire. When he wore khaki, he'd teach us how to build fires.

4   "Country," Scoutmaster Brenkman said in answer to my question, "is anywhere that has lots of trees and is not the city. Many boys camp in the Palisades."

5   "Where's that?"

6   "Just north of the city. It's a park in Jersey."

7   "Isn't that a zillion miles from here?"

8   "Take the subway to the George Washington Bridge, then hike across."

9   I thought for a moment, then asked, "How do I prove I went?"

10   Mr. Brenkman looked deeply shocked. "You wouldn't *lie*, would you? What about Scout's honor?"

11   "Yes, sir," I replied meekly.

12　My two best friends were Philip Hossfender, whom we nicknamed Horse, and Richard Macht, called Max because we were not great spellers. They were also Scouts, Tenderfoots like me.

13　Horse was a skinny little kid about half my size whose way of arguing was to ball up his fist and say, "Are you saying. . .?" in a threatening tone.

14　Max was on the pudgy side, but he could talk his way out of a locked room. More importantly, he always seemed to have pocket money, which gave his talk real power.

15　I wasn't sure why, but being best friends meant we were rivals too. One of the reasons for my wanting to be tougher was a feeling that Horse was a lot tougher than I was, and that Max was a little tougher.

16　"I'm going camping in the Palisades next weekend," I casually informed them.

17　"How come?" Max challenged.

18　"Scout Craft," I replied.

19　"Oh, *that,*" Horse said with a shrug.

20　"Look," I said, "I don't know about you, but I don't intend to be a Tenderfoot all my life. Anyway, doing stuff in the city is for sissies. Scouting is real camping. Besides, I like roughing it."

21　"You saying I don't?" Horse snapped.

22　"I'm not saying nothing," I said.

23　They considered my idea. Finally, Horse said, "Yeah, well, I was going to do that, but I didn't think you guys were ready for it."

24　"I've been ready for *years,*" Max protested.

25　"Then we're going, right?" I said.

26　They looked around at me. "If you can do it, I can do it," Max said.

27　"Yeah," Horse said thoughtfully.

28　The way they agreed made me nervous. Now I really was going to have to be tough.

29　We informed our folks that we were going camping overnight (which was true) and that the Scoutmaster was going with us—which was a lie. We did remember what Mr. Brenkman said about honesty, but we were baseball fans too, and since we were prepared to follow Scout law—being loyal, helpful, friendly, **courteous,** kind, obedient, cheerful, thrifty, brave, clean *and* reverent—we figured a 900 batting average was not bad.

NOTES

Skill:
Plot

These early paragraphs tell me that the plot will involve friends who are trying to prove they're tough. I think it is the inciting incident because it seems to set up the rest of the story.

Please note that excerpts and passages in the StudySync® library and this workbook are intended as touchstones to generate interest in an author's work. The excerpts and passages do not substitute for the reading of entire texts, and StudySync® strongly recommends that students seek out and purchase the whole literary or informational work in order to experience it as the author intended. Links to online resellers are available in our digital library. In addition, complete works may be ordered through an authorized reseller by filling out and returning to StudySync® the order form enclosed in this workbook.

NOTES

30 So Saturday morning we met at the High Street subway station. I got there first. Stuffed in my dad's army surplus knapsack was a blanket, a pillow, and a paper bag with three white-bread peanut-butter-and-jelly sandwiches—that is, lunch, supper, and Sunday breakfast. My pockets were full of stick matches. I had an old flashlight, and since I lived by the Scout motto—Be Prepared—I had brought along an umbrella. Finally, being a serious reader, I had the latest Marvel Family comics.

31 Horse arrived next, his arms barely managing to hold on to a mattress that seemed twice his size. As for food, he had four cans of beans jammed into his pockets.

32 Max came last. He was lugging a new knapsack that contained a cast-iron frying pan, a packet of hot dogs, and a box of saltine crackers—plus two bottles. One bottle was mustard, the other, celery soda. He also had a bag of Tootsie Rolls and a shiny hatchet. "To build a lean-to," he explained.

33 Max's prize **possession,** however, was an official Scout compass. "It's really swell," he told us. "You can't ever get lost with it. Got it at the Scout store."

34 "I hate that place," Horse informed us. "It's all new. Nothing real."

35 "This compass is real," Max retorted. "Points north all the time. You can get cheaper ones, but they point all different directions."

36 "What's so great about the north?" Horse said.

37 "That's always the way to go," Max insisted.

38 "Says who?" I demanded.

39 "Mr. Brenkman, dummy," Horse cried. "Anyway, there's always an arrow on maps pointing the way north."

40 "Cowboys live out west," I reminded them. They didn't care.

41 On the subway platform, we realized we did not know which station we were heading for. To find out, we studied the system map, which looked like a noodle factory hit by a bomb. The place we wanted to go (north) was at the top of the map, so I had to hoist Horse onto my shoulders for a closer look. Since he refused to let go of his mattress—or the tin cans in his pockets—it wasn't easy. I asked him—in a kindly fashion—to put the mattress down.

42 No sooner did he find the station—168th Street—than our train arrived. We rushed on, only to have Horse scream, "My mattress!" He had left it on the platform. Just before the doors shut, he and I leaped off. Max, however, remained on the train. Helplessly, we watched as his horror-stricken face slid away from us. "Wait at the next station!" I bellowed. "Don't move!"

43 The next train took forever to come. Then it took even longer to get to the next stop. There was Max. All around him—like fake snow in a glass ball—were crumbs. He'd been so nervous he had eaten all his crackers.

44 "Didn't that make you thirsty?"

45 "I drank my soda."

46 I noticed streaks down his cheeks. Horse noticed them too. "You been crying?" he asked.

47 "Naw," Max said. "There was this water dripping from the tunnel roof. But, you said don't move, right? Well, I was just being obedient."

48 By the time we got on the next train—with all our possessions—we had been traveling for an hour. But we had managed to go only one stop.

49 During the ride, I got hungry. I pulled out one of my sandwiches. With the jelly soaked through the bread, it looked like a limp scab.

50 Horse, **envious,** complained *he* was getting hungry.

51 "Eat some of your canned beans," I suggested.

52 He got out one can without ripping his pocket too badly. Then his face took on a mournful look.

53 "What's the matter?" I asked.

54 "Forgot to bring a can opener."

55 Max said, "In the old days, people opened cans with their teeth."

56 "You saying my teeth aren't strong?"

57 "I'm just talking about history!"

58 "You saying I don't know history?"

59 Always kind, I plopped half my sandwich into Horse's hand. He squashed it into his mouth and was quiet for the next fifteen minutes. It proved something I'd always believed: The best way to stop arguments is to get people to eat peanut butter sandwiches. They can't talk.

60 Then we became so **absorbed** in our Marvel Family comics we missed our station. We got to it only by coming back the other way. When we reached street level, the sky was dark.

61 "I knew it," Max announced. "It's going to rain."

Skill:
Plot

I see that the boys' adventure is going from bad to worse. Max began by being brave, but now I see that he has been crying. This is the conflict, and it suggests to me that there will be more challenges ahead before a resolution is reached.

NOTES

62 "Don't worry," Horse said. "New Jersey is a whole other state. It probably won't be raining there."

63 "I brought an umbrella," I said smugly, though I wanted it to sound helpful.

64 As we marched down 168th Street, heading for the George Washington Bridge, we looked like European war refugees. Every few paces, Horse cried, "Hold it!" and adjusted his arms around his mattress. Each time we paused, Max pulled out his compass, peered at it, then announced, "Heading north!"

65 I said, "The bridge goes from east to west."

66 "Maybe the bridge does," Max insisted with a show of his compass, "but guaranteed, *we* are going north."

67 About then, the heel of my left foot, encased in a heavy rubber boot over an earth-crushing Buster Brown shoe, started to get sore. Things weren't going as I had hoped. Cheerfully, I tried to ignore the pain.

68 The closer we drew to the bridge, the more **immense** it seemed. And the clouds had become so thick, you couldn't see the top of the far side.

69 Max eyed the bridge with deep suspicion. "I'm not so sure we should go," he said.

70 "Why?"

71 "Maybe it doesn't have another side."

72 We looked at him.

73 "No, seriously," Max explained, "they could have taken the Jersey side away, you know, for repairs."

74 "Cars are going across," I pointed out.

75 "They could be dropping off," he suggested.

76 "You would hear them splash," Horse argued.

77 "I'm going," I said. Trying to look brave, I started off on my own. My bravery didn't last for long. The walkway was narrow. When I looked down, I saw only fog. I could feel the bridge tremble and sway. It wasn't long before I was convinced the bridge was about to collapse. Then a ray of hope struck me: Maybe the other guys had chickened out. If they had, I could quit because of *them*. I glanced back. My heart sank. They were coming.

78 After they caught up, Horse looked me in the eye and said, "If this bridge falls, I'm going to kill you."

Skill: Story Structure

I think the boys are trying to prove that they're tough. I think this event is important to the theme since the narrator wants to prove he's brave in front of his friends. I wonder if this attitude will continue throughout the whole story.

NOTES

79 A quarter of a mile farther across, I gazed around. We were completely fogged in.

80 "I think we're lost," I announced.

81 "What do we do?" Horse whispered. His voice was jagged with panic. That made me feel better.

82 "Don't worry," Max said. "I've got my compass." He pulled it out. "North is that way," he said, pointing in the direction we had been going.

83 Horse said, "You sure?"

84 "A Scout compass never lies," Max insisted.

85 "*We* lied," I reminded him.

86 "Yeah, but this is an *official* Scout compass," Max returned loyally.

87 "Come on," Max said and marched forward. Horse and I followed. In moments, we crossed a metal bar on the walkway. On one side, a sign proclaimed: NEW YORK; on the other, it said: NEW JERSEY.

88 "Holy smoke," Horse said with reverence as he straddled the bar. "Talk about being tough. We're in two states at the same time."

89 It began to rain. Max said, "Maybe it'll keep us clean."

90 "You saying I'm not clean?" Horse shot back.

91 Ever friendly, I put up my umbrella.

92 We went on—Max on one side, Horse on the other, me in the middle—trying to avoid the growing puddles. After a while, Max said, "Would you move the umbrella? Rain is coming down my neck."

93 "We're supposed to be roughing it," I said.

94 "Being in the middle isn't roughing it," Horse reminded me.

95 I folded the umbrella up so we could all get soaked equally.

96 "Hey!" I cried. "Look!" Staring up ahead, I could make out tollbooths and the dim outlines of buildings.

97 "Last one off the bridge is a rotten egg!" Horse shouted and began to run. The next second, he tripped and took off like an F-36 fighter plane. Unfortunately, he landed like a Hell-cat dive-bomber as his mattress unspooled before him and then slammed into a big puddle.

98 Max and I ran to help. Horse was damp. His mattress was soaked. When he tried to roll it up, water cascaded like Niagara Falls.

99 "Better leave it," Max said.

100 "It's what I sleep on at home," Horse said as he slung the soaking, dripping mass over his shoulder.

101 When we got off the bridge, we were in a small plaza. To the left was the roadway, full of roaring cars. In front of us, aside from the highway, there was nothing but buildings. Only to the right were there trees.

102 "North is that way," Max said, pointing toward the trees. We set off.

103 "How come you're limping?" Horse asked me. My foot *was* killing me. All I said, though, was, "How come you keep rubbing your arm?"

104 "I'm keeping the blood moving."

105 We **approached** a grove of trees. "Wow," Horse exclaimed. "Country." But as we drew closer, what we found were discarded cans, bottles, and newspapers—plus an old mattress spring.

106 "Hey," Max cried, sounding relieved, "this is just like Brooklyn."

107 I said, "Let's find a decent place, make camp, and eat."

108 It was hard to find a campsite that didn't have junk. The growing dark didn't help. We had to settle for the place that had the least amount of garbage.

109 Max said, "If we build a lean-to, it'll keep us out of the rain." He and Horse went a short distance with the hatchet.

110 Seeing a tree they wanted, Max whacked at it. The hatchet bounced right out of his hand. There was not even a dent in the tree. Horse retrieved the hatchet and checked the blade. "Dull," he said.

111 "Think I'm going to carry something sharp and cut myself?" Max protested. They contented themselves with picking up branches.

112 I went in search of firewood, but everything was wet. When I finally gathered some twigs and tried to light them, the only thing that burned was my fingers.

113 Meanwhile, Horse and Max used their branches to build a lean-to directly over me. After many collapses—which didn't help my work—they finally got the branches to stand in a shaky sort of way.

114 "Uh-oh," Horse said. "We forgot to bring something for a cover."

115 Max eyed me. "Didn't you say you brought a blanket?"

NOTES

116   "No way!" I cried.

117   "All in favor of using the blanket!"

118   Horse and Max both cried, "Aye."

119   Only after I built up a mound of partially burned match sticks and lit *them*, did I get the fire going. It proved that where there's smoke there doesn't have to be much fire. The guys meanwhile draped my blanket over their branch construction. It collapsed twice.

120   About an hour after our arrival, the three of us were gathered inside the tiny space. There was a small fire, but more light came from my flickering flashlight.

121   "No more rain," Horse said with pride.

122   "Just smoke," I said, rubbing my stinging eyes.

123   "We need a vent hole," Horse pointed out.

124   "I could cut it with the hatchet," Max said.

125   "It's my mother's favorite blanket."

126   "And you took it?" Max said.

127   I nodded.

128   "You *are* tough," Horse said.

129   Besides having too much smoke in our eyes and being wet, tired, and in pain, we were starving. I almost said something about giving up, but as far as I could see, the other guys were still tough.

130   Max put his frying pan atop my smoldering smoke. After dumping in the entire contents of his mustard bottle, he threw in the franks. Meanwhile, I bolted down my last sandwich.

131   "What am I going to eat?" Horse suddenly said.

132   "Your beans," I reminded him.

133   Max offered up his hatchet. "Here. Just chop off the top end of the can."

134   "Oh, right," Horse said. He selected a can, set it in front of him, levered himself onto his knees, then swung down—hard. There was an explosion. For a stunned moment, we just sat there, hands, face, and clothing dripping with beans.

135   Suddenly Max shouted, "Food fight! Food fight!" and began to paw the stuff off and fling it around.

136   Having a food fight in a cafeteria is one thing. Having one in the middle of a soaking wet lean-to with cold beans during a dark, wet New Jersey night is another. In seconds, the lean-to was down, the fire kicked over, and Max's frankfurters dumped on the ground.

137   "The food!" Max screamed, and began to snatch up the franks. Coated with mustard, dirt, grass, and leaves, they looked positively prehistoric. Still, we wiped the franks clean on our pants then ate them—the franks, that is. Afterward, we picked beans off each other's clothes—the way monkeys help friends get rid of lice.

138   For dessert, Max shared some Tootsie Rolls. After Horse swallowed his sixteenth piece, he announced, "I don't feel so good."

139   The thought of his getting sick was too much. "Let's go home," I said, ashamed to look at the others. To my surprise—and relief—nobody objected.

140   Wet and cold, our way lit by my fast-fading flashlight, we gathered our belongings—most of them, anyway. As we made our way back over the bridge, gusts of wind-blown rain pummeled us until I felt like a used-up punching bag. By the time we got to the subway station, my legs were melting fast. The other guys looked bad too. Other riders moved away from us. One of them murmured, "Juvenile delinquents." To cheer us up, I got out my comic books, but they had congealed into a lump of red, white, and blue pulp.

141   With the subways running slow, it took hours to get home. When we emerged from the High Street Station, it was close to midnight.

142   Before we split up to go to our own homes, we just stood there on a street corner, embarrassed, trying to figure out how to end the day gracefully. I was the one who said, "Okay, I admit it. I'm not as tough as you guys. I gave up first."

143   Max shook his head. "Naw. I wanted to quit, but I wasn't tough enough to do it." He looked to Horse.

144   Horse made a fist. "You saying I'm the one who's tough?" he demanded. "I hate roughing it!"

145   "Me too," I said quickly.

146   "Same for me," Max said.

147   Horse said, "Only thing is, we just have to promise not to tell Mr. Brenkman."

148 Grinning with relief, we **simultaneously** clasped hands. "No matter what," Max reminded us.

149 To which I added, "Scout's Honor."

"Scout's Honor" by Avi. Copyright ©1996 by Avi. Originally appeared in WHEN I WAS YOUR AGE: Original Stories About Growing Up, published by Candlewick Press. Used by permission of Brandt & Hochman Literary Agents, Inc. All rights reserved.

First Read

Read "Scout's Honor." After you read, complete the Think Questions below.

☁ THINK QUESTIONS

1. Where did the narrator grow up? How does that influence his idea of the "country"? Cite textual evidence from the selection to support your answer.

2. What happens to Max on the subway? What does the event reveal about their friendship?

3. How do Max and Horse react when the narrator suggests they head back home? Why does this surprise the narrator? Cite textual evidence from the selection to support your answer.

4. Find the word **absorbed** in paragraph 60 of "Scout's Honor." Use context clues in the surrounding sentences, as well as the sentence in which it appears, to determine the word's meaning. Write your definition here and identify clues that helped you figure out its meaning.

5. Use context clues to determine the meaning of **simultaneously** as it is used in paragraph 148 of "Scout's Honor." Write your definition here and identify clues that helped you figure out its meaning. Then check the meaning in a dictionary.

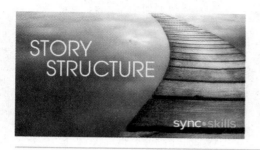

Skill:
Story Structure

Use the Checklist to analyze Story Structure in "Scout's Honor." Refer to the sample student annotations about Story Structure in the text.

••• CHECKLIST FOR STORY STRUCTURE

In order to identify how a particular sentence, chapter, or scene fits into the overall structure of a text, note the following:

✓ the author's use of description, dialogue, and narration and how each develops the events of the plot

✓ the pattern the author uses to organize the events within a story or chapter

  • chronological, or in time order

  • events out of time order

✓ any literary devices the author uses, such as flashback, a part of a story that shows something that happened in the past

✓ any particular sentence, chapter, or scene that contributes to the development of the setting, the plot, and the theme

✓ how a particular sentence, chapter, or scene fits into the overall structure

To analyze how a particular sentence, chapter, or scene fits into the overall structure of a text and contributes to the development of the theme, setting, or plot, consider the following questions:

✓ What are the key events in the story and when did they take place?

✓ What impact does the order of events that take place in the story have on the theme, setting, or plot?

✓ What literary devices does the author use? How do they affect the development of the plot?

✓ How does a particular sentence, chapter, or scene fit into the overall structure? How does it contribute to the development of the theme, setting, or plot?

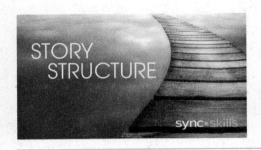

Skill:
Story Structure

Reread paragraphs 80–98 of "Scout's Honor." Then, using the Checklist on the previous page, answer the multiple-choice questions below.

🔄 YOUR TURN

1. Reread paragraph 81. Based on this paragraph, what can the reader conclude about the narrator?

   ○ A. The narrator is irritated with Horse because he does not know how to proceed bravely in this situation.

   ○ B. Although he attempts to be brave, the narrator is still feeling anxious about the journey to the country.

   ○ C. The narrator understands that Horse is unable to stay calm and tries to comfort him in his time of need.

   ○ D. Horse's anxiety creates a sense of tension between the boys, thus the narrator is unsettled.

2. Which of the following best describes the theme based on the passage provided?

   ○ A. Desperate times call for desperate measures.

   ○ B. In dark times, friends can offer the best support.

   ○ C. Blindly following others can cause trouble.

   ○ D. In life, we sometimes take on more than we can handle.

3. How does this passage contribute to the rest of the story's plot?

   ○ A. The events in the passage highlight the turning point of the plot because the boys are afraid.

   ○ B. The dialogue in the passage conveys a sense of urgency because the boys are not sure they will survive.

   ○ C. The passage emphasizes key, humbling events in the story that support the overall theme.

   ○ D. The narration in the passage highlights a dark tone that is maintained throughout the plot.

PLOT

Skill:
Plot

Use the Checklist to analyze Plot in "Scout's Honor." Refer to the sample student annotations about Plot in the text.

••• CHECKLIST FOR PLOT

In order to determine the plot and how a particular story's or drama's plot unfolds, note the following:

- ✓ specific plot events as they occur in the story

- ✓ the series of episodes as they occur

- ✓ ways characters respond or change as the plot moves toward a resolution

- ✓ dialogue between or among characters or actions that reveal their growth or change

To describe how a particular story's or drama's plot unfolds in a series of episodes as well as how the characters respond or change as the plot moves toward a resolution, consider the following questions:

- ✓ What is the plot? What are the key events in the plot?

- ✓ How does the series of episodes in the story help the plot unfold?

- ✓ How do the characters respond or change as the plot moves through the conflict and toward a resolution?

PLOT

Skill:
Plot

Reread paragraphs 129–139 from the text. Then, using the Checklist on the previous page, answer the multiple-choice questions below.

⟲ YOUR TURN

1. Based on the narrator's thoughts in paragraph 129, the reader can conclude that —

   ○ A. the narrator's friends are close to giving up.
   ○ B. the narrator still doesn't think he's tough enough.
   ○ C. the boys are out of food.
   ○ D. the narrator is going to tell his friends that he gives up and wants to go home.

2. The turning point of the story is when —

   ○ A. Max shouts "food fight!"
   ○ B. the lean-to is knocked down.
   ○ C. the can of beans explodes all over them.
   ○ D. the boys eat the dirty franks.

3. Which paragraph includes the resolution of the story's conflict?

   ○ A. 138
   ○ B. 136
   ○ C. 139
   ○ D. 135

Close Read

Reread "Scout's Honor." As you reread, complete the Skills Focus questions below. Then use your answers and annotations from the questions to help you complete the Write activity.

◎ SKILLS FOCUS

1. Think about how the narrator reacts to the challenges the characters face. Identify what these reactions tell you about his personality.

2. Think about the beginning of the "Scout's Honor" when the narrator tells his friends he's going camping. Using textual evidence, explain why this scene is important to the rest of the story.

3. How boys can prove they are tough: this is the central conflict of Avi's story. Identify how each character reacts to key events in the plot as the

boys try to resolve the conflict through their camping trip.

4. Use key events, including the inciting incident and moments of conflict, to determine how the resolution of the conflict contributes to the meaning of the story.

5. Identify how the development of the characters and plot in "Scout's Honor" connects to the Essential Question: "What do we do when life gets hard?"

✏ WRITE

LITERARY ANALYSIS: There are many challenges in "Scout's Honor" that the boys face. How do the characters' responses to these challenges help develop the plot and help readers interpret the events in the plot—such as the inciting incident, conflict, turning point and resolution—as they take place? Support your writing with evidence from the text.

Please note that excerpts and passages in the StudySync® library and this workbook are intended as touchstones to generate interest in an author's work. The excerpts and passages do not substitute for the reading of entire texts, and StudySync® strongly recommends that students seek out and purchase the whole literary or informational work in order to experience it as the author intended. Links to online resellers are available in our digital library. In addition, complete works may be ordered through an authorized reseller by filling out and returning to StudySync® the order form enclosed in this workbook.

Reading & Writing Companion   **65**

The Good Samaritan

FICTION
René Saldaña, Jr.
2007

Introduction

René Saldaña, Jr.'s 2003 collection of short stories, *Finding Our Way*, features adolescents and young adults searching for answers wherever they are to be found. Encompassing universal experiences and rites of passage, Saldaña, Jr.'s stories take place in Hispanic neighborhoods ranging from Georgia to the south of Texas, where the author was born and raised. The collection's opening story, "The Good Samaritan," is told through the eyes of teenage Rey. As Rey's relationship with a neighborhood family turns sour, he soon finds himself faced with an age-old

"Let him do his own dirty work for once. He could stay out there and melt in this heat for all I cared."

1   I know he's in there, I thought. I saw the curtains of his bedroom move, only a little, yes, but they moved.

2   Yesterday Orlie told me, "Come over tomorrow afternoon. We'll hang out by the pool."

3   I rang the doorbell again. Then I knocked.

4   The door creaked open. The afternoon light crept into the dark living room inch by slow inch. Mrs. Sánchez, Orlie's mom, stuck her head through the narrow opening, her body hidden behind the door. "Hi, Rey, how can I help you?"

5   "Ah, Mrs. Sánchez, is Orlando here?" I tried looking past her but only saw a few pictures hanging on the wall. One of the Sánchez family all dressed up fancy and smiling, standing in front of a gray marble background.

6   "No, he's not. He went with his father to Mission."

7   "Oh, because Orlando said he would be here, and told me to come over."

8   "They won't be back until later tonight," she said. "You can come by tomorrow and see if he's here. You know how it is in the summer. He and his dad are always doing work here and there. Come back tomorrow, but call first."

9   "It's just that he said I could come by and swim in your pool. Dijo, 'Tomorrow, come over. I'll be here. We'll go swimming.'"

10 "I'm sorry he told you that, but without him or my husband here, you won't be able to use the pool," me dijo Mrs. Sánchez.

11 "Okay," I said.

12 "Maybe tomorrow?"

13 "Yeah, maybe."

14 But there was no maybe about it. I wouldn't be coming back. Because I knew that Orlando was in the house, he just didn't want to hang out. Bien codo con

su pool. Plain stingy. And tricky. This guy invited me and a few others over all summer to help his dad with some yard work because Mr. Sánchez told us, "If you help clean up the yard, you boys can use the pool any time you want so long as one of us is here." And we cleaned up his yard. On that hot day the water that smelled of chlorine looked delicious to me. And after a hard day's work cleaning his yard, I so looked forward to taking a dip. I'd even worn my trunks under my work clothes. Then Mr. Sánchez said, "Come by tomorrow. I don't want you fellas to track all this dirt into the pool."

15   "We can go home and shower and be back," said Hernando.

16   "No, mejor que regresen mañana. I'll be here tomorrow and we can swim. After lunch, okay. For sure we'll do it tomorrow," said Mr. Sánchez.

**Skill:
Summarizing**

Rey recalls that he and his friends have been taken advantage of by Mr. Sánchez in the past.

The setting is a yard opposite Mr. Sánchez's house. It is so untidy and overgrown that Mr. Sánchez is afraid it will shame him in front of his guests.

Rey explains that he and his friends were promised a reward for their efforts, but the reward was smaller than Mr. Sánchez promised. They had to share a snack meant for a few people between the ten of them.

17   The following day he was there, but he was headed out right after lunch and he didn't feel safe leaving us behind without **supervision.** "If one of you drowns, your parents will be angry at me and…" He didn't say it, but he didn't need to. One of our parents could sue him. And he needed that like I needed another F in my Geometry I class!

18   Or, we figured out later, he could have just said, "I used you saps to do my dirty work. And I lied about the pool, suckers!"

19   I don't know why we hadn't learned our lesson. Twice before he had **hustled** us this way of our time and effort. Always dangling the carrot in front of our eyes, then snatching it away last second.

20   One of those times he promised us soft drinks and snacks if we helped clean up a yard across the street from his house. It wasn't his yard to worry about, but I guess he just didn't like to see the weeds growing as tall as dogs. What if he had company? What would they think? And he was angling for a position on the school board. How could a politico live in such filth!

21   Well, we did get a soft drink and chips, only it was one two-liter bottle of Coke and one bag of chips for close to ten of us. We had no cups, and the older, stronger boys got dibs on most of the eats. "I didn't know there'd be so many of you," he said. "Well, share. And thanks. You all are good, strong boys."

22   The next time was real hard **labor.** He said, "Help me dig these holes here, then we can put up some basketball rims. Once the cement dries on the court itself, you all can come over and play anytime since it's kind of your court too. That is, if you help me dig the holes."

23   And we did. We dug and dug and dug for close to six hours straight until we got done, passing on the shovel from one of us to the next. But we got it done. We had our court. Mr. Sánchez kept his word. He reminded us we could come over to play anytime, and we took special care not to dunk and grab hold of the rim. Even the shortest kid could practically dunk it because

the baskets were so low. But we'd seen the rims all bent down at the different yards at school. And we didn't want that for our court.

24   One day, we wanted to play a little three on three. After knocking on the different doors several times and getting no answer, we figured the Sánchez family had gone out. We decided that it'd be okay to play. We weren't going to do anything wrong. The court was far enough from the house that we couldn't possibly break a window. And Mr. Sánchez had said we could come over any time we wanted. It was our court, after all. Those were his words exactly.

25   A little later in the afternoon, Mr. Sánchez drove up in his truck, honking and honking at us. "Here they come. Maybe Orlando and Marty can play with us," someone said.

26   Pues, it was not to be. The truck had just come to a standstill when Mr. Sánchez shot out of the driver's side. He ran up to us, waving his hands in the air like a crazy man, first saying, then screaming, "What are you guys doing here? You all can't be here when I'm not here."

27   "But you told us we could come over anytime. And we knocked and knocked, and we were being very careful.'

28   "It doesn't matter. You all shouldn't be here when I'm not home. What if you had broken something?" he said.

29   "But we didn't," I said.

30   "But if you had, then who would have been responsible for paying to replace it? I'm sure every one of you would have denied breaking anything."

31   "Este vato!" said Hernando.

32   "Vato? Is that what you called me? I'm no street punk, no hoodlum. I'll have you know, I've worked my whole life, and I won't be called a vato. It's Mr. Sánchez. Got that? And you boys know what—from now on, you are not allowed to come here whether I'm home or not! You all messed it up for yourselves. You've shown me so much disrespect today you don't deserve to play on my court. It was a **privilege** and not a right, and you messed it up. Now leave!"

33   Hernando, who was fuming, said, "Orale, guys, let's go." He took the ball from one of the smaller boys and began to run toward the nearest basket. He slowed down the closer he came to the basket and leapt in the air. I'd never seen him jump with such grace. He floated from the foul line, his long hair like wings, all the way to the basket. He grabbed the ball in both his hands and let go of it at the last moment. Instead of dunking the ball, he let it shoot up to the sky; then he wrapped his fingers around the rim and pulled down as hard as

Skill:
Summarizing

Mr. Sánchez angrily kicks the boys off the basketball court. He feels disrespected. Mr. Sánchez says the boys were wrong to let themselves onto his property when he wasn't home.

he could, hanging on for a few seconds. Then the rest of us walked after him, dejected. He hadn't bent the rim even a millimeter. Eventually Orlie talked us into going back when his dad wasn't home. His baby brother, Marty, was small and slow, and Orlie wanted some competition on the court.

34 Today was it for me, though. I made up my mind never to go back to the Sánchezes'. I walked to the little store for a Fanta Orange. That and a grape Popsicle would cool me down. I sat on the bench outside, finished off the drink, returned the bottle for my nickel refund, and headed for home.

35 As soon as I walked through our front door, my mother said, "Mi'jo, you need to go pick up your brother at summer school. He missed the bus."

36 "Again? He probably missed it on purpose, Ama. He's always walking over to Leo's Grocery to talk to his little girlfriends, then he calls when he needs a ride." I turned toward the bedroom.

37 "Come back here," she said. So I turned and took a seat at the table. "Have you forgotten the times we had to go pick you up? Your brother always went with us, no matter what time it was."

38 "Yeah, but I was doing school stuff. Football, band. He's in summer school just piddling his time away!"

39 She looked at me as she brushed sweat away from her face with the back of her hand and said, "Just go pick him up, and hurry home. On the way back, stop at Circle Seven and buy some tortillas. There's money on the table."

40 I shook my head in disgust. Here I was, already a senior, having to be my baby brother's chauffeur.

41 I'd driven halfway to Leo's Grocery when I saw Mr. Sánchez's truck up ahead by the side of the road. I could just make him out sitting under the shade of his truck. Every time he heard a car coming his way, he'd raise his head slightly, try to catch the driver's attention by staring at him, then he'd hang his head again when the car didn't stop.

42 I slowed down as I **approached.** Could he tell it was me driving? When he looked up at my car, I could swear he almost smiled, thinking he had been saved. He had been leaning his head between his bent knees, and I could tell he was tired; his white shirt stuck to him because of all the sweat. His sock on one leg was bunched up at his ankle like a carnation. He had the whitest legs I'd ever seen on a Mexican. Whiter than even my dad's. I kept on looking straight; that is, I made like I was looking ahead, not a care in the world, but out of the corner of my eye I saw that he had a flat tire, that he had gotten two of the lug nuts off but hadn't gotten to the others, that the crowbar lay half on his other foot and half on the ground beside him, that his hair was matted by sweat to his forehead.

43   I knew that look. I'd probably looked just like that digging those holes for our basketball court, cleaning up his yard and the one across the street from his house. I wondered if he could use a cold two-liter Coke right about now! If he was dreaming of taking a dip in his pool!

44   I drove on. No way was I going to help him out again! Let him do his own dirty work for once. He could stay out there and melt in this heat for all I cared. And besides, someone else will stop, I thought. Someone who doesn't know him like I do.

45   And I knew that when Mr. Sánchez got home, he'd stop at my house on his walk around the barrio. My dad would be watering the plants, his evening ritual to relax from a hard day at work, and Mr. Sánchez would mention in passing that I had probably not seen him by the side of the road so I hadn't stopped to help him out; "Kids today" he would say to my dad, "not a care in the world, their heads up in the clouds somewhere." My dad would call me out and ask me to tell him and Mr. Sánchez why I hadn't helped out a neighbor when he needed it most. I'd say, to both of them, "That was you? I thought you and Orlie were in Mission taking care of some business, so it never **occurred** to me to stop to help a neighbor. Geez, I'm so sorry." Or I could say, "You know, I was in such a hurry to pick up my brother in La Joya that I didn't even notice you by the side of the road."

46   I'd be off the hook. Anyways, why should I be the one to extend a helping hand when he's done every one of us in the barrio wrong in one way or another! He deserves to sweat a little. A taste of his own bad medicine. Maybe he'll learn a lesson.

47   But I remembered the look in his eyes as I drove past him. That same tired look my father had when he'd get home from work and he didn't have the strength to take off his boots. My father always looked like he'd been working for centuries without any rest. He'd sit there in front of the television on his favorite green vinyl sofa chair and stare at whatever was on TV. He'd sit there for an hour before he could move, before he could eat his supper and take his shower, that same look on his face Mr. Sánchez had just now.

48   What if this were my dad stranded on the side of the road? I'd want someone to stop for him.

49   "My one good deed for today," I told myself. "And I'm doing it for my dad really, not for Mr. Sánchez."

50   I made a U-turn, drove back to where he was still sitting, turned around again, and pulled up behind him.

51   "I thought that was you, Rey," he said. He wiped at his forehead with his shirtsleeve. "And when you drove past, I thought you hadn't seen me. Thank

NOTES

goodness you stopped. I've been here for close to forty-five minutes and nobody's stopped to help. Thank goodness you did. I just can't get the tire off."

52 Thank my father, I thought. If it weren't for my father, you'd still be out here.

53 I had that tire changed in no time. All the while Mr. Sánchez stood behind me and a bit to my left saying, "Yes, thank God you came by. Boy, it's hot out here. You're a good boy, Rey. You'll make a good man. How about some help there?"

54 "No, I've got it," I answered. "I'm almost done."

55 "Oyes, Rey, what if you come over tomorrow night to my house? I'm having a little barbecue for some important people here in town. You should come over. We're even going to do some swimming. What do you say?"

56 I tightened the last of the nuts, replaced the jack, the flat tire, and the crowbar in the bed of his truck, looked at him, and said, "Thanks. But I'll be playing football with the vatos."

First Read

Read "The Good Samaritan." After you read, complete the Think Questions below.

☁ THINK QUESTIONS

1. Why is Rey upset with Orlie at the beginning of the story? Cite textual evidence from the selection to support your answer.

2. Why does Rey hold a grudge against Mr. Sánchez? Cite textual evidence from the selection to support your answer.

3. What is the main problem Rey faces at the end of the story? What actions does he take? Cite textual evidence from the selection to support your answer.

4. Find the word **labor** in paragraph 22 of "The Good Samaritan." Use context clues in the surrounding sentences, as well as the sentence in which the word appears, to determine the word's meaning. Write your definition here and identify clues that helped you figure out its meaning.

5. Use context clues to determine the meaning of **approached** as it is used in paragraph 42 of "The Good Samaritan." Write your definition here and identify clues that helped you figure out its meaning. Then check the meaning in a dictionary.

Please note that excerpts and passages in the StudySync® library and this workbook are intended as touchstones to generate interest in an author's work. The excerpts and passages do not substitute for the reading of entire texts, and StudySync® strongly recommends that students seek out and purchase the whole literary or informational work in order to experience it as the author intended. Links to online resellers are available in our digital library. In addition, complete works may be ordered through an authorized reseller by filling out and returning to StudySync® the order form enclosed in this workbook.

Reading & Writing Companion 73

Skill:
Summarizing

Use the Checklist to analyze Summarizing in "The Good Samaritan." Refer to the sample student annotations about Summarizing in the text.

••• CHECKLIST FOR SUMMARIZING

In order to determine how to write an objective summary of a text, note the following:

✓ in literature, note the setting, characters, and events in the plot, taking into account the main problem the characters face and how it is solved

✓ answers to the basic questions *who, what, where, when, why,* and *how*

✓ stay objective, and do not add your own personal thoughts, judgments, or opinions to the summary

To provide an objective summary of a text not influenced by personal opinions or judgments, consider the following questions:

✓ What are the answers to basic *who, what, where, when, why,* and *how* questions in literature?

✓ Are all of the details I have included in my summary of a work of literature important?

✓ Is my summary objective, or have I added my own thoughts, judgments, or personal opinions?

Skill:
Summarizing

Reread paragraphs 42–44 of "The Good Samaritan." Then, using the Checklist on the previous page, answer the multiple-choice questions below.

⟳ YOUR TURN

1. Which of the following best describes Rey's relationship with Mr. Sánchez in this selection?

   ○ A. Mr. Sánchez is like a father figure to Rey.

   ○ B. Rey thinks that Mr. Sánchez treats him unfairly.

   ○ C. Mr. Sánchez relies on Rey to do things that he cannot.

   ○ D. Rey pities Mr. Sánchez as he wishes he could help.

2. Which of the following answer choices provides the best summary of this selection?

   ○ A. Rey recalls times when Mr. Sánchez has used him and does not want to help him fix the flat tire.

   ○ B. Mr. Sánchez gets a flat tire and wishes he hadn't taken advantage of Rey in the past.

   ○ C. Rey sees Mr. Sánchez struggling to fix a flat tire and decides to help him out.

   ○ D. Mr. Sánchez observes Rey passing him up in his time of need.

Please note that excerpts and passages in the StudySync® library and this workbook are intended as touchstones to generate interest in an author's work. The excerpts and passages do not substitute for the reading of entire texts, and StudySync® strongly recommends that students seek out and purchase the whole literary or informational work in order to experience it as the author intended. Links to online resellers are available in our digital library. In addition, complete works may be ordered through an authorized reseller by filling out and returning to StudySync® the order form enclosed in this workbook.

Reading & Writing
Companion

75

Close Read

Reread "The Good Samaritan." As you reread, complete the Skills Focus questions below. Then use your answers and annotations from the questions to help you complete the Write activity.

◎ SKILLS FOCUS

1. Summarize the lessons Rey learns as he deals with the Sánchez family without giving your personal opinion.

2. Think about how Rey makes decisions in "The Good Samaritan." Use evidence of Rey's decision-making to explain his character.

3. Use textual evidence to explain why making the decision to help Mr. Sánchez was hard for Rey.

✏ WRITE

DEBATE: Rey lives up to the story's title, "The Good Samaritan," when he stops to help Mr. Sánchez. However, do you think Rey made the right decision in stopping to help? Summarize Rey's experiences dealing with the Sánchez family and use them to prepare an argument for a debate. Use evidence from the text to support your position.

Jabberwocky

POETRY
Lewis Carroll
1872

Introduction

This whimsical poem about a heroic quest was first published in its entirety in author Lewis Carroll's *Through the Looking Glass*. Carroll (1832–1898) is best known for his fanciful stories and his contributions to the genre of literary nonsense. His most famous work, *Alice's Adventures in Wonderland*, has been adapted for film and television, and continues to be well-beloved today. In its sequel, *Through the Looking Glass*, Alice finds "Jabberwocky" in a curious book after she steps through a mirror into an odd new world. The poem's fantastical characters, invented language, and formal structure have made it a classic in its own right.

"'Beware the Jabberwock, my son! The jaws that bite, the claws that catch! . . .'"

from Chapter 1: "Looking-Glass House"

1 'Twas brillig, and the slithy toves
2 Did gyre and gimble in the wabe;
3 All mimsy were the borogoves,
4 And the mome raths outgrabe.

5 'Beware the Jabberwock, my son!
6 The jaws that bite, the claws that catch!
7 Beware the Jubjub bird, and **shun**
8 The frumious Bandersnatch!'

9 He took his vorpal sword in hand:
10 Long time the manxome **foe** he **sought**—
11 So rested he by the Tumtum tree
12 And stood awhile in thought.

13 And, as in uffish thought he stood,
14 The Jabberwock, with eyes of flame,
15 Came whiffling through the tulgey wood,
16 And burbled as it came!

17 One, two! One, two! And through and through
18 The vorpal blade went snicker-snack!
19 He left it dead, and with its head
20 He went **galumphing** back.

21 'And hast thou slain the Jabberwock?
22 Come to my arms, my beamish boy!
23 O frabjous day! Callooh! Callay!'
24 He **chortled** in his joy.

25 'Twas brillig, and the slithy toves
26 Did gyre and gimble in the wabe;
27 All mimsy were the borogoves,
28 And the mome raths outgrabe.

The Jabberwock

WRITE

POETRY: The poem "Jabberwocky" uses nonsense language to describe a heroic battle. Choose two nonsensical words from the first stanza of "Jabberwocky" and create a definition for each based on context, sound, and the image you picture in your head. Then write a poem about a time you overcame an obstacle incorporating each of the two words.

Please note that excerpts and passages in the StudySync® library and this workbook are intended as touchstones to generate interest in an author's work. The excerpts and passages do not substitute for the reading of entire texts, and StudySync® strongly recommends that students seek out and purchase the whole literary or informational work in order to experience it as the author intended. Links to online resellers are available in our digital library. In addition, complete works may be ordered through an authorized reseller by filling out and returning to StudySync® the order form enclosed in this workbook.

Reading & Writing Companion **79**

Gathering Blue

FICTION
Lois Lowry
2000

Introduction

Lois Lowry (b. 1937) has written more than 30 novels for children and young adults in her long career. The novel excerpted here, *Gathering Blue*, takes place in the same universe as several other novels of Lowry's, including 1993's Newbery-winning *The Giver*. Prior to this excerpt from Chapter 5, a young girl, Kira, has been left an orphan after her mother's death. Having been born with a twisted leg in a place where the weak and disabled are typically left in the fields to die, Kira fears she will be forced to leave—unless her talent for embroidery can earn her a role in society. She awaits judgment from Jamison and the Council of Guardians over a dispute between her and Vandara, an enemy of hers who seeks her expulsion from the village.

"The proceedings are complete. We have reached our decision."

NOTES

from Chapter 5

1   Kira noticed for the first time that a large box had been placed on the floor behind the seats of the Council of Guardians.

2   It had not been there before the lunchtime break.

3   As she and Vandara watched, one of the guards, responding to a nod from the chief guardian, lifted the box to the table and raised its lid. Her defender, Jamison, removed and unfolded something that she recognized immediately.

4   "The Singer's robe!" Kira spoke aloud in delight.

5   "This has no **relevance**," Vandara muttered. But she too was leaning forward to see.

6   The magnificent robe was laid out on the table in display. Ordinarily it was seen only once a year, at the time when the village gathered to hear the Ruin Song, the lengthy history of their people. Most citizens, crowded into the auditorium for the occasion, saw the Singer's robe only from a distance; they shoved and pushed, trying to nudge closer for a look.

7   But Kira knew the robe well from watching her mother's meticulous work on it each year. A guardian had always stood nearby, attentive. Warned not to touch, Kira had watched, marveling at her mother's skill, at her ability to choose just the right shade.

8   There, on the left shoulder! Kira remembered that spot, where just last year some threads had pulled and torn and her mother had carefully coaxed the broken threads free. Then she had selected pale pinks, slightly darker roses, and other colors darkening to crimson, each hue only a hint deeper than the one before; and she had stitched them into place, blending them flawlessly into the edges of the **elaborate** design.

9   Jamison watched Kira as she remembered. Then he said, "Your mother had been teaching you the art."

10 Kira nodded. "Since I was small," she acknowledged aloud.

NOTES

11 "Your mother was a skilled worker. Her dyes were **steadfast.** They have not faded."

12 "She was careful," Kira said, "and thorough."

13 "We are told that your skill is greater than hers."

14 *So they knew.* "I still have much to learn," Kira said.

15 "And she taught you the coloring, as well as the stitches?"

16 Kira nodded because she knew he expected her to. But it was not exactly true. Her mother had planned to teach her the art of the dyes, but the time had not yet come before the illness struck. She tried to be honest in her answer. "She was beginning to teach me," Kira said. "She told me that she had been taught by a woman named Annabel."

17 "Annabella now," Jamison said.

18 Kira was startled. "She is still alive? And four syllables?"

19 "She is very old. Her sight is somewhat **diminished.** But she can still be used as a **resource.**"

20 *Resource for what?* But Kira stayed silent. The scrap in her pocket was warm against her hand.

21 Suddenly Vandara stood. "I request that these proceedings continue," she said abruptly and harshly. "This is a delaying tactic on the part of the defender."

22 The chief guardian rose. Around him, the other guardians, who had been murmuring among themselves, fell silent.

23 His voice, directed at Vandara, was not unkind. "You may go," he said. "The proceedings are complete. We have reached our decision."

24 Vandara stood silent, unmoving. She glared at him defiantly. The chief guardian nodded, and two guards moved forward to escort her from the room.

25 "I have a right to know your decision!" Vandara shouted, her face twisted with rage. She wrested her arms free of the guards' grasp and faced the Council of Guardians.

26 "Actually," the chief guardian said in a calm voice, "you have no rights at all. But I am going to tell you the decision so that there will be no misunderstanding.

27 "The orphan girl Kira will stay. She will have a new role."

28 He gestured toward the Singer's robe, still spread out on the table. "Kira," he said, looking at her, "you will continue your mother's work. You will go beyond her work, actually, since your skill is far greater than hers was. First, you will repair the robe, as your mother always did. Next, you will restore it. Then your true work will begin. You will *complete* the robe." He gestured toward the large undecorated expanse of fabric across the shoulders. He raised one eyebrow, looking at her as if he were asking a question.

29 Nervously Kira nodded in reply and bowed slightly.

30 "As for you?" The chief guardian looked again at Vandara, who stood sullenly between the guards. He spoke politely to her. "You have not lost. You demanded the girl's land, and you may have it, you and the other women. Build your pen. It would be wise to pen your tykes; they are troublesome and should be better contained.

31 "Go now," he commanded.

32 Vandara turned. Her face was a mask of fury. She shrugged away the hands of the guards, leaned forward, and whispered harshly to Kira, "You will fail. Then they will kill you."

33 She smiled coldly at Jamison. "So, that's it, then," she said. "The girl is yours." She stalked down the aisle and went through the broad door.

34 The chief guardian and the other Council members ignored the outburst, as if it were merely an annoying insect that had finally been swatted away. Someone was refolding the Singer's robe.

35 "Kira," Jamison said, "go and gather what you need. Whatever you want to bring with you. Be back here when the bell rings four times. And we will take you to your quarters, to the place where you will live from now on."

36 Puzzled, Kira waited a moment. But there were no other instructions. The guardians were straightening their papers and collecting their books and belongings. They seemed to have forgotten she was there. Finally she stood, straightened herself against her walking stick, and limped from the room.

37 Emerging from the Council Edifice into bright sunlight and the usual chaos of the village central plaza, she realized that it was still midafternoon, still an ordinary day in the existence of the people, and that no one's life had changed except her own.

Excerpted from *Gathering Blue* by Lois Lowry, published by Ember.

WRITE

PERSONAL RESPONSE: Think back to a challenge that you've faced in your life. How did you feel facing it? How were you able to respond? With that memory in mind, what advice would you give Kira from *Gathering Blue* to help her with the challenge she faces now?

A Wrinkle in Time

FICTION
Madeleine L'Engle
1962

Introduction

Meg Murry and her precocious younger brother, Charles Wallace, will do anything they can to find their father. Did their father's top-secret experiments with time-travel cause his mysterious disappearance? What evil forces are holding him hostage? In *A Wrinkle in Time* by Madeleine L'Engle (1918–2007), Meg and Charles embark on a dangerous journey to find the answers, joined by their young neighbor, Calvin. In the excerpt, they have arrived on distant planet Camazotz, where they encounter a strange man with a fixed, red-eyed gaze. Telepathically, he urges them to merge their thoughts with his. First published in 1963, L'Engle's beloved novel won a Newbery Medal, the Sequoyah Book Award, and the Lewis Carroll Shelf Award, and it remains a classic to this day.

"The only reason we are here is because we think our father is here. Can you tell us where to find him?"

NOTES

from Chapter 7: The Man with Red Eyes

1 "Once ten is ten. Once eleven is eleven. Once twelve is twelve."

2 The number words pounded insistently against Meg's brain. They seemed to be boring their way into her skull.

3 "Twice one is two. Twice two is four. Twice three is six."

4 Calvin's voice came out in an angry shout. "Fourscore and seven years ago our fathers brought forth on this continent a new nation, **conceived** in liberty, and dedicated to the proposition that all men are created equal."

5 "Twice four is eight. Twice five is ten. Twice six is twelve."

6 "Father!" Meg screamed. "Father!" The scream, half involuntary, jerked her mind back out of darkness.

7 The words of the multiplication table seemed to break up into laughter. "Splendid! Splendid! You have passed your **preliminary** tests with flying colors."

8 "You didn't think we were as easy as all that, falling for that old stuff, did you?" Charles Wallace demanded.

9 "Ah, I hoped not. I most sincerely hoped not. But after all you are very young and very impressionable, and the younger the better, my little man. The younger the better."

10 Meg looked up at the fiery eyes, at the light pulsing above them, and then away. She tried looking at the mouth, at the thin, almost colorless lips, and this was more possible, even though she had to look obliquely, so that she was not sure exactly what the face really looked like, whether it was young or old, cruel or kind, human or alien.

11 "If you please," she said, trying to sound calm and brave. "The only reason we are here is because we think our father is here. Can you tell us where to find him?"

Skill:
Context Clues

Meg seems to be having a hard time looking directly at the man. The words "not sure exactly what the face really looked like" suggest that she is looking at him sideways, or indirectly. So obliquely must mean "indirectly." Meg can't tell whether he is young or old or if he's even human!

12 "Ah, your father!" There seemed to be a great chortling of delight. "Ah, yes, your father! It is not *can* I, you know, young lady, but *will* I?"

13 "Will you, then?"

14 "That depends on a number of things. Why do you want your father?"

15 "Didn't you ever have a father yourself?" Meg demanded. "You don't want him for a *reason*. You want him because he's your *father*."

16 "Ah, but he hasn't been *acting* very like a father, lately, has he? **Abandoning** his wife and his four little children to go gallivanting off on wild adventures of his own."

17 "He was working for the government. He'd never have left us otherwise. And we want to see him, please. Right now."

18 "My, but the little miss is impatient! Patience, patience, young lady."

19 Meg did not tell the man on the chair that patience was not one of her virtues.

20 "And by the way, my children," he continued blandly, "you don't need to vocalize verbally with me, you know. I can understand you quite as well as you can understand me."

21 Charles Wallace put his hands on his hips defiantly. "The spoken word is one of the triumphs of man," he proclaimed, "and I intend to continue using it, particularly with people I don't trust." But his voice was shaking. Charles Wallace, who even as an infant had seldom cried, was near tears.

22 "And you don't trust me?"

23 "What reason have you given us to trust you?"

24 "What cause have I given you for distrust?" The thin lips curled slightly.

25 Suddenly Charles Wallace darted forward and hit the man as hard as he could, which was fairly hard, as he had had a good deal of coaching from the twins.

26 "Charles!" Meg screamed.

27 The men in dark smocks moved smoothly but with swiftness to Charles. The man in the chair casually raised one finger, and the men dropped back.

28 "Hold it—" Calvin whispered, and together he and Meg darted forward and grabbed Charles Wallace, pulling him back from the platform.

29 The man gave a wince and the thought of his voice was a little breathless, as though Charles Wallace's punch had succeeded in winding him. "May I ask why you did that?"

30 "Because you aren't you," Charles Wallace said. "I'm not sure what you are, but you"—he pointed to the man on the chair—"aren't what's talking to us. I'm sorry if I hurt you. I didn't think you were real. I thought perhaps you were a robot, because I don't feel anything coming directly from you. I'm not sure where it's coming from, but it's coming through you. It isn't you."

31 "Pretty smart, aren't you?" the thought asked, and Meg had an uncomfortable feeling that she detected a snarl.

32 "It's not that I'm smart," Charles Wallace said, and again Meg could feel the palm of his hand sweating inside hers.

33 "Try to find out who I am, then," the thought probed.

34 "I have been trying," Charles Wallace said, his voice high and troubled.

35 "Look into my eyes. Look deep within them and I will tell you."

36 Charles Wallace looked quickly at Meg and Calvin, then said, as though to himself, "I have to," and focused his clear blue eyes on the red ones of the man in the chair. Meg looked not at the man but at her brother. After a moment it seemed that his eyes were no longer focusing. The pupils grew smaller and smaller, as though he were looking into an **intensely** bright light, until they seemed to close entirely, until his eyes were nothing but an opaque blue. He slipped his hands out of Meg's and Calvin's and started walking slowly toward the man on the chair.

37 "No!" Meg screamed. "No!"

38 But Charles Wallace continued his slow walk forward, and she knew that he had not heard her.

39 "No!" she screamed again, and ran after him. With her inefficient flying tackle she landed on him. She was so much larger than he that he fell sprawling, hitting his head a sharp crack against the marble floor. She knelt by him, sobbing. After a moment of lying there as though he had been knocked out by the blow, he opened his eyes, shook his head, and sat up. Slowly the pupils of his eyes dilated until they were back to normal, and the blood came back to his white cheeks.

40 The man on the chair spoke directly into Meg's mind, and now there was a **distinct** menace to the words. "I am not pleased," he said to her. "I could very easily lose patience with you, and that, for your information, young lady, would not be good for your father. If you have the slightest desire to see your father again, you had better cooperate."

Excerpted from *A Wrinkle in Time* by Madeleine L'Engle, published by Farrar, Straus and Giroux.

First Read

Read *A Wrinkle in Time*. After you read, complete the Think Questions below.

 THINK QUESTIONS

1. The voice says that Meg, Calvin, and Charles have passed their "preliminary tests." What tests have they passed, and how? Cite textual evidence from the selection to support your answer.

2. Write two or three sentences contrasting Charles Wallace with Meg and Calvin.

3. The author alludes to the saying "Patience is a virtue." How does Meg demonstrate a lack of patience in the text? Cite textual evidence from the selection to support your answer.

4. Find the word **abandoning** in paragraph 16 of *A Wrinkle in Time*. Use context clues in the surrounding sentences, as well as the sentence in which the word appears, to determine the word's meaning. Write your definition here and identify clues that helped you figure out its meaning.

5. Use context clues to determine the meaning of **intensely** as it is used in paragraph 36 of *A Wrinkle in Time*. Write your definition here and identify clues that helped you figure out its meaning. Then check the meaning in the dictionary.

Skill:
Context Clues

Use the Checklist to analyze Context Clues in *A Wrinkle in Time*. Refer to the sample student annotations about Context Clues in the text.

••• CHECKLIST FOR CONTEXT CLUES

In order to use context as a clue to infer the meaning of a word, note the following:

- ✓ clues about the word's part of speech

- ✓ clues in the surrounding text about the word's meaning

- ✓ signal words that cue a type of context clue, such as:

  - • *for example* or *for instance* to signal an example context clue
  - • *like, similarly,* or *just as* to signal a comparison clue
  - • *but, however,* or *unlike* to signal a contrast context clue

To determine the meaning of a word as it is used in a text, consider the following questions:

- ✓ What is the overall sentence, paragraph, or text about?

- ✓ How does the word function in the sentence?

- ✓ What clues can help me determine the word's part of speech?

- ✓ What textual clues can help me figure out the word's definition?

- ✓ Are there any examples that show what the word means?

- ✓ What do I think the word means?

To verify the preliminary determination of the meaning of the word based on context, consider the following questions:

- ✓ Does the definition I inferred make sense within the context of the sentence?

- ✓ Which of the dictionary's definitions makes sense within the context of the sentence?

Skill:
Context Clues

Reread paragraphs 20–24 of *A Wrinkle in Time*. Then, using the Checklist on the previous page, answer the multiple-choice questions below.

↻ YOUR TURN

1. This question has two parts. First, answer Part A. Then answer Part B.

   Part A: Which of the following words or phrases most closely matches the definition of **defiantly** as it is used in the passage?

   ○ A. in a manner that shows open resistance
   ○ B. in a manner that shows fear
   ○ C. in a manner that shows sadness
   ○ D. in a manner that shows entertainment

   Part B: Which of the following words or phrases from the passage best supports the answer to Part A?

   ○ A. "triumph"
   ○ B. "voice was shaking"
   ○ C. "infant"
   ○ D. "put his hands on his hips"

Please note that excerpts and passages in the StudySync® library and this workbook are intended as touchstones to generate interest in an author's work. The excerpts and passages do not substitute for the reading of entire texts, and StudySync strongly recommends that students seek out and purchase the whole literary or informational work in order to experience it as the author intended. Links to online resellers are available in our digital library. In addition, complete works may be ordered through an authorized reseller by filling out and returning to StudySync® the order form enclosed in this workbook.

Reading & Writing
Companion

91

Close Read

Reread *A Wrinkle in Time*. As you reread, complete the Skills Focus questions below. Then use your answers and annotations from the questions to help you complete the Write activity.

◎ SKILLS FOCUS

1. Think about the word choices Madeleine L'Engle makes in *A Wrinkle in Time*. Identify examples of unknown words and what context clues you used to understand them.

2. Identify the words and phrases the author uses to describe the setting, and explain how you used context clues to understand them.

3. Using context clues, identify how the characters in *A Wrinkle in Time* feel and how you would feel if you were in their situation. Support your description with textual evidence.

4. In "Jabberwocky," Lewis Carroll uses nonsensical words. In *Gathering Blue*, Lois Lowry uses descriptive language. Identify passages in *A Wrinkle in Time* where L'Engle uses language in similar ways to Carroll's or Lowry's.

5. Meg, Calvin, and Charles Wallace are dealing with the challenge of understanding the unknown in *A Wrinkle in Time*. Explain how their experiences change their perspectives of the Man with Red Eyes. Support your explanation with textual evidence.

✏ WRITE

COMPARE AND CONTRAST: "Jabberwocky" and *A Wrinkle in Time* both have eerie language. *A Wrinkle in Time* and *Gathering Blue* both feature settings and events that make the reader feel uncertain. How does using context clues help you understand these unique selections? Compare the language and context clues you used in *A Wrinkle in Time* with those in one of the other two selections. Remember to support your ideas with evidence from the texts.

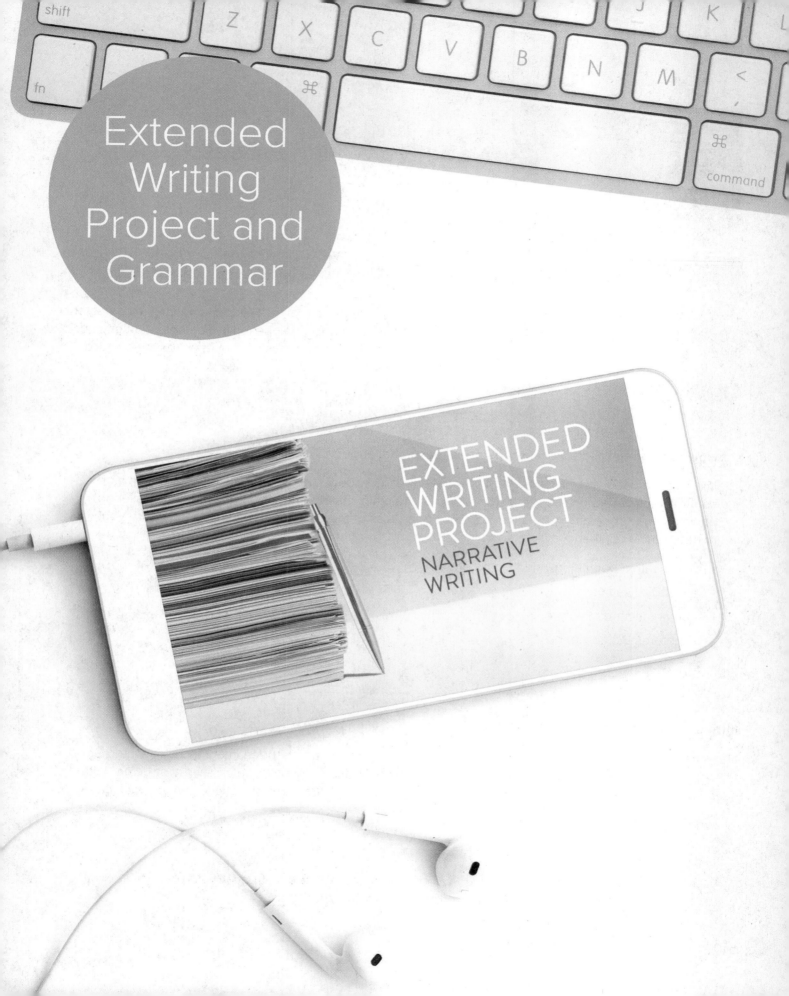

Extended
Writing
Project and
Grammar

EXTENDED
WRITING
PROJECT
NARRATIVE
WRITING

Narrative Writing Process: Plan

PLAN	DRAFT	REVISE	EDIT AND PUBLISH

The challenges that a character faces in a story are what make the story interesting. Sometimes a character is faced with a major challenge that is a matter of life and death, like Brian Robeson in *Hatchet*. At other times the challenge might be something small and seemingly insignificant, but it has a major effect on the character.

WRITING PROMPT

How can an unexpected event turn into a major challenge?

Imagine the very worst possible day. What event or individual makes that day so terrible? How do your characters respond? Write a story in which the main character faces an unexpected challenge on what was supposed to be a normal day. Regardless of the challenge you choose, be sure your narrative includes the following:

- a plot with a beginning, middle, and end
- a detailed setting
- characters and dialogue
- an interesting challenge
- a clear theme

Introduction to Narrative Writing

Narrative writing tells a story. It includes experiences or events that have been imagined by a writer. Good fiction writing uses effective techniques. These include relevant descriptive details and a structure with a series of events that contain a beginning, middle, and end. The characteristics of fiction writing include:

- setting
- characters
- plot
- theme
- point of view

As you continue with this Extended Writing Project, you'll receive more instruction and practice at crafting each of the characteristics of fiction writing to create your own narrative.

Before you get started on your own narrative, read this narrative that one student, Nik, wrote in response to the writing prompt. As you read the Model, highlight and annotate the features of narrative writing that Nik included in his narrative.

An Unexpected Challenge

1   Even before he opened his eyes that Saturday morning, Tyler could hear the sirens. He tried to turn over and go back to sleep, but the piercing sound grew louder. Then he smelled smoke. Was his house on fire? Where were his parents? Tyler leaped out of bed and ran to the window. He gripped the windowsill tightly as he took in the scene. Smoke was pouring out of the house across the way. Three fire trucks, their lights blinking, were parked in the street. Mr. Molano stood on the curb in his pajamas, gesturing wildly.

2   Tyler flew to his bedroom door and flung it open. "Dad?!" he yelled, looking around wildly. "DAD!"

3   "Tyler? I could use your help down here!"

4   Tyler dashed down the stairs. His father was standing in the kitchen. He was holding the Molanos' infant daughter, Tonya. She was trying hard to keep her eyes open. Next to him, their 8-year-old son Max stood staring. He looked like he was in shock.

5   "I was just going to get you," Tyler's father said. "You saw the fire? Luckily no one has been seriously hurt. Look, I know this is a lot to ask, but I need your help here. Mrs. Molano has been taken to the hospital. I think she'll be fine, but Mr. Molano is too upset to drive. I have to take him to the hospital, and I need you to watch Tonya and Max until I get back."

6   Suddenly Tyler looked like *he* was in shock. "Look after *Tonya?* Dad, is she even a year old? I don't know how to. . ."

7   Tyler's father cut him off. "Tyler, I know this is a lot to ask. But your mom is at her office seeing patients until noon. There's no one else who can do this right now. Mr. Molano's sister is coming to see to their house, but she lives an hour away."

8   "But . . ."

9   "Tonya will probably sleep until we get back, Tyler. I'll place her in your bed and surround her with pillows so she'll be safe. See if you can get Max to eat some breakfast. Then take him up to your room so you can watch Tonya."

10   Almost before Tyler knew it, his father had swept up the stairs and then out the door. Tyler just stood there. Slowly, he looked down at Max. "Um, would you like some breakfast, Max?" he said. The boy just nodded, and Tyler led him over to the kitchen table.

11   Tyler thought about making pancakes. He had watched his father make them often enough. But it would take too long. He opened a cabinet and pulled out some cereal.

12   "Is this okay, Max?" Tyler asked.

13   The boy nodded again. Then, unexpectedly, he burst into tears. "I want my mom!" he wailed.

14   Tyler froze. What should he do? Then he remembered what his father had said—Mrs. Molano would be all right.

15   Tyler patted the boy on the shoulder. As he poured some cereal into a bowl, he said, "Don't worry, buddy. Your mom will be okay. The doctors at the hospital will take good care of her. My dad said he thought she would be fine. You'll see."

16   Max looked up at Tyler. He sniffed a few times and then smiled weakly. Tyler went to get him some tissues so Max could wipe his eyes.

17   After Max finished his cereal, Tyler said, "Let's go check on Tonya. Also, I've got a big picture book about space pirates I think you're going to like!"

18   Max grinned and Tyler felt a flood of relief. He wasn't sure how he would deal with Max if he started crying again.

19   Soon Max was sitting on the floor reading. For a moment, everything was wonderfully quiet. Tyler walked over to the window and peered out. The fire seemed under control. There was no more smoke at least. Best of all, it didn't seem as if the house had been damaged very much.

NOTES

20 Then, suddenly, Tonya woke up. It was as if someone had flipped a switch. The tiny baby went from a sound sleep to full-on crying mode. Tyler's eyes widened and he looked at Max. "What should I do?" he asked.

21 "Mom always picks her up," Max said.

22 Tyler bent over and carefully picked up the baby. He was terrified that he might drop her. But she still cried.

23 "Okay, now what?" Tyler asked.

24 "You should walk around with her."

25 Tyler walked around the bedroom and into the hallway with the baby. The motion seemed to calm her down. But anytime Tyler stopped walking, Tonya began crying again. "Okay, Tonya, you're the boss. I'll keep walking," Tyler said.

26 After Tyler had circled the hallway for what felt like the five-hundredth time, his mom came home. Tyler had never been so glad to see her in his life.

27 "Well, look at you!" Mom said. "You're an expert baby walker. May I hold her?"

28 "You bet. Boy, my arms are tired!"

29 As his mother scooped Tonya into her arms, she said, "Great job, Tyler. Dad called me from the hospital and told me what was going on. I got here as soon as I could, but it looks like you didn't even need my help. I'm really proud of you for rising to the challenge and helping out."

30 "Dad and Max were the real experts," Tyler said. "I just did what they told me to do."

31 Tyler's mother turned to smile at Max. "Your mom's going to be fine, Max," she said. "She'll be home tomorrow."

32 Max clapped and at the same time Tonya started crying again. Tyler's mother placed the baby back in Tyler's arms.

33 "Here," she laughed. "You're the champion baby walker!"

✏ WRITE

Writers often take notes about story ideas before they sit down to write. Think about what you've learned so far about organizing narrative writing to help you begin prewriting.

- **Genre:** In what sort of genre would you like to write? Most any genre can include focus on an unexpected challenge. Genres include realistic fiction, science fiction, fantasy, or mystery, to name some examples.

- **Characters:** What kinds of characters will you include in your narrative?

- **Plot:** What would a normal day be like for your character or characters? What could happen that would pose a challenge for them?

- **Plot/Character:** How will your character or characters respond to the challenge?

- **Setting:** How might the setting of your story affect the characters and the challenges they face?

- **Point of View:** From which point of view should your story be told, and why?

Response Instructions

Use the questions in the bulleted list to write a one-paragraph summary. Your summary should describe what will happen in your narrative, like the one above.

Don't worry about including all of the details now; focus only on the most essential and important elements. You will refer back to this short summary as you continue through the steps of the writing process.

Skill:
Organizing Narrative Writing

••• CHECKLIST FOR ORGANIZING NARRATIVE WRITING

As you consider how to organize your writing for your narrative, use the following questions as a guide:

- Who is the narrator and who are the characters in the story?
- Where will the story take place?
- What conflict or problem will the characters have to resolve?
- Have I created a series of plot events that flow logically and naturally from one event to the next?

Here are some strategies to help you organize your narrative:

- Introduce a narrator and/or characters.

  > Characters can be introduced all at once or throughout the narrative.

  > Choose the role each character will play.

- Establish a context.

  > Begin with your **exposition**—decide what background information your readers need to know about the characters, setting, and conflict.

  > List the events of the **rising action**—be sure that these events build toward the climax.

  > Describe what will happen during the **climax** of the story—make sure that this is the point of highest interest, conflict, or suspense in your story.

  > List the events of the **falling action**—make sure that these events show what happens to the characters as a result of the climax.

  > Explain the **resolution** of the main conflict in your story.

⟳ YOUR TURN

Complete the chart below by matching each event to its correct place in the narrative sequence.

Event Options	
A	Her parents take out a boat at dusk to go fishing. They tell her to call for help if they're not back an hour after it gets dark.
B	They find Chloe's parents sitting on some rocks, their boat having capsized.
C	Chloe, her parents, and the man all get back to their cabins safely.
D	Chloe is on vacation with her parents.
E	When her parents still haven't come back after dark, Chloe asks a man in a neighboring cabin for help. They take his boat out to look for them.

Narrative Sequence	Event
Exposition	
Rising Action	
Climax	
Falling Action	
Resolution	

⟳ YOUR TURN

Complete the chart below by writing a short summary of what will happen in each section of your narrative.

Narrative Sequence	Event
Exposition	
Rising Action	
Climax	
Falling Action	
Resolution	

Narrative Writing Process: Draft

| PLAN | DRAFT | REVISE | EDIT AND PUBLISH |

You have already made progress toward writing your narrative. Now it is time to draft your narrative.

✏️ WRITE

Use your Plan and other responses in your Binder to draft your narrative. You may also have new ideas as you begin drafting. Feel free to explore those new ideas as they occur to you. You can also ask yourself these questions:

- Have I included specifics about my setting, characters, plot, theme, and point of view?
- Have I made the conflict in the story clear to readers?
- Does the sequence of events in my story make sense?
- Does my main character face a challenge in the story?

Before you submit your draft, read it over carefully. You want to be sure that you've responded to all aspects of the prompt.

Here is Nik's short story draft. As you read, identify details that Nik includes in his inciting incident. As Nik continues to revise and edit his narrative, he will find and improve weak spots in his writing, as well as correct any language, punctuation, or spelling mistakes.

☰ STUDENT MODEL: FIRST DRAFT

An Unexpected Challenge

~~Tyler heard sirens. Then he smelled smoke. He wonder what was going on. He looked out the window. He saw smoke and fire trucks below. Mr. Molano was standing on the curb waveing her arms.~~

~~Tyler opened his bedroom door. "Dad?" he yelled, looking around wildly. "DAD!"~~

Even before he opened his eyes that Saturday morning, Tyler could hear the sirens. He tried to turn over and go back to sleep, but the piercing sound grew louder. Then he smelled smoke. Was his house on fire? Where were his parents? Tyler leaped out of bed and ran to the window. He gripped the windowsill tightly as he took in the scene. Smoke was pouring out of the house across the way. Three fire trucks, their lights blinking, were parked in the street. Mr. Molano stood on the curb in his pajamas, gesturing wildly.

Tyler flew to his bedroom door and flung it open. "Dad?" he yelled, looking around wildly. "DAD!"

Tyler went down the stairs. Him father was standing in the kitchen he was holding the Molanos' infant daughter, Tonya. Next to him, their 8-year-old son Max stood staring.

~~"You saw the fire? Mrs. Molano has been taken to the hospital. I think she'll be fine, but Mr. Molano is too upset to drive. I have to take him to the hospital, and I need you to watch Tonya and Max until I get back."~~

~~"I don't know how to. . ."~~

~~"I know this is a lot to ask. But you mom is at her office seeing patients until noon."~~

~~"But . . ."~~

Skill:
Story Beginnings

To engage readers in the story, Nik has them experience the fire the way Tyler does. Nik uses the action method to grab readers' attention and set an urgent tone in the first paragraph.

Skill:
Descriptive Details

Nik adds descriptive details to his draft so that readers can better imagine what is happening during this part of the story. Sound details like "the piercing sound grew louder" help readers imagine what Tyler hears in this specific event.

Skill: Narrative
Techniques

*Nik decides that the
reason for dialogue in
this section is to
advance the plot and
show why the
characters, Tyler and
his father, are under
pressure. He adds
dialogue tags to make it
clear who is talking.*

~~"Tonya will probably sleep until we get back. I'll place her in your bed and surround her with pillows so her will be safe. See if you can get Max to eat some breakfast. Then take he up to your room so you can watch Tonya."~~

"I was just going to get you," Tyler's father said. "You saw the fire? Luckily no one has been seriously hurt. Look, I know this is a lot to ask, but I need your help here. Mrs. Molano has been taken to the hospital. I think she'll be fine, but Mr. Molano is too upset to drive. I have to take him to the hospital, and I need you to watch Tonya and Max until I get back."

Suddenly Tyler looked like *he* was in shock. "Look after *Tonya?* Dad, is she even a year old? I don't know how to . . ."

Tyler's father cut him off. "Tyler, I know this is a lot to ask. But your mom is at her office seeing patients until noon. There's no one else who can do this right now. Mr. Molano's sister is coming to see to their house, but she lives an hour away."

"But . . ."

"Tonya will probably sleep until we get back, Tyler. I'll place her in your bed and surround her with pillows so she'll be safe. See if you can get Max to eat some breakfast. Then take him up to your room so you can watch Tonya."

~~His father had gone up the stairs. Then out the door. Tyler just stood there. Slowly, he looked down at Max. "Um, would you like some breakfast, Max"? he said. The boy just nodded, and Tyler led them over to the kitchen table.~~

~~Tyler thought about making pancakes. He had watched his father make them often enough. Sometimes on Saturday mornings the whole family would sit in the kitchen and watch as Dad mixed the batter and cooked each pancake. But it would take too long. He opened a cabinet and found some cereal.~~

~~"Is this okay?"~~

Almost before Tyler knew it, his father had swept up the stairs and then out the door. Tyler just stood there. Slowly, he looked down at Max. "Um, would you like some breakfast, Max?" he said. The boy just nodded, and Tyler led him over to the kitchen table.

Tyler thought about making pancakes. He had watched his father make them often enough. But it would take too long. He opened a cabinet and pulled out some cereal.

"Is this okay, Max?" Tyler asked.

The boy nodded again. Then, unexpectedly, he burst into tears. "I want my mom!" he wailed.

Tyler froze. What should she do? Then he remembered. What his father had said—Mrs. Molano would be all right.

Tyler patted the boy on the shoulder. As he poared some cereal into the bowl, he said "Don't worry, buddy. Your mom will be okay, the doctors at the hospital will take good care of them. My dad said he thought she would be fine. You'll see".

Max looked up at Tyler. He sniffed a few times. Then smiled weakly. Tyler went to get him some tissue so Max could wipe their eyes.

After Max finished his cerael, Tyler said "Let's go check on Tonya. Also, I've got a big picture book about space pirates I think you're going to like"!

Max grins and Tyler felt a flood of relief. He wasn't sure how he would deal with Max if he started crying again.

Soon Max was sitting on the floor reading. For a moment, everything was wonderfully quiet. Tyler walked over to the window and peared out. The fire seemed under control. There was no more smoke at least. Best of all, it didn't seem as if the house had been damaged very much. If it had been, Tyler wondered where the Molano would stay. Would they live in Tyler's house until their house was repaired?

Skill:
Transitions

Nik continues to add transitions throughout the rest of the story to show relationships between ideas from one paragraph to the next in his narrative. He decides to use the transitional phrase "almost before Tyler knew it" before "his father had swept up the stairs . . ." This signals a shift in time and how quickly the events are taking place.

Please note that excerpts and passages in the StudySync® library and this workbook are intended as touchstones to generate interest in an author's work. The excerpts and passages do not substitute for the reading of entire texts, and StudySync® strongly recommends that students seek out and purchase the whole literary or informational work in order to experience it as the author intended. Links to online resellers are available in our digital library. In addition, complete works may be ordered through an authorized reseller by filling out and returning to StudySync® the order form enclosed in this workbook.

Reading & Writing Companion   **105**

NOTES

Then, suddenly, Tonya woke up. It was as if someone had flipped a switch. The tiny baby goes from a sound sleep to full-on crying mode. Tyler's eyes widened and he looked at Max. "What should I do"? him asked. "Mom always picks her up," Max said.

Tyler bent over and carefully picks up the baby he was terrified that he might drop her. But she still cried.

"Okay, now what?" Tyler asked.

"You should walk around with her."

Tyler walks around the bedroom and into the hallway with the baby. The motion seemed to calm her down. But anytime Tyler stopped walking Tonya began crying again. "Okay, Tonya, you the boss. I'll keep walking" Tyler said.

~~After Tyler had circled the hallway yet again, his mom came home. Tyler was so happy to see her.~~

~~"Well, look at you!" Mom said. "May I hold her?"~~

~~"You bet. Boy, my arms are tired!"~~

~~As his mother took Tonya into her arms, she said, "Great job, Tyler."~~

After Tyler had circled the hallway for what felt like the five-hundredth time, his mom came home. Tyler had never been so glad to see her in his life.

"Well, look at you!" Mom said. "You're an expert baby walker! May I hold her?"

"You bet. Boy, my arms are tired!"

As his mother scooped Tonya into her arms, she said, "Great job, Tyler. Dad called me from the hospital and told me what was going on. I got here as soon as I could, but it looks like you didn't even need my help. I'm really proud of you for rising to the challenge and helping out."

Skill:
Conclusions

Nik revises these concluding events through character dialogue between Tyler and his mom. He sums up the story with how Tyler has changed and what his mom thinks about him.

"Dad and Max were the real experts," Tyler said. "I just did what them told me to do."

Tyler's mother was smiling at Max. "Your mom's going to be fine, Max," she said. "She'll be home tomorrow."

Max clapped and at the same time Tonya started crying again. Tyler's mother placed the baby in he arms.

"Here. Your the champion baby walker!"

Skill:
Story Beginnings

••• CHECKLIST FOR STORY BEGINNINGS

Before you begin to write the beginning of your narrative, ask yourself the following questions:

- What kind of information does my reader need to know at the beginning of the story about the main character, the setting, and the character's conflict?
- What will happen to my character in the story?

There are many ways to engage and orient the reader to your narrative. Here are four methods to consider to help you establish a context and introduce the narrator and/or characters:

- Action

  > What action could help reveal information about my character or conflict?

  > How might an exciting moment grab my reader's attention?

  > How could a character's reaction help set the mood of my narrative?

- Description

  > Does my story take place in a special location or specific time period?

  > How can describing a location or character grab my reader's attention?

- Dialogue

  > What dialogue would help my reader understand the setting or the conflict?

  > How could a character's internal thoughts provide information for my reader?

- Information

  > Would a surprising statement grab my reader's attention?

  > What details will help my reader understand the character, conflict, or setting?

YOUR TURN

Read the beginning of each story below. Then, complete the chart by writing the type of story beginning that correctly matches each paragraph.

Story Beginning Options			
Description	Action	Information	Dialogue

Story Beginning	Type of Story Beginning
Back in 1946, when I was nine, I worried that I wasn't tough enough. That's why I became a Boy Scout. Scouting, I thought, would make a man of me. It didn't take long to reach Tenderfoot rank. You got that for joining. To move up to Second Class, however, you had to meet three requirements. Scout Spirit and Scout Participation were a cinch. The third requirement, Scout Craft, meant I had to go on an overnight hike in the country. In other words, I had to leave Brooklyn, on my own, for the first time in my life. "Scout's Honor"	
"Sit down, sit down. Don't be afraid." Chairman Jin pointed to the empty chair. "These comrades from your father's work unit are just here to have a study session with you. It's nothing to worry about." *Red Scarf Girl*	
I know he's in there, I thought. I saw the curtains in his bedroom move—only a little, yes, but they moved. "The Good Samaritan"	
They would look for him, look for the plane. His father and mother would be frantic. They would tear the world apart to find him. Brian had seen searches on the news, seen movies about lost planes. When a plane went down, they mounted extensive searches and almost always they found the plane within a day or two. *Hatchet*	

 WRITE

Use the questions in the checklist to revise the beginning of your narrative.

Skill:
Descriptive Details

••• CHECKLIST FOR DESCRIPTIVE DETAILS

First, reread the draft of your narrative and identify the following:

- where descriptive details are needed to convey experiences and events
- vague, general, or overused words and phrases
- places where you want to tell how something looks, sounds, feels, smells, or tastes, such as:

  > experiences

  > events

Use precise words and phrases, relevant descriptive details, figurative language such as metaphors and similes, and sensory language to convey experiences and events, using the following questions as a guide:

- What experiences and events do I want to convey in my writing?
- Have I included descriptive details that are relevant and make sense in my story?
- Where can I add descriptive details to describe the characters and the events of the plot?
- Have I told how something looks, sounds, feels, smells, or tastes in order to help the reader picture the story in their mind?
- Could I use a metaphor, simile, or some other kind of figurative language to make my description more engaging?
- What can I refine or revise in my word choice to make sure that the reader can picture what is taking place?

↻ YOUR TURN

Choose the best answer to each question.

1. The following section is from an earlier draft of Nik's story. In the underlined sentence, Nik did not use the most appropriate word to describe the sound of the sirens. Which of the following is the best replacement for the word *crazy*?

> When he woke up, Tyler could hear the sirens. <u>The crazy sound grew louder and louder.</u> He could no longer go back to sleep.

- ○ A. dull
- ○ B. red
- ○ C. ear-splitting
- ○ D. large

2. Nik wants to add a descriptive sensory visual detail to this sentence from a previous draft. Which sentence BEST adds sight detail to his sentence?

> The fire looked like it was under control.

- ○ A. The bright orange flames got fainter and fainter against the bright blue sky and the fire finally looked like it was under control.
- ○ B. As Tyler took a deep breath in, the scent of smoke seemed less extreme—the fire looked like it was under control.
- ○ C. The fire looked like it was under control and Tyler could no longer hear the welcome sound of the firehose blasting the raging flames.
- ○ D. With the syrupy sweet taste of soda still circulating in his mouth, Tyler noticed that the fire finally looked like it was under control.

YOUR TURN

Complete the chart by writing a descriptive detail that appeals to each sense for your narrative.

Sense	Descriptive Detail
sight	
smell	
touch	
taste	
sound	

Skill:
Narrative Techniques

••• CHECKLIST FOR NARRATIVE TECHNIQUES

As you begin to develop the techniques you will use in your narrative, ask yourself the following questions:

- Which characters are talking? How am I organizing the dialogue?

- How quickly or slowly do I want the plot to move? Why?

- Which literary devices can be added to strengthen the characters or plot? How can I better engage the reader?

There are many techniques you can use in a narrative. Here are some methods that can help you write dialogue, pacing, and description, to develop experiences, events, and/or characters:

- Use dialogue between characters to explain events or move the action forward.

  > Set all dialogue off in quotation marks.

  > Include identifying names as needed before or after quotation marks.

- Include description to engage the reader and help them visualize the characters, setting, and other elements in the narrative.

  > Include only those descriptions relevant to the reader's understanding of the element being described.

- Use pacing effectively to convey a sense of urgency or calm in a narrative.

  > To speed up the pace, try using limited description, short paragraphs, brief dialogue, and simpler sentences.

  > To slow down the pace, try using detailed description, longer paragraphs, and more complex sentence structures.

- Use any combination of the above narrative techniques to develop experiences, events, and/or characters.

↻ YOUR TURN

Choose the best answer to each question.

1. The following section is from a previous draft of Nik's story. What change, if any, needs to be made in the underlined sentence?

> Before Tyler knew it, his father had run up the stairs and out the door. Tyler stood there nervously and then looked down at Max. <u>Um, would you like me to refill your water bottle, Max?" he said.</u> The boy nodded, so Tyler walked him over to the sink.

- ○ A. Change *your* to *you're*.
- ○ B. Insert quotation marks at the beginning of the sentence.
- ○ C. Change *said* to *says*.
- ○ D. The underlined sentence does not need to be changed.

2. The following section is from a previous draft of Nik's story. Which of the following is a description of how Tyler feels?

> Before Tyler knew it, his father had run up the stairs and out the door. Tyler stood there nervously and then looked down at Max. Um, would you like me to refill your water bottle, Max?" he said. The boy nodded, so Tyler walked him over to the sink.

- ○ A. "looked down at Max"
- ○ B. "walked him over to the sink"
- ○ C. "stood there nervously"
- ○ D. "before Tyler knew it"

3. The following sentences are from a previous draft of Nik's story. What is the correct way to write the sentences?

> "The real experts are Dad and Max," Tyler said. "I just did what I was asked."

○ A. The real experts are Dad and Max," Tyler said. "I just did what I was asked."

○ B. "The real experts are Dad and Max," Tyler said. I just did what I was asked."

○ C. "The real experts are Dad and Max, Tyler said. I just did what I was asked."

○ D. The sentences are written correctly in the story.

✏ WRITE

Use the questions in the checklist to add narrative techniques, such as writing new dialogue, for your narrative.

Skill:
Transitions

••• CHECKLIST FOR TRANSITIONS

Before you revise your current draft to include transitions, think about:

- the order of events including the rising action, climax, falling action, and resolution
- moments where the time or setting changes

Next, reread your current draft and note areas in your story where:

- the order of events is unclear or illogical
- when changes in time or setting are confusing or unclear. Look for:

  > sudden jumps in time and setting

  > missing or illogical plot events

  > places where you could add more context or exposition, such as important background information about the narrator, setting, characters, and conflict, to help the reader understand where and when plot events are happening

Revise your draft to use a variety of transition words, phrases, and clauses to convey sequence and signal shifts from one time frame or setting to another, using the following questions as a guide:

- Does my exposition provide necessary background information?
- Do the events of the rising action, climax, falling action, and resolution flow naturally and logically?
- Did I include a variety of transition words and phrases that show sequence and signal setting and time changes?

  > transitions such as *that night* or *on the first sunny day* can indicate changes in time periods

  > phrases such as *a week later, Bob boarded a train to Iowa* can indicate shifts in setting and time

YOUR TURN

Choose the best answer to each question.

1. Which of the following is a transition word that signals a shift in time in this sentence?

> After Max finished his cereal, Tyler said, "Let's go check on Tonya. Also, I've got a big picture book about space pirates I think you're going to like!"

○ A. "After"
○ B. "check"
○ C. "Also"
○ D. "finished"

2. Which of the following phrases includes transition words that signal a shift in action?

> Then, suddenly, Tonya woke up. It was as if someone had flipped a switch. The tiny baby went from a sound sleep to full-on crying mode. Tyler's eyes widened and he looked at Max. "What should I do?" he asked.

○ A. "as if someone had flipped a switch"
○ B. "from a sound sleep"
○ C. "Then, suddenly"
○ D. "Tyler's eyes widened."

 YOUR TURN

Complete the chart by adding transitions that organize the structure of your draft and show the relationship between ideas.

Transitions that organize the story structure	Transitions that show the relationship between ideas

Skill:
Conclusions

••• CHECKLIST FOR CONCLUSIONS

Before you write your conclusion, ask yourself the following questions:

- What important details should I include in the summary in my conclusion?
- What other thoughts and feelings could the characters share with readers in the conclusion?
- Should I express the importance of the events in my narrative through dialogue or a character's actions?

Below are two strategies to help you provide a conclusion that follows from the narrated experiences or events:

- Peer Discussion

  > After you have written your introduction and body paragraphs, talk with a partner about possible endings for your narrative, writing notes about your discussion.

  > Review your notes and think about how you want to end your story.

  > Briefly summarize the events in the narrative through the narrator or one of the characters.

  > Describe how the narrator feels about the events they experienced.

  > Reveal to readers why the experiences in the narrative matter through a character's reflections or dialogue.

  > Write your conclusion.

- Freewriting

  > Freewrite for 10 minutes about what you might include in your conclusion. Don't worry about grammar, punctuation, or having fully formed ideas. The point of freewriting is to discover ideas.

  > Review your notes and think about how you want to end your story.

  > Briefly summarize the events in the narrative through the narrator or one of the characters.

  > Describe how the narrator feels about the events they experienced.

  > Reveal to readers why the experiences in the narrative matter through a character's reflections or dialogue.

  > Write your conclusion.

 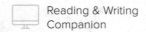

YOUR TURN

Read the conclusions below. Then, complete the chart by sorting them into those that are strong conclusions and those that are not.

Conclusion Options	
A	"You're the champion baby walker!"
B	As his mother scooped Tonya into her arms, she said, "Great job, Tyler. Dad called me from the hospital and told me what was going on. I got here as soon as I could, but it looks like you didn't even need my help. I'm really proud of you for rising to the challenge and helping out."
C	Max clapped and at the same time Tonya started crying again.
D	But anytime Tyler stopped walking, Tonya began crying again.

Strong Conclusion	Not Strong Conclusion

WRITE

Use the questions in the checklist to add a conclusion: use details, dialogue, action, and character feelings or thoughts to conclude your narrative.

Narrative Writing Process: Revise

PLAN	DRAFT	REVISE	EDIT AND PUBLISH

You have written a draft of your narrative. You have also received input from your peers about how to improve it. Now you are going to revise your draft.

◄◄ REVISION GUIDE

Examine your draft to find areas for revision. Keep in mind your purpose and audience as you revise for clarity, development, organization, and style. Use the guide below to help you review.

Review	Revise	Example
Clarity		
Label each piece of dialogue so you know who is speaking. Annotate any places where it is unclear who is speaking.	Use the character's name to show who is speaking or add description about the speaker.	"Is this okay, Max?" Tyler asked. The boy nodded again. Then, unexpectedly, he burst into tears. "I want my mom!" he wailed.
Development		
Identify key moments leading up to the climax. Annotate places that don't move the story along toward the climax or the resolution.	Focus on a single event and think carefully about whether it drives the story forward or keeps it standing still. If it doesn't move the story forward, you might consider adding or subtracting details to make it more important to the plot.	Tyler thought about making pancakes. He had watched his father make them often enough. ~~Sometimes on Saturday mornings the whole family would sit in the kitchen and keep Dad company while he mixed the batter and cooked each pancake.~~ But it would take too long. He opened a cabinet and pulled out some cereal.

Review	Revise	Example

Organization

Explain your story in one or two sentences. Reread and annotate any parts that don't match your explanation.	Rewrite the events in the correct sequence. Delete events that are not essential to the story.	Soon Max was sitting on the floor reading. For a moment, everything was wonderfully quiet. Tyler walked over to the window and peered out. The fire seemed under control. There was no more smoke at least. Best of all, it didn't seem as if the house had been damaged very much. ~~If it had been, Tyler wondered where the Molanos would stay. Would they live in Tyler's house until their house was repaired?~~

Style: Word Choice

Identify every pronoun that takes the place of a noun in your story.	Select sentences to rewrite using consistent pronoun use and correct pronoun and antecedent agreement.	Mr. Molano was standing on the curb waving ~~her~~ his arms.

Style: Sentence Variety

Think about a key event where you want your reader to feel a specific emotion. Long sentences can draw out a moment and make a reader think; short sentences can show urgent actions or danger.	Rewrite a key event making your sentences longer or shorter to achieve the emotion you want your reader to feel.	After Tyler had circled the hallway ~~yet again,~~ for what felt like the five-hundredth time, his mom came home. Tyler ~~was so happy to see her~~ had never been so glad to see her in his life.

✏ WRITE

Use the guide above, as well as your peer reviews, to help you evaluate your narrative to determine areas that should be revised.

Grammar:
Personal Pronouns

Personal pronouns are pronouns used to refer to persons or things. Two cases, or forms, that pronouns take are nominative case, or subject, and objective case, or object. Each case is determined by how the pronoun functions in a sentence.

Subject Pronouns:
Singular: *I, you, he, she, it*
Plural: *we, you, they*

Object Pronouns:
Singular: *me, you, him, her*
Plural: *us, you, them*

They might come today. Hatchet	The subject pronoun *they* is the subject of the sentence.
In this manner, stopping to rest when I was tired, I carried **him** to the headland. Island of the Blue Dolphins	The object pronoun *him* is the object of the verb *carried*.
There were threats against **me** and my family and even out-and-out attempts at physical harm to **me**. I Never Had It Made: An Autobiography of Jackie Robinson	The object pronoun *me* is the object of the prepositions *against* and *to*.

When writing, make sure to use pronouns in the correct case.

Correct	Incorrect
I walk one mile to school every day.	Me walk one mile to school every day.
Paula asked them for help.	Paula asked they for help.

↻ YOUR TURN

1. How should this sentence be changed?

> Them mow lawns during summer vacation.

- ○ A. Change **Them** to **Her**.
- ○ B. Change **Them** to **They**.
- ○ C. Change **Them** to **Him**.
- ○ D. No change needs to be made to this sentence.

2. How should this sentence be changed?

> She told he a funny joke.

- ○ A. Change **he** to **him**.
- ○ B. Change **she** to **her**.
- ○ C. Change **he** to **they**.
- ○ D. No change needs to be made to this sentence.

3. How should this sentence be changed?

> We nervously watched the big, brown dog approach us.

- ○ A. Change **We** to **Us**.
- ○ B. Change **We** to **Him**.
- ○ C. Change **us** to **we**.
- ○ D. No change needs to be made to this sentence.

4. How should this sentence be changed?

> Her brought Cara for a visit.

- ○ A. Change **Cara** to **she**.
- ○ B. Change **Her** to **Us**.
- ○ C. Change **Her** to **She**.
- ○ D. No change needs to be made to this sentence.

Please note that excerpts and passages in the StudySync® library and this workbook are intended as touchstones to generate interest in an author's work. The excerpts and passages do not substitute for the reading of entire texts, and StudySync® strongly recommends that students seek out and purchase the whole literary or informational work in order to experience it as the author intended. Links to online resellers are available in our digital library. In addition, complete works may be ordered through an authorized reseller by filling out and returning to StudySync® the order form enclosed in this workbook.

Reading & Writing Companion   **123**

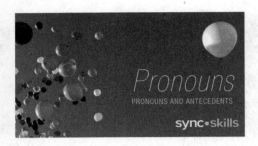

Grammar: Pronouns and Antecedents

Pronouns and Antecedents

A pronoun is a word that takes the place of a noun mentioned earlier. The noun is the pronoun's antecedent. A pronoun must agree in number and gender with its antecedent.

Text	Pronoun	Antecedent
The morning after my **teacher** came she led me into **her** room and gave me a doll. The Story of My Life	her	teacher
Some of the **Dodgers** who swore **they** would never play with a black man had a change of mind, when **they** realized I was a good ballplayer who could be helpful in **their** earning a few thousand more dollars in world series money. I Never Had It Made: An Autobiography of Jackie Robinson	they their	Dodgers
On this bus on that day, **Rosa Parks** initiated a new era in the American quest for freedom and equality. **She** sat near the middle of the bus, just behind the 10 seats reserved for whites. The Story Behind the Bus	she	Rosa Parks

A pronoun's antecedent should always be clear.

Clear	Unclear	Explanation
Andrea and her sister baked bread. **Her sister** had a special talent for it.	Andrea and her sister baked bread. **She** had a special talent for it.	The pronoun *she* in the second sentence could refer to either Andrea or her sister.
The diplomats, who had traveled from Puerto Rico, met with the reporters.	The diplomats met with the reporters. **They** had traveled from Puerto Rico.	The pronoun *they* could refer to either the diplomats or the reporters.

⟳ YOUR TURN

1. How should this sentence be changed?

   > My brother has a test tomorrow, so it is going to study after dinner.

   ○ A. Change the word **it** to **we**.
   ○ B. Change the word **it** to **he**.
   ○ C. Change the word **it** to **she**.
   ○ D. No change needs to be made to this sentence.

2. How should this sentence be changed?

   > John Adams disagreed with Thomas Jefferson, but he later changed his opinions.

   ○ A. Change **he** to **Adams**.
   ○ B. Change **he** to **they**.
   ○ C. Change **he** to **it**.
   ○ D. No change needs to be made to this sentence.

3. How should these sentences be changed?

   > The Sistine Chapel is in Rome. Michelangelo painted it.

   ○ A. Change **Michelangelo** to **He**.
   ○ B. Change **The Sistine Chapel** to **It**.
   ○ C. Change **it** to **her**.
   ○ D. No changes need to be made to these sentences.

4. How should this sentence be changed?

   > All of the teams promote its star players.

   ○ A. Change **teams** to **team**.
   ○ B. Change **its** to **their**.
   ○ C. Change **its** to **his**.
   ○ D. No change needs to be made to this sentence.

Grammar:
Consistent Pronoun Use

An antecedent is the word or group of words to which a pronoun refers or that a pronoun replaces. A pronoun must agree with its antecedent in number (singular or plural) and gender (masculine, feminine, or neutral). A pronoun's antecedent may be a noun, another pronoun, or a phrase or clause acting as a noun.

Text	Explanation
I even move **my** chair a little to the right. Not **mine**, not **mine**, not **mine**. Eleven	The pronoun *I* is the antecedent of the pronouns *my* and *mine*. The pronouns agree in person and number.
"Oh, I forgot to show you my pigs!" **he** exclaimed, the gleam returning to **his** eyes. The Pigman	The pronoun *he* is the antecedent of the pronoun *his*. The pronouns agree in person and number.

Pronouns should be used with consistency, so avoid shifting pronoun number and person within a sentence or passage.

Correct	Incorrect
Many older Americans know the exact date **they** started their first job.	Many older Americans know the exact date it started their first job.
My friends and I attended the football game; then **we** walked uptown.	My friends and I attended the football game; then he walked uptown.

Do not use *you* and *they* as indefinite pronouns, and avoid pronouns with no clear antecedent. If clearer, name the person or group to which you are referring.

Correct	Incorrect
As the old adage says: Better safe than sorry.	You know what they say: Better safe than sorry.
People in the community like to attend weekly basketball games. Anybody can have a great time.	People in the community like to attend weekly games. You don't have to love basketball to have a great time.

⟳ YOUR TURN

1. How should this sentence be changed?

> Penelope likes the game of soccer; it plays often.

- ○ A. Change **it** to **they**.
- ○ B. Change **it** to **he**.
- ○ C. Change **it** to **she**.
- ○ D. No change needs to be made to this sentence.

2. How should this sentence be changed?

> Maria and Sean thought the computer was just what he needed to make their business work.

- ○ A. Change **he** to **they**.
- ○ B. Change **he** to **she**.
- ○ C. Change **he** to **it**.
- ○ D. No change needs to be made to this sentence.

3. How should this sentence be changed?

> Jason was spending the week with his dad in Boston, where you were going to watch two Celtics games.

- ○ A. Change **his** to **its**.
- ○ B. Change **you** to **they**.
- ○ C. Change **you** to **he**.
- ○ D. No change needs to be made to this sentence.

4. How should this sentence be changed?

> Sidney moved to the city of Seattle and became a member of its city council.

- ○ A. Change **its** to **your**.
- ○ B. Change **its** to **their**.
- ○ C. Change **its** to **our**.
- ○ D. No change needs to be made to this sentence.

Reading & Writing Companion

Narrative Writing Process: Edit and Publish

| PLAN | DRAFT | REVISE | EDIT AND PUBLISH |

You have revised your narrative based on your peer feedback and your own examination.

Now, it is time to edit your narrative. When you revised, you focused on the content of your narrative. You probably looked at the story's beginning, descriptive details, and dialogue. When you edit, you focus on the mechanics of your story, paying close attention to things like grammar and punctuation.

Use the checklist below to guide you as you edit:

☐ Have I followed all the rules for punctuating dialogue?

☐ Have I used correct pronoun and antecedent agreement throughout the story?

☐ Have I used correct and consistent pronouns throughout the story?

☐ Do I have any sentence fragments or run-on sentences?

☐ Have I spelled everything correctly?

Notice some edits Nik has made:

- Changed a pronoun to agree with the antecedent.

- Fixed a sentence fragment.

- Corrected spelling.

- Added a comma before a piece of dialogue.

- Fixed a run-on sentence.

- Changed a pronoun to maintain consistency.

- Moved a period inside quotation marks.

Tyler froze. What should ~~she~~ **he** do? Then he ~~remembered. What~~ **remembered what** his father had said—Mrs. Molano would be all right.

Tyler patted the boy on the shoulder. As he ~~poared~~ **poured** some cereal into the bowl, he ~~said "Don't~~ **said, "Don't** worry, buddy. Your mom will be ~~okay the~~ **okay. The** doctors at the hospital will take good care of ~~them~~ **her**. My dad said he thought she would be fine. You'll ~~see".~~ **see."**

 ## WRITE

Use the questions on the previous page, as well as your peer reviews, to help you evaluate your narrative to determine areas that need editing. Then edit your narrative to correct those errors.

Once you have made all your corrections, you are ready to publish your work. You can distribute your writing to family and friends, hang it on a bulletin board, or post it on your blog. If you publish online, share the link with your family, friends, and classmates.

Please note that excerpts and passages in the StudySync® library and this workbook are intended as touchstones to generate interest in an author's work. The excerpts and passages do not substitute for the reading of entire texts, and StudySync® strongly recommends that students seek out and purchase the whole literary or informational work in order to experience it as the author intended. Links to online resellers are available in our digital library. In addition, complete works may be ordered through an authorized reseller by filling out and returning to StudySync® the order form enclosed in this workbook.

Reading & Writing Companion   **129**

Lost Island

FICTION

Introduction

Mariana wakes up alone, thirsty, and hungry on a deserted island. How did she get here, and why is her head throbbing? As she slowly recalls a large wave smashing into Uncle Merlin's fishing boat, Mariana takes her first steps

V VOCABULARY

damp

wet

capsized

tipped over in the water

intense

very strong

rescuer

someone who saves a person from harm or danger

anchored

held in place firmly

cautioned

gave a warning

☰ READ

NOTES

1 Mariana woke up slowly.

2 She was on her back. She felt sand in her mouth. The air was hot and **damp**. Where am I? Her head was throbbing. Was that the smell of salt in the air? Did I hear a seagull cry?

3 Mariana turned her head and slowly opened her eyes. The bright light was too **intense** for her. At first, she saw only damp yellow sand. She looked around. She saw stones, weeds, and a few palm trees. She could see the entire island. It was no larger than a soccer field.

4 Then Mariana remembered. She remembered fishing with Uncle Merlin. They found a good spot, so they **anchored** their boat near a little island. In the warm morning sun, the bay was calm. Mariana and Merlin got their fishing lines ready, when suddenly an enormous, thundering wave came out of nowhere. The wave overturned the boat, tossing them into the water. Mariana

NOTES

remembered rising to the surface and seeing land. She swam toward it; she swam and swam. An eternity seemed to have passed. She remembered thinking: Why don't I just give up? What had motivated her to keep swimming? She had finally reached the shore and had crawled up onto the sand. Exhausted.

5   Mariana looked at her surroundings now and thought. She must have passed out and slept on the beach for hours. The boat had **capsized** in early morning, but now the sun was high in the sky. It must be noon.

6   Noon, and hot.

7   Mariana wondered where her uncle was. Why hasn't he come to get me? What is he waiting for? She felt hungry; her mouth was dry. She thought of the lunch her uncle had packed. A cool drink and a sandwich would be perfect right now!

8   Then she realized something. Maybe her uncle wasn't coming to get her because maybe he had drowned. Maybe no **rescuer** was coming to get her. She was trapped. Stuck. Alone. Was she going to die on this island?

9   Mariana started to cry, but she stopped herself quickly. Wait. She **cautioned** herself. Don't be a baby. Use your head. That's what Uncle Merlin always said: "Use your head!"

10   Slowly turning her body, she then lifted herself onto her elbows. Next, she got onto her knees and finally stood up. Her head throbbed, but she looked into the island and took a step.

First Read

Read the story. After you read, answer the Think Questions below.

☁ **THINK QUESTIONS**

---

1. Who is the main character in the story? Where is she?

   _____ is the main character.

   She is _____.

2. What happened that tipped the boat over?

   The boat tipped over because _____.

3. How can you tell that Mariana is getting more worried as time passes?

   Mariana is getting more worried because _____

   _____.

4. Use context to confirm the meaning of the word *rescuer* as it is used in "Lost Island." Write your definition of *rescuer* here.

   Rescuer means _____.

   A context clue is _____.

5. What is another way to say that a boat *capsized*?

   A boat _____.

Please note that excerpts and passages in the StudySync® library and this workbook are intended as touchstones to generate interest in an author's work. The excerpts and passages do not substitute for the reading of entire texts, and StudySync® strongly recommends that students seek out and purchase the whole literary or informational work in order to experience it as the author intended. Links to online resellers are available in our digital library. In addition, complete works may be ordered through an authorized reseller by filling out and returning to StudySync® the order form enclosed in this workbook.

Reading & Writing Companion **133**

Skill:
Analyzing Expressions

 DEFINE

When you read, you may find English **expressions** that you do not know. An expression is a group of words that communicates an idea. Three types of expressions are idioms, sayings, and figurative language. They can be difficult to understand because the meanings of the words are different from their **literal**, or usual, meanings.

An **idiom** is an expression that is commonly known among a group of people. For example: "It's raining cats and dogs" means it is raining heavily. **Sayings** are short expressions that contain advice or wisdom. For instance: "Don't count your chickens before they hatch" means do not plan on something good happening before it happens. **Figurative** language is when you describe something by comparing it with something else, either directly (using the words *like* or *as*) or indirectly. For example, "I'm as hungry as a horse" means I'm very hungry. None of the expressions are about actual animals.

••• CHECKLIST FOR ANALYZING EXPRESSIONS

To determine the meaning of an expression, remember the following:

✓ If you find a confusing group of words, it may be an expression. The meaning of words in expressions may not be their literal meaning.

  • Ask yourself: Is this confusing because the words are new? Or because the words do not make sense together?

✓ Determining the overall meaning may require that you use one or more of the following:

  • context clues

  • a dictionary or other resource

  • teacher or peer support

✓ Highlight important information before and after the expression to look for clues.

YOUR TURN

Read paragraphs 9–10 from "Lost Island." Then complete the multiple-choice questions below.

---

from **"Lost Island"**

Mariana started to cry, but she stopped herself quickly. Wait. She cautioned herself. Don't be a baby. Use your head. That's what Uncle Merlin always said: "Use your head!"

Slowly turning her body, she then lifted herself onto her elbows. Next, she got onto her knees and finally stood up. Her head throbbed, but she looked into the island and took a step.

---

1. What does Mariana mean when she says "use your head" in paragraph 9?

    ○ A. find her uncle

    ○ B. to be cautious exploring

    ○ C. to use her head as a tool

    ○ D. to think about a solution

2. Which context clue helped you determine the meaning of the expression?

    ○ A. "Mariana started to cry . . ."

    ○ B. "That's what Uncle Merlin always said."

    ○ C. "Slowly turning her body . . ."

    ○ D. ". . . she got onto her knees and finally stood up."

Please note that excerpts and passages in the StudySync® library and this workbook are intended as touchstones to generate interest in an author's work. The excerpts and passages do not substitute for the reading of entire texts, and StudySync strongly recommends that students seek out and purchase the whole literary or informational work in order to experience it as the author intended. Links to online resellers are available in our digital library. In addition, complete works may be ordered through an authorized reseller by filling out and returning to StudySync® the order form enclosed in this workbook.

Reading & Writing Companion

135

Skill:
Conveying Ideas

 ★ **DEFINE**

Conveying ideas means communicating a **message** to another person. When speaking, you might not know what word to use to convey your ideas. When you do not know the exact English word, you can try different strategies. For example, you can ask for help from classmates or your teacher. You may use gestures and physical movements to act out the word. You can also try using **synonyms** or **defining** and describing the meaning you are trying to express.

••• CHECKLIST FOR CONVEYING IDEAS

To convey ideas for words you do not know, try the following strategies:

- ✓ Request help.

- ✓ Use gestures or physical movements.

- ✓ Use a synonym for the word.

- ✓ Describe what the word means using other words.

- ✓ Give an example of the word you want to use.

YOUR TURN

Read the following excerpt from the story. Then imagine that someone is trying to convey the idea of the boat *overturning*. Find the correct example for each strategy to complete the chart below.

---

from "**Lost Island**"

Then Mariana remembered. She remembered fishing with Uncle Merlin. They found a good spot, so they anchored their boat near a little island. In the warm morning sun, the bay was calm. Mariana and Merlin got their fishing lines ready, when suddenly an enormous, thundering wave came out of nowhere. The wave overturned the boat, tossing them into the water. Mariana remembered rising to the surface and seeing land.

	Examples
A	The person explains that the word means "to roll over."
B	The person turns her or his hand upside-down.
C	The person uses the similar words *tip* over.
D	The person says this when you knock a glass over and it spills.

Strategies	Examples
Use gestures or physical movements.	
Use a synonym for the word.	
Describe what the word means using other words.	
Give examples of when you would use the word.	

Please note that excerpts and passages in the StudySync® library and this workbook are intended as touchstones to generate interest in an author's work. The excerpts and passages do not substitute for the reading of entire texts, and StudySync® strongly recommends that students seek out and purchase the whole literary or informational work in order to experience it as the author intended. Links to online resellers are available in our digital library. In addition, complete works may be ordered through an authorized reseller by filling out and returning to StudySync® the order form enclosed in this workbook.

Reading & Writing Companion   **137**

Close Read

✎ **WRITE**

PERSONAL RESPONSE: Mariana faces dangers that few people her age ever see. How would you react if you were faced with the same situation? How would your response be like Mariana's? How would it be different? Recount the events that Mariana experienced, and describe what you might feel and do in her situation. Pay attention to spelling patterns as you write.

Use the checklist below to guide you as you write:

☐ What happens to Mariana in the story?

☐ What dangers does Mariana face?

☐ How does she act and feel?

☐ How would I be like Mariana?

☐ How would I be different from Mariana?

Use the sentence frames to organize and write your personal response.

If I were Mariana, _____.

First, I would _____.

Like Mariana, I would _____.

Unlike Mariana, I might _____.

Connected

FICTION

Introduction

What would you do if a friend went missing? What if you learned that a powerful, maybe even scary, secret lay behind the disappearance? In the story "Connected," three friends search for a missing person—and learn of a tantalizing force that could threaten the world as they know it.

V VOCABULARY

habitually
done regularly or often

digits
symbols for the numbers 0 to 9

froze
stopped in a position and without further movement

whirlpool
a place in a body of water, such as a river or a stream, where the water moves very fast in a circle

virus
a software program that is created to cause harm to a computer or network

 NOTES

≡ READ

1 Joshua was late. At first, his friends were not surprised. Joshua was **habitually** late. Joshua liked to stay connected to the Internet. His friends thought he was *too* connected.

2 But it was opening night for the biggest movie of the summer. Joshua should have met them hours ago.

3 "Did you hear from him today?" Victoria asked. Ibrahim and Mateo shook their heads.

4 She frowned. "Something's not right. We need to see what's going on."

5 "I know where he could be," Ibrahim said.

6 "His computer," they all exclaimed.

. . .

NOTES

7   Ibrahim opened the door to Joshua's room and **froze**. Clothes, food wrappers, and comic books were on the floor. A blue light glowed on Joshua's computer. He wasn't there.

8   "Start looking," Victoria said.

9   "For what?" Ibrahim asked.

10   "I don't know," Victoria answered, "but I think we'll find a clue."

11   Mateo stood behind his friends.

12   Ibrahim searched Joshua's backpack. Victoria checked some notebooks. She saw Mateo's eyes before he glanced down.

13   "What's wrong? Aren't you going to help us?"

14   Mateo mumbled something but didn't look up.

15   "What is it?" Ibrahim asked.

16   Mateo answered, "A few days ago Joshua told me he discovered a **virus**. He said it was different. It could take over any computer."

17   "But there was more," Mateo continued. "Joshua said the virus could take over *anyone*. He was going to find out who created it. He asked me not to tell."

18   Victoria and Ibrahim were shocked. Mateo stepped forward.

19   "What about his computer?" he asked. "Maybe he left something there."

20   "Yes!" said Victoria.

21   The three friends gathered around the computer. Ibrahim took the mouse and clicked.

22   They saw white numbers moving across the screen. Soon, the **digits** moved faster. First, they moved diagonally, like rippling water. Then, they moved in circles like a **whirlpool**. The three friends moved closer to the screen. They couldn't look away. The numbers blurred and four words appeared:

23   *Enter, if you wish*

24   Ibrahim pressed [Enter].

Copyright © BookheadEd Learning, LLC

NOTES

25 They saw a bright flash and had to close their eyes. When they opened their eyes, they were in a long hallway.

26 They could see a shape. It was the figure of a man, moving toward them.

27 "That was an interesting choice, wouldn't you say?" the figure said coolly. The words hung in the air like icicles.

28 Victoria spoke first. "Who are you?" she asked, her voice shivering.

29 "We will get to that. And we will get to your friend. But first you must do something for us."

CONNECTED   First Read

Read the story. After you read, answer the Think Questions below.

☁ THINK QUESTIONS

1. What is Joshua late for at the beginning of the story?

    Joshua is late for _____.

2. Where did Joshua's friends go to find him? What did they find?

    Joshua's friends went to _____.

    They found _____.

3. What happened when Ibrahim pressed [Enter] on the computer?

    There was _____.

4. Use context to confirm the meaning of the word *habitually* as it is used in "Connected." Write your definition of *habitually* here.

    Habitually means _____.

    A context clue is _____.

5. What is another way to say that Ibrahim *froze*?

    Ibrahim was _____.

Please note that excerpts and passages in the StudySync® library and this workbook are intended as touchstones to generate interest in an author's work. The excerpts and passages do not substitute for the reading of entire texts, and StudySync® strongly recommends that students seek out and purchase the whole literary or informational work in order to experience it as the author intended. Links to online resellers are available in our digital library. In addition, complete works may be ordered through an authorized reseller by filling out and returning to StudySync® the order form enclosed in this workbook.

Reading & Writing Companion   **143**

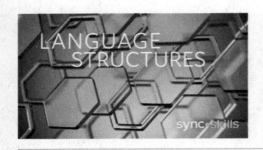

Skill:
Language Structures

 ## ★ DEFINE

In every language, there are rules that tell how to **structure** sentences. These rules define the correct order of words. In the English language, for example, a **basic** structure for sentences is subject, verb, and object. Some sentences have more **complicated** structures.

You will encounter both basic and complicated **language structures** in the classroom materials you read. Being familiar with language structures will help you better understand the text.

••• CHECKLIST FOR LANGUAGE STRUCTURES

To improve your comprehension of language structures, do the following:

✓ Monitor your understanding.

- Ask yourself: Why do I not understand this sentence? Is it because I do not understand some of the words? Or is it because I do not understand the way the words are ordered in the sentence?

✓ Break down the sentence into its parts.

✓ In English, most sentences share the same pattern: subject + verb + object.

- The **subject** names who or what is doing the action.
- The **verb** names the action or state of being.
- The **object** answers questions such as "Who?," "What?," "Where?," and "When?"

✓ Ask yourself: What is the subject and the verb of this sentence? What details do the other words provide?

✓ Confirm your understanding with a peer or teacher.

YOUR TURN

Read the following excerpt from "Connected." Then, complete the chart by writing the words and phrases into the "Subject," "Verb," and "Object" columns. The first row has been done as an example.

---

from **"Connected"**

Mateo stood behind his friends.

Ibrahim searched Joshua's backpack. Victoria checked some notebooks. She saw Mateo's eyes before he glanced down.

Sentence	Subject	Verb	Object
Mateo stood behind his friends.	Mateo	stood	behind his friends
Ibrahim searched Joshua's backpack.			
Victoria checked some notebooks.			
She saw Mateo's eyes before he glanced down.			

Skill: Retelling and Summarizing

★ DEFINE

You can retell and summarize a text after reading to show your understanding. **Retelling** is telling a story again in your own words. **Summarizing** is giving a short explanation of the most important ideas in a text.

Keep your retelling or summary **concise**. Only include important information and keywords from the text. By summarizing and retelling a text, you can improve your comprehension of the text's ideas.

••• CHECKLIST FOR RETELLING AND SUMMARIZING

In order to retell or summarize text, note the following:

✓ Identify the main events of the text.

- Ask yourself: What happens in this text? What are the main events that happen at the beginning, the middle, and the end of the text?

✓ Identify the main ideas in a text.

- Ask yourself: What are the most important ideas in the text?

✓ Determine the answers to the 6 *Wh-* questions.

- Ask yourself: After reading this text, can I answer Who? What? Where? When? Why? and How? questions.

YOUR TURN

Read the following excerpt from "Connected." Then, write the events in the beginning, middle, and end of the excerpt to retell what happened.

---

from **"Connected"**

They saw white numbers moving across the screen. Soon, the digits moved faster. First, they moved diagonally, like rippling water. Then, they moved in circles like a whirlpool. The three friends moved closer to the screen. They couldn't look away. The numbers blurred and four words appeared: *Enter, if you wish.*

Event Options		
The friends moved closer to the screen.	The words "Enter, if you wish" appeared on the screen.	They saw numbers moving across the screen.

Beginning	
Middle	
End	

Close Read

 WRITE

PERSONAL RESPONSE: Would you have pressed [Enter] like Joshua's friends did? Write a short paragraph that explains your reasoning. Support your explanation with details and evidence from the text. Pay attention to subject-verb agreement as you write.

Use the checklist below to guide you as you write.

☐ What happened at the beginning and middle of the story?

☐ Why did Joshua's friends press [Enter] at the end of the story?

☐ What would you have done that is the same?

☐ What would you have done that is different?

Use the sentence frames to organize and write your personal response.

In the beginning, Joshua's friends realized that Joshua was _____.

They went to his room to look for _____.

Matteo remembered Joshua talking about a _____.

The friends decided to look at Joshua's _____.

Like Joshua's friends, I would have _____

because _____.

However, I would not have _____

because _____.

:::studysync®

ASSIGNMENTS   BINDER   LIBRARY

You and Me

UNIT 2

You and Me

How do relationships shape us?

Genre Focus: **POETRY**

Texts

 Paired Readings

Extended Writing Project and Grammar

English Language Learner Resources

Copyright © BookheadEd Learning, LLC

How do relationships shape us?

SHARON CREECH

In a suburb of Cleveland, Ohio, Sharon Creech (b. 1945) grew up in a house filled with visiting relatives and friends, along with her parents, sister, and three brothers. Each summer, Creech's parents would pile all five children into the family car to go on a long road trip. On one of these trips, when Creech was twelve years old, they went to Idaho, and that experience became the basis of the story told in the novel *Walk Two Moons* (1994).

COUNTEE CULLEN

In 1918, at the age of fifteen, Countee Cullen (1903-1946) lost the woman who cared for him: his grandmother. His new guardian would be the pastor of Salem Methodist Episcopal Church, which hosted the largest congregation in Harlem. Cullen's poetry is regarded as a significant voice of the Harlem Renaissance, a vibrant period that ushered in an innovative generation of African American writers in New York City. Cullen often expressed that he believed art could transcend race, and hoped his poems would bring together people from all walks of life.

NIKKI GIOVANNI

Nikki Giovanni (b. 1943) is an African American poet who grew up during the civil rights movement and launched her career at the age of twenty-five with her collection of poems, *Black Feeling Black Talk* (1968), published shortly after the assassination of Dr. Martin Luther King Jr. Around the same time, Giovanni was a preeminent author in the Black Arts Movement and was friends with Rosa Parks and Muhammad Ali. She went on to develop a distinguished career as a poet and activist, and is currently a college professor in Virginia.

FRANCISCO JIMÉNEZ

Francisco Jiménez (b. 1943) is a Chicano writer of fiction and memoir who moved from his home in Mexico to California and back several times before he reached adulthood. Along with his family, Jiménez was a migrant field-worker, moving through California to pick crops: Corcoran for cotton, Santa Maria for strawberries, and Fresno for grapes. Despite facing many hardships, including not having a permanent home or consistent education, Jiménez excelled in school and went on to become a college professor and a successful author.

JACKI JING

NCAA Division I athlete Jacki Jing (b. 1986) grew up playing volleyball in Centennial, Colorado. She received a full athletic scholarship to the State University of New York at Binghamton, where she earned degrees in political science and English, and was later inducted into their Athletic Hall of Fame in 2014. Jing went on to become a television journalist, reporting and anchoring for stations in Colorado, New York, Massachusetts, and Louisiana.

DAVID KHERDIAN

"What we learn in childhood is carved in stone. What we learn as adults is carved in ice," writes David Kherdian (b. 1931). The poet, biographer, and editor was born to two survivors of the Armenian Genocide and raised in Wisconsin near Root River. He excelled at sports, especially basketball, football, and softball, and also loved to read and draw. From an early age, he was exposed to and fought against the discrimination he experienced as a child of immigrants.

WALTER DEAN MYERS

Walter Dean Myers (1937–2004) was raised in Harlem by his adopted family. As a child, he was a gifted student and athlete but was teased for having a speech impediment and was known to have a quick temper. He found solace in reading and writing, and would grow up to become an award-winning author of books for young adults and children. His first book, *Where Does the Day Go* (1969), was written for a contest for African American writers, and marked the start of a career-long mission to write literature for and about people of color.

MILDRED TAYLOR

Mildred Taylor (b. 1943) moved with her family from Jackson, Mississippi, to newly-integrated Toledo, Ohio, when she was only three months old. She describes herself as a quiet child in a family of prodigious storytellers. The family visited Mississippi every year, where her great-grandfather had purchased land in the late 1800s that the family still owns. Taylor used those visits to the American South and family lore as the basis for her stories. *Roll of Thunder, Hear My Cry*, the second novel of the saga, won the 1977 Newbery Award.

HOLLY WARLICK

When Holly Warlick (b. 1958) was named head coach of the University of Tennessee's women's basketball team, her predecessor Pat Summitt admitted that Warlick had already been leading the team in her role as assistant coach. The legendary Summitt passed her whistle to Warlick after receiving a diagnosis of Alzheimer's Disease in 2011. Warlick was formerly a player on Summitt's team, and was the first player in Tennessee sports history to have her jersey retired at the end of her playing career.

PAT MORA

Mexican American author Pat Mora (b. 1942) grew up surrounded by books in El Paso, Texas, and fell in love with reading and writing at an early age. Her poetry and stories explore Chicana identity in the region of the border and are written in both English and Spanish. Mora grew up with bilingual parents and says that switching between English and Spanish was the rhythm of her childhood. She went on to replicate a book-loving, bilingual home for her own three children.

Walk Two Moons

FICTION
Sharon Creech
1994

Introduction

On a trip with her grandparents, Salamanca, or Sal, tells them the story of her best friend, Phoebe Winterbottom. Sal met Phoebe when she and her father left their farm in Kentucky and moved to Ohio, where Margaret Cadaver lives. Sal's father befriended Margaret after her mother disappeared. Phoebe is certain that Mrs. Cadaver, who lives next door to her family, is somehow sinister, and is responsible for the strange notes that appear on her family's doorstep. They wind up having a magical effect on the grief that surrounds Phoebe's mother, and help Sal understand her own identity. A beloved classic, this novel by Sharon Creech (b. 1945) has won numerous awards, including the Newbery Medal.

"In the course of a lifetime, what does it matter?"

1   A few days after Phoebe and I had seen Mr. Birkway and Mrs. Cadaver whacking away at the rhododendron, I walked home with Phoebe after school. She was as **crotchety** and **sullen** as a three-legged mule, and I was not quite sure why. She had been asking me why I had not said anything to my father about Mrs. Cadaver and Mr. Birkway, and I told her that I was waiting for the right time.

2   "Your father was over there yesterday," Phoebe said. "I saw him. He'd better watch out. What would you do if Mrs. Cadaver chopped up your father? Would you go live with your mother?"

3   It surprised me when she said that, reminding me that I had told Phoebe nothing about my mother. "Yes, I suppose I would go live with her." That was impossible and I knew it, but for some reason I could not tell Phoebe that, so I lied.

4   Phoebe's mother was sitting at the kitchen table when we walked in. In front of her was a pan of burned brownies. She blew her nose. "Oh sweetie," she said, "you startled me. How was it?"

5   "How was what?" Phoebe asked.

6   "Why, sweetie, school of course. How was it? How were your classes?"

7   "Okay."

8   "Just okay?" Mrs. Winterbottom suddenly leaned over and kissed Phoebe's cheek.

9   "I'm not a baby, you know," Phoebe said, wiping off the kiss.

10 Mrs. Winterbottom stabbed the brownies with a knife. "Want one?" she asked.

11 "They're burned," Phoebe said. "Besides, I'm fat."

NOTES

Skill: Language, Style, and Audience

The author chooses words like sullen to show the audience that Sal is smart because this is not a word kids often use. After reading this paragraph, I also know that Sal is from the country because she mentions a mule. She's funny, and she's tolerant because she doesn't get mad that Phoebe is grouchy.

Copyright © BookheadEd Learning, LLC

12 "Oh sweetie, you're not fat," Mrs. Winterbottom said.

13 "I am."

14 "No, you're not."

15 "I am, I am, I am!" Phoebe shouted at her mother. "You don't have to bake things for me. I'm too fat. And you don't have to wait here for me to come home. I'm thirteen now."

16 Phoebe marched upstairs. Mrs. Winterbottom offered me a brownie, so I sat down at the table. What I started doing was remembering the day before my mother left. I did not know it was to be her last day home. Several times that day, my mother asked me if I wanted to walk up in the fields with her. It was drizzling outside, and I was cleaning out my desk, and I just did not feel like going. "Maybe later," I kept saying. When she asked me for about the tenth time, I said, "No! I don't want to go. Why do you keep asking me?" I don't know why I did that. I didn't mean anything by it, but that was one of the last memories she had of me, and I wished I could take it back.

17 Phoebe's sister, Prudence, stormed into the house, slamming the door behind her. "I blew it. I just know it!" she wailed.

18 "Oh sweetie," her mother said.

19 "I did!" Prudence said. "I did, I did, I did."

Skill: Textual Evidence

Using textual evidence, I can make inferences about Mrs. Winterbottom's sadness. I think Mrs. Winterbottom and Prudence have a rocky relationship. I can also infer Sal's guilt for how she treated her mother on their last day together.

20 Mrs. Winterbottom half-heartedly chipped away at the burned brownies and asked Prudence if she would have another chance at cheerleading **tryouts.**

21 "Yes, tomorrow. But I know I'm going to blow it!"

22 Her mother said, "Maybe I'll come along and watch." I could tell that Mrs. Winterbottom was trying to rise above some awful sadness she was feeling, but Prudence couldn't see that. Prudence had her own **agenda**, just as I had had my own agenda that day my mother wanted me to walk with her. I couldn't see my own mother's sadness.

23 "What?" Prudence said. "Come along and *watch*?"

24 "Yes, wouldn't that be nice?"

25 "No!" Prudence said. "No, no, no. You can't. It would be awful."

26 I heard the front door open and shut and Phoebe came in the kitchen waving a white envelope. "Guess what was on the steps?" she said.

27   Mrs. Winterbottom took the envelope and turned it over and over before she slowly unsealed it and slipped out the message.

28   "Oh," she said. "Who is doing this?" She held out the piece of paper: *In the course of a lifetime, what does it matter?*

29   Prudence said, "Well, I have more important things to worry about, I can **assure** you. I know I'm going to blow those cheerleading tryouts, I just know it."

30   On and on she went, until Phoebe said, "Cripes, Prudence, in the course of a lifetime, what does it matter?"

31   At that moment, it was as if a switch went off in Mrs. Winterbottom's brain. She put her hand to her mouth and stared out the window. She was invisible to Prudence and Phoebe, though. They did not notice.

32   Phoebe said, "Are these cheerleading tryouts such a big deal? Will you even remember them in five years?"

33   "Yes!" Prudence said. "Yes, I most certainly will."

34   "How about ten years? Will you remember them in ten?"

35   "Yes!" Prudence said.

36   As I walked home, I thought about the message. *In the course of a lifetime, what does it matter?* I said it over and over. I wondered about the mysterious messenger, and I wondered about all the things in the course of a lifetime that would not matter. I did not think cheerleading tryouts would matter, but I was not so sure about yelling at your mother. I was certain, however, that if your mother left, it would be something that mattered in the whole long course of your lifetime.

Excerpted from *Walk Two Moons* by Sharon Creech, published by HarperCollins Publishers.

First Read

Read *Walk Two Moons*. After you read, complete the Think Questions below.

1. What kind of relationship does Mrs. Winterbottom have with her daughters Prudence and Phoebe? Cite evidence from the text to support your answer.

2. What message does Phoebe find on the steps? What effect does it have on the narrator? Be sure to cite textual evidence to support your answer.

3. Mood is the emotional quality or atmosphere of a story. What is the mood in Mrs. Winterbottom's kitchen in this excerpt from *Walk Two Moons*? Which words and descriptions contribute to this mood?

4. Find the word **agenda** in paragraph 22 of *Walk Two Moons*. Use context clues in the surrounding sentences, as well as the sentence in which the word appears, to determine the word's meaning. Write your definition here and identify clues that helped you figure out its meaning.

5. Use context clues to determine the meaning of **assure** as it is used in paragraph 29 of *Walk Two Moons*. Write your definition here and identify clues that helped you figure out its meaning. Then check the meaning in a dictionary.

Skill:
Language, Style, and Audience

Use the Checklist to analyze Language, Style, and Audience in *Walk Two Moons*. Refer to the sample student annotations about Language, Style, and Audience in the text.

••• CHECKLIST FOR LANGUAGE, STYLE, AND AUDIENCE

In order to determine an author's style, do the following:

- ✓ identify and define any unfamiliar words or phrases

- ✓ use context, including the meaning of surrounding words and phrases

- ✓ note specific words and phrases that the author uses to create a response in the reader

- ✓ note the tone that the author is communicating through the word choices

To analyze the impact of specific word choice on meaning and tone, ask the following questions:

- ✓ How did the language impact your understanding of the meaning of the text?

- ✓ What stylistic choices can you identify in the text? How does the style influence your understanding of the language?

- ✓ How could various audiences interpret this language? What different possible emotional responses can you list?

- ✓ How does the writer's choice of words impact or create a specific tone in the text?

Please note that excerpts and passages in the StudySync® library and this workbook are intended as touchstones to generate interest in an author's work. The excerpts and passages do not substitute for the reading of entire texts, and StudySync® strongly recommends that students seek out and purchase the whole literary or informational work in order to experience it as the author intended. Links to online resellers are available in our digital library. In addition, complete works may be ordered through an authorized reseller by filling out and returning to StudySync® the order form enclosed in this workbook.

Reading & Writing Companion   **159**

Skill:
Language, Style, And Audience

Reread paragraphs 17–25 of *Walk Two Moons*. Then, using the Checklist on the previous page, answer the multiple-choice questions below.

⟳ YOUR TURN

1. How does the author use the words *stormed* and *wailed* in paragraph 17 to characterize Prudence?

   ○ A. Prudence is dramatic and self-absorbed.
   ○ B. Prudence is quiet and respectful.
   ○ C. Prudence is loud, but interested in others.
   ○ D. Prudence is distracted, but caring.

2. What does the author's repetition of words in paragraphs 19 and 25 reveal about Prudence?

   ○ A. Prudence wants to make sure she's being heard.
   ○ B. Prudence accommodates her mother's poor hearing.
   ○ C. Prudence is childish, and she throws tantrums.
   ○ D. Prudence is a good speaker, and she emphasizes her points.

3. What is the effect of the author's use of italics in paragraph 23?

   ○ A. The italics show gratitude in Prudence's tone.
   ○ B. The italics show horror in Prudence's tone.
   ○ C. The italics show humor in Prudence's tone.
   ○ D. The italics show sorrow in Prudence's tone.

Skill:
Textual Evidence

Use the Checklist to analyze Textual Evidence in *Walk Two Moons*. Refer to the sample student annotations about Textual Evidence in the text.

••• CHECKLIST FOR TEXTUAL EVIDENCE

In order to support analysis and ideas by citing textual evidence that is explicitly stated in the text, do the following:

- ✓ read the text closely and critically

- ✓ identify what the text says explicitly

- ✓ find the most relevant textual evidence that supports your analysis and ideas

- ✓ consider why an author explicitly states specific details and information

- ✓ cite the specific words, phrases, sentences, or paragraphs from the text that support your analysis and ideas

In order to interpret implicit meanings in a text by making inferences, do the following:

- ✓ combine information directly stated in the text with your own knowledge, experiences, and observations

- ✓ cite the specific words, phrases, sentences, or paragraphs from the text that support these inferences

In order to cite textual evidence to support an analysis of what the text says explicitly as well as inferences drawn from the text, consider the following questions:

- ✓ Have I read the text closely and critically?

- ✓ What inferences am I making about the text? What textual evidence am I using to support these inferences?

- ✓ Am I quoting the evidence from the text correctly?

- ✓ Does my textual evidence logically relate to my analysis?

Please note that excerpts and passages in the StudySync® library and this workbook are intended as touchstones to generate interest in an author's work. The excerpts and passages do not substitute for the reading of entire texts, and StudySync® strongly recommends that students seek out and purchase the whole literary or informational work in order to experience it as the author intended. Links to online resellers are available in our digital library. In addition, complete works may be ordered through an authorized reseller by filling out and returning to StudySync® the order form enclosed in this workbook.

Reading & Writing Companion   161

Skill:
Textual Evidence

Reread paragraphs 27–36 of *Walk Two Moons*. Then, using the Checklist on the previous page, answer the multiple-choice questions below.

⟳ YOUR TURN

1. What evidence explicitly stated in the text best describes Prudence's reaction to the letter?

   ○ A. "'Cripes, Prudence, in the course of a lifetime, what does it matter?'"
   ○ B. "'Well, I have more important things to worry about, I can assure you.'"
   ○ C. "She put her hand to her mouth and stared out the window."
   ○ D. "I wondered about all the things in the course of a lifetime that would not matter."

2. In paragraph 31, what is the effect of the letter on Mrs. Winterbottom, and how is this effect revealed by the author?

   ○ A. Mrs. Winterbottom continues to be confused by the letter, which the author reveals by having Mrs. Winterbottom put her hand to her mouth.
   ○ B. Mrs. Winterbottom doesn't show interest in the letter, which the author reveals with the narration that Mrs. Winterbottom stares out the window.
   ○ C. Mrs. Winterbottom suddenly figures something out about the letter, which the author reveals with the narration that a switch went off in Mrs. Winterbottom's brain.
   ○ D. Mrs. Winterbottom opens the letter and disappears from the kitchen, which the author reveals with the narration that Mrs. Winterbottom is invisible to her daughters.

3. Which message can be inferred from this scene of *Walk Two Moons*?

   ○ A. The past and the present remain separate time periods in one's life.
   ○ B. The present is more important than the past.
   ○ C. The past can invade the present through triggered memories.
   ○ D. Past events determine future events through present choices.

Close Read

Reread *Walk Two Moons*. As you reread, complete the Skills Focus questions below. Then use your answers and annotations from the questions to help you complete the Write activity.

◎ SKILLS FOCUS

1. Identify evidence that shows how the author contrasts Sal's treatment of her own mother with the way Phoebe and Prudence respond to their mother, Mrs. Winterbottom.

2. Identify evidence that shows what Sal learns about herself after witnessing the scene between Mrs. Winterbottom, Phoebe, and Prudence.

3. Phoebe finds a note on the doorstep that asks, "In the course of a lifetime, what does it matter?" What inference can you draw from the text to explain Mrs. Winterbottom's reaction to the note? What evidence explicitly stated in the text explains Prudence's reaction?

4. Explain how the author's word choice influenced the reader's understanding of the characters of Phoebe and Mrs. Winterbottom.

5. Identify evidence in the last paragraph that reveals what Sal realizes when she reflects back about her own mother leaving home.

✏ WRITE

NARRATIVE: Rewrite this excerpt from *Walk Two Moons* with Phoebe, Prudence, or Mrs. Winterbottom as the narrator instead of Sal. Use evidence explicitly stated in the text, as well as inferences drawn from the text, to identify the narrator's relationship with the other characters. In your narrative, select language that reflects an appropriate tone for the narrator you choose.

Roll of Thunder, Hear My Cry

FICTION

Mildred D. Taylor

1976

Introduction

Written by Mildred D. Taylor (b. 1943), *Roll of Thunder, Hear My Cry* is the gripping story of the Logans, a land-owning black family in the Deep South struggling to keep things together during a tumultuous year in the 1930s. Largely insulated from the injustices of the world around her, but raised with a strong sense of fairness, nine-year-old Cassie is only beginning to understand the realities of racism and the everyday terror it brings to the grown-ups in her community. In the excerpt here, neighbors bring bad news for her father. Published in 1976, Taylor's novel won the Newbery Medal the following year.

"We keep doing what we gotta, and we don't give up. We can't. . . ."

1   When supper was ready, I eagerly grabbed the iron bell before Christopher-John or Little Man could claim it, and ran onto the back porch to summon Papa, Mr. Morrison, and Stacey from the fields. As the three of them washed up on the back porch, Mama went to the end of the porch where Papa stood alone. "What did Mr. Jamison want?" she asked, her voice barely **audible.**

2   Papa took the towel Mama handed him, but did not reply immediately. I was just inside the kitchen dipping out the butter beans. I moved closer to the window so that I could hear his answer.

3   "Don't keep anything from me, David. If there's trouble, I want to know."

4   Papa looked down at her. "Nothing to worry 'bout, honey . . . . just seems that Thurston Wallace been in town talking 'bout how he's not gonna let a few smart colored folks ruin his business. Says he's gonna put a stop to this shopping in Vicksburg. That's all."

5   Mama sighed and stared out across the plowed field to the sloping pasture land. "I'm feeling scared, David," she said.

6   Papa put down the towel. "Not yet, Mary. It's not time to be scared yet. They're just talking."

7   Mama turned and faced him. "And when they stop talking?"

8   "Then . . . then maybe it'll be time. But right now, pretty lady," he said, leading her by the hand toward the kitchen door, "right now I've got better things to think about."

Copyright © BookheadEd Learning, LLC

NOTES

Skill:
Story Structure

I see that Mama is nervous because the narrator can hardly hear her ask the question about Mr. Jamison. This seems to be part of the conflict.

Papa does not seem worried about the situation with Mr. Jamison, but the problem seems serious. How will the family solve this problem?

Skill: Connotation and Denotation

I am not sure what this word means, but I can tell that Papa is very happy because he seems excited about the dinner. In this context, it seems like he is looking down at the table because he sees the dinner as he comes into the room. I think the word beamed means that he has a big smile on his face because he is very happy about seeing the dinner.

Skill: Theme

Mama is still scared and anxious, but Cassie hopes for a solution. This hope starts to go away though, which can be seen by the way her words keep getting interrupted. Her desperation and Mama's fear show the theme: fear can make people lose hope even though they try not to.

9   Quickly I poured the rest of the butter beans into the bowl and hurried across the kitchen to the table. As Mama and Papa entered, I slid onto the bench beside Little Man and Christopher-John. Papa beamed down at the table.

10   "Well, look-a-here!" he exclaimed. "Good ole butter beans and cornbread! You better come on, Mr. Morrison! You too, son!" he called. "These womenfolks done gone and fixed us a feast."

11   After school was out, spring drooped quickly toward summer; yet Papa had not left for the railroad. He seemed to be waiting for something, and I secretly hoped that whatever that something was, it would never come so that he would not leave. But one evening as he, Mama, Big Ma, Mr. Morrison, and Stacey sat on the front porch while Christopher-John, Little Man, and I dashed around the yard chasing fireflies, I overheard him say, "Sunday I'm gonna have to go. Don't want to though. I got this gut feeling it ain't over yet. It's too easy."

12   I released the firefly **imprisoned** in my hand and sat beside Papa and Stacey on the steps. "Papa, please," I said, leaning against his leg, "don't go this year." Stacey looked out into the falling night, his face resigned, and said nothing.

13   Papa put out his large hand and caressed my face. "Got to, Cassie girl," he said softly. "Baby, there's bills to pay and ain't no money coming in. Your mama's got no job come fall and there's the **mortgage** and next year's taxes to think of."

14   "But, Papa, we planted more cotton this year. Won't that pay the taxes?"

15   Papa shook his head. "With Mr. Morrison here we was able to plant more, but that cotton is for living on; the railroad money is for the taxes and the mortgage."

16   I looked back at Mama wanting her to speak, to persuade him to stay, but when I saw her face I knew that she would not. She had known he would leave, just as we all had known.

17   "Papa, just another week or two, couldn't you—"

18   "I can't, baby. May have lost my job already."

19   "But Papa—"

20   "Cassie, that's enough now," Mama said from the deepening shadows.

21 I grew quiet and Papa put his arms around Stacey and me, his hands falling casually over our shoulders. From the edge of the lawn where Little Man and Christopher-John had **ventured** after lightning bugs, Little Man called, "Somebody's coming!" A few minutes later Mr. Avery and Mr. Lanier emerged from the dusk and walked up the sloping lawn. Mama sent Stacey and me to get more chairs for the porch, then we settled back beside Papa still sitting on the steps, his back propped against a pillar facing the visitors.

22 "You goin' up to the store tomorrow, David?" Mr. Avery asked after all the amenities had been said. Since the first trip in January, Mr. Morrison had made one other trip to Vicksburg, but Papa had not gone with him.

23 Papa motioned to Mr. Morrison. "Mr. Morrison and me going the day after tomorrow. Your wife brought down that list of things you need yesterday."

24 Mr. Avery cleared his throat nervously. "It's—it's that list I come 'bout, David. . . . I don't want them things no more."

25 The porch grew silent.

26 When no one said anything, Mr. Avery glanced at Mr. Lanier, and Mr. Lanier shook his head and continued. "Mr. Granger making it hard on us, David. Said we gonna have to give him sixty percent of the cotton, 'stead of fifty . . . now that the cotton's planted and it's too late to plant more. . . . Don't s'pose though that it makes much difference. The way cotton sells these days, seems the more we plant, the less money we gets anyways—"

27 Mr. Avery's coughing interrupted him and he waited patiently until the coughing had stopped before he went on. "I'm gonna be hard put to pay that debt in Vicksburg, David, but I'm gonna. . . . I want you to know that."

• • •

28 Mr. Avery's coughing started again and for a while there was only the coughing and the silence. But when the coughing ceased, Mr. Lanier said, "I pray to God there was a way we could stay in this thing, but we can't go on no chain gang, David."

29 Papa nodded. "Don't expect you to, Silas."

30 Mr. Avery laughed softly. "We sure had 'em goin' for a time though, didn't we?"

31 "Yes," agreed Papa quietly, "we sure did."

32 When the men had left, Stacey snapped, "They got no right pulling out! Just 'cause them Wallaces threaten them one time they go jumping all over themselves to get out like a bunch of scared jackrabbits—"

33 Papa stood suddenly and grabbed Stacey upward. "You, boy, don't you get so grown you go to talking 'bout more than you know. Them men, they doing what they've gotta do. You got any idea what a risk they took just to go shopping in Vicksburg in the first place? They go on that chain gang and their families got nothing. They'll get kicked off that plot of land they tend and there'll be no place for them to go. You understand that?"

34 "Y-yessir," said Stacey. Papa released him and stared moodily into the night. "You were born blessed, boy, with land of your own. If you hadn't been, you'd cry out for it while you try to survive . . . like Mr. Lanier and Mr. Avery. Maybe even do what they doing now. It's hard on a man to give up, but sometimes it seems there just ain't nothing else he can do."

35 "I . . . I'm sorry, Papa," Stacey muttered.

36 After a moment, Papa reached out and draped his arm over Stacey's shoulder.

37 "Papa," I said, standing to join them, "we giving up too?"

38 Papa looked down at me and brought me closer, then waved his hand toward the drive. "You see that fig tree over yonder, Cassie? Them other trees all around . . . that oak and walnut, they're a lot bigger and they take up more room and give so much shade they almost **overshadow** that little ole fig. But that fig tree's got roots that run deep, and it belongs in that yard as much as that oak and walnut. It keeps on blooming, bearing good fruit year after year, knowing all the time it'll never get as big as them other trees. Just keeps on growing and doing what it gotta do. It don't give up. It give up, it'll die. There's a lesson to be learned from that little tree, Cassie girl, 'cause we're like it. We keep doing what we gotta, and we don't give up. We can't."

Excerpted from *Roll of Thunder, Hear My Cry* by Mildred D. Taylor, published by Puffin Books.

First Read

Read *Roll of Thunder, Hear My Cry*. After you read, complete the Think Questions below.

1. Why are Thurston Wallace and Mr. Granger angry with the black farmers? Cite textual evidence from the selection to support your answer.

2. Write two or three sentences describing why Papa is in a better position than Mr. Avery and Mr. Lanier to stand up to Thurston Wallace. Cite textual evidence from the selection to support your answer.

3. Voice is the use of language that conveys the distinctive personality of the writer or speaker, the narrator, or a particular character. In paragraph 33, what words or phrases does Papa use when talking with Stacey that give you a sense of his personality? How would you describe his personality? Cite textual evidence from the selection to support your answer.

4. Find the word **imprisoned** in paragraph 12 of *Roll of Thunder, Hear My Cry*. Use context clues in the surrounding sentences, as well as the sentence in which the word appears, to determine the word's meaning. Write your definition here and identify clues that helped you figure out its meaning.

5. Use context to determine the meaning of the word **ventured** as it is used in *Roll of Thunder, Hear My Cry* in paragraph 21. Write your definition here and identify clues that helped you figure out its meaning. Then check the meaning in a dictionary.

Please note that excerpts and passages in the StudySync® library and this workbook are intended as touchstones to generate interest in an author's work. The excerpts and passages do not substitute for the reading of entire texts, and StudySync® strongly recommends that students seek out and purchase the whole literary or informational work in order to experience it as the author intended. Links to online resellers are available in our digital library. In addition, complete works may be ordered through an authorized reseller by filling out and returning to StudySync® the order form enclosed in this workbook.

Reading & Writing Companion **169**

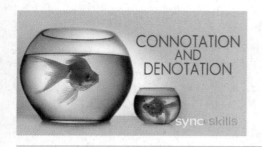

Skill:
Connotation and Denotation

Use the Checklist to analyze Connotation and Denotation in *Roll of Thunder, Hear My Cry.* Refer to the sample student annotations about Connotation and Denotation in the text.

••• CHECKLIST FOR CONNOTATION AND DENOTATION

In order to identify the denotative meanings of words and phrases, use the following steps:

- ✓ first, note unfamiliar words and phrases; key words used to describe important characters, events, and ideas; or words that inspire an emotional reaction

- ✓ next, verify the denotative meaning of words by consulting a reference material such as a dictionary, glossary, or thesaurus

To better understand the meaning of words and phrases as they are used in a text, including connotative meanings, use the following questions:

- ✓ What is the genre or subject of the text? How does that affect the possible meaning of a word or phrase?

- ✓ Does the word create a positive, negative, or neutral emotion?

- ✓ What synonyms or alternative phrasing help you describe the connotative meaning of the word?

To determine the meaning of words and phrases as they are used in a text, including connotative meanings, use the following questions:

- ✓ What is the meaning of the word or phrase? What is the connotation as well as the denotation?

- ✓ If I substitute a synonym based on denotation, is the meaning the same? How does it change the meaning of the text?

Skill:
Connotation and Denotation

Reread paragraph 21 of *Roll of Thunder, Hear My Cry*. Then, using the Checklist on the previous page, answer the multiple-choice questions below.

⟳ YOUR TURN

1. This question has two parts. First, answer Part A. Then, answer Part B.

   Part A: What is the denotative meaning of the word **ventured** as it is used in the context of paragraph 21?

   ○ A. set out
   ○ B. yelled loudly
   ○ C. remembered
   ○ D. caught

   Part B: Based on your answer to Part A, what is the intended connotation of the word *venture* below? Which definition BEST supports the conclusion drawn in Part A?

   ○ A. Positive - the boys are having fun venturing out after the bugs.
   ○ B. Negative - the boys are afraid to go after the bugs.
   ○ C. Negative - the boys are sad about hunting the bugs.
   ○ D. Neither positive nor negative - the boys have no feelings about chasing the bugs.

Please note that excerpts and passages in the StudySync® library and this workbook are intended as touchstones to generate interest in an author's work. The excerpts and passages do not substitute for the reading of entire texts, and StudySync® strongly recommends that students seek out and purchase the whole literary or informational work in order to experience it as the author intended. Links to online resellers are available in our digital library. In addition, complete works may be ordered through an authorized reseller by filling out and returning to StudySync® the order form enclosed in this workbook.

Reading & Writing
Companion

171

Skill:
Theme

Use the Checklist to analyze Theme in *Roll of Thunder, Hear My Cry*. Refer to the sample student annotations about Theme in the text.

••• CHECKLIST FOR THEME

In order to identify a theme or central idea in a text, note the following:

- ✓ the topic of the text

- ✓ whether or not the theme is stated directly in the text

- ✓ details in the text that may reveal the theme

  - • the title and chapter headings

  - • details about the setting

  - • a narrator's or speaker's tone

  - • characters' thoughts, actions, and dialogue

  - • the central conflict in the story's plot

  - • the resolution of the conflict

  - • what the characters learn through their experiences

- ✓ analyze how characters are affected by the setting, the other characters, and the problems they face and what impact these may have on how the theme is developed

To determine a theme or central idea of a text and how it is conveyed through particular details, consider the following questions:

- ✓ What theme, message, or central idea is being communicated in the text?

- ✓ What details helped to reveal that theme or central idea?

- ✓ When did you become aware of that theme? For instance, did the story's conclusion reveal the theme?

Skill:
Theme

Reread paragraphs 1–8 of *Roll of Thunder, Hear My Cry*. Then, using the Checklist on the previous page, answer the multiple-choice questions below.

⟳ YOUR TURN

1. What can the reader infer about Mrs. Logan from these lines of dialogue?

   ○ A. She is shy about speaking to her husband.
   ○ B. She is not afraid to confront problems head on.
   ○ C. She expects her husband to protect her.
   ○ D. She feels easily scared over small events.

2. What can the reader infer about Mr. Logan from these lines of dialogue?

   ○ A. He doesn't trust his wife with information.
   ○ B. He is often silent during a conflict.
   ○ C. He remains reasonable in the face of conflict.
   ○ D. He is quick to anger.

3. What theme can readers infer from the dialogue between Mr. and Mrs. Logan?

   ○ A. It's best for a family if secrets are kept from the children.
   ○ B. When a person feels fear, he or she should back down from a conflict.
   ○ C. Don't go looking for trouble, but don't shy away from defending your rights either.
   ○ D. It's best to ignore problems until they work themselves out or go away on their own.

Please note that excerpts and passages in the StudySync® library and this workbook are intended as touchstones to generate interest in an author's work. The excerpts and passages do not substitute for the reading of entire texts, and StudySync® strongly recommends that students seek out and purchase the whole literary or informational work in order to experience it as the author intended. Links to online resellers are available in our digital library. In addition, complete works may be ordered through an authorized reseller by filling out and returning to StudySync® the order form enclosed in this workbook.

Reading & Writing
Companion

173

Skill:
Story Structure

Use the Checklist to analyze Story Structure in *Roll of Thunder, Hear My Cry*. Refer to the sample student annotations about Story Structure in the text.

••• CHECKLIST FOR STORY STRUCTURE

In order to identify how a particular sentence, chapter, scene or stanza fits into the overall structure of a text, note the following:

✓ the author's use of description, dialogue, and narration and how each develops the events of the plot

✓ the pattern the author uses to organize the events within a story or chapter

  • chronological, or in time order

  • events out of time order

✓ any literary devices the author uses, such as flashback, a part of a story that shows something that happened in the past

✓ any particular sentence, chapter, scene, or a stanza in a poem that contributes to the development of the setting, the plot, and the theme

✓ how a particular sentence, chapter, scene, or a stanza in a poem fit into the overall structure

To analyze how a particular sentence, chapter, scene, or stanza fits into the overall structure of a text and contributes to the development of the theme, setting, or plot, consider the following questions:

✓ What are the key events in the story and when did they take place?

✓ What impact does the order of events that take place in the story have on the theme, setting, or plot?

✓ What literary devices does the author use? How does it affect the development of the plot?

✓ How does a particular sentence, chapter, scene, or a stanza in a poem fits into the overall structure? How do they contribute to the development of the theme, setting, or plot?

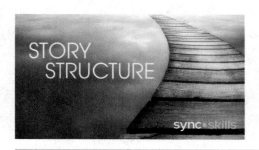

Skill:
Story Structure

Reread paragraphs 22–26 of *Roll of Thunder, Hear My Cry*. Then, using the Checklist on the previous page, answer the multiple-choice questions below.

🔁 YOUR TURN

1. This question has two parts. First, answer Part A. Then, answer Part B.

   Part A: Which of the following statements best summarizes how the dialogue in this passage moves the plot forward?

   ○ A. Farmers are making less money even though they're planting more cotton.

   ○ B. Mr. Avery doesn't need anything from Vicksburg on this trip.

   ○ C. Mr. Avery and Mr. Lanier need to give Mr. Granger 60 percent of their cotton.

   ○ D. Mr. Avery is backing out of shopping in Vicksburg because Mr. Granger is threatening him.

   Part B: Which of the following lines of dialogue BEST supports the summary selected in Part A?

   ○ A. "You goin' to the store tomorrow, David?"

   ○ B. "Your wife brought down that list of things you need yesterday."

   ○ C. "It's—it's that list I come 'bout, David... I don't want them things no more."

   ○ D. "The way cotton sells these days, seems the more we plant, the less money we gets anyways."

Close Read

Reread *Roll of Thunder, Hear My Cry*. As you reread, complete the Skills Focus questions below. Then use your answers and annotations from the questions to help you complete the Write activity.

◎ SKILLS FOCUS

1. Reread the last paragraph of the excerpt. Analyze how the trees in the Logans' backyard symbolize, or represent, their relationship with people like Thurston Wallace.

2. Identify parts of *Roll of Thunder, Hear My Cry* where the author uses specific words and phrases to create a tense atmosphere and how this relates to the overall plot.

3. Locate the word *sloping*. Analyze how the word functions in the sentence to help you determine which dictionary definition best represents the meaning of *sloping* in this context.

4. Identify parts in the story that show how Cassie's relationship with her family impacts her life and helps her see things in a new way.

✎ WRITE

DISCUSSION: In this excerpt, the author builds and releases tension through events in the plot. With each new challenge that the characters have to face, a new theme is revealed or suggested. Overall, do you feel that the author's themes, or messages, are positive or negative? As you prepare for your discussion, use specific parts of the text as well as supporting details to help you form an opinion. Additionally, include any lingering questions you have regarding characters and events.

Teenagers

POETRY
Pat Mora
1991

Introduction

Pat Mora (b. 1942) is a celebrated Mexican-American author whose bilingual works explore themes of culture and identity among families in Texas and along the Southwestern border, where Mora was born and raised. Her 1991 poem "Teenagers" is written from the point of view of a parent who feels they have lost touch with their teenage children. In this brief, fourteen-line poem, Mora reflects upon a universal experience both parents and children endure as they age.

"Doors and lips shut and we become strangers in our own home."

1 One day they disappear
2 into their rooms.
3 Doors and lips shut
4 and we become strangers
5 in our own home.

6 I **pace** the hall, hear whispers,
7 a **code** I knew but can't remember,
8 mouthed by mouths I taught to speak.

9 Years later the door opens.
10 I see faces I once held,
11 open as sunflowers in my hands. I see
12 **familiar** skin now stretched on long bodies
13 that move past me
14 glowing almost like pearls.

"Teenagers" by Pat Mora is reprinted with permission from the publisher of "Communion" (© 1991 Arte Público Press - University of Houston)

NOTES

Skill: Figurative Language

The poet uses a simile. The speaker describes the children's faces "as" sunflowers. A sunflower's petals are not closed up like a rose. I think this means the speaker's children were open to learning from her when they were younger.

First Read

Read "Teenagers." After you read, complete the Think Questions below.

☁ THINK QUESTIONS

1. In lines 4 and 5, the speaker says that "we become strangers in our own home." Who are the strangers in this home? Cite textual evidence to support your answer.

2. Write two or three sentences that explain what happens to the "strangers" when "years later, the door opens"?

3. "Voice" is the way an author uses word choice, tone, and speech patterns to show the personality of a speaker, narrator, or character. Voice gives the sense that a real person is talking to the reader or to other characters. Whose voice is talking in this poem? Cite words and phrases that support your answer.

4. Find the word **code** in the second stanza of "Teenagers." Use context clues in the surrounding stanzas, as well as the stanza in which the word appears, to determine the word's meaning. Write your definition here and identify clues that helped you figure out its meaning.

5. Read the following dictionary entry:

familiar
fa•mil•iar \fə 'mil yər\ *adjective*

1. closely acquainted
2. sociable
3. having personal knowledge

Which definition most closely matches the meaning of **familiar** as it is used in the last stanza? Explain how you chose the correct meaning.

Skill:
Figurative Language

Use the Checklist to analyze Figurative Language in "Teenagers." Refer to the sample student annotations about Figurative Language in the text.

••• CHECKLIST FOR FIGURATIVE LANGUAGE

To determine the meaning of figures of speech in a text, note the following:

✓ words that mean one thing literally and suggest something else

✓ similes, such as "strong as an ox"

✓ metaphors, such as "her eyes were stars"

✓ personification, such as "the daisies danced in the wind"

In order to interpret the meaning of a figure of speech in context, ask the following questions:

✓ Does any of the descriptive language in the text compare two seemingly unlike things?

✓ Do any descriptions include the words "like" or "as" that indicate a simile?

✓ Is there a direct comparison that suggests a metaphor?

✓ Is a human quality used to describe an animal, object, force of nature or idea in a way that suggests personification?

✓ How does the use of this figure of speech change your understanding of the thing or person being described?

In order to analyze the impact of figurative language on the meaning of a text, use the following questions as a guide:

✓ Where does figurative language appear in the text? What does it mean?

✓ Why does the author use figurative language rather than literal language?

Copyright © BookheadEd Learning, LLC

 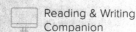

Skill:
Figurative Language

Reread "Teenagers." Then, using the Checklist on the previous page, answer the multiple-choice questions below.

↻ YOUR TURN

1. The poet uses a metaphor comparing whispers to a code for the purpose of —

   ○ A. showing that the speaker cannot hear the voices.

   ○ B. illustrating that the language the teenagers use is not something she understands.

   ○ C. suggesting that the teenagers are writing secret notes.

   ○ D. saying the speaker fears that the teenagers are talking about her.

2. Based on the examples of figurative language in the poem, you can infer that the speaker—

   ○ A. is afraid to admit that her children are grown and are now moving out into the wider world as adults.

   ○ B. still does not understand her children even though they are now familiar again and have grown into strong and tall young adults.

   ○ C. enjoyed holding her children's faces and teaching them when they were younger, but is gratified that they have grown into fine young adults.

   ○ D. is angry that so much time has passed with her teenagers behind closed doors and unwilling to communicate.

Close Read

Reread "Teenagers." As you reread, complete the Skills Focus questions below. Then use your answers and annotations from the questions to help you complete the Write activity.

⊙ SKILLS FOCUS

1. Use textual evidence to infer what the speaker means when she writes "a code I knew but can't remember."

2. Identify examples of similes and metaphors in the poem and explain what purpose the poet achieves by using this figurative language.

3. Identify and explain the ways in which the poem explores how relationships impact our lives.

✏ WRITE

LITERARY ANALYSIS: In the poem "Teenagers," a parent talks about her teenage children and how they have changed over time. How does the poem show the speaker's character? Identify examples of figurative language that help the reader understand the speaker. Respond using evidence from the text.

Tableau

POETRY
Countee Cullen
1925

Introduction

"Tableau" was published in 1925 during the peak of the Harlem Renaissance. Its author, Countee Cullen (1903–1946), was one of the leading poetic voices throughout the African American neighborhood's cultural explosion, and would go on to publish multiple books during his lifetime. In "Tableau," Cullen speaks to his unique perspective of walking through both white and black universes, and the joys and challenges that sprang from blacks and whites attempting to forge relationships during this time.

"The golden splendor of the day
The sable pride of night."

Skill: Poetic Elements and Structure

This Stanza helps me to understand the setting. Two boys are walking together outside. The poet describes the white boy as "golden splendor of the day," while the black boy is the "sable pride of night."

This Stanza helps me understand that some people were not happy to see boys of two different races walking together as friends. I think one theme of the poem is that not everyone celebrates diversity.

1   Locked arm in arm they cross the way
2   The black boy and the white,
3   The golden **splendor** of the day
4   The sable pride of night.

5   From lowered blinds the dark folk stare
6   And here the **fair** folk talk,
7   **Indignant** that these two should dare
8   In **unison** to walk.

9   **Oblivious** to look and word
10   They pass, and see no wonder
11   That lightning brilliant as a sword
12   Should blaze the path of thunder.

First Read

Read "Tableau." After you read, complete the Think Questions below.

☁ THINK QUESTIONS

1. How does the poet contrast the two boys in the first stanza? Cite textual evidence from the poem to support your answer.

2. Write two to three sentences explaining what people likely think about the two boys in the second stanza.

3. A metaphor is a figure of speech that compares two seemingly unlike things but implies a comparison instead of stating it directly with the words "like" or "as." In stanza 3, what is the boys' passing compared to? What do you think the metaphor means?

4. Find the word **oblivious** in line 9 of "Tableau." Use context clues in the surrounding lines, as well as the line in which the word appears, to determine the word's meaning. Write your definition here and identify clues that helped you figure out its meaning.

5. Read the following dictionary entry:

   unison
   u•ni•son \ˈyü-nə-sən\ noun

   1. singing parts of a song together
   2. at the same time
   3. all elements in one place

   Which definition most closely matches the meaning of **unison** as it is used in the second stanza? Write the correct definition of *unison* here. Then explain how you figured out the correct meaning.

Please note that excerpts and passages in the StudySync® library and this workbook are intended as touchstones to generate interest in an author's work. The excerpts and passages do not substitute for the reading of entire texts, and StudySync® strongly recommends that students seek out and purchase the whole literary or informational work in order to experience it as the author intended. Links to online resellers are available in our digital library. In addition, complete works may be ordered through an authorized reseller by filling out and returning to StudySync® the order form enclosed in this workbook.

Reading & Writing Companion   **185**

Skill:
Poetic Elements and Structure

Use the Checklist to analyze Poetic Elements and Structure in "Tableau." Refer to the sample student annotations about Poetic Elements and Structure in the text.

••• CHECKLIST FOR POETIC ELEMENTS AND STRUCTURE

In order to identify elements of poetic structure, note the following:

- ✓ how the words and lines are arranged

- ✓ the form and overall structure of the poem

- ✓ the rhyme, rhythm, and meter, if present

- ✓ how the arrangement of lines and stanzas in the poem contribute to the poem's theme, or message

To analyze how a particular stanza fits into the overall structure of a poem and contributes to the development of the theme, consider the following questions:

- ✓ What poetic form does the poet use? What is the structure?

- ✓ How do the lengths of the lines and stanzas affect the meaning?

- ✓ How does a poem's stanza fit into the structure of the poem overall?

- ✓ How does the form and structure affect the poem's meaning?

- ✓ In what way does a specific stanza contribute to the poem's theme?

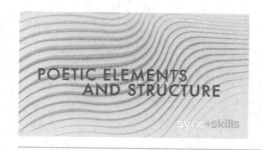

Skill:
Poetic Elements and Structure

Reread lines 9–12 of "Tableau." Then, using the Checklist on the previous page, answer the multiple-choice questions below.

♻ YOUR TURN

1. Lines 9–10 reveal . . .

   ○ A. the boys are impolite as they ignore their neighbors.
   ○ B. the conflict in the poem.
   ○ C. the boys' proud nature as they walk together.
   ○ D. the importance of the setting in the poem.

2. What theme does stanza 3 reveal?

   ○ A. Don't judge a book by its cover.
   ○ B. Be confident when doing the right thing.
   ○ C. Ignoring others leads to the path of justice.
   ○ D. Gossiping is wrong.

Close Read

Reread "Tableau." As you reread, complete the Skills Focus questions below. Then use your answers and annotations from the questions to help you complete the Write activity.

◎ SKILLS FOCUS

1. Identify lines in the poem that help contribute to the poem's overall theme.

2. Identify places in the poem where Cullen uses figurative language, and explain how this language contributes to the poem's meaning.

3. Countee Cullen's poem "Tableau" reads like a story. Identify and explain the events in the poem and how they explore the way relationships impact our lives.

✏ WRITE

LITERARY ANALYSIS: In "Tableau," the poet Countee Cullen describes an unlikely pair of friends. How does the poet use specific stanzas and lines to focus on the theme of friendship? Use evidence from the text to support your response.

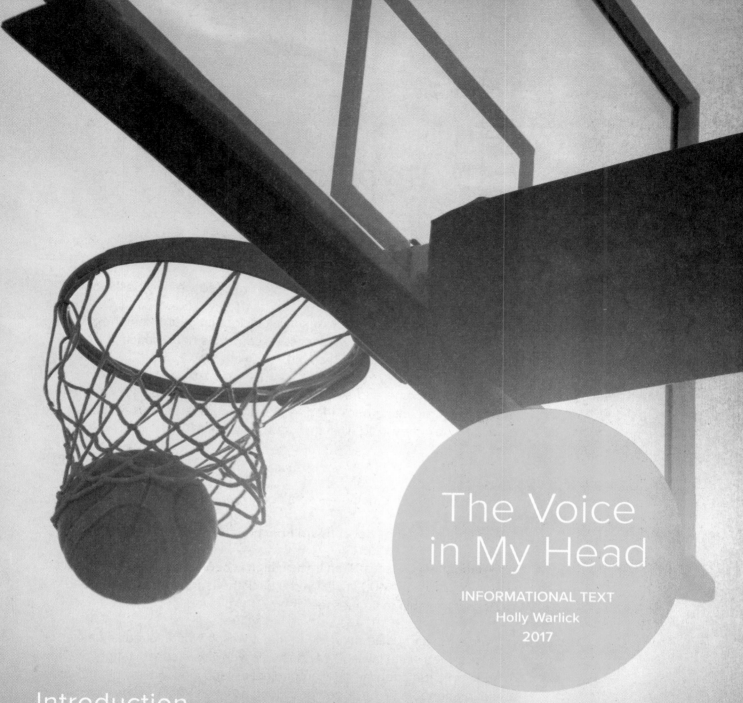

The Voice in My Head

INFORMATIONAL TEXT
Holly Warlick
2017

Introduction

n this essay from *The Players' Tribune*, Tennessee Lady Vols women's basketball coach Holly Warlick (b. 1958) speaks to her profound and life-altering relationship with her mentor, legendary coach Pat Summitt (1952–2016). Summitt's eight NCAA titles place her among the winningest college basketball coaches of all time. Yet she is remembered as much for her advocacy for women's sports—and her deep regard for the development of her players outside of the sport—as she is for her impressive championship record.

"She'd break you down . . . and yet you'd show up the next day."

1   I remember the first time Pat Summitt ever watched me play basketball.

2   I was a senior in high school — a small, quick point guard from the Knoxville area — and Pat was the new Tennessee Lady Vols head coach. It was 1975. She was only six years older than me.

3   "You've got to come and see this girl play," someone had told her. There wasn't much recruiting back then — not like there is today. A coach would show up, and if they liked what they saw, that was it.

4   Pat didn't like what she saw.

5   I didn't even finish the game — I sprained my ankle real bad.

6   She left the gym, and I never heard from her again.

7   It's a good thing I was fast. I ran track in high school as well, and won the state championship in the 400 (it was yards back then, not meters). My speed got me the scholarship to Tennessee.

8   But while running came naturally to me, it wasn't what I loved — basketball was. I'd played since I was 10. My dad, Bill, who was a coach, taught me how to dribble. I'd run dribbling drills around chairs, and play with my older brother and our neighbors in the street for as long as it was light outside.

9   Back then, girls weren't allowed to play full-court basketball — just half-court, three-on-three. It was thought that girls' bodies couldn't handle the strain and physicality of full-court basketball. But I knew otherwise. I knew that I could handle it, and that playing with the boys only made me tougher, and made me better. My dad knew it, too. He encouraged it.

10 I tried to walk on to the basketball team my freshman year before my track career even started. I hadn't seen Pat since I had blown it in high school. I'd met some of her players, though, and asked about her — asked what to expect.

11   "She's hard."

12   "She's tough."

13   Every single player said the same thing. Not that I cared — I just wanted to play. And, I figured, at least I was in shape. How bad could it be?

14   I walked into the gym on the first day of tryouts. *Does she remember me? I thought. Nope, no recognition.* Pat put us on the line and blew her whistle.

15   Suicides. A lot of suicides. Then she put 30 minutes on the clock for a continuous four-on-two fast break.

16   And that was just the warmup.

17   "That woman is crazy," I said to myself after walking out of the gym that day. "What am I getting myself into?"

18   But I went back the next day, and the day after that. She had that way about her. She'd break you down . . . and yet you'd show up the next day. You wanted to prove to her that you could take it. It took me years to realize that she didn't care about players proving it to her.

19   She cared about players proving it to themselves.

• • •

20   I made the team.

21   "You didn't even recruit her," people would say to Pat years later.

22   "Yeah, I recruited her," Pat would deadpan. "She wasn't very good."

23   She had one drill in practice that she named after me. "This is a Holly day!" she'd yell. Everyone would line up and run suicides, while I had to make 10 layups in a row, sprinting from one end of the court to the other. I was notorious for missing layups because I was too fast — I'd run full speed and my momentum would carry me too far under the basket. I'd make eight in a row and then miss. Every single one of us would have to start over again. It was brutal.

24   She was brutal.

25   But she was building us. She was also building her own legacy, though it probably didn't feel like that at the time. She made $250 a month to coach, recruit, wash our uniforms and drive the team van. (She had a habit of

Please note that excerpts and passages in the StudySync® library and this workbook are intended as touchstones to generate interest in an author's work. The excerpts and passages do not substitute for the reading of entire texts, and StudySync® strongly recommends that students seek out and purchase the whole literary or informational work in order to experience it as the author intended. Links to online resellers are available in our digital library. In addition, complete works may be ordered through an authorized reseller by filling out and returning to StudySync® the order form enclosed in this workbook.

Reading & Writing Companion   191

multitasking behind the wheel generally: speeding, applying mascara and — when cellphones became a thing — talking on the phone.) She was also fighting for equal opportunities for women's basketball — not just our program — at every turn. She demanded the best from people and her players. It was the only way she knew, and it worked. Wins and championships followed.

26   In 1985, a few years after I graduated, I got a call from Pat. In that time, I'd played professionally in the Women's Professional Basketball League for a year, and was working at the University of Nebraska as an assistant coach.

27   "Would you be interested in coming here to coach?" she asked me.

28   "I can be there in 18 hours," I said.

29   The coaching dynamic between us — head coach and assistant — wasn't all that different from the dynamic between us when I was a player and she was my coach. As a player, Pat pushed me harder than others because she knew I could take it. She would give me the hardest defensive assignments, or yell at me a little louder than she would at everybody else. When I became her assistant, she kept challenging me. Our basketball philosophy was the same — how could it not be? But she knew when, how and just how far to push me.

30   She called me Warlick. I called her Summitt.

31   Eventually, through all the time we spent together, especially traveling to road games or going on recruiting trips, that dynamic shifted to something more like friendship. Everyone knows about Pat's icy stare and tough persona, but she was also a loving matriarch with a quick wit. She was someone you always wanted to be around because you never knew what was going to come out of her mouth or happen next.

. . .

32   I was the buffer between Pat and the players.

33   I'm not sure how it got started, but that's how it worked: She'd chew them out, and I'd remind them that they were O.K. I "survived" Pat myself. Everyone survives.

34   Our players — they were just kids — would come in knowing that she was going to be tough. But they still didn't really *know*. Not until they got here. So, that was my role: to listen and reassure. Over time, I slowly started to lead some practices, handle scouting and sit in on meetings with parents.

35   And when Pat got sick, I slowly started to take the lead on everything.

36   She was suffering from dementia before any of us knew it. We all knew something was wrong, but we just covered for her. It was *Pat Summitt*, you know? No one ever asked. But when she was diagnosed in 2011, we weren't surprised. She told the staff one night, not long before the news broke, on the back porch at her house. We sat quietly for a minute after that before she cut through the silence:

37   "Now, I can drink all I want because I won't remember," she said.

38   That's Pat, for you. One of the worst days of our lives, and there she was, cracking jokes.

39   I remember being in the locker room with Pat later that season. Her illness had been announced publicly, and as a coaching staff, we were just trying to keep our focus on the game. I was going to be acting as head coach that night.

40   "What do you want to see?" I asked Pat. "Do you want to see a press?"

41   "I want to see you not sweat tonight," she said. "I'm gonna be sittin' beside you, and you sweat so much."

42   We laughed our way through it.

43   Together, over time, Pat and I talked about the **transition** of me becoming the head coach quite a bit. But the truth is . . . she was planning on being here forever. I was planning on it, too.

44   I inherited a lot. How do you fill those shoes? Pat Summitt is a basketball icon who not only built a championship program at Tennessee — but she also made it known the world over. She set the standard for other programs. She created opportunities for women when there had been none before, and her monumental **influence** on the game of basketball made little girls all over the world — little girls who may never have seen the Lady Vols play — feel seen and strong.

45   The expectation for the Lady Vols is to win a championship. It's a wonderful burden — to be known and celebrated for greatness, but to be disappointed in anything that falls short of another championship banner. I wouldn't be truthful if I said it's not a challenge. I've had to grow more in the last five years than the 25 plus that came before.

46   Someone was always going to have to follow Pat.

47   Pat Summitt is a mountain. We're all standing in her shadow.

48   I visited her often after she stepped down. We'd take rides on her boat or just spend time on the beach. Pat loved the beach. We'd talk, but rarely about basketball. Just . . . life. Her health was **declining** and I was traveling more, so when I couldn't visit, I'd call.

49   "Pat, turn to channel 25 — so-and-so is playing," I'd tell her. Or, I'd ask, "Hey, Pat, what are you up to?"

50   "You know I'm not doing anything," she'd say.

51   She always made me laugh.

52   Our conversations got more difficult as the years passed. She didn't know she was struggling, but I could see it grow. When people who hadn't seen her in a while would visit, I could see the shock on their faces. Pat Summitt was supposed to be invincible.

53   Last June, I'd gotten a call saying she was in bad condition. I went to the hospice where she was staying. Nikki Fargas and Mickie DeMoss were there — both former assistants — and we sat in Pat's room while she lay quietly. I stepped out for a bit while Nikki and Mickie were telling old stories, laughing up a riot.

54   When I came back, there was Pat, sitting up straight while those two were laughing their way through the past. I walked over to the side of her bed and listened. Pat grabbed my shirt and pulled me close to her.

55   "Pat, you know I love you," I said.

56   She'd been hanging on for so many people. Her whole life was about other people.

57   "You gotta let go," I said.

58   That's one of the last things I remember — her gripping my shirt, pulling me close . . . and letting me go.

59   She knew what was coming.

. . .

60   People say grief is like the ocean — that it comes in waves. But waves is too soft of a description. It feels more like lightning. Sometimes, I'll be driving somewhere and suddenly be struck, crying on my way to the grocery. Grief splits you open. I swear you spend your whole life trying to sew yourself back up.

61   I see her statue every day just outside of our facility. Our court is named after her. There's an empty chair on our bench in her memory. I'm confronted by her loss — personally and professionally — in so many visceral ways. On some level, it's comforting. I'm glad she's still around. She's the voice in my head.

62   Pat's presence when she was alive was so big that the void she left was **inevitably** going to be **vast**. As the Lady Vols' head coach, I am trying now to continue her legacy but when I'm not on the sideline — when I go home and sit with everything — I'm just someone who lost their best friend.

63   I carry the weight of that loss, and the weight of the program. But I'll do that every day with gratitude for her life and all that she imparted. And I'll do it with pride for this team and program, which I love with every fiber of my being.

64   I want to make a difference in these kids' lives — because that's what Pat made in mine.

© 2017 by Holly Warlick. Reproduced by permission of *The Players' Tribune*.

✏ WRITE

PERSONAL RESPONSE: Why do you think it's important to have mentors in your life? Write a response to this question that represents your own point of view. Use examples from the essay "The Voice in My Head" to support your response.

We're on the Same Team

ARGUMENTATIVE TEXT
Jacki Jing
2017

Introduction

Jacki Jing was an NCAA Division I volleyball player at Binghamton University, where she was inducted into the school's Athletic Hall of Fame. Here, she draws from personal experiences to respond to a newspaper article that questioned the difficulty of mastering the sport.

"I had to bleed and I had to sweat just as hard as any other elite athlete."

Jacki Jing
562 Maple St.
Dallas, TX 75215

March 21, 2018

SportsNews
854 Commerce St.
New York, NY 10103

Dear Editor,

1   I was pretty excited recently when I saw a SportsNews article titled, "Why Volleyball Is So Popular." As a former NCAA Division I volleyball player, I was excited to see my favorite sport featured on your website. My excitement quickly turned to disbelief as I read your article.

2   In particular, I was insulted when I read the following passage:

   Athletes go where they find success. Basketball is a difficult sport to master. Unless you're willing to put in the time and effort and have a certain level of athleticism and hand-eye skills, you will not be successful. You will be pushed out of the sport because of what it demands. In volleyball, those barriers are lower.

3   Basketball is an incredible sport. It requires talent and athletic ability. Yet the exact same is true of volleyball.

4   Just like basketball, it takes years to hone volleyball skills. Volleyball requires long practices in the gym (or in the sand) multiple times a week. Approaching, hitting, serving, passing—these aspects of volleyball may not look hard. However, playing at a high level requires an athlete to master a very specific **technique** for each skill. In this regard, volleyball is no different than basketball. Anyone can pick up a ball and shoot it at the basket. But it takes a lifetime of practice to be as good as the best NBA and WNBA players. The ladies on the

Skill: Summarizing

Jacki Jing, a former college volleyball player, writes a letter to the editor of SportsNews to say that she has a problem with an article she recently read on the website called "Why Volleyball Is So Popular."

According to Jing, mastering volleyball skills and techniques requires years of practice, especially for high level players. Jing insists that volleyball is an intensely difficult sport to learn and play, and I am neither supporting nor opposing her opinion.

Olympic volleyball teams might make it look easy. That's because years of practice have **refined** their movements so they appear fluid and graceful.

5   I remember being a gangly, awkward teen. I had to choose between volleyball and basketball. Every person chooses his or her own path for different reasons. I don't think one sport is better or harder than the other. Personally, I chose volleyball because it **required** work. I had to learn how to control my body. I had to learn how to do more than just jump high. I had to learn how to swing hard and sharp. I had to think fast, move quickly, and use strategy. I had to bleed and I had to sweat just as hard as any other **elite** athlete.

6   I am tired of hearing that volleyball is easy. I resent that this article **implies** volleyball players have somehow chosen an "easier" path. More young women are choosing to play volleyball because it is tough. It is competitive. It is fierce and fun. That's it.

7   As for the young women out there who are thinking about volleyball, I can tell you right now it is my life and my passion. I was not able to become an Olympian. Yet at 30 years old I still play as much as I can. And believe me, I still have not mastered it. I am always refining my skills and my knowledge of the game.

8   Volleyball changed my life. When I think about playing in high school and college, it brings back memories that make me tear up. My teammates are my sisters. I am still friends with some of my biggest rivals from college. The relationships you form when working that hard at something stay with you forever.

Women's volleyball: A tough, but fun, sport

9   I still hold close to my heart some of my biggest wins and hardest losses. I've learned what is necessary to perform under pressure. I've learned how to push myself mentally and physically. I've learned how to work with a large group of people. I've learned what it takes to achieve what I want. I have experienced the highest highs of my life on the volleyball court.

10   SportsNews, volleyball is not girly. It is not any less athletic. It is just awesome.

Sincerely,
Jacki Jing

First Read

Read "We're on the Same Team." After you read, complete the Think Questions below.

☁ THINK QUESTIONS

1. What is the author of the letter's main problem with the SportsNews article? Cite evidence from the selection to support your answer.

2. Why did the author choose to play volleyball? Cite textual evidence from the text to explain the author's reasoning.

3. According to the author, why do young women choose to play volleyball? Provide evidence from the text to support your answer.

4. Find the word **refined** in paragraph 4 of "We're on the Same Team." Use context clues in the surrounding sentences, as well as the sentence in which the word appears, to determine the word's meaning. Write your definition here and identify clues that helped you figure out its meaning.

5. Use context clues to determine the meaning of **implies** in paragraph 6. Write your definition here and identify clues that helped you figure out its meaning. Then check the meaning in a dictionary.

Skill:
Summarizing

Use the Checklist to analyze Summarizing in "We're on the Same Team." Refer to the sample student annotations about Summarizing in the text.

••• CHECKLIST FOR SUMMARIZING

In order to determine how to write an objective summary of a text, note the following:

- ✓ in a nonfiction text, examine details to identify the main idea, making notations in a notebook or graphic organizer

- ✓ answers to the basic questions *who, what, where, when, why,* and *how*

- ✓ stay objective, and do not add your own personal thoughts, judgments, or opinions to the summary

To provide an objective summary of a text free of personal opinions or judgments, consider the following questions:

- ✓ What are the answers to basic *who, what, where, when, why,* and *how* questions in literature and works of nonfiction?

- ✓ In what order should I put the main ideas and most important details in a work of nonfiction to make my summary logical?

- ✓ Is my summary objective, or have I added my own thoughts, judgments, or personal opinions?

Skill:
Summarizing

Reread paragraphs 5–6 of "We're on the Same Team." Then, using the Checklist on the previous page, answer the multiple-choice questions below.

↻ YOUR TURN

1. What is the best summary of paragraph 5?

   ○ A. Jing states that she chose to play volleyball because she was awkward.
   ○ B. Jing states that she chose to play volleyball because it was challenging.
   ○ C. Jing states that she chose to play volleyball because it involved jumping.
   ○ D. Jing states that she chose to play volleyball because she got to swing hard.

2. What is the best summary of paragraph 6?

   ○ A. Jing believes young women choose to play volleyball because it is fun not because it is easy.
   ○ B. Jing believes that young women play volleyball because it is tough and competitive not because it is easy.
   ○ C. While Jing knows that many people think volleyball is an easy sport, she believes volleyball is tough.
   ○ D. Jing knows that young women find out that volleyball is tough and competitive after thinking it was an easy sport.

Please note that excerpts and passages in the StudySync® library and this workbook are intended as touchstones to generate interest in an author's work. The excerpts and passages do not substitute for the reading of entire texts, and StudySync® strongly recommends that students seek out and purchase the whole literary or informational work in order to experience it as the author intended. Links to online resellers are available in our digital library. In addition, complete works may be ordered through an authorized reseller by filling out and returning to StudySync® the order form enclosed in this workbook.

Reading & Writing
Companion   **201**

WE'RE ON THE
SAME TEAM

Close Read

Reread "We're on the Same Team." As you reread, complete the Skills Focus questions below. Then use your answers and annotations from the questions to help you complete the Write activity.

◎ SKILLS FOCUS

1. Identify textual evidence that supports Jacki Jing's argument in favor of volleyball.

2. Select a paragraph in Jing's argument. Identify the most important details in the paragraph. Then use the details to summarize the main ideas in your own words.

3. Identify evidence in the letter that indicates how sports relationships affected Jing's life. Use details to summarize the impact of these relationships.

✎ WRITE

INFORMATIVE: In the essay "The Voice in My Head" by Holly Warlick and the letter to the editor "We're On the Same Team" by Jacki Jing, both authors write about the ways they have worked hard in athletics and in life. In a blog post of your own, summarize the ways that each author had to work hard, including challenges they faced and what helped them succeed. Then, explain a situation where you had to work hard to achieve a goal. Include any setbacks you had and how you finally managed to succeed. Be sure to provide textual evidence from the two texts and your own personal experiences to convey your ideas.

The Treasure of Lemon Brown

FICTION
Walter Dean Myers
1983

Introduction

Award-winning writer and former National Ambassador for Young People's Literature, Walter Dean Myers (1937–2014) once said, "I write to give hope to those kids who are like the ones I knew—poor, troubled, treated indifferently by society." Myers was raised in Harlem, New York, and grew up loving stories—both the ones his family told him and the ones he read in books. Much of what he writes is based on experiences from his own life. In the short story "The Treasure of Lemon Brown," teenager Greg Ridley meets a homeless man who teaches him a valuable lesson.

"Didn't I tell you every man got a treasure?"

Skill:
Point of View

The narrator is describing what happens from outside the story because I see a character's name and the pronoun he. I know how Greg feels, but not what his father feels. So the point of view must be third-person limited.

1 The dark sky, filled with angry, swirling clouds, reflected Greg Ridley's mood as he sat on the **stoop** of his building. His father's voice came to him again, first reading the letter the principal had sent to the house, then lecturing endlessly about his poor efforts in math.

2 "I had to leave school when I was thirteen," his father had said, "that's a year younger than you are now. If I'd had half the chances you have, I'd . . ."

3 Greg sat in the small, pale green kitchen listening, knowing the lecture would end with his father saying he couldn't play ball with the Scorpions. He had asked his father the week before, and his father had said it depended on his next report card. It wasn't often the Scorpions took on new players, especially fourteen-year-olds, and this was a chance of a lifetime for Greg. He hadn't been allowed to play high school ball, which he had really wanted to do, but playing for the Community Center team was the next best thing. Report cards were due in a week, and Greg had been hoping for the best. But the principal had ended the suspense early when she sent the letter saying Greg would probably fail math if he didn't spend more time studying.

4 "And you want to play *basketball?*" His father's brows knitted over deep brown eyes. "That must be some kind of a joke. Now you just get into your room and hit those books."

5 That had been two nights before. His father's words, like the distant thunder that now echoed through the streets of Harlem, still rumbled softly in his ears.

6 It was beginning to cool. Gusts of wind made bits of paper dance between the parked cars. There was a flash of nearby lightning, and soon large drops of rain splashed onto his jeans. He stood to go upstairs, thought of the lecture that probably awaited him if he did anything except shut himself in his room with his math book, and started walking down the street instead. Down the block there was an old tenement that had been abandoned for some months. Some of the guys had held an **impromptu** checker tournament there the week before, and Greg had noticed that the door, once boarded over, had been slightly ajar.

7   Pulling his collar up as high as he could, he checked for traffic and made a dash across the street. He reached the house just as another flash of lightning changed the night to day for an instant, then returned the graffiti-scarred building to the grim shadows. He vaulted over the outer stairs and pushed **tentatively** on the door. It was open, and he let himself in.

8   The inside of the building was dark except for the dim light that filtered through the dirty windows from the streetlamps. There was a room a few feet from the door, and from where he stood in the entrance, Greg could see a squarish patch of light on the floor. He entered the room, frowning at the musty smell. It was a large room that might have been someone's parlor at one time. Squinting, Greg could see an old table on its side against one wall, what looked like a pile of rags or a torn mattress in the corner, and a couch, with one side broken, in front of the window.

9   He went to the couch. The side that wasn't broken was comfortable enough, though a little creaky. From the spot he could see the blinking neon sign over the bodega on the corner. He sat awhile, watching the sign blink first green then red, allowing his mind to drift to the Scorpions, then to his father. His father had been a postal worker for all Greg's life, and was proud of it, often telling Greg how hard he had worked to pass the test. Greg had heard the story too many times to be interested now.

10 For a moment Greg thought he heard something that sounded like a scraping against the wall. He listened carefully, but it was gone.

11 Outside the wind had picked up, sending the rain against the window with a force that shook the glass in its frame. A car passed, its tires hissing over the wet street and its red tail lights glowing in the darkness.

12 Greg thought he heard the noise again. His stomach tightened as he held himself still and listened intently. There weren't any more scraping noises, but he was sure he had heard something in the darkness—something breathing!

13 He tried to figure out just where the breathing was coming from; he knew it was in the room with him. Slowly he stood, tensing. As he turned, a flash of lightning lit up the room, frightening him with its sudden brilliance. He saw nothing, just the overturned table, the pile of rags and an old newspaper on the floor. Could he have been imagining the sounds? He continued listening, but heard nothing and thought that it might have just been rats. Still, he thought, as soon as the rain let up he would leave. He went to the window and was about to look when he heard a voice behind him.

14 "Don't try nothin' 'cause I got a razor sharp enough to cut a week into nine days!"

15 Greg, except for an **involuntary** tremor in his knees, stood stock still. The voice was high and brittle, like dry twigs being broken, surely not one he had ever heard before. There was a shuffling sound as the person who had been speaking moved a step closer. Greg turned, holding his breath, his eyes straining to see in the dark room.

16 The upper part of the figure before him was still in darkness. The lower half was in the dim rectangle of light that fell unevenly from the window. There were two feet, in cracked, dirty shoes from which rose legs that were wrapped in rags.

17 "Who are you?" Greg hardly recognized his own voice.

18 "I'm Lemon Brown," came the answer. "Who're you?"

19 "Greg Ridley."

20 "What you doing here?" The figure shuffled forward again, and Greg took a small step backward.

21 "It's raining," Greg said.

22 "I can see that," the figure said.

23 The person who called himself Lemon Brown peered forward, and Greg could see him clearly. He was an old man. His black, heavily wrinkled face was surrounded by a halo of crinkly white hair and whiskers that seemed to separate his head from the layers of dirty coats piled on his smallish frame. His pants were bagged to the knee, where they were met with rags that went down to the old shoes. The rags were held on with strings, and there was a rope around his middle. Greg relaxed. He had seen the man before, picking through the trash on the corner and pulling clothes out of a Salvation Army box. There was no sign of a razor that could "cut a week into nine days."

24 "What are you doing here?" Greg asked.

25 "This is where I'm staying," Lemon Brown said. "What you here for?"

26 "Told you it was raining out," Greg said, leaning against the back of the couch until he felt it give slightly.

27 "Ain't you got no home?"

28 "I got a home," Greg answered.

29 "You ain't one of them bad boys looking for my treasure, is you?"

30 Lemon Brown cocked his head to one side and squinted one eye.

31 "Because I told you I got me a razor."

32 "I'm not looking for your treasure," Greg answered, smiling. "*If* you have one."

33 "What you mean, if I have one." Lemon Brown said. "Every man got a treasure. You don't know that, you must be a fool!"

34 "Sure," Greg said as he sat on the sofa and put one leg over the back. "What do you have, gold coins?"

35 "Don't worry none about what I got," Lemon Brown said. "You know who I am?"

36 "You told me your name was orange or lemon or something like that."

37 "Lemon Brown," the old man said, pulling back his shoulders as he did so," they used to call me Sweet Lemon Brown."

38 "Sweet Lemon?" Greg asked.

39 "Yessir. Sweet Lemon Brown. They used to say I sung the blues so sweet that if I sang at a funeral, the dead would **commence** to rocking with the beat. Used to travel all over Mississippi and as far as Monroe, Louisiana, and east on over to Macon, Georgia. You mean you ain't never heard of Sweet Lemon Brown?"

40 "Afraid not," Greg said. "What . . . happened to you?"

41 "Hard times, boy. Hard times always after a poor man. One day I got tired, sat down to rest a spell and felt a tap on my shoulder. Hard times caught up with me."

42 "Sorry about that."

43 "What you doing here? How come you don't go in home when the rain come? Rain don't bother you young folks none."

44 "Just didn't." Greg looked away.

45 "I used to have a knotty-headed boy just like you." Lemon Brown had half walked, half shuffled back to the corner and sat down against the wall. "Had them big eyes like you got. I used to call them moon eyes. Look into them moon eyes and see anything you want."

NOTES

46   "How come you gave up singing the blues?" Greg asked.

47   "Didn't give it up," Lemon Brown said. "You don't give up the blues; they give you up. After a while you do good for yourself, and it ain't nothing but foolishness singing about how hard you got it. Ain't that right?"

48   "I guess so."

49   "What's that noise?" Lemon Brown asked, suddenly sitting upright.

50   Greg listened, and he heard a noise outside. He looked at Lemon Brown and saw the old man pointing toward the window. Greg went to the window and saw three men, neighborhood thugs, on the stoop. One was carrying a length of pipe. Greg looked back toward Lemon Brown, who moved quietly across the room to the window. The old man looked out, then beckoned frantically for Greg to follow him. For a moment Greg couldn't move. Then he found himself following Lemon Brown into the hallway and up the darkened stairs. Greg followed as closely as he could. They reached the top of the stairs, and Greg felt Lemon Brown's hand first lying on his shoulder, then probing down his arm until he took Greg's hand into his own as they crouched in the darkness.

51   "They's bad men," Lemon Brown whispered. His breath was warm against Greg's skin.

52   "Hey! Rag man!" A voice called. "We know you in here. What you got up under them rags? You got any money?"

53   Silence.

54   "We don't want to have to come in and hurt you, old man, but we don't mind if we have to."

55   Lemon Brown squeezed Greg's hand in his own hard, gnarled fist.

56   There was a banging downstairs and a light as the men entered. They banged around noisily, calling for the rag man.

57   "We heard you talking about your treasure." The voice was slurred.

58   "We just want to see it, that's all."

59   "You sure he's here?" One voice seemed to come from the room with the sofa.

60   "Yeah, he stays here every night."

61 "There's another room over there; I'm going to take a look. You got that flashlight?"

62 "Yeah, here, take the pipe too."

63 Greg opened his mouth to quiet the sound of his breath as he sucked it in uneasily. A beam of light hit the wall a few feet opposite him, then went out.

64 "Ain't nobody in that room," a voice said. "You think he gone or something?"

65 "I don't know," came the answer. "All I know is that I heard him talking about some kind of treasure. You know they found that shopping bag lady with that load of money in her bags."

66 "Yeah. You think he's upstairs?"

67 "HEY, OLD MAN, ARE YOU UP THERE?"

68 Silence.

69 "Watch my back. I'm going up."

70 There was a footstep on the stairs, and the beam from the flashlight danced crazily along the peeling wallpaper. Greg held his breath. There was another step and a loud crashing noise as the man banged the pipe against the wooden banister. Greg could feel his temples throb as the man slowly neared them. Greg thought about the pipe, wondering what he would do when the man reached them—what he *could* do.

71 Then Lemon Brown released his hand and moved toward the top of the stairs. Greg looked around and saw stairs going up to the next floor. He tried waving to Lemon Brown, hoping the old man would see him in the dim light and follow him to the next floor. Maybe, Greg thought, the man wouldn't follow them up there. Suddenly, though, Lemon Brown stood at the top of the stairs, both arms raised high above his head.

72 "There he is!" A voice cried from below.

73 "Throw down your money, old man, so I won't have to bash your head in!"

74 Lemon Brown didn't move. Greg felt himself near panic. The steps came closer, and still Lemon Brown didn't move. He was an **eerie** sight, a bundle of rags standing at the top of the stairs, his shadow on the wall looming over him. Maybe, the thought came to Greg, the scene could be even eerier.

Skill:
Point of View

The speaker describes Greg's feelings and actions. He seems scared and doesn't know what to do.

Greg doesn't know what Lemon Brown plans to do, so neither do I. That's what happens with third-person limited point of view. Is Lemon Brown trying to protect Greg? Or scare the men? Not knowing creates suspense in the story.

Copyright © BookheadEd Learning, LLC

Copyright © BookheadEd Learning, LLC

75　Greg wet his lips, put his hands to his mouth and tried to make a sound. Nothing came out. He swallowed hard, wet his lips once more and howled as evenly as he could.

76　"What's that?"

77　As Greg howled, the light moved away from Lemon Brown, but not before Greg saw him hurl his body down the stairs at the men who had come to take his treasure. There was a crashing noise, and then footsteps. A rush of warm air came in as the downstairs door opened, then there was only an ominous silence.

78　Greg stood on the landing. He listened, and after a while there was another sound on the staircase.

79　"Mr. Brown?" he called.

80　"Yeah, it's me," came the answer. "I got their flashlight."

81　Greg exhaled in relief as Lemon Brown made his way slowly back up the stairs.

82　"You OK?"

83　"Few bumps and bruises," Lemon Brown said.

84　"I think I'd better be going," Greg said, his breath returning to normal. "You'd better leave, too, before they come back."

85　"They may hang around for a while," Lemon Brown said, "but they ain't getting their nerve up to come in here again. Not with crazy rag men and howling spooks. Best you stay a while till the coast is clear. I'm heading out west tomorrow, out to east St. Louis."

86　"They were talking about treasures," Greg said. "You really have a treasure?"

87　"What I tell you? Didn't I tell you every man got a treasure?" Lemon Brown said. "You want to see mine?"

88　"If you want to show it to me," Greg shrugged.

89　"Let's look out the window first, see what them scoundrels be doing," Lemon Brown said.

90　They followed the oval beam of the flashlight into one of the rooms and looked out the window. They saw the men who had tried to take the treasure sitting on the curb near the corner. One of them had his pants leg up, looking at his knee.

NOTES

91 "You sure you're not hurt?" Greg asked Lemon Brown.

92 "Nothing that ain't been hurt before," Lemon Brown said. "When you get as old as me all you say when something hurts is, 'Howdy, Mr. Pain, sees you back again.' Then when Mr. Pain see he can't worry you none, he go on mess with somebody else."

93 Greg smiled.

94 "Here, you hold this." Lemon Brown gave Greg the flashlight.

95 He sat on the floor near Greg and carefully untied the strings that held the rags on his right leg. When he took the rags away, Greg saw a piece of plastic. The old man carefully took off the plastic and unfolded it. He revealed some yellowed newspaper clippings and a battered harmonica.

96 "There it be," he said, nodding his head. "There it be."

97 Greg looked at the old man, saw the distant look in his eye, then turned to the clippings. They told of Sweet Lemon Brown, a blues singer and harmonica player who was appearing at different theaters in the South. One of the clippings said he had been the hit of the show, although not the headliner. All of the clippings were reviews of shows Lemon Brown had been in more than fifty years ago. Greg looked at the harmonica. It was dented badly on one side, with the reed holes on one end nearly closed.

98 "I used to travel around and make money to feed my wife and Jesse—that's my boy's name. Used to feed them good, too. Then his mama died, and he stayed with his mama's sister. He growed up to be a man, and when the war come he saw fit to go off and fight in it. I didn't have nothing to give him except these things that told him who I was, and what he come from. If you know your pappy did something, you know you can do something too.

99 "Anyway, he went off to war, and I went off still playing and singing. 'Course by then I wasn't as much as I used to be, not without somebody to make it worth the while. You know what I mean?"

100 "Yeah." Greg nodded, not quite really knowing.

101 "I traveled around, and one time I come home, and there was this letter saying Jesse got killed in the war. Broke my heart, it truly did.

102   "They sent back what he had with him over there, and what it was is this old mouth fiddle and these clippings. Him carrying it around with him like that told me it meant something to him. That was my treasure, and when I give it to him he treated it just like that, a treasure. Ain't that something?"

103   "Yeah, I guess so," Greg said.

104   "You guess so?" Lemon Brown's voice rose an octave as he started to put his treasure back into the plastic. "Well, you got to guess 'cause you sure don't know nothing. Don't know enough to get home when it's raining."

105   "I *guess* . . . I mean, you're right."

106   "You OK for a youngster," the old man said as he tied the strings around his leg, "better than those scalawags what come here looking for my treasure. That's for sure."

107   "You really think that treasure of yours was worth fighting for?" Greg asked. "Against a pipe?"

108   "What else a man got 'cepting what he can pass on to his son, or his daughter, if she be his oldest?" Lemon Brown said. "For a big-headed boy you sure do ask the foolishest questions."

109   Lemon Brown got up after patting his rags in place and looked out the window again.

110   "Looks like they're gone. You get on out of here and get yourself home. I'll be watching from the window so you'll be all right."

111   Lemon Brown went down the stairs behind Greg. When they reached the front door the old man looked out first, saw the street was clear and told Greg to scoot on home.

112   "You sure you'll be OK?" Greg asked.

113   "Now didn't I tell you I was going to east St. Louis in the morning?"

114   Lemon Brown asked. "Don't that sound OK to you?"

115   "Sure it does," Greg said. "Sure it does. And you take care of that treasure of yours."

116   "That I'll do," Lemon said, the wrinkles around his eyes suggesting a smile. "That I'll do."

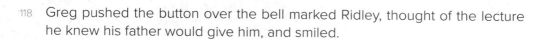

NOTES

117   The night had warmed and the rain had stopped, leaving puddles at the curbs. Greg didn't even want to think how late it was. He thought ahead of what his father would say and wondered if he should tell him about Lemon Brown. He thought about it until he reached his stoop, and decided against it. Lemon Brown would be OK, Greg thought, with his memories and his treasure.

118   Greg pushed the button over the bell marked Ridley, thought of the lecture he knew his father would give him, and smiled.

Please note that excerpts and passages in the StudySync® library and this workbook are intended as touchstones to generate interest in an author's work. The excerpts and passages do not substitute for the reading of entire texts, and StudySync® strongly recommends that students seek out and purchase the whole literary or informational work in order to experience it as the author intended. Links to online resellers are available in our digital library. In addition, complete works may be ordered through an authorized reseller by filling out and returning to StudySync® the order form enclosed in this workbook.

Reading & Writing
Companion

213

First Read

Read "The Treasure of Lemon Brown." After you read, complete the Think Questions below.

THINK QUESTIONS

1. Why does Lemon Brown consider a harmonica and some newspaper clippings his "treasure"? Cite textual evidence from the selection to support your answer.

2. Write two or three sentences describing how Lemon's heart got broken and how this event contributes to his life as an older man.

3. Figurative language is language used for descriptive effect, often to illustrate or imply ideas indirectly. Expressions of figurative language are not literally true, but express some truth beyond the literal level. What does the figurative expression "the dead would commence to rocking with the beat" tell readers about Lemon's talent as a blues musician? Cite textual evidence from the selection to support your answer.

4. Use context clues to determine the meaning of **commence** as it is used in paragraph 39 of "The Treasure of Lemon Brown." Write your definition here and identify clues that helped you figure out its meaning.

5. Read the following dictionary entry:

eerie
ee·rie \'ir-ē\ adjective

1. mysterious
2. strange
3. unexpected
4. causing fright

Which definition most closely matches the meaning of **eerie** as it is used in paragraph 74? Write the correct definition of *eerie* here and explain how you figured out the correct meaning.

Skill:
Point Of View

Use the Checklist to analyze Point Of View in "The Treasure of Lemon Brown." Refer to the sample student annotations about Point Of View in the text.

••• CHECKLIST FOR POINT OF VIEW

In order to identify how an author develops the point of view of the narrator or speaker in a text, note the following:

- ✓ the speaker or narrator

- ✓ what pronouns the narrator or speaker uses to describe characters or events, such as *I, me, he, she,* or *they*

- ✓ how much the narrator or speaker knows and reveals

- ✓ what the narrator or speaker says or does that reveals how they feel about other characters and events in the poem or story

To explain how an author develops the point of view of the narrator or speaker in a text, consider the following questions:

- ✓ Is the narrator or speaker objective and honest? Or do they mislead the reader? How?

- ✓ What is the narrator's or the speaker's point of view?

  - Is the narrator or speaker "all-knowing," or omniscient?

  - Is the narrator or speaker limited to revealing the thoughts and feelings of just one character?

  - Are there multiple narrators or speakers telling the story?

  - Is the narrator a character within the story or telling the story from the "outside"?

- ✓ How does the narrator or speaker reveal their thoughts about the events or the other characters in the story or poem? How does the narrator's or speaker's experiences and cultural background affect his or her thoughts?

Skill:
Point Of View

Reread paragraphs 71–77 of "The Treasure of Lemon Brown." Then, using the Checklist on the previous page, answer the multiple-choice questions below.

↻ YOUR TURN

1. Based on the text in paragraphs 74 and 75, what can you infer about how the author develops the point of view of the narrator in the story?

   ○ A. The narrator describes only what Greg and Lemon Brown are doing, not thinking.
   ○ B. The reader knows how Greg and Lemon Brown are feeling because the narrator is Greg.
   ○ C. The author reveals only what Greg is feeling and thinking.
   ○ D. The reader knows why the characters are acting as they do because the narrator is Lemon Brown.

2. How would the story be different if it were told only from Lemon Brown's point of view?

   ○ A. The narrator would only describe what the men were thinking as they called out from below.
   ○ B. One of the men would be using the pronoun I to reveal his thoughts.
   ○ C. The narrator would be asking the reader what he or she thought of the scene.
   ○ D. Only Lemon Brown's thoughts would be revealed to the reader.

3. Which paragraph best reveals Greg's thoughts and feelings about the sight of Lemon Brown on the stairs?

   ○ A. 71
   ○ B. 74
   ○ C. 75
   ○ D. 77

Close Read

Reread "The Treasure of Lemon Brown." As you reread, complete the Skills Focus questions below. Then use your answers and annotations from the questions to help you complete the Write activity.

◎ SKILLS FOCUS

1. Identify the setting of "The Treasure of Lemon Brown" and explain how the setting affects the tone at the beginning of the story.

2. Identify key events in the plot and how Greg's response to Lemon Brown changes throughout the story.

3. Identify the advantages and disadvantages of the author's choice of point of view when trying to understand the scene with the three bad men.

4. Identify how Greg's thoughts, words, and actions help the plot unfold throughout the story.

5. Explain how Greg Ridley's brief encounter with Lemon Brown impacts his life and how it may shape his relationship with his father.

✏ WRITE

ARGUMENTATIVE: Three men, one carrying a length of pipe, arrive at the abandoned building to steal Lemon Brown's treasure. Lemon, with Greg's help, scares them off. Does the author reveal enough about Lemon Brown's treasure for the reader to understand its importance? Do you think Lemon Brown's treasure is worth fighting for? Why or why not? Defend your point of view with evidence from the text.

The Circuit: Stories from the Life of a Migrant Child

FICTION
Francisco Jiménez
1997

Introduction

When Francisco Jiménez (b. 1943) was four years old, he and his family immigrated to the United States. At the age of six, he began working on farms, like other members of his family. Now a professor of literature at Santa Clara University in California, Jiménez said, "I came to realize that learning and knowledge were the only stable things in my life. Whatever I learned in school, that knowledge would stay with me no matter how many times we moved." *The Circuit: Stories from the Life of a Migrant Child* is Jiménez's autobiographical novel about migrant farm workers in 1950s California. It describes how migrant workers would go from farm to farm picking fruits and vegetables—also known as traveling the circuit.

"My mouth was dry. My eyes began to water. I could not begin. . . ."

from the Chapter: **The Circuit**

1   It was that time of year again. Ito, the strawberry sharecropper[1], did not smile. It was natural. The peak of the strawberry season was over and the last few days the workers, most of them *braceros,* were not picking as many boxes as they had during the months of June and July.

2   As the last days of August disappeared, so did the number of braceros. Sunday, only one—the best picker—came to work. I liked him. Sometimes we talked during our half-hour lunch break. That is how I found out he was from Jalisco, the same state in Mexico my family was from. That Sunday was the last time I saw him.

3   When the sun had tired and sunk behind the mountains, Ito signaled us that it was time to go home. "*Ya esora,*" he yelled in his broken Spanish. Those were the words I waited for twelve hours a day, every day, seven days a week, week after week. And the thought of not hearing them again saddened me.

4   As we drove home Papá did not say a word. With both hands on the wheel, he stared at the dirt road. My older brother, Roberto, was also silent. He leaned his head back and closed his eyes. Once in a while he cleared from his throat the dust that blew in from outside.

5   Yes, it was that time of year. When I opened the front door to the shack, I stopped. Everything we owned was neatly packed in cardboard boxes. Suddenly I felt even more the weight of hours, days, weeks, and months of work. I sat down on a box. The thought of having to move to Fresno and knowing what was in store for me there brought tears to my eyes.

6   That night I could not sleep. I lay in bed thinking about how much I hated this move.

7   A little before five o'clock in the morning, Papá woke everyone up. A few minutes later, the yelling and screaming of my little brothers and sisters, for

---

1. **sharecropper** a farmer who farms someone else's land, and in exchange, is allowed to live there

Copyright © BookheadEd Learning, LLC

whom the move was a great adventure, broke the silence of dawn. Shortly, the barking of the dogs accompanied them.

8   While we packed the breakfast dishes, Papá went outside to start the "*Carcachita.*" That was the name Papá gave his old black Plymouth. He bought it in a used-car lot in Santa Rosa. Papá was very proud of his little jalopy[2]. He had a right to be proud of it. He spent a lot of time looking at other cars before buying this one. When he finally chose the *Carcachita,* he checked it thoroughly before driving it out of the car lot. He examined every inch of the car. He listened to the motor, tilting his head from side to side like a parrot, trying to **detect** any noises that spelled car trouble. After being satisfied with the looks and sounds of the car, Papá then insisted on knowing who the original owner was. He never did find out from the car salesman, but he bought the car anyway. Papá figured the original owner must have been an important man because behind the rear seat of the car he found a blue necktie.

9   Papá parked the car out in front and left the motor running. "*Listo,*" he yelled. Without saying a word, Roberto and I began to carry the boxes out to the car. Roberto carried the two big boxes and I carried the two smaller ones. Papá then threw the mattress on top of the car roof and tied it with ropes to the front and rear bumpers.

10 Everything was packed except Mamá's pot. It was on old large galvanized pot she had picked up at an army surplus store in Santa Maria. The pot had many dents and nicks, and the more dents and nicks it **acquired** the more Mamá liked it. "*Mi olla,*" she used to say proudly.

11 I held the front door open as Mamá carefully carried out her pot by both handles, making sure not to spill the cooked beans. When she got to the car, Papá reached out to help her with it. Roberto opened the rear car door and Papá gently placed it on the floor behind the front seat. All of us then climbed in. Papá sighed, wiped the sweat off his forehead with his sleeve, and said wearily: "*Es todo.*"

12 As we drove away, I felt a lump in my throat. I turned around and looked at our little shack for the last time.

13 At sunset we drove into a labor camp near Fresno. Since Papá did not speak English, Mamá asked the camp **foreman** if he needed any more workers. "We don't need no more," said the foreman, scratching his head. "Check with Sullivan down the road. Can't miss him. He lives in a big white house with a fence around it."

---

2. **jalopy** an old automobile, usually in disrepair

14   When we got there, Mamá walked up to the house. She went through a white gate, past a row of rose bushes, up the stairs to the front door. She rang the doorbell. The porch light went on and a tall husky man came out. They exchanged a few words. After the man went in, Mamá clasped her hands and hurried back to the car. "We have work! Mr. Sullivan said we can stay there the whole season," she said, gasping and pointing to an old garage near the stables.

15   The garage was worn out by the years. It had no windows. The walls, eaten by termites, strained to support the roof full of holes. The dirt floor, populated by earthworms, looked like a gray road map.

16   That night, by the light of a kerosene lamp[3], we unpacked and cleaned our new home. Roberto swept away the loose dirt, leaving the hard ground. Papá plugged the holes in the walls with old newspapers and tin can tops. Mamá fed my little brothers and sisters. Papá and Roberto then brought in the mattress and placed it on the far corner of the garage. "Mamá, you and the little ones sleep on the mattress. Roberto, Panchito, and I will sleep outside under the trees," Papá said.

17   Early next morning Mr. Sullivan showed us where his crop was, and after breakfast, Papá, Roberto, and I headed for the vineyard to pick.

18   Around nine o'clock the temperature had risen to almost one hundred degrees. I was completely soaked in sweat and my mouth felt as if I had been chewing on a handkerchief. I walked over to the end of the row, picked up the jug of water we had brought, and began drinking. "Don't drink too much; you'll get sick," Roberto shouted. No sooner had he said that than I felt sick to my stomach. I dropped to my knees and let the jug roll off my hands. I remained motionless with my eyes glued on the hot sandy ground. All I could hear was the drone of insects. Slowly I began to recover. I poured water over my face and neck and watched the dirty water run down my arms to the ground.

19   I still felt a little dizzy when we took a break to eat lunch. It was past two o'clock and we sat underneath a large walnut tree that was on the side of the road. While we ate, Papá jotted down the number of boxes we had picked. Roberto drew designs on the ground with a stick. Suddenly I noticed Papá's face turn pale as he looked down the road. "Here comes the school bus," he whispered loudly in alarm. Instinctively, Roberto and I ran and hid in the vineyards. We did not want to get in trouble for not going to school. The neatly dressed boys about my age got off. They carried books under their arms. After they crossed the street, the bus drove away. Roberto and I came out from hiding and joined Papá. "*Tienen que tener cuidado,*" he warned us.

3. **kerosene lamp** a handheld lamp that burned liquid fuel for light

20   After lunch we went back to work. The sun kept beating down. The buzzing insects, the wet sweat, and the hot dry dust made the afternoon seem to last forever. Finally the mountains around the valley reached out and swallowed the sun. Within an hour it was too dark to continue picking. The vines blanketed the grapes, making it difficult to see the bunches. "*Vámanos,*" said Papá, signaling to us that it was time to quit work. Papá then took out a pencil and began to figure out how much we had earned our first day. He wrote down numbers, crossed some out, wrote down some more, "*Quince,*" he murmured.

21   When we arrived home, we took a cold shower underneath a water hose. We then sat down to eat dinner around some wooden crates that served as a table. Mamá had cooked a special meal for us. We had rice and tortillas with *carne con chile,* my favorite dish.

22   The next morning I could hardly move. My body ached all over. I felt little control over my arms and legs. This feeling went on every morning for days until my muscles finally got used to the work.

23   It was Monday, the first week of November. The grape season was over and I could now go to school. I woke up early that morning and lay in bed, looking at the stars and **savoring** the thought of not going to work and of starting sixth grade for the first time that year. Since I could not sleep, I decided to get up and join Papá and Roberto at breakfast. I sat at the table across from Roberto, but I kept my head down. I did not want to look up and face him. I knew he was sad. He was not going to school today. He was not going tomorrow, or next week, or next month. He would not go until the cotton season was over, and that was sometime in February. I rubbed my hands together and watched the dry, acid stained skin fall to the floor in little rolls.

24   When Papá and Roberto left for work, I felt relief. I walked to the top of a small grade next to the shack and watched the *Carcachita* disappear in the distance in a cloud of dust.

25   Two hours later, around eight o'clock, I stood by the side of the road waiting for school bus number twenty. When it arrived I climbed in. Everyone was busy either talking or yelling. I sat in an empty seat in the back.

26   When the bus stopped in front of the school, I felt very nervous. I looked out the bus window and saw boys and girls carrying books under their arms. I put my hands in my pant pockets and walked to the principal's office. When I entered I heard a woman's voice say: "May I help you?" I was startled. I had not heard English for months. For a few seconds I remained speechless. I looked at the lady who waited for an answer. My first instinct was to answer her in Spanish, but I held back. Finally, after struggling for English words, I

managed to tell her that I wanted to enroll in the sixth grade. After answering many questions, I was led to the classroom.

27 Mr. Lema, the sixth grade teacher, greeted me and assigned me a desk. He then introduced me to the class. I was so nervous and scared at that moment when everyone's eyes were on me that I wished I were with Papá and Roberto picking cotton. After taking roll, Mr. Lema gave the class the assignment for the first hour. "The first thing we have to do this morning is finish reading the story we began yesterday," he said enthusiastically. He walked up to me, handed me an English book, and asked me to read. "We are on page 125," he said politely. When I heard this, I felt my blood rush to my head; I felt dizzy. "Would you like to read?" he asked **hesitantly**. I opened the book to page 125. My mouth was dry. My eyes began to water. I could not begin. "You can read later," Mr. Lema said understandingly.

28 For the rest of the reading period I kept getting angrier and angrier with myself. I should have read, I thought to myself. During recess I went into the restroom and opened my English book to page 125. I began to read in a low voice, pretending I was in class. There were many words I did not know. I closed the book and headed back to the classroom.

29 Mr. Lema was sitting at his desk correcting papers. When I entered he looked up at me and smiled. I felt better. I walked up to him and asked if he could help me with the new words. "Gladly," he said.

30 The rest of the month I spent my lunch hours working on English with Mr. Lema, my best friend at school.

31 One Friday, during lunch hour, Mr. Lema asked me to take a walk with him to the music room. "Do you like music?" he asked me as we entered the building. "Yes, I like *corridos*[4]," I answered. He then picked up a trumpet, blew on it, and handed it to me. The sound gave me goose bumps. I knew that sound. I had heard it in many *corridos*. "How would you like to learn how to play it?" he asked. He must have read my face because before I could answer, he added: "I'll teach you how to play it during our lunch hours."

---

4. **corridos** a traditional Mexican ballad, usually with lyrics describing an actual historical event

32   That day I could hardly wait to tell Papá and Mamá the great news. As I got off the bus, my little brothers and sisters ran up to meet me. They were yelling and screaming. I thought they were happy to see me, but when I opened the door to our shack, I saw that everything we owned was neatly packed in cardboard boxes.

✎ WRITE

PERSONAL RESPONSE: In *The Circuit*, Francisco and his family are constantly moving. Each time Francisco's family moves, he feels sad to leave yet another place behind. At school, Francisco finds stability with a teacher, Mr. Lema, who helps him with reading.

Have you ever moved? If so, how did it make you feel? If not, think about something in your life that is stable and consistent. How does it contribute to your happiness? How do your feelings compare or contrast with Francisco's? Use newly-acquired vocabulary and evidence from the text to support your response.

That Day

POETRY
David Kherdian
1978

Introduction

David Kherdian (b. 1931) is an Armenian American writer and poet who is best known for penning an account of his mother's childhood during the Armenian Genocide called *The Road from Home*. In total, he has published more than 75 books in numerous genres, from creative nonfiction to poetry, and has also worked as an editor of numerous literary journals and anthologies. In his poem "That Day," presented here, Kherdian reflects on a special memory of his father.

"Just once
and the day stands out forever
in my memory"

1 Just once
2 my father stopped on the way
3 into the house from work
4 and joined in the softball game
5 we were having in the street,
6 and **attempted** to play in *our*
7 game that *his* country had never
8 known.
9 Just once
10 and the day stands out forever
11 in my memory
12 as a father's living **gesture**
13 to his son,
14 that in playing even the fool
15 or the clown, he would **reveal**
16 that the lines of their lives
17 were sewn from a tougher **fabric**
18 than the son had **previously** known.

© 1978 by David Kherdian, "That Day" from I Remember Root River. Used by permission of David Kherdian.

 WRITE

PERSONAL RESPONSE: Using "That Day" as an inspiration, write about a memory of an experience from which you learned something valuable about a family member or friend. Borrow key language from the poem to describe what you saw and felt, along with details and descriptions of your own.

A Poem for
My Librarian,
Mrs. Long

POETRY
Nikki Giovanni
2007

Introduction

Nikki Giovanni (b. 1943) calls herself a "Black American, a daughter, a mother, a professor of English." She is also the recipient of 25 honorary degrees, as well as an award-winning poet, writer, and activist who gives voice to issues of social justice and identity. In this poem, she adopts the persona of a "troubled little girl" in need of a book to demonstrate how reading can be a revolutionary act.

"You never know what troubled little girl needs a book. . ."

A Poem for My Librarian, Mrs. Long
(You never know what troubled little girl needs a book)

1 At a time when there was not tv before 3:00 P.M.
2 And on Sunday none until 5:00
3 We sat on the front porches watching
4 The jfg sign go on and off greeting
5 The neighbors, discussing the political
6 **Situation** congratulating the preacher
7 On his sermon
8 There was always the radio which brought us
9 Songs from wlac in nashville and what we would now call
10 Easy listening or smooth jazz but when I listened
11 Late at night with my **portable** (that I was so proud of)
12 Tucked under my pillow
13 I heard nat king cole and matt dennis, june christy and ella
14 Fitzgerald
15 And sometimes sarah vaughan sing
16 Black coffee
17 Which I now drink
18 It was just called music

19 There was a bookstore uptown on gay street
20 Which I visited and inhaled that wonderful odor
21 Of new books
22 Even today I read hardcover as a preference paperback only
23 As a last resort

24 And up the hill on vine street
25 (The main black corridor) sat our carnegie library
26 Mrs. Long always glad to see you
27 The stereoscope always ready to show you faraway
28 Places to dream about

29 Mrs. Long asking what are you looking for today
30 When I wanted Leaves of Grass or Alfred North Whitehead
31 She would go to the big library uptown and I now know
32 Hat in hand to ask to borrow so that I might borrow
33 Probably they said something **humiliating** since southern
34 Whites like to humiliate southern blacks

35 But she **nonetheless** brought the books
36 Back and I held them to my chest
37 Close to my heart
38 And happily skipped back to grandmother's house
39 Where I would sit on the front porch
40 In a gray **glider** and dream of a world
41 Far away

42 I love the world where I was
43 I was safe and warm and grandmother gave me neck kisses
44 When I was on my way to bed

45 But there was a world
46 Somewhere
47 Out there
48 And Mrs. Long opened that **wardrobe**
49 But no lions or witches scared me
50 I went through
51 Knowing there would be
52 Spring

"A Poem for My Librarian, Mrs: Long" from ACOLYTES by NIKKI GIOVANNI
Used by permission of HarperCollins Publishers

First Read

Read "A Poem for My Librarian, Mrs. Long." After you read, complete the Think Questions below.

 THINK QUESTIONS

1. Describe the setting of the poem. Cite textual evidence from the selection to support your answer.

2. Why is Mrs. Long important to the speaker of the poem? Cite textual evidence from the selection to support your answer.

3. Poetic structure describes the organization of words and lines in a poem. Examine Giovanni's line breaks. One line often runs into the next. What ideas about the speaker do you get from the way lines 13 and 14 run together? Cite textual evidence from the selection to support your answer.

4. Use context clues to determine the meaning of **portable** as it is used in line 11 of "A Poem for My Librarian, Mrs. Long."

5. Read the following dictionary entry:

nonetheless
none•the•less \ˌnən-thə-'les\ adverb

1. in spite of that
2. by any means
3. without care

Which definition most closely matches the meaning of **nonetheless** as it is used in line 35? Write the correct definition of *nonetheless* here and explain how you figured out the correct meaning.

Skill:
Compare and Contrast

Use the Checklist to analyze Compare and Contrast in "A Poem for My Librarian, Mrs. Long." Refer to the sample student annotations about Compare and Contrast in the text.

••• CHECKLIST FOR COMPARE AND CONTRAST

In order to determine how to compare and contrast texts in different forms or genres, use the following steps:

- ✓ first, choose texts with similar subjects or topics

- ✓ next, identify the qualities or characteristics of each genre

- ✓ after, identify the theme or topic in each work

- ✓ finally, analyze ways in which the texts are similar and different in the way they approach similar themes and topics

  - think about what the characters or narrators do and say

  - think about what happens as a result of the characters or narrators' words and actions

To compare and contrast texts in different forms or genres in terms of their approaches to similar themes and topics, consider the following questions:

- ✓ How does each text approach the theme and topic? How does the form or genre of the text affect this approach?

- ✓ What are the similarities and differences in the subjects or topics of the texts I have chosen?

Please note that excerpts and passages in the StudySync® library and this workbook are intended as touchstones to generate interest in an author's work. The excerpts and passages do not substitute for the reading of entire texts, and StudySync strongly recommends that students seek out and purchase the whole literary or informational work in order to experience it as the author intended. Links to online resellers are available in our digital library. In addition, complete works may be ordered through an authorized reseller by filling out and returning to StudySync® the order form enclosed in this workbook.

Reading & Writing
Companion

231

COMPARE AND CONTRAST

sync skills

Skill:
Compare and Contrast

Reread paragraphs 28–30 of *The Circuit*, lines 45–52 of "A Poem for My Librarian, Mrs. Long" and lines 9–18 of "That Day." Then, using the Checklist on the previous page, complete the chart below to compare and contrast the passages.

⟳ YOUR TURN

	Observation Options
A	A librarian's special interest in a girl who loves to read prepares the girl to enter the wider world unafraid.
B	Through the help of an understanding adult all the characters find ways to bridge their world with the wider world.
C	A teacher becomes a friend and helps the main character work on his English.
D	A father's willingness to seem foolish shows his son the strength needed to live in a new and strange home.

The Circuit	A Poem for My Librarian, Mrs. Long	That Day	All

Close Read

Reread "A Poem for My Librarian, Mrs. Long." As you reread, complete the Skills Focus questions below. Then use your answers and annotations from the questions to help you complete the Write activity.

◎ SKILLS FOCUS

1. Identify the theme of "A Poem for My Librarian, Mrs. Long." Use textual evidence to explain the theme.

2. Nikki Giovanni writes from her own point of view as a child. How does this help the reader relate to her? Use textual evidence from the poem to support your answer.

3. In *The Circuit*, Mr. Lema gives up his lunch hour to help Francisco improve his reading. Identify evidence in "A Poem for My Librarian, Mrs. Long" where Mrs. Long steps in to help the young Nikki Giovanni. Use textual evidence to compare and contrast what the two authors want their audience to understand when they read about these actions.

4. The boy in "That Day" is deeply touched when his father joins his softball game. Identify evidence in "A Poem for My Librarian, Mrs Long" that reveals how Nikki Giovanni also appreciated Mrs. Long's efforts. Use textual evidence to compare and contrast the responses of the two young people.

5. The impact of relationships on people's lives is one of the messages in *The Circuit*. Grateful for Mr. Lema's guidance, Francisco considers him his best friend at school. Identify textual evidence in "A Poem for My Librarian, Mrs. Long" that shows Nikki Giovanni is delivering a similar message about the importance of relationships. Use textual evidence to explain how relationships have impacted Giovanni's life.

✏ WRITE

COMPARE AND CONTRAST: What theme do *The Circuit*, "That Day," and "A Poem for My Librarian, Mrs. Long" have in common? Write a response in which you compare and contrast each text's theme. Remember to support your ideas with evidence from all three texts, and use newly-acquired vocabulary as appropriate.

Extended Writing Project and Grammar

EXTENDED WRITING PROJECT
ARGUMENTATIVE WRITING

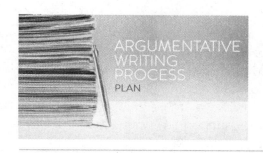

Argumentative Writing Process: Plan

PLAN	DRAFT	REVISE	EDIT AND PUBLISH

In this unit, you have read and learned about how relationships can shape people's lives. Sometimes, the way a relationship influences our lives goes unnoticed, like Phoebe's dismissive, uncaring behavior toward her mother in *Walk Two Moons*. In other cases, a relationship may leave an impression that lasts from childhood to adulthood, as in Nikki Giovanni's "A Poem for My Librarian, Mrs. Long."

WRITING PROMPT

Can relationships shape your future?

Think about the ways in which relationships shaped the lives of characters and individuals in the texts you have read in this unit. Then reflect on your own life. Think of a person who has influenced you in a positive way. Would your life be different if this person were not in your life? Based on your personal experience and at least one text from the unit, do you think relationships can actually shape people's futures? Why or why not? Support your argument with evidence from at least one text and your personal experience.

- an introduction
- a thesis statement
- coherent body paragraphs
- reasons and relevant evidence, which includes textual evidence
- a conclusion that follows from this argument

Writing to Sources

As you gather ideas and information from the texts in the unit, be sure to:

- include a claim;
- address counterclaims;
- use evidence from multiple sources; and
- avoid overly relying on one source.

Introduction to Argumentative Writing

Argumentative writing is meant to convince readers of the writer's position or point of view on a subject. To best support an opinion in argumentative writing, the writer introduces claims, which are statements that explain why he or she agrees or disagrees with the prompt. In order to make a convincing argument, writers may address opposing points of view, or counterclaims, and explain why these are not true in their opinion. Argumentative writing also relies on reasons and relevant evidence to support the writer's point of view. Without specific examples or evidence, an argument wouldn't be very strong.

A successful argument should have the following characteristics:

- an introduction
- a clear thesis statement summarizing the argument's main idea or central claim
- body paragraphs containing specific claims
- reasons and relevant evidence to support the claims
- a conclusion

As you continue with this Extended Writing Project, you'll receive more instruction and practice at crafting each of the characteristics of argumentative writing in order to develop your opinion about whether or not relationships can truly impact people's futures.

Before you get started on your own argument, read the essay that one student, Ellie, wrote in response to the writing prompt. As you read the Model, highlight and annotate the features of argumentative writing that Ellie included in her argument.

☰ STUDENT MODEL

NOTES

1   Has someone ever helped you achieve a goal? While friends, family members, and mentors cannot prewrite our futures for us, they can help us shape them. In Nikki Giovanni's "A Poem for My Librarian, Mrs. Long," the speaker describes how a librarian named Mrs. Long helped her overcome the limits that a segregated city tried to put on her learning. This relationship changed the speaker's life. While I have not faced such a difficult barrier, I did make a connection to my own experience as I read Giovanni's poem. I thought of Mr. Lin because he helped me discover an interest in acting even though I was shy. Based on Giovanni's poem and my experience, I believe that relationships can help shape your future when people provide you with the support you need to overcome barriers and achieve goals.

2   People can run into challenges or difficulties, and other people can impact their futures by helping them find ways to make progress in spite of them. This is evident in "A Poem for My Librarian, Mrs. Long" because Mrs. Long helped the speaker gain knowledge even though Mrs. Long and the speaker both faced segregation. For example, Mrs. Long gave the speaker the means to explore the world: "Mrs. Long always glad to see you / The stereoscope always ready to show you faraway / Places to dream about." The speaker emphasizes that Mrs. Long always encouraged her to pursue her interests in the library. For example, detail about the stereoscope also shows that Mrs. Long provided the speaker with technology that let her learn about many different parts of the world. These efforts helped the speaker find ways to work around barriers that were meant to limit what she could do and discover.

3   In addition to helping others overcome barriers, people can also impact individuals' futures by helping them achieve their goals. For example, in "A Poem for My Librarian, Mrs. Long," the speaker shares her childhood goal of wanting to read more books. She writes, "I wanted *Leaves of Grass* or Alfred North Whitehead." Mrs. Long helped the speaker achieve her goal by going to "the big library uptown" with her "hat in hand to ask to borrow so that I might borrow." After traveling

Copyright © BookheadEd Learning, LLC

Reading & Writing Companion

to the main library, Mrs. Long endured "humiliating" remarks from the white librarians. Yet Mrs. Long did not let this stop her. She "nonetheless brought the books" back to the speaker, who read and loved the books. The speaker remembers that after getting the books "I held them to my chest / Close to my heart." Mrs. Long's determination and assistance helped the speaker to achieve her goal of reading more books and encouraged the speaker to continue reading.

4   Although my goals and circumstances are different from the poem, I have been able to achieve a goal due to support from another person. I am extremely shy and feel nervous when I am in groups of people. My hands get sweaty and my voice shakes. Despite my shyness, I have always dreamed of becoming an actress. When our local community center announced they were putting on a production of *Peter Pan*, I wanted to audition for the role of Wendy. I shared this goal with my drama teacher Mr. Lin and explained that I was nervous. Mr. Lin helped me to overcome this barrier by offering me encouragement. He told me that I did not need to be an expert actor. Instead, I just needed to be the best Wendy I could be. He suggested that we start with small steps and had me read the school announcements at the beginning of class. After a couple of weeks, reading the announcements felt like second nature! Once we addressed this first barrier, Mr. Lin suggested that I perform a scene from *Peter Pan* in front of my drama class. Then, he and my classmates gave me helpful feedback that made my final audition much stronger. When I heard I got the part, I knew Mr. Lin's support helped me to achieve my goal.

5   Mr. Lin's mentorship has taught me that I can overcome personal challenges to pursue my dreams. Likewise, the poem "A Poem for My Librarian, Mrs. Long," shows that relationships can have a positive impact on individuals' futures. The speaker explains that: "Mrs. Long opened that wardrobe / But no lions or witches scared me / I went through / Knowing there would be / Spring." In other words, Mrs. Long helped the speaker to open up doors to other worlds and view the future with confidence and optimism. Based on the speaker's experiences in the poem and my own experiences, I believe that relationships can help us to overcome challenges that might otherwise make achieving goals seem impossible. Perhaps they might even inspire us to dream of new and bigger goals, creating a positive and long-lasting effect on our lives.

WRITE

Writers often take notes about their ideas before they sit down to write. Think about what you've learned so far about argumentative writing to help you begin prewriting.

- Who has influenced you? In what way?

- Would your life be different without this person? Why or why not?

- Drawing from your own experiences and relationships, do you believe that relationships can actually shape people's futures? Why or why not?

Response Instructions

Use the questions in the bulleted list to write a one-paragraph summary. Your summary should include a personal example of a relationship that has influenced you, if your life would be different without this person, as well as your opinion about whether or not relationships can truly shape someone's future.

Don't worry about including all of the details now; focus only on the most essential and important elements. You will refer to this short summary as you continue through the steps of the writing process.

Skill: Organizing Argumentative Writing

••• CHECKLIST FOR ORGANIZING ARGUMENTATIVE WRITING

As you consider how to organize your writing for your argumentative essay, use the following questions as a guide:

- What is my position on this topic?
- Have I chosen the best organizational structure to present my information?
- Can my claim be supported by logical reasoning and relevant evidence?
- Do I have enough evidence to support my claim?

Follow these steps to plan out the organization of your argumentative essay, including organizing your reasons and evidence clearly:

- Identify your claim.
  - > Write a statement that will present your claim in the first paragraph.

- Choose an organizational structure that will present your claim effectively.
- identify reasons and evidence that support your claim.

YOUR TURN

Read the statements below. Then, complete the chart by matching each statement to its correct place in the outline.

	Statement Options
A	People can run into challenges or difficulties, and other people can impact their futures by helping them find ways to make progress in spite of them.
B	While friends, family members, and mentors cannot prewrite our futures for us, they can help us shape them.
C	Mr. Lin's mentorship has taught me that I can overcome personal challenges to pursue my dreams.

Outline	Statement
Position	
Claim	
Reason/Evidence	

✏️ WRITE

Use the questions in the checklist section to write an outline for your argument.

Skill:
Thesis Statement

••• CHECKLIST FOR THESIS STATEMENT

Before you begin writing your thesis statement, ask yourself the following questions:

- What is the prompt asking me to write about?
- What is the topic of my argument or essay?
- What claim do I want to make about the topic of this argument or essay? Is my opinion clear to my reader?
- Does my thesis statement introduce the body of my argument or essay?
- Where should I place my thesis statement?

Here are some methods to introduce and develop your claim and topic:

- Think about the topic and central idea of your essay.
  - > The central idea of an argument is stated as a claim, or what will be proven or shown to be true.
  - > Identify as many claims as you intend to prove.

- Write a clear statement about the central idea or claim. Your thesis statement should:
  - > let the reader anticipate the body of your essay.
  - > respond completely to the writing prompt.

- Consider the best placement for your thesis statement.
  - > If your response is short, you may want to get right to the point. Your thesis statement may be presented in the first sentence of the argument or essay.
  - > If your response is longer (as in a formal argument or essay), you can build up to your thesis statement. In this case, you can place your thesis statement at the end of your introductory paragraph.

↻ YOUR TURN

Read the thesis statement questions and responses below. Then, complete the chart by correctly matching each thesis statement question with the appropriate response.

	Response Options
A	The topic of my argument is that my life would be very different if it weren't for my basketball coach, Mr. Montgomery, because he helped me decide that I want to be a basketball player when I grow up.
B	The prompt is asking whether or not relationships can shape people's futures. The prompt is also asking me to argue if my life would be different if a certain person were not in my life.
C	My argument will have an introduction, three body paragraphs, and a conclusion. Since it's a formal argument, I will put my thesis statement as the last sentence of the introduction.
D	My thesis statement tells the reader that I will list reasons for how Coach Montgomery helped shape my future, so it sets up the rest of the argument very well.
E	My main claim is that I think that relationships can shape people's futures because Coach Montgomery shaped mine. My thesis statement will be something like this: Special people in your life can definitely shape your future, just like Coach Montgomery helped shape mine.

Thesis Statement Question	Response
What is the prompt asking me to write about?	
What is the topic of my argument?	
What is the main claim I want to make in my argument, and how can I turn this into a thesis statement?	
Does my thesis statement set up the rest of the argument?	
Where should I place my thesis statement?	

⟳ YOUR TURN

Complete the chart by answering each of the questions about your thesis statement.

Thesis Statement Question	Response
What is the prompt asking me to write about?	
What is the topic of my argument?	
What is the main claim I want to make in my argument, and how can I turn this into a thesis statement?	
Does my thesis statement set up the rest of the argument?	
Where should I place my thesis statement?	

Skill: Reasons and Relevant Evidence

••• CHECKLIST FOR REASONS AND RELEVANT EVIDENCE

As you begin to determine what reasons and relevant evidence will support your claim(s), use the following questions as a guide:

- What is the claim (or claims) that I am making in my argument?

- Are the reasons I have included clear and easy to understand?

- What relevant evidence (specific examples) am I using to support this claim?

Use the following steps as a guide to help you determine how you will support your claim(s) with clear reasons and relevant evidence:

- Identify the claim(s) you will make in your argument.

- Establish clear reasons for making your claim(s).

- Explain the connection between your claim(s) and the evidence/examples selected.

⟳ YOUR TURN

Choose the best answer to each question.

1. The following is a section from a previous draft of Ellie's argument. Ellie would like to add an example to support the claim she has presented. Which of these would BEST follow and support her claim sentence?

> In addition to helping others overcome barreirs, people can also impact individual's futures by helping them achieve their goals.

- ○ A. I pretended I was acting the part of a volcano expert in a play.
- ○ B. I conducted a research project for my social studies class.
- ○ C. Mrs. Long worked at a library.
- ○ D. Mrs. Long helped the speaker achieve her goal by going to "the big library uptown" with her "hat in hand to ask to borrow" books so that the speaker could read them.

2. The following is a paragraph from a previous draft of Ellie's argument. Ellie has included an unnecessary example that does not support her claim. Which sentence should be deleted from this paragraph?

> (1) Although my goals and circumstances are different from the poem, I have been able to achieve a goal due to support from another person. (2) I am extremely shy and feel nervous when I am in groups of people. My hands get sweaty and my voice shakes. Despite my shyness, I have always dreamed of becoming an actress. (3) Except when I was really little I wanted to be a princess. (4) When our local community center announced they were putting on a production of Peter Pan, I wanted to audition for the role of Wendy.

- ○ A. Sentence 1
- ○ B. Sentence 2
- ○ C. Sentence 3
- ○ D. Sentence 4

✐ WRITE

Use the three questions in the checklist to revise the first few paragraphs of your argument by adding one or more reasons and/or relevant evidence to support your claim(s) and overall opinion.

Argumentative Writing Process: Draft

| PLAN | DRAFT | REVISE | EDIT AND PUBLISH |

You have already made progress toward writing your argument. Now it is time to draft your argument.

✏ WRITE

Use your Plan and other responses in your Binder to draft your argument. You may also have new ideas as you begin drafting. Feel free to explore those new ideas as you have them. You can also ask yourself these questions:

- Have I clearly stated if I agree or disagree with the prompt's question?
- Have I clearly provided claims about whether or not relationships can truly shape one's future?
- Do I provide enough reasons and relevant evidence to support my claims?
- Does the organization of the argument make sense?

Before you submit your draft, read it over carefully. You want to be sure that you've responded to all aspects of the prompt.

Here is Ellie's argument draft. Notice her thesis statement. As you read, identify how she supported her claim through reasons and relevant evidence. As she continues to revise and edit her argument, she will find and improve weak spots in her writing, as well as correct any language, punctuation, or spelling mistakes.

NOTES

STUDENT MODEL: FIRST DRAFT

Skill:
Introductions

Ellie decides that although her introduction has a clear claim and thesis statement, it doesn't grab the attention of the reader. Ellie connects her relationship with Mr. Lin to the poem "A Poem for My Librarian, Mrs. Long" by Nikki Giovanni. She decides that this connection would make a perfect "hook" for her introduction.

~~While friends, family members, and mentors cannot prewrite our futures for us, they can help us shape them. I thought of Mr. Lin because he helped me discover an interest in acting even though I was shy. Based on Giovanni's poem and my experience, I believe that relationships can help shape your future when people provide you with the support you need to overcome barriers and achieve goals.~~

Has someone ever helped you achieve a goal? While friends, family members, and mentors cannot prewrite our futures for us, they can help us shape them. In Nikki Giovanni's "A Poem for My Librarian, Mrs. Long," the speaker describes how a librarian named Mrs. Long helped her overcome the limits that a segregated city tried to put on her learning. This relationship changed the speaker's life. While I have not faced such a difficult barrier, I did make a connection to my own experience as I read Giovanni's poem. I thought of Mr. Lin because he helped me discover an interest in acting even though I was shy. Based on Giovanni's poem and my experience, I believe that relationships can help shape your future when people provide you with the support you need to overcome barriers and achieve goals.

~~In addition to helping others overcome barreirs, people can also impact individual's futures by helping them achieve their goals. In "A Poem for My Librarian, Mrs. Long," the speaker chats about her childhood goal of wanting to read more books. She writes, "I wanted Leaves of Grass or Alfred North Whitehead." Mrs. Long helped the speaker achieve her goal by going to "the big library uptown" with her "hat in hand to ask to borrow so that I might borrow" because Mrs. Long wanted to borrow a book at the library. Mrs. Long endured "humiliating" remarks from the white librarians. Mrs. Long did not let this stop her.~~

In addition to helping others overcome barriers, people can also impact individuals' futures by helping them achieve their goals. For example, in "A Poem for My Librarian, Mrs. Long," the speaker shares her childhood goal of wanting to read more books. She writes, "I wanted Leaves of Grass or Alfred North Whitehead." Mrs. Long helped the speaker achieve her goal by going to "the big library uptown" with her "hat in hand to ask to borrow so that I might borrow." After traveling to the main library, Mrs. Long endured "humiliating" remarks from the white librarians. Yet Mrs. Long did not let this stop her. She "nonetheless brought the books" back to the speaker, who read and loved the books. The speaker remembers that after getting the books "I held them to my chest / Close to my heart." Mrs. Long's determination and assistance helped the speaker to achieve her goal of reading more books and encouraged the speaker to continue reading.

~~Some people think that you make your own future, so the relationships you have with people don't make much of a difference. I like totally disagree. Relationships help you work hard to acheive your goals. Without Mr. Lin's advice, I still would have been afraid to try my hardest. Although my goals and circumstances are different from the poem, I've been able to acheive a goal due to support from another person. I am super shy and feel totally spooked when I am in groups of people. My hands get sweaty and my voice shakes. Despite my shiness, I have always dreamed of becoming an actress. Even though Mr. Lin was my theater teacher, his helped me to become a better student in my other classes. It was so crazy because I did my research, but I felt nervous, I wanted a good grad. I really really didn't want to get laughed at. In front of the class, I made mine fears go away by remembering what Mr. Lin taught me. I pertended I was acting the part of a volcano expert in a play. I was like the most excited person ever when I got an A. Thanks to Mr. Lin, I'm a great student in all of my classes. He helped me believe in myself.~~

Although my goals and circumstances are different from the poem, I have been able to achieve a goal due to support from another person. I am extremely shy and feel nervous when I am in groups of people. My hands get sweaty and my voice shakes. Despite my shyness, I have always dreamed of becoming an actress. When our local community center announced they were putting on a production of *Peter Pan*, I wanted to audition for the role of Wendy. I shared this goal with my drama teacher Mr. Lin and explained that I was nervous. Mr. Lin helped me to overcome this barrier by offering me encouragement. He told me that I did not need to be an expert actor. Instead, I just needed to be the best Wendy I could be. He suggested that we start with small steps and had me read the school announcements at the beginning of class. After a couple of weeks, reading the announcements

NOTES

Skill:
Transitions

Ellie adds the transitional phrase "For example" to make the connection between her evidence and claim clearer. Ellie also adds "Yet" to highlight how Mrs. Long chose to help the speaker, in spite of the "humiliating" remarks she received.

Skill:
Style

Since this argument is an academic assignment, it requires formal language, not slang or a conversational tone. Ellie changed several instances of informal or conversational language. For instance, she changed "super shy" to "extremely shy," as well as "totally spooked" to "nervous." Eliminating her conversational tone helps her essay to sound formal and professional.

felt like second nature! Once we addressed this first barrier, Mr. Lin suggested that I perform a scene from *Peter Pan* in front of my drama class. Then, he and my classmates gave me helpful feedback that made my final audition much stronger. When I heard I got the part, I knew Mr. Lin's support helped me to achieve my goal.

People can influence your future by helping you realize what you're meant to be. Although some may argue that people's influence on our lives often goes innoticed, I don't think that's true. Because of Mr. Lin's influence in my life, I decid what I want to be when I grow up. I realized I wanted to be an actor when I had to give a speech at a dinner for ours team's soccer coach. I wanted to say something from mine heart, but it was pounding in my chest. I remembered what Mr. Lin taught me about speaking, so I took a deep breath and just started talking about how great Coach Healy was and how much we'd miss hers. It felt like I talked forever about all the things she had done for us and all of the reasons we would miss her. Everybody was inpresed with my speaking skills and told me I would be a great actor one day. Because of my relationship with Mr. Lin, I know I *will* be a great actor one day.

~~Mr. Lin could have had a big acting career instaed of being a theater camp teacher. But, I am really glad he was my teacher. Just like Mrs. Long changed Nikki Giovanni's life, I think Mr. Lin was part of my life for a reason. My life would have been very different without him. He showed me how to face my fears and act like my words matter. He taught me how to be a good actor and a brave person. He changed how I felt about myself and the goals I have for mine future. And, it's true that relationships with people can really shape your future. I'll never forget the lessons I learned from my favorite teacher, Mr. Lin.~~

Mr. Lin could have had a big acting career instead of being a theater camp teacher. Likewise, the poem "A Poem for my Librarian, Mrs. Long," shows that relationships can have a positive impact on individuals' futures. The speaker explains that: "Mrs. Long opened that wardrobe / But no lions or witches scared me / I went through / Knowing there would be / Spring." In other words, Mrs. Long helped the speaker to open up doors to other worlds and view the future with confidence and optimism. Based on the speaker's experiences in the poem and my own experiences, I believe that relationships can help us to overcome challenges that might otherwise make achieving goals seem impossible. Perhaps they might even inspire us to dream of new and bigger goals, creating a positive and long-lasting effect on our lives.

Skill:
Conclusions

Ellie needs to remind her reader of her opinion about the prompt's question: Can relationships actually shape your future? After restating her thesis, Ellie decides to end her conclusion with a memorable closing comment: "Perhaps they might even inspire us to dream of new and bigger goals, creating a positive and long-lasting effect on our lives."

Skill: Introductions

••• CHECKLIST FOR INTRODUCTIONS

Before you write your introduction, ask yourself the following questions:

- What is my claim? How can I introduce my claim(s) so it is clear to readers?

- What is the best way to organize my ideas, concepts, reasons, and evidence in a clear and logical order?

- How will I "hook" my reader's interest? I might:

  > start with an attention-grabbing statement.

  > begin with an intriguing question.

  > use descriptive words to set a scene.

Below are two strategies to help you introduce your topic and claim, and organize reasons and evidence clearly in an introduction:

- Peer Discussion

  > Talk about your topic with a partner, explaining what you already know and your ideas about your topic.

  > Write notes about the ideas you have discussed and any new questions you may have.

  > Review your notes and think about what will be your claim or controlling idea.

  > Briefly state your claim or thesis.

  > Organize your reasons and evidence in an order that is clear to readers, presenting your reasons first, followed by evidence.

  > Write a possible "hook."

Please note that excerpts and passages in the StudySync® library and this workbook are intended as touchstones to generate interest in an author's work. The excerpts and passages do not substitute for the reading of entire texts, and StudySync® strongly recommends that students seek out and purchase the whole literary or informational work in order to experience it as the author intended. Links to online resellers are available in our digital library. In addition, complete works may be ordered through an authorized reseller by filling out and returning to StudySync® the order form enclosed in this workbook.

Reading & Writing Companion   **251**

- Freewriting

  > Freewrite for 10 minutes about your topic. Don't worry about grammar, punctuation, or having fully formed ideas. The point of freewriting is to discover ideas.

  > Review your notes and think about what will be your claim or controlling idea.

  > Briefly state your claim or thesis.

  > Organize your reasons and evidence in an order that is clear to readers, presenting your reasons first, followed by evidence.

  > Write a possible "hook."

YOUR TURN

Choose the best answer for each question.

1. Below is a section from a previous draft of Ellie's introduction. Keeping in mind the organization of the introduction, which sentence does not belong?

> (1) People can run into challenges or difficulties, and other people can impact their futures by helping them find ways to make progress in spite of them. (2) I'm a lot like Nikki Giovanni because the relationship she had with her librarian changed her life. (3) This is evident because Mrs. Long helped the speaker gain knowledge even though Mrs. Long and the speaker both faced segregation. (4) For example, Mrs. Long gave the speaker the means to explore the world: "Mrs. Long always glad to see you / The stereoscope always ready to show you faraway / Places to dream about."

- ○ A. Sentence 1
- ○ B. Sentence 2
- ○ C. Sentence 3
- ○ D. Sentence 4

2. Which "hook" could Ellie add to improve the introduction of her argumentative essay?

- ○ A. Relationships are important.
- ○ B. Mr. Lin was the best teacher.
- ○ C. Have you ever gotten through a tough time with the help of a mentor?
- ○ D. Some people don't value relationships as much as I do.

WRITE

Use the questions and notes in the checklist to revise the introduction of your argumentative essay.

Skill:
Transitions

Before you revise your current draft to include transitions, think about:

- the key ideas you discuss in your body paragraphs.
- the organizational structure of your essay.
- the relationships among claim(s) and reasons.

Next, reread your current draft and note areas in your essay where:

- the relationships between your claim(s) and the reasons and evidence are unclear, identifying places where you could add linking words or other transitional devices to make your argument more clear and complete. Look for:
  - > sudden jumps in your ideas.
  - > breaks between paragraphs where the ideas in the next paragraph are not connected to the previous.

Revise your draft to use words, phrases, and clauses to clarify the relationships among claim(s) and reasons, using the following questions as a guide:

- Are there relationships between the claims, reasons, and the evidence in my argument?
- Have I clarified, or made clear, these relationships?
- What linking words (such as conjunctions), phrases, or clauses could I add to my argument to clarify the relationships between the claims, reasons, and evidence I present?

YOUR TURN

Choose the best answer to each question.

1. The following section is from an earlier draft of Ellie's argument. Ellie has not used the most effective transition (underlined). Which of the following could replace *On the other hand* in the following sentence?

> Mr. Lin's mentorship has taught me that I can overcome personal challenges to pursue my dreams. <u>On the other hand</u>, the poem "A Poem for my Librarian, Mrs. Long," shows that relationships can have a positive impact on individuals' futures.

- ○ A. Likewise
- ○ B. However
- ○ C. Below
- ○ D. Nearby

2. The following section is from an earlier draft of Ellie's argument. Ellie would like to add a transition word or phrase to unify sentences 1 and 2. Which of these is the most effective transition to add between sentences 1 and 2?

> (1) The speaker emphasizes that Mrs. Long always encouraged her to pursue her interests in the library. (2) The detail about the stereoscope also shows that Mrs. Long provided the speaker with technology that let her learn about many different parts of the world.

- ○ A. In contrast,
- ○ B. For example,
- ○ C. Lastly,
- ○ D. But,

↻ YOUR TURN

Complete the chart by writing a transitional sentence that connects ideas with or between sentences or paragraphs in your argument.

Transition	Transitional Sentence
Transitions that clarify a relationship between a claim and reasons/evidence	
Transitions that make writing more coherent, or clear	
Transitions that provide cohesion, or a logical flow of ideas	

Skill:
Style

••• CHECKLIST FOR STYLE

First, reread the draft of your argumentative essay and identify the following:

- places where you use slang, contractions, abbreviations, and a conversational tone
- areas where you could use subject-specific or academic language in order to help persuade or inform your readers
- areas where sentence structure lacks variety
- incorrect uses of the conventions of standard English for grammar, spelling, capitalization, and punctuation

Establish and maintain a formal style in your essay, using the following questions as a guide:

- Have I avoided slang in favor of academic language?
- Have I varied my sentence structure and the length of my sentences? Apply these specific questions where appropriate:
  - > Where should I make some sentences longer by using conjunctions to connect independent clauses, dependent clauses, and phrases?
  - > Where should I make some sentences shorter by separating any independent clauses?
- Did I follow the conventions of standard English including:
  - > grammar?
  - > spelling?
  - > capitalization?
  - > punctuation?

Please note that excerpts and passages in the StudySync® library and this workbook are intended as touchstones to generate interest in an author's work. The excerpts and passages do not substitute for the reading of entire texts, and StudySync® strongly recommends that students seek out and purchase the whole literary or informational work in order to experience it as the author intended. Links to online resellers are available in our digital library. In addition, complete works may be ordered through an authorized reseller by filling out and returning to StudySync® the order form enclosed in this workbook.

Reading & Writing Companion   257

⟳ YOUR TURN

Read the words and phrases below. Then, complete the chart by sorting them into those that maintain a formal style and those that do not.

	Word and Phrase Options
A	It was like, the best day ever!?
B	researched
C	It was totally crazy that I felt nervous and stuff, caus oh boy, I was ready!
D	believe
E	resaerchd
F	Mr. lin who was my theater camp teacher was the COOLEST teacher ever, dont ya think?
G	It was unusual that I felt nervous because I was prepared.
H	beleive
I	Mr. Lin, my theater camp teacher, helped me become a great student.
J	It was the best day of my life!

Maintaining a Formal Style	Informal Style/Containing Errors

↻ YOUR TURN

Edit the sentences to fix the style mistakes.

Sentence	Corrected Sentence
The assignment was turned in totally too late for my teacher to be impresed?	
even though I erned a poor grad in science I stil wantted to be a doctor.	
He put him notes undernaeth the book.	
It was the craziest thing ever when mrs. Long unnounced the field trip.	
Marissa ate she lunch with me class on Wednesday.	

Skill:
Conclusions

••• CHECKLIST FOR CONCLUSIONS

Before you write your conclusion, ask yourself the following questions:

- How can I restate the thesis or main idea in my concluding section or statement? What impression can I make on my reader?

- How can I write my conclusion so that it follows logically from my argument?

- Should I include a call to action?

- How can I conclude with a memorable comment?

Below are two strategies to help you provide a concluding statement or section that follows from the argument presented:

- Peer Discussion

  > After you have written your introduction and body paragraphs, talk with a partner and tell them what you want readers to remember, writing notes about your discussion.

  > Review your notes and think about what you wish to express in your conclusion.

  > Do not simply restate your claim or thesis statement. Rephrase your main idea to show the depth of your knowledge, the importance of your idea, and encourage readers to adopt your view.

  > Write your conclusion.

- Freewriting

  > Freewrite for 10 minutes about what you might include in your conclusion. Don't worry about grammar, punctuation, or having fully formed ideas. The point of freewriting is to discover ideas.

  > Review your notes and think about what you wish to express in your conclusion.

  > Do not simply restate your claim or thesis statement. Rephrase your main idea to show the depth of your knowledge, the importance of your idea, and encourage readers to adopt your view.

  > Write your conclusion.

YOUR TURN

Choose the best answer to each question.

1. Ellie knows that her conclusion will be stronger if she can summarize how her personal experiences support the claim that other people can help us achieve our goals. Which of the following statements can be added to strengthen her conclusion?

> Mr. Lin could have had a big acting career instead of being a theater camp teacher. Likewise, the poem "A Poem for my Librarian, Mrs. Long," shows that relationships can have a positive impact on individuals' futures. The speaker explains that: "Mrs. Long opened that wardrobe / But no lions or witches scared me / I went through / Knowing there would be / Spring." In other words, Mrs. Long helped the speaker to open up doors to other worlds and view the future with confidence and optimism.

- ○ A. He was the best ever.
- ○ B. Mr. Lin's mentorship has taught me that I can overcome personal challenges to pursue my dreams.
- ○ C. I'll never forget my favorite teacher Mr. Lin and his fun acting classes.
- ○ D. Hopefully, one day you will have a teacher like Mr. Lin!

2. Ellie wants to improve the conclusion of her argumentative draft. One of these sentences can be removed to make her conclusion more logically follow her argument. Which sentence can be removed?

> (1) Mr. Lin could have had a big acting career instead of being a theater camp teacher. (2) Mr. Lin's mentorship has taught me that I can overcome personal challenges to pursue my dreams. (3) Likewise, the poem "A Poem for my Librarian, Mrs. Long," shows that relationships can have a positive impact on individuals' futures. The speaker explains that: "Mrs. Long opened that wardrobe / But no lions or witches scared me / I went through / Knowing there would be / Spring." (4) In other words, Mrs. Long helped the speaker to open up doors to other worlds and view the future with confidence and optimism.

- ○ A. Sentence 1
- ○ B. Sentence 2
- ○ C. Sentence 3
- ○ D. Sentence 4

 WRITE

Use the questions in the checklist to revise the conclusion of your argumentative essay.

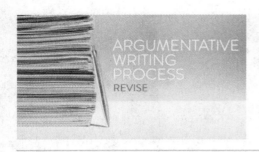

Argumentative Writing Process: Revise

| PLAN | DRAFT | REVISE | EDIT AND PUBLISH |

You have written a draft of your argument. You have also received input from your peers about how to improve it. Now you are going to revise your draft.

◀ REVISION GUIDE

Examine your draft to find areas for revision. Keep in mind your purpose and audience as you revise for clarity, development, organization, and style. Use the guide below to help you review:

Review	Revise	Example
Clarity		
Highlight the first few sentences in a paragraph, ensuring that the topic or claim is clearly stated first.	Identify the title, author, speaker or narrator, and names of characters.	This is evident in "A Poem for My Librarian, Mrs. Long" because Mrs. Long helped the speaker gain knowledge even though Mrs. Long and the speaker both faced segregation.
Development		
Identify places where you identify claims. Note reasons, relevant evidence, or specific examples you could incorporate to add support.	Add reasons, relevant evidence, or examples to support your ideas.	But Mrs. Long did not let this stop her. She "nonetheless brought the books" back to the speaker, who read and loved the books. The speaker remembers that after getting the books "I held them to my chest / Close to my heart."

Review	Revise	Example
Organization		
Examine the first sentence in each paragraph. Annotate any paragraph that does not transition smoothly from the previous paragraph.	Add a transitional phrase or sentence to provide coherence among body paragraphs.	When I heard I got the part, I knew Mr. Lin's support helped me to achieve my goal.
Style: Word Choice		
Identify informal words and phrases that do not help convey your purpose or opinion in an effective manner.	Select sentences to rewrite using more formal language.	Mrs. Long's determination and assistance helped the speaker to achieve her goal of reading ~~tons of~~ more books and encouraged the speaker to ~~keep at it~~ continue reading.
Style: Sentence Variety		
Annotate paragraphs, sentences, and words that are unusually long.	Separate long sentences into two sentences or shorten sentences by deleting information that is repetitive or unnecessary.	Mrs. Long helped the speaker achieve her goal by going to "the big library uptown" with her "hat in hand to ask to borrow so that I might borrow." ~~because Mrs. Long wanted to borrow a book at the library.~~ After traveling to the main library, Mrs. Long endured "humiliating" remarks from the white librarians.

✏ WRITE

Use the guide above, as well as your peer reviews, to help you evaluate your argument to determine areas that should be revised.

Grammar:
Basic Spelling Rules I

Suffixes and the Silent *e*

Spelling Conventions	Base Words	Correct	Incorrect
When adding a suffix that begins with a consonant to a word that ends with a silent *e*, keep the *e*.	place hope	placement hopeful	placment hopful
When adding a suffix that begins with a vowel or *y* to a word that ends with a silent *e*, usually drop the *e*.	race pore	racism porous	raceism poreous
When adding *-ly* to a word that ends with an *l* plus a silent *e*, drop the *le*.	probable humble	probably humbly	probablely humblely

Suffixes and the Final *y*

Spelling Conventions	Base Words	Correct	Incorrect
When a word ends in a consonant + *y*, change the *y* to *i* before adding a suffix. However, if the suffix begins with *i*, do not change the *y* to *i*.	bounty duty fry	bountiful dutiful frying	bountyful dutyful friing
When a word ends in a vowel + *y*, keep the *y*.	essay joy	essayist joyous	essaist joious

Spelling *ie* and *ei*

Spelling Conventions	Correct	Incorrect
Usually, when *i* and *e* appear together in one syllable, the *i* comes before the *e*.	yield friend	yeild freind
When *i* and *e* appear after a *c*, the *e* usually comes before the *i*.	receive conceit	recieve conciet
However, there are exceptions to these patterns.	seizure weird weigh	siezure wierd wiegh

↻ YOUR TURN

1. How should the spelling error in this sentence be corrected?

> *Dragonwings* is about the expereinces of a young boy from China who goes to America to join his father, a maker of kites that are beautiful enough to be heirlooms.

- ○ A. Change **expereinces** to **experiences**.
- ○ B. Change **beautiful** to **beautyful**.
- ○ C. Change **heirlooms** to **hierlooms**.
- ○ D. No change needs to be made to this sentence.

2. How should the spelling error in this sentence be corrected?

> A person's heart was weighed right after death to determine whether the person had been guilty of deceit or other sins—that was the beleif of the ancient Egyptians.

- ○ A. Change **weighed** to **wieghed**.
- ○ B. Change **deceit** to **deciet**.
- ○ C. Change **beleif** to **belief**.
- ○ D. No change needs to be made to this sentence.

3. How should the spelling error in this sentence be corrected?

> Because of their stark portraial of the thin, pitiful faces of the poor, Dorothea Lange's photographs changed the way the public perceived the Depression.

- ○ A. Change **portraial** to **portrayal**.
- ○ B. Change **pitiful** to **pityful**.
- ○ C. Change **perceived** to **percieved**.
- ○ D. No change needs to be made to this sentence.

4. How should the spelling error in this sentence be corrected?

> When Rosa Parks courageously refused to give up her bus seat, she committed an incredibly dangerous act, but her bravry helped launch the civil rights movement.

- ○ A. Change **courageously** to **couragously**.
- ○ B. Change **incredibly** to **incredibley**.
- ○ C. Change **bravry** to **bravery**.
- ○ D. No change needs to be made to this sentence.

Grammar: Possessive Pronouns

Possessive pronouns are a kind of personal pronoun. A possessive pronoun takes the place of a person or thing that owns or possesses something. It can come before the noun that is possessed, or it can stand alone in a sentence.

USED BEFORE NOUNS	USED ALONE
Singular: my, your, her, his, its	Singular: mine, yours, hers, his, its
Plural: our, your, their	Plural: ours, yours, theirs
Ever since I can remember, I had wanted to know about the Land of the Golden Mountain, but **my** mother had never wanted to talk about it. Dragonwings	Athene claimed that she had the better right, for the beauty of wisdom such as **hers** surpassed all else. Black Ships Before Troy: The Story of the Iliad

When using a personal pronoun to show possession, make sure the pronoun is in the possessive case.

Correct	Incorrect
The computer quickly stores information in **its** huge memory.	The computer quickly stores information in **it** huge memory.
Our dog is a Labrador retriever.	**We** dog is a Labrador retriever.
The clever idea was **theirs**.	The clever idea was **their**.

⟳ YOUR TURN

1. How should this sentence be changed?

> The red house on the corner is our.

- ○ A. Change **our** to **ours**.
- ○ B. Change **our** to **they**.
- ○ C. Change **our** to **their**.
- ○ D. No change needs to be made to this sentence.

2. How should this sentence be changed?

> She hand shot up when the teacher asked for volunteers.

- ○ A. Change **she** to **him**.
- ○ B. Change **she** to **her**.
- ○ C. Change **she** to **hers**.
- ○ D. No change needs to be made to this sentence.

3. How should this sentence be changed?

> Yours is the third seat in the first row.

- ○ A. Change **your** to **you**.
- ○ B. Change **yours** to **they**.
- ○ C. Change **yours** to **their**.
- ○ D. No change needs to be made to this sentence.

4. How should this sentence be changed?

> Will strummed him guitar and invited everyone to sing.

- ○ A. Change **him** to **he**.
- ○ B. Change **him** to **his**.
- ○ C. Change **him** to **we**.
- ○ D. No change needs to be made to this sentence.

Grammar: Formal and Informal Language

Different types of language are appropriate for different situations. Follow these rules when using formal and informal language:

Rules	Informal	Formal
Using a contraction makes language sound more informal.	I can't do it.	I cannot do it.
When writing an academic essay, it is necessary to use formal language.	We should totally focus on how crazy fast animals are disappearing.	The most important fact to consider about endangered animal species is the rate of their disappearance.
When conversing with a friend, it is appropriate to use informal language.	What's up, Sam?	Hello, Sam. How are you doing today?

The type of language you use affects the tone of your writing or speaking.

Formal	Informal
Papa took the towel Mama handed him, but did not reply immediately. I was just inside the kitchen dipping out the butter beans. I moved closer to the window so that I could hear his answer. Roll of Thunder, Hear My Cry	You ain't one of them bad boys looking for my treasure, is you? The Treasure of Lemon Brown
I resent that this article implies volleyball players have somehow chosen an "easier" path. We're on the Same Team	She was as crotchety and sullen as a three-legged mule, and I was not quite sure why. Walk Two Moons

⟳ YOUR TURN

1. How could this sentence be changed from informal to formal language?

> Hey dude, what's happenin' today?

○ A. Hey, what's gonna happen today?

○ B. Hello, what's going on today?

○ C. Hello. What are you doing today?

○ D. Dude, what's going on today?

2. How could these sentences be changed from formal to informal language?

> Good afternoon. Please include an example in your essay.

○ A. Hey dude, also do an example when you write that essay.

○ B. Please include an example in your essay.

○ C. Include an example in your essay.

○ D. Hello. Make sure to include an example.

3. How can this sentence be changed to eliminate contractions?

> I'm thinking there's a good chance you won't be able to try the cake today.

○ A. I am thinking there is a good chance you won't be able to try the cake today.

○ B. I think there is a good chance you will not be able to try the cake today.

○ C. I'm thinking there is a good chance you will not be able to try the cake today.

○ D. I'm thinking there's a good chance you will not be able to try the cake today.

Please note that excerpts and passages in the StudySync® library and this workbook are intended as touchstones to generate interest in an author's work. The excerpts and passages do not substitute for the reading of entire texts, and StudySync® strongly recommends that students seek out and purchase the whole literary or informational work in order to experience it as the author intended. Links to online resellers are available in our digital library. In addition, complete works may be ordered through an authorized reseller by filling out and returning to StudySync® the order form enclosed in this workbook.

Reading & Writing Companion   269

Argumentative Writing Process: Edit and Publish

PLAN	DRAFT	REVISE	EDIT AND PUBLISH

You have revised your argument based on your peer feedback and your own examination.

Now it is time to edit your argumentative essay. When you revised, you focused on the content of your argument. You looked at your use of reasons, evidence, specific examples, and transitions. When you edit, you focus on the mechanics of your essay, paying close attention to things like grammar, spelling, and punctuation.

Use the checklist below to guide you as you edit:

☐ Have I followed basic spelling rules for words with *ie/ei*, unstressed vowels, suffixes, and prefixes?

☐ Have I correctly used possessive pronouns?

☐ Have I used formal language and eliminated informal language?

☐ Have I spelled everything correctly?

☐ Do I have any sentence fragments or run-on sentences?

Notice some edits Ellie has made:

- Used basic spelling rules to correct spelling errors.

- Fixed errors with possessive pronouns.

- Corrected informal language, changing it to have a more formal and appropriate tone.

In addition to helping others overcome ~~barreirs~~ barriers, people can also impact ~~individual's~~ individuals' futures by helping them achieve their goals. For example, in "A Poem for My Librarian, Mrs. Long," the speaker ~~chats about~~ shares her childhood goal of wanting to read more books.

✏ WRITE

Use the questions on the previous page, as well as your peer reviews, to help you evaluate your argumentative essay to determine areas that need editing. Then edit your argument to correct those errors.

Once you have made all your corrections, you are ready to publish your work. You can distribute your writing to family and friends, hang it on a bulletin board, or post it on your blog. If you publish online, share the link with your family, friends, and classmates.

The Other Side

FICTION

Introduction

Many of us know what it's like to wish for superpowers. We might sometimes wish we could do things nobody else can do, or know things nobody else could know. But if we did have these powers, would anyone else understand? For the narrator of the short story "The Other Side," an extraordinary experience leads to complicated feelings and big questions.

V VOCABULARY

glanced
looked quickly

instant
a moment; a very short span of time

frowned
turned corners of the mouth down to show displeasure

reached
moved arm to touch or hold

creak
make a sound when moved or stepped on

grasped
held tightly

motionless
not moving

☰ READ

Copyright © BookheadEd Learning, LLC

  NOTES

1 I **glanced** at my sister, Alexandria, swaying under the tree in our backyard. How could I explain it? I couldn't keep it a secret. She knew there was more.

2 "What aren't you telling me?" she **frowned**. "This doesn't just happen. What did you do?"

3 In most ways, last Wednesday was normal. The sun took its place in the sky, and like countless times before, our neighborhood slowly came alive.

4   What was unusual was that I woke up early. I can't remember the last time I was up before sunrise. That Wednesday something had woken me. I knew that there was no going back because I would be different.

5   I didn't mention that when I told Alexandria before. Now her eyes were asking me to help her understand.

6   "Listen," I pleaded. "I'm trying to explain."

7   That morning, I slipped out of my bedroom and walked slowly down the hallway. The house was silent and my mom and sister slept peacefully. Our dog, Bella, was curled up somewhere.

8   There was darkness in the hallway but I knew where I had to go. I waited for the floorboards to **creak** but they didn't.

9   I arrived at the front door, standing there **motionless**. At first, I felt the presence on the other side. Something was calling to me and waiting for me. I don't know how long the presence had been there, but it wasn't going anywhere. I didn't try to understand. How could I?

10 I couldn't breathe. I looked at the doorknob for a long, long time. I knew that once I opened the door, I wouldn't be the same. I thought of my family and wondered if they would understand. I wished I'd just stayed in bed.

11 I tried to collect myself, but my heart was racing. I turned the knob and stepped forward.

12 In an **instant** I was aware of *everything*: The colors, the wind, and the earth below me — I understood it and could feel it more than ever.

13 I **reached** out to touch it and I changed forever.

14 I looked at Alexandria, as she **grasped** the tree trunk, her mouth open in amazement. I couldn't imagine how this sounded. I felt guilty for burdening her. At the same time, I felt relieved.

15 "Does anyone else know?" Alexandria asked frantically, not even trying to hide her concern.

16 I shook my head. Who could understand – let alone believe – what I could do now?

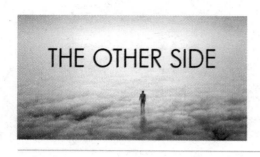

First Read

Read the story. After you read, answer the Think Questions below.

☁ THINK QUESTIONS

1. Who is the story about? How are they related?

   The story is about _____.

   They are _____.

2. Where does the story take place?

   The story takes place _____.

3. How does Alexandria feel at the end of the story?

   Alexandria feels _____.

4. Use context to confirm the meaning of the word *motionless* as it is used in "The Other Side." Write your definition of *motionless* here.

   Motionless means _____.

   A context clue is _____.

5. What is another way to say that the boy *glanced* at Alexandria?

   The boy _____.

Please note that excerpts and passages in the StudySync® library and this workbook are intended as touchstones to generate interest in an author's work. The excerpts and passages do not substitute for the reading of entire texts, and StudySync® strongly recommends that students seek out and purchase the whole literary or informational work in order to experience it as the author intended. Links to online resellers are available in our digital library. In addition, complete works may be ordered through an authorized reseller by filling out and returning to StudySync® the order form enclosed in this workbook.

Reading & Writing Companion   275

Skill:
Analyzing Expressions

★ DEFINE

When you read, you may find English expressions that you do not know. An **expression** is a group of words that communicates an idea. Three types of expressions are **idioms**, **sayings,** and **figurative language**. They can be difficult to understand because the meanings of the words are different from their **literal**, or usual, meanings.

An **idiom** is an expression that is commonly known among a group of people. For example, "It's raining cats and dogs" means it is raining heavily. **Sayings** are short expressions that contain advice or wisdom. For instance: "Don't count your chickens before they hatch" means do not plan on something good happening before it happens. **Figurative** language is when you describe something by comparing it with something else, either directly (using the words like or as) or indirectly. For example, "I'm hungry as a horse" means I'm very hungry. None of the expressions are about actual animals.

••• CHECKLIST FOR ANALYZING EXPRESSIONS

To determine the meaning of an expression, remember the following:

✓ If you find a confusing group of words, it may be an expression. The meaning of words in expressions may not be their literal meaning.

   • Ask yourself: Is this confusing because the words are new? Or because the words do not make sense together?

✓ Determining the overall meaning may require that you use one or more of the following:

   • context clues

   • a dictionary or other resource

   • teacher or peer support

✓ Highlight important information before and after the expression to look for clues.

YOUR TURN

Read the following excerpt from the "The Other Side." Then complete the multiple-choice questions below.

---

from **"The Other Side"**

I couldn't breathe. I looked at the doorknob for a long, long time. I knew that once I opened the door, I wouldn't be the same. I thought of my family and wondered if they would understand. I wished I'd just stayed in bed.

I tried to collect myself, but my heart was racing. I turned the knob and stepped forward.

In an instant I was aware of *everything*: The colors, the wind, and the earth below me — I understood it and could feel it more than ever.

I reached out to touch it and I changed forever.

---

1. What does the narrator mean when he says "my heart was racing"?

   ○ A. He is in a competition.
   ○ B. He is in love.
   ○ C. He is nervous.
   ○ D. He is excited.

2. Which context clue helped you determine the meaning of the expression?

   ○ A. "I couldn't breathe. I looked at the doorknob for a long, long time."
   ○ B. "I thought of my family and wondered if they would understand."
   ○ C. "I turned the knob and stepped forward."
   ○ D. "I reached out to touch it and I changed forever."

Skill:
Sharing Information

★ DEFINE

Sharing information involves asking for and giving information. The process of sharing information with other students can help all students learn more and better understand a text or a topic. You can share information when you participate in **brief** discussions or **extended** speaking assignments.

••• CHECKLIST FOR SHARING INFORMATION

When you have to speak for an extended period of time, as in a discussion, you ask for and share information. To ask for and share information, you may use the following sentence frames:

✓ To ask for information:

• What do you think about _____?

• Do you agree that _____?

• What is your understanding of _____?

✓ To give information:

• I think _____.

• I agree because _____.

• My understanding is _____.

YOUR TURN

Watch the "The Lightning Thief" StudySyncTV episode . After watching, sort the following statements from the episode into the appropriate columns:

	Statements
A	Makes me feel bad for him.
B	But Percy is not normal.
C	Do you think he is lying?
D	How do you know Percy is lonely?
E	I can feel it.
F	Can you prove it?

Asking for Information	Giving Information

Please note that excerpts and passages in the StudySync® library and this workbook are intended as touchstones to generate interest in an author's work. The excerpts and passages do not substitute for the reading of entire texts, and StudySync® strongly recommends that students seek out and purchase the whole literary or informational work in order to experience it as the author intended. Links to online resellers are available in our digital library. In addition, complete works may be ordered through an authorized reseller by filling out and returning to StudySync® the order form enclosed in this workbook.

Reading & Writing
Companion

279

Close Read

THE OTHER SIDE

 WRITE

NARRATIVE: Think about the end of the story. How has the main character changed? What do you think happens next? Recount the events at the end of the story and describe what you think would happen if the story continued. Pay attention to the *IE* and *EI* spelling rule as you write.

Use the checklist below to guide you as you write.

☐ How was the boy changed?

☐ How does Alexandria feel and what does she do?

☐ How does it end?

Use the sentence frames to organize and write your narrative.

I shook my head. Who could understand — let alone believe — what I could do now?

I couldn't believe that now I _____.

Alexandria was _____.

Then, _____.

Suddenly, _____.

I decided _____.

A Role to Play

FICTION

Introduction

On a day like any other day in science class, Bryan gets unwelcome news. He is assigned a role for a group project. He doubts his own abilities as he thinks back to a role he was assigned for a group project in sixth grade. He had wanted to do well, but he let his group down. Now Bryan must confront his fears and fulfill his role. Can he do it?

V VOCABULARY

environment
the natural world

nervous
anxious, agitated, worried

conservation
protection of the natural environment

webmaster
a person who maintains a website

erratically
moving or behaving in a way that is not usual or predictable

 NOTES

☰ READ

1 Bryan sat in science class. "Next week, we will be finishing our unit on the **environment** and **conservation**," Mrs. Jesky said. "So it's time to show what you have learned. You will complete a group project on conservation. I will be assigning each person in the group a role. Your role will help the group complete the project."

2 At once, Bryan felt his palms get damp. He told himself to breathe. He could feel his heart thumping **erratically**. *Group project? Roles?* he thought. *Anything but that.* It was like being back in sixth-grade language arts. Bryan and his group had to prepare a presentation on their book. Their teacher, Mr. Mack, gave each person a role. Bryan's role was to pick important passages from the text and explain their significance. Bryan was **nervous**. He wasn't sure how to do his task. His group asked a few times about his progress. He said he was almost done. But it was a lie. A year later, he still felt guilty for letting his group down.

3   Back in science class, Bryan tried to focus. He looked about the room tentatively. Mrs. Jesky was explaining the project. "With your group, you will be creating a Web page to explain your idea for a community conservation project. Your role will be based on what you're good at and like to do."

4   Bryan was preoccupied with the science project. Mrs. Jesky gave Bryan the role of **webmaster**. It was his job to take the group's ideas and put them into a website. *Why webmaster? Why not researcher? Why not spokesperson?* He wasn't sure he could do it. It was just like sixth-grade language arts.

5   Bryan walked slowly into science class the next day. He usually showed more energy. Mrs. Jesky noticed the change in his demeanor. "Bryan, what's wrong?" she asked.

6   "It's the project," he said. "I don't think I can do it."

7   Mrs. Jesky said, "Bryan, I gave you that role for a good reason. Those videos and presentations you are making for Ms. Reed's art club are great! You are good at presenting information in a way that people understand."

8   Bryan thought about that. Finally, he smiled. "Maybe you're right," he said. "I do really like making those videos. And people have told me they are good. Maybe I can be a good webmaster."

9   Mrs. Jesky smiled. "I know you can."

First Read

Read the story. After you read, answer the Think Questions below.

☁ THINK QUESTIONS

1. **What role does Mrs. Jesky give Bryan?**

    Mrs. Jesky gives Bryan _____.

2. **Why did Mrs. Jesky give Bryan that role?**

    She gave him that role because _____.

3. **What happened to Bryan when he participated in a group project in sixth grade?**

    When Bryan participated in the group project _____

    _____.

4. **Use context to confirm the meaning of the word *webmaster* as it is used in "A Role to Play." Write your definition of *webmaster* here.**

    Webmaster means _____.

    A context clue is _____.

5. **What is another way to say that your heart is thumping *erratically*?**

    Your heart is thumping _____.

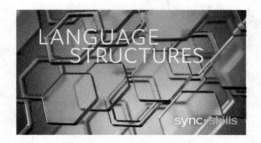

Skill:
Language Structures

★ DEFINE

In every language, there are rules that tell how to **structure** sentences. These rules define the correct order of words. In the English language, for example, a **basic** structure for sentences is subject, verb, and object. Some sentences have more **complicated** structures.

You will encounter both basic and complicated **language structures** in the classroom materials you read. Being familiar with language structures will help you better understand the text.

••• CHECKLIST FOR LANGUAGE STRUCTURES

To improve your comprehension of language structures, do the following:

✓ Monitor your understanding.

- Ask yourself: Why do I not understand this sentence? Is it because I do not understand some of the words? Or is it because I do not understand the way the words are ordered in the sentence?

✓ Break down the sentence into its parts.

✓ Confirm your understanding with a peer or teacher.

✓ In English, adjectives almost always come before the noun. Example: *He had a **big dog**.*

- A **noun** names a person, place, thing, or idea.

- An **adjective** modifies, or describes, a noun or a pronoun

- If there is more than one adjective, they usually appear in the following order separated by a comma: quantity or number, quality or opinion, size, age, shape, color. Example: *He had a **big, brown dog**.*

- If there is more than one adjective from the same category, include the word *"and."* Example: *He had a **brown and white dog**.*

✓ Ask yourself: What are the nouns in this sentence? What adjectives describe them? In what order are the nouns and adjectives?

Please note that excerpts and passages in the StudySync® library and this workbook are intended as touchstones to generate interest in an author's work. The excerpts and passages do not substitute for the reading of entire texts, and StudySync® strongly recommends that students seek out and purchase the whole literary or informational work in order to experience it as the author intended. Links to online resellers are available in our digital library. In addition, complete works may be ordered through an authorized reseller by filling out and returning to StudySync® the order form enclosed in this workbook.

Reading & Writing Companion   **285**

↻ YOUR TURN

Read each sentence in the first column. Then complete the chart by writing the words and phrases into the "Adjective" and "Noun" columns. The first row has been done as an example.

Sentence	Adjective	Noun
You will complete a group project on conservation.	group	project
Bryan's role was to pick important passages from the text and explain their significance.		
His group asked a few times about his progress.		
Back in science class, Bryan tried to focus.		
Bryan, I gave you that role for a good reason.		

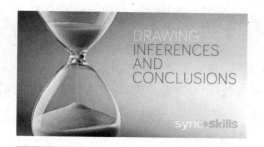

Skill: Drawing Inferences and Conclusions

★ DEFINE

Making **inferences** means connecting your experiences with what you read. Authors do not always tell readers directly everything that takes place in a story or text. You need to use clues to infer, or make a guess, about what is happening. To make an inference, first find facts, details, and examples in the text. Then think about what you already know. Combine the **textual evidence** with your **prior knowledge** to draw a **conclusion** about what the author is trying to communicate.

Making inferences and drawing conclusions can help you better understand what you are reading. It may also help you search for and find the author's message in the text.

••• CHECKLIST FOR DRAWING INFERENCES AND CONCLUSIONS

In order to make inferences and draw conclusions, do the following:

✓ Look for information that is missing from the text or that is not directly stated.

  • Ask yourself: What is confusing? What is missing?

✓ Think about what you already know about the topic.

  • Ask yourself: Have I had a similar experience in my life? Have I learned about this subject in another class?

✓ Combine clues from the text with prior knowledge to make an inference and draw a conclusion.

  • Think: I can conclude _____, because the text says _____ and I know that _____.

✓ Use textual evidence to support your inference and make sure that it is valid.

⟳ YOUR TURN

Read the following excerpt from "A Role to Play." Then, complete the multiple-choice questions below.

---

from "A Role to Play"

Back in science class, Bryan tried to focus. He looked about the room tentatively. Mrs. Jesky was explaining the project. "With your group, you will be creating a Web page to explain your idea for a community conservation project. Your role will be based on what you're good at and like to do."

Bryan was preoccupied with the science project. Mrs. Jesky gave Bryan the role of webmaster. It was his job to take the group's ideas and put them into a website. *Why webmaster? Why not researcher? Why not spokesperson?* He wasn't sure he could do it. It was just like sixth-grade language arts.

---

1. At the beginning of this excerpt, Bryan feels:

   ○ A. embarrassed by his lack of talent
   ○ B. anxious and unable to concentrate
   ○ C. angry at his teacher and classmates
   ○ D. frightened by the events in the room

2. A detail that best supports this conclusion is:

   ○ A. "tried to focus"
   ○ B. "Mrs. Jesky was explaining"
   ○ C. "With your group"
   ○ D. "what you're good at"

3. At the end of the excerpt, Bryan wonders whether:

   ○ A. Mrs. Jesky will let him quit
   ○ B. he belongs in a different class
   ○ C. other students are laughing at him
   ○ D. another role would suit him better

4. A detail that best supports this conclusion is:

   ○ A. "preoccupied with the science project"
   ○ B. "take the group's ideas"
   ○ C. *"Why not researcher?"*
   ○ D. "like sixth-grade language arts"

Close Read

✏ WRITE

LITERARY ANALYSIS: Why is Bryan nervous? How does the author show that something in his past is worrying him now? Write a short paragraph explaining why Bryan is nervous about working on a class project. Support your writing with evidence and specific details from the text, along with your personal experience. Pay attention to matching pronouns and antecedents as you write.

Use the checklist below to guide you as you write.

☐ How does Bryan feel?

☐ How do you know?

☐ Why does Bryan feel this way?

☐ How do you know?

Use the sentence frames to organize and write your literary analysis.

I believe that Bryan feels _____

because _____.

The passage supports my conclusion about _____

by telling about _____.

Please note that excerpts and passages in the StudySync® library and this workbook are intended as touchstones to generate interest in an author's work. The excerpts and passages do not substitute for the reading of entire texts, and StudySync® strongly recommends that students seek out and purchase the whole literary or informational work in order to experience it as the author intended. Links to online resellers are available in our digital library. In addition, complete works may be ordered through an authorized reseller by filling out and returning to StudySync® the order form enclosed in this workbook.

Reading & Writing Companion   **289**

studysync®

ASSIGNMENTS   BINDER   LIBRARY

In the Dark

UNIT 3

In the Dark

How do you know what to do when there are no instructions?

Genre Focus: **INFORMATIONAL**

Texts

 Paired Readings

Extended Writing Project and Grammar

English Language Learner Resources

How do you know what to do when there are no instructions?

CARL HIAASEN

Carl Hiaasen (b. 1953) has been a regular columnist for the *Miami Herald* since 1985, reporting and commenting on everything from the Everglades to local politics to Facebook to raccoons. He has also written a number of novels for adults and for younger audiences, all set in Florida. In an interview with *Strand Magazine*, Hiassen stated, "Every writer's obligation is to create enough suspense to keep the readers turning the pages, and it's doubly hard if you're trying to make them laugh along the way."

LANGSTON HUGHES

The final line of the poem "I, Too," by Langston Hughes (1902 – 1967) is chiseled in the stone wall of the National Museum of African American History and Culture in Washington, D.C.: "I, too, am America." Hughes first wrote these words in 1926 as a young poet at the forefront of the Harlem Renaissance in New York. Through the lasting impact of his poems, Hughes continues to edify and give voice to the African American experience in the United States.

MADELEINE L'ENGLE

American author Madeleine L'Engle (1918–2007) is known primarily for her works of fiction for young adults, including the novels *A Wrinkle in Time* and *A Wind in the Door*. She also wrote poetry and memoir, and served a long career as a librarian in New York. In her acceptance speech for the 1963 Newbery award, L'Engle commented on how she wrote such resonant, popular work, stating: "Most of what is best in writing isn't done deliberately."

HAMILTON WRIGHT MABIE

After a short time practicing law, Hamilton Wright Mabie (1846–1916) terminated his career as an attorney in 1879 to become an editor at a magazine called *The Outlook*, published weekly in New York City, where he worked alongside Theodore Roosevelt. The first of over thirty books he published in his lifetime was *Norse Stories Retold* (1882), which he later expanded on by writing versions of myths, fairy tales, heroes, and legends for children.

RANDALL MUNROE

From an early age, Randall Munroe (b. 1984) loved reading *Calvin and Hobbes*. Years later, he would himself become a cartoonist after earning a degree in physics and working at NASA. He is most famous for *xkcd*, a stick figure webcomic that draws on technology, math, and science for content. Munroe writes a blog called *What If?* (and has published a book by the same name) which answers questions sent in by fans of his comics, such as: What if a rainstorm dropped all of its water in a single giant drop?

RICK RIORDAN

When Rick Riordan (b. 1964) moved to San Francisco from his native San Antonio around the age of thirty, he began missing Texas so much he was compelled to write a story set in his home state. Not long after, his first book *Big Red Tequila* (1997) was published, and his life as an author began. Riordan was a middle school teacher at the time, who transitioned into being a full-time writer when he started writing a popular series about Percy Jackson, a twelve-year-old boy who discovers he is the son of Poseidon.

CATHERINE M. ANDRONIK

Catherine M. Andronik (b. 1958) is a high school librarian and author who shares her Connecticut home with an array of rescue parrots. She primarily writes biographies for a young adult audience, animating such historical figures as England's King Arthur, the mathematician and astronomer Copernicus, the former American president Abraham Lincoln, and the Egyptian pharaoh Hatshepsut. In her spare time, she likes to read, travel, and ride horses.

PAT MORA

Born and raised in El Paso, Texas, as a child of two first-generation Mexican American immigrants, Pat Mora (b. 1942) received her BA from Texas Western College and her MA from the University of Texas at El Paso. She is the author of over forty books, including YA literature, poetry, and children's books. She is a champion of bilingual literacy, and an advocate for "Children's Day, Book Day," which promotes literacy and a love of books. It takes place each year on April 30. She lives in Santa Fe, New Mexico.

Heroes Every Child Should Know: Perseus

FICTION
Hamilton Wright Mabie
1914

Introduction

Perseus, the son of a mortal woman, Danaë, and Zeus, the king of the gods, faced challenges from the day he was born. Locked in a wooden chest, the infant and his mother are set adrift in the sea. They wash up safely on a remote island, where a fisherman takes them in and Perseus grows into a fine, able-bodied young man. One fateful day, he is visited by the goddess Athene, who has chosen him for the task of killing her bitter enemy Medusa, the snake-haired Gorgon whose gaze turns a beholder to stone. Perseus is all too willing to take on the mission,

"It is better to die like a hero than to live like an ox in a stall."

from Chapter I: Perseus

1   Then Athene smiled and said:

2   "Be patient, and listen; for if you forget my words, you will indeed die. You must go northward to the country of the Hyperboreans[1], who live beyond the pole, at the sources of the cold north wind, till you find the three Grey Sisters, who have but one eye and one tooth between them. You must ask them the way to the Nymphs, the daughters of the Evening Star, who dance about the golden tree, in the Atlantic island of the west. They will tell you the way to the Gorgon[2], that you may slay her, my enemy, the mother of monstrous beasts. Once she was a maiden as beautiful as morn, till in her pride she sinned a sin at which the sun hid his face; and from that day her hair was turned to vipers, and her hands to eagle's claws; and her heart was filled with shame and rage, and her lips with bitter venom; and her eyes became so terrible that whosoever looks on them is turned to stone; and her children are the winged horse and the giant of the golden sword; and her grandchildren are Echidna the witch-adder, and Geryon the three-headed tyrant, who feeds his herds beside the herds of hell. So she became the sister of the Gorgons, the daughters of the Queen of the Sea. Touch them not, for they are **immortal;** but bring me only Medusa's head."

3   "And I will bring it!" said Perseus; "but how am I to escape her eyes? Will she not freeze me too into stone?"

4   "You shall take this polished shield," said Athene, "and when you come near her look not at her yourself, but at her image in the brass; so you may strike her safely. And when you have struck off her head, wrap it, with your face turned away, in the folds of the goatskin on which the shield hangs. So you will bring it safely back to me, and win to yourself **renown,** and a place among the heroes who feast with the Immortals upon the peak where no winds blow."

5   Then Perseus said, "I will go, though I die in going. But how shall I cross the seas without a ship? And who will show me my way? And when I find her, how shall I slay her, if her scales be iron and brass?"

---

1. **Hyperboreans** giants in Greek myth who lived in the extreme north
2. **Gorgons** three monster-women of Greek myth, the most famous of whom is Medusa

Skill:
Word Meaning

I am not sure what the word pride means, but I can tell it's a noun. Pride is the feeling of the once beautiful maiden.

There are more nouns to describe aspects of the maiden throughout the paragraph, such as shame and rage. I wonder if this will help me understand the meaning of pride in this paragraph?

NOTES

6   Now beside Athene appeared a young man more light-limbed than the stag, whose eyes were like sparks of fire. By his side was a **scimitar** of diamond, all of one clear precious stone, and on his feet were golden sandals, from the heels of which grew living wings.

7   Then the young man spoke: "These sandals of mine will bear you across the seas, and over hill and dale like a bird, as they bear me all day long; for I am Hermes, the far-famed Argus-slayer, the messenger of the Immortals who dwell on Olympus."

8   Then Perseus fell down and worshipped, while the young man spoke again:

9   "The sandals themselves will guide you on the road, for they are divine and cannot stray; and this sword itself the Argus-slayer, will kill her, for it is divine, and needs no second stroke. Arise, and gird them on, and go forth."

10   So Perseus arose, and girded on the sandals and the sword.

11   And Athene cried, "Now leap from the cliff and be gone."

12   But Perseus **lingered**.

13   "May I not bid farewell to my mother and to Dictys? And may I not offer burnt offerings to you, and to Hermes the far-famed Argus-slayer, and to Father Zeus above?"

14   "You shall not bid farewell to your mother, lest your heart **relent** at her weeping. I will comfort her and Dictys until you return in peace. Nor shall you offer burnt offerings to the Olympians; for your offering shall be Medusa's head. Leap, and trust in the armour of the Immortals."

15   Then Perseus looked down the cliff and shuddered; but he was ashamed to show his dread. Then he thought of Medusa and the renown before him, and he leapt into the empty air.

16   And behold, instead of falling he floated, and stood, and ran along the sky. He looked back, but Athene had vanished, and Hermes; and the sandals led him on northward ever, like a crane who follows the spring toward the Ister fens.

17   So Perseus started on his journey, going dry-shod over land and sea; and his heart was high and joyful, for the winged sandals bore him each day a seven days' journey. And he turned neither to the right hand nor the left, till he came to the Unshapen Land, and the place which has no name.

18   And seven days he walked through it on a path which few can tell, till he came to the edge of the everlasting night, where the air was full of feathers, and the soil was hard with ice; and there at last he found the three Grey Sisters, by the shore of the freezing sea, nodding upon a white log of

Skill:
Character

Perseus's thoughts show that he's afraid to leap from the cliff. He's embarrassed by his fear, but his desire for fame is stronger, so he leaps. This action brings him closer to the climax of the plot when he will battle with Medusa.

driftwood, beneath the cold white winter moon; and they chanted a low song together, "Why the old times were better than the new."

19 There was no living thing around them, not a fly, not a moss upon the rocks. Neither seal nor sea gull dare come near, lest the ice should clutch them in its claws. The surge broke up in foam, but it fell again in flakes of snow; and it frosted the hair of the three Grey Sisters, and the bones in the ice cliff above their heads. They passed the eye from one to the other, but for all that they could not see; and they passed the tooth from one to the other, but for all that they could not eat; and they sat in the full glare of the moon, but they were none the warmer for her beams. And Perseus pitied the three Grey Sisters; but they did not pity themselves.

20 So he said, "Oh, venerable mothers, wisdom is the daughter of old age. You therefore should know many things. Tell me, if you can, the path to the Gorgon."

21 Then one cried, "Who is this who **reproaches** us with old age?" And another, "This is the voice of one of the children of men."

22 Then one cried, "Give me the eye, that I may see him"; and another, "Give me the tooth, that I may bite him." But Perseus, when he saw that they were foolish and proud, and did not love the children of men, left off pitying them. Then he stepped close to them, and watched till they passed the eye from hand to hand. And as they groped about between themselves, he held out his own hand gently, till one of them put the eye into it, fancying that it was the hand of her sister. Then he sprang back, and laughed, and cried:

23 "Cruel and proud old women, I have your eye; and I will throw it into the sea, unless you tell me the path to the Gorgon, and swear to me that you tell me right."

24 Then they wept, and chattered, and scolded; but in vain. They were forced to tell the truth, though, when they told it, Perseus could hardly make out the road.

25 "You must go," they said, "foolish boy, to the southward, into the ugly glare of the sun, till you come to Atlas the Giant, who holds the heaven and the earth apart. And you must ask his daughters, the Hesperides, who are young and foolish like yourself. And now give us back our eye, for we have forgotten all the rest."

26 So Perseus gave them back their eye. And he leaped away to the southward, leaving the snow and the ice behind. And the terns and the sea gulls swept laughing round his head, and called to him to stop and play, and the dolphins gambolled up as he passed, and offered to carry him on their back. And all night long the sea nymphs sang sweetly. Day by day the sun rose higher and leaped more swiftly into the sea at night, and more swiftly out of the sea at dawn; while Perseus skimmed over the billows like a sea gull, and his feet were never wetted; and leapt on from wave to wave, and his limbs were never weary, till he saw far away a mighty mountain, all rose-red in the setting

Skill:
Character

Perseus really is clever. He figures out what is going on with the Grey Sisters and gains control of the eye.

He uses the eye as a way to get the information he wants in his quest to kill Medusa, which is the main conflict of the story.

I notice how Perseus has changed. He is brave and strong now. He is tough with the Grey Sisters.

sun. Perseus knew that it was Atlas, who holds the heavens and the earth apart.

27   He leapt on shore, and wandered upward, among pleasant valleys and waterfalls. At last he heard sweet voices singing; and he guessed that he was come to the garden of the Nymphs, the daughters of the Evening Star. They sang like nightingales among the thickets, and Perseus stopped to hear their song; but the words which they spoke he could not understand. So he stepped forward and saw them dancing, hand in hand around the charmed tree, which bent under its golden fruit; and round the tree foot was coiled the dragon, old Ladon the sleepless snake, who lies there for ever, listening to the song of the maidens, blinking and watching with dry bright eyes.

28   Then Perseus stopped, not because he feared the dragon, but because he was bashful before those fair maids; but when they saw him, they too stopped, and called to him with trembling voices:

29   "Who are you, fair boy? Come dance with us around the tree in the garden which knows no winter, the home of the south wind and the sun. Come hither and play with us awhile; we have danced alone here for a thousand years, and our hearts are weary with longing for a playfellow."

30   "I cannot dance with you, fair maidens; for I must do the errand of the Immortals. So tell me the way to the Gorgon, lest I wander and perish in the waves."

31   Then they sighed and wept; and answered:

32   "The Gorgon! she will freeze you into stone."

33   "It is better to die like a hero than to live like an ox in a stall. The Immortals have lent me weapons, and they will give me wit to use them."

34   Then they sighed again and answered: "Fair boy, if you are bent on your own ruin, be it so. We know not the way to the Gorgon; but we will ask the giant Atlas above upon the mountain peak." So they went up the mountain to Atlas their uncle, and Perseus went up with them. And they found the giant kneeling, as he held the heavens and the earth apart.

35   They asked him, and he answered mildly, pointing to the sea board with his mighty hand, "I can see the Gorgons lying on an island far away, but this youth can never come near them, unless he has the hat of darkness, which whosoever wears cannot be seen."

36   Then cried Perseus, "Where is that hat, that I may find it?"

37   But the giant smiled. "No living mortal can find that hat, for it lies in the depths of Hades, in the regions of the dead. But my nieces are immortal, and they shall fetch it for you, if you will promise me one thing and keep your faith."

38 Then Perseus promised; and the giant said, "When you come back with the head of Medusa, you shall show me the beautiful horror, that I may lose my feeling and my breathing, and become a stone for ever; for it is weary labour for me to hold the heavens and the earth apart."

39 Then Perseus promised, and the eldest of the Nymphs went down, and into a dark cavern among the cliffs, out of which came smoke and thunder, for it was one of the mouths of hell.

40 And Perseus and the Nymphs sat down seven days and waited trembling, till the Nymph came up again; and her face was pale, and her eyes dazzled with the light for she had been long in the dreary darkness; but in her hand was the magic hat.

The Arming of Perseus

41 Then all the Nymphs kissed Perseus, and wept over him a long while; but he was only impatient to be gone. And at last they put the hat upon his head, and he vanished out of their sight.

42 But Perseus went on boldly, past many an ugly sight, far away into the heart of the Unshapen Land, till he heard the rustle of the Gorgons' wings and saw the glitter of their **brazen** talons; and then he knew that it was time to halt, lest Medusa should freeze him into stone.

43 He thought awhile with himself, and remembered Athene's words. He arose aloft into the air, and held the mirror of the shield above his head, and looked up into it that he might see all that was below him.

44 And he saw the three Gorgons sleeping. He knew that they could not see him, because the hat of darkness hid him; and yet he trembled as he sank down near them, so terrible were those brazen claws.

45 Two of the Gorgons were foul as swine, and lay sleeping heavily, with their mighty wings outspread; but Medusa tossed to and fro restlessly, and as she tossed Perseus pitied her. But as he looked, from among her tresses the vipers' heads awoke, and peeped up with their bright dry eyes, and showed their fangs, and hissed; and Medusa, as she tossed, threw back her wings and showed her brazen claws.

46 Then Perseus came down and stepped to her boldly, and looked steadfastly on his mirror, and struck with Herpe stoutly once; and he did not need to strike again.

47   Then he wrapped the head in the goat-skin, turning away his eyes, and sprang into the air aloft, faster than he ever sprang before.

48   For Medusa's wings and talons rattled as she sank dead upon the rocks; and her two foul sisters woke, and saw her lying dead.

49   Into the air they sprang yelling, and looked for him who had done the deed. They rushed, sweeping and flapping, like eagles after a hare; and Perseus's blood ran cold as he saw them come howling on his track; and he cried, "Bear me well now, brave sandals, for the hounds of Death are at my heels!"

50   And well the brave sandals bore him, aloft through cloud and sunshine, across the shoreless sea; and fast followed the hounds of Death. But the sandals were too swift, even for Gorgons, and by nightfall they were far behind, two black specks in the southern sky, till the sun sank and he saw them no more.

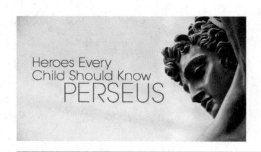

First Read

Read *Heroes Every Child Should Know: Perseus*. After you read, complete the Think Questions below.

☁ THINK QUESTIONS

1. How do Athene and Hermes help prepare Perseus for his journey? Cite textual evidence from the selection to support your answer.

2. Who else helps Perseus in his quest? How do they help him? Cite specific evidence from the text in your response.

3. How does Perseus feel about Medusa? Cite textual evidence from the selection to support your answer.

4. Find the word **renown** in paragraph 4 of "Heroes Every Child Should Know: Perseus." Use context clues in the surrounding sentences, as well as the sentence in which the word appears, to determine the word's meaning. Write your definition here and identify clues that helped you figure out its meaning.

5. Use context to determine the meaning of the word **scimitar** as it is used in the text. Write your definition here and identify clues that helped you figure out its meaning. Then check the meaning in a dictionary.

Skill:
Character

Use the Checklist to analyze Character in *Heroes Every Child Should Know: Perseus*. Refer to the sample student annotations about Character in the text.

••• CHECKLIST FOR CHARACTER

In order to determine how the characters respond or change as the plot moves toward a resolution, note the following:

✓ the characters in the story, including the protagonist and antagonist

✓ key events or series of episodes in the plot, especially events that cause characters to react, respond, or change in some way

✓ characters' responses as the plot reaches a climax, and moves toward a resolution of the problem facing the protagonist

✓ the resolution of the conflict in the plot and the ways that affects each character

To describe how a particular story's or drama's plot unfolds in a series of episodes as well as how the characters respond or change as the plot moves toward a resolution, consider the following questions:

✓ How do the characters' responses change or develop from the beginning to the end of the story?

✓ Do the characters in the story change? Which event or events in the story causes a character to change?

✓ Is there an event in the story that provokes, or causes, a character to make a decision?

✓ Do the characters' problems reach a resolution? How?

✓ How does the resolution affect the characters?

Skill:
Character

Reread paragraphs 46–50 of *Heroes Every Child Should Know: Perseus*. Then, using the Checklist on the previous page, answer the multiple-choice questions below.

↻ YOUR TURN

1. Based on Perseus's actions in paragraphs 46 through 47, the reader can conclude that—

   ○ A. Athene will be pleased with the resolution of the plot's conflict.
   ○ B. Athene will be displeased with the resolution of the plot's conflict.
   ○ C. Hermes will be saddened over the resolution of the plot's conflict.
   ○ D. Hermes will be angry over the resolution of the plot's conflict.

2. When Perseus's blood runs cold in paragraph 49, it reveals that he has—

   ○ A. full confidence in Athene's plan.
   ○ B. no fear of death in the Unshapen Land.
   ○ C. brief doubt in Athene's plan.
   ○ D. no fear of Medusa's sisters.

Skill:
Word Meaning

Use the Checklist to analyze Word Meaning in *Heroes Every Child Should Know: Perseus*. Refer to the sample student annotations about Word Meaning in the text.

↻ CHECKLIST FOR WORD MEANING

In order to find the pronunciation of a word or determine or clarify its precise meaning or its part of speech, do the following:

- ✓ try to determine the word's part of speech from context

- ✓ consult reference materials, both print and digital, to find the pronunciation of a word or determine or clarify its precise meaning or its part of speech

In order to verify the preliminary determination of the meaning of a word or phrase, do the following:

- ✓ use context clues to make an inference about the word's meaning

- ✓ consult a dictionary to verify your preliminary determination of the meaning

- ✓ be sure to read all of the definitions, and then decide which definition makes sense within the context of the text

To determine a word's precise meaning or part of speech, ask the following questions:

- ✓ What is the word describing?

- ✓ How is the word being used in the phrase or sentence?

- ✓ Have I consulted my reference materials?

Skill:
Word Meaning

Reread paragraphs 6–7 from *Heroes Every Child Should Know: Perseus*. Then, using the Checklist on the previous page as well as the dictionary entries below, answer the multiple-choice questions.

⟳ YOUR TURN

precious \ˈpreSHəs\

adjective
1. of great value; not to be wasted
2. excessively refined

noun
3. a term used to address a beloved person

adverb
4. very; extremely

origin: from Old French *precios*, from Latin *pretiosus* meaning "of great value"

bear \ber\

verb
1. to assume or accept
2. to carry

noun
3. a large, heavy mammal
4. something difficult to deal with

origin: Old English *beran* meaning "to bring forth"

1. Which definition best matches the way the word *precious* is used in paragraph 6? Remember to pay attention to the word's part of speech as you make your decision.

   ○ A. Definition 1   ○ C. Definition 3
   ○ B. Definition 2   ○ D. Definition 4

2. Which definition best matches the way the word *bear* is used in paragraph 7? Remember to pay attention to the word's part of speech as you make your decision.

   ○ A. Definition 1   ○ C. Definition 3
   ○ B. Definition 2   ○ D. Definition 4

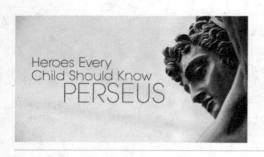

Close Read

Reread *Heroes Every Child Should Know: Perseus*. As you reread, complete the Skills Focus questions below. Then use your answers and annotations from the questions to help you complete the Write activity.

◎ SKILLS FOCUS

1. Many of Perseus's actions in his quest are prescribed by Athene. Identify one of his thoughts and one of his actions that surprise you. Then identify one of his responses that is not directed by Athene.

2. Identify actions of Perseus that reveal something about who he is and what he wants. Explain what the actions reveal.

3. Identify the resolution of the conflict in the story. Explain how this resolution contributes to the meaning of myth.

4. Identify textual evidence that indicates from what point of view the myth is told. Explain what the point of view is and how you know.

5. As he tells the Nymphs, Perseus is on an errand for the immortals. Identify situations in the quest that test Perseus's inner strength.

✎ WRITE

LITERARY ANALYSIS: How do Perseus's responses to individuals and events drive the action of the plot forward? Support your writing with evidence from the text.

The Lightning Thief

FICTION
Rick Riordan
2005

Introduction

Greek gods come to life in Rick Riordan's fantasy novel, *The Lightning Thief*. After being kicked out of boarding school, again, 12-year-old Percy Jackson learns that his father is Poseidon, God of the Sea. Before long, Percy and his friends are off on a dangerous mission to find Zeus's missing lightning bolt, which must be returned before Mount Olympus erupts into war. Here, Percy questions his mother about the father who abandoned him, and then reflects on the odd things that seem to happen to him wherever he goes. This award-winning novel by Rick Riordan (b. 1964) has been adapted into a series of films. Riordan has also written other fictional series based on mythology, including *The Trials of Apollo* and

". . . For your own good. I have to send you away."

from Chapter 3

1   Our rental cabin was on the south shore, way out at the tip of Long Island. It was a little pastel box with faded curtains, half sunken into the dunes. There was always sand in the sheets and spiders in the cabinets, and most of the time the sea was too cold to swim in.

2   I loved the place.

3   We'd been going there since I was a baby. My mom had been going even longer. She never exactly said, but I knew why the beach was special to her. It was the place where she'd met my dad.

4   As we got closer to Montauk, she seemed to grow younger, years of worry and work disappearing from her face. Her eyes turned the color of the sea.

5   We got there at sunset, opened all the cabin's windows, and went through our usual cleaning routine. We walked on the beach, fed blue corn chips to the seagulls, and munched on blue jelly beans, blue saltwater taffy, and all the other free samples my mom had brought from work.

6   I guess I should explain about the blue food.

7   See, Gabe had once told my mom there was no such thing. They had this fight, which seemed like a really small thing at the time. But ever since, my mom went out of her way to eat blue. She baked blue birthday cakes. She mixed blueberry smoothies. She bought blue-corn tortilla chips and brought home blue candy from the shop. This—along with keeping her maiden name, Jackson, rather than calling herself Mrs. Ugliano—was proof that she wasn't totally suckered by Gabe. She did have a **rebellious** streak, like me.

8   When it got dark, we made a fire. We roasted hot dogs and marshmallows. Mom told me stories about when she was a kid, back before her parents died in the plane crash. She told me about the books she wanted to write someday, when she had enough money to quit the candy shop.

9   Eventually, I got up the nerve to ask about what was always on my mind whenever we came to Montauk—my father. Mom's eyes went all misty. I

Skill:
Story Structure

This flashback tells me that both Percy and his mother are rebellious. Percy admires his mom for not giving in to Gabe. This might be a clue that Percy is also not one to back down. It helps us learn more about the characters' personalities.

NOTES

figured she would tell me the same things she always did, but I never got tired of hearing them.

10   "He was kind, Percy," she said. "Tall, handsome, and powerful. But gentle, too. You have his black hair, you know, and his green eyes."

11   Mom fished a blue jelly bean out of her candy bag. "I wish he could see you, Percy. He would be so proud."

12   I wondered how she could say that. What was so great about me? A **dyslexic, hyperactive** boy with a D+ report card, kicked out of school for the sixth time in six years.

13   "How old was I?" I asked. "I mean . . . when he left?"

14   She watched the flames. "He was only with me for one summer, Percy. Right here at this beach. This cabin."

15   "But . . . he knew me as a baby."

16   "No, honey. He knew I was expecting a baby, but he never saw you. He had to leave before you were born."

17   I tried to square that with the fact that I seemed to remember . . . something about my father. A warm glow. A smile.

18   I had always **assumed** he knew me as a baby. My mom had never said it outright, but still, I'd felt it must be true. Now, to be told that he'd never even seen me . . .

19   I felt angry at my father. Maybe it was stupid, but I **resented** him for going on that ocean voyage, for not having the guts to marry my mom. He'd left us, and now we were stuck with Smelly Gabe.

20   "Are you going to send me away again?" I asked her. "To another boarding school?"

21   She pulled a marshmallow from the fire.

22   "I don't know, honey." Her voice was heavy. "I think . . . I think we'll have to do something."

23   "Because you don't want me around?" I regretted the words as soon as they were out.

24   My mom's eyes welled with tears. She took my hand, squeezed it tight. "Oh, Percy, no. I—I *have* to, honey. For your own good. I have to send you away."

25   Her words reminded me of what Mr. Brunner had said—that it was best for me to leave Yancy.

26   "Because I'm not normal," I said.

Skill:
Story Structure

The word *remember* signals another flashback. Percy recalls something he associates with his father. But Percy's mother suggests this memory is false. Maybe the story might be about Percy's missing dad.

27 "You say that as if it's a bad thing, Percy. But you don't realize how important you are. I thought Yancy Academy would be far enough away. I thought you'd finally be safe."

28 "Safe from what?"

29 She met my eyes, and a flood of memories came back to me—all the weird, scary things that had ever happened to me, some of which I'd tried to forget.

30 During third grade, a man in a black trench coat had stalked me on the playground. When the teachers threatened to call the police, he went away growling, but no one believed me when I told them that under his broad-brimmed hat, the man only had one eye, right in the middle of his head.

31 Before that—a really early memory. I was in preschool, and a teacher accidentally put me down for a nap in a cot that a snake had slithered into. My mom screamed when she came to pick me up and found me playing with a limp, scaly rope I'd somehow managed to strangle to death with my meaty toddler hands.

32 In every single school, something creepy had happened, something unsafe, and I was forced to move.

33 I knew I should tell my mom about the old ladies at the fruit stand, and Mrs. Dodds at the art museum, about my weird **hallucination** that I had sliced my math teacher into dust with a sword. But I couldn't make myself tell her. I had a strange feeling the news would end our trip to Montauk, and I didn't want that.

34 "I've tried to keep you as close to me as I could," my mom said. "They told me that was a mistake. But there's only one other option, Percy—the place your father wanted to send you. And I just . . . I just can't stand to do it."

35 "My father wanted me to go to a special school?"

36 "Not a school," she said softly. "A summer camp."

37 My head was spinning. Why would my dad—who hadn't even stayed around long enough to see me born—talk to my mom about a summer camp? And if it was so important, why hadn't she ever mentioned it before?

38 "I'm sorry, Percy," she said, seeing the look in my eyes. "But I can't talk about it. I—I couldn't send you to that place. It might mean saying good-bye to you for good."

39 "For good? But if it's only a summer camp . . ."

40 She turned toward the fire, and I knew from her **expression** that if I asked her any more questions she would start to cry.

Excerpted from *The Lightning Thief* by Rick Riordan, published by Miramax Books/Hyperion Books for Children.

First Read

Read *The Lightning Thief*. After you read, complete the Think Questions below.

☁ THINK QUESTIONS

1. How does Percy describe himself? Is his view of himself mostly positive or negative? Cite textual evidence from the selection to support your answer.

2. What's unusual about Percy's school attendance? Use details from the text in your response.

3. What does Percy discover about his father? How does this discovery make Percy feel? Cite textual evidence from the selection to support your answer.

4. Find the word **assumed** in paragraph 18 of *The Lightning Thief.* Use context clues in the surrounding sentences, as well as the sentence in which the word appears, to determine the word's meaning. Write your definition here and identify clues that helped you figure out its meaning.

5. Use context clues to determine the meaning of **resented** as it is used in paragraph 19 of *The Lightning Thief.* Write your definition here and identify clues that helped you figure out the meaning. Then check the meaning in a dictionary.

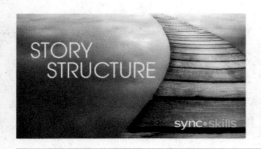

Skill:
Story Structure

Use the Checklist to analyze Story Structure in *The Lightning Thief*. Refer to the sample student annotations about Story Structure in the text.

••• CHECKLIST FOR STORY STRUCTURE

In order to identify how a particular sentence, chapter, scene, or stanza fits into the overall structure of a text, note the following:

- ✓ the author's use of description, dialogue, and narration and how each develops the events of the plot

- ✓ the pattern the author uses to organize the events within a story or chapter

  - • chronological, or in time order

  - • events out of time order

- ✓ any literary devices the author uses, such as flashback, a part of a story that shows something that happened in the past

- ✓ any particular sentence, chapter, scene, or a stanza in a poem that contributes to the development of the setting, the plot, and the theme

- ✓ how a particular sentence, chapter, scene, or a stanza in a poem fits into the overall structure

To analyze how a particular sentence, chapter, scene, or stanza fits into the overall structure of a text and contributes to the development of the theme, setting, or plot, consider the following questions:

- ✓ What are the key events in the story, and when did they take place?

- ✓ What impact does the order of events that take place in the story have on the theme, setting, or plot?

- ✓ What literary devices does the author use? How do they affect the development of the plot?

- ✓ How does a particular sentence, chapter, scene, or a stanza in a poem fit into the overall structure? How does it contribute to the development of the theme, setting, or plot?

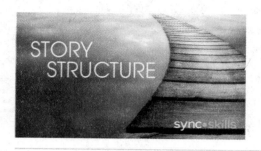

Skill:
Story Structure

Reread paragraphs 29–32 of *The Lightning Thief*. Then, using the Checklist on the previous page, answer the multiple-choice questions below.

⟳ YOUR TURN

1. Which phrase from paragraph 29 best signals the author's use of flashback?

   ○ A. she met my eyes
   ○ B. flood of memories came back to me
   ○ C. weird, scary things
   ○ D. had ever happened to me

2. Why might the author choose to use the flashbacks in paragraphs 30 and 31?

   ○ A. to explain Percy's earlier anger toward his missing father
   ○ B. to describe Percy's mother's irrational fear that Percy isn't safe
   ○ C. to support Mr. Brunner's earlier claim that it's best for Percy to leave Yancy
   ○ D. to reinforce the idea that Percy is different and unique

3. Which sentence or phrase from the passage gives the clearest understanding that the story will be about Percy's struggles?

   ○ A. "She met my eyes, and a flood of memories came back to me . . ."
   ○ B. "In every single school, something creepy had happened, something unsafe, and I was forced to move."
   ○ C. "I was in preschool, and a teacher accidentally put me down for a nap in a cot that a snake had slithered into."
   ○ D. "My mom screamed when she came to pick me up and found me playing with a limp, scaly rope I'd somehow managed to strangle to death with my meaty toddler hands.

Close Read

Reread *The Lightning Thief*. As you reread, complete the Skills Focus questions below. Then use your answers and annotations from the questions to help you complete the Write activity.

◎ SKILLS FOCUS

1. Explain how the author's use of flashbacks about Percy's childhood help develop the plot.

2. Identify examples of Percy's thoughts that reveal how he feels about himself. Explain how these thoughts help establish Percy as an outsider.

3. Identify textual evidence that illustrates how the author uses dialogue between Percy and his mother to develop the plot and theme. Explain your reasoning.

4. In the ninth paragraph, Percy finally gets up the nerve to ask about his father. How is this an example of a turning point in the story, and how does it further develop the plot? Explain your reasoning.

5. Percy has many challenges and few instructions on how to resolve them. Identify evidence of these challenges and explain how they contribute to the story's conflict.

✏ WRITE

DISCUSSION: How does this excerpt from *The Lightning Thief* connect to the overall structure of the story? What hints does the author provide about the overall plot and theme? Think about how the author uses flashbacks to describe Percy's past, Percy's thoughts, and Percy's dialogue with his mother. As you prepare for your discussion, be sure to find plenty of textual evidence to support your ideas.

Elena

POETRY
Pat Mora
1994

Introduction

Pat Mora (b. 1942) is a celebrated Mexican American author whose bilingual works explore themes of culture and identity in families across Texas and along the Southwestern border, where Mora was born and raised. The poem presented here, "Elena," is told from the perspective of a mother who has emigrated from Mexico to the United States with her husband and their children. After some time in the States, her kids have adapted and now speak English even at home—a language in which Elena has little fluency. In direct and confessional language, she worries about the increasing cultural divide between her and her children.

"I stand at the stove and feel dumb, alone."

NOTES

1   My Spanish isn't good enough.
2   I remember how I'd smile
3   listening to my little ones,
4   understanding every word they'd say,
5   their jokes, their songs, their **plots.**
6   *Vamos a pedirle dulces a mamá. Vamos.*
7   But that was in Mexico.
8   Now my children go to American high schools.
9   They speak English. At night they sit around
10   the kitchen table, laugh with one another.
11   I stand at the stove and feel dumb, alone.
12   I bought a book to learn English.
13   My husband **frowned**, drank more beer.
14   My oldest said, "*Mamá*, he doesn't want you
15   to be smarter than he is." I'm forty,
16   **embarrassed** at **mispronouncing** words,
17   embarrassed at the laughter of my children,
18   the grocer, the mailman. Sometimes I take
19   my English book and lock myself in the bathroom,
20   say the thick words softly,
21   for if I stop trying, I will be **deaf**
22   when my children need my help.

"Elena" from "Chants" by Pat Mora (©1994 Arte Público Press - University of Houston)

✏ WRITE

POETRY: The poem "Elena" is told from the mother's point of view. Write a poem in response to the mother from the perspective of one of her children.

Hatshepsut: His Majesty, Herself

INFORMATIONAL TEXT
Catherine M. Andronik
2001

studysync TV

Introduction

In Egypt's 18th dynasty, during the mid-to-late 1400s BCE, a long pattern of male dominance was interrupted when Hatshepsut, the widow of Pharaoh Tuthmosis II, and daughter of the previous pharaoh, Tuthmosis I, took the throne. Hatshepsut's reign lasted 22 years, during which time she built great monuments, sent an expedition to the little-known land of Punt, and handed over a peaceful Egypt to her nephew, Tuthmosis III, who subsequently attempted to erase Hatshepsut's historical

"Hatshepsut took a bold and unprecedented step: She had herself crowned pharaoh . . ."

NOTES

1   Hatshepsut, royal daughter of **Pharaoh** Tuthmosis and his Great Wife Ahmose, grew up in an Egypt that was peaceful, **prosperous,** and respected throughout the known world.

2   Despite this prosperity, all but one of Hatshepsut's siblings died. Fatal diseases were common, deadly creatures such as scorpions flourished in the Egyptian desert, accidents happened, and a doctor's treatment was often more superstitious than scientific. When the time came for Pharaoh Tuthmosis to name an **heir** to his throne, only one son remained: Tuthmosis, son of Mutnofret, a woman of the pharaoh's harem[1]. When he became pharaoh, young Tuthmosis would have little choice but to marry a woman of the royal blood. Marriages between close relatives were customary within ancient Egypt's royal family, so Hatshepsut was destined to become her half brother's wife. As the sole child of the pharaoh and the God's Wife, Hatshepsut was her dynasty's last hope to keep the royal bloodlines of Egypt intact.

3   Hatshepsut's father, Pharaoh Tuthmosis I, died at the relatively old age of fifty. His secret tomb, the first underground chamber to be hidden in the towering cliffs of the Valley of the Kings, just northwest of Thebes[2], had been excavated years in advance. The fine sarcophagus (sar-KOFF-ah-guss), or stone coffin, which would hold his body, was also ready. The pharaoh's mummy was carefully prepared, as befitted a great and beloved king. After seventy days, with solemn ceremony, Tuthmosis was laid in a tomb filled with all the choice food and drink, games and furniture, clothing and jewelry, and the little clay servant figures, called shawabtis (shah-WAHB-tees), that he could possibly need in the afterlife.

4   Following her father's death, Hatshepsut married her half brother, and the young man was crowned Pharaoh Tuthmosis II. Hatshepsut may have been only about twelve years old. As queen, she received a variety of new titles. Her favorite was God's Wife. Tuthmosis II and Hatshepsut had one child, a daughter named Neferure (neh-feh-ROO-ray).

Skill: Informational Text Elements

I notice that the author introduces the character Hatshepsut through an anecdote about her marrying her half-brother. That seems weird to me that Hatshepsut would have to marry her half-brother, but the author explains that this was "customary," or normal, in ancient Egypt. Plus, she really didn't have a choice. Hatshepsut was her family's last hope to keep the family as royalty.

---

1. **harem** a household of wives and/or servants attached to one man
2. **Thebes** a city on the banks of the Nile that was the capital of ancient Egypt when Hatshepsut was pharaoh

5   The reign of Tuthmosis II was unremarkable. It was also brief, for he was a sickly young man. Within a few years of his coronation, Hatshepsut's husband had died.

6   With the death of Tuthmosis II, Egypt was left without a king to ensure that the many gods would look kindly upon the fragile desert land. *Maat* was a delicate thing, and without a pharaoh to tend to its preservation, it was in danger of collapsing.

7   Although Hatshepsut had been Tuthmosis II's Great Wife, he'd had other wives in his harem, including one named Isis. Isis had borne the pharaoh a baby boy, who was also named Tuthmosis. Since Isis was not royal, neither was her baby. But like his father, he could grow up to be pharaoh if he married a princess of the royal blood: his half sister, Neferure.

8   Until Tuthmosis III was mature enough to be crowned pharaoh, what Egypt needed was a regent[3], an adult who could take control of the country. The regent would have to be someone familiar with palace life and **protocol**. He would need to conduct himself with the proper authority around the royal advisors. He should be prepared to wield power if it became necessary, and he should feel comfortable around visiting dignitaries from other lands. He needed to know his place among the priests of the various gods.

9   It was a job Hatshepsut, perhaps just fifteen years old, had been training for since her earliest days by her father's side. Women had acted as regents for infants at other times in Egypt's history, and the gods had not frowned upon them.

10   So until Tuthmosis III was ready to be crowned as pharaoh, the acting ruler of Egypt would be his aunt, the royal widow of the king, Hatshepsut.

11   At first, little Tuthmosis III was considered the pharaoh, with Hatshepsut just his second-in-command. But a small child could not be an effective ruler. As Hatshepsut settled into her role as regent, she gradually took on more and more of the royal decision-making. She appointed officials and advisors; dealt with the priests; appeared in public ceremonies first behind, then beside, and eventually in front of her nephew. Gradually, over seven years, her power and influence grew. In the end, Hatshepsut was ruling Egypt in all but name.

12   There is no reliable record of exactly when or how it happened, but at some point, Hatshepsut took a bold and unprecedented step: She had herself crowned pharaoh with the large, heavy, red-and-white double crown of the two Egypts, north and south. Since all pharaohs took a throne name, a sort of symbolic name, upon their coronation, Hatshepsut chose Maatkare (maht-KAH-ray). *Maat,* that crucial cosmic order, was important to Hatshepsut. Egypt required a strong pharaoh to ensure *maat*. Hatshepsut could be that pharaoh—even if she did happen to be a woman.

---

3. **regent** a person who exercises power temporarily on behalf of a ruler or monarch

---

NOTES

Skill: Central or Main Idea

This seems to be the most important idea in the text, or the main idea. The whole text seems to be about how Hatshepsut became the pharaoh even though a woman had never been a king of Egypt before.

I think this statement goes along with the main idea. It seems to be important that she is a woman because pharaohs had only ever been men.

Skill: Informational Text Elements

Hatshepsut is trying hard to be like a man in order to keep up with tradition and please her people. She even dresses like a man and is called "pharaoh," or king. I think this shows that she is determined.

Skill: Greek and Latin Affixes and Roots

I noticed the word inscribed and found that scrib is a Latin root word that means "to write." The prefix in- must mean "inside." The verb inscribed must mean to have written inside something, such as Hatshepsut's bracelets and cosmetic pots.

13 A few women had tried to rule Egypt before, but never with such a valid claim to the throne or at such a time of peace and prosperity. When Queens Nitocris and Sobekneferu had come to the throne in earlier dynasties, Egypt had been suffering from political problems, and there had been no male heirs. These women had not ruled long or well, and neither had had the audacity to proclaim herself pharaoh. Hatshepsut would be different.

14 There was no word in the language of ancient Egypt for a female ruler; a queen was simply the wife of a king. Hatshepsut had no choice: she had to call herself pharaoh, or king—a male title. She was concerned with preserving and continuing traditional order as much as possible, so to the people of Egypt she made herself look like a man in her role as pharaoh. In ceremonies, she wore a man's short kilt instead of a woman's long dress, much as she had as a child. Around her neck she wore a king's broad collar. She even fastened a false golden beard to her chin. When she wrote about herself as pharaoh, sometimes she referred to herself as he, other times as she. This would be very confusing for historians trying to uncover her identity thousands of years later.

15 Since Hatshepsut could not marry a queen, her daughter Neferure acted as God's Wife in public rituals. It was good training for Neferure, who would in time be expected to marry her half brother, Tuthmosis III, and be his royal consort. But Hatshepsut never seems to have considered that her daughter could succeed her as pharaoh.

16 Hatshepsut might have had to look and act like a man in public, but she never gave up feminine pleasures. Archaeologists have uncovered bracelets and alabaster cosmetic pots with Hatshepsut's cartouche (kar-TOOSH), or hieroglyphic name symbol, inscribed on each. Both men and women in Egypt used cosmetics. They needed creams and oils to keep their skin and hair from drying out under the brutal desert sun. And the kohl, a kind of makeup made from powdered lead that people applied around their eyes, did more than make them attractive; it also helped block out the sun's glare. But Hatshepsut was especially particular about her appearance. One inscription describes her as "more beautiful than anything."

17 With the exception of one military campaign against Nubia, Hatshepsut's reign was peaceful. Instead of expanding Egypt's borders through war and conquest, Hatshepsut built monuments within her country to proclaim its power. Her masterpiece was the magnificent temple at the site known today as Deir el-Bahri. The temple was dedicated to Amen, the

The Temple of Hatshepsut in the Valley of the Kings

god who was supposed to be the divine father of every pharaoh, the god to whom Hatshepsut felt she owed her good fortune. The temple at Deir el-Bahri was said to be Hatshepsut's own mortuary temple. The building is set into the side of a mountain and rises gracefully in three beautifully proportioned tiers, each supported by columns like those to be seen centuries later in Greek temples. Its design was far ahead of its time. Hatshepsut called it Djeser-Djeseru (JEH-sir jeh-SEH-roo)—"Holy of Holies."

18   On the walls of this temple, Hatshepsut had artists carve and paint her biography. According to the story told on the walls of Djeser-Djeseru, she had been chosen as pharaoh by the gods themselves, even before her birth. Perhaps, even after years on the throne, she still felt a need to **justify** a woman's right to rule. The gods in the pictures on the temple walls do not seem to care whether Hatshepsut is a man or a woman—in fact, some of the paintings show her as a boy.

First Read

Read *Hatshepsut: His Majesty, Herself*. After you read, complete the Think Questions below.

☁ THINK QUESTIONS

1. Before Hatshepsut became pharaoh, what experience does the text say she had for the job? Include evidence from the text to support your answer.

2. How was Hatshepsut's reign different from the reigns of the two earlier queens who had ruled Egypt? Use evidence from the text to support your answer.

3. What evidence does the text give to support the idea that Hatshepsut cared about her appearance? Refer to details from the text in your response.

4. Remembering that the Latin suffix *-ous* means "having, characterized by," use the context clues provided in the passage to determine the meaning of **prosperous**. Write your definition of "prosperous" here and tell how you were able to figure it out. In your answer, identify any relationships between words that helped you understand the meaning of "prosperous."

5. Use context to determine the meaning of the word **protocol** as it is used in the text. Then write your definition of *protocol* here and explain how you discovered the meaning of the word.

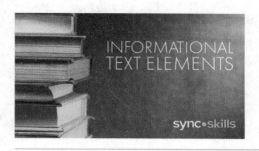

Skill:
Informational Text Elements

Use the Checklist to analyze Informational Text Elements in *Hatshepsut: His Majesty, Herself*. Refer to the sample student annotations about Informational Text Elements in the text.

••• CHECKLIST FOR INFORMATIONAL TEXT ELEMENTS

In order to identify a key individual, event, or idea in a text, note the following:

✓ examples that describe or explain important ideas, events, or individuals in the text

✓ anecdotes in the text. An anecdote is a personal story an author has passed on to readers

✓ how a key individual, event, or idea is introduced or illustrated

✓ other features, such as charts, maps, sidebars, and photos that might provide additional information outside of the main text

To analyze in detail how a key individual, event, or idea is introduced, illustrated, and elaborated in a text, consider the following questions:

✓ How does the author introduce or illustrate a key individual, event, or idea?

✓ What key details does the author include to describe or elaborate on important information in the text?

✓ Does the author include any anecdotes? What do they add to the text?

✓ What other features, if any, help readers to analyze the events, ideas, or individuals in the text?

Please note that excerpts and passages in the StudySync® library and this workbook are intended as touchstones to generate interest in an author's work. The excerpts and passages do not substitute for the reading of entire texts, and StudySync® strongly recommends that students seek out and purchase the whole literary or informational work in order to experience it as the author intended. Links to online resellers are available in our digital library. In addition, complete works may be ordered through an authorized reseller by filling out and returning to StudySync® the order form enclosed in this workbook.

Reading & Writing
Companion   **325**

Skill:
Informational Text Elements

Reread paragraph 16 from *Hatshepsut: His Majesty, Herself*. Then, using the Checklist on the previous page, answer the multiple-choice questions below.

⟳ YOUR TURN

1.   This question has two parts. First, answer Part A. Then, answer Part B.

Part A: What does this paragraph reveal about Hatshepsut as an individual?

- ○ A.   She was obsessed with her looks.
- ○ B.   She was tired of acting like a man.
- ○ C.   She was true to herself in private.
- ○ D.   She hid her true gender from her people.

Part B: Which of the following details from the text best supports your answer to Part A?

- ○ A.   "Hatshepsut might have had to look and act like a man in public, but she never gave up feminine pleasures."
- ○ B.   "Archaeologists have uncovered bracelets and alabaster cosmetic pots with Hatshepsut's cartouche. . ."
- ○ C.   "They needed creams and oils to keep their skin and hair from drying out under the brutal desert sun."
- ○ D.   "One inscription describes her as 'more beautiful than anything.'"

2. Why does the author write that "both men and women in Egypt used cosmetics"?

○ A. to explain why Hatshepsut used cosmetics both in public and in private

○ B. to highlight an opinion concerning the use of cosmetics in ancient Egypt

○ C. to provide a factual detail that illustrates what ancient Egypt was like

○ D. to emphasize the anecdote about Hatshepsut and why she chose to dress like a man in public

Skill:
Central or Main Idea

Use the Checklist to analyze Central or Main Idea in *Hatshepsut: His Majesty, Herself*. Refer to the sample student annotations about Central or Main Idea in the text.

••• CHECKLIST FOR CENTRAL OR MAIN IDEA

In order to identify a central idea of a text, note the following:

- ✓ the topic or subject of the text

- ✓ the central or main idea, if it is explicitly stated

- ✓ details in the text that convey the theme

To determine a central idea of a text and how it is conveyed through particular details consider the following questions:

- ✓ What main idea do the details in one or more paragraphs explain or describe?

- ✓ What bigger idea do all the paragraphs support?

- ✓ What is the best way to state the central idea? How might you summarize the text and message?

- ✓ How do particular details in the text convey the central idea?

Skill:
Central or Main Idea

Reread paragraph 17 from *Hatshepsut: His Majesty, Herself*. Then, using the Checklist on the previous page, answer the multiple-choice questions below.

⟳ YOUR TURN

1. This question has two parts. First, answer Part A. Then, answer Part B.

Part A: Which of the following statements best portrays the central idea of the paragraph?

- ○ A. Hatshepsut valued military campaigns to keep the peace.
- ○ B. The temple Deir el-Bahri was dedicated to the god Amen.
- ○ C. Hatshepsut's use of dynamic temple designs blazed a trail for future leaders.
- ○ D. Hatshepsut promoted a peaceful reign of Egypt by building monuments, not starting wars.

Part B: Which line from the paragraph best supports your answer to Part A?

- ○ A. "With the exception of one military campaign against Nubia, Hatshepsut's reign was peaceful."
- ○ B. "Instead of expanding Egypt's borders through war and conquest, Hatshepsut built monuments within her country to proclaim its power."
- ○ C. "Her masterpiece was the magnificent temple at the site known today as Deir el-Bahri."
- ○ D. "The building is set into the side of a mountain and rises gracefully in three beautifully proportioned tiers . . ."

Please note that excerpts and passages in the StudySync® library and this workbook are intended as touchstones to generate interest in an author's work. The excerpts and passages do not substitute for the reading of entire texts, and StudySync® strongly recommends that students seek out and purchase the whole literary or informational work in order to experience it as the author intended. Links to online resellers are available in our digital library. In addition, complete works may be ordered through an authorized reseller by filling out and returning to StudySync® the order form enclosed in this workbook.

Reading & Writing
Companion

329

Skill: Greek and Latin Affixes and Roots

Use the Checklist to analyze Greek and Latin Affixes and Roots in *Hatshepsut: His Majesty, Herself*. Refer to the sample student annotations about Greek and Latin Affixes and Roots in the text.

••• CHECKLIST FOR GREEK AND LATIN AFFIXES AND ROOTS

In order to identify Greek and Latin affixes and roots, note the following:

✓ the root

✓ the prefix and/or suffix

To use common, grade-appropriate Greek or Latin affixes and roots as clues to the meaning of a word, use the following questions as a guide:

✓ Can I identify the root of this word? Should I look in a dictionary or other resource?

✓ What is the meaning of the root?

✓ Can I identify the prefix and/or suffix of this word? Should I look in a dictionary or other resource?

✓ What is the meaning of the prefix and/or suffix?

✓ Does this suffix change the word's part of speech?

✓ How do the word parts work together to define the word's meaning and part of speech?

Skill: Greek and Latin Affixes and Roots

Reread paragraph 8 from *Hatshepsut: His Majesty, Herself*. Then, using the Checklist on the previous page, answer the multiple-choice questions.

⟳ YOUR TURN

1. The Latin root *reg* means "guide or rule." Therefore, the most likely meaning of *regent* is—

   ○ A. a counselor
   ○ B. a merchant
   ○ C. a governing body
   ○ D. a university

2. Stemming from the Latin root *auctor*, the word *authority* means "the power or right to give orders." Based on this meaning, which word can you substitute for *authority* in the paragraph?

   ○ A. permission
   ○ B. loyalty
   ○ C. respect
   ○ D. command

Close Read

Reread *Hatshepsut: His Majesty, Herself*. As you reread, complete the Skills Focus questions below. Then use your answers and annotations from the questions to help you complete the Write activity.

⊚ SKILLS FOCUS

1. Find evidence that supports the author's main idea in *Hatshepsut: His Majesty, Herself.* Explain how this evidence supports the main idea.

2. Identify at least two informational text elements (such as anecdotes or examples) that introduce, illustrate, or elaborate the life of the pharaoh Hatshepsut.

3. Identify evidence of Hatshepsut's leadership skills and explain how you would restate the main

ideas and the most important details of the text in your own words.

4. The Essential Question asks: "How do you know what to do when there are no instructions?" Identify evidence in *Hatshepsut: His Majesty, Herself* that reveals how Hatshepsut made history by breaking tradition.

✎ WRITE

COMPARE AND CONTRAST: In "Elena," a woman strives to learn English in order to benefit her children, despite her family's lack of support. Similarly, in *Hatshepsut: His Majesty, Herself,* a woman defies all odds and many years of tradition by becoming a pharaoh in Egypt to benefit her family and keep their royal lineage intact. Keeping these women in mind, respond to the following prompt: What central or main idea does the author of *Hatshepsut: His Majesty, Herself* convey about female empowerment? How does this idea compare and contrast with that of "Elena"? In your response, use evidence from the text to support your claim.

I, Too

POETRY
Langston Hughes
1925

Introduction

Born in Joplin, Missouri, James Mercer Langston Hughes (1902–1967) was an influential figure during the Harlem Renaissance, where he helped pioneer a new literary art form called jazz poetry. Inspired by Carl Sandburg and Walt Whitman, Hughes wrote poems that gave voice to his own experiences and the shared experiences of other African Americans during the era of segregation. "I, Too" starts as a personal statement and extends to inspire future generations.

"I, too, am America."

Skill: Poetic
Elements and
Structure

*The speaker says he is
the "darker brother." I
think this means he is
black. But by calling
himself "brother" he
must mean that he is
still in some way
connected to the
people who send him to
eat in the kitchen.*

Skill:
Media

*The audio version of
the poem emphasizes
the speaker's upbeat
tone. He has a sing-
song tone to his voice
when he speaks these
lines. I think this is
because he knows that
change is coming and
that he will be
considered equal.*

1 I, too, sing America.

2 I am the **darker** brother.
3 They send me to eat in the kitchen
4 When **company** comes,
5 I laugh,
6 And eat well,
7 And grow strong.

8 **Tomorrow,**
9 I'll be at the table
10 When company comes.
11 Nobody'll **dare**
12 Say to me,
13 "Eat in the kitchen,"
14 Then.

15 Besides,
16 They'll see how beautiful I am
17 And be **ashamed** —

18 I, too, am America.

"I, Too" from THE COLLECTED POEMS OF LANGSTON HUGHES by Langston
Hughes, edited by Arnold Rampersad with David Roessel, Associate Editor,
copyright ©1994 by the Estate of Langston Hughes. Used by permission of
Alfred A. Knopf, an imprint of the Knopf Doubleday Publishing Group, a
division of Random House LLC. All rights reserved.

By permission of Harold Ober Associates Incorporated.
Copyright ©1994 by The Estate of Langston Hughes.

First Read

Read "I, Too." After you read, complete the Think Questions below.

1. Who is the speaker of the poem? How do you know? Refer to one or more details from the beginning of the text to support your response.

2. What is the speaker comparing in lines 2–4 and 8–10? How are these two sets of lines similar? How are they different? Cite specific evidence from the text to support your answer.

3. Why will those who make the speaker "eat in the kitchen," in line 3, "be ashamed" in the future? Cite specific evidence from the text to support your response.

4. Read the following dictionary entry:

   company

   com•pa•ny \kəmp(ə)nē\ *noun*

   1. a business or other commercial organization
   2. a visiting person or group
   3. a group of soldiers

   Which definition most closely matches the meaning of **company** as it is used in line 4? Write the correct definition of *company* here and explain how you figured out the correct meaning.

5. Based on the context of the poem, what do you think the word **dare** means in line 11? Write your definition of *dare* here and confirm the meaning in a print or digital dictionary.

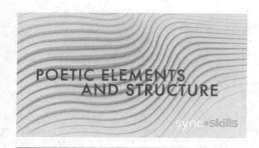

Skill:
Poetic Elements and Structure

Use the Checklist to analyze Poetic Elements and Structure in "I, Too." Refer to the sample student annotations about Poetic Elements and Structure in the text.

••• CHECKLIST FOR POETIC ELEMENTS AND STRUCTURE

In order to identify elements of poetic elements and structure, note the following:

- ✓ how the words and lines are arranged
- ✓ the form and overall structure of the poem
- ✓ the rhyme, rhythm, and meter, if present
- ✓ how the arrangement of lines and stanzas in the poem contribute to the poem's theme, or message

To analyze how a particular stanza fits into the overall structure of a text and contributes to the development of the theme, consider the following questions:

- ✓ What poetic form does the poet use? What is the structure?
- ✓ How do the lengths of the lines and stanzas affect the meaning?
- ✓ How does a poem's stanza fit into the structure of the poem overall?
- ✓ How does the form and structure affect the poem's meaning?
- ✓ In what way does a specific stanza contribute to the poem's theme?

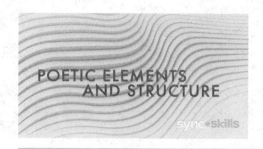

Skill:
Poetic Elements and Structure

Reread lines 8–18 of "I, Too." Then, using the Checklist on the previous page, answer the multiple-choice questions below.

YOUR TURN

1. How does the stanza from lines 8–14 convey a message to the reader?

   ○ A. It suggests that what the speaker hopes for will never happen.
   ○ B. It sends a message of hope for equality in America.
   ○ C. It implies that the speaker will continue to wait.
   ○ D. It suggests that the speaker has given up.

2. What clues tell you the poem is open form?

   ○ A. The poem has a predictable rhythm scheme.
   ○ B. The words rhyme at the end of the lines.
   ○ C. It doesn't have consistent meter, rhyme, or stanza length.
   ○ D. There is a pattern of stressed and unstressed syllables.

3. How do the lines and line breaks, when read aloud, help to convey the theme of the poem?

   ○ A. Each idea is spoken calmly, with hope, and with confidence.
   ○ B. The speaker sounds angry, rushing to express something upsetting.
   ○ C. The short lines and line breaks suggest the speaker is tired and depressed.
   ○ D. Each line seems to express a threatening demand.

Skill:
Media

Use the Checklist to analyze Media in "I, Too." Refer to the sample student annotations about Media in the text.

••• CHECKLIST FOR MEDIA

In order to determine how to compare and contrast reading a story, drama, or poem to listening to or viewing an audio, video, or live version of a text, do the following:

- ✓ think about the key features of the different media presentations

- ✓ consider how different kinds of media treat story or poetic elements in different ways

- ✓ note which details are emphasized or missing in each medium

- ✓ think about what you "see"—or visualize—as well as "hear" when you read a story, drama, or poem and how it compares to seeing it as a film, or hearing it read aloud

To compare and contrast the experience of reading a story, drama, or poem to listening to or viewing an audio, video, or live version of the text, including contrasting what you "see" and "hear" when reading the text to what you perceive when you listen or watch, consider the following questions:

- ✓ What features of each medium are the most important?

- ✓ Do you listen to it or view it? Do you hear one voice or many? How do these affect the written work?

- ✓ Which details are missing or emphasized in each medium? What do you think are the reasons behind these choices, and what effect do they have?

- ✓ How is the way you picture a character or narrator in your mind as you read similar to the way that same character or narrator is portrayed in a filmed or audio version of the same text? How is it different?

Skill:
Media

Reread lines 4–10 of "I, Too." Then, using the Checklist on the previous page, answer the multiple-choice questions below.

↻ YOUR TURN

1. How can comparing and contrasting different forms of media be useful for analyzing the theme of "I, Too"?

   ○ A. Varying themes help the reader understand how the piece connects to the world today.
   ○ B. A shift in mood helps the reader draw further conclusions about the speaker.
   ○ C. Analyzing tone and use of pronouns helps the reader to better understand theme.
   ○ D. A shift in tone can help the reader visualize the events in the piece.

2. How are the audio and printed versions of the poem "I, Too" different?

   ○ A. The textual difference between the spoken and written versions influences the audience's understanding of the poem's theme
   ○ B. The difference in the rhyming lines between the spoken and written versions impacts how the reader imagines the speaker.
   ○ C. The difference in the theme between the spoken and written versions allows the reader to relate to the speaker.
   ○ D. The student is better able to analyze the narrator's tone in the printed version.

I, TOO

Close Read

Reread "I, Too." As you reread, complete the Skills Focus questions below. Then use your answers and annotations from the questions to help you complete the Write activity.

⊚ SKILLS FOCUS

1. Explain the effect of two or three lines, or a stanza, on the poem's theme.

2. Hughes uses a dining table as a metaphor to explain American racism. Explain how this metaphor causes readers to think about the topic in a new way.

3. Compare and contrast the experience of reading the poem and listening to the audio version as it relates to meaning. Explain your thinking using textual evidence.

4. Explain why it's important for the speaker to sit at the table, even though he was instructed to sit in the kitchen. Cite traits of the speaker that will help him achieve this goal.

✎ WRITE

LITERARY ANALYSIS: How does Langston Hughes use poetic elements and structure to explore the theme of change in his poem "I, Too"? Write a response in which you analyze the effect of the poem's poetic structure. Did the effect change when you listened to the poem? Be sure to use evidence from the text to support your response.

Everybody Jump

(from 'What If?')

INFORMATIONAL TEXT
Randall Munroe
2014

Introduction

Randall Munroe (b. 1984) once worked as a roboticist at NASA. He currently writes *xkcd*, "A Webcomic of Sarcasm, Math, and Language." In all of his writing, Munroe combines scientific and mathematical expertise with humor and finely drawn stick figures to give concrete answers to far-out questions. He has written two books, *What If? Serious Scientific Answers to Absurd Hypothetical Questions* and *The Thing Explainer: Complicated Stuff in Simple Words*. In "Everybody Out," Munroe takes a premise common in science fiction—all humans must leave Earth due to environmental or nuclear disaster—and puts it to the test. Is it actually physically possible, with the technology we currently have, to evacuate

"At the stroke of noon, everyone jumps."

Skill: Technical Language

I think the subject of the text is "science" because the author mentions ScienceBlogs. I can guess that "kinematics" has to do with motion because everyone will jump. If the text is about motion, the type of science is probably physics.

1   *What would happen if everyone on earth stood as close to each other as they could and jumped, everyone landing on the ground at the same instant?*
    —Thomas Bennett (and many others)

2   This is one of the most popular questions submitted to this blog. It's been examined before, including by a ScienceBlogs post and a Straight Dope article. They cover the kinematics pretty well. However, they don't tell the whole story.

3   Let's take a closer look.

4   At the start of the **scenario,** the entire Earth's population has been magically transported together into one place.

5   This crowd takes up an area the size of Rhode Island. But there's no reason to use the vague phrase "an area the size of Rhode Island." This is our scenario; we can be specific. They're *actually* in Rhode Island.

6   At the stroke of noon, everyone jumps.

7   As discussed elsewhere, it doesn't really affect the planet. Earth outweighs us by a factor of over ten trillion. On average, we humans can vertically jump maybe half a meter on a good day. Even if the Earth were **rigid** and responded instantly, it would be pushed down by less than an atom's width[1].

8   Next, everyone falls back to the ground.

9   Technically, this delivers a lot of energy into the Earth, but it's spread out over a large enough area that it doesn't do much more than leave footprints in a lot of gardens. A slight pulse of pressure spreads through the North American continental crust and dissipates with little effect. The sound of all those feet hitting the ground creates a loud, drawn-out roar which lasts many seconds.

10   Eventually, the air grows quiet.

11   Seconds pass. Everyone looks around.

Skill: Informational Text Structure

Next is one of the key signal words for sequential order, so I know to look out for other words or phrases that signal events are happening in a specific order, like *eventually* and *seconds pass* below. The sequential order helps me understand what's going to happen next in the scenario.

---

1. **atom's width** The atom is the smallest unit, or part, of matter.

12 There are a lot of uncomfortable glances. Someone coughs.

The author is using cause-and-effect structure here to develop the story. The cause is that everybody tries to use their cell phones at the same time. The effect is that the cell networks stop working. This helps me understand the consequences of the jump.

13 A cell phone comes out of a pocket. Within seconds, the rest of the world's five billion phones follow. All of them—even those **compatible** with the region's towers—are displaying some version of "NO SIGNAL." The cell networks have all collapsed under the unprecedented load.

14 The T. F. Green airport in Warwick, Rhode Island handles a few thousand passengers a day. Assuming they got things organized (including sending out scouting missions to retrieve fuel), they could run at 500% **capacity** for years without making a dent in the crowd.

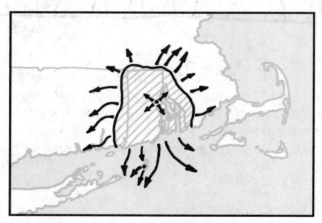

15 The addition of all the nearby airports doesn't change the equation much. Nor does the region's light rail system. Crowds climb on board container ships in the deepwater port of Providence, but stocking sufficient food and water for a long sea voyage proves a challenge.

16 Rhode Island's half-million cars are commandeered. Moments later, I-95, I-195, and I-295 become the sites of the largest traffic jam in the history of the planet. Most of the cars are engulfed by the crowds, but a lucky few get out and begin wandering the abandoned road network.

17 Some make it past New York or Boston before running out of fuel. Since the electricity is probably not on at this point, rather than find a working gas pump, it's easier to just abandon the car and steal the new one. Who can stop you? All the cops are in Rhode Island.

18 The edge of the crowd spreads outward into southern Massachusetts and Connecticut. Any two people who meet are unlikely to have a language in common, and almost nobody knows the area. The state becomes a patchwork chaos of **coalescing** and collapsing social hierarchies[2]. Violence is common. Everybody is hungry and thirsty. Grocery stores are emptied. Fresh water is hard to come by and there's no efficient system for distributing it.

19 Within weeks, Rhode Island is a graveyard of billions.

20 The survivors spread out across the face of the world and struggle to build a new civilization atop the pristine ruins of the old. Our species staggers on, but our population has been greatly reduced. Earth's orbit is completely unaffected—it spins along exactly as it did before our species-wide jump.

21 But at least now we know.

Everybody Jump" from WHAT IF?: Serious Scientific Answers to Absurd Hypothetical Questions by Randall Munroe. Copyright ©2014 by xked Inc. Reprinted by permission of Houghton Mifflin Harcourt Publishing Company. All rights reserved.

2. **hierarchies** systems of ranking according to status, power, or importance

First Read

Read the essay "Everybody Jump." After you read, complete the Think Questions below.

1. Why does the author of this essay choose to answer this seemingly absurd question? What is his purpose in doing so? Explain by citing textual evidence from the selection to support your answer.

2. According to the author, how would a coordinated jump affect the Earth's orbit? Describe in your own words what would happen, referring to specific details from the text.

3. Why is the outcome of this imaginary scenario surprising? Discuss how things turn out a little differently than expected. Be sure to cite examples.

4. The prefix *com-* means "together" or "in association with" something. Based on this clue and any other common affixes, what is the meaning of **compatible** as it is used in paragraph 13 of the excerpt? Write your definition here, explaining its roots and/or affixes.

5. According to paragraph 14, the T. F. Green airport "could run at 500% **capacity** for years." Based on context, what does the word *capacity* mean? Write your best definition here and explain how you figured out its meaning.

Skill:
Informational Text Structure

Use the Checklist to analyze Informational Text Structure in "Everybody Jump." Refer to the sample student annotations about Informational Text Structure in the text.

••• CHECKLIST FOR INFORMATIONAL TEXT STRUCTURE

In order to determine the overall structure of a text, note the following:

- ✓ the topic(s) and how the author organizes information about the topic(s)

- ✓ patterns in a paragraph or section of text that reveal the text structure, such as:

  - sequences, including the order of events or steps in a process

  - problems and their solutions

  - cause-and-effect relationships

  - comparisons

- ✓ the overall structure of the text and how each section contributes to the development of ideas

To analyze how a particular sentence, paragraph, chapter, or section fits into the overall structure of a text and contributes to the development of the ideas, use the following questions as a guide:

- ✓ What organizational patterns reveal the text structure the author uses to present information?

- ✓ How does a particular sentence, paragraph, chapter, or section fit into the overall structure of the text? How does it affect the development of the author's ideas?

- ✓ In what ways does the text structure contribute to the development of ideas in the text?

Skill:
Informational Text Structure

Reread paragraphs 14–18 of "Everybody Jump." Then, using the Checklist on the previous page, answer the multiple-choice questions below.

⟳ YOUR TURN

1. In paragraphs 14 and 15, the author uses a problem-and-solution structure. What problem are the suggested solutions trying to solve?

   ○ A. how to get people home from Rhode Island after the jump

   ○ B. how to find fuel for airplanes

   ○ C. how to direct people to the nearest train station

   ○ D. how to prepare ships for a long sea voyage

2. In paragraph 16, what text structure do the phrases "moments later" and "begin wandering" suggest?

   ○ A. classify information

   ○ B. compare and contrast

   ○ C. sequential order

   ○ D. order of important ideas

3. Which of the following ideas discussed in paragraph 18 is most relevant to the central idea of the text?

   ○ A. the disadvantages of knowing multiple languages

   ○ B. the effects of collapsing social hierarchies

   ○ C. the common problems when people don't know an area

   ○ D. the crowds in Massachusetts and Connecticut

Skill:
Technical Language

Use the Checklist to analyze Technical Language in "Everybody Jump." Refer to the sample student annotations about Technical Language in the text.

••• CHECKLIST FOR TECHNICAL LANGUAGE

In order to determine the meaning of words and phrases as they are used in a text, note the following:

- ✓ the subject of the book or article

- ✓ any unfamiliar words that you think might be technical terms

- ✓ words have multiple meanings that change when used with a specific subject

- ✓ the possible contextual meaning of a word, or the definition from a dictionary

To determine the meaning of words and phrases as they are used in a text, including technical meanings, consider the following questions:

- ✓ What is the subject of the informational text?

- ✓ Are there any unfamiliar words that look as if they might be technical language?

- ✓ Do any of the words in the text have more than one meaning?

- ✓ Can you identify the contextual meaning of any of the words?

Skill:
Technical Language

Reread paragraphs 19–21 of "Everybody Jump." Then, using the Checklist on the previous page, answer the multiple-choice questions below.

↻ YOUR TURN

1. Which of the following best defines "species" as it is used in the passage?

   ○ A. coined money

   ○ B. humans inhabiting the earth

   ○ C. animals of the same biological classification

   ○ D. plants of the same group

2. Which line helps you best determine the meaning of "orbit" in paragraph 20?

   ○ A. "The survivors spread out across the face of the world. . ."

   ○ B. "Our species staggers on. . ."

   ○ C. ". . . it spins along exactly as it did before our species-wide jump."

   ○ D. ". . . but our population has been greatly reduced."

Close Read

Reread "Everybody Jump." As you reread, complete the Skills Focus questions below. Then use your answers and annotations from the questions to help you complete the Write activity.

◎ SKILLS FOCUS

1. Identify examples of the author's use of a cause-and-effect text structure. Explain what details or signal words reveal the text structure.

2. Identify a place in the text where the author uses another text structure that helps develop the central idea of the text. Explain what details or signal words reveal the text structure.

3. Identify a technical meaning of a word in the text and the context clues you used to help you define it.

4. Think about the unit's essential question: How do you know what to do when there are no instructions? Identify textual evidence in Munroe's scenario that answers this question, and explain your reasoning.

✏ WRITE

NARRATIVE: Randall Munroe describes the effect of everyone on Earth jumping at the same time as they stand close together. Imagine that you are one of these jumping individuals. Write a scene describing the incident from your point of view. What do you see? How do you maneuver yourself and others through the chaos? Draw inspiration for your narrative using evidence from the various informational text structures in Munroe's essay as you write your narrative.

Please note that excerpts and passages in the StudySync® library and this workbook are intended as touchstones to generate interest in an author's work. The excerpts and passages do not substitute for the reading of entire texts, and StudySync® strongly recommends that students seek out and purchase the whole literary or informational work in order to experience it as the author intended. Links to online resellers are available in our digital library. In addition, complete works may be ordered through an authorized reseller by filling out and returning to StudySync® the order form enclosed in this workbook.

Reading & Writing Companion   351

Hoot

FICTION
Carl Hiaasen
2002

Introduction

studysync tv

After a move from Montana to Florida, Roy is the new kid in town, with no friends and no allies—not yet, anyway. One day, with his face smashed against the school bus window courtesy of the school bully, Roy sees something that attracts his curiosity. This coming-of-age novel, written by Carl Hiaasen (b. 1953), was awarded the Newbery Honor in 2003.

"... Roy lowered the window and stuck out his head. The strange boy was gone."

Excerpted from Chapter 1

1   Roy would not have noticed the strange boy if it weren't for Dana Matherson, because Roy ordinarily didn't look out the window of the school bus. He preferred to read comics and mystery books on the morning ride to Trace Middle.

2   But on this day, a Monday (Roy would never forget), Dana Matherson grabbed Roy's head from behind and pressed his thumbs into Roy's temple, as if he were squeezing a soccer ball. The older kids were supposed to stay in the back of the bus, but Dana had snuck up behind Roy's seat and **ambushed** him. When Roy tried to wriggle free, Dana mushed his face against the window.

3   It was then, squinting through the smudged glass, that Roy spotted the strange boy running along the sidewalk. It appeared as if he was hurrying to catch the school bus, which had stopped at a corner to pick up more kids.

4   The boy was straw-blond and wiry, and his skin was nutbrown from the sun. The **expression** on his face was **intent** and serious. He wore a faded Miami Heat basketball jersey and dirty khaki shorts, and here was the odd part: no shoes. The soles of his bare feet looked as black as barbecue coals.

5   Trace Middle School didn't have the world's strictest dress code, but Roy was pretty sure that some sort of footwear was **required**. The boy might have been carrying sneakers in his backpack, if only he'd been wearing a backpack. No shoes, no backpack, no books—strange, indeed, on a school day.

6   Roy was sure that the barefoot boy would catch all kinds of grief from Dana and the other big kids once he boarded the bus, but that didn't happen. . . .

7   Because the boy kept running—past the corner, past the line of students waiting to get on the bus; past the bus itself. Roy wanted to shout, "Hey, look at that guy!" but his mouth wasn't working so well. Dana Matherson still had him from behind, pushing his face against the window.

**Skill:
Theme**

Here, the mysterious boy reminds Roy of his best friend back in Montana. I wonder if the novel will explore themes related to friendship and whether Roy and this mysterious boy will become friends.

8 As the bus pulled away from the intersection, Roy hoped to catch another glimpse of the boy farther up the street. However, he had turned off the sidewalk and was now cutting across a private yard—running very fast, much faster than Roy could run and maybe even faster than Richard, Roy's best friend back in Montana. Richard was so fast that he got to work out with the high school track squad when he was only in seventh grade.

9 Dana Matherson was digging his fingernails into Roy's scalp, trying to make him squeal, but Roy barely felt a thing. He was gripped with curiosity as the running boy dashed through one neat green yard after another, getting smaller in Roy's vision as he put a wider distance between himself and the school bus.

10 Roy saw a big pointy-eared dog, probably a German shepherd, **bound** off somebody's porch and go for the boy. Incredibly, the boy didn't change his course. He vaulted over the dog, crashed through a cherry hedge, and then disappeared from view.

11 Roy gasped.

12 "Whassamatter, cowgirl? Had enough?"

13 This was Dana, hissing in Roy's right ear. Being the new kid on the bus, Roy didn't expect any help from the others. The "cowgirl" remark was so lame, it wasn't worth getting mad about. Dana was a well-known idiot, on top of which he outweighed Roy by at least fifty pounds. Fighting back would have been a complete waste of energy.

14 "Had enough yet? We can't hear you, Tex." Dana's breath smelled like stale cigarettes. Smoking and beating up smaller kids were his two main hobbies.

15 "Yeah, okay," Roy said impatiently. "I've had enough."

16 As soon as he was freed, Roy lowered the window and stuck out his head. The strange boy was gone.

17 Who was he? What was he running from?

18 Roy wondered if any of the other kids on the bus had seen what he'd seen. For a moment he wondered if he'd really seen it himself.

Excerpted from *Hoot* by Carl Hiaasen, published by Alfred A. Knopf.

First Read

Read *Hoot*. After you read, complete the Think Questions below.

☁ THINK QUESTIONS

1. Why is Roy looking out the window? Cite textual evidence from the selection to support your answer.

2. Based on paragraph 4, what inferences can you make about the mysterious boy? What clues does the text give?

3. Describe the relationship between Dana and Roy, using specific examples from the text.

4. Find the word **required** in paragraph 5 of *Hoot*. Use context clues in the surrounding sentences, as well as the sentence in which the word appears, to determine the word's meaning.

5. Use context clues to determine the meaning of **bound** as it is used in paragraph 10 of *Hoot*. Write your definition here and identify clues that helped you figure out its meaning. Then check the meaning in the dictionary.

Skill:
Theme

Use the Checklist to analyze Theme in *Hoot*. Refer to the sample student annotations about Theme in the text.

In order to identify a theme or central idea in a text, note the following:

✓ the topic of the text

✓ whether or not the theme is stated directly in the text

✓ details in the text that may reveal the theme

- the title and chapter headings

- details about the setting

- a narrator's or speaker's tone

- characters' thoughts, actions, and dialogue

- the central conflict in the story's plot

- the resolution of the conflict

- what the characters learn through their experiences

✓ how characters are affected by the setting, the other characters, and the problems they face, and what impact these may have on how the theme is developed

Even when you first start reading a novel, you can pay attention to details and think about what themes might be developed in the novel. Consider the following questions:

✓ What conflict is the main character facing?

✓ What do I learn about the main character?

✓ What themes might the novel develop based on the main character's conflict and personality traits?

Skill:
Theme

Reread paragraphs 16–18 from *Hoot*. Then, using the Checklist on the previous page, answer the multiple-choice questions below.

YOUR TURN

1. How does this passage create a sense of mystery surrounding the running boy that intrigues Roy?

   ○ A. The boy's identity is unknown.
   ○ B. The boy helped Roy escape Dana's bullying.
   ○ C. The boy disappears, and Roy questions whether he was real.
   ○ D. None of the other characters know what the boy looks like.

2. What does this passage suggest about Roy that suggests he would be a fun and interesting friend?

   ○ A. Roy is the new kid on the bus and is hoping to make friends.
   ○ B. Roy is curious and fascinated by mysteries.
   ○ C. Roy questions his own perceptions.
   ○ D. Roy is no longer afraid of Dana.

Close Read

Reread *Hoot*. As you reread, complete the Skills Focus questions below. Then use your answers and annotations from the questions to help you complete the Write activity.

◎ SKILLS FOCUS

1. Dealing with Dana's bullying is one of the challenges Roy faces in the story. Identify evidence of how Roy responds to this challenge. Explain what the response helps you infer about a theme in the story.

2. Dana's bullying is not the only plot event in the chapter. Identify evidence about the other event the author describes and about Roy's reaction to it. Explain how the two plot events are related and how this helps you infer the theme.

3. The author uses Roy's thoughts and actions to develop the plot. Identify examples of Roy's responses that help you understand his character. Explain how these responses help develop the plot.

4. Roy is new to Trace Middle School, so he is on his own in figuring out how to handle Dana's bullying. Identify textual evidence that highlights Roy's methods. Explain what the evidence tells you about Roy's character.

✎ WRITE

LITERARY ANALYSIS: How does the author use details and description to communicate a theme? Do you agree or disagree with the author's message in this part of the story? Use evidence from the text to support your response.

Donna O'Meara: The Volcano Lady

INFORMATIONAL TEXT
McGraw Hill Education
2017

Introduction

Donna O'Meara is an explorer and adventurer like few others. As a photographer of some of the world's biggest volcanoes, her job is often quite perilous. In the face of danger, however, O'Meara often risks her life to obtain some of the most amazing up-close footage of volcanoes the world has ever witnessed. This short biography profiles O'Meara's life, from her time growing up in New England to how she came to be known as the "volcano lady."

"They were stuck on a narrow ledge just 200 feet above a fiery, smoking pit."

NOTES

1   After a blistering hot day, a cold storm suddenly whipped the top of Mt. Stromboli, a volcano on an island off the coast of Sicily. The temperature quickly dropped more than 60 degrees. Donna O'Meara and her husband, Steve, didn't dare try to climb down the steep slopes in the dark. They were stuck on a narrow ledge just 200 feet above a fiery, smoking pit.

2   They huddled together, shivering nonstop in the cold air. Thundering blasts from the volcano and falling rocks the size of basketballs kept them awake and fearful. When the sun came up, Donna felt cinder burns on her face. There were sharp pieces of rock tangled in her hair.

3   Frightening experiences on top of a volcano are not unusual for Donna O'Meara. For over 25 years, she has worked with Steve to photograph and study volcanoes all over the world. They hope their documentation will someday be a written and visual record of information that helps scientists to better **predict** volcanic **eruptions.**

4   O'Meara grew up in the New England countryside. There are no volcanoes in Connecticut, but in the spring and summer there were fierce thunder and lightning storms that thrilled Donna. In school, her favorite classes were earth science and biology. However, instead of turning her love for science into a career after graduation, she became an artist, photographer, and writer. As she worked on different magazines and books, she gradually began to realize that something was missing in her life.

5   When Donna went back to school at the age of 32 to study science, her passion for volcanoes began. She took geology classes to learn more about what rocks and soil tell us about the earth. She found out that volcanism is one of the most **dynamic** forces in nature. Volcanoes constantly shape and change the earth. Many islands, such as the islands that make up Hawaii, were formed by volcanic activity.

6   In 1986, Donna visited her first volcano as Steve's research assistant. After dodging lava bombs and feeling the heat from underground lava melting her shoes, Donna was hooked. The following year, she and Steve were married

on lava that had oozed from Kilauea on Hawaii and hardened. Lava that hardens creates new landforms, and some volcanoes, such as Surtsey off the coast of Iceland, actually create new islands!

7   Today, Donna can't imagine what her life would be like without volcanoes. She loves them so much she lives on one. Her home is on top of Kilauea, where she was married. This is one of the most **active** volcanoes in the world.

Kilauea, in Hawaii

8   From their home, Donna and Steve run Volcano Watch International (VWI). The O'Mearas' organization is dedicated to understanding how Earth's active volcanoes work. VWI uses photos and video to educate people about the dangers of volcanoes. Their mission is to travel to active volcanoes and **document** the eruptions. The first volcano Donna studied was Kilauea, which is a shield volcano.

9   Mt. Stromboli is a stratovolcano. A stratovolcano has the common cone shape people usually picture when they think of a volcano. It is formed from explosive eruptions that build layers of ash, lava, and cinders at the top of the mountain.

10   Donna says the experience of being stranded on Mt. Stromboli for one freezing night was the scariest experience of her life. Since the sides of this volcano are steep, it was impossible for the O'Mearas to travel down the slopes until the sun rose in the morning. So they were trapped on a ledge in the freezing cold with scalding rocks flying around them.

11   Donna O'Meara escaped from her scary night of Mt. Stromboli safe and sound. Now she and Steve hope that the knowledge they gather photographing and studying volcanoes will help save the lives of people who live near them. The O'Mearas' volcano photographs, videos, and samples of volcanic rock are part of the permanent collection of the Smithsonian Institution located in Washington, D.C.

12   Donna believes they have the best jobs on Earth, even though their work may be the most dangerous as well.

Used with permission of McGraw-Hill Education.

WRITE

PERSONAL RESPONSE: Donna O'Meara and her husband, Steve, risk their lives to collect close-up photos of volcanoes from around the world. If you were a scientist or researcher, what kind of natural phenomenon would you want to explore? Why? Support your response with evidence from the text and from your personal experience. As you make connections between Donna O'Meara's dream and your own, include any information that may have changed your understanding or opinion of what it means to be a scientist or researcher.

Dare to be creative!

INFORMATIONAL TEXT
Madeleine L'Engle
1983

Introduction

I n 1983, renowned young adult author Madeleine L'Engle (1918–2007) delivered this lecture before the Library of Congress. "Dare to be creative!" is heralded as an inspirational manifesto on the beauty and power of words, the magic of reading, as well as a stunning rebuke of literary censorship. L'Engle is the author of such young adult classics as *A Wrinkle in Time* and *A Wind in the Door*.

"My books push me and prod me and make me ask questions I might otherwise avoid."

1 We need to dare disturb the universe by not being **manipulated** or frightened by judgmental groups who assume the right to insist that if we do not agree with them, not only do we not understand but we are wrong. How dull the world would be if we all had to feel the same way about everything, if we all had to like the same books, dislike the same books. For my relaxing reading I enjoy English murder mysteries, but my husband prefers spy thrillers. I like beet greens and he likes beet root. We would be a society of ants if we couldn't have personal tastes and honest differences. And how sad it would be if we had to give up all sense of mystery for the limited world of provable fact. I still can't read *The Happy Prince* or *The Selfish Giant* aloud without a lump coming into my throat, but I suppose that talking statues and giants are on someone's hit list.

2 Perhaps some of this zeal is caused by fear. But, as Bertrand Russell warns, "Zeal is a bad mark for a cause. Nobody had any zeal about arithmetic. It was the anti-vaccinationists[1], not the vaccinationists, who were **zealous.**" Yet because those who were not threatened by the idea of vaccination ultimately won out, we have **eradicated** the horror of smallpox[2] from the planet.

3 It is hard for us to understand the zeal of the medical **establishment** when Dr. Semmelweis sensibly suggested that it might be a good idea if surgeons washed their hands after dissecting a cadaver, before going to deliver a woman in labor. This, to us, obvious suggestions of cleanliness was so threatening to the medical establishment of the day that they zealously set about persecuting

Despite overzealous critics, Dr. Semmelweis convinced doctors to wash their hands when dealing with patients, which saved many lives.

1. **anti-vaccinationists** activists or individuals who oppose the practice of giving vaccinations or shots
2. **smallpox** a lethal and disfiguring infectious virus eradicated in 1980

Semmelweis. But, thanks to him, many of us are alive because doctors now wash their hands. If the zealots had won, women would still be dying of septicemia[3] after childbirth.

4   Russell suggests that people are zealous when they are not completely certain they are right. I agree with him. When I find myself hotly defending something, when I am, in fact, zealous, it is time for me to step back and examine whatever it is that has me so hot under the collar. Do I think it's going to threaten my comfortable **rut?** Make me change and grow?—and growing always causes growing pains. Am I afraid to ask questions?

5   Sometimes. But I believe that good questions are more important than answers, and the best children's books ask questions, and make the reader ask questions. And every new question is going to disturb someone's universe.

6   Writing fiction is definitely a universe disturber, and for the writer, first of all. My books push me and prod me and make me ask questions I might otherwise avoid. I start a book, having lived with the characters for several years, during the writing of other books, and I have a pretty good idea of where the story is going and what I hope it's going to say. And then, once I get deep into the writing, unexpected things begin to happen, things which make me question, and which sometimes really shake my universe.

By Madeleine L'Engle, 1983. Used by permission of Crosswicks Ltd., c/o Aaron M. Priest Literary Agency

3. **septicemia** a bacterial infection of the blood, skin or lungs

✏ WRITE

PERSONAL RESPONSE: In the speech "Dare to be creative!," Madeleine L'Engle urges listeners to not be scared of thinking independently. Write about a time when you took a risk to do something creative or unexpected, and it turned out well. Then explain how this connects to the speech. Support your response with evidence from the text as well as personal experience.

Please note that excerpts and passages in the StudySync® library and this workbook are intended as touchstones to generate interest in an author's work. The excerpts and passages do not substitute for the reading of entire texts, and StudySync® strongly recommends that students seek out and purchase the whole literary or informational work in order to experience it as the author intended. Links to online resellers are available in our digital library. In addition, complete works may be ordered through an authorized reseller by filling out and returning to StudySync® the order form enclosed in this workbook.

Reading & Writing Companion   365

Margaret Bourke-White:
Fearless Photographer

INFORMATIONAL TEXT
McGraw Hill Education
2017

Introduction

Margaret Bourke-White (1904–1971) was an American photographer who gained fame for traveling around the world and snapping photographs for high-profile magazines. As the first American female war photojournalist, her photographs earned her a spot on the cover of *Life* magazine and can be viewed to this day in museums nationwide, including the Library of Congress. This short biography of her life describes some of the challenges she faced and feats she accomplished throughout her career.

"... Margaret made the production of steel look magnificent, mysterious, and awe-inspiring."

1 In 1904, girls weren't supposed to dream of careers that took them flying into the sky on airplanes or climbing out onto ledges at the top of skyscrapers. And they certainly weren't encouraged to think about competing with men for the opportunity to photograph important people and events.

2 Joseph White and Minnie Bourke, however, never told their daughter what to think and dream about. Instead, young Margaret, or "Peg" as her friends called her, got plenty of attention and encouragement from her parents to explore her world. Early on, they taught her to work hard and to go after what she wanted. They even gave her a motto: "You can." It's no wonder Margaret Bourke-White grew up to be one of the most accomplished women and talked-about photographers of the twentieth century.

Margaret Bourke-White paved the way for female photographers.

3 Many photographers today owe thanks to Margaret. From the time she started taking photographs and recognized that they could stir up feelings to the **culmination** of her long career as a photojournalist, Margaret was a trailblazer[1]. She shaped the art of photography and the profession of photojournalism and showed that women photographers could travel all over the world and work alongside men in dangerous situations.

A Star Photographer

4 Her mother gave Margaret her first camera in 1921, when she was 17 years old. Her interest in photography grew as a result of her father's enthusiasm for cameras. A few years later, Margaret's classmates at Cornell University became her first admirers when photos she took of the campus appeared in

NOTES

Skill:
Textual Evidence

I can find evidence explicitly in the text that supports the idea that Margaret was a trailblazer. I will highlight the "firsts" in her career.

---

1. **trailblazer** someone who does things for the first time, metaphorically burning a trail for others

Skill: Technical Language

I know the word technique can have many different meanings, like having a certain technique for cooking or skateboarding! I can use the subject of the text to understand that the word technique here refers to Margaret's skills in photography. I also know that technical problems is a term that probably means that there were challenges Margaret had to overcome in her work.

the school newspapers. A year after graduating, Margaret moved to Cleveland, Ohio and opened a commercial photography studio.

5   One of Margaret's first clients was the Otis Steel Company. Her success was due both to her technique and her skills in dealing with people. At first, several people at the company wondered if a woman could stand up to the intense heat and generally dirty and gritty conditions inside a steel mill[2]. When Margaret finally got permission, the technical problems began. Black-and-white film at that time was sensitive to blue light, not the reds and oranges of hot steel. The pictures came out all black. Margaret solved this problem by bringing along a new style of flare (which produces white light) and having assistants hold them to light her scenes. Her abilities resulted in some of the best steel factory pictures of that era, and these earned her national attention.

6   The city's powerful businessmen soon began calling on her to take pictures of their mills, factories, and buildings. In the steel mills, she wanted to be right next to the melted metal. The extreme heat sometimes burned her face and damaged the paint on her camera. In her first well-known photographs, Margaret made the production of steel look magnificent, mysterious, and awe-inspiring. Her photos, filled with streams of melted steel and flying sparks, caught the eye of someone who would change her life.

A New Sort of Storytelling

7   Henry Luce was a powerful and important American publisher. In the 1920s and 1930s he started a series of magazines that would change journalism and the reading habits of Americans. Luce's magazine called *Time* summarized and **interpreted** the week's news. *Life* was a picture magazine of politics, culture and society that became very popular in the years before television, and *Fortune* explored the economy and the world of business. *Sports Illustrated* investigated the teams and important players of popular sports such as baseball and football.

8   In 1929, Henry Luce invited Margaret to work at *Fortune* Magazine. She jumped at the chance and became the first woman in a new field called photojournalism, in which photographers reported the news through images.

9   As Margaret snapped artistic shots of workplaces, she was able to find beauty in simple objects. Over time she **adapted** her techniques to photograph people and was **adept** at catching expressions and showing hardship. In 1930, she was the first photographer from a Western country to be allowed

---

2. **steel mill** a plant where part or all of the steelmaking process is done

into the Soviet Union (now Russia), where she took pictures of the workers in what was then a communist[3] country.

World War II and After

10   When World War II broke out in 1939, Margaret became the first female war correspondent. This is a journalist who covers stories first hand from a war zone. In 1941, she traveled to the Soviet Union again and was the only foreign photographer in Moscow when German forces invaded. Taking shelter in the U.S. Embassy,[4] she then captured much of the fierce battle on camera.

11   As the war continued, Margaret joined the U.S. Army Air Force in North Africa and then traveled with the U.S. Army in Italy and later Germany. She repeatedly came under fire in Italy as she traveled through areas of intense fighting.

12   After the war, Margaret continued to make the world's most complex events understandable. Her photos reflected stirring social issues of the time. She photographed South Africans laboring in gold mines and civil rights leader Mahatma Gandhi's nonviolent work in India.

A Lasting Influence

13   During the 1930s and 1940s, Margaret's adventurous attitude and perseverance paved the way for women to take on roles beyond the **norm**. Rather than snapping photos of high-society parties as other female photographers had done before her, she marched into steel plants and combat zones. She proved to women that they had every right to pursue the careers they wanted.

14   Through her work, Margaret became a role model for working women as well as a strong voice for the poor and powerless. She earned the respect of powerful businessmen when women were discouraged from working. When she died in 1971, she left behind not only an amazing photographic record of the human experience. She also left a message for women all over the world who wanted to make an impact: "You can."

Used with permission by McGraw Hill Education.

Skill:
Textual Evidence

These "firsts" in Margaret Bourke-White's career are evidence that she was a trailblazer.

3. **communist** referring to the political and economic theory in which the government takes over the means of production, and people live without social classes or private property
4. **U.S. Embassy** the office of the United States in any other country

MARGARET
BOURKE-WHITE
FEARLESS PHOTOGRAPHER

First Read

Read "Margaret Bourke-White: Fearless Photographer." After you read, complete the Think Questions below.

☁ THINK QUESTIONS

1. Describe one example of when Margaret Bourke-White's hardworking attitude helped advance her career. Refer to specific passages or quotations from the text in your answer.

2. What was special about how Margaret Bourke-White photographed steel mills? Use evidence from the text in your response.

3. What made Margaret Bourke-White different from other photojournalists of her time? Identify several ways in which Margaret stood out from the crowd, citing textual evidence.

4. Which context clues helped you determine the meaning of the word **adapted** in paragraph 9? Write your definition of *adapted* and describe which words in the paragraph led you to your understanding of the word. Then look up the word in a print or online dictionary to confirm your definition.

5. The word **norm** is derived from the Latin *norma*, meaning "precept" or "rule." Knowing this, try to infer the meaning of *norm* as it is used in paragraph 13. Write your best definition here, along with any other words you know that could be derived from the same Latin root.

Skill:
Textual Evidence

Use the Checklist to analyze Textual Evidence in "Margaret Bourke-White: Fearless Photographer." Refer to the sample student annotations about Textual Evidence in the text.

⟳ CHECKLIST FOR TEXTUAL EVIDENCE

In order to support an analysis by citing textual evidence that is explicitly stated, do the following:

- ✓ read the text closely and critically

- ✓ identify what the text says explicitly

- ✓ find the most relevant textual evidence that supports your analysis

- ✓ consider why the author explicitly states specific details and information

- ✓ cite the specific words, phrases, sentences, or paragraphs from the text that support your analysis

In order to interpret implicit meanings in a text by making inferences, do the following:

- ✓ combine information directly stated in the text with your own knowledge, experiences, and observations

- ✓ cite the specific words, phrases, sentences, or paragraphs from the text that support this inference

In order to cite textual evidence to support an analysis of what the text says explicitly as well as inferences drawn from the text, consider the following questions:

- ✓ Have I read the text closely and critically?

- ✓ What inferences am I making about the text? What textual evidence am I using to support these inferences?

- ✓ Am I quoting the evidence from the text correctly?

- ✓ Does my textual evidence logically relate to my analysis?

Skill:
Textual Evidence

Reread paragraphs 13–14 of "Margaret Bourke-White: Fearless Photographer." Then, using the Checklist on the previous page, answer the multiple-choice questions below.

↻ YOUR TURN

1. Using the textual evidence in paragraph 13, what is most likely an inference you can make about Margaret Bourke-White?

   ○ A. She was unable to become an advocate for women because of her profession.
   ○ B. She was able to become successful because her father was a powerful businessman.
   ○ C. She encouraged other women to pursue photography as a way to support equal rights.
   ○ D. She was an innovator and a symbol for women's rights and equality.

2. Which textual evidence best supports the author's claim in paragraph 14 that Margaret Bourke-White was "a strong voice for the poor and powerless"?

   ○ A. "Margaret's classmates at Cornell University became her first admirers when photographs she took of the campus appeared in the school newspapers."
   ○ B. "The city's powerful businessmen soon began calling on her to take pictures of their mills, factories, and buildings."
   ○ C. "As Margaret snapped artistic shots of workplaces, she was able to find beauty in simple objects."
   ○ D. "She photographed South Africans laboring in gold mines and civil rights leader Mahatma Gandhi's nonviolent work in India."

Skill:
Technical Language

Use the Checklist to analyze Technical Language in "Margaret Bourke-White: Fearless Photographer." Refer to the sample student annotations about Technical Language in the text.

⟳ CHECKLIST FOR TECHNICAL LANGUAGE

In order to determine the meaning of words and phrases as they are used in a text, note the following:

- ✓ the subject of the book or article

- ✓ any unfamiliar words that you think might be technical terms

- ✓ words have multiple meanings that change when used with a specific subject

- ✓ the possible contextual meaning of a word, or the definition from a dictionary

To determine the meaning of words and phrases as they are used in a text, including technical meanings, consider the following questions:

- ✓ What is the subject of the informational text?

- ✓ Are there any unfamiliar words that look as if they might be technical language?

- ✓ Do any of the words in the text have more than one meaning?

- ✓ Can you identify the contextual meaning of any of the words?

Skill:
Technical Language

Reread paragraph 5 of "Margaret Bourke-White: Fearless Photographer." Then, using the Checklist on the previous page, answer the multiple-choice questions below.

⟳ YOUR TURN

1. Which of the following context clues in the text help you to define the technical term "flare"?

   ○ A. "produces white light"
   ○ B. "came out all black"
   ○ C. "light her scenes"
   ○ D. "national attention"

2. Which of the following best defines "scenes" as it's used in the passage?

   ○ A. a type of camera
   ○ B. the subjects/locations of her photographs
   ○ C. a theater production
   ○ D. the film used

Close Read

Reread "Margaret Bourke-White: Fearless Photographer." As you reread, complete the Skills Focus questions below. Then use your answers and annotations from the questions to help you complete the Write activity.

◎ SKILLS FOCUS

1. "Margaret Bourke-White: Fearless Photographer" claims that Bourke-White "became a role model for working women." Identify textual evidence that supports this claim. Explain your reasoning.

2. Identify technical terms in "Margaret Bourke-White: Fearless Photographer" that relate to the subject of photography. Cite the evidence that helped you identify the terms' meanings.

3. In "Donna O'Meara: The Volcano Lady," the author presents textual evidence that suggests that O'Meara is attracted to the adventure of photographing volcanoes. Identify evidence in "Margaret Bourke-White: Fearless Photographer" that suggests that Bourke-White was also motivated by a sense of adventure. Use the evidence to compare and contrast the career motivations of the two women.

4. "Margaret Bourke-White: Fearless Photographer" calls Bourke-White a trailblazer. Identify textual evidence that supports this claim. Explain how the evidence relates to the unit's essential question: How do you know what to do when there are no instructions?

✎ WRITE

COMPARE AND CONTRAST: "Donna O'Meara: The Volcano Lady," "Dare to be creative!," and "Margaret Bourke-White: Fearless Photographer" each describe a person motivated to do something other people see as impossible. These artists refuse to be manipulated into one way of thinking or living. Some people are motivated by role models or successes, while other people derive motivation from their experiences. Compare and contrast the main motivation of each individual in these three texts, using technical language when possible. Remember to use evidence from all three texts to support your ideas.

Please note that excerpts and passages in the StudySync® library and this workbook are intended as touchstones to generate interest in an author's work. The excerpts and passages do not substitute for the reading of entire texts, and StudySync® strongly recommends that students seek out and purchase the whole literary or informational work in order to experience it as the author intended. Links to online resellers are available in our digital library. In addition, complete works may be ordered through an authorized reseller by filling out and returning to StudySync® the order form enclosed in this workbook.

Reading & Writing Companion · 375

Extended Writing Project and Grammar

EXTENDED WRITING PROJECT
INFORMATIVE WRITING

Informative Writing Process: Plan

PLAN	DRAFT	REVISE	EDIT AND PUBLISH

The texts in this unit feature individuals who are driven to act without instructions, a clear plan, or a certain outcome. Margaret Bourke-White became the first female war photojournalist, sacrificing her safety in order to capture important moments in history. In one of the most popular Greek myths, Perseus sets out on a quest to defeat the snake-haired Gorgon, Medusa. He does not know if he'll survive the battle. Hatshepsut became the first female leader in ancient Egypt to call herself "pharaoh," breaking tradition and gender barriers throughout her reign. What motivates, or moves, these individuals to attempt something no one has done before?

WRITING PROMPT

What motivates us to conquer feelings of uncertainty?

Think about the individuals from this unit who take action even when they are unsure of what lies ahead. Identify three of these individuals and write an informative essay explaining what drives them to respond, take action, or make a decision when there are no guidelines to help them. Be sure your informative essay includes the following:

- an introduction
- a thesis or controlling idea
- coherent body paragraphs
- supporting details
- a conclusion

Writing to Sources

As you gather ideas and information from the texts in the unit, be sure to:

- use evidence from multiple sources; and
- avoid overly relying on one source.

Please note that excerpts and passages in the StudySync® library and this workbook are intended as touchstones to generate interest in an author's work. The excerpts and passages do not substitute for the reading of entire texts, and StudySync® strongly recommends that students seek out and purchase the whole literary or informational work in order to experience it as the author intended. Links to online resellers are available in our digital library. In addition, complete works may be ordered through an authorized reseller by filling out and returning to StudySync® the order form enclosed in this workbook.

Reading & Writing Companion **377**

Introduction to Informative Writing

Writers of informative texts provide facts and details related to historical, scientific, and cultural topics. An informative text presents readers with information, facts, and ideas about real people, places, things, and events. The text should include an introduction with a thesis statement, or the main idea about the topic, body paragraphs that include details that support the main idea, and a conclusion.

Text structure refers to the way a writer organizes the information in a nonfiction text. It is an organizational pattern that is used to present facts and other information clearly. There are several different types of informative text structures. For instance, a writer may:

- describe a process or a series of steps to follow in sequential order
- tell about events in chronological order
- discuss ideas in order of importance
- compare and contrast information
- present cause and effect relationships
- list advantages and disadvantages
- describe a problem and offer a solution
- define the essential, or most important, qualities of a subject
- classify, or organize, information into categories and subcategories

A writer may use more than one organizational pattern within the same text. In addition, a text structure can be used to organize information about more than one topic.

Analyzing the structure of an informative text helps a reader to follow what a writer is trying to say and understand how different facts and details are related. It can also help a reader identify the main, or controlling, idea.

As you continue with this Extended Writing Project, you'll receive more instruction and practice at crafting each of the characteristics of informative writing. This will help you to create your own informative text.

Before you get started on your own informative text, read this informative essay that one student, Colin, wrote in response to the writing prompt. As you read the Model, highlight and annotate the features of informative writing that Colin included in his text.

☰ STUDENT MODEL

NOTES

1 Sometimes people are motivated to take action without really knowing why. It could be a feeling, a goal, or a person that encourages them. Scientist Donna O'Meara is motivated by a desire to understand something dangerous. She also wants to help others. The character Roy in Carl Hiaasen's book *Hoot* is motivated by curiosity. His quick-witted thinking helps him out. Author Randall Munroe is motivated by mathematical reasoning. He wants to answer what seems to be an impossible question. Each of these people or characters has a different motivation and faces different obstacles and problems, but they all learn something important.

2 Donna O'Meara's desire to understand how volcanoes work has sometimes put her in danger. Most people would probably be afraid to get close to a volcano. There's a lot we don't know about them. But O'Meara has risked her life to study them. During her first visit to a volcano, she dodged "lava bombs," and hot lava melted her shoes. Another time, she and her husband Steve "were trapped on a ledge in the freezing cold with scalding rocks flying around them." The desire for knowledge has pushed O'Meara to conquer the unknown and hazardous world of volcanoes. Now she's an expert on volcanoes. She shares her knowledge to help keep others safe when volcanoes erupt. She hopes her work will "help save the lives of people who live near" volcanoes.

3 Like Donna O'Meara, the character Roy in *Hoot* is motivated by a desire for knowledge. He's also clever when it comes to dealing with problems. These qualities help Roy, who's the new kid at school, deal with Dana the bully. Dana is attacking Roy on his way to school when Roy sees a boy running past the school bus. Even though Dana is hurting him, Roy is "gripped with curiosity" about the boy: "Who was he? What was he running from?" Roy doesn't care about the pain. He just wants Dana to stop bothering him, and he is smarter than Dana. Although Roy might not know the boy running past the

NOTES

bus, he does know that Dana is "a well-known idiot." Roy also knows that fighting back would be "a complete waste of energy." When Roy tells Dana "I've had enough," Dana lets him go. Now Roy, released from the grip of Dana's hands, is free to wonder about the strange boy. Roy's curiosity and his intelligence help him get out of a bad situation.

4   In "Everybody Jump," scientist Randall Munroe is motivated to use mathematical reasoning to answer a difficult question: "What would happen if everyone on earth stood as close to each other as they could and jumped . . . at the same instant?" This could never happen in real life, but Munroe takes the question seriously. He knows that "many others" are curious about this topic and uncertain about the answer. Munroe uses mathematical reasoning, or logic, to explain the unknown. In his conclusion, he says that everyone jumping at once in the same place would have "little effect" on the planet. But then some terrible things would happen. When these billions of people tried to go back to their homes, they would run out of food, water, and fuel. They would probably become violent and die "within weeks." Munroe paints an ugly picture, but it's where his reasoning takes him. He ends by stating certainly, "at least now we know."

5   Donna O'Meara could have been hurt as she tried to find answers to her questions about volcanoes, but her wish to learn more and help others kept her pushing forward. Curiosity and intelligence help Roy get through the experience of being bullied. Randall Munroe's logic leads him to conquer feelings of uncertainty about a frightening event. Each person or character is motivated by a desire to know something for certain. Even though none of them is sure what will happen next, they are all motivated into action. As a result, they learn something about themselves and the world.

WRITE

Writers often take notes about their ideas before they sit down to write. Think about what you've learned so far about informative writing to help you begin prewriting.

- Which three individuals from this unit will you focus on in your informative text?

- What steps did they take in order to move forward even when they felt uncertain?

- Were there any cause and effect relationships that set each individual's story in motion?

- How will you compare and contrast each individual's situation?

- Which texts will you use to support your ideas? Will you need to do more research?

Response Instructions

Use the questions in the bulleted list to write a one-paragraph summary. Your summary should describe what your informative essay will be about.

Don't worry about including all of the details now; focus only on the most essential and important elements. You will refer back to this short summary as you continue through the steps of the writing process.

Skill:
Thesis Statement

••• CHECKLIST FOR THESIS STATEMENT

Before you begin writing your thesis statement, ask yourself the following questions:

- What is the prompt asking me to write about?
- What is the topic of my essay?
- What claim do I want to make about the topic of this essay? Is my opinion clear to my reader?
- Does my thesis statement introduce the body of my essay?
- Where should I place my thesis statement?

Here are some methods to introduce and develop your claim and topic:

- Think about the topic and central idea of your essay.
  - > The central idea of an argument is stated as a claim, or what will be proven or shown to be true.
  - > Identify as many claims as you intend to prove.
- Write a clear statement about the central idea or claim. Your thesis statement should:
  - > Let the reader anticipate the body of your essay.
  - > Respond completely to the writing prompt.
- Consider the best placement for your thesis statement.
  - > If your response is short, you may want to get right to the point. Your thesis statement may be presented in the first sentence of the essay.
  - > If your response is longer (as in a formal essay), you can build up your thesis statement. In this case, you can place your thesis statement at the end of your introductory paragraph.

Copyright © BookheadEd Learning, LLC

YOUR TURN

Read the excerpts from *Donna O'Meara: Volcano Lady* below. Then, complete the chart by sorting them into those that are thesis statements and those that are not. Write your answer in the second column.

Excerpts	Thesis Statement or Not Thesis Statement?
When Donna went back to school at the age of 32 to study science, her passion for volcanoes began.	
For over 25 years, she has worked with Steve to photograph and study volcanoes all over the world. They hope their documentation will someday be a written and visual record of information that helps scientists to better predict volcanic eruptions.	
Donna says the experience of being stranded on Mt. Stromboli for one freezing night was the scariest experience of her life.	
The following year, she and Steve were married on lava that had oozed from Kilauea on Hawaii and hardened. Lava that hardens creates new landforms, and some volcanoes, such as Surtsey off the coast of Iceland, actually create new islands!	

✏️ WRITE

Use the list and questions from the checklist to write a thesis statement for your essay.

Skill:
Organizing Informative Writing

••• CHECKLIST FOR ORGANIZING INFORMATIVE WRITING

As you consider how to organize your writing for your informative essay, use the following questions as a guide:

* What is my topic? How can I summarize the main idea?

* What is the logical order of my ideas, concepts, and information? Do I see a pattern that is similar to a specific text structure?

* Which organizational structure should I use to present my information?

* How might using graphics, headings, or some form of multimedia help to present my information?

Here are some strategies to help you organize ideas, concepts, and information and aid comprehension:

* definition is useful for:

  > defining a difficult idea or concept

  > defining the essential qualities of a subject

  > teaching readers about a topic or how to do something

  > providing examples

  > restating a definition in different ways to help readers understand the subject

* classification is useful for:

  > dividing larger ideas and concepts into subcategories that are easier to understand

  > sorting information into subcategories

  > using subcategories to clarify ideas and provide detailed descriptions

* compare and contrast is useful for:

  > comparing the similarities and differences between two texts, ideas, or concepts

* cause and effect is useful for:

  > explaining what and why something happened

  > understanding how things change over time

- visual elements are useful for:

  > using headings to organize your essay into groups of information

  > using graphics, such as charts or tables, to visually represent large amounts of information

  > using multimedia, such as video, sound, and hypertext links, to help readers understand complex ideas and concepts

YOUR TURN

Read the thesis statements and descriptions of each writer's overall purpose for writing, below. Then, complete the chart by writing the organizational structure that would best develop the thesis and achieve the writer's overall purpose.

Organizational Structure Options

Cause and Effect   Steps in a Process in Sequential Order   Compare and Contrast   Problem and Solution

Thesis	Purpose	Organizational Structure
The Civil War reshaped American ideas about freedom by resolving the question of slavery.	to show how the Civil War caused Americans to change the way they think about freedom	
Although many people prefer cats, some people find dogs to be the best companions.	to show the differences and similarities between cat ownership and dog ownership	
Bullying is a serious issue for some students, but with support from teachers, parents, and administrators, we can eliminate the problem.	to present a possible solution for the problem of bullying in schools	
The Hudson River is the longest glacial river in America, and the way it was formed is quite fascinating.	to explain how the Hudson River was formed	

 WRITE

Use the steps in the checklist to plan out the organization of your informative essay.

Skill:
Supporting Details

••• CHECKLIST FOR SUPPORTING DETAILS

As you look for supporting details to develop your topic, claim, or thesis statement, ask yourself the following questions:

- What is my main idea about this topic?

- What does a reader need to know about the topic in order to understand the main idea?

- What details will support my thesis?

- Is this information necessary to the reader's understanding of the topic?

- Does this information help to develop and refine my key concept or idea?

- Does this information relate closely to my thesis or claim?

- Where can I find better evidence that will provide stronger support for my point?

- Which details that I've already included need further explanation?

Here are some suggestions for how you can develop your topic:

- review your thesis or claim

- consider your main idea

- note what the reader will need to know in order to understand the topic

- be sure to consult credible sources

- use different types of supporting details, such as:

  > facts that are specific to your topic and enhance your discussion to establish credibility with your reader and build information

  > definitions to explain difficult concepts, terms, or ideas in your topic, claim, or thesis statement

  > concrete details that will add descriptive and detailed material to your topic

  > quotations to directly connect your thesis statement or claim to the text

  > examples and other information to deepen your claim, topic, or thesis statement

YOUR TURN

Choose the best answer to each question.

1. The following is a section from a previous draft of Colin's essay. Colin would like to add a sentence to support the idea that he has presented in the underlined sentence. Which of these would BEST follow and support the underlined sentence?

> In "Everybody Jump," scientist Randall Munroe is motivated to use logic to answer a difficult question: "What would happen if everyone on earth stood as close to each other as they could and jumped . . . at the same instant?" <u>He knows that this could never really happen, but Munroe takes the question seriously.</u>

- ○ A. He knows that other people are curious about this topic and uncertain about the answer.
- ○ B. It's an interesting scenario, even if it can't happen in real life.
- ○ C. It's a chance for him to impress readers with his ability to use mathematical reasoning to solve real-life problems.
- ○ D. He hopes to advance the science of kinematics.

2. The following is a paragraph from a previous draft of Colin's informative essay. Colin has included an irrelevant sentence in the paragraph. Which sentence should be deleted from this paragraph?

> (1) Roy is motivated by a desire for knowledge. (2) He's also clever at dealing with problems. (3) These qualities help Roy—who's the new kid at school—deal with Dana the bully. (4) Roy's family has recently moved from Montana to Florida. (5) Dana is attacking Roy on the way to school when Roy sees a boy running past the school bus. (6) Even though Dana is hurting him, Roy is curious about the boy: "Who was he? What was he running from?" (7) Roy doesn't care about the pain. (8) He just wants Dana to stop bothering him. (9) When Roy tells Dana "I've had enough," Dana lets him go. (10) Now Roy is free to wonder about the strange boy.

- ○ A. Sentence 2
- ○ B. Sentence 4
- ○ C. Sentence 6
- ○ D. Sentence 9

✏ **WRITE**

Use the steps and questions in the checklist to revise the body of your informative essay.

Informative Writing
Process: Draft

| PLAN | DRAFT | REVISE | EDIT AND PUBLISH |

You have already made progress toward writing your informative essay. Now it is time to draft your informative essay.

✏️ WRITE

Use your Plan and other responses in your Binder to draft your informative essay. You may also have new ideas as you begin drafting. Feel free to explore those new ideas as they occur to you. You can also ask yourself these questions:

☐ Does my essay fully address the prompt?

☐ Have I included a clear thesis statement or controlling idea?

☐ Does my thesis statement let readers know what to expect in the body of my essay?

☐ Does the organizational text structure support my purpose for writing? Would another text structure be more effective?

Before you submit your draft, read it over carefully. You want to be sure you've responded to all aspects of the prompt.

Please note that excerpts and passages in the StudySync® library and this workbook are intended as touchstones to generate interest in an author's work. The excerpts and passages do not substitute for the reading of entire texts, and StudySync® strongly recommends that students seek out and purchase the whole literary or informational work in order to experience it as the author intended. Links to online resellers are available in our digital library. In addition, complete works may be ordered through an authorized reseller by filling out and returning to StudySync® the order form enclosed in this workbook.

Reading & Writing Companion

389

Here is Colin's informative essay draft. As you read, identify how effectively he has presented his thesis statement or controlling idea and organized his information. As he continues to revise and edit his essay, he will find and improve weak spots in his writing, as well as correct any language or punctuation mistakes.

 Skill:
Introductions

By adding a "hook" to his introduction, Colin has made his essay more interesting to readers. He has also made his thesis more concise while keeping important details.

 Skill:
Precise Language

Colin notices that he's using some inexact words. He replaces the phrase "triumph over" with the more precise word "conquer."

 Skill:
Style

In order to make his writing have an academic tone, Colin decides to replace the words "scary job" with more sophisticated vocabulary, such as "the unknown and hazardous world of volcanoes."

≡ STUDENT MODEL: FIRST DRAFT

~~Scientist Donna O'Meara is motivated by a desire to understand something dangerous. She also wants to help others. The character Roy in Carl Hiaasen's book Hoot is motivated by curiosity. His quick-witted thinking helps him out. Author Randall Munroe is motivated by mathematical reasoning to answer what seems to be an impossible question. Each of these people or characters has a different motivation. Each of them faces different obstacles and problems. But each of them learns something important.~~

Sometimes people are motivated to take action without really knowing why. It could be a feeling, a goal, or a person that encourages them. Scientist Donna O'Meara is motivated by a desire to understand something dangerous. She also wants to help others. The character Roy in Carl Hiaasen's book *Hoot* is motivated by curiosity. His quick-witted thinking helps him out. Author Randall Munroe is motivated by mathematical reasoning. He wants to answer what seems to be an impossible question. Each of these people or characters has a different motivation and faces different obstacles and problems, but they all learn something important.

~~Donna O'Meara's desire to understand how volcanoes work has sometimes put her in danger. Most people would probably be afraid to get close to a volcano. There's a lot we don't know about them. But O'meara has risked her life to study them. The desire for knowledge has pushed O'Meara to triumph over her scary job. Now she's an expert on volcanoes and shares her knowledge to help keep others safe. She hopes her work will "help (save the lives) of people who live near" volcanoes.~~

Donna O'Meara's desire to understand how volcanoes work has sometimes put her in danger. Most people would probably be afraid to get close to a volcano. There's a lot we don't know about them. But O'Meara has risked her life to study them. During her first visit to a volcano, she dodged "lava bombs," and hot lava melted her shoes. Another time, she and her husband Steve "were trapped on a ledge in the freezing cold with scalding rocks flying around them." The desire for knowledge has pushed O'Meara to conquer the unknown and hazardous world of volcanoes. Now she's an expert on volcanoes. She shares her knowledge to help keep others safe when volcanoes erupt. She hopes her work will "help save the lives of people who live near" volcanoes.

~~The character Roy is motivated by a desire for knowledge. He's also clever when it comes to dealing with problems. These qualities help Roy who's the new kid at school deal with Dana the bully. Dana is attacking Roy on his way to school, when Roy sees a boy running past the school bus. Roy is "griped with curiousity" about the boy: "… Who was he? What was he runing from?" Roy doesn't care about the pain. He just wants Dana to stop bothering him, and he is smarter than Dana. He does know that Dana is "a well-known [idiot]." Roy also knows that fighting back would be "a complete waste of (energy)." When Roy tells Dana "I've had enough," Dana lets him go. Now Roy, released from the grip of Dana's hands, are free to wonder about the strange boy. Roy's curiousity and his intelligence help him get out of a bad situation~~

Like Donna O'Meara, the character Roy in *Hoot* is motivated by a desire for knowledge. He's also clever when it comes to dealing with problems. These qualities help Roy, who's the new kid at school, deal with Dana the bully. Dana is attacking Roy on his way to school when Roy sees a boy running past the school bus. Even though Dana is hurting him, Roy is "gripped with curiosity" about the boy: "Who was he? What was he running from?" Roy doesn't care about the pain. He just wants Dana to stop bothering him, and he is smarter than Dana. Although Roy might not know the boy running past the bus, he does know that Dana is "a well-known idiot." Roy also knows that fighting back would be "a complete waste of energy." When Roy tells Dana "I've had enough," Dana lets him go. Now Roy, released from the grip of Dana's hands, is free to wonder about the strange boy. Roy's curiosity and his intelligence help him get out of a bad situation.

In "Everybody Jump," scientist Randall Munroe is motivated to use mathematical reasoning to answer a difficult question: "What would happen if everyone on earth stood as close to each other as they

Skill:
Transitions

Colin continues to add transitions to his draft in order to clarify ideas between paragraphs and make apparent his organizational structure. He realizes that there is no connection between the paragraph about Donna O'Meara and the one about Roy from Hoot. Therefore, he adds the transitional phrase "Like Donna O'Meara" before introducing the character Roy. Colin also adds cohesion and clarity to the ideas within this paragraph by adding other transitions, such as "Even though Dana is hurting him" and "Although Roy might not know the boy running past the bus."

NOTES

could and jumpped . . . at the same instant?" This could never sucsede in real life since it would totally be unpossible to get everyone in the same place at the same time, but Munroe takes the question seriously. He knows that "many others" are curious about this topic and discertain about the answer. Munroe uses mathematical reasoning, or logic, to explain the inknown. In his conclusion, he says that everyone jumping at once in the same place. Would have "little effect" on the planet. But then some terrible things would happen. When these billions of people tried to go back to their homes, they would be come violent and die "within weeks." Munroe paints an ugly picture, but it's where his reasoning takes him. He ends by stating certainly, "at least now we know."

Donna O'Meara could have been hurt as she tried to find answers to her questions about volcanoes, but her wish to learn more and help others kept her pushing forward. Curiosity and intelligence help Roy get through the experience of being bullied. Randall Munroe's logic leads him to conquer feelings of uncertainty about a frightening event. Each person or character is motivated by a desire to know something for certain. Even though none of them is sure what will happen next, they are all motivated into action. As a result, they learn something about themselves and the world.

Skill:
Conclusions

Colin decides that his conclusion does a good job of wrapping up his main points about each person. However, he realizes that he has not rephrased his main idea, or thesis. Thus, he adds several sentences that show his depth of knowledge about his main idea.

Skill:
Introductions

Before you write your introduction, ask yourself the following questions:

- What is my claim? How can I introduce my claim(s) so it is clear to my reader?

- What is the best way to organize my ideas, concepts, reasons, and evidence in a clear and logical order?

- How will you "hook" your reader's interest? You might:

  > start with an attention-grabbing statement

  > begin with an intriguing question

  > use descriptive words to set a scene

Below are two strategies to help you introduce your topic and claim, and organize reasons and evidence clearly in an introduction:

- Peer Discussion

  > Talk about your topic with a partner, explaining what you already know and your ideas about your topic.

  > Write notes about the ideas you have discussed and any new questions you may have.

  > Review your notes and think about what will be your claim.

  > Briefly state your claim or thesis.

  > Organize your reasons and evidence in an order that is clear to readers, presenting your reasons first, followed by evidence.

  > Write a possible "hook."

- Freewriting

  > Freewrite for 10 minutes about your topic. Don't worry about grammar, punctuation, or having fully formed ideas. The point of freewriting is to discover ideas.

  > Review your notes and think about what will be your claim.

Please note that excerpts and passages in the StudySync® library and this workbook are intended as touchstones to generate interest in an author's work. The excerpts and passages do not substitute for the reading of entire texts, and StudySync® strongly recommends that students seek out and purchase the whole literary or informational work in order to experience it as the author intended. Links to online resellers are available in our digital library. In addition, complete works may be ordered through an authorized reseller by filling out and returning to StudySync® the order form enclosed in this workbook.

Reading & Writing
Companion

393

> Briefly state your claim or thesis.

> Organize your reasons and evidence in an order that is clear to readers, presenting your reasons first, followed by evidence.

> Write a possible "hook."

⟳ YOUR TURN

Choose the best answer to each question.

1. Below is the introduction from a previous draft of Colin's essay. The first sentence is a weak "hook." How could Colin rewrite the sentence to better grab the reader's attention?

> <u>Lots of things motivate people.</u> Scientist Donna O'Meara is motivated to understand volcanoes, even if it means putting herself in danger. Roy in Carl Hiaasen's novel *Hoot* is motivated by curiosity. Author Randall Munroe is motivated by the challenge of using mathematical reasoning to answer a seemingly impossible question.

- ○ A. People are motivated by different things.
- ○ B. A quest for understanding, a keen sense of curiosity, a sharp mind—many different things motivate people to act.
- ○ C. Motivation comes from surprising places.
- ○ D. Motivation—the reason or reasons that drive people to take action—comes from many sources.

2. Colin wants to improve the introduction in an earlier draft of his informative essay. Which of these revisions to the following three sentences makes a more concise thesis?

> Each of these people or characters has a different motivation. Each of them faces different obstacles and problems. But each of them learns something important.

- ○ A. Each person learns something important through a different motivation.
- ○ B. In each case, they all learn something different.
- ○ C. Despite unique motivations and different obstacles, each of them learns something important.
- ○ D. In each case, they face different problems and overcome uncertainty.

✏ WRITE

Use the questions in the checklist to revise the introduction of your informative essay.

Please note that excerpts and passages in the StudySync® library and this workbook are intended as touchstones to generate interest in an author's work. The excerpts and passages do not substitute for the reading of entire texts, and StudySync® strongly recommends that students seek out and purchase the whole literary or informational work in order to experience it as the author intended. Links to online resellers are available in our digital library. In addition, complete works may be ordered through an authorized reseller by filling out and returning to StudySync® the order form enclosed in this workbook.

Reading & Writing Companion

395

Skill:
Transitions

••• CHECKLIST FOR TRANSITIONS

Before you revise your current draft to include transitions, think about:

- the key ideas you discuss in your body paragraphs

- the organizational structure of your essay

- the relationships among ideas and concepts

Next, reread your current draft and note areas in your essay where:

- the organizational structure is not yet apparent

  > For example, if you are comparing and contrasting two texts, your explanations about how two texts are similar and different should be clearly stated.

- the relationship between ideas from one paragraph to the next is unclear

  > For example, an essay that describes a process in sequential order should make clear the order of steps using transitional words like *first, then, next,* and *finally.*

- the relationship between ideas within a paragraph is unclear

  > For example, when providing evidence to support an idea in a topic sentence, you should introduce the evidence with a transition such as *for example* or *to illustrate.*

Revise your draft to use appropriate transitions to clarify the relationships among ideas and concepts, using the following questions as a guide:

- What kind of transitions should I use to make the organizational structure clear to readers?

- Which transition best connects the ideas within a paragraph?

- Which transition best connects ideas across paragraphs?

YOUR TURN

Choose the best answer to the question.

Below is a section from Colin's essay. Which transition would make the most sense to add to the beginning of sentence 3?

> (1) Munroe uses mathematical reasoning, or logic, to explain the unknown. (2) In his conclusion, he says that everyone jumping at once in the same place would have "little effect" on the planet. (3) Some terrible things would happen.

- ○ A. However,
- ○ B. To illustrate,
- ○ C. In addition,
- ○ D. Finally,

YOUR TURN

Complete the chart by adding the following transitions to sentences of your informative essay.

Transition	Rewritten Sentence
However	
To illustrate	
In addition	
For example	

Please note that excerpts and passages in the StudySync® library and this workbook are intended as touchstones to generate interest in an author's work. The excerpts and passages do not substitute for the reading of entire texts, and StudySync® strongly recommends that students seek out and purchase the whole literary or informational work in order to experience it as the author intended. Links to online resellers are available in our digital library. In addition, complete works may be ordered through an authorized reseller by filling out and returning to StudySync® the order form enclosed in this workbook.

Reading & Writing Companion   **397**

Skill:
Precise Language

••• CHECKLIST FOR PRECISE LANGUAGE

As you consider precise language and domain-specific vocabulary related to a subject or topic, use the following questions as a guide:

- What information am I trying to convey or explain to my audience?

- Are there any key concepts that need to be explained or understood?

- What domain-specific vocabulary is relevant to my topic and explanation?

- Where can I use more precise vocabulary in my explanation?

Here are some suggestions that will help guide you in using precise language and domain-specific vocabulary to inform about or explain a topic:

- determine the topic or area of study you will be writing about

- identify key concepts that need explanation in order to inform readers

- research any domain-specific vocabulary that you may need to define

- substitute vague, general, or overused words and phrases for more precise, descriptive, and domain-specific language with clear connotative meaing

- reread your writing to refine and revise if needed

⟳ YOUR TURN

Choose the best answer to the question.

Below is a section from a previous draft of Colin's essay. How could Colin change sentence 2 to add more precise language?

> (1) In "Everybody Jump," scientist Randall Munroe is motivated to use mathematical reasoning to answer a difficult question: "What would happen if everyone on earth stood as close to each other as they could and jumped . . . at the same instant?" (2) This could never happen in real life, but Munroe takes the question seriously.

○ A. This could never happen in fantasy, but Munroe takes the question seriously.

○ B. This could never happen in reality, but Munroe considers the query seriously.

○ C. This could never happen in real life, but Munroe takes the debate seriously.

○ D. This could never happen in real life, but Munroe takes the question totally seriously.

⟳ YOUR TURN

Complete the chart by adding an example of precise language and domain-specific language to your essay.

Type of Language	Rewritten Sentence
precise language	
domain-specific vocabulary	

Please note that excerpts and passages in the StudySync® library and this workbook are intended as touchstones to generate interest in an author's work. The excerpts and passages do not substitute for the reading of entire texts, and StudySync® strongly recommends that students seek out and purchase the whole literary or informational work in order to experience it as the author intended. Links to online resellers are available in our digital library. In addition, complete works may be ordered through an authorized reseller by filling out and returning to StudySync® the order form enclosed in this workbook.

Reading & Writing Companion   399

Skill:
Style

••• CHECKLIST FOR STYLE

First, reread the draft of your informative essay and identify the following:

- places where you use slang, contractions, abbreviations, and a conversational tone

- areas where you could use subject-specific or academic language in order to help persuade or inform your readers

- moments where you use first-person (*I*) or second person (*you*)

- areas where sentence structure lacks variety

- incorrect uses of the conventions of standard English for grammar, spelling, capitalization, and punctuation

Establish and maintain a formal style in your essay, using the following questions as a guide:

- Have I avoided slang in favor of academic language?

- Did I consistently use a third-person point of view, using third-person pronouns (*he, she, they*)?

- Have I varied my sentence structure and the length of my sentences? Apply these specific questions where appropriate:

  > Where should I make some sentences longer by using conjunctions to connect independent clauses, dependent clauses, and phrases?

  > Where should I make some sentences shorter by separating any independent clauses?

- Did I follow the conventions of standard English, including:

  > grammar?

  > spelling?

  > capitalization?

  > punctuation?

Copyright © BookheadEd Learning, LLC

 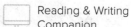

YOUR TURN

Choose the best answer to the question.

Below is a section from a previous draft of Colin's essay. Which of the following revisions shows correct conventions of English?

> Now Roy, released from the grip of Dana's hands, are free to wonder about the strange boy. Roy's curiousity and his intelligence help him get out of a bad situation.

○ A. Now Roy released from the grip of Dana's hands is free to wonder about the strange boy. Roy's curiosity and his intelligence help him get out of a bad situation.

○ B. Now Roy, released from the grip of Dana's hands, is free to wonder about the strange boy. Roy's curiosity and him intelligence help he get out of a bad situation.

○ C. Now Roy, released from the grip of Dana's hands, is free to wonder about the strange boy and Roy's curiosity and his intelligence help him get out of a bad situation.

○ D. Now Roy, released from the grip of Dana's hands, is free to wonder about the strange boy. Roy's curiosity and his intelligence help him get out of a bad situation.

YOUR TURN

Complete the chart by making style changes within your informative essay.

Style Change	Rewritten Sentence
Eliminate slang, contractions, abbreviations, or a conversational tone.	
Use domain-specific or academic language.	
Vary sentence structure and the length of sentences.	

Please note that excerpts and passages in the StudySync® library and this workbook are intended as touchstones to generate interest in an author's work. The excerpts and passages do not substitute for the reading of entire texts, and StudySync® strongly recommends that students seek out and purchase the whole literary or informational work in order to experience it as the author intended. Links to online resellers are available in our digital library. In addition, complete works may be ordered through an authorized reseller by filling out and returning to StudySync® the order form enclosed in this workbook.

Reading & Writing Companion   **401**

Skill:
Conclusions

••• CHECKLIST FOR CONCLUSIONS

Before you write your conclusion, ask yourself the following questions:

- How can I restate the thesis or main idea in my concluding section or statement? What impression can I make on my reader?

- How can I write my conclusion so that it follows logically from the information I presented?

- Have I left out any important information in my concluding statement that I have presented in my essay?

Below are two strategies to help you provide a concluding statement or section that follows from the information or explanation presented:

- Peer Discussion

  > After you have written your introduction and body paragraphs, talk with a partner and tell them what you want readers to remember, writing notes about your discussion.

  > Review your notes and think about what you wish to express in your conclusion.

  > Do not simply restate your claim or thesis statement. Rephrase your main idea to show the depth of your knowledge.

  > Write your conclusion.

- Freewriting

  > Freewrite for 10 minutes about what you might include in your conclusion. Don't worry about grammar, punctuation, or having fully formed ideas. The point of freewriting is to discover ideas.

  > Review your notes and think about what you wish to express in your conclusion.

  > Do not simply restate your claim or thesis statement. Rephrase your main idea to show the depth of your knowledge.

  > Write your conclusion.

YOUR TURN

Choose the best answer to each question.

1. Below is the conclusion from a previous draft of Colin's essay. What key component is Colin missing from his conclusion?

> Donna O'Meara could have been hurt as she tried to find answers to her questions about volcanoes, but her wish to learn more and help others kept her pushing forward. Curiosity and intelligence help Roy get through the experience of being bullied. Randall Munroe's logic leads him to conquer feelings of uncertainty about a frightening event.

- ○ A. restating all three people or characters
- ○ B. restating the essay's thesis
- ○ C. a "hook"
- ○ D. descriptions of the motivation of each person or character

2. Colin wants to improve the conclusion to an earlier draft of his informative essay. What is the most effective revision to make to the underlined sentence in order to end with a memorable comment that expresses the essay's thesis?

> Donna O'Meara could be hurt trying to understand volcanoes, but her wish to learn more spurs her on. Curiosity helps Roy cope with being bullied. Randall Munroe's logic leads him to overcome uncertainty about a frightening event. <u>In each case, the person or character learns something.</u>

- ○ A. In each case, the person learns something important through motivation.
- ○ B. In each case, the desire to push past uncertainty leads to knowledge about themselves and the world.
- ○ C. In each case, the desire to know something pushes the person or character past uncertainty to learn something about themselves and the world.
- ○ D. In each case, knowledge of the world helps them overcome uncertainty.

 WRITE

Use the questions in the checklist to revise the conclusion of your informative essay.

Informative Writing
Process: Revise

PLAN	DRAFT	REVISE	EDIT AND PUBLISH

You have written a draft of your informative essay. You have also received input from your peers about how to improve it. Now you are going to revise your draft.

← REVISION GUIDE

Examine your draft to find areas for revision. Keep in mind your purpose and audience as you revise for clarity, development, organization, and style. Use the guide below to help you review:

Review	Revise	Example
Clarity		
Highlight any place in your essay where there are unnecessary details that lack a formal style and hinder clarity.	Remove irrelevant information and informal language from sentences.	This could never happen in real life ~~since it would totally be impossible to get everyone in the same place at the same time~~, but Munroe takes the question seriously.
Development		
Identify places where you give details in support of your thesis. Note reasons, descriptions, and examples you could incorporate to add support.	Focus on a single idea and add reasons, descriptions, or examples to support your idea.	In his conclusion, he says that everyone jumping at once in the same place. Would have "little effect" on the planet. But then some terrible things would happen. When these billions of people tried to go back to their homes, they would run out of food, water, and fuel. They ~~they~~ would become violent and die "within weeks."

Review	Revise	Example
Organization		
Review whether your text structure supports your purpose. Annotate places where the organization can be improved.	Rewrite the transition between paragraphs to make the text structure clear to readers.	She shares her knowledge to help keep others safe when volcanoes erupt. She hopes her work will "help save the lives of people who live near" volcanoes. Like Donna O'Meara, the ~~The~~ character Roy is motivated by a desire for knowledge. He's also clever when it comes to dealing with problems.
Style: Word Choice		
Identify prefixes in your writing (such as *in-* and *un-*).	Select sentences to rewrite using correct prefixes.	Munroe uses mathematical reasoning, or logic, to explain the ~~inknown~~ unknown.
Style: Sentence Variety		
Review your essay for precise language. Create comprehensible sentences by using language that is specific to the text.	Rewrite sentences to include domain-specific vocabulary.	The desire for knowledge has pushed O'Meara to conquer ~~her scary job~~ the unknown and hazardous world of volcanoes.

 WRITE

Use the guide above, as well as your peer reviews, to help you evaluate your informative essay to determine areas that should be revised.

Grammar: Parentheses, Brackets, and Ellipses

Parentheses

Parentheses ( ) are punctuation marks used to set off supplemental or explanatory material that is not part of the main sentence. Supplemental material often includes words that define or explain another word.

Text	Explanation
The fine sarcophagus **(sar-KOFF-ah-guss)**, or stone coffin, which would hold his body was also ready. His Majesty, Herself	The pronunciation is explanatory material, so it is set off in parentheses.

Brackets

Brackets [ ] are punctuation marks used in quotations to set off information inserted by someone besides the original writer or speaker in order to clarify the quotation.

Text	Explanation
Hail, Ari-em-ab-f, who comest forth from Tebu, I have never stopped **[the flow of]** water. Book of the Dead	The words *the flow of* clarify the sentence and were inserted by someone besides the original writer. Therefore, they are set off in brackets.

Ellipses

When writers quote other texts, sometimes they need to leave out some of the material. They use ellipses [. . .], or three spaced points, to indicate that material from a quotation has been left out.

Text	Explanation
"Troy . . . was sacked twice," modern archaeologists remark, "once by the Greeks and once by Heinrich Schliemann." The Hero Schliemann: The Dreamer Who Dug for Troy	The ellipses indicate the omission of material from the middle or end of a quotation.

↻ YOUR TURN

1. How should this sentence be changed?

> Their property consists of one-half acre 21,780 square feet.

- ○ A. Insert brackets around the words *one-half acre*.
- ○ B. Insert brackets around the words *21,780 square feet*.
- ○ C. Insert parentheses around the words *21,780 square feet*.
- ○ D. No change needs to be made to this sentence.

2. Which revision of the quotation uses ellipses correctly?

> The news anchor explained, "Although his lawyer presented an eloquent defense, he was found guilty and sentenced to life in prison."

- ○ A. The news anchor explained, "Although his lawyer presented an eloquent defense, he was found guilty . . ."
- ○ B. The news anchor explained, "Although his lawyer presented an eloquent defense, he was . . . life in prison."
- ○ C. The news anchor explained, "Although his lawyer presented an eloquent defense, he was . . . sentenced to life in prison."
- ○ D. None of the above.

3. How should this sentence be changed?

> According to Anika's history book, "she (Susan B. Anthony) played a major role in winning American women the right to vote."

- ○ A. Remove the parentheses around the words *Susan B. Anthony*.
- ○ B. Remove the parentheses and insert brackets around the words *Susan B. Anthony*.
- ○ C. Remove the parentheses and insert commas around the words *Susan B. Anthony*.
- ○ D. No change needs to be made to this sentence.

Grammar: Prefixes

A prefix is a word part that is added to the beginning of a base word and changes its meaning. Prefixes help develop meaning in words and sentences. An understanding of prefixes and their meanings will help you learn new words.

Prefix	Meaning	Examples	Meaning
in-	not	**in**direct **in**visible	not direct not visible
non-	without, not	**non**stop **non**fiction	without stop not fiction
un-	opposite of, not, reverse	**un**clean **un**tie	not clean to loosen
pre-	before	**pre**pay **pre**heat	to pay in advance to heat in advance
de-	remove from, reduce	**de**grade **de**throne	to make lower to remove from the throne
dis-	opposite of, not, remove from	**dis**agree **dis**appear	to not agree to vanish

⟳ YOUR TURN

1. Which word with a prefix best replaces the **bolded words** in the following sentence?

> His actions were **not kind**.

○ A. cruel
○ B. insane
○ C. unkind
○ D. None of the above.

2. Which word with a prefix best replaces the **bolded words** in the following sentence?

> When playing this card game, after each turn you must **remove a card** from your hand.

○ A. discard
○ B. disallow
○ C. draw
○ D. None of the above.

3. Which word with a prefix best replaces the **bolded words** in the following sentence?

> Passengers may **remove themselves from the plane** upon landing.

○ A. disrobe
○ B. disagree
○ C. deplane
○ D. None of the above.

4. Which word with a prefix best replaces the **bolded words** in the following sentence?

> The team got together to enjoy a **before the game** snack.

○ A. pregame
○ B. early
○ C. preapproved
○ D. None of the above.

Please note that excerpts and passages in the StudySync® library and this workbook are intended as touchstones to generate interest in an author's work. The excerpts and passages do not substitute for the reading of entire texts, and StudySync® strongly recommends that students seek out and purchase the whole literary or informational work in order to experience it as the author intended. Links to online resellers are available in our digital library. In addition, complete works may be ordered through an authorized reseller by filling out and returning to StudySync® the order form enclosed in this workbook.

Reading & Writing
Companion

409

Grammar: Basic Spelling Rules II

Doubled Consonants

Spelling Conventions	Correct Spelling	Incorrect Spelling
Before adding -*ed* or a suffix: When a word ends in a single consonant following one vowel, double the final consonant if the word is one syllable.	slap + -*ed* = slapped sit + -*ing* = sitting	slaped siting
Before adding -*ed* or a suffix: Double the final consonant if the last syllable of the word is accented and the accent stays there after the suffix is added.	refer + -*ed* = referred occur + -*ence* = occurrence deter + -*ing* = deterring admit + -*ed* = admitted	refered occurence detering admited
Before adding -*ly* to a double *l*: When adding -*ly* to a word that ends in *ll*, drop one *l*.	full + -*ly* = fully dull + -*ly* = dully	fullly dullly

Compound Words

Spelling Conventions	Original Words	Compound Words
Compound words are made up of two or more words. When forming compound words, maintain all original spellings.	back + pack honey + bee fly + wheel	backpack honeybee flywheel

Spelling -*cede*, -*ceed*, and -*sede*

Spelling Conventions	Correct Spelling	Incorrect Spelling
The only English word ending in -*sede* is *supersede*.	supersede	superceed
Three words end in -*ceed: proceed, exceed,* and *succeed*.	proceed exceed succeed	procede exsede succede
All other words ending with the "seed" sound are spelled with -*cede*.	precede recede	preceed receed

↻ YOUR TURN

1. How should the spelling error in this sentence be corrected?

> No one in our class has ever experienced a naturally occuring disaster such as an earth quake.

- ○ A. Change *occuring* to *occurring* and *earth quake* to *earthquake*.
- ○ B. Change *occuring* to *occurring*.
- ○ C. Change *earth quake* to *earthquake*.
- ○ D. No change needs to be made to this sentence.

2. How should the spelling error in this sentence be corrected?

> If you look very carefully you will succede in finding the book some where in this room.

- ○ A. Change *succede* to *succeed*.
- ○ B. Change *some where* to *somewhere*.
- ○ C. Change *succede* to *succeed* and *some where* to *somewhere*.
- ○ D. No change needs to be made to this sentence.

3. How should the spelling error in this sentence be corrected?

> The founders of the religion believed that the new faith would fully superceed all existing forms of belief.

- ○ A. Change *superceed* to *supersede*.
- ○ B. Change *fully* to *fullly*.
- ○ C. Change *fully* to *fuly*.
- ○ D. No change needs to be made to this sentence.

4. How should the spelling error in this sentence be corrected?

> When the rock hit the windshield, the driver slammed on the brakes, and then she proceeded through the traffic light.

- ○ A. Change *windshield* to *wind shield*.
- ○ B. Change *slammed* to *slamed*.
- ○ C. Change *proceeded* to *proceded*.
- ○ D. No change needs to be made to this sentence.

Informative Writing
Process: Edit and Publish

PLAN	DRAFT	REVISE	EDIT AND PUBLISH

You have revised your informative essay based on your peer feedback and your own examination.

Now, it is time to edit your informative essay. When you revised, you focused on the content of your essay. You probably looked at your essay's thesis statement, introduction, organizational text structure, supporting details, transitions, precise language, style, and conclusion. When you edit, you focus on the mechanics of your essay, and pay close attention to things like grammar and punctuation.

Use the checklist below to guide you as you edit:

- ☐ Have I correctly used parentheses, brackets, and ellipses?

- ☐ Have I correctly used prefixes?

- ☐ Did I follow spelling rules, especially regarding doubled consonants, compound words, and words ending with the "seed" sound?

- ☐ Do I have any sentence fragments or run-on sentences?

- ☐ Have I spelled everything correctly?

Notice some edits Colin has made:

- Corrected the incorrect use of parentheses.

- Corrected incorrect prefixes.

- Used basic spelling rules to correct spelling errors, especially in words with doubled consonants and compound words.

- Changed a verb so that it matches the subject.

- Corrected a sentence fragment.

Roy also knows that fighting back would be "a complete waste of ~~(energy)~~ energy." When Roy tells Dana "I've had enough," Dana lets him go. Now Roy, released from the grip of Dana's hands, ~~are~~ is free to wonder about the strange boy. Roy's ~~curiousity~~ curiosity and his intelligence help him get out of a bad situation.

In "Everybody Jump," scientist Randall Munroe is motivated to use mathematical reasoning to answer a difficult question: "What would happen if everyone on earth stood as close to each other as they could and ~~jumpped~~ jumped . . . at the same instant?" This could never happen in real life, but Munroe takes the question seriously. He knows that "many others" are curious about this topic and ~~discertain~~ uncertain about the answer. Munroe uses mathematical reasoning, or logic, to explain the ~~inknown~~ unknown. In his conclusion, he says that everyone jumping at once in the same place. ~~W~~ would have "little effect" on the planet. But then some terrible things would happen. When these billions of people tried to go back to their homes, they would run out of food, water, and fuel. They would probably ~~be come~~ become violent and die "within weeks."

✏ WRITE

Use the questions on the previous page, as well as your peer reviews, to help you evaluate your informative essay to determine areas that need editing. Then edit your essay to correct those errors.

Once you have made all your corrections, you are ready to publish your work. You can distribute your writing to family and friends, hang it on a bulletin board, or post it on your blog. If you publish online, share the link with your family, friends, and classmates.

Please note that excerpts and passages in the StudySync® library and this workbook are intended as touchstones to generate interest in an author's work. The excerpts and passages do not substitute for the reading of entire texts, and StudySync® strongly recommends that students seek out and purchase the whole literary or informational work in order to experience it as the author intended. Links to online resellers are available in our digital library. In addition, complete works may be ordered through an authorized reseller by filling out and returning to StudySync® the order form enclosed in this workbook.

Reading & Writing Companion   413

Tracking Down Typhoid Mary

INFORMATIONAL TEXT

Introduction

This true-life mystery tells about a serious illness and the man who tracked down its source. The story is set in the early 1900s, when people were just

VOCABULARY

mansion

a large and impressive house

thoroughly

completely; in a detailed way

carrier

a person or animal that transmits a disease without suffering from or showing signs of the disease

isolation

the condition of being alone

inspector

someone whose job is to examine something closely

READ

NOTES

1   It was a lovely day in Oyster Bay. The sun was shining. The sky was blue. At Charles Warren's **mansion** on the shore, though, all was not well. Six people in the house were fighting for their lives. All were very ill with symptoms that included a very high fever. One of them was Charles's little daughter.

2   As it turned out, the six people had typhoid fever. In 1906 it was a common illness, found in crowded parts of the city. However, no one had ever seen it in rich Oyster Bay homes. How did it get there? Where had it come from? Charles wanted to know.

3   Charles hired a man named George Soper. George had an unusual job. He was a sanitation engineer. He worked to make buildings cleaner because making them cleaner kept sickness from spreading. Dirty water and dirty hands made germs spread. One of those germs caused typhoid fever. George set to work in the Warrens' house, looking for the cause of disease.

4   George found nothing wrong with the water pipes. Nothing was wrong with the drains. Could bad seafood be making people sick? George checked the kitchen. Everything seemed fresh and clean. He talked to everyone in the household. By spring, he had the answer. He tracked the fever to one woman. She had worked in the house as a cook. She had worked in other homes before that, and people at those homes had become sick. The woman's name was Mary Mallon.

5   Mary had never been sick herself. Others became sick, but she did not. She was a **carrier** of the disease. She did not believe that she had made anyone sick. She was angry. In fact, she chased George away with a fork!

6   Mary was still a cook. Now she worked for a different family. George was worried. Would she make them sick, too? He called the Health Department. An **inspector** came to talk to Mary, but she ran away. Finally, the police picked her up. They took her to a hospital. There, doctors tested her blood. She was loaded with the germ that caused typhoid fever.

7   How did Mary make people sick? The doctors figured it out. Mary made great peach ice cream. She did not wash her hands **thoroughly**, so germs could spread. The peaches were raw, so cooking did not kill the germs.

8   The Health Department locked Mary away in **isolation**. She lived alone on an island for three years. She went to court. The judge agreed that she was dangerous. Finally, in 1910, she was freed.

9   Mary continued to work as a cook. Everywhere she worked, people got sick. Many people got typhoid fever from Mary Mallon. At least three people died from her cooking.

10   In 1915, the courts locked Mary up again. She died on the island 23 years later. She had never once had typhoid fever. Even so, people everywhere called her "Typhoid Mary."

First Read

Read the text. After you read, answer the Think Questions below.

☁ THINK QUESTIONS

1. Whom did Charles Warren hire? Why did he hire that person?

   Charles Warren hired _____.

   He hired him _____.

2. How did Mary get people sick?

   Mary got people sick because _____.

3. What happened to Mary after she was freed in 1910?

   After Mary was freed she _____.

4. Use context to confirm the meaning of the word *isolation* as it is used in "Tracking Down Typhoid Mary." Write your definition of *isolation* here.

   Isolation means _____.

   A context clue is _____.

5. What is another way to say that you cleaned your room *thoroughly*?

   I cleaned my room _____.

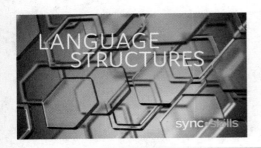

Skill:
Language Structures

★ DEFINE

In every language, there are rules that tell how to **structure** sentences. These rules define the correct order of words. In the English language, for example, a **basic** structure for sentences is subject, verb, and object. Some sentences have more **complicated** structures.

You will encounter both basic and complicated **language structures** in the classroom materials you read. Being familiar with language structures will help you better understand the text.

••• CHECKLIST FOR LANGUAGE STRUCTURES

To improve your comprehension of language structures, do the following:

✓ Monitor your understanding.

- Ask yourself: Why do I not understand this sentence? Is it because I do not understand some of the words? Or is it because I do not understand the way the words are ordered in the sentence?

✓ Pay attention to verbs followed by prepositions.

- A **verb** names an action.

  > Example: I **sit** on my chair.

  > This tells the reader what the subject of the sentence is doing (sitting).

- A **preposition** defines the relationship between two or more nouns or verbs in a sentence.

  > Example: I sit **on** my chair.

  > This tells the reader where the subject is doing the action (on a chair).

- Sometimes the preposition comes directly after the verb, but it can also be separated by another word.

    Example: I **took** it **to** school with me.

- Sometimes the preposition changes the meaning of the verb. This is called a **phrasal verb**.

    > Example: The teacher liked to **call on** the students in the front of the class.

    > The phrasal verb *call on* means "to select someone to share information."

✓ Break down the sentence into its parts.

- Ask yourself: What words make up the verbs in this sentence? Is the verb followed by a preposition? How does this affect the meaning of the sentence?

✓ Confirm your understanding with a peer or teacher.

↻ YOUR TURN

Read each sentence from the text. Find the verb and preposition that goes along with it. Then, write the verb in the center column and the preposition in the last column. Remember, the preposition may not always directly follow the verb.

Sentences	Verbs	Prepositions
At least three people died from her cooking.		
He tracked the fever to one woman.		
She lived alone on an island for three years.		
She went to court.		

Skill:
Main Ideas and Details

★ DEFINE

The **main ideas** are the most important ideas of a paragraph, a section, or an entire text. The **supporting details** are details that describe or explain the main ideas.

To **distinguish** between the main ideas and the supporting details, you will need to decide what information is the most important—this is the main idea. Then identify the facts that support or explain the main idea—these are the supporting details.

••• CHECKLIST FOR MAIN IDEAS AND DETAILS

In order to distinguish between main ideas and supporting details, do the following:

✓ Preview the text. Look at headings, topic sentences, and boldface vocabulary.

- Ask yourself: What seems to be the main idea in this text?

✓ Read the text.

- Ask yourself: What are the most important ideas? What details support or explain the most important ideas?

✓ Take notes or use a graphic organizer to distinguish between main ideas and supporting details.

YOUR TURN

Read the following excerpt from the text. Then, complete the multiple-choice questions below.

---

from "Tracking Down Typhoid Mary"

How did Mary make people sick? The doctors figured it out. Mary made great peach ice cream. She did not wash her hands thoroughly, so germs could spread. The peaches were raw, so cooking did not kill the germs.

---

1. What is the main idea of the paragraph?

   ○ A. Mary never learned to clean her tools.
   ○ B. Mary wanted to make people sick.
   ○ C. Mary's peach ice cream made people sick.
   ○ D. Mary's ice cream needed further cooking.

2. Which detail supports the main idea?

   ○ A. Mary made great ice cream.
   ○ B. Cooking did not kill the germs.
   ○ C. Peaches may be used in ice cream.
   ○ D. Germs spread when Mary washed up.

3. Which other detail supports the main idea of the paragraph?

   ○ A. Mary did not wash her hands properly.
   ○ B. Peaches are often loaded with germs.
   ○ C. Mary forgot to cook the peaches.
   ○ D. Ice cream can cause stomach pains.

Close Read

✏️ WRITE

PERSONAL RESPONSE: Imagine that you were Mary Mallon in this story. How would you feel about George? How would you react to being told you were spreading disease, and why? Write about your experience as Mary. Recount details from the original story in your response. Pay attention to spelling patterns and rules as you write.

Use the checklist below to guide you as you write.

☐ How do you think Mary Mallon feels?

☐ Why does George look for Mary?

☐ What information from the text supports your ideas?

Use the sentence frames to organize and write your personal response.

Mary is not sure why George _____.

I would feel _____ if _____.

I think I would _____.

Spreading germs is bad because _____.

I practice healthy habits to _____.

The Notice

FICTION

Introduction

New York City in the 1930s was home to immigrant families who traveled there from every corner of the world in search of a happy life. At times, they faced a less-than-warm welcome. In the story "The Notice," two Czech families experience a dilemma: can they keep their livelihood when their landlord

VOCABULARY

impatient

unwilling to wait for someone or something

property

a piece of land or a building that is owned by a person or business

counter

a flat surface over which goods are bought or food is served.

admit

to tell the truth, but in an unwilling way

glassware

objects made of glass

☰ READ

NOTES

1   The last customer put on her coat and left. It was a cold January night. My *táta* locked the door and looked out. He stood there for a while. I began to grow **impatient**. I wanted to see his warm smile. I saw that smile every day, after he closed our shop for the day.

2   He turned at last, but he didn't look happy. He placed his hand on my shoulder and walked past me.

3   My *máma* and I watched him stand behind the **counter**. He took out a folded piece of paper from a small wooden box. He spread the paper out before him. Delicate glass vases, bowls, and plates sparkled in the display case below. Our family and the Vaceks made them in the back of the shop. We used to make the same **glassware** in Prague. The Vaceks were watching my *táta* too.

4   "What can we do, Dominik?" Josefa asked. Her husband, Miroslav, winced slightly.

5   Eventually my *táta* looked up. Josefa's question brought him back from some faraway place.

6   "Mr. Davis hasn't given us much of a choice." There was anger in his voice. "He has already made his choice. He will give our shop to anyone who didn't pass through Ellis Island. Or, he will *allow* us to pay extra for letting us work on his **property**."

7   *Máma* knew what my *táta* said was true.

8   *Táta* gripped the edges of the display case. Like the glassware the case contained, his expression was easy for everyone to see.

9   Mr. Vacek read the notice again. Mr. Davis left it on our shop door this morning. He didn't even hand it to my *táta* or Mr. Vacek.

10   I glanced at it. Mr. Davis blamed the doubling of our rent on hard times. It was difficult to imagine that he knew about hard times.

11   Mr. Vacek cleared his throat and said, "Josefa and I, we need this place." He didn't want to **admit** it, but it was true.

12   My *táta* looked at Mr. Vacek and nodded. They had known each other since they were children. My *táta* didn't want to hear his friend say that. But I knew my *táta* wasn't going to abandon him now.

13   "Whatever we decide, we will decide it together," my *táta* said.

First Read

Read the text. After you read, answer the Think Questions below.

☁ THINK QUESTIONS

1. Who are the main characters in the story? What is their relationship?

   The main characters are _____.

   They are _____.

2. Write two or three sentences describing the setting of the story.

   The setting _____.

   _____.

3. At the end of the story, why does the narrator still have hope?

   The narrator still has hope because _____.

4. Use context to confirm the meaning of the word *admit* as it is used in "The Notice." Write your definition of *admit* here.

   Admit means _____.

   A context clue is _____.

5. What is another way to say the word *abandon*?

   Another way to say *abandon* is _____.

Skill:
Analyzing Expressions

★ **DEFINE**

When you read, you may find English expressions that you do not know. An **expression** is a group of words that communicates an idea. Three types of expressions are idioms, sayings, and figurative language. They can be difficult to understand because the meanings of the words are different from their **literal**, or usual, meanings.

An **idiom** is an expression that is commonly known among a group of people. For example: "It's raining cats and dogs" means it is raining heavily. **Sayings** are short expressions that contain advice or wisdom. For instance: "Don't count your chickens before they hatch" means do not plan on something good happening before it happens. **Figurative** language is when you describe something by comparing it with something else, either directly (using the words *like* or *as*) or indirectly. For example, "I'm as hungry as a horse" means I'm very hungry. None of these expressions are about actual animals.

••• **CHECKLIST FOR ANALYZING EXPRESSIONS**

To determine the meaning of an expression, remember the following:

✓ If you find a confusing group of words, it may be an expression. The meaning of words in expressions may not be their literal meaning.

- Ask yourself: Is this confusing because the words are new? Or because the words do not make sense together?

✓ Determining the overall meaning may require that you use one or more of the following:

- context clues

- a dictionary or other resource

- teacher or peer support

✓ Highlight important information before and after the expression to look for clues.

⟳ YOUR TURN

Read paragraphs 5–6 and 10–11 from the text. Then complete the multiple-choice questions below.

---

from **"The Notice"**

Eventually my *táta* looked up. Josefa's question brought him back from some faraway place.

"Mr. Davis hasn't given us much of a choice." There was anger in his voice. "He has already made his choice. He will give our shop to anyone who didn't pass through Ellis Island. Or, he will allow us to pay extra for letting us work on his property."

. . .

I glanced at it. Mr. Davis blamed the doubling of our rent on hard times. It was difficult to imagine that he knew about hard times.

Mr. Vacek cleared his throat and said, "Josefa and I, we need this place." He didn't want to admit it, but it was true.

---

1. What does the narrator mean by "brought him back from a faraway place" in paragraph 5?

   ○ A. He came back from a distant country.

   ○ B. Josefa brought *táta* from a distant place.

   ○ C. Josefa's question rescued *táta*.

   ○ D. The question brought *táta's* attention back.

2. Which context clue helped you determine the meaning of the expression?

   ○ A. "Mr. Davis hasn't given us much of a choice."

   ○ B. "He has already made his choice."

   ○ C. "There was anger in his voice."

   ○ D. "…Eventually my *táta* looked up…"

Please note that excerpts and passages in the StudySync® library and this workbook are intended as touchstones to generate interest in an author's work. The excerpts and passages do not substitute for the reading of entire texts, and StudySync® strongly recommends that students seek out and purchase the whole literary or informational work in order to experience it as the author intended. Links to online resellers are available in our digital library. In addition, complete works may be ordered through an authorized reseller by filling out and returning to StudySync® the order form enclosed in this workbook.

Reading & Writing Companion   **429**

3. What does the narrator mean when she says "hard times" in paragraph 10?

○ A. a time where people need money

○ B. a strong, solid period of time

○ C. events that happened long ago

○ D. the due date for paying your bills

4. Which context clue helped you determine the meaning of the expression?

○ A. "Josefa and I, we need this place"

○ B. "I glanced at it."

○ C. "He has already made his choice."

○ D. "Mr. Davis blamed the doubling of our rent …"

Skill:
Comparing and Contrasting

★ DEFINE

To **compare** is to show how two or more pieces of information or literary elements in a text are similar. To **contrast** is to show how two or more pieces of information or literary elements in a text are different. By comparing and contrasting, you can better understand the **meaning** and the **purpose** of the text you are reading.

••• CHECKLIST FOR COMPARING AND CONTRASTING

In order to compare and contrast, do the following:

✓ Look for information or elements that you can compare and contrast.

- Ask yourself: How are these two things similar? How are they different?

✓ Look for signal words that indicate a compare-and-contrast relationship.

- Ask yourself: Are there any words that indicate the writer is trying to compare and contrast two or more things?

✓ Use a graphic organizer, such as a Venn diagram or chart, to compare and contrast information.

↻ YOUR TURN

Read the following excerpt from the text. Then complete the Compare-and-Contrast chart by writing the letter of the correct example in chart below.

> from **"The Notice"**
>
> Mr. Vacek read the notice again. Mr. Davis left it on our shop door this morning. He didn't even hand it to my *táta* or Mr. Vacek.
>
> I glanced at it. Mr. Davis blamed the doubling of our rent on hard times. It was difficult to imagine that he knew about hard times.
>
> Mr. Vacek cleared his throat and said, "Josefa and I, we need this place." He didn't want to admit it, but it was true.
>
> My *táta* looked at Mr. Vacek and nodded. They had known each other since they were children. My *táta* didn't want to hear his friend say that. But I knew my *táta* wasn't going to abandon him now.

Examples	
A	know Mr. Vacek
B	would never abandon his friend
C	left a notice without talking in person

Mr. Davis	Both	Táta

Close Read

✏️ **WRITE**

INFORMATIONAL: Beginning a new life in a new country can be difficult. Imagine that like the families in "The Notice," you are starting over in a new country and trying to find a job. However, even though you are qualified, no one wants to hire you because you weren't born in their country. Think about the types of information you would need to provide in order to prove that you are able to do the work. Explain why that information is important. Pay attention to verb tenses as you write.

Use the checklist below to guide you as you write.

☐ How would you react if you weren't being hired because of where you were from?

☐ What could you do to show you were qualified?

☐ Who could you have the employer talk to?

☐ What other information could help you get the job?

Use the sentence frames to organize and write your informational paragraph.

If I couldn't get a job because I was from another country, I would feel _____ . I would try my

best to _____ the boss that I could do the work. I would _____ letters from

my old boss. I would also show the boss any papers, like a school diploma or degree, that prove that I am

_____ . This information is important because it proves that just because I'm from another

country, I'm as _____ and deserving of the job as anyone.

studysync

ASSIGNMENTS   BINDER   LIBRARY

Personal Best

UNIT 4

Personal Best

What qualities of character matter most?

Genre Focus: **ARGUMENTATIVE TEXT**

Texts

 Paired Readings

Extended Writing Project and Grammar

What qualities of character matter most?

RAY BRADBURY

American author Ray Bradbury (1920–2012) was fourteen when his family moved from Illinois to an apartment in the middle of Hollywood. Bradbury roller-skated to movie premieres and dreamed of becoming a writer. A few years later, he published his first story and began his distinguished career as an author of fantasy, horror, mystery, and science fiction. Bradbury's influence extended beyond literature, and he was consulted by Disney in the design of Epcot and flown to Cape Canaveral by NASA to lecture astronauts.

RUSSELL FREEDMAN

As a reporter and editor for the Associated Press in San Francisco, Russell Freedman (1929–2018) gained experience in research and writing that prepared him for his second career as an author of nonfiction, which he began in the 1950s when he moved to New York City. His biographies illuminated the lives of historical figures—Abraham Lincoln, Marco Polo, Tasunke Witco (more commonly known as Crazy Horse), and Eleanor Roosevelt, to name a few—who were motivated to challenge injustice.

NAOMI SHIHAB NYE

"Where we live in the world is never one place," writes Naomi Shihab Nye (b. 1952), who grew up between Ferguson, Missouri, near where her American mother was raised, and Jerusalem, her father's Palestinian homeland. The poet, essayist, and songwriter currently lives in San Antonio, Texas. Nye began writing poems at the age of six, and says she loves to write anywhere—at home, outdoors, or even at the airport.

RICHARD PECK

Novelist Richard Peck (1934–2018) gathered material for some of his stories from his brief career as an English teacher at a junior high in Illinois. "Ironically, it was my students who taught me to be a writer, though I was hired to teach them," Peck said after winning the Newbery Medal in 2001 for his book *A Year Down Yonder*. For nearly fifty years Peck lived in New York City, writing for children and young adults, and composing all of his works on the typewriter.

KURT VONNEGUT

Kurt Vonnegut (1922–2007) was an American author of novels, short stories, plays, and essays from Indianapolis, Indiana. In 1943, he dropped out of Cornell University and enlisted in the US Army to fight in World War II. He was captured during the Battle of the Bulge and taken to a prison camp in Dresden, where took refuge in the meat locker of a slaughterhouse during the bombing of the city by Allied forces. This experience forms the plot of the first chapter of his most famous novel, *Slaughterhouse-Five* (1969).

MALALA YOUSAFZAI

When Malala Yousafzai (b. 1997) was just eleven years old, she said goodbye to her classmates in Mingora, Pakistan, unsure when or if she would ever see them again. It was 2008, and the Taliban had just seized control of Yousafzai's village in Swat Valley, and, among many new rules, girls were no longer allowed to go to school. Yousafzai, an activist, writer, and Nobel laureate, has since dedicated her life to creating "a world where girls are empowered to reach their potential through a quality education."

LYNNE OLSON

Former US Secretary of State Madeleine Albright called American author and historian Lynne Olson (b. 1949) "our era's foremost chronicler of World War II politics and diplomacy." Olson, who was born in Hawaii, was a journalist for a decade before becoming a full-time author. She wrote national features for the Associated Press and reported on national politics and the White House for the *Baltimore Sun*. She currently lives in Washington, DC.

I Am Malala:
The Girl Who Stood Up
for Education and
Was Shot by the Taliban

INFORMATIONAL TEXT
Malala Yousafzai
2013

Introduction

studysync tv

A champion of education from an early age, Malala Yousafzai (b. 1997) survived a gunshot wound to the head at age 15 inflicted by a Taliban gunman. At age 17, Malala became the youngest person to receive the Nobel Peace Prize. In this excerpt from her memoir, Malala, age 11, lives with her parents and two younger brothers in the Swat Valley of Northern Pakistan, which has come under control of Taliban extremists. Incensed by the Taliban's mandate that all girls' schools in the Swat Valley must close by January 15, 2009, Malala takes a risky, conspicuous public stance against the Taliban, using radio, TV, a blog, and a diary written under the pseudonym Gul Makai (for which this chapter is titled) to relay her message.

"Education is neither Eastern nor Western. It is human."

from Chapter 13: The Diary of Gul Makai

1   We had a special assembly that final morning, but it was hard to hear with the noise of helicopters overhead. Some of us spoke out against what was happening in our valley. The bell rang for the very last time, and then Madam Maryam announced it was winter vacation. But unlike in other years no date was announced for the start of next term. Even so, some teachers still gave us homework. In the yard I hugged all my friends. I looked at the honors board and wondered if my name would ever appear on it again. Exams were due in March, but how could they take place? Coming first didn't matter if you couldn't study at all. When someone takes away your pens you realize quite how important education is.

2   Before I closed the school door I looked back as if it were the last time I would ever be at school. That's the closing door in one part of the documentary. In reality I went back inside. My friends and I didn't want that day to end, so we decided to stay on for a while longer. We went to the primary school where there was more space to run around and played cops and robbers. Then we played mango mango, where you make a circle and sing, then when the song stops everyone has to freeze. Anyone who moves or laughs is out.

3   We came home from school late that day. Usually we leave at 1 p.m., but that day we stayed till three. Before we left, Moniba and I had an argument over something so silly I can't remember what it was. Our friends couldn't believe it. "You two always argue when there's an important occasion!" they said. It wasn't a good way to leave things.

4   I told the documentary makers, "They cannot stop me. I will get my education if it's at home, school, or somewhere else. This is our request to the world—to save our schools, save our Pakistan, save our Swat."

5   When I got home, I cried and cried. I didn't want to stop learning. I was only eleven years old, but I felt as though I had lost everything. I had told everyone in my class that the Taliban wouldn't go through with it. "They're just like our politicians—they talk the talk, but they won't do anything," I'd said. But then

Skill:
Connotation
and Denotation

I can look at context clues to determine the denotation of the word cut. I notice that Malala says that the school closing is a loss of business for her dad, and she mentions fees, money and bills that her dad had to take care of. I think cut means a decrease or loss.

Skill: Author's
Purpose and
Point of View

Malala's purpose is to criticize the Taliban and persuade readers to agree with her views about education. She thinks education should be available to all. She makes it clear by using short, clear sentences full of emotion to share her opinion.

they went ahead and closed our school and I felt embarrassed. I couldn't control myself. I was crying, my mother was crying, but my father insisted, "You will go to school."

6 For him the closing of the schools also meant the loss of business. The boys' school would reopen after the holidays, but the loss of the girls' school **represented** a big cut in our income. More than half the school fees were overdue, and my father spent the last day chasing money to pay the rent, the utility bills and the teachers' salaries.

7 That night the air was full of artillery fire and I woke up three times. The next morning everything had changed. I began to think that maybe I should go to Peshawar[1] or abroad or maybe I could ask our teachers to form a secret school in our home, as some Afghans had done during Taliban rule. Afterward I went on as many radio and TV channels as possible. "They can stop us going to school, but they can't stop us learning," I said. I sounded hopeful, but in my heart I was worried. My father and I went to Peshawar and visited lots of places to tell people what was happening. I spoke of the irony of the Taliban wanting female teachers and doctors for women yet not letting girls go to school to qualify for these jobs.

8 Once Muslim Khan had said girls should not go to school and learn Western ways. This from a man who had lived so long in America! He insisted he would have his own education system. "What would Muslim Khan use instead of the stethoscope and the thermometer?" my father asked. "Are there any Eastern instruments that will treat the sick?" The Taliban is against education because they think that when a child reads a book or learns English or studies science he or she will become Westernized.

9 But I said, "Education is education. We should learn everything and then choose which path to follow." Education is neither Eastern nor Western. It is human."

10 My mother used to tell me to hide my face when I spoke to the media because at my age I should be in purdah[2] and she was afraid for my safety. But she never banned me from doing anything. It was a time of horror and fear. People often said the Taliban would kill my father but not me. "Malala is a child," they would say, "and even the Taliban don't kill children."

11 But my grandmother wasn't so sure. Whenever my grandmother saw me speaking on television, or leaving the house, she would pray, "Please God make Malala like Benazir Bhutto but do not give her Benazir's short life."

---

1. **Peshawar** Pakistani city near the Khyber Pass
2. **purdah** the practice of covering and segregation of women in Muslim and Hindu cultures

12   After my school closed down, I continued to write the blog. Four days after the ban on girls' schools, five more were destroyed. "I'm quite surprised," I wrote, "because these schools had closed, so why did they also need to be destroyed? No one has gone to school following the Taliban's deadline. The army is doing nothing about it. They are sitting in their bunkers on top of the hills. They slaughter goats and eat with pleasure." I also wrote about people going to watch the **floggings** announced on Mullah FM, and the fact that the army and police were nowhere to be seen.

13   One day we got a call from America, from a student at Stanford University. Her name was Shiza Shahid and she came from Islamabad. She had seen the *New York Times* documentary *Class Dismissed in Swat Valley* and tracked us down. We saw then the power of the media and she became a great support to us. My father was almost bursting with pride at how I came across in the documentary. "Look at her," he told Adam Ellick. "Don't you think she is meant for the skies?" Fathers can be very embarrassing.

14   Adam took us to Islamabad. It was the first time I had ever visited. Islamabad was a beautiful place with nice white bungalows and broad roads, though it has none of the natural beauty of Swat. We saw the Red Mosque where the **siege** had taken place, the buildings of the Parliament House and the Presidency, where Zardari now lived. General Musharraf was in exile in London.

15   We went to shops where I bought school books and Adam bought me DVDs of American TV programs like *Ugly Betty,* which was about a girl with big braces and a big heart. I loved it and dreamed of one day going to New York and working on a magazine like her. We visited the Lok Virsa museum, and it was a joy to celebrate our national **heritage** once again. Our own museum in Swat had closed. On the steps outside an old man was selling popcorn. He was a Pashtun[3] like us, and when my father asked if he was from Islamabad he replied, "Do you think Islamabad can ever belong to us Pashtuns?" He said he came from Mohmand, one of the tribal areas, but had to flee because of a military operation. I saw tears in my parents' eyes.

16   Lots of buildings were surrounded by concrete blocks, and there were checkpoints for incoming vehicles to guard against suicide bombs. When our bus hit a pothole on our way back my brother Khushal, who had been asleep, jerked awake. "Was that a bomb blast?" he asked. This was the fear that filled our daily lives. Any small disturbance or noise could be a bomb or gunfire.

 Skill: Author's Purpose and Point of View

Malala's attitude toward the police is clear. Her point of view is that the police and army were failing in their duty to protect the people by allowing the Taliban to terrorize her city.

Excerpted from I Am Malala: The Girl Who Stood Up for Education and Was Shot by the Taliban by Malala Yousafzai, published by Back Bay Books

---

3. **Pashtun** members of the Pashto people living in Afghanistan and Pakistan

First Read

Read "I Am Malala: The Girl Who Stood Up for Education and Was Shot by the Taliban." After you read, complete the Think Questions below.

 THINK QUESTIONS

1. How does Malala respond to the closing of her school? Use specific examples from the text in your answer.

2. Based on the text, why does the Taliban condemn the education of girls and not the education of boys? What can you infer about the Taliban's values?

3. How do Malala's relatives feel about her choice to speak up for the right of girls to education? Use specific examples from the text in your answer.

4. Read the following dictionary entry:

   siege

   siege /sēj/ *noun*

   1. An attack in which an army surrounds a group of people or city to get them to surrender
   2. An illness
   3. Any general attempt to gain control

   Which definition most closely matches the meaning of **siege** as it is used in paragraph 14? Write the correct definition of *siege* here and explain how you figured out the correct meaning.

5. Use context clues to determine the meaning of the word **heritage** as it is used in paragraph 15. Write your definition of *heritage* here and explain how context clues in the paragraph led to your understanding of the word's meaning.

Copyright © BookheadEd Learning, LLC

Skill: Author's Purpose and Point of View

Use the Checklist to analyze Author's Purpose and Point of View in "I Am Malala: The Girl Who Stood Up for Education and Was Shot by the Taliban." Refer to the sample student annotations about Author's Purpose and Point of View in the text.

••• CHECKLIST FOR AUTHOR'S PURPOSE AND POINT OF VIEW

In order to identify an author's purpose and point of view, note the following:

- ✓ facts, statistics, and graphic aids as these indicate that the author is writing to inform

- ✓ the author's use of emotional or figurative language, which may indicate that the author is trying to persuade readers or stress an opinion

- ✓ descriptions that present a complicated process in plain language, which may indicate that the author is writing to explain

- ✓ the language the author uses, as figurative and emotional language can be clues to the author's point of view on a subject or topic

To determine the author's purpose and point of view in a text, consider the following questions:

- ✓ How does the author convey, or communicate, information in the text?

- ✓ Does the author use figurative or emotional language? For what purpose?

- ✓ Does the author make use of charts, graphs, maps and other graphic aids?

Skill: Author's Purpose and Point of View

Reread paragraphs 14–15 from "I Am Malala: The Girl Who Stood Up for Education and Was Shot by the Taliban." Then, using the Checklist on the previous page, answer the multiple-choice questions below.

⟳ YOUR TURN

1. What is the author's purpose in telling readers about Islamabad in paragraph 14?

   ○ A. to persuade readers to visit the city

   ○ B. to describe the city so readers can visualize it

   ○ C. to inform readers about the origin of the city

   ○ D. to explain why Adam took the family to the city

2. Which of the following best describes the author's point of view in paragraph 15?

   ○ A. Malala feels safer in Islamabad.

   ○ B. Malala is angry that Islamabad is different from Swat.

   ○ C. Malala wishes her parents had not come with her to Islamabad.

   ○ D. Malala loves Islamabad and wishes her city could be more like it.

Skill:
Connotation and Denotation

Use the Checklist to analyze Connotation and Denotation in "I Am Malala: The Girl Who Stood Up for Education and Was Shot by the Taliban." Refer to the sample student annotations about Connotation and Denotation in the text.

••• CHECKLIST FOR CONNOTATION AND DENOTATION

In order to identify the denotative meanings of words and phrases, use the following steps:

✓ first, note unfamiliar words and phrases: key words used to describe important individuals, events or ideas, and words that inspire an emotional reaction

✓ next, verify the denotative meaning of unfamiliar words by consulting reference material such as a dictionary, glossary, or thesaurus

To better understand the meaning of words and phrases as they are used in a text, including connotative meanings, use the following questions:

✓ What is the genre or subject of the text? How does that affect the possible meaning of a word or phrase?

✓ Does the word create a positive, negative, or neutral emotion?

✓ What synonyms or alternative phrasings help you describe the connotative meaning of the word?

To determine the meaning of words and phrases as they are used in a text, including connotative meanings, use the following questions:

✓ What is the meaning of the word or phrase? What is the connotation as well as the denotation?

✓ If I substitute a synonym based on denotation, is the meaning the same? How does it change the meaning of the text?

Please note that excerpts and passages in the StudySync® library and this workbook are intended as touchstones to generate interest in an author's work. The excerpts and passages do not substitute for the reading of entire texts, and StudySync® strongly recommends that students seek out and purchase the whole literary or informational work in order to experience it as the author intended. Links to online resellers are available in our digital library. In addition, complete works may be ordered through an authorized reseller by filling out and returning to StudySync® the order form enclosed in this workbook.

Reading & Writing Companion 447

Skill:
Connotation and Denotation

Reread paragraphs 10–11 from "I Am Malala: The Girl Who Stood Up for Education and Was Shot by the Taliban." Then, using the Checklist on the previous page, answer the multiple-choice questions below.

⟳ YOUR TURN

1. Based on the context clues in paragraph 10, what is most likely the denotative meaning of "purdah"?

   ○ A. being in a mosque
   ○ B. being out in the open
   ○ C. being with her mother
   ○ D. being in seclusion

2. Which of the following is most likely the intended connotation of "pray" in paragraph 11?

   ○ A. positive - her grandmother is showing her adoration for God.
   ○ B. negative - her grandmother is pleading and begging God to keep her safe.
   ○ C. negative - neither positive nor negative - her grandmother is asking a question of God.
   ○ D. neither positive nor negative - her grandmother is just speaking to God.

Close Read

Reread "I Am Malala: The Girl Who Stood Up for Education and Was Shot by the Taliban." As you reread, complete the Skills Focus questions below. Then use your answers and annotations from the questions to help you complete the Write activity.

◎ SKILLS FOCUS

1. Identify places in the text where Malala's purpose is to persuade readers to accept her point of view on conditions in Swat. Explain what Malala wants readers to understand.

2. Identify specific words and phrases in the text that indicate Malala's negative feelings about the Taliban.

3. Identify passages in the text where Malala's purpose is to persuade readers that the media both supports her cause and endangers her at the same time.

4. Not everyone would stand up to the Taliban. Identify examples of the character qualities you think were most important in driving Malala to act. Explain your reasoning.

✎ WRITE

ARGUMENTATIVE: What message is Malala trying to convey about the media? According to the author, did it help or injure her, or both? In your response, cite specific examples of Malala's word choice that help the reader understand how she views the media.

Malala Yousafzai— Nobel Lecture

ARGUMENTATIVE TEXT
Malala Yousafzai
2013

Introduction

The 2014 Nobel Peace Prize was awarded to two advocates for children's rights, one of them a Pakistani teenager named Malala Yousafzai. At 17, Malala was the youngest Nobel laureate in history. Malala had captured the world's attention two years earlier when a Taliban gunman shot her at close range as she was on her way home from school. She was targeted because she had long been speaking out against the Taliban's policy of forbidding education for girls; in fact, the Taliban had been bombing schools to make their point. In her Nobel Prize acceptance speech, Malala delivers a passionate rebuke to the Taliban's brutal anti-education policy and lays out her mission to promote a worldwide commitment to guaranteeing education for all children, surmounting the barriers of poverty, child labor, social taboos, and terrorist bullying.

"I had two options. One was to remain silent and wait to be killed. And the second was to speak up and then be killed."

1   *Bismillah hir rahman ir rahim. In the name of God, the most merciful, the most beneficent.*

2   Your Majesties, Your royal highnesses, distinguished members of the Norwegian Nobel Committee,

3   Dear sisters and brothers, today is a day of great happiness for me. I am humbled that the Nobel Committee has selected me for this precious award.

4   Thank you to everyone for your continued support and love. Thank you for the letters and cards that I still receive from all around the world. Your kind and encouraging words strengthens and inspires me.

5   I would like to thank my parents for their **unconditional** love. Thank you to my father for not clipping my wings and for letting me fly. Thank you to my mother for inspiring me to be patient and to always speak the truth — which we strongly believe is the true message of Islam. And also thank you to all my wonderful teachers, who inspired me to believe in myself and be brave.

6   I am proud, well in fact, I am very proud to be the first Pashtun, the first Pakistani, and the youngest person to receive this award. Along with that, along with that, I am pretty certain that I am also the first recipient of the Nobel Peace Prize who still fights with her younger brothers. I want there to be peace everywhere, but my brothers and I are still working on that.

7   I am also honoured to receive this award together with Kailash Satyarthi, who has been a champion for children's rights for a long time. Twice as long, in fact, than I have been alive. I am proud that we can work together, we can work together and show the world that an Indian and a Pakistani, they can work together and achieve their goals of children's rights.

8   Dear brothers and sisters, I was named after the inspirational Malalai of Maiwand who is the Pashtun Joan of Arc. The word Malala means "grief stricken", "sad", but in order to lend some happiness to it, my grandfather

NOTES

Skill: Arguments
and Claims

*Malala's opening
remarks make it clear
that she believes all
children deserve and
want peace and
education. She makes
the claim that all people
need to act to make
sure all children have
access to education.*

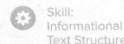
Skill:
Informational
Text Structure

*Malala first lists how
others describe her.
Then, she contrasts
this list using
"However," saying how
her brothers describe
her. Malala's
description of herself is
different from the rest
because she says what
she believes in. This is a
compare and contrast
text structure.*

would always call me Malala — "The happiest girl in the world" and today I am very happy that we are together fighting for an important cause.

9   This award is not just for me. It is for those forgotten children who want education. It is for those frightened children who want peace. It is for those voiceless children who want change.

10   I am here to stand up for their rights, to raise their voice. . . it is not time to pity them. It is not time to pity them. It is time to take action so it becomes the last time, the last time, so it becomes the last time that we see a child **deprived** of education.

11   I have found that people describe me in many different ways.

12   Some people call me the girl who was shot by the Taliban.

13   And some, the girl who fought for her rights.

14   Some people, call me a "Nobel Laureate" now.

15   However, my brothers still call me that annoying bossy sister. As far as I know, I am just a committed and even stubborn person who wants to see every child getting quality education, who wants to see women having equal rights and who wants peace in every corner of the world.

16   Education is one of the blessings of life — and one of its necessities. That has been my experience during the 17 years of my life. In my paradise home, Swat, I always loved learning and discovering new things. I remember when my friends and I would decorate our hands with henna[1] on special occasions. And instead of drawing flowers and patterns we would paint our hands with mathematical formulas and equations.

17   We had a thirst for education, we had a thirst for education because our future was right there in that classroom. We would sit and learn and read together. We loved to wear neat and tidy school uniforms and we would sit there with big dreams in our eyes. We wanted to make our parents proud and prove that we could also excel in our studies and achieve those goals, which some people think only boys can.

18   But things did not remain the same. When I was in Swat, which was a place of tourism and beauty, suddenly changed into a place of terrorism. I was just ten that more than 400 schools were destroyed. Women were flogged. People were killed. And our beautiful dreams turned into nightmares.

1. **henna** dye from the henna tree and/or the practice of making designs on the skin with it

19 Education went from being a right to being a crime.

20 Girls were stopped from going to school.

21 When my world suddenly changed, my priorities changed too.

22 I had two options. One was to remain silent and wait to be killed. And the second was to speak up and then be killed.

23 I chose the second one. I decided to speak up.

24 We could not just stand by and see those injustices of the terrorists denying our rights, ruthlessly killing people and misusing the name of Islam. We decided to raise our voice and tell them: Have you not learnt, have you not learnt that in the Holy Quran[2] Allah says: if you kill one person it is as if you kill the whole **humanity**?

25 Do you not know that Mohammad, peace be upon him, the prophet of mercy, he says, do not harm yourself or others".

26 And do you not know that the very first word of the Holy Quran is the word "Iqra", which means "read"?

27 The terrorists tried to stop us and attacked me and my friends who are here today, on our school bus in 2012, but neither their ideas nor their bullets could win.

28 We survived. And since that day, our voices have grown louder and louder.

29 I tell my story, not because it is unique, but because it is not.

30 It is the story of many girls.

31 Today, I tell their stories too. I have brought with me some of my sisters from Pakistan, from Nigeria and from Syria, who share this story. My brave sisters Shazia and Kainat who were also shot that day on our school bus. But they have not stopped learning. And my brave sister Kainat Soomro who went through severe abuse and extreme violence, even her brother was killed, but she did not **succumb**.

32 Also my sisters here, whom I have met during my Malala Fund campaign. My 16-year-old courageous sister, Mezon from Syria, who now lives in Jordan as refugee and goes from tent to tent encouraging girls and boys to learn. And

Skill:
Informational
Text Structure

Malala is using words like "suddenly changed" to show what happened after the terrorists took over her district. The sequential text structure helps me understand the order of events and why Malala took action.

Skill:
Media

Reading this part of the speech without watching and listening to Malala isn't the same. From the video, you can hear the audience begin to applaud her before she can finish her last sentence. The video shows the impact of her courage.

---

2. **Quran** the Holy Book of Islam

my sister Amina, from the North of Nigeria, where Boko Haram[3] threatens, and stops girls and even kidnaps girls, just for wanting to go to school.

33   Though I appear as one girl, though I appear as one girl, one person, who is 5 foot 2 inches tall, if you include my high heels. (It means I am 5 foot only) I am not a lone voice, I am not a lone voice, I am many.

34   I am Malala. But I am also Shazia.

35   I am Kainat.

36   I am Kainat Soomro.

37   I am Mezon.

38   I am Amina. I am those 66 million girls who are deprived of education. And today I am not raising my voice, it is the voice of those 66 million girls.

39   Sometimes people like to ask me why should girls go to school, why is it important for them. But I think the more important question is why shouldn't they, why shouldn't they have this right to go to school.

40   Dear sisters and brothers, today, in half of the world, we see rapid progress and development. However, there are many countries where millions still suffer from the very old problems of war, poverty, and injustice.

41   We still see conflicts in which innocent people lose their lives and children become orphans. We see many people becoming refugees in Syria, Gaza and Iraq. In Afghanistan, we see families being killed in suicide attacks and bomb blasts.

42   Many children in Africa do not have access to education because of poverty. And as I said, we still see, we still see girls who have no freedom to go to school in the north of Nigeria.

43   Many children in countries like Pakistan and India, as Kailash Satyarthi mentioned, many children, especially in India and Pakistan are deprived of their right to education because of social **taboos**, or they have been forced into child marriage or into child labour.

44   One of my very good school friends, the same age as me, who had always been a bold and confident girl, dreamed of becoming a doctor. But her dream remained a dream. At the age of 12, she was forced to get married. And then

---

3. **Boko Haram** Islamic jihadi group active in West Africa responsible for murders and kidnappings

soon she had a son, she had a child when she herself was still a child — only 14. I know that she could have been a very good doctor.

45 But she couldn't . . . because she was a girl.

46 Her story is why I dedicate the Nobel Peace Prize money to the Malala Fund, to help give girls quality education, everywhere, anywhere in the world and to raise their voices. The first place this funding will go to is where my heart is, to build schools in Pakistan — especially in my home of Swat and Shangla.

47 In my own village, there is still no secondary school for girls. And it is my wish and my commitment, and now my challenge to build one so that my friends and my sisters can go there to school and get quality education and to get this opportunity to fulfil their dreams.

48 This is where I will begin, but it is not where I will stop. I will continue this fight until I see every child, every child in school.

49 Dear brothers and sisters, great people, who brought change, like Martin Luther King and Nelson Mandela, Mother Teresa and Aung San Suu Kyi, once stood here on this stage. I hope the steps that Kailash Satyarthi and I have taken so far and will take on this journey will also bring change — lasting change.

50 My great hope is that this will be the last time, this will be the last time we must fight for education. Let's solve this once and for all.

51 We have already taken many steps. Now it is time to take a leap.

52 It is not time to tell the world leaders to realise how important education is — they already know it — their own children are in good schools. Now it is time to call them to take action for the rest of the world's children.

53 We ask the world leaders to unite and make education their top priority.

54 Fifteen years ago, the world leaders decided on a set of global goals, the Millennium Development Goals. In the years that have followed, we have seen some progress. The number of children out of school has been halved, as Kailash Satyarthi said. However, the world focused only on primary education, and progress did not reach everyone.

55 In year 2015, representatives from all around the world will meet in the United Nations to set the next set of goals, the **Sustainable** Development Goals. This will set the world's ambition for the next generations.

Copyright © BookheadEd Learning, LLC

56 The world can no longer accept, the world can no longer accept that basic education is enough. Why do leaders accept that for children in developing countries, only basic literacy is sufficient, when their own children do homework in Algebra, Mathematics, Science and Physics?

57 Leaders must seize this opportunity to guarantee a free, quality, primary and secondary education for every child.

58 Some will say this is impractical, or too expensive, or too hard. Or maybe even impossible. But it is time the world thinks bigger.

59 Dear sisters and brothers, the so-called world of adults may understand it, but we children don't. Why is it that countries which we call strong" are so powerful in creating wars but are so weak in bringing peace? Why is it that giving guns is so easy but giving books is so hard? Why is it, why is it that making tanks is so easy, but building schools is so hard?

60 We are living in the modern age and we believe that nothing is impossible. We have reached the moon 45 years ago and maybe will soon land on Mars. Then, in this 21st century, we must be able to give every child quality education.

61 Dear sisters and brothers, dear fellow children, we must work. . . not wait. Not just the politicians and the world leaders, we all need to contribute. Me. You. We. It is our duty.

62 Let us become the first generation to decide to be the last, let us become the first generation that decides to be the last that sees empty classrooms, lost childhoods, and wasted potentials.

63 Let this be the last time that a girl or a boy spends their childhood in a factory.

64 Let this be the last time that a girl is forced into early child marriage.

65 Let this be the last time that a child loses life in war.

66 Let this be the last time that we see a child out of school.

67 Let this end with us.

68 Let's begin this ending . . . together . . . today . . . right here, right now. Let's begin this ending now.

69 Thank you so much.

© The Nobel Foundation 2014

First Read

Read "Malala Yousafzai - Nobel Lecture." After you read, complete the Think Questions below.

☁ THINK QUESTIONS

1. How does Malala feel about education? Cite textual evidence from the selection to support your answer.

2. What is the significance Malala places on the first word of the Quran?

3. Who are the "sisters" Malala describes? What challenges do the "sisters" face? Support your answer with textual evidence.

4. The word **deprive** comes, in part, from the Latin root *de-*, which means "away" or "against," and the Latin *privus,* which means "individual" or "single." With this in mind, what do you think the word *deprive* means? Write your best definition here and explain how you arrived at its meaning.

5. Use context clues to determine the meaning of the word **succumb** as it is used in the text. Write your definition here and tell how you got it.

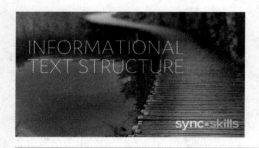

Skill:
Informational Text Structure

Use the Checklist to analyze Informational Text Structure in "Malala Yousafzai - Nobel Lecture." Refer to the sample student annotations about Informational Text Structure in the text.

••• CHECKLIST FOR INFORMATIONAL TEXT STRUCTURE

In order to determine the overall structure of a text, note the following:

✓ the topic(s) and how the author organizes information about the topic(s)

✓ patterns in a paragraph or section of text that reveal the text structure, such as:

- sequences, including the order of events or steps in a process

- problems and their solutions

- cause-and-effect relationships

- comparisons

✓ the overall structure of the text and how each section contributes to the development of ideas

To analyze how a particular sentence, paragraph, chapter, or section fits into the overall structure of a text and contributes to the development of the ideas, use the following questions as a guide:

✓ What organizational patterns reveal the text structure the author uses to present information?

✓ How does a particular sentence, paragraph, or section fit into the overall structure of the text? How does it affect the development of the author's ideas?

✓ In what ways does the text structure contribute to the development of ideas in the text?

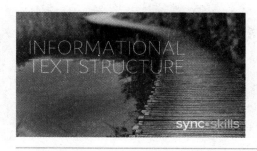

Skill:
Informational Text Structure

Reread paragraphs 27–38 from "Malala Yousafzai - Nobel Lecture." Then, using the Checklist on the previous page, answer the multiple-choice questions below.

↻ YOUR TURN

1. Which informational text structure is used in paragraph 28?

   ○ A. compare and contrast
   ○ B. cause and effect
   ○ C. problem and solution
   ○ D. advantage and disadvantage

2. How does the pattern of saying "I am" in paragraphs 34–38 contribute to the development of ideas in the speech?

   ○ A. It shows that all of those girls have been shot.
   ○ B. It shows that all of those girls were forced to flee their countries.
   ○ C. It shows that Malala stands up for all girls and their education.
   ○ D. It shows that all of those girls have been kidnapped.

Skill:
Media

Use the Checklist to analyze Media in "Malala Yousafzai - Nobel Lecture." Refer to the sample student annotations about Media in the text.

••• CHECKLIST FOR MEDIA

In order to determine how information is presented in different media or formats, note the following:

- ✓ how the same topic can be treated, or presented, in more than one medium, including visual and audio

- ✓ how treatments of a topic through different kinds of media can give you more information about the topic

- ✓ details that are emphasized or missing in each medium and the reasons behind these choices

- ✓ how, if different details are stressed by different media, a reader or viewer may begin to think about the subject in a new way

To integrate information presented in different media or formats, consider the following questions:

- ✓ Which details are missing or emphasized in each medium? What do you think are the reasons behind these choices, and what effect do they have?

- ✓ What information can you learn by analyzing and comparing these two sources?

- ✓ How can you integrate the information presented in different media or formats?

- ✓ How does integrating information from different media and formats help you to develop a fuller and more coherent understanding of a topic?

Skill:
Media

Analyze characteristics of digital text in the following video clips from "Media." Then, using the Checklist on the previous page, answer the multiple-choice questions below.

⟳ YOUR TURN

1. Which of the following best describes how the video enhances the audio, and therefore, the watcher/listener's comprehension of this part of the speech?

   ○ A. The video shows how Malala's body language emphasizes what she is saying

   ○ B. The video shows a close-up of how people in the audience react to her speech

   ○ C. The video reveals the facial expressions of various committee members.

   ○ D. The video shows a contrast between Malala's gestures and her quiet voice.

2. What information communicated in this audio/visual clip would add to the text of Malala's speech?

   ○ A. The audio gives details about the girls, which makes their stories more important.

   ○ B. The video shows the girls who are named in Malala's speech.

   ○ C. The video and audio replicate the same information that is in the text without adding any details.

   ○ D. The video and audio give the girls' stories greater impact by showing who they are and telling what happened to them.

Please note that excerpts and passages in the StudySync® library and this workbook are intended as touchstones to generate interest in an author's work. The excerpts and passages do not substitute for the reading of entire texts, and StudySync® strongly recommends that students seek out and purchase the whole literary or informational work in order to experience it as the author intended. Links to online resellers are available in our digital library. In addition, complete works may be ordered through an authorized reseller by filling out and returning to StudySync® the order form enclosed in this workbook.

Reading & Writing Companion   **461**

Skill:
Arguments and Claims

Use the Checklist to analyze Arguments and Claims in "Malala Yousafzai - Nobel Lecture." Refer to the sample student annotations about Arguments and Claims in the text.

••• CHECKLIST FOR ARGUMENTS AND CLAIMS

In order to trace the argument and specific claims, do the following:

✓ identify clues that reveal the speaker's opinion in the title, opening remarks, or concluding statement

✓ note the first and last sentence of each body paragraph for specific claims that help to build the speaker's argument

✓ listen for declarative statements that come before or follow an anecdote or story

✓ list the information that the speaker introduces in sequential order

✓ use different colored highlights to distinguish the speaker's argument, claims, reasoning, and evidence

✓ describe the speaker's argument in your own words

To evaluate the argument and specific claims, consider the following questions:

✓ Does the speaker support each claim with reasoning and evidence?

✓ In what order does the speaker introduce arguments and claims?

✓ Am I able to distinguish claims that are supported by reasoning and evidence from those that are not?

✓ Do the speaker's claims work together to support her overall argument?

✓ Which claims are not supported, if any?

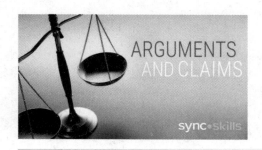

Skill:
Arguments and Claims

Reread paragraphs 57–61 and listen to 23:31–26:16 in the video of the speech of "Malala Yousafzai - Nobel Lecture." Then, using the Checklist on the previous page, answer the multiple-choice questions below.

⟳ YOUR TURN

1. This question has two parts. First, answer Part A. Then, answer Part B.

Part A: Which of the following most closely reflects the argument of this section of the speech?

- ○ A. It is up to regular people to make sure all children have access to education.
- ○ B. All children deserve access to education regardless of where they live.
- ○ C. It is up to everybody to work together to make sure all children have access to education.
- ○ D. It is up to world leaders to make sure all children have access to education.

Part B: Which of following claims from the speech does NOT specifically contribute to the argument identified in Part A?

- ○ A. "Leaders must seize this opportunity to guarantee a free, quality, primary and secondary education for every child."
- ○ B. "We have reached the moon 45 years ago and maybe will soon land on Mars."
- ○ C. "Then, in this 21st century, we must be able to give every child quality education."
- ○ D. "Not just the politicians and the world leaders, we all need to contribute."

Close Read

Reread "Malala Yousafzai - Nobel Lecture." As you reread, complete the Skills Focus questions below. Then use your answers and annotations from the questions to help you complete the Write activity.

◎ SKILLS FOCUS

1. Identify places where Malala uses a cause and effect text structure to present information. Identify details or signal words that reveal the text structure.

2. Malala uses a variety of text structures in her speech. Identify places in the speech where she employs text structures other than cause and effect to get her message across. Explain how you determined the text structures.

3. Having experienced "Malala Yousafzai - Nobel Lecture" as a mixed-media presentation, identify and explain passages of the speech in which audio or video contributes to the meaning of Malala's words.

4. The Nobel Committee identified qualities in Malala that they believed made her worthy of receiving the Nobel Peace Prize in 2014. Identify evidence in the speech that illustrates qualities of character that help Malala in her efforts to promote education for all. Explain why you think these qualities matter.

✏ WRITE

ARGUMENTATIVE: Near the end of her speech, Malala gives a call to action. She says, "Dear sisters and brothers, dear fellow children, we must work . . . not wait. Not just the politicians and the world leaders, we all need to contribute. Me. You. We. It is our duty." Malala uses a combination of informational text structures in the course of her speech to communicate the idea contained in this call to action. Which do you think is the most effective, and why? Write a response using specific examples from the text and the video to support your claims.

Priscilla and the Wimps

FICTION
Richard Peck
1984

Introduction

Richard Peck (b. 1934) is a Newbery Medal-winning author who has written more than a dozen young adult novels in a prolific career spanning five decades. Peck first worked as a middle school teacher before his writing career began. He has said that his experiences with students inspired many of the characters and situations within his young adult books. In his story "Priscilla and the Wimps," Peck paints a vivid portrait of a school being ruled by a bully named Monk Klutter and his gang, known as Klutter's Kobras. Monk thinks he has the entire school under his thumb until he runs into someone even bigger than him—a girl

"I admit this, too:
I paid up on a regular basis.
And I might add: so would you."

1   Listen, there was a time when you couldn't even go to the *rest room* in this school without a pass. And I'm not talking about those little pink tickets made out by some teacher. I'm talking about a pass that could cost anywhere up to a buck, sold by Monk Klutter.

2   Not that Mighty Monk ever touched money, not in public. The gang he ran, which ran the school for him, was his collection agency. They were Klutter's Kobras, a name spelled out in nailheads on six well-known black plastic windbreakers.

3   Monk's threads were more . . . **subtle.** A pile-lined suede battle jacket with lizard-skin flaps over tailored Levis and a pair of ostrich-skin boots, brassed-toed and suitable for kicking people around. One of his Kobras did nothing all day but walk a half step behind Monk, carrying a fitted bag with Monk's gym shoes, a roll of restroom passes, a cashbox, and a switchblade that Monk gave himself manicures with at lunch over at the Kobras' table.

4   Speaking of lunch, there were a few cases of advanced malnutrition among the newer kids. The ones who were a little slow in handing over a cut of their lunch money and were therefore barred from the cafeteria. Monk ran a tight ship.

5   I admit it. I'm five foot five, and when the Kobras slithered by, with or without Monk, I shrank. I admit this, too: I paid up on a regular basis. And I might add: so would you.

6   This school was old Monk's Garden of Eden. Unfortunately for him, there was a serpent in it. The reason Monk didn't recognize trouble when it was staring him in the face is that the serpent in the Kobras' Eden was a girl.

7   Practically every guy in school could show you his scars. Fang marks from Kobras, you might say. And they were all highly **visible** in the shower room: lumps, lacerations, blue bruises, you name it. But girls usually got off with a warning.

8 Except there was this one girl named Priscilla Roseberry. Picture a girl named Priscilla Roseberry, and you'll be light years off. Priscilla was, hands down, the largest student in our particular institution of learning. I'm not talking fat. I'm talking big. Even beautiful, in a bionic way. Priscilla wasn't **inclined** toward organized crime. Otherwise, she could have put together a gang that would turn Klutter's Kobras into garter snakes.

9 Priscilla was basically a loner except she had one friend. A little guy named Melvin Detweiler. You talk about The Odd Couple. Melvin's one of the smallest guys above midget status ever seen. A really nice guy, but, you know—little. They even had lockers next to each other, in the same bank as mine. I don't know what they had going. I'm not saying this was a romance. After all, people deserve their privacy.

10 Priscilla was sort of above everything, if you'll pardon the pun. And very calm, as only the very big can be. If there was anybody who didn't notice Klutter's Kobras, it was Priscilla.

11 Until one winter day after school when we were all grabbing our coats out of our lockers. And hurrying, since Klutter's Kobras made sweeps of the halls for after-school shakedowns.

12 Anyway, up to Melvin's locker swaggers one of the Kobras. Never mind his name. Gang members don't need names. They've got group identity. He reaches down and grabs little Melvin by the neck and slams his head against his locker door. The sound of skull against steel rippled all the way down the locker row, speeding the crowds on their way.

13 "Okay, let's see your pass," snarls the Kobra.

14 "A pass for what this time?" Melvin asks, probably still dazed.

15 "Let's call it a pass for very short people," says the Kobra, "a dwarf tax." He wheezes a little Kobra chuckle at his own wittiness. And already he's reaching for Melvin's wallet with the hand that isn't circling Melvin's windpipe. All this time, of course, Melvin and the Kobra are standing in Priscilla's big shadow.

16 She's taking her time shoving her books into her locker and pulling on a very large-size coat. Then, quicker than the eye, she brings the side of her **enormous** hand down in a chop that breaks the Kobra's hold on Melvin's throat. You could hear a pin drop in that hallway. Nobody'd ever laid a finger on a Kobra, let alone a hand the size of Priscilla's.

17 Then Priscilla, who hardly ever says anything to anybody except Melvin, says to the Kobra, "Who's your leader, wimp?" This practically blows the Kobra

Copyright © BookheadEd Learning, LLC

away. First he's chopped by a girl, and now she's acting like she doesn't know Monk Klutter, the Head Honcho of the World. He's so amazed, he tells her. "Monk Klutter."

18 "Never heard of him," Priscilla mentions. "Send him to see me." The Kobra just backs away from her like the whole **situation** is too big for him, which it is.

19 Pretty soon Monk himself slides up. He jerks his head once, and his Kobras slither off down the hall. He's going to handle this interesting case personally. "Who is it around here doesn't know Monk Klutter?"

20 He's standing inches from Priscilla, but since he'd have to look up at her, he doesn't. "Never heard of him," says Priscilla. Monk's not happy with this answer, but by now he's spotted Melvin, who's grown smaller in spite of himself. Monk breaks his own rule by reaching for Melvin with his own hands. "Kid," he says, "you're going to have to educate your girl friend."

21 His hands never quite make it to Melvin. In a move of pure poetry Priscilla has Monk in a hammerlock. His neck's popping like gunfire, and his head's bowed under the immense weight of her forearm. His suede jacket's peeling back, showing pile.

22 Priscilla's behind him in another easy motion. And with a single mighty thrust forward, frog-marches Monk into her own locker. It's incredible. His ostrich-skin boots click once in the air. And suddenly he's gone, neatly wedged into the locker, a perfect fit. Priscilla bangs the door shut, twirls the lock, and strolls out of school. Melvin goes with her, of course, trotting along below her shoulder. The last stragglers leave quietly.

23 Well, this is where fate, an even bigger force than Priscilla, steps in. It snows all that night, a blizzard. The whole town ices up. And school closes for a week.

"Priscilla and the Wimps" by Richard Peck from *Sixteen: Short Stories by Outstanding Writers for Young Adults* edited by Donald R. Gallo. Copyright © 1984. Used with permission of New York: Dell Publishing Company, Inc.

WRITE

PERSONAL RESPONSE: Write about a time that you have seen someone stand up to a bully or a threat, similar to the way Priscilla confronts Monk and the Kobras. In your response, compare the situation, the confrontation, and the result after the bully or threat was challenged.

Please note that excerpts and passages in the StudySync® library and this workbook are intended as touchstones to generate interest in an author's work. The excerpts and passages do not substitute for the reading of entire texts, and StudySync® strongly recommends that students seek out and purchase the whole literary or informational work in order to experience it as the author intended. Links to online resellers are available in our digital library. In addition, complete works may be ordered through an authorized reseller by filling out and returning to StudySync® the order form enclosed in this workbook.

Reading & Writing Companion   469

All Summer in a Day

FICTION
Ray Bradbury
1954

Introduction

studysync

Ray Bradbury (1920–2012) was an American writer best known for his works of science fiction. In Bradbury's short story "All Summer in a Day," the inhabitants of Venus live underground to avoid falling victim to the constant onslaught of rain. Only once every seven years does the rain stop and the sun comes out. Set in an elementary school classroom, a group of children await the sun's arrival. Only one of the kids, a girl named Margot who spent the first four years of her life on Earth, recalls the appearance of the sun. Rather than appreciating her knowledge, the other children in the class grow jealous and mean.

"I think the sun is a flower, That blooms for just one hour."

1 "Ready?"

2 "Ready."

3 "Now?"

4 "Soon."

5 "Do the scientists really know? Will it happen today, will it?"

6 "Look, look; see for yourself!"

7 The children pressed to each other like so many roses, so many weeds, intermixed, peering out for a look at the hidden sun.

8 It rained.

9 It had been raining for seven years; thousands upon thousands of days compounded and filled from one end to the other with rain, with the drum and gush of water, with the sweet crystal fall of showers and the concussion[1] of storms so heavy they were tidal waves come over the islands. A thousand forests had been crushed under the rain and grown up a thousand times to be crushed again. And this was the way life was forever on the planet Venus, and this was the schoolroom of the children of the rocket men and women who had come to a raining world to set up civilization and live out their lives.

10 "It's stopping, it's stopping!"

11 "Yes, yes!"

12 Margot stood apart from them, from these children who could not ever remember a time when there wasn't rain and rain and rain. They were all nine years old, and if there had been a day, seven years ago, when the sun came out for an hour and showed its face to the stunned world, they could not

---

1. **concussion** injury to the brain caused by a blow; usually resulting in loss of consciousness

Skill:
Point of View

The narrator uses a character's name and the pronouns they and she, and seems to stand outside the story. The narrator also knows what Margot and the other children feel and think. Therefore, the point of view must be omniscient. The narrator is not a character in the story.

Reading & Writing Companion

471

recall. Sometimes, at night, she heard them stir, in remembrance, and she knew they were dreaming and remembering gold or a yellow crayon or a coin large enough to buy the world with. She knew they thought they remembered a warmness, like a blushing in the face, in the body, in the arms and legs and trembling hands. But then they always awoke to the tatting drum, the endless shaking down of clear bead necklaces upon the roof, the walk, the gardens, the forests, and their dreams were gone.

13 All day yesterday they had read in class about the sun. About how like a lemon it was, and how hot. And they had written small stories or essays or poems about it: I think the sun is a flower, That blooms for just one hour. That was Margot's poem, read in a quiet voice in the still classroom while the rain was falling outside.

14 "Aw, you didn't write that!" protested one of the boys.

15 "I did," said Margot. "I did."

16 "William!" said the teacher.

17 But that was yesterday. Now the rain was slackening, and the children were crushed in the great thick windows.

18 "Where's teacher?"

19 "She'll be back."

20 "She'd better hurry, we'll miss it!"

21 They turned on themselves, like a feverish wheel, all tumbling spokes. Margot stood alone. She was a very frail girl who looked as if she had been lost in the rain for years and the rain had washed out the blue from her eyes and the red from her mouth and the yellow from her hair. She was an old photograph dusted from an album, whitened away, and if she spoke at all her voice would be a ghost. Now she stood, separate, staring at the rain and the loud wet world beyond the huge glass.

22 "What're you looking at?" said William.

23 Margot said nothing.

24 "Speak when you're spoken to."

25 He gave her a shove. But she did not move; rather she let herself be moved only by him and nothing else. They edged away from her, they would not look at her. She felt them go away. And this was because she would play no games with them in the echoing tunnels of the underground city. If they tagged her and ran,

she stood blinking after them and did not follow. When the class sang songs about happiness and life and games her lips barely moved. Only when they sang about the sun and the summer did her lips move as she watched the drenched windows. And then, of course, the biggest crime of all was that she had come here only five years ago from Earth, and she remembered the sun and the way the sun was and the sky was when she was four in Ohio. And they, they had been on Venus all their lives, and they had been only two years old when last the sun came out and had long since forgotten the color and heat of it and the way it really was. But Margot remembered.

26   "It's like a penny," she said once, eyes closed.

27   "No it's not!" the children cried.

28   "It's like a fire," she said, "in the stove."

29   "You're lying, you don't remember!" cried the children.

30   But she remembered and stood quietly apart from all of them and watched the patterning windows. And once, a month ago, she had refused to shower in the school shower rooms, had clutched her hands to her ears and over her head, screaming the water mustn't touch her head. So after that, dimly, dimly, she sensed it, she was different and they knew her difference and kept away. There was talk that her father and mother were taking her back to Earth next year; it seemed **vital** to her that they do so, though it would mean the loss of thousands of dollars to her family. And so, the children hated her for all these reasons of big and little **consequence**. They hated her pale snow face, her waiting silence, her thinness, and her possible future.

31   "Get away!" The boy gave her another push. "What're you waiting for?"

32   Then, for the first time, she turned and looked at him. And what she was waiting for was in her eyes.

33   "Well, don't wait around here!" cried the boy **savagely**. "You won't see nothing!"

34   Her lips moved.

35   "Nothing!" he cried. "It was all a joke, wasn't it?" He turned to the other children. "Nothing's happening today. *Is* it?"

36   They all blinked at him and then, understanding, laughed and shook their heads.

37   "Nothing, nothing!"

Skill:
Point of View

An omniscient narrator allows Bradbury to get across both Margot's and the other children's feelings. I think he wants readers to think about why there is conflict, not just about how Margot feels.

**Skill:
Media**

The text emphasizes how silent it is once the rain stops. In the video, the children are silent, and there's music playing. We get to see how confused they are because we can see their faces. When I visualized the story, I hadn't considered that they would be confused.

**Skill:
Media**

In the text, the sun is described in detail. In the video, there are close-ups of the children's faces as the sun peeks through. The video shows each child with a unique reaction. Like in the text, they scatter when the sun comes out.

38   "Oh, but," Margot whispered, her eyes helpless. "But this is the day, the scientists predict, they say, they *know*, the sun. . ."

39   "All a joke!" said the boy, and seized her roughly. "Hey, everyone, let's put her in a closet before the teacher comes!"

40   "No," said Margot, falling back.

41   They surged about her, caught her up and bore her, protesting, and then pleading, and then crying, back into a tunnel, a room, a closet, where they slammed and locked the door. They stood looking at the door and saw it tremble from her beating and throwing herself against it. They heard her muffled cries. Then, smiling, they turned and went out and back down the tunnel, just as the teacher arrived.

42   "Ready, children?" She glanced at her watch.

43   "Yes!" said everyone.

44   "Are we all here?"

45   "Yes!"

46   The rain slacked still more.

47   They crowded to the huge door.

48   The rain stopped.

49   It was as if, in the midst of a film concerning an avalanche, a tornado, a hurricane, a volcanic eruption, something had, first, gone wrong with the sound apparatus, thus muffling and finally cutting off all noise, all of the blasts and repercussions and thunders, and then, second, ripped the film from the projector and inserted in its place a beautiful tropical slide which did not move or tremor. The world ground to a standstill. The silence was so **immense** and unbelievable that you felt your ears had been stuffed or you had lost your hearing altogether. The children put their hands to their ears. They stood apart. The door slid back and the smell of the silent, waiting world came into them.

50   The sun came out.

51   It was the color of flaming bronze and it was very large. And the sky around it was a blazing blue tile color. And the jungle burned with sunlight as the children, released from their spell, rushed out, yelling into the springtime.

52 "Now, don't go too far," called the teacher after them. "You've only two hours, you know. You wouldn't want to get caught out!"

53 But they were running and turning their faces up to the sky and feeling the sun on their cheeks like a warm iron; they were taking off their jackets and letting the sun burn their arms. "Oh, it's better than the sun lamps, isn't it?"

54 "Much, much better!"

55 They stopped running and stood in the great jungle that covered Venus, that grew and never stopped growing, tumultuously, even as you watched it. It was a nest of octopi, clustering up great arms of flesh-like weed, wavering, flowering in this brief spring. It was the color of rubber and ash, this jungle, from the many years without sun. It was the color of stones and white cheeses and ink, and it was the color of the moon.

56 The children lay out, laughing, on the jungle mattress, and heard it sigh and squeak under them **resilient** and alive. They ran among the trees, they slipped and fell, they pushed each other, they played hide-and-seek and tag, but most of all they squinted at the sun until the tears ran down their faces; they put their hands up to that yellowness and that amazing blueness and they breathed of the fresh, fresh air and listened and listened to the silence which suspended them in a blessed sea of no sound and no motion. They looked at everything and savored everything. Then, wildly, like animals escaped from their caves, they ran and ran in shouting circles. They ran for an hour and did not stop running.

57 And then —

58 In the midst of their running one of the girls wailed.

59 Everyone stopped.

60 The girl, standing in the open, held out her hand.

61 "Oh, look, look," she said, trembling.

62 They came slowly to look at her opened palm. In the center of it, cupped and huge, was a single raindrop. She began to cry, looking at it. They glanced quietly at the sun.

63 "Oh. Oh."

64 A few cold drops fell on their noses and their cheeks and their mouths. The sun faded behind a stir of mist. A wind blew cold around them. They turned and started to walk back toward the underground house, their hands at their sides, their smiles vanishing away.

NOTES

65 A boom of thunder startled them and like leaves before a new hurricane, they tumbled upon each other and ran. Lightning struck ten miles away, five miles away, a mile, a half mile. The sky darkened into midnight in a flash.

66 They stood in the doorway of the underground for a moment until it was raining hard. Then they closed the door and heard the gigantic sound of the rain falling in tons and avalanches, everywhere and forever.

67 "Will it be seven more years?"

68 "Yes. Seven." Then one of them gave a little cry.

69 "Margot!"

70 "What?"

71 "She's still in the closet where we locked her."

72 "Margot."

73 They stood as if someone had driven them, like so many stakes, into the floor. They looked at each other and then looked away. They glanced out at the world that was raining now and raining and raining steadily. They could not meet each other's glances. Their faces were solemn and pale. They looked at their hands and feet, their faces down.

74 "Margot."

75 One of the girls said, "Well. . .?"

76 No one moved.

77 "Go on," whispered the girl.

78 They walked slowly down the hall in the sound of cold rain. They turned through the doorway to the room in the sound of the storm and thunder, lightning on their faces, blue and terrible. They walked over to the closet door slowly and stood by it.

79 Behind the closet door was only silence.

80 They unlocked the door, even more slowly, and let Margot out.

Reprinted by permission of Don Congdon Associates, Inc. Copyright (c) 1954, renewed 1982 by Ray Bradbury.

First Read

Read "All Summer in a Day." After you read, complete the Think Questions below.

☁ THINK QUESTIONS

1. How does Bradbury describe the sun? Citing at least two descriptive passages that you find in the text, explain what the sun means to the characters in the story.

2. Based on the text, how has life on Venus affected Margot? Cite specific evidence from the text to support your answer.

3. How do the children react to seeing the sun? Cite specific evidence from the text to support your answer.

4. Use context to determine the meaning of the word **immense** as it is used in paragraph 49. In your own words, define *immense* and explain how you found its meaning.

5. Read the following dictionary entry:

   consequence
   con•se•quence \ˈkän(t)-sə-ˌkwen(t)s\ *noun*

   1. a result or effect of an action or condition
   2. importance or relevance
   3. a conclusion reached by a line of reasoning

   Which definition most closely matches the meaning of **consequence** as it is used in paragraph 30? Write the correct definition of *consequence* here and explain how you figured out the correct meaning.

Reading & Writing Companion

Skill:
Point of View

Use the Checklist to analyze Point of View in "All Summer in a Day." Refer to the sample student annotations about Point of View in the text.

••• CHECKLIST FOR POINT OF VIEW

In order to identify the point of view of the narrator or speaker in a text, note the following:

- ✓ the speaker or narrator

- ✓ how much the narrator or speaker knows and reveals

- ✓ what the narrator or speaker says or does that reveals how they feel about other characters and events in the poem or story

To explain how an author develops the point of view of the narrator or speaker in a text, consider the following questions:

- ✓ Is the narrator or speaker objective and honest? Or do they mislead the reader? How?

- ✓ What is the narrator's or the speaker's point of view?

  - Is the narrator or speaker "all-knowing"; i.e., omniscient?

  - Is the narrator or speaker limited to revealing the thoughts and feelings of just one character?

  - Are there multiple narrators or speakers telling the story?

  - Are there multiple narrators or speakers telling the story?

  - Is the narrator a character within the story or telling the story from the "outside"?

- ✓ How does the narrator or speaker reveal his or her thoughts about the events or about the other characters in the story or poem? How do his or her experiences or cultural background affect those thoughts?

Skill:
Point of View

Reread paragraphs 56–62 from "All Summer in a Day." Then, using the Checklist on the previous page, answer the multiple-choice questions below.

1. If the story were told from a limited point of view from the perspective of Margot, how might paragraphs 56–62 be different?

   ○ A. The narrator would describe how the other children feel about being out in the sun.
   ○ B. The narrator would not be able to describe how the children feel, but only what they do or say.
   ○ C. The children would have to use the pronoun / to explain their own feelings.
   ○ D. The narrator would be asking the reader what he or she thought about the scene.

2. The author uses an omniscient point of view to achieve which of the following purposes?

   ○ A. To allow readers to empathize with the girl who catches the raindrop in her hand.
   ○ B. To reveal to readers the emotions the children feel about the sun.
   ○ C. To show the weather through one child's perspective.
   ○ D. To show the resilient quality of the rain.

Please note that excerpts and passages in the StudySync® library and this workbook are intended as touchstones to generate interest in an author's work. The excerpts and passages do not substitute for the reading of entire texts, and StudySync® strongly recommends that students seek out and purchase the whole literary or informational work in order to experience it as the author intended. Links to online resellers are available in our digital library. In addition, complete works may be ordered through an authorized reseller by filling out and returning to StudySync® the order form enclosed in this workbook.

Reading & Writing
Companion

479

Skill: Theme

Use the Checklist to analyze Theme in "All Summer in a Day ." Refer to the sample student annotations about Theme in the text.

••• CHECKLIST FOR THEME

In order to *infer* a theme in a text, note the following:

- ✓ the topic of the text

- ✓ whether or not the theme is stated directly in the text

- ✓ details in the text that may reveal the theme

    - the title and chapter headings

    - details about the setting

    - a narrator's or speaker's tone

    - a narrator's or speaker's point of view

    - characters' thoughts, actions, and dialogue

    - the central conflict in the story's plot

    - the resolution of the conflict

    - what the characters learn through their experiences

- ✓ analyze how characters are affected by the setting, the other characters and the problems they face, and what impact these may have on how the theme is developed

To determine a theme or central idea of a text and how it is conveyed through particular details, consider the following questions:

- ✓ What theme, message, or central idea is being communicated in the text?

- ✓ What details helped to reveal that theme or central idea?

- ✓ When did you become aware of that theme? For instance, did the story's conclusion reveal the theme?

Skill:
Theme

Reread paragraphs 13–15 of "Priscilla and the Wimps" and paragraphs 12–15 of "All Summer in a Day." Then, using the Checklist on the previous page, answer the multiple-choice questions below.

⟳ YOUR TURN

1. This question has two parts. First, answer Part A. Then, answer Part B.

Part A: From the excerpts above, the reader can infer that another theme across both texts is

- ○ A. Violence is not a successful way to solve problems.
- ○ B. People are often unkind toward those they perceive as different from themselves.
- ○ C. Sometimes people hide their fear by being mean to others.
- ○ D. It's better to avoid or hide from a bully than try to confront one.

Part B: The sentences from each text that best suggest this theme are —

- ○ A. From "Priscilla and the Wimps": "Okay, let's see your pass," snarls the Kobra. From "All Summer in a Day": "Aw, you didn't write that!" protested one of the boys.
- ○ B. From "Priscilla and the Wimps": He wheezes a little Kobra chuckle at his own wittiness. From "All Summer in a Day": That was Margot's poem, read in a quiet voice in the still classroom while the rain was falling outside.
- ○ C. From "Priscilla and the Wimps": "Let's call it a pass for very short people," says the Kobra, "a dwarf tax." From "All Summer in a Day": Margot stood apart from them, from these children who could not ever remember a time when there wasn't rain and rain and rain.
- ○ D. From "Priscilla and the Wimps": And already he's reaching for Melvin's wallet with the hand that isn't circling Melvin's windpipe. From "All Summer in a Day": But then they always awoke to the tatting drum, the endless shaking down of clear bead necklaces upon the roof, the walk, the gardens, the forests, and their dreams were gone.

Reading & Writing Companion **481**

Skill:
Media

Use the Checklist to analyze Media in "All Summer in a Day." Refer to the sample student annotations about Media in the text.

••• CHECKLIST FOR MEDIA

In order to determine how to compare and contrast reading a story, drama, or poem to listening to or viewing an audio, video, or live version of a text, do the following:

✓ think about the key features of the different media presentations

✓ consider how different kinds of media treat story elements in different ways

✓ note which details are emphasized or missing in each medium

✓ think about what you "see"—or visualize—as well as "hear" when you read a story, drama, or poem and how it compares to seeing it as a film, or hearing it read aloud

To compare and contrast the experience of reading a story, drama, or poem to listening to or viewing an audio, video, or live version of the text, including contrasts between what they "see" and "hear" as they are reading the text and what they perceive as they are listening or watching. Consider the following questions:

✓ What features of each medium are the most important?

✓ Do you listen to it or view it? Do you hear one voice or many? How do these affect the written work?

✓ Which details are missing or emphasized in each medium? What do you think are the reasons behind these choices, and what effect do they have?

✓ How is the way you picture a character in your mind as you read similar to the way that same character is portrayed in a filmed version of the same story? How is it different?

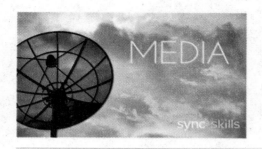

Skill:
Media

Reread paragraphs 53–56 from "All Summer in a Day." Then, using the Checklist on the previous page, answer the multiple-choice questions below.

⟳ YOUR TURN

1. What is the most significant difference between paragraphs 53–56 of the printed version and the video clip of the story "All Summer in a Day"?

   ○ A. The children speak in the story and they don't in the video clip.
   ○ B. The setting is different: the children are in a jungle in the story, but not in the video.
   ○ C. There are no differences.
   ○ D. The children don't lie down in the video, which they do in the text.

2. What is the most significant similarity between paragraphs 53–56 of the printed version and the video clip of the story "All Summer in a Day"?

   ○ A. Both versions emphasize that the sun is out.
   ○ B. Both versions emphasize how cruel the children are to Margot.
   ○ C. Both versions emphasize how excited the children are by having them run wildly.
   ○ D. They are not similar at all.

Close Read

Reread "All Summer in a Day." As you reread, complete the Skills Focus questions below. Then use your answers and annotations from the questions to help you complete the Write activity.

◎ SKILLS FOCUS

1. Identify places in "All Summer in a Day" where an omniscient point of view helps the author to achieve a specific purpose.

2. Identify a theme that is common to both "Priscilla and the Wimps" and "All Summer in a Day." Support your answer with evidence from both texts.

3. Although the narrator occasionally addresses the reader, "Priscilla and the Wimps" is told from the point of view of a character within the story. Highlight a passage in "All Summer in a Day" that deals with bullying. Compare the effectiveness of the point of view in that passage with the effectiveness of the

narrator's descriptions of bullying in "Priscilla and the Wimps."

4. Compare and contrast the scene in which the children experience the sun in "All Summer in a Day" in the printed text with the same scene in the video clip. Be sure to use textual evidence to support your response.

5. Identify evidence in "All Summer in a Day" that reveals how the children born on Venus change by the end of the story, and develop new character traits, or qualities. Explain what these new qualities are, what brings about the change, and why these new qualities are important.

✏ WRITE

COMPARE AND CONTRAST: Compare and contrast the points of view in "Priscilla and the Wimps" and "All Summer in a Day." Explain how the point of view in each text illustrates important themes about bullying. In your response, be sure to cite evidence from both texts.

Bullying in Schools

ARGUMENTATIVE TEXT
2014

Introduction

The writers of these two articles each believe that bullying is a serious problem that needs to be addressed. However, the writers disagree on the issue of whether schools are currently doing enough to face the challenge. One writer argues that schools have not invested nearly enough effort in creating safeguards and programs to protect students and prevent bullying. The other writer argues that most schools now take bullying very seriously and have initiated enough programs to address the problem effectively. Both writers present strong arguments and support their claims with evidence. Which argument do you feel is more convincing?

"Without getting to the root of the situation, the problem of bullying can never truly be solved."

Skill:
Arguments and
Claims

The writer restates the claim made in the title and follows with reasons why not enough is being done. In the last sentence, the writer makes another claim to convince readers why bullying is such a serious and immediate problem.

Skill:
Reasons and
Evidence

The statistic cited in paragraph 2 is evidence that supports the claim the author makes in the first sentence of the paragraph.

Bullying in Schools: Are we doing enough?

Point: Schools Are Not Doing Enough to Prevent Bullying

1   Although the media continues to raise public awareness of student bullying, many schools are still not doing enough to solve the problem. Most teachers and school administrators do not witness bullying. Sometimes they don't know how to recognize it. Sometimes they ignore it. They may also hold the age-old attitude that bullying is just something children do or go through. They think it's a normal part of growing up. But we know now that the **repercussions** of bullying can be lasting and **severe.** Sometimes they even end in tragedy.

2   The fact that a huge amount of bullying still happens demonstrates that not enough is being done about the issue. The exact number of victims is hard to determine because many incidents go unreported. The National Center for Education Statistics reported in 2013 that one of three students is bullied either in school or through social media. This statistic includes both physical and emotional harassment. Either form can leave lasting scars on victims. Students who are bullied often become very stressed. They can have trouble sleeping and begin to do poorly in school. Furthermore, victims are at a greater risk of suffering from low self-esteem, anxiety, and depression. These effects can even continue well into adulthood.

3   One way in which schools are failing to keep pace with the problem is in adequately supervising school property. Bullying usually happens in unsupervised areas like bathrooms, cafeterias, and school buses. The simplest solution would be for schools to put teachers, monitors, or aides in these areas. Unfortunately, many schools do not have enough staff to ensure that these areas are supervised.

4   An even harder venue to monitor for bullying is the Internet. Cyber-bullying, or bullying that happens over social media, is often extremely hard to track. It is easy to delete comments or pictures before authority figures can see them. In many cases there is little evidence to go on. Students, teachers, and administrators all need to be educated about how to deal with the challenge

of cyber-bullying. There are not currently enough programs that address this issue.

5 Most schools also do not have a clear procedure or policy for investigating bullying. This means that if a victim is brave enough to come forward and ask for help, he or she often does not receive it. This is because administrators and authorities do not have a set path for examining the situation. They do not have a plan for ending harmful situations.

Cyber-bulling can be hard for schools to monitor.

6 In addition to educating teachers and administrators about bullying, schools need more programs to help students themselves address the problem. Top-down approaches that simply dole out punishments for bullies are not enough to solve the problem. Students need to be taught more about the ways their words and actions can hurt others. They also need to learn that cases of bullying are often more complex than a "perpetrator" and a "victim." Often, a situation of **perceived** "bullying" is actually made up of several smaller events. Different students may have played different roles. A student may be bullied one day and become the bully the next. These complicated interactions and behavior can make it difficult to find a solution that will satisfy all parties.

7 Many schools have "zero-**tolerance**" policies regarding bullying. These policies are often not sensitive enough to students' particular needs and reasons for behaving the way they do. Every school is different, and student issues can vary widely. Teachers and administrators need to listen carefully to students' problems and perceived injustices, and be sensitive to them. If a student is punished for being a bully when he or she has a different perspective on the situation, that student may feel unfairly persecuted or "ganged-up on." Casting bullies as one-sided villains can be just as damaging to a student as being bullied.

8 Another issue with these "zero-tolerance" policies is that they can often encourage teachers and administrators to over-discipline students. Sometimes one-time or casual conflicts between students can be blown out of proportion. Students may be punished needlessly.

9 We need more policies and programs in place to educate students, teachers, administrators, and parents about what bullying is and how to recognize it. Policies and programs need to show how to end bullying, and, most importantly, what *causes* it. Most schools that do have anti-bullying strategies only deal with the surface of the problem. They don't address the underlying causes. Without getting to the root of the situation, the problem of bullying can never truly be solved.

Skill:
Arguments and Claims

The writer argues that programs and policies should be designed to help people understand fully what bullying is, why it happens, and how it can be stopped. He claims that existing anti-bullying strategies fail to go to the root of the problem, and until we understand what causes bullying the problem will remain unsolved.

"Some of the effort needs to be made on the part of the parents."

NOTES

Skill: Word Patterns and Relationships

The author mentions a workshop, then goes on to explain that Dave Seaburg delivers lessons and heads a program about bullying and how to empower students. I think that the program and lessons mentioned are part of the workshop, so a workshop must be "a presentation of helpful information to a larger group.

Counterpoint: Most Schools Are Doing Their Best to Stop Bullying

10   A group of students is playing on the playground. One boy pokes another in the back while waiting in line for the swings. "Knock it off," says the boy. "That's not nice."

11   "Oh, sorry," says the first boy, and stops. "I didn't really mean that."

12   This is the sort of response you might hear on the playground at a school in Forest Lakes, Minnesota, where Dave Seaburg is a teacher. In many schools across the country, bullying is being reduced or eliminated thanks to anti-bullying programs and policies. These programs are carried out by dedicated teachers like Mr. Seaburg. As part of an anti-bullying program, he leads workshops and provides lessons designed to teach students about the harmful effects of bullying. Students also learn ways to empower themselves against it. The school district where Dave Seaburg works has seen a steady decline in bullying since anti-bullying programs were implemented.

13   Schools across the United States are in fact doing an enormous amount to meet the challenge of bullying. As the media has heightened awareness of the issue, the attention devoted to solving the problem has been growing steadily. One example would be schools in the state of New Jersey. The first law against bullying in New Jersey schools was passed by the state legislature a little more than a decade ago. Within a few years, school districts were required to appoint an anti-bullying coordinator in every school. Today, according to the *Asbury Park Press,* each New Jersey school district spends more than thirty thousand dollars a year on supplies, software, additional personnel, and staff and teacher training devoted to anti-bullying measures.

14   How many school districts are expending this kind of effort? Certainly, many hundreds. More than forty-five states currently have laws on the books that direct school districts to adopt anti-bullying programs. Organizations from the National Education Association to the National Association of Student Councils are developing initiatives aimed at preventing bullying.

15 What exactly do school programs to prevent bullying do, and how do they work? There is no one single profile. A New Hampshire law states that all school staff must be trained to know what bullying looks like. People learn to spot the signs, and those who see bullying must report it. In Midland, Texas, police officers visit the schools to let students know that bullying is a crime. A school district in Miami, Florida has implemented several anti-bullying programs including Challenge Day and Girls Day Out. Girls Day Out teaches girls how they can deal with social issues in a positive way rather than resorting to bullying.

16 When it comes to cyberbullying, it can be extremely difficult for a school to monitor and police students' activity on social media. Some of the effort needs to be made on the part of the parents. When parents take an active role in their children's social media usage, it becomes much easier to keep track of what's going on. Also, students are less likely to cyberbully if they know their Internet activity is being supervised and they are being held accountable for their actions. Even in the arena of cyberbullying, however, there is a role schools can and do play. In more than a dozen states, schools have been authorized to take disciplinary action against students who engage in bullying that takes place off of school property.

17 For example, the state of California recently passed Seth's Law. This new law strengthens the anti-bullying legislation that is already in place. It requires all California public schools to regularly update their anti-bullying programs and policies. There are even provisions for cyber-bullying. Seth's Law also focuses on protecting students who are victims of bullying due to their race, gender, sexual orientation, religion, or disabilities. Seth's Law makes it mandatory for teachers and authority figures to take action against any bullying behavior that they witness.

18 If school anti-bullying programs vary widely, are there any general guidelines that can be recommended? Certainly controversial issues exist where school policies are concerned. Should bullies be suspended or otherwise punished, or should they be helped with counseling and anger management programs? Should bystanders who witness bullying and fail to report it be reprimanded? Should schools be involved at all, or is bullying a family matter, as some people contend?

19 The federal government hosts a website, http://stopbullying.gov, with information for students, parents, and teachers on the issue of bullying. It suggests a number of different measures that schools can implement. For teachers and staff, these measures include finding out why, when, and where bullying takes place; launching awareness campaigns; creating school safety committees; and building information into the student curriculum. The website

also recommends something that can be useful everywhere at all times—creating a culture of **civility** and tolerance.

20   Most schools are doing all they can to raise awareness, prevent, and ultimately eliminate bullying. If they devote any more time to anti-bullying education than they already do, it will take time away from core subjects like math and language arts. Anti-bullying programs are expensive for schools to run and they require highly trained staff.

21   Still, even with the very best anti-bullying programs and policies, it can take a long time for change to come about. It may be as many as three to ten years before an anti-bullying culture becomes standard all over the country. Though it may not seem like schools are doing enough because bullying still **persists**, even the most effective programs will take time to bring about the sort of change people are looking for.

First Read

Read "Bullying in Schools." After you read, complete the Think Questions below.

☁ THINK QUESTIONS

1. Use details from the text to explain the Point author's response to the issue of "Bullying in Schools." Cite the Point author's main claim and one reason why the author makes the claim. What evidence does the author use to support this position?

2. Use details from the text to explain the Counterpoint author's response to the issue of "Bullying in Schools." Cite the Counterpoint author's main claim and one reason why the author makes this claim. What evidence does the author use to support this position?

3. The Point author acknowledges that some schools have "zero-tolerance policies," but he or she is critical of them. Explain why the author criticizes these policies. Use textual evidence to support your answer.

4. Use context to determine the meaning of the word **severe** as it is used in "Point: Schools Are Not Doing Enough to Prevent Bullying." Write your definition of *severe* here and explain how you determined its meaning. Then, check your inferred definition both in context and with a dictionary.

5. The Latin root *per-* means "through or during" and the Latin *sistere* means "to stand." With this in mind, try to infer the meaning of the word **persists** as it is used in the final paragraph. Write your definition of *persists* here and explain how you determined its meaning.

Skill:
Arguments and Claims

Use the Checklist to analyze Arguments and Claims in "Bullying in Schools." Refer to the sample student annotations about Arguments and Claims in the text.

••• CHECKLIST FOR ARGUMENTS AND CLAIMS

In order to trace the argument and specific claims, do the following:

- ✓ identify clues that reveal the author's opinion in the title, introduction, or conclusion

- ✓ note the first and last sentence of each body paragraph for specific claims that help to build the author's argument

- ✓ list the information that the writer introduces in sequential order

- ✓ use a different color highlight to distinguish the writer's argument, claims, reasoning, and evidence

- ✓ describe the speaker's argument in your own words

To evaluate the argument and specific claims, consider the following questions:

- ✓ Does the writer support each claim with reasoning and evidence?

- ✓ Am I able to distinguish claims that are supported by reasons and evidence from those that are not?

- ✓ Do the writer's claims work together to support the writer's overall argument?

- ✓ Which claims are not supported, if any?

Skill:
Arguments and Claims

Reread paragraphs 13, 16, and 21 of the second writer's Counterpoint from "Bullying in Schools." Then, using the Checklist on the previous page, answer the multiple-choice questions below.

⟳ YOUR TURN

1. What claim does the writer make about the topic in paragraph 13?

   ○ A. The media is focusing on the issue of bullying.
   ○ B. Schools are making a big effort to meet the challenge of bullying.
   ○ C. Anti-bullying programs have been in schools for more than ten years.
   ○ D. New Jersey spends a lot of time and money on anti-bullying programs.

2. In paragraph 16, what claim does the writer make about addressing cyberbullying?

   ○ A. Parents need to be involved in monitoring social media usage.
   ○ B. Social media usage cannot be monitored.
   ○ C. Students will not cyberbully if Internet usage is supervised.
   ○ D. Schools cannot discipline bullying off school property.

3. In the conclusion of the counterpoint, in paragraph 21, what does the writer want readers to believe?

   ○ A. Effective bullying programs in schools are rare, even after ten years.
   ○ B. Bullying will persist no matter how effective programs are.
   ○ C. The best anti-bullying programs take effect in a short time.
   ○ D. It takes a long time for anti-bullying programs to work, so people need to be patient.

Skill:
Reasons and Evidence

Use the Checklist to analyze Reasons and Evidence in "Bullying in Schools." Refer to the sample student annotations about Reasons and Evidence in the text.

••• CHECKLIST FOR REASONS AND EVIDENCE

In order to identify claims that are supported by reasons and evidence, do the following:

✓ look for the argument the author is making

✓ identify the claim or the main idea of the argument

✓ find the reasons and evidence that support the claim

To distinguish claims that are supported by reasons and evidence from claims that are not, consider the following questions:

✓ What reasons does the author give to support his claim?

✓ What kinds of evidence does the author include to support his or her reasons?

✓ Does each piece of evidence support the claim? Why or why not?

✓ Are there any claims that are not supported by reasons and evidence? If so, what kinds of reasons or evidence would the author need to include?

Skill:
Reasons and Evidence

Reread paragraphs 4–5 of the Counterpoint argument. from "Bullying in Schools." Then, using the Checklist on the previous page, answer the multiple-choice questions below.

⟳ YOUR TURN

1. Which of the following best supports the claim that New Jersey is doing a lot to prevent bullying?

   ○ A. Every school must appoint an anti-bullying coordinator.

   ○ B. The news and media have covered the issue of bullying.

   ○ C. 45 states have created anti-bullying programs.

   ○ D. Teacher training for anti-bullying procedures are available.

2. Which of the following claims is NOT supported by evidence in the second paragraph of this passage?

   ○ A. Laws that attempt to prevent bullying in schools are in effect in many states.

   ○ B. New Jersey spends money each year on their anti-bullying platform.

   ○ C. There are extensive efforts being made in an attempt to prevent bullying.

   ○ D. Hundreds of other school districts are putting forth effort.

Skill: Word Patterns and Relationships

Use the Checklist to analyze Word Patterns and Relationships in "Bullying in Schools." Refer to the sample student annotations about Word Patterns and Relationships in the text.

••• CHECKLIST FOR WORD PATTERNS AND RELATIONSHIPS

In order to determine the relationship between particular words to better understand each of the words, note the following:

- ✓ any unfamiliar words in the text
- ✓ the surrounding words and phrases in order to better understand the meanings or possible relationships between words
- ✓ examples of part/whole, item/category, or other relationships between words, such as cause/effect, where what happens is a result of something
- ✓ the meaning of a word

To use the relationship between particular words to better understand each of the words, consider the following questions:

- ✓ Are these words related to each other in some way? How?
- ✓ What kind of relationship do these words have?
- ✓ Can any of these words be defined by using a part/whole, item/category, or cause/effect relationship?

Skill: Word Patterns and Relationships

Reread paragraphs 7–8 of the Counterpoint article in "Bullying in Schools." Then, using the Checklist on the previous page, answer the multiple-choice questions below.

🔁 YOUR TURN

1. In paragraph 7, the author explains that schools are allowed to take *disciplinary action* against bullies. Then, the author goes on to describe the intended results of *disciplinary action* in paragraph 8. This is an example of what kind of word relationship?

   ○ A. Word patterns
   ○ B. Cause/effect relationship
   ○ C. Part/whole relationship
   ○ D. Item/category relationship

2. How does recognizing the relationship between *disciplinary action* and the intended results help you to better understand the text?

   ○ A. The relationship between the term *disciplinary action* and the intended results allows the reader to understand the severity of cyberbullying and the necessity of prevention.
   ○ B. The relationship between *disciplinary action* and its intended results provides the reader with insight concerning how laws are made.
   ○ C. The relationship between *disciplinary action* and the intended results emphasizes the idea that there is not enough being done in school to prevent bullying.
   ○ D. The relationship between *disciplinary action* and the intended results highlights the understanding that schools don't have a bullying problem.

Please note that excerpts and passages in the StudySync® library and this workbook are intended as touchstones to generate interest in an author's work. The excerpts and passages do not substitute for the reading of entire texts, and StudySync® strongly recommends that students seek out and purchase the whole literary or informational work in order to experience it as the author intended. Links to online resellers are available in our digital library. In addition, complete works may be ordered through an authorized reseller by filling out and returning to StudySync® the order form enclosed in this workbook.

Reading & Writing Companion   **497**

Close Read

Reread "Bullying in Schools." As you reread, complete the Skills Focus questions below. Then use your answers and annotations from the questions to help you complete the Write activity.

◎ SKILLS FOCUS

1. Identify evidence that supports the claim made in the Point argument that many schools are not doing enough to prevent bullying. Explain how the evidence supports the claim.

2. Identify the evidence the writer of the Counterpoint argument uses to support the claim that schools are doing a lot to meet the challenges of bullying. Then, identify claims that are not supported by reasons or evidence.

3. Identify evidence from the Point and Counterpoint arguments that claims students can be taught not to bully and to protect themselves from being bullied. Explain how the evidence relates to the Essential Question: Which qualities of character matter most?

✏ WRITE

DEBATE: Which of the two arguments do you consider to be more persuasive? As you prepare for your debate, use the graphic organizer to consider how the arguments develop and if you think their claims will convince the readers. After choosing a position, justify your claims by citing reasons and evidence from the text in the debate with your classmates. After your debate, you will write a reflection in the space below.

Freedom Walkers:
The Story of the Montgomery Bus Boycott

INFORMATIONAL TEXT
Russell Freedman
2006

Introduction

studysync

Rosa Parks's famous refusal to give up her seat on a Montgomery, Alabama bus was part of a planned civil action. Nine months earlier, 15-year-old Claudette Colvin spontaneously made the same decision, confronting a Montgomery bus driver who told her to move.

"Claudette had been studying the U.S. Constitution and the Bill of Rights, and she had taken those lessons to heart."

NOTES

Chapter 2: Claudette Colvin

1   *"It's my constitutional right!"*

2   Two youngsters from New Jersey-sixteen-year-old Edwina Johnson and her brother Marshall, who was fifteen-arrived in Montgomery to visit relatives during the summer of 1949. No one told them about the city's segregation laws for buses, and one day they boarded a bus and sat down by a white man and boy.

3   The white boy told Marshall to get up from the seat beside him. Marshall refused. Then the bus driver ordered the black teenagers to move, but they continued to sit where they were. Up North, they were accustomed to riding integrated buses and trains. They didn't see now why they should give up their seats.

4   The driver called the police, and Edwina and Marshall were arrested. Held in jail for two days, they were convicted at a court hearing of violating the city's segregation laws. Judge Wiley C. Hill threatened to send them to reform school until they were twenty-one, but relatives managed to get them an attorney. They were fined and sent back to New Jersey.

5   During the next few years, other black riders were arrested and convicted for the same offense-sitting in seats reserved for whites. They paid their fines quietly and continued to ride the public buses. It took a spunky fifteen-year-old high school student to bring matters to a head.

6   Claudette Colvin was an A student at all-black Booker T. Washington High. She must have been paying attention in her **civics** classes, for she insisted on applying the lessons she had learned after boarding a city bus on March 2, 1955.

7   Claudette was on her way home from school that day. She found a seat in the middle of the bus, behind the section reserved for whites. As more riders got

on, the bus filled up until there were no empty seats left. The aisle was jammed with passengers standing, mostly blacks and a few whites.

8   The driver stopped the bus and ordered black passengers seated behind the white section to get up and move further back, making more seats available for whites. Reluctantly, black riders gave up their seats and moved into the crowded aisle as whites took over the vacated seats.

9   Claudette didn't move. She knew she wasn't sitting in the **restricted** white section. She felt that she was far enough back to be **entitled** to her seat. A pregnant black woman was sitting next to her. When the driver insisted that the woman get up and stand in the aisle, a black man in the rear offered her his seat, then quickly left the bus to avoid trouble.

10 Claudette was now occupying a double seat alone. "Hey, get up!" the bus driver ordered. Still she refused to move. None of the white women standing would sit in the empty seat next to Claudette. It was against the law for blacks to sit in the same row as a white person.

11 The driver refused to move the bus. "This can't go on," he said. "I'm going to call the cops." He did, and when the police arrived, he demanded that Claudette be arrested.

12 "Aren't you going to get up?" one of the police officers asked.

13 "No," Claudette replied. "I don't have to get up. I paid my fare, so I don't have to get up." At school, Claudette had been studying the U.S. Constitution and the Bill of Rights, and she had taken those lessons to heart. "It's my constitutional right to sit here just as much as that [white] lady," she told the police. "It's my constitutional right!"

14 Blacks had been arrested before for talking back to white officials. Now it was Claudette's turn. She was crying and madder than ever when the police told her she was under arrest. "You have no right to do this," she protested. She struggled as they knocked her books aside, grabbed her wrists, and dragged her off the bus, and she screamed when they put on the handcuffs.

15 "I didn't know what was happening," she said later. "I was just angry. Like a teenager might be, I was just downright angry. It felt like I was helpless." She remained locked up at the city jail until she was bailed out later that day by the pastor of her church.

16 Under Montgomery's segregation laws, Claudette was in fact entitled to her seat behind the whites-only section. If no seats were available for blacks to move back to as additional white passengers boarded the bus, then they

were not required to give up their seats. That was the official **policy.** But in actual practice, whenever a white person needed a seat, the driver would order blacks to get up and move to the back of the bus, even when they had to stand in the aisle.

Skill:
Compare and Contrast

I see similarities to Freedom's Daughters. The author mentions the NAACP and segregation. The author of Freedom Walkers describes how Claudette stood up for her rights and got others to join her, much like Barbara Johns did when she gathered student leaders for a strike in Freedom's Daughters.

17   Prosecutors threw the book at Claudette. She was charged not only with violating the segregation laws, but also with assault and **battery** for resisting arrest. "She insisted she was colored and just as good as white," the surprised arresting officer told the judge at the court hearing.

18   Claudette's arrest galvanized the black community. E.D. Nixon, an influential black leader, came to the teenager's defense. Nixon was employed as a railroad sleeping car porter, but his passion was working to advance human rights. A rugged man with a forceful manner and commanding voice, he founded the Montgomery chapter of the National Association for the Advancement of Colored People (NAACP). Nixon was recognized by blacks and whites alike as a powerful presence in the black community, a vital force to be reckoned with. It was said that he knew every white policeman, judge, and government clerk in town, and he was always ready to help anyone in trouble.

19   When Nixon heard about Claudette Colvin's arrest, he got in touch with Clifford Durr, a liberal white attorney in Montgomery. Together they contacted Fred Gray, a twenty-four-year-old black lawyer who agreed to represent Colvin in court. Gray had grown up in Montgomery, attended Alabama State, and gone to Ohio for law school, because Alabama didn't have a law school for blacks. He was one of only two black attorneys in town.

20   After a brief trial in juvenile court, Claudette was found guilty of assault. She was fined and placed on probation in her parents' custody. She had expected to be cleared, and when the judge announced his verdict, she broke into agonized sobs that shook everyone in the crowded courtroom.

21   "The verdict was a bombshell!" Jo Ann Robinson recalled. "Blacks were as near a breaking point as they had ever been."

22   E.D. Nixon and other black leaders wanted to take the entire bus segregation issue into federal court. They hoped to demonstrate that segregated buses were illegal under the U.S. Constitution. But first they needed the strongest possible case-the arrest of a black rider who was above reproach, a person of unassailable character and reputation who could withstand the closest scrutiny. Claudette Colvin, Nixon felt, was too young and immature, too prone to emotional outbursts, to serve as standard-bearer for a long and expensive constitutional test case. As Nixon pointed out, she had fought with police, she came from the poorer side of black Montgomery, and it was later rumored

that she was pregnant. "I had to be sure I had somebody I could win with. . . to ask people to give us a half million dollars to fight discrimination on a bus line," Nixon said later.

23   In October 1955, several months after Claudette was convicted, Mary Louise Smith, an eighteen-year-old black girl, was arrested when she refused to move to the back of the bus so a white woman could take her seat. "[The driver] asked me to move three times," Smith recalled. "And I refused. I told him, 'I am not going to move out of my seat. I am not going to move anywhere. I got the privilege to sit here like anybody else does.'"

24   Smith's case did not create the furor that the Colvin case did, because Smith chose to plead guilty. She was fined five dollars. Once again, Nixon decided that Smith, like Colvin, wasn't the right person to inspire a battle against bus segregation.

25   Two months later, on December 1, 1955, another black woman boarded a city bus and found an empty seat just behind the white section. She was Rosa Parks.

✎ WRITE

PERSONAL RESPONSE: Referring to the story of Claudette Colvin, and to your own experience, write a speech about courage. Before you write, think about the following questions: What motivates courage? How is it driven by emotion? How is courage influenced by one's values and strong beliefs? How is it driven by conditions in our society?

Please note that excerpts and passages in the StudySync® library and this workbook are intended as touchstones to generate interest in an author's work. The excerpts and passages do not substitute for the reading of entire texts, and StudySync® strongly recommends that students seek out and purchase the whole literary or informational work in order to experience it as the author intended. Links to online resellers are available in our digital library. In addition, complete works may be ordered through an authorized reseller by filling out and returning to StudySync® the order form enclosed in this workbook.

Reading & Writing Companion   **503**

Letter to Xavier High School

ARGUMENTATIVE TEXT
Kurt Vonnegut
2013

Introduction

Kurt Vonnegut (1922–2007) is one of the most celebrated and influential American novelists of the postmodern era. His works include the classic novels *Slaughterhouse-Five* and *Breakfast of Champions*. In 2006, a group of students at Xavier High School wrote a letter to Vonnegut trying to convince him to visit their school. Though age prevented him from attending in person, his written response was quintessential Vonnegut. "[D]o art and do it for the rest of your lives," he wrote, even if it means singing in the shower, writing and then destroying a poem, or pretending to be Count Dracula. Create for the sake of creating. Vonnegut passed away less than six months later at the age of 84.

"... starting right now, do art and do it for the rest of your lives"

1 Dear Xavier High School, and Ms. Lockwood, and Messrs Perin, McFeely, Batten, Maurer and Congiusta:

2 I thank you for your friendly letters. You sure know how to cheer up a really old geezer (84) in his sunset years. I don't make public appearances any more because I now **resemble** nothing so much as an iguana.

3 What I had to say to you, moreover, would not take long, to wit: **Practice** any art, music, singing, dancing, acting, drawing, painting, sculpting, poetry, fiction, essays, reportage, no matter how well or badly, not to get money and fame, but to experience becoming, to find out what's inside you, to make your soul grow.

4 Seriously! I mean starting right now, do art and do it for the rest of your lives. Draw a funny or nice picture of Ms. Lockwood, and give it to her. Dance home after school, and sing in the shower and on and on. Make a face in your mashed potatoes. Pretend you're Count Dracula.

5 Here's an assignment for tonight, and I hope Ms. Lockwood will flunk you if you don't do it: Write a six line poem, about anything, but rhymed. No fair tennis without a net. Make it as good as you possibly can. But don't tell anybody what you're doing. Don't show it or **recite** it to anybody, not even your girlfriend or parents or whatever, or Ms. Lockwood. OK?

6 Tear it up into teeny-weeny pieces, and **discard** them into widely separated trash recepticals [sic]. You will find that you have already been gloriously rewarded for your poem. You have experienced becoming, learned a lot more about what's inside you, and you have made your soul grow.

7 God bless you all!

Kurt Vonnegut

WRITE

PERSONAL RESPONSE: Vonnegut claims that any creative pursuit, whether as a hobby or career, has a significant and positive impact on a person's life. In your opinion, do you think schools today do enough to nurture and promote creativity? Support your response with evidence from the text as well as your own experiences.

Freedom's Daughters

The Unsung Heroines of the Civil Rights Movement from 1830 to 1970

INFORMATIONAL TEXT
Lynne Olson
2001

Introduction

Lynne Olson (b. 1949) is an American author and historian who includes the story of Barbara Johns in *Freedom's Daughters*, her book about the female champions of civil rights frequently neglected in history books. In 1950, Barbara Johns was a high school student in Farmville, Virginia who ran out of patience with the collection of tar-paper shacks they called a high school, and organized a student strike to take action.

"For six months, the students planned their strategy. They put it into effect on April 23, 1951."

From Chapter 4: Lighting the Fuse

1   Although she had spent much of her early life there, Farmville was a place where Barbara Johns never really felt she belonged. The seat of Prince Edward County, Farmville was a trading center for tobacco and lumber, a town that didn't seem to have changed much since Robert E. Lee and Ulysses S. Grant had separately stopped there in April 1865 on their way to end the Civil War at Appomattox Court House. In 1951, local blacks were barred from the hotel where the generals had rested, just as they were barred from Farmville's restaurants, its drugstore counters, and its only movie theater, bowling alley, and swimming pool. And, of course, its all-white public schools. The school Barbara Johns attended, Moton High School, featured "temporary" buildings that were really just tar-paper shacks, and classrooms that were usually too stuffy and hot in the fall and spring and too cold in the winter. For years, the all-white school district had been promising the black community a new school, but somehow it was never built. The blacks, despite their resentment, did not dare complain too loudly.

2   Barbara Johns could not understand such **docility**. Pretty and bright, she had always been an outspoken child; family members said she took after her uncle Vernon, the pastor of the Dexter Avenue Baptist Church in Montgomery, Alabama. The family didn't mean that as much of a compliment, but Barbara, who idolized her uncle, took it as one anyway. Vernon Johns was a hot-tempered crusader for civil rights, who railed at his congregation and other blacks for their **complacency** in the face of racial and other social injustice. Not much loved by the **affluent** black members of his church, he was destined to have a powerful influence on his young successor at Dexter Avenue, Martin Luther King, Jr.

3   When Johns visited Farmville, Barbara loved to hear him talk. "He was beyond the intellectual **scope** of everyone around the county," she said. "I remember that white men would . . . listen to him speak and shake their heads, not understanding his language." As much as she hero-worshipped her uncle,

Copyright © BookheadEd Learning, LLC

however, she didn't shy away from disagreeing with him. "We'd always be on opposite sides in an argument. I'm afraid we were both very **antagonistic**."

4   At Moton High School, Barbara Johns participated in the drama club, the chorus, and the student council. Those activities made it possible for her to travel to other black high schools around the state. Many, she couldn't help noticing, were in better shape than Moton. What bothered Johns and her fellow students most about their school were the tar-paper shacks, with their leaky roofs and pathetic woodstoves. An occasional motorist, driving by the school, would stop to ask the students what the shacks were. One man, told they were part of the school, responded: "School? Looks like a poultry farm!"

5   In the fall of 1950, Johns decided to take action on her own. She brought five other student leaders together for a **clandestine** student meeting in the bleachers of the school's athletic field. Farmville's black adults, she said, had made no headway in getting a new school. "Then," recalled one of the other students at the meeting, "she said our parents ask us to follow them but in some instances—and I remember her saying this very vividly—a little child shall lead them. She said we could make a move that would broadcast Prince Edward County all over the world."

6   For six months, the students planned their strategy. They put it into effect on April 23, 1951. Late that morning, Moton's principal, Boyd Jones, received a phone call from one of the conspirators, advising him that two of his students were about to be arrested by police at the Greyhound bus station. Jones left school in a hurry, never suspecting that the summons was a **ploy** to get him safely away so that a note with Jones's forged signature could be sent to each classroom, announcing an immediate school assembly. After the teachers and the school's 450 students gathered in the auditorium, the curtains on the stage parted and revealed Barbara Johns, not Boyd Jones, standing at the podium. She declared that the meeting was for students only and asked the teachers to leave. When some teachers protested, Johns removed one of her shoes and smacked it on a bench, "I want you out of here!" she shouted. At that, all the teachers left, some with student escorts. Then Johns got down to business. The time had come, she said, for dramatic action. Joined by the other student organizers, she called for a student strike and produced hand-lettered picket signs proclaiming "We Want a New School or None at All" and "Down with the Tar-Paper Shacks." The students cheered and marched out of the auditorium, with Barbara Johns in the vanguard.

7   The strike leaders sent a letter to the NAACP in Richmond that same afternoon. "We hate to impose as we are doing," the letter began, "but under the circumstances we are facing, we have to ask for your help." Three days later, two top civil rights lawyers were on their way to Farmville. By this time, the

Skill:
Central or Main
Idea

I can see that Barbara makes a decision to do something about the horrible conditions of her school, so she is a leader. I think the central idea of this text is that a young, African American girl stood up to injustice and was going to help get a better school.

Skill:
Central or Main
Idea

I believe these details support the idea that Barbara is standing up for injustice as she attempts to accomplish her goal.

NOTES

Skill:
Compare and
Contrast

The author of
Freedom's Daughters
also mentions the
NAACP and
segregation, so these
terms must be
important to know
when reading about the
civil rights movement.

NAACP had already decided to challenge "separate but equal" in favor of total desegregation. Although there may have been, as Richard Kluger has written, "no less promising place in all Virginia to wage the fight for equal schools," the NAACP lawyers were willing to try. In a shabby basement meeting room of a local church, they told the students and some parents that the NAACP would help them *only* if they were prepared to go for broke—desegregation or nothing—and then only if the students could demonstrate that they had the support of the adults in the black community. The strikers were stunned but enthusiastic. "It seemed like reaching for the moon," said Barbara Johns.

Excerpted from *Freedom's Daughters: The Unsung Heroines of the Civil Rights Movement from 1830 to 1970* by Lynne Olson, published by Touchstone.

First Read

Read *Freedom's Daughters: The Unsung Heroines of the Civil Rights Movement from 1830 to 1970.* After you read, complete the Think Questions below.

 THINK QUESTIONS

1. How was Barbara Johns similar to her uncle Vernon? What was their relationship like? Support your response with evidence from the text.

2. What can you infer about the people in the Farmville school district? Support your response with textual evidence.

3. Why did Barbara Johns decide to plan a student boycott? Cite evidence from the text in your response.

4. Use context to determine the meaning of the word **ploy** as it is used in *Freedom's Daughters.* Write your definition of *ploy* here and include an explanation of how details in the text helped your understanding.

5. Compare the meaning of **complacency** with words that are slightly different in meaning: *contentment, satisfaction, delight,* and *euphoria.* Check the different connotations in a dictionary.

Please note that excerpts and passages in the StudySync® library and this workbook are intended as touchstones to generate interest in an author's work. The excerpts and passages do not substitute for the reading of entire texts, and StudySync® strongly recommends that students seek out and purchase the whole literary or informational work in order to experience it as the author intended. Links to online resellers are available in our digital library. In addition, complete works may be ordered through an authorized reseller by filling out and returning to StudySync® the order form enclosed in this workbook.

Reading & Writing Companion **511**

Skill:
Central or Main Idea

Use the Checklist to analyze Central or Main Idea in *Freedom's Daughters: The Unsung Heroines of the Civil Rights Movement from 1830 to 1970.* Refer to the sample student annotations about Central or Main Idea in the text.

••• CHECKLIST FOR CENTRAL OR MAIN IDEA

In order to identify the central idea of a text, note the following:

- ✓ the topic or subject of the text
- ✓ the central or main idea, if it is explicitly stated
- ✓ details in the text that convey the theme

To determine the central idea of a text and how it is conveyed through particular details consider the following questions:

- ✓ What main idea do the details in one or more paragraphs explain or describe?
- ✓ What bigger idea do all the paragraphs support?
- ✓ What is the best way to state the central idea? How might you summarize the text and message?
- ✓ How do particular details in the text convey the central idea?

Skill:
Central or Main Idea

Reread paragraphs 2–3 of *Freedom's Daughters: The Unsung Heroines of the Civil Rights Movement from 1830 to 1970*. Then, using the Checklist on the previous page, answer the multiple-choice questions below.

⟳ YOUR TURN

1. This question has two parts. First, answer Part A. Then, answer Part B

Part A: Which of the following best represents the central or main idea of the excerpt?

- ○ A. Barbara Johns was meant to stand up and fight injustice.
- ○ B. Martin Luther King, Jr. was a strong influencer.
- ○ C. Barbara Johns admired her uncle Vernon's speeches.
- ○ D. Montgomery, Alabama was central to the civil rights movement.

Part B: Which of the following details best supports the central or main idea in Part A?

- ○ A. ". . . she had always been an outspoken child; family members said she took after her uncle Vernon . . ."
- ○ B. "The family didn't mean that as much of a compliment, but Barbara, who idolized her uncle, took it as one anyway."
- ○ C. "Not much loved by the affluent black members of his church, he was destined to have a powerful influence . . ."
- ○ D. "He was beyond the intellectual scope of everyone around the county . . .'"

Please note that excerpts and passages in the StudySync® library and this workbook are intended as touchstones to generate interest in an author's work. The excerpts and passages do not substitute for the reading of entire texts, and StudySync® strongly recommends that students seek out and purchase the whole literary or informational work in order to experience it as the author intended. Links to online resellers are available in our digital library. In addition, complete works may be ordered through an authorized reseller by filling out and returning to StudySync® the order form enclosed in this workbook.

Reading & Writing Companion   **513**

Skill:
Compare and Contrast

Use the Checklist to analyze Compare and Contrast in *Freedom's Daughters: The Unsung Heroines of the Civil Rights Movement from 1830 to 1970*. Refer to the sample student annotations about Compare and Contrast in the text.

••• CHECKLIST FOR COMPARE AND CONTRAST

In order to determine how to compare and contrast one author's presentation of events with that of another, use the following steps:

✓ first, choose two texts with similar subjects or topics, such as an autobiography and a biography of the same person, or a news report of an event and a narrative nonfiction account of the same event

✓ next, identify the author's approach to the subject in each genre

✓ after, explain how the point of view changes in each text

✓ finally, analyze ways in which the texts are similar and different in their presentation of specific events and information

  • whether the nonfiction narrative account contains dialogue that may not have been spoken, or may have been altered in some way

  • what the author of an autobiography might know that a biographer might never be able to uncover or research

To compare and contrast one author's presentation of events with that of another, consider the following questions:

✓ How does the author approach each topic or subject?

✓ What are the similarities and differences in the presentation of events in each text?

Skill:
Compare and Contrast

Reread paragraphs 5 and 6 of *Freedom Walkers: The Story of the Montgomery Bus Boycott* and paragraph 4 of *Freedom's Daughters: The Unsung Heroines of the Civil Rights Movement from 1830 to 1970*. Then, using the Checklist on the previous page, answer the multiple-choice questions below.

↻ YOUR TURN

1. Which of the following do both passages have in common?

   ○ A. They both present information about young men who were activists in the civil rights movement.

   ○ B. They both present information about women who came from families that were involved in the Civil Rights Movement

   ○ C. They both present information about teenage girls who stood up against racism during the civil rights movement.

   ○ D. They both highlight the unfair treatment of African Americans in regard to the poor condition of schools during the civil rights movement

Read the textual evidence from *Freedom Walkers* and *Freedom's Daughters* below. Then, using the Checklist on the previous page, complete the chart by choosing which piece of textual evidence contrasts the author's presentation in each text.

⟳ YOUR TURN

	Textual Evidence
A	"What bothered Johns and her fellow students most about their school were the tar-paper shacks, with their leaky roofs and pathetic woodstoves."
B	"During the next few years, other black riders were arrested and convicted for the same offense-sitting in seats reserved for whites."

Discrimination in *Freedom Walkers*	Discrimination in *Freedom's Daughters*

Close Read

Reread *Freedom's Daughters: The Unsung Heroines of the Civil Rights Movement from 1830 to 1970*. As you reread, complete the Skills Focus questions below. Then use your answers and annotations from the questions to help you complete the Write activity.

◎ SKILLS FOCUS

1. Determine the main idea of *Freedom's Daughters: The Unsung Heroines of the Civil Rights Movement from 1830 to 1970* and identify the details that support it.

2. Find evidence in *Freedom's Daughters: The Unsung Heroines of the Civil Rights Movement from 1830 to 1970 and Freedom Walkers: The Story of the Montgomery Bus Boycott*, in order to compare and contrast how each author presents events of the civil rights movement.

3. Describe how Barbara Johns would answer the question, "What qualities of character matter most?" Use evidence from the text to support your response.

✏ WRITE

COMPARE AND CONTRAST: In *Freedom Walkers: The Story of the Montgomery Bus Boycott*, fifteen-year-old Claudette Colvin refuses to give up her seat on a bus. By staying seated, she stood up for the rights of all African Americans. In *Freedom's Daughters: The Unsung Heroines of the Civil Rights Movement from 1830 to 1970*, another teenager, Barbara Johns, notices the unfair school conditions for African Americans and organizes a strike until the condition of her school is improved. Compare and contrast the main ideas of these two texts, noting how the authors present events in the civil rights movement. Be sure to use evidence from both texts in your response.

Celebrities as Heroes

ARGUMENTATIVE TEXT
2015

Introduction

There is no question that celebrities are frequently idolized as heroes, especially by young people. But do they deserve such admiration? The authors of these two articles have different opinions. One claims that most celebrities have not done enough to be called heroic, while the other argues that many celebrities do qualify as heroes for their achievements and cultural influence. Both writers present strong arguments and support their claims with evidence.

"They may think that if they act like their idol, they too will become famous."

Celebrities as Heroes: What makes someone a hero?

Point: Celebrities Should Not Be Idolized as Heroes

1. "Did you read what he said on Twitter? He's my hero!"

2. "Do you know what she did on vacation? She's my hero!"

3. "Did you hear how they finally tracked down the gang in the latest podcast? They're my heroes!"

4. "Did you see what she wore to that awards show? She's my hero!"

5. Today, many people use the word "hero" too lightly. They confuse the word "hero" with the word "celebrity." Right now, almost anyone can be a celebrity. But money, **notoriety**, and flamboyant behavior don't make someone a hero. Neither does playing the role of a hero on TV or in the movies. In fact, most celebrities don't deserve to be called heroes because they aren't heroes. They're people who are "celebrities" or "celebrated" for no other reason than because their fame has spread by word of mouth, the press, or social media. They may go to a thousand parties a month and are famous for being famous. We cannot regard these people as heroes in any way because they are all frivolous.

6. What makes a hero? Heroes have been defined as people who have admirable qualities. These can include strength, honesty, courage, and perseverance. They have done something that helped others in some way. For example, by refusing to give up her seat on a bus, Rosa Parks became a hero for **civil** rights, and her action inspired others to fight for equality. Firefighters, police officers, soldiers, and regular citizens have often acted heroically, and they have saved people from attacks and natural disasters. Heroes can also be individuals who have made a difference in people's lives. These people might include teachers, parents, coaches, and mentors.

NOTES

Skill:
Reasons and
Evidence

The writer has made the claim that celebrities should not be idolized as heroes. This is because most celebrities are not heroes. Then the writer adds to that reason by giving a definition of a celebrity as evidence.

NOTES

7   When celebrities are idolized just because they play heroes in movies and on television, they can end up overshadowing real heroes. They may get our attention, but they don't do much to change the world. This leaves young people with heroes who have little substance. The increase in this kind of hero worship is because more teenagers are using social media.

8   Psychologist Abby Aronowitz, Ph.D., says that the media is partly to blame for the hero worship of celebrities. She says that the media gives celebrities a lot of attention. However, many who work in the media claim that news about their idols is what people want to watch and read about. Celebrity sells.

9   Dr. Stuart Fischoff of the American Psychological Association says it's normal for people to idolize those who have fame and fortune. "We are sociologically preprogrammed to 'follow the leader,'" he says. However, if young people choose to idolize a celebrity who **indulges** in risky behavior, then they might be inspired to do the same. They may think that if they act like their idol, they too will become famous.

10   Many celebrities love that the media turns them into heroes, but some celebrities criticize these false images, and they don't want to be heroes. They don't want the pressure of being seen as role models. They don't want any mistakes they make to be reported. This will likely upset those who idolize them. However, young fans will continue to turn celebrities into heroes.

11   Convincing young people that celebrities do not make good role models or heroes will be difficult. So the media needs to focus on real heroes. Many can be found in history. Examples include Martin Luther King Jr., Eleanor Roosevelt, Gandhi, and Abraham Lincoln. There are also many everyday men and women who have acted heroically. Even though they have flaws as all humans do, their courage can inspire others. These people will still be heroes long after some celebrities are no longer remembered.

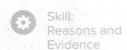

Skill:
Reasons and
Evidence

The writer is trying to support his claim that celebrities are not heroes by saying that celebrities don't want to be labeled that way. However, the writer doesn't provide any evidence to back up this claim. This point would be stronger if he had a quote from a real celebrity.

"If fans confuse mere celebrities with real heroes, they rob themselves of good role models."

Counterpoint: Celebrities Can Be Cultural Heroes

NOTES

12 After the baseball game is over, young fans line up to get autographs from their favorite players. The player who hit the home run that won the game is greeted with cheers. One fan yells, "You're my hero!"

13 Many actors, singers, and television stars are also idolized. They are all famous celebrities, but are they also heroes? Do they deserve or even want such admiration?

14 Society can be quick to sneer at celebrities who are idolized. Many people say that any contribution a celebrity makes is minor. Some people dismiss celebrities just because they *are* celebrities. Yet, there are many celebrities who are true heroes. These individuals may have struggled courageously to reach their goals and made outstanding achievements in their fields—sports, movies, music, fashion—that can inspire others.

Celebrities might be considered heroes because of their outstanding achievements, like winning the World Series.

15 Striving to be the best one can be at a sport or profession is not easy. It can require extraordinary skill. It takes determination, self-sacrifice, and dedication. Celebrities who struggle and work to be the best in their field can set good examples as role models.

16 Dr. Eric Hollander at the Mt. Sinai School of Medicine in New York City says "Celebrities can have a positive **influence** on our lives, with positive messages." This is especially true when fans appreciate a celebrity's abilities and achievements. They may idolize a soccer player's genuine ability to play well and score points. This admiration may lead young fans to work harder when they play soccer. They want to be like their hero.

 Skill: Arguments and Claims

The first and last sentences of paragraph 15 claim that celebrities who work hard should be admired, which supports the argument that celebrities can be heroes.

Copyright © BookheadEd Learning, LLC

Skill:
Arguments and
Claims

In paragraph 17, the
author lists two actors
and explains how they
have helped others. The
specific examples of
charitable celebrities
support the argument
that some celebrities
are heroic.

17 In addition, some celebrities have made outstanding contributions to charitable causes. Paul Newman was called one of the best actors of his time, but he also founded a food company that donates all of its profits to charity. In 2010 actress Sandra Bullock gave money to several charitable organizations. This was to help survivors of the 2010 earthquake in Haiti. Celebrities like these have a positive effect on people. Helping others is definitely something that heroes do.

18 Still, it's up to the fans to choose their heroes carefully. Fans need to know what qualities real heroes have and to look for these qualities in celebrities. They need to ask themselves if they are worshiping celebrities just because these people are famous or because they are true heroes. If fans confuse mere celebrities with real heroes, they rob themselves of good role models.

19 It's also up to the media to pay more attention to celebrities who are true role models. This is not always easy. Some celebrities are not necessarily looking for the media to shine a spotlight on their actions. They are involved in helping refugees, fighting for **conservation**, or working on other issues important to them. They aren't doing these things to increase their fame or to be admired as heroes.

20 Do people need heroes? Do dogs bark? All people need someone they can look up to and admire. If we are clear about the qualities we admire, we will be able to find many true role models among people we think of as "celebrities." But the individuals we choose to call our "heroes" can't be just any celebrities. They should be people who, by example or action, are trying to make a difference in other people's lives. Still, if you really believe in freedom, you should support the rights of people to choose whatever heroes they want.

First Read

Read "Celebrities as Heroes." After you read, complete the Think Questions below.

☁ THINK QUESTIONS

1. What is the main claim in the Point article? Use specific evidence from the text to support your answer.

2. What is the main claim in the Counterpoint article? Use specific evidence from the text to support your answer.

3. Why might celebrities want or not want to be viewed as heroes? Use specific evidence from the text to support your answer.

4. Use context clues to determine the meaning of the word **indulges** as it is used in paragraph 9 of the Point essay. Write your definition of *indulges* here and explain how you figured it out.

5. Read the following dictionary entry:

   civil
   civ•il \siv(ə)l\ *adjective*

   1. related to the people living in a country
   2. polite or courteous
   3. relating to public business or gatherings

   Which definition most closely matches the meaning of **civil** as it is used in paragraph 6? Write the correct definition of *civil* here and explain how you figured out the proper meaning.

Please note that excerpts and passages in the StudySync® library and this workbook are intended as touchstones to generate interest in an author's work. The excerpts and passages do not substitute for the reading of entire texts, and StudySync® strongly recommends that students seek out and purchase the whole literary or informational work in order to experience it as the author intended. Links to online resellers are available in our digital library. In addition, complete works may be ordered through an authorized reseller by filling out and returning to StudySync® the order form enclosed in this workbook.

Reading & Writing Companion   **523**

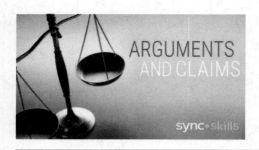

Skill:
Arguments and Claims

Use the Checklist to analyze Arguments and Claims in "Celebrities as Heroes ." Refer to the sample student annotations about Arguments and Claims in the text.

••• CHECKLIST FOR ARGUMENTS AND CLAIMS

In order to trace the argument and specific claims, do the following:

- ✓ identify clues that reveal the author's opinion in the title, introduction, or conclusion
- ✓ note the first and last sentence of each body paragraph for specific claims that help to build the author's argument
- ✓ list the information that the writer introduces in sequential order
- ✓ use a different color highlight to distinguish the writer's argument, claims, reasoning, and evidence
- ✓ describe the speaker's argument in your own wordsr

To evaluate the argument and specific claims, consider the following questions:

- ✓ Does the writer support each claim with reasoning and evidence?
- ✓ Am I able to distinguish claims that are supported by reasons and evidence from those that are not?
- ✓ Do the writer's claims work together to support the writer's overall argument?
- ✓ Which claims are not supported, if any?

Skill:
Arguments and Claims

Reread paragraphs 8 and 9 of the Counterpoint argument. of "Celebrities as Heroes." Then, using the Checklist on the previous page, answer the multiple-choice questions below.

⟲ YOUR TURN

1. This question has two parts. First, answer Part A. Then, answer Part B.

Part A: What claim is the author making in paragraph 8?

○ A. We should pay attention to the celebrities who try to make the world a better place.

○ B. All celebrities are heroes.

○ C. Most celebrities do not work on important issues, but should be considered heroes.

○ D. We should pay attention to celebrities who do not work on important issues.

Part B: Which of the following sentences best supports the claim from Part A?

○ A. "Do people need heroes?"

○ B. "They should be people who, by example or action, are trying to make a difference in other people's lives."

○ C. "All people need someone they can look up to and admire."

○ D. "Still, if you really believe in freedom, you should support the rights of people to choose whatever heroes they want."

Skill:
Reasons and Evidence

Use the Checklist to analyze Reasons and Evidence in "Celebrities as Heroes." Refer to the sample student annotations about Reasons and Evidence in the text.

••• CHECKLIST FOR REASONS AND EVIDENCE

In order to identify claims that are supported by reasons and evidence, do the following:

- ✓ look for the argument the author is making
- ✓ identify the claim or the main idea of the argument
- ✓ find the reasons and evidence that support the claim

To distinguish claims that are supported by reasons and evidence from claims that are not, consider the following questions:

- ✓ What reasons does the author give to support his claim?
- ✓ What kinds of evidence does the author include to support his or her reasons?
- ✓ Does each piece of evidence support the claim? Why or why not?
- ✓ Are there any claims that are not supported by reasons and evidence? If so, what kinds of reasons or evidence would the author need to include?

Skill:
Reasons and Evidence

Reread paragraphs 7–9 from the Point argument from "Celebrities as Heroes." Then, using the Checklist on the previous page, answer the multiple-choice questions below.

⟳ YOUR TURN

1. The kind of evidence used in paragraph 9 is —

   ○ A. a specific example
   ○ B. a quotation and expert opinion
   ○ C. numerical data
   ○ D. facts

2. How does the writer use the evidence in paragraph 9?

   ○ A. to support a claim that idolizing celebrities is not normal behavior
   ○ B. to warn that all celebrities indulge in risky behavior
   ○ C. to show how young people's normal behavior can turn into risky behavior
   ○ D. to emphasize that many young people need psychiatric help

3. Which of these three paragraphs supports the writer's argument the least?

   ○ A. paragraph 7
   ○ B. paragraph 8
   ○ C. paragraph 9
   ○ D. they all equally support the argument

Close Read

Reread "Celebrities as Heroes." As you reread, complete the Skills Focus questions below. Then use your answers and annotations from the questions to help you complete the Write activity.

◎ SKILLS FOCUS

1. Identify evidence that supports the Point claim that celebrities should not be idolized as heroes and the Counterpoint claim that celebrities can be cultural heroes. Explain how well the evidence or reasons support each claim.

2. Identify examples of claims that aren't supported by reasons or evidence in the Point and Counterpoint arguments. Explain what effect those unsupported claims have on the authors' arguments.

3. Highlight evidence from the Point or Counterpoint argument that suggests that character matters when determining whether a celebrity might qualify as a hero. Explain how the evidence supports the claim.

✎ WRITE

ARGUMENTATIVE: Which of the two arguments is less persuasive? In your response, include an analysis of the arguments, claims, reasons, and evidence the author uses in the argument you feel is less persuasive. Explain why you cannot commit to that argument by citing textual evidence from both texts to support your opinion.

Famous

POETRY
Naomi Shihab Nye
1995

Introduction

The word "famous" is used a dozen times over in Naomi Shihab Nye's relatively short poem of the same title. Yet the words "star," "celebrity," and even "fans" are not found anywhere in Nye's (b. 1952) nine stanzas. Instead, Nye creates a new definition of her titular word based on relationships that exist in nature and everyday life. Nye is an American poet and the daughter of a Palestinian refugee, born in St. Louis and raised in San Antonio and Jerusalem. She is known for exploring the mundane and overlooked elements around us, both on full display in "Famous,"

"The tear is famous, briefly, to the cheek."

NOTES

Skill:
Poetic Elements
and Structure

Nye uses the same pattern in these stanzas. First, she names an item. Then, she tells to whom or what the item is famous. This repetition creates a pattern that in turn, creates the structure of the poem.

Skill:
Poetic Elements
and Structure

The structure of the poem changes at line 15. Instead of naming an item and saying to what or whom it is famous, Nye starts the last two stanzas with the phrase "I want to be famous."

1 The river is famous to the fish.

2 The loud voice is famous to silence,
3 which knew it would **inherit** the earth
4 before anybody said so.

5 The cat sleeping on the fence is famous to the birds
6 watching him from the birdhouse.

7 The tear is famous, **briefly**, to the cheek.

8 The idea you carry close to your **bosom**
9 is famous to your bosom.

10 The boot is famous to the earth,
11 more famous than the dress shoe,
12 which is famous only to floors.

13 The bent photograph is famous to the one who carries it
14 and not at all famous to the one who is pictured.

15 I want to be famous to shuffling men
16 who smile while crossing streets,
17 sticky children in grocery lines,
18 famous as the one who smiled back.

19 I want to be famous in the way a pulley is famous,
20 or a buttonhole, not because it did anything **spectacular,**
21 but because it never forgot what it could do.

"Famous" from *Words Under the Words: Selected Poems* by Naomi Shihab Nye, copyright © 1995. Reprinted with the permission of Far Corner Books.

First Read

Read "Famous." After you read, complete the Think Questions below.

☁ THINK QUESTIONS

1. By the standards of the speaker, what does it mean to be famous? Cite two of the examples the speaker calls "famous" and explain why they are.

2. Why is the boot more famous than the dress shoe? Explain the meaning behind this description.

3. What makes the speaker want to be famous "the way a pulley is famous, / or a buttonhole" in the final stanza of the poem? What is significant about these objects?

4. Find the word **inherit** in stanza 2 of "Famous." Use context clues in the surrounding lines, as well as the line in which the word appears, to determine the word's meaning. Write your definition here and identify clues that helped you to figure out the meaning.

5. Which context clues helped you determine the meaning of **spectacular** in the last stanza? Use these to write your own definition of the word, and then check a dictionary to confirm.

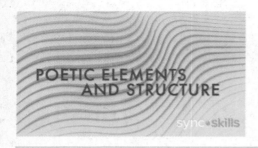

Skill:
Poetic Elements and Structure

Use the Checklist to analyze Poetic Elements and Structure in "Famous." Refer to the sample student annotations about Poetic Elements and Structure in the text.

••• CHECKLIST FOR POETIC ELEMENTS AND STRUCTURE

In order to identify elements of poetic structure, note the following:

- ✓ how the words and lines are arranged
- ✓ the form and overall structure of the poem
- ✓ the rhyme, rhythm, and meter, if present
- ✓ how the arrangement of lines and stanzas in the poem contribute to the poem's theme, or message

To analyze how a particular stanza fits into the overall structure of a text and contributes to the development of the theme, consider the following questions:

- ✓ What poetic form does the poet use? What is the structure?
- ✓ How do the lengths of the lines and stanzas affect the meaning?
- ✓ How does a poem's stanza fit into the structure of the poem overall?
- ✓ How does the form and structure affect the poem's meaning?
- ✓ In what way does a specific stanza contribute to the poem's theme?

Skill:
Poetic Elements and Structure

Reread lines 19–21 from "Famous." Then, using the Checklist on the previous page, answer the multiple-choice questions below.

↻ YOUR TURN

1. How does the final stanza affect the meaning of the poem?

   ○ A. The speaker shows that not everyone can be famous.
   ○ B. The speaker shows value for traditional fame.
   ○ C. The speaker shows that everyone can be important to someone.
   ○ D. The speaker shows the unimportance of fame.

2. Which line from the poem best describes the theme?

   ○ A. None of the lines from this stanza describe the theme.
   ○ B. Line 19: I want to be famous in the way a pulley is famous,
   ○ C. Line 20: or a buttonhole, not because it did anything spectacular,
   ○ D. Line 21: But because it never forgot what it could do

Close Read

Reread "Famous." As you reread, complete the Skills Focus questions below. Then use your answers and annotations from the questions to help you complete the Write activity.

◎ SKILLS FOCUS

1. Examine Nye's open-form poem. Explain how this structure and other poetic elements contribute to the poem's theme.

2. A poem's theme is the message the poet is trying to deliver. Identify how the poet's use of comparing and contrasting help you infer a theme in "Famous." Explain the theme using specific lines or stanzas from the poem.

3. Think about the message Nye is delivering about the true nature of fame. Highlight evidence in the poem that reveals the qualities of character that represent true fame. Explain what these qualities are.

✏ WRITE

LITERARY ANALYSIS: In her poem, Naomi Shihab Nye shakes up most people's ideas about what it means to be famous. Fame isn't about celebrity; it's about what's important. How does Nye's use of poetic elements and structure contribute to this theme? Be sure to cite evidence from the poem in your response.

Extended
Writing
Project and
Grammar

EXTENDED
WRITING
PROJECT
LITERARY ANALYSIS
WRITING

Literary Analysis Writing Process: Plan

PLAN	DRAFT	REVISE	EDIT AND PUBLISH

Reading true stories about influential people, such as Malala Yousafzai, can help us identify characteristics and actions that we consider noble or just. Reading about fictional characters who must face familiar and realistic struggles, like Margot in "All Summer in a Day," can help us develop empathy, or understanding. The texts in this unit feature a mix of the two—individuals demonstrating their personal best and authors and poets who share their ideas on the qualities of character that matter most.

WRITING PROMPT

As part of a school-wide character-building initiative, your school will be hosting a book club. The purpose of this club is to give all students an opportunity to read and discuss two texts (one informational and one literary) that help teach the qualities of character that matter most. To choose the texts you will read, your school has decided to let students submit proposals.

After reading the texts from the *Personal Best* unit, write a proposal in which you argue which texts would be the most effective for a school-wide book club. In your proposal, choose one informational and one literary text. Use textual evidence to help support an argument and explain how both of the texts you have chosen develop a theme or a main idea that communicates the qualities of character that matter most. Make sure your proposal includes the following:

- an introduction
- a thesis statement
- coherent body paragraphs with claims
- reasons and relevant evidence

- transitions
- a formal style
- a conclusion

Writing to Sources

As you gather ideas and information from the texts or sources in the unit, be sure to:

- include a claim about each one
- use evidence from each one

- avoid overly relying on one text or source

Introduction to Argumentative Writing

An argumentative essay is a form of persuasive writing where the writer makes a claim about a topic and then provides evidence—facts, details, examples, and quotations—to convince readers to accept and agree with the writer's claim. In order to provide convincing supporting evidence for an argumentative essay, the writer must often do outside research as well as cite the sources of the evidence that are presented in the essay.

A **literary analysis** is a form of argumentative writing that tries to persuade readers to accept the writer's interpretation of a literary text. Good literary analysis writing builds an argument with a strong claim, convincing reasons, relevant textual evidence, and a clear structure with an introduction, body paragraphs, and a conclusion. The characteristics of argumentative and literary analysis writing include:

- an introduction

- a claim or thesis

- textual evidence

- transitions

- a formal style

- a conclusion

As you continue with this Extended Writing Project, you'll receive more instruction and practice at crafting each of the characteristics of argumentative writing to create your own literary analysis.

Before you get started on your own literary analysis text, read this argument that one student, Samrah, wrote in response to the writing prompt. As you read the Model, highlight and annotate the features of argumentative writing that Samrah included in her literary analysis.

NOTES

☰ STUDENT MODEL

1   One quality of character that matters is bravery. Sometimes bravery means standing up for an idea or taking on bullies. That's what Malala Yousafzai did. The Taliban said she couldn't go to school. She went anyway and got shot. Now she speaks out for the right of all kids to go to school. For example, Malala says, "Education is education. We should learn everything and then choose which path to follow. Education is neither Eastern nor Western. It is human." Similarly, Priscilla, in "Priscilla and the Wimps," also stands up to bullies. Only these bullies are actually at her school. She's a loner but she takes action and speaks up when her friend gets bullied. Both Malala and Priscilla bravely stand up for what's right. Therefore, I nominate "Malala Yousafzai - Nobel Lecture" and the short story "Priscilla and the Wimps."

2   First, students will relate to the gripping story Malala tells about standing up to the Taliban. Malala is a young person with "a thirst for education" that the Taliban tried to end. When they said she and her classmates couldn't go to school anymore, Malala had two options. She could "remain silent and wait to be killed" or she could "speak up and then be killed." The Taliban shot her on her school bus, but she says "neither their ideas nor their bullets could win." Students will be inspired by her courage and strong beliefs.

3   "Priscilla and the Wimps" is an entertaining short story about a girl named Priscilla who stands up to a gang called "Klutter's Kobras." The gang, led by Monk Klutter, forces kids to pay up so they don't get "barred from the cafeteria" or worse. Most of the boys have "blue bruises" from getting beaten up. When one of the Kobras attacks Priscilla's only friend, Melvin, she steps in. Priscilla is quiet, large, and strong. With one "chop," she "breaks the Kobra's hold on Melvin's throat." She calls the Kobra a "wimp" and says she doesn't even know who Monk Klutter is. When Monk tries to grab Melvin, Priscilla puts him in a hammerlock. Students will laugh out loud reading this story while witnessing bravery in action.

Copyright © BookheadEd Learning, LLC

4   Both of these texts tell a story that will affect readers. However, what is most important is how each text teaches a message: You don't have to be an adult or big and powerful to be brave. We kids complain a lot about school; however, Malala's speech might make us see things differently. Malala recovered. She won the Nobel Peace Prize. Now she travels around the world fighting for the right of children to go to school. She tells the stories of children who live in Nigeria, India, and Syria. These are places where war or certain beliefs keep kids, especially girls, from going to school. Her speech is worth reading because it's a reminder that an education is a right not every kid in the world enjoys. Its message might make us feel more grateful for our school.

5   Priscilla, from "Priscilla and the Wimps," is also young and brave. In the text it states she "hardly ever says anything to anybody," but she takes action and speaks up when her friend gets bullied. Sometimes standing up to other kids can be intimidating. The narrator of the story, one of the scared kids, calls Priscilla's actions "a move of pure poetry." Priscilla inspires the narrator because she isn't afraid to take on the bad guys. Priscilla will certainly have that effect on readers, too. Any kid who's ever been bullied or just felt like an underdog will find this story interesting and satisfying to read.

6   These texts are the best fit for our book club because they show different ways of being brave. Malala faced threats and was nearly killed for wanting to go to school. She survived and now speaks to the world. In the text it states that when she speaks, it's in "the voice of those 66 million girls" that can't go to school. She is determined and brave. Priscilla is different. She's a loner who "was sort of above everything," but when her one friend is threatened, she takes on the school bully. Her act of bravery helps out the other kids. We should read these texts in our book club because they show how you have to be brave to stand up for what's right. If you want to get an education, you might have to fight for it. If you want freedom from bullies, sometimes you have to get tough. These are lessons in bravery that we can all benefit from.

✏ WRITE

Writers often take notes about their ideas before they sit down to write. Think about what you've learned so far about organizing literary analysis writing to help you begin prewriting.

- Which two texts will you choose to write about in your proposal?

- What about each of these texts suggests the qualities of character that matter most?

- What textual evidence will you include to make your proposal convincing?

- What kind of text structure would best suit your purpose for writing?

Response Instructions

Use the questions in the bulleted list to write a one-paragraph summary. Your summary should describe what you will include in your essay.

Don't worry about including all of the details now; focus only on the most essential and important elements. You will refer back to this short summary as you continue through the steps of the writing process.

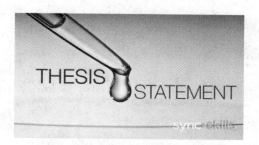

Skill:
Thesis Statement

••• CHECKLIST FOR THESIS STATEMENT

Before you begin writing your thesis statement, ask yourself the following questions:

- What is the prompt asking me to write about?

- What is the topic of my essay?

- What claim do I want to make about the topic of this essay? Is my opinion clear to my reader?

- Does my thesis statement introduce the body of my essay?

- Where should I place my thesis statement?

Here are some methods to introduce and develop your claim and topic:

- Think about the topic and central idea of your essay.

  > The central idea of an argument is stated as a claim, or what will be proven or shown to be true.

  > Identify as many claims as you intend to prove.

- Write a clear statement about the central idea or claim. Your thesis statement should:

  > let the reader anticipate the body of your essay.

  > respond completely to the writing prompt.

- Consider the best placement for your thesis statement.

  > If your response is short, you may want to get right to the point. Your thesis statement may be presented in the first sentence of the essay.

  > If your response is longer (as in a formal essay), you can build up your thesis statement. In this case, you can place your thesis statement at the end of your introductory paragraph.

Please note that excerpts and passages in the StudySync® library and this workbook are intended as touchstones to generate interest in an author's work. The excerpts and passages do not substitute for the reading of entire texts, and StudySync® strongly recommends that students seek out and purchase the whole literary or informational work in order to experience it as the author intended. Links to online resellers are available in our digital library. In addition, complete works may be ordered through an authorized reseller by filling out and returning to StudySync® the order form enclosed in this workbook.

Reading & Writing Companion   541

⟳ YOUR TURN

Read the sentences below from a paragraph of a previous draft of Samrah's proposal. Choose the sentence that best states the main idea of the paragraph.

Sentences
A. Her speech is worth reading because it reminds us that an education is a right that not every kid in the world enjoys.
B. We kids complain a lot about school; however, Malala's speech might make us see things differently.
C. However, what is most important is how each text teaches a message that you don't have to be a grown-up or big and powerful to be brave.
D. It might make us feel more grateful for our school.

Main Idea	Not the Main Idea

✏ WRITE

Use the questions in the checklist to write a thesis statement for your proposal.

Skill: Organizing Argumentative Writing

••• CHECKLIST FOR ORGANIZING ARGUMENTATIVE WRITING

As you consider how to organize your writing for your argumentative essay, use the following questions as a guide:

- What is my position on this topic?
- Have I chosen the best organizational structure to present my information?
- Can my claim be supported by logical reasoning and relevant evidence?
- Do I have enough evidence to support my claim?

Follow these steps to plan out the organization of your argumentative essay, including organizing your reasons and evidence clearly:

- identify your claim
  - > write a statement that will present your claim in the first paragraph
- choose an organizational structure that will present your claim effectively
- identify reasons and evidence that support your claim
- note that textual evidence can be proven to be true in other sources, and may be in the form of:
  - > numbers or statistics
  - > quotes from experts
  - > names or dates
  - > reference sources

YOUR TURN

Read each claim and the descriptions of each writer's overall purpose for writing below. Then, complete the chart by writing the organizational text structure that would best develop the thesis and achieve the writer's overall purpose.

Organizational Text Structure Options			
listing advantages and disadvantages	problem and solution	cause and effect	compare and contrast

Claim	Purpose	Organizational Text Structure
To deal with the problem of vandalism in schools, surveillance cameras should be placed in several locations.	to show how the problem of vandalism can be solved	
Although many people prefer dogs, cats are really the best pet a person can have.	to show the differences and similarities between cat ownership and dog ownership	
To combat the issue of bullying, the administration has proposed a zero-tolerance policy, but there are some disadvantages with this policy.	to explain why a zero-tolerance-for-bullying policy might not be the best solution	
If the mayor agrees to allow the factory to be built beside the river, the effects on the environment could be terrible.	to explain what will happen if a factory is built next to a river	

 WRITE

Use the steps in the checklist to plan out the organization of your argumentative essay/literary analysis.

Skill: Reasons and Relevant Evidence

••• CHECKLIST FOR REASONS AND RELEVANT EVIDENCE

As you begin to determine what reasons and relevant evidence will support your claim(s), use the following questions as a guide:

* What is the claim (or claims) that I am making in my argument?
* Are the reasons I have included clear and easy to understand?
* What relevant evidence am I using to support this claim?
* Have I selected evidence from credible sources, and are they relevant to my claim?
* Am I quoting the source evidence accurately?

Use the following steps as a guide to help you determine how you will support your claim(s) with clear reasons and relevant evidence, using credible sources:

* identify the claim(s) you will make in your argument
* establish clear reasons for making your claim(s)
* select evidence from credible sources that will convince others to accept your claim(s)

  > look for reliable and relevant sources of information online, such as government or educational websites

  > search print resources such as books written by an expert or authority on a topic

* explain the connection between your claim(s) and the evidence selected

YOUR TURN

Choose the best answer to each question.

1. The following is a section of text from a previous draft of Samrah's proposal. Samrah would like to add a sentence to support the idea that she has presented in the underlined sentence. Which of these could BEST follow and support the underlined sentence?

> In "Priscilla and the Wimps," Priscilla stands up to the bully Monk Klutter and his gang, the "Kobras."
> All the kids at the school are terrified of the gang because the Kobras collect money from them.
> <u>The kids pay up so they don't get "barred from the cafeteria" or worse.</u>

○ A. Priscilla is not afraid of Monk or the Kobras.

○ B. Most of the boys have "blue bruises" from getting beaten up.

○ C. Priscilla's friend Melvin is definitely afraid of the Kobras.

○ D. Any kid who has been bullied understands why.

2. The following is a paragraph from a previous draft of Samrah's proposal. Samrah has included a sentence that is not relevant to her literary analysis. Which sentence should be deleted from this paragraph?

> (1) When one of the Kobras attacks Melvin, Priscilla's only friend, she steps in. (2) Priscilla has difficulty making friends. (3) Large and strong, she "breaks the Kobra's hold on Melvin's throat" with one "chop." (4) She calls the Kobra a "wimp" and claims not to know who Monk Klutter is. (5) Priscilla puts Monk in a hammerlock when he tries to grab Melvin. (6) The narrator calls it "a move of pure poetry." (7) Then she stuffs Monk in a locker and walks away. (8) Priscilla isn't afraid to take on the bad guys.

○ A. sentence 2

○ B. sentence 3

○ C. sentence 5

○ D. sentence 8

 WRITE

Use the questions in the checklist to revise your proposal.

Literary Analysis Writing Process: Draft

| PLAN | DRAFT | REVISE | EDIT AND PUBLISH |

You have already made progress toward writing your proposal. Now it is time to draft your proposal.

WRITE

Use your plan and other responses in your Binder to draft your proposal. You may also have new ideas as you begin drafting. Feel free to explore those new ideas as you have them. You can also ask yourself these questions:

- Have I organized my ideas in a way that makes my argument clear to readers and responsive to the prompt?

- Is my thesis statement clearly stated, responsive to the prompt, and correctly placed?

- Have I supported my position with convincing reasons, evidence, and examples?

Before you submit your draft, read it over carefully. You want to be sure that you've responded to all aspects of the prompt.

Here is Samrah's draft of her proposal. As you read, identify details that Samrah includes in support of her thesis. As she continues to revise and edit her proposal, she will find and improve weak spots in her writing, as well as correct any language or punctuation mistakes.

STUDENT MODEL: FIRST DRAFT

~~One quality of character that matters is bravery. Sometimes bravery means standing up for an idea or taking on bullies. That's what Malala Yousafzai did. The Taliban said her couldn't go to school. She went anyway and got shot. Now she speaks out for the right of all kids to go to school. Priscilla in "Priscilla and the Wimps" stands up to the bullies at her school. She's a loner, but she takes action and speaks up when they friend gets bullied. Both Malala and Priscilla bravely stand up for what's right. That's why I nominate "Malala Yousafzai - Nobel Lecture" and the short story "Priscilla and the Wimps."~~

One quality of character that matters is bravery. Sometimes bravery means standing up for an idea or taking on bullies. That's what Malala Yousafzai did. The Taliban said she couldn't go to school. She went anyway and got shot. Now she speaks out for the right of all kids to go to school. For example, Malala says, "Education is education. We should learn everything and then choose which path to follow. Education is neither Eastern nor Western. It is human." Similarly, Priscilla, in "Priscilla and the Wimps," also stands up to bullies. Only these bullies are actually at her school. She's a loner but she takes action and speaks up when her friend gets bullied. Both Malala and Priscilla bravely stand up for what's right. Therefore, I nominate "Malala Yousafzai - Nobel Lecture" and the short story "Priscilla and the Wimps."

~~In her speach Malala shows that you don't have to be a grown up or big and powerful to be brave. She is still a young person. But she "had a thirst for education" that the Taliban tried to end. The Taliban shot her on her school bus, but Malala recovered. She won the Nobel Peace Prize. Now she travels around the world fighting for the write of children to go to school in her country of Pakistan and all around the world. We kids complain a lot about school but Malala's speech might make we see things differently. It's message might make us feel more grateful for our school.~~

Skill:
Introductions

Samrah reads her introduction. She wants to add a hook to grab the reader's attention. Therefore, Samrah adds a quote from Malala to clearly inform the reader of Malala's goal, and it provides an interesting hook for the reader.

First, students will relate to the gripping story Malala tells about standing up to the Taliban. Malala is a young person with "a thirst for education" that the Taliban tried to end. When they said she and her classmates couldn't go to school anymore, Malala had two options. She could "remain silent and wait to be killed" or she could "speak up and then be killed." The Taliban shot her on her school bus, but she says "neither their ideas nor the bullets could win." Students will be inspired by her courage and strong beliefs.

"Priscilla and the Wimps" is a entertaining short story, written by Richard Peck, about a girl, Priscilla, who stands up to a gang called "Klutter's Kobras." The Kobras are led by Monk Klutter, who terrifies the kids at school by collecting money from them. They're afraid of Monk and his gang. They pay up so they don't get "barred from the cafeteria" or worse. Most of the boys have "blue bruises" from getting beaten up. Priscilla is quiet, large, and strong. When one of the Kobras attacks Priscilla's only friend Melvin she steps in. With one "chop," she "breaks the Kobra's hold on Melvin's throat." She calls the Kobra a "wimp." She says she doesn't know who Monk Klutter is. When Monk tries to grab Melvin Priscilla puts he in a hammer lock. The narrator one of the scared kids calls it "a move of pure poetry." Then she stuffs Monk in a locker and walks away. Priscilla isn't afraid to take on the bad guys. Its like it doesn't effect her. Any kid who's ever been bullied or just felt left out will find this story interesting and satisfying to read.

Both of these texts tell a story that will affect readers. However, what is most important is how each text teaches a message: You don't have to be an adult or big and powerful to be brave. We kids complain a lot about school; however, Malala's speech might make us see things differently. Malala recovered. She won the Nobel Peace Prize. Now she travels around the world fighting for the right of children to go to school. She tells the stories of children who live in Nigeria, India, and Syria. These are places where war or certain beliefs keep kids, especially girls, from going to school. Her speech is worth reading because it's a reminder that an education is a right not every kid in the world enjoys. Its message might make us feel more grateful for our school.

Skill:
Style

Samrah wants to use domain-specific language in her writing. She decides to be specific and mention the Taliban by name. She also includes the phrase "and strong beliefs" in the last sentence because this language strongly relates to Malala's passion for education.

Skill:
Transitions

Samrah wants to use transitions to connect her ideas about what Malala went through, the message she is spreading, and why she is a great example for the quality of bravery. Samrah adds a paragraph to highlight these ideas and decides to use the word however *in two places to create cohesion among her ideas.*

Please note that excerpts and passages in the StudySync® library and this workbook are intended as touchstones to generate interest in an author's work. The excerpts and passages do not substitute for the reading of entire texts, and StudySync® strongly recommends that students seek out and purchase the whole literary or informational work in order to experience it as the author intended. Links to online resellers are available in our digital library. In addition, complete works may be ordered through an authorized reseller by filling out and returning to StudySync® the order form enclosed in this workbook.

Reading & Writing Companion   **549**

NOTES

Skill:
Conclusions

Samrah decides to add "because they show different ways of being brave" to her first sentence in order to restate the thesis more clearly. She also adds quotes about Malala and Priscilla to include details that show the depth of her knowledge about bravery. Finally, Samrah concludes her paragraph with a strong statement relating to the quality of character at the center of her analysis: bravery.

~~These texts are the best fit for we book club. Malala faced threats and was nearly killed for wanting to go to school. She survived and now speaks to the world. She is determined and brave. Priscilla is different. When her one friend is threatened, she takes on the school bully. She act of bravery helps out the other kids. We should read these texts in our book club because they show how you have to be brave to stand up for what's right.~~

These texts are the best fit for our book club because they show different ways of being brave. Malala faced threats and was nearly killed for wanting to go to school. She survived and now speaks to the world. In the text it states that when she speaks, it's in "the voice of those 66 million girls" that can't go to school. She is determined and brave. Priscilla is different. She's a loner who "was sort of above everything," but when her one friend is threatened, she takes on the school bully. Her act of bravery helps out the other kids. We should read these texts in our book club because they show how you have to be brave to stand up for what's right. If you want to get an education, you might have to fight for it. If you want freedom from bullies, sometimes you have to get tough. These are lessons in bravery that we can all benefit from.

Skill:
Introductions

Before you write your introduction, ask yourself the following questions:

- What is my claim? How can I introduce my claim(s) so it is clear to readers?

- What is the best way to organize my ideas, concepts, reasons, and evidence in a clear and logical order?

- How will you "hook" your reader's interest? You might:

  > start with an attention-grabbing statement

  > begin with an intriguing question

  > use descriptive words to set a scene

Below are two strategies to help you introduce your topic and claim, and organize reasons and evidence clearly in an introduction:

- Peer Discussion

  > Talk about your topic with a partner, explaining what you already know and your ideas about your topic.

  > Write notes about the ideas you have discussed and any new questions you may have.

  > Review your notes and think about what will be your claim or controlling idea.

  > Briefly state your claim or thesis.

  > Organize your reasons and evidence in an order that is clear to readers, presenting your reasons first followed by evidence.

  > Write a possible "hook."

- Freewriting

  > Freewrite for 10 minutes about your topic. Don't worry about grammar, punctuation, or having fully formed ideas. The point of freewriting is to discover ideas.

  > Review your notes and think about what will be your claim or controlling idea.

  > Briefly state your claim or thesis.

  > Organize your reasons and evidence in an order that is clear to readers, presenting your reasons first followed by evidence.

  > Write a possible "hook."

YOUR TURN

Choose the best answer to each question.

1. The following introduction is from an earlier draft of Samrah's proposal. Which sentence should Samrah add at the beginning to hook her reader?

> Malala Yousafzai was brave. The Taliban said her couldn't go to school. She went anyway and got shot. Now she speaks out for the right of all kids to go to school. Priscilla in "Priscilla and the Wimps" stands up to the bullies at her school. She's a loner, but she takes action and speaks up when they friend gets bullied. Both Malala and Priscilla bravely stand up for what's right. Therefore, I nominate "Malala Yousafzai - Nobel Lecture" and the short story "Priscilla and the Wimps."

- ○ A. Have you ever been brave?
- ○ B. Bravery, the most important quality of character, can be shown by standing up to all types of bullies.
- ○ C. Priscilla was brave, but Malala was even braver.
- ○ D. Bravery is shown in many ways.

2. Samrah would like to add transitions in order to organize the ideas of her introduction more clearly. Which transition or transitional phrase could be added to the beginning of sentence 5?

> (1) Malala Yousafzai was brave. (2) The Taliban said her couldn't go to school. (3) She went anyway and got shot. (4) Now she speaks out for the right of all kids to go to school. (5) Priscilla in "Priscilla and the Wimps" stands up to the bullies at her school.

- ○ A. Likewise,
- ○ B. Then,
- ○ C. Finally,
- ○ D. However,

 WRITE

Use the questions in the checklist to revise the introduction of your literary analysis.

Skill:
Transitions

••• CHECKLIST FOR TRANSITIONS

Before you revise your current draft to include transitions, think about:

- the key ideas you discuss in your body paragraphs
- the organizational structure of your essay
- the relationships among claim(s) and reasons

Next, reread your current draft and note areas in your essay where:

- the relationships between your claim(s) and the reasons and evidence are unclear, identifying places where you could add linking words or other transitional devices to make your argument clear and complete. Look for:

  > sudden jumps in your ideas

  > breaks between paragraphs where the ideas in the next paragraph are not connected to the previous

Revise your draft to use words, phrases, and clauses to clarify the relationships among claim(s) and reasons, using the following questions as a guide:

- Are there relationships between the claims, reasons, and evidence in my argument?
- Have I clarified, or made clear, these relationships?
- What linking words (such as conjunctions), phrases, or clauses could I add to my argument to clarify the relationships between the claims, reasons, and evidence I present?

YOUR TURN

Which transition would be most effective for each category of writing?

Transition Options	
A	meanwhile
B	for example
C	on the other hand

Type of Writing	Transition
informative	
narrative	
argumentative	

 YOUR TURN

Complete the chart by adding transitions into your literary analysis.

Transition	Transitional Sentence
although	
on the other hand	
however	
for example	

Skill: Style

••• CHECKLIST FOR STYLE

First, reread the draft of your argumentative essay and identify the following:

- places where you use slang, contractions, abbreviations, and a conversational tone
- areas where you could use subject-specific or academic language in order to help persuade or inform your readers
- moments where you use first-person (*I*) or second person (*you*)
- areas where sentence structure lacks variety
- incorrect uses of the conventions of standard English for grammar, spelling, capitalization, and punctuation

Establish and maintain a formal style in your essay, using the following questions as a guide:

- Have I avoided slang in favor of academic language?

- Did I consistently use a third-person point of view, using third-person pronouns (*he*, *she*, *they*)?

- Have I varied my sentence structure and the length of my sentences? Apply these specific questions where appropriate:

  > Where should I make some sentences longer by using conjunctions to connect independent clauses, dependent clauses, and phrases?

  > Where should I make some sentences shorter by separating any independent clauses?

- Did I follow the conventions of standard English including:

  > grammar?

  > spelling?

  > capitalization?

  > punctuation?

⟳ YOUR TURN

Choose the best answer to each question.

1. The following is from a previous draft of Samrah's proposal. How can the underlined sentence be rewritten in a more formal style?

> When Monk tries to grab Melvin, Priscilla puts him in a hammer lock. <u>If this doesn't make you laugh, I don't know what will.</u>

- ○ A. This is definitely the funniest part of the book.
- ○ B. Priscilla is brave.
- ○ C. You will laugh when reading this part.
- ○ D. Students will laugh out loud reading this story while witnessing bravery in action.

2. How can the following sentences be rewritten into more varied sentences, in keeping with a formal style?

> Priscilla is from "Priscilla and the Wimps." She is also young and brave. In the text it states she "hardly ever says anything to anybody." But she takes action and speaks up. She does this when her friend gets bullied.

- ○ A. Priscilla is. From "Priscilla and the Wimps." She is also young and brave. In the text it states she "hardly ever says anything to anybody," but she takes action and speaks up when her friend gets bullied.
- ○ B. Priscilla is from "Priscilla and the Wimps." She is also young and brave. But she takes action and speaks up when her friend gets bullied. Don't you think standing up to other kids is intimidating?
- ○ C. Priscilla, from "Priscilla and the Wimps," is also young and brave. In the text it states she "hardly ever says anything to anybody," but she takes action and speaks up when her friend gets bullied.
- ○ D. Priscilla, from "Priscilla and the Wimps," is also young and brave and in the text it states she "hardly ever says anything to anybody" but she takes action and speaks up when her friend gets bullied.

⟳ YOUR TURN

Complete the chart below by revising your draft to use a more formal and academic style. Look for areas in your draft in which you can vary the length of your sentences and use domain-specific language.

Style	Revised Sentence
academic/formal style	
varied sentence length and structure	
domain-specific language	

Skill:
Conclusions

••• CHECKLIST FOR CONCLUSIONS

Before you write your conclusion, ask yourself the following questions:

- How can I restate the thesis or main idea in my concluding section or statement? What impression can I make on my reader?

- How can I write my conclusion so that it follows logically from my argument?

- Should I include a call to action?

- How can I conclude with a memorable comment?

Below are two strategies to help you provide a concluding statement or section that follows from the argument presented:

- Peer Discussion

  > After you have written your introduction and body paragraphs, talk with a partner and tell them what you want readers to remember, writing notes about your discussion.

  > Review your notes and think about what you wish to express in your conclusion.

  > Do not simply restate your claim or thesis statement. Rephrase your main idea to show the depth of your knowledge, the importance of your idea, and encourage readers to adopt your view.

  > Write your conclusion.

- Freewriting

  > Freewrite for 10 minutes about what you might include in your conclusion. Don't worry about grammar, punctuation, or having fully formed ideas. The point of freewriting is to discover ideas.

  > Review your notes and think about what you wish to express in your conclusion.

  > Do not simply restate your claim or thesis statement. Rephrase your main idea to show the depth of your knowledge, the importance of your idea, and encourage readers to adopt your view.

  > Write your conclusion.

Please note that excerpts and passages in the StudySync® library and this workbook are intended as touchstones to generate interest in an author's work. The excerpts and passages do not substitute for the reading of entire texts, and StudySync® strongly recommends that students seek out and purchase the whole literary or informational work in order to experience it as the author intended. Links to online resellers are available in our digital library. In addition, complete works may be ordered through an authorized reseller by filling out and returning to StudySync® the order form enclosed in this workbook.

Reading & Writing
Companion

559

YOUR TURN

Choose the best answer to each question.

1. The following conclusion is from an earlier draft of Samrah's proposal. How can she rewrite the first, underlined sentence to better restate her thesis?

> <u>Both of these texts should be read by the book club.</u> Malala faced threats and was nearly killed for wanting to go to school. She survived and now speaks to the world. In the text it states that when she speaks, it's in "the voice of those 66 million girls" that can't go to school. She is determined and brave. Priscilla is different. She's a loner who "was sort of above everything," but when her one friend is threatened, she takes on the school bully. Her act of bravery helps out the other kids. We should read these texts in our book club because they show how you have to be brave to stand up for what's right. If you want to get an education, you might have to fight for it. If you want freedom from bullies, sometimes you have to get tough. These are lessons in bravery that we can all benefit from.

- ○ A. These texts are the best for learning about bravery.
- ○ B. These texts teach about bravery, and therefore are the best choice for our book club.
- ○ C. If you want to learn about bravery, you should totally pick these books for the book club.
- ○ D. Have you ever wanted to learn how to be brave?

2. Which sentence includes a call to action?

> (1) Her act of bravery helps out the other kids. (2) We should read these texts in our book club because they show how you have to be brave to stand up for what's right. (3) If you want to get an education, you might have to fight for it. (4) These are lessons in bravery that we can all benefit from.

- ○ A. sentence 1
- ○ B. sentence 2
- ○ C. sentence 3
- ○ D. sentence 4

 WRITE

Use the questions in the checklist to revise the conclusion of your literary analysis.

Literary Analysis Writing Process: Revise

PLAN	DRAFT	REVISE	EDIT AND PUBLISH

You have written a draft of your proposal. You have also received input from your peers about how to improve it. Now you are going to revise your draft.

← REVISION GUIDE

Examine your draft to find areas for revision. Keep in mind your purpose and audience as you revise for clarity, development, organization, and style. Use the guide below to help you review:

Review	Revise	Example
Clarity		
Highlight any place in your proposal where irrelevant information or sentence structure hinders clarity.	Revise sentences to remove irrelevant information and make the meaning clear.	"Priscilla and the Wimps" is an entertaining short story, ~~written by Richard Peck,~~ about a girl, named Priscilla, who stands up to a gang called "Klutter's Kobras." ~~The Kobras are led by Monk Klutter, who terrifies the kids at school by collecting money from them. They're afraid of Monk and his gang. They~~ The gang, led by Monk Klutter, forces kids to pay up so they don't get "barred from the school cafeteria" or worse.

Please note that excerpts and passages in the StudySync® library and this workbook are intended as touchstones to generate interest in an author's work. The excerpts and passages do not substitute for the reading of entire texts, and StudySync® strongly recommends that students seek out and purchase the whole literary or informational work in order to experience it as the author intended. Links to online resellers are available in our digital library. In addition, complete works may be ordered through an authorized reseller by filling out and returning to StudySync® the order form enclosed in this workbook.

Reading & Writing Companion   **561**

Review	Revise	Example
Development		
Identify places where you need to provide additional reasons or relevant evidence to support your thesis or main idea.	Focus on a single idea and add reasons, descriptions, details, evidence, or examples to support your idea.	Now she travels around the world fighting for the right of children to go to school. ~~in her country of Pakistan and all around the world.~~ She tells the stories of children who live in Nigeria, India, and Syria. These are places where war or certain beliefs keep kids, especially girls, from going to school.
Organization		
Review whether your text structure supports your purpose. Annotate places where the organization can be improved.	Rewrite information within paragraphs to improve organization.	~~Priscilla is quiet, large, and strong.~~ When one of the Kobras attacks Priscilla's only friend, Melvin, she steps in. Priscilla is quiet, large, and strong. With one "chop," she "breaks the Kobra's hold on Melvin's throat."
Style: Word Choice		
Identify places where stronger words or phrases would make your arguments more persuasive.	Select sentences to rewrite using words or phrases that appeal to emotions or logic.	Any kid who's ever been bullied or just felt ~~left out~~ like an underdog will find this story interesting and satisfying to read.
Style: Sentence Variety		
Review your proposal for choppiness. Create a better flow by combining some short sentences with transitions.	Rewrite choppy sentences to form more complex ones, using transitions when applicable.	She calls the Kobra a ~~"wimp." She~~ "wimp" and says she doesn't even know who Monk Klutter is.

✏ WRITE

Use the guide above, as well as your peer reviews, to help you evaluate your proposal to determine areas that should be revised.

Grammar: Commas with Nonessential Elements

Commas with Nonessential Elements

Use commas to set off the nonessential elements of a sentence. Nonessential elements are not necessary to understand the meaning of a sentence. Use commas to set off nonessential adjective clauses. Adjective clauses modify a noun or pronoun, and often start with the words *which, whom, who,* and *whose.*

	Example	Explanation
Nonessential	Now beside Athene appeared a young man more light-limbed than the stag, **whose eyes were like sparks of fire**. From Chapter I: Perseus	The adjective clause gives additional information about the young man. The clause is **nonessential**, so it is set off with commas.
Essential	So you will bring it safely back to me, and win to yourself renown, and a place among the heroes **who feast with the Immortals** upon the peak **where no winds blow."** From Chapter I: Perseus	The adjective clauses are necessary to make clear to which heroes and which peak the author is referring. The clauses are **essential**, so they require no commas.

Use commas to set off nonessential participles and participial phrases. Participles are verb forms that can function as adjectives.

	Example	Explanation
Nonessential	"You didn't think we were as easy as all that, **falling for that old stuff,** did you?" Charles Wallace demanded. A Wrinkle in Time	The present participle *falling* and its phrase give information about *we.* The participial phrase is **nonessential**, so it is set off with commas.

Use commas to set off words that interrupt the flow of thought in a sentence.

	Example	Explanation
Nonessential	Heinrich, **of course,** was looking for Homer's Troy. The Hero Schliemann: The Dreamer Who Dug for Troy	The phrase *of course* interrupts the flow of thought in the sentence. It is a **nonessential** element, and so it is set off with commas.

♺ YOUR TURN

1. Which, if any, change should be made to the sentence to punctuate it correctly?

> One lonely leaf shriveled by winter wind remained on the vine.

- ○ A. One lonely leaf, shriveled by winter wind remained on the vine.
- ○ B. One lonely leaf shriveled by winter wind, remained on the vine.
- ○ C. One lonely leaf, shriveled by winter wind, remained on the vine.
- ○ D. No change is needed.

2. Which, if any, change should be made to the sentence to punctuate it correctly?

> I am looking for a large house covered in ivy.

- ○ A. I am looking for a large house, covered, in ivy.
- ○ B. I am looking, for a large house covered in ivy.
- ○ C. I am looking, for a large house, covered in ivy.
- ○ D. No change is needed.

3. Which, if any, change should be made to the sentence to punctuate it correctly?

> The snow, drifting practically up to the rooftops blocked the sun.

- ○ A. The snow drifting practically up to the rooftops, blocked the sun.
- ○ B. The snow, drifting practically up to the rooftops, blocked the sun.
- ○ C. The snow drifting practically up to the rooftops blocked the sun.
- ○ D. No change is needed.

4. Which, if any, change should be made to the sentence to punctuate it correctly?

> If that is what you think, then hey you should say something.

- ○ A. If that is what you think, then hey, you should say something.
- ○ B. If that is what you think, then, hey, you should say something.
- ○ C. If that is what you think, then, hey you should say something.
- ○ D. No change is needed.

Grammar:
Using Pronouns

Pronouns should have a clear antecedent when taking the place of a noun the second time it appears in a sentence. Make sure that the antecedent of a pronoun is clearly stated and that a pronoun cannot possibly refer to more than one antecedent. Do not use the pronouns *this*, *that*, *which*, and *it* without a clearly stated antecedent. If a pronoun seems to refer to more than one antecedent, either reword the sentence to make the antecedent clear or eliminate the pronoun. Avoid the indefinite use of the pronouns *you* and *they*.

Text	Text with Unclear Pronoun-Antecedent Agreement	Explanation
While Feng Ru is little known in the United States, **his** fame in China is equivalent to the Wright brothers'. The Father of Chinese Aviation	Feng Ru, Orville Wright, and Wilbur Wright all accomplished flight, but **he** is little known in the United States.	In the second sentence, *he* could refer to either Feng Ru, Orville Wright, or Wilbur Wright.
Today, **many people** use the word "hero" too lightly. Celebrities as Heroes	Today, **they** use the word "hero" too lightly.	In the second sentence, it is unclear to whom *they* refers.

Consider these additional examples:

Clear	Unclear	Explanation
Some stagecoaches crossed this land, but **stagecoach travel** was very slow.	Some stagecoaches crossed this land, **which** was very slow.	In the unclear sentence, the antecedent of *which* is ambiguous. The first sentence clearly shows that *stagecoach travel* was very slow.
When the "Hallelujah Chorus" is performed, **everyone** should rise.	When the "Hallelujah Chorus" is performed, **you** should rise.	The pronouns *you* and *they* should not be used as indefinite pronouns. Instead, name the performer of the action.

↻ YOUR TURN

1. How should this sentence be rewritten?

> This was called the "great American desert," where they didn't live.

- ○ A. Change **where they didn't live** to **where few Americans lived**.
- ○ B. Change **where they didn't live** to **where you didn't live**.
- ○ C. Change **where they didn't live** to **where it didn't live**.
- ○ D. No change needs to be made to this sentence.

2. How should this sentence be rewritten?

> Then the mail carriers had to cross the plains to get to the western towns, which stretched for 1,500 miles.

- ○ A. Then the mail carriers had to cross the plains to get to the western towns, it stretched for 1,500 miles.
- ○ B. Then the mail carriers had to cross the plains, which stretched for 1,500 miles, to get to the western towns.
- ○ C. Then the mail carriers had to cross the plains to get to the western towns, you stretched for 1,500 miles.
- ○ D. No change needs to be made to this sentence.

3. How should this sentence be rewritten?

> Then in 1861, the first telegraph lines were stretched across the country, which allowed you to send messages.

- ○ A. Then in 1861, the first telegraph lines were stretched across the country, that allowed you to send messages faster.
- ○ B. Then in 1861, the first telegraph lines were stretched across the country, it allowed you to send messages faster.
- ○ C. Then in 1861, the first telegraph lines, which allowed messages to be sent faster, were stretched across the country.
- ○ D. No changes need to be made to this sentence.

commonly confused words

sync-skills

Grammar: Commonly Confused Words

Its vs. It's

Words that look and sound alike are sometimes misused or misspelled:

- *Its* is the possessive form of *it*.
- *It's* is a contraction of *it is* or *it has*.

Word	Text	Explanation
its	Troy was **its** name, a great city surrounded by strong walls. . . Black Ships Before Troy	*It* stands in for *Troy*. The name belongs to *Troy*, so the possessive form *its* is used.
it's	You open your eyes and everything's just like yesterday, only **it's** today. Eleven	The contraction *it's* can be replaced by *it is* without changing the meaning of the sentence.

Affect vs. Effect

Words that are similar are sometimes misused:

- *Affect* is a verb that means "to cause a change in."
- *Effect* is a noun that means "a result."

Word	Text	Explanation
affect	The breakdown of discipline likewise **affected** the dogs in their relations with one another. The Call of the Wild	*Affected* is the past tense of the verb *affect*, and it means "caused a change in."
effect	As part of an anti-bullying program, he leads workshops and provides lessons designed to teach students about the harmful **effects** of bullying. Bullying in Schools	*Effects* is used as a noun, and it means "results."

↻ YOUR TURN

1. Which sentence is written correctly?

    > 1. It's not easy to go to school and work a part-time job, but it is possible.
    >
    > 2. Ted's pet turtle is hiding in it's shell.
    >
    > 3. This old wooden chair lost it's legs when I sat on it.

    ○ A. 1
    ○ B. 2
    ○ C. 3
    ○ D. All sentences are written correctly.

2. Which sentence is written correctly?

    > 1. Its dangerous to walk on thin ice.
    >
    > 2. The coat is on its usual hook.
    >
    > 3. Its time to get ready for the holidays again.

    ○ A. 1
    ○ B. 2
    ○ C. 3
    ○ D. All sentences are written correctly.

3. Which sentence is written correctly?

    > 1. Beautiful falling snow can effect the view out the window.
    >
    > 2. Building a snowman can have an effect on the kids' excitement.
    >
    > 3. The snow had no affect on the school's decision to close early.

    ○ A. 1
    ○ B. 2
    ○ C. 3
    ○ D. All sentences are written correctly.

Literary Analysis Writing Process: Edit and Publish

PLAN	DRAFT	REVISE	EDIT AND PUBLISH

You have revised your proposal based on your peer feedback and your own examination.

Now, it is time to edit your proposal. When you revised, you focused on the content of your proposal. You probably looked at your proposal's thesis statement, introduction, and conclusion; organizational structure; style; transitions; reasons; and relevant evidence. When you edit, you focus on the mechanics of your proposal, paying close attention to things like grammar and punctuation.

Use the checklist below to guide you as you edit:

☐ Have I used commas correctly with nonessential elements?

☐ Have I used pronouns correctly?

☐ Have I been careful not to confuse *its* and *it's*, as well as *affect* and *effect*?

☐ Do I have any sentence fragments or run-on sentences?

☐ Have I spelled everything correctly?

Notice some edits Samrah has made:

- Added commas to set off nonessential elements.

- Replaced incorrect pronouns.

- Replaced *effect* with *affect* and *its* with *it's*.

Please note that excerpts and passages in the StudySync® library and this workbook are intended as touchstones to generate interest in an author's work. The excerpts and passages do not substitute for the reading of entire texts, and StudySync® strongly recommends that students seek out and purchase the whole literary or informational work in order to experience it as the author intended. Links to online resellers are available in our digital library. In addition, complete works may be ordered through an authorized reseller by filling out and returning to StudySync® the order form enclosed in this workbook.

Reading & Writing Companion 569

Both of these texts tell a story that will ~~effect~~ affect readers. However, what is most important is how each text teaches a message: You don't have to be an adult or big and powerful to be brave. We kids complain a lot about school; however, Malala's speech might make ~~them~~ us see things differently. Malala recovered. She won the Nobel Peace Prize. Now she travels around the world fighting for the right of children to go to school. She tells the stories of children who live in Nigeria, India, and Syria. These are places where war or certain beliefs keep kids, especially girls, from going to school. Her speech is worth reading because ~~its~~ it's a reminder that an education is a right not every kid in the world enjoys. ~~It's~~ Its message might make us feel more grateful for our school.

Priscilla, from "Priscilla and the Wimps," is also young and brave. In the text it states she "hardly says anything to anybody," but ~~he~~ she takes action and speaks up when her friend gets bullied. Sometimes standing up to other kids can be intimidating. The narrator of the story, one of the scared kids, calls Priscilla's actions "a move of pure poetry." Priscilla inspires the narrator because she isn't afraid to take on the bad guys. Priscilla will certainly have that ~~affect~~ effect on readers, too. Any kid who's ever been bullied or just felt like an underdog will find this story interesting and satisfying to read.

✏ WRITE

Use the questions above, as well as your peer reviews, to help you evaluate your proposal to determine areas that need editing. Then edit your proposal to correct those errors.

Once you have made all your corrections, you are ready to publish your work. You can distribute your writing to family and friends, hang it on a bulletin board, or post it on your blog. If you publish online, share the link with your family, friends, and classmates.

A Story of the South

Introduction

Imagine moving to another state and suddenly being ordered to leave a train station or sit at the back of a bus simply because of the color of your skin. How would you feel? How would you respond? These are the experiences and challenges faced by thirteen-year-old James Roberson, an African American boy growing up in the 1950's, whose family is forced to move from Ohio to Alabama at a time when the South was deeply segregated.

V VOCABULARY

treatment
the way that someone acts toward another person

surrender
to give up control or possession of

whim
a sudden desire

rebellion
uprisings against a government

elderly
older

terrifying
extremely frightening

NOTES

≡ READ

1 James Roberson's mother wanted to leave the South. She could not bear the racial hostility of the 1950s. The family moved to Ohio. There, James was judged by his southern accent rather than the color of his skin. The kids nicknamed him "Alabama," and they respected him because he was a good student. Then James and his family had to return to the South. James' dad could not find a job.

2 The train stopped in Decatur, Alabama, on the way back. James got off the train. He went into the station to get a snack. A woman suddenly shouted, "Get out of here!" James was stunned by this **treatment**. The woman had judged him on the color of his skin. He dashed back to the train and told his mother what had happened. She explained that black people in the South were not allowed in "all white" areas like the train station.

3   James quickly learned about discrimination. City buses in Birmingham, Alabama, were segregated based on city laws and the **whim** of the bus driver. Each bus had a green, wooden board. It fit on the back of bus seats. The board said, "Colored, do not sit beyond this board." The driver could decide any time to move the board. He could move it closer to the back of the bus. Then blacks sitting in front had to give up their seats to white people. An **elderly** black person might have to **surrender** his seat to a healthy white child.

4   When James was a teenager, he and his friends would throw the board away. They did this in **rebellion** against segregation. Sometimes they would sit right behind the bus driver. The driver would tell them to move. When they wouldn't, he would get off the bus and call for help. James and his friends would sneak off and disappear.

5   James was a member of a church led by Reverend Shuttlesworth. In 1956, the church parsonage was bombed. James lived nearby. The **terrifying** explosion broke windows in his house. The reverend surprisingly escaped injury. Armed blacks quickly gathered. James listened as the reverend urged people not to be violent.

First Read

Read the story. After you read, answer the Think Questions below.

☁ THINK QUESTIONS

1. Who is the main character in the story?

   The main character in the story is _____.

2. Write two or three sentences describing the setting of the story.

   The setting of the story_____

   _____.

3. At the end of the story, why were people worried?

   People were worried because _____

   _____.

4. Use context to confirm the meaning of the word *rebellion* as it is used in "A Story of the South." Write your definition of *rebellion* here.

   Rebellion means _____.

   A context clue is _____.

5. What is another way to say that a person is *elderly*?

   A person is _____.

Copyright © BookheadEd Learning, LLC

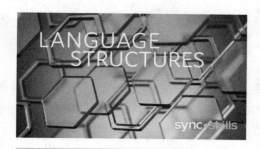

Skill:
Language Structures

★ **DEFINE**

In every language, there are rules that tell how to **structure** sentences. These rules define the correct order of words. In the English language, for example, a **basic** structure for sentences is subject, verb, and object. Some sentences have more **complicated** structures.

You will encounter both basic and complicated **language structures** in the classroom materials you read. Being familiar with language structures will help you better understand the text.

••• **CHECKLIST FOR LANGUAGE STRUCTURES**

To improve your comprehension of language structures, do the following:

✓ Monitor your understanding.

- Ask yourself: Why do I not understand this sentence? Is it because I do not understand some of the words? Or is it because I do not understand the way the words are ordered in the sentence?

✓ Pay attention to **perfect tenses** as you read. There are three perfect tenses in the English language: the present perfect, past perfect, and future perfect.

- **Present perfect tense** can be used to indicate a situation that began at a prior point in time and continues into the present.

  > Combine *have* or *has* with the past participle of the main verb.
  > Example: **I have played** basketball for three years.

- **Past perfect tense** can describe an action that happened before another action or event in the past.

  > Combine *had* with the past participle of the main verb.
  > Example: **I had learned** how to dribble a ball before I could walk!

> **Future perfect tense** expresses one future action that will begin and end before another future event begins or before a certain time.

> Use *will have* or *shall have* with the past participle of a verb.
>
> Example: Before the end of the year, **I will have played** more than 100 games!
>
> Example: By the time you play your first game, **I will have played** 100 games!

✓ Break down the sentence into its parts.

- Ask yourself: What actions are expressed in this sentence? Are they completed or are they ongoing? What words give me clues about when an action is taking place?

✓ Confirm your understanding with a peer or teacher.

YOUR TURN

Read each sentence in the first column. Write the action that happened first into the middle column. Write the action that happened second into the last column.

Sentences	First Past Action	Second Past Action
The class had stopped talking when the teacher walked into the room.		
When you arrived at the table, I had already finished my lunch.		
Jack likes Brazil's soccer team, so I gave him the jersey that I had bought in Brazil last month.		
My sister and I had cleaned our rooms before our mother asked us.		

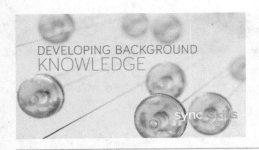

Skill: Developing Background Knowledge

★ DEFINE

Developing background knowledge is the process of gaining information about different topics. By developing your background knowledge, you will be able to better understand a wider variety of texts.

First, preview the text to determine what the text is about. To **preview** the text, read the title, headers, and other text features and look at any images or graphics. As you are previewing, identify anything that is unfamiliar to you and that seems important.

While you are reading, you can look for clues that will help you learn more about any unfamiliar words, phrases, or topics. You can also look up information in another resource to increase your background knowledge.

••• CHECKLIST FOR DEVELOPING BACKGROUND KNOWLEDGE

To develop your background knowledge, do the following:

- ✓ Preview the text. Read the title, headers, and other features. Look at any images and graphics.

- ✓ Identify any words, phrases, or topics that you do not know a lot about.

- ✓ As you are reading, try to find clues in the text that give you information about any unfamiliar words, phrases, or topics.

- ✓ If necessary, look up information in other sources to learn more about any unfamiliar words, phrases, or topics. You can also ask a peer or teacher for information or support.

- ✓ Think about how the background knowledge you have gained helps you better understand the text.

↻ YOUR TURN

Read each quotation from "A Story of the South." Imagine how you could develop your background knowledge. Write the letter of each strategy into the correct row.

Strategy	
A	You read an article about the Montgomery Bus Boycott.
B	You look at a map of the United States and find 'Ohio' and 'Alabama.'
C	You learn that your grandmother used trains to travel in 1950s.

Quotation	Strategy
"The family moved to Ohio. There, James was judged by his southern accent rather than the color of his skin. The kids nicknamed him 'Alabama,' and they respected him because he was a good student."	
"The train stopped in Decatur, Alabama, on the way back. James got off the train. He went into the station to get a snack."	
"City buses in Birmingham, Alabama, were segregated based on city laws and the whim of the bus driver."	

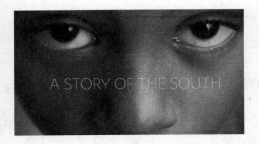

Close Read

✏️ **WRITE**

INFORMATIVE: In this text, James and his friends participated in several forms of "nonviolent protests" when riding the bus. Write a paragraph explaining what it means to participate in a nonviolent protest. Use details and examples from the text and your own background knowledge to support your ideas. Pay attention to spelling patterns and rules as you write.

Use the checklist below to guide you as you write.

☐ What is an injustice you experienced?

☐ How did you feel while it was happening?

☐ How did you react? What did you do?

Use the sentence frames to organize and write your informative paragraph.

An unjust experience that I had is _____.

It happened when _____.

I felt very _____.

I thought _____.

I reacted by _____.

It helped me _____.

Who's the Real Hero?

ARGUMENTATIVE TEXT

Introduction

Two writers try to answer the question: What is a hero? The first writer believes that a hero must be special. Many of the people we call heroes are merely human, but a real hero must have more. After all, heroes from history fought and died for others. The second writer believes that heroes may simply be good people who do good things. That writer does not believe that heroes belong to an exclusive club. Instead, we may find heroes right in our own backyards!

V VOCABULARY

designated
called by a particular name or title

venerate
to treat with great respect and admiration

merely
only; and nothing more

exclusive
open only to a select group

charitable
merciful or kind

NOTES

≡ READ

1   **Pro: Heroes Should Be Extraordinary**

2   It is boring to read yet another story about a local hero. The track star who runs like the wind is a hero. The woman who saved her own dog from a pond is a hero. Even a dog can be **designated** a hero, come to think of it. People love stories about brave dogs. The smoke alarm beeps. The dog barks. That doesn't seem heroic. It's more about saving oneself!

3   We should pick our heroes more carefully. Once, heroes were kings. They fought and died for others. Heroes' actions should be bold and brilliant. Did you invent a cure for cancer? You could be a hero. Did you yell, "Watch out for the car?" Not so much.

4   If an action is **merely** human, let's not call it heroic. If you see a falling brick, it's human to warn someone. If your dog falls in the water, it is **charitable** to help it out. These are acts that are part of being human. We should all be capable of such acts.

5   Rosa Parks was a hero. She risked her freedom to help others gain theirs. Stephen Hawking is a hero. He does amazing science from a wheelchair. Salvatore Guinta is a hero. He risked his life to save the members of his army squad. He won the Medal of Honor for his actions. Can you live up to their examples? You could be a hero. Did you make a basket that won the game? Not so much.

6   **Con: A Hero May Be Quite Ordinary**

7   For good reason, we **venerate** the work of soldiers. We admire firefighters. We appreciate our Founders. However, they aren't the only heroes we have. We should not set the bar too high. We might miss the heroes right in our own backyard.

8   Imagine a single mom. Her dreams are on hold, but her children are well fed and educated. She is a hero. Imagine a student athlete. He does well in school and on the ball field. He is a hero. Heroism is about honor, sacrifice, and excellence. It shouldn't be an **exclusive** club. Many people have what it takes to be heroes.

9   A true hero should be a mirror that we hold up to ourselves. A true hero should make us want to be better than we are. The ordinary hero gives us something to live up to. We want to be like him or her, and we can.

First Read

Read the story. After you read, answer the Think Questions below.

☁ THINK QUESTIONS

1. Whom does the first writer name as true heroes?

    The writer names _____

    _____.

2. Write two or three sentences describing why a single mom and a student athlete can be heroes.

    A single mom and a student athlete can be heroes because _____

    _____.

3. According to the second writer, what should a true hero do?

    A true hero should _____

    _____.

4. Use context to confirm the meaning of the word *exclusive* as it is used in "Who's the Real Hero?" Write your definition of *exclusive* here.

    Exclusive means _____.

    A context clue is _____.

5. What is another way to say that a person is *charitable*?

    A person is _____.

Skill:
Analyzing Expressions

★ **DEFINE**

When you read, you may find English expressions that you do not know. An **expression** is a group of words that communicates an idea. Three types of expressions are idioms, sayings and figurative language They can be difficult to understand because the meanings of the words are different from their **literal**, or usual, meanings.

An **idiom** is an expression that is commonly known among a group of people. For example: "It's raining cats and dogs" means it is raining heavily. **Sayings** are short expressions that contain advice or wisdom. For instance, "Don't count your chickens before they hatch" means do not plan on something good happening before it happens. **Figurative** language is when you describe something by comparing it with something else, either directly (using the words *like* or *as*) or indirectly. For example, "I'm hungry as a horse" means I'm very hungry. None of these expressions are about actual animals.

••• **CHECKLIST FOR ANALYZING EXPRESSIONS**

To determine the meaning of an expression, remember the following:

✓ If you find a confusing group of words, it may be an expression. The meaning of words in expressions may not be their literal meaning.

- Ask yourself: Is this confusing because the words are new? Or because the words do not make sense together?

✓ Determining the overall meaning may require that you use one or more of the following:

- context clues
- a dictionary or other resource
- teacher or peer support

✓ Highlight important information before and after the expression to look for clues.

Please note that excerpts and passages in the StudySync® library and this workbook are intended as touchstones to generate interest in an author's work. The excerpts and passages do not substitute for the reading of entire texts, and StudySync® strongly recommends that students seek out and purchase the whole literary or informational work in order to experience it as the author intended. Links to online resellers are available in our digital library. In addition, complete works may be ordered through an authorized reseller by filling out and returning to StudySync® the order form enclosed in this workbook.

Reading & Writing Companion   **585**

YOUR TURN

Read the following excerpt from the text. Then, complete the multiple-choice questions below.

---

from **"Who's the Real Hero?"**

It is boring to read yet another story about a local hero. The track star who <u>runs like the wind</u> is a hero. The woman who saved her own dog from a pond is a hero. Even a dog can be designated a hero, come to think of it. People love stories about brave dogs. The smoke alarm beeps. The dog barks. That doesn't seem heroic. It's more about saving oneself!

---

1. What does it mean to "run like the wind"?

    ○ A. make noise as you run

    ○ B. run where the wind blows

    ○ C. run extremely quickly

    ○ D. use your arms to help you run

2. A context clue that helps you understand the expression "runs like the wind" is:

    ○ A. another story

    ○ B. local hero

    ○ C. track star

    ○ D. saved her own dog

Skill:
Supporting Evidence

★ DEFINE

In some informational or argumentative texts, the author may share an opinion. This **opinion** may be the author's **claim** or **thesis**. The author must then provide readers with **evidence** that supports their opinion. Supporting evidence can be details, examples, or facts that agree with the author's claim or thesis.

Looking for supporting evidence can help you confirm your understanding of what you read. Finding and analyzing supporting evidence can also help you form your own opinions about the subject.

••• CHECKLIST FOR SUPPORTING EVIDENCE

In order to find and analyze supporting evidence, do the following:

✓ Identify the topic and the author's claim or thesis.

- Ask yourself: What is this mostly about? What is the author's opinion?

✓ Find details, facts, and examples that support the author's claim or thesis.

- Ask yourself: Is this detail important? How does this detail relate to the thesis or claim?

✓ Analyze the supporting evidence.

- Ask yourself: Is this evidence strong? Do I agree with the evidence?

Please note that excerpts and passages in the StudySync® library and this workbook are intended as touchstones to generate interest in an author's work. The excerpts and passages do not substitute for the reading of entire texts, and StudySync® strongly recommends that students seek out and purchase the whole literary or informational work in order to experience it as the author intended. Links to online resellers are available in our digital library. In addition, complete works may be ordered through an authorized reseller by filling out and returning to StudySync® the order form enclosed in this workbook.

Reading & Writing Companion **587**

YOUR TURN

Read the following excerpt from the text. Then, complete the multiple choice questions below.

---

from "Who's the Real Hero?"

Imagine a single mom. Her dreams are on hold, but her children are well fed and educated. She is a hero. Imagine a student athlete. He does well in school and on the ball field. He is a hero. Heroism is about honor, sacrifice, and excellence. It shouldn't be an exclusive club. Many people have what it takes to be heroes.

---

1. What is the author's claim?

   ○ A. Heroes are athletic and strong.
   ○ B. Heroes can be ordinary people.
   ○ C. Heroes are in an exclusive club.
   ○ D. Heroes should be well educated.

2. What examples does the author give as evidence?

   ○ A. Children who are well fed
   ○ B. A single mom and a student athlete
   ○ C. Many people who have what it takes
   ○ D. Anyone who has sacrificed for others

3. What actions are provided as evidence of "sacrifice"?

   ○ A. Putting dreams on hold for one's children
   ○ B. Feeding children while she goes hungry
   ○ C. Succeeding on the baseball field
   ○ D. Doing well in school and getting an education

4. What actions are provided as evidence of "excellence"?

   ○ A. Making sure that children are well fed
   ○ B. Attending the best possible schools
   ○ C. Surviving as a single mother
   ○ D. Being successful in academics and athletics

WHO'S
THE REAL
HERO?

Close Read

 WRITE

ARGUMENTATIVE: What do you think it takes to be a hero? Write a paragraph explaining your opinion. Use evidence from the text and from your own personal experience to support your argument. Pay attention to using negatives and contractions correctly as you write.

Use the checklist below to guide you as you write.

☐ Who are some of your personal heroes?

☐ Which text argument do your personal heroes more closely match?

☐ How would you describe heroism?

Use the sentence frames to organize and write your argument.

To be a hero, you should _____

_____.

For example, heroes should be _____

_____.

In my experience, real heroes _____

_____.

An example of a true hero, in my opinion, might be _____

_____

_____, because _____

_____.

studysync®

ASSIGNMENTS   BINDER   LIBRARY

Making Your Mark

UNIT 5

Making Your Mark

What's your story?

Genre Focus: **DRAMA**

Texts

Paired Readings

Extended Oral Project and Grammar

What's your story?

MELBA PATTILLO BEALS

Melba Pattillo Beals (b. 1941) was twelve years old when segregation in public schools was ruled unconstitutional by the Supreme Court in *Brown v. Board of Education* in 1954. Three years later, Beals would go down in history as among the first to integrate Little Rock Central High School as part of the Little Rock Nine. For weeks, Beals made headline news all around the country, and as she navigated a relationship with the media, she decided to pursue a career as a journalist and news reporter.

WILLIAM GIBSON

William Gibson (1914–2008) was a playwright who grew up in the Bronx. He prepared to write for the theater by first working as an actor, stage manager, and a prop person for the Topeka Civic Theater in Kansas. When his writing career took off in the 1950s, he garnered worldwide recognition for two plays, *The Miracle Worker* (1957) and *Two for the Seesaw* (1958). Both plays featured women at their center, and, like many of Gibson's scripts, dealt with historical eras and characters.

LANGSTON HUGHES

Poet, playwright, short story writer, and essayist Langston Hughes (1902–1967) was born in Joplin, Missouri. In 1926, his first book of poetry, *The Weary Blues*, marked the start of his renowned and prolific career as a writer. His writing pursued honest portraits of the African American working class and engaged the rhythms of jazz music through unadorned language. A prominent figure in the Harlem Renaissance, Hughes died in New York City in 1967.

SHIRLEY JACKSON

When American writer Shirley Jackson (1916–1965) broke onto the literary scene in 1948 with the publication of her short story, "The Lottery," readers of the *New Yorker* sent more letters than the magazine had ever received in response to a piece. The gruesome ritual of a New England community that Jackson described had been mistaken for truth. Later in Jackson's career, she turned toward stories that drew on her experience as a mother, often crafting stories about ordinary domestic life.

HELEN KELLER

Helen Keller (1880–1968) spent most of her life advocating for social and political issues, and co-founded the American Civil Liberties Union in 1920. Her autobiography, *The Story of My Life* (1903), tells of the illness that took Keller's sight and hearing at nineteen months old, and of the remarkable triumphs over adversity that would make her the first deaf-blind individual to receive a bachelor of arts degree.

PIRI THOMAS

Born to a Puerto Rican mother and Cuban father, Piri Thomas (1928–2011) grew up in Spanish Harlem in New York City. In his best-selling memoir *Down These Mean Streets* (1967), Thomas explored how the pressures of a childhood infused with racism and gang violence drew him into drug addiction, crime, and eventually prison. After serving his seven-year sentence, Thomas channeled his life experience toward helping at-risk youth through stories, lectures, and workshops.

DIANA CHANG

Diana Chang (1924-2009) was an author from New York City. She spent most of her childhood in China, and returned with her family to the United States to attend college and begin her career as a literary editor, and an author of fiction and poetry. Chang's first novel, *The Frontiers of Love* (1994), is considered the first major Chinese American literary work, and, like much of her writing, explores and challenges cross-cultural identity.

FAN KISSEN

Fan Kissen (1904–1978) was an American author of biographies of historical figures such as Sacagawea, Thomas Jefferson, Benjamin Franklin, and Clara Barton. In the 1940s and 1950s, Kissen had a radio series called *Tales from the Four Winds*, in which she transformed folktales from around the world into "plays for the loudspeaker," which were broadcast directly into classrooms at the time. Before becoming an author, Kissen taught elementary school in her home in New York City.

THANHHÀ LAI

Poet and novelist Thanhhà Lai (b. 1965) writes memorably about both of her homes—Vietnam and the United States. Lai fled Saigon in 1975 to live in Alabama and eventually earn college and graduate degrees in Texas and New York. She dedicated her first book to the millions of refugees in the world because she believes that stories of the displaced are "essential to understanding who we are, how we arrived in our home, and what responsibilities we have toward those still searching for a home."

LENSEY NAMIOKA

Lensey Namioka (b. 1929) cites adventure stories as her first love. At the age of nine, she moved with her family from China to the United States and initially excelled in math because numerals were the same in the English classroom as in her native country. She even became a professor of mathematics, before steering her career back to the creation of fiction. Namioka is best known for the Zenta and Matsuzo Samurai series, which follows the adventures of two 16th-century samurai warriors.

Warriors Don't Cry

INFORMATIONAL TEXT
Melba Pattillo Beals
1994

Introduction

In 1954, the Supreme Court decision *Brown v. Board of Education* declared that segregation was unconstitutional and schools must be integrated. To thwart the efforts of the Arkansas governor to keep the first nine black students, including Melba Pattillo Beals, out of Central High School, President Eisenhower sent federal troops to Little Rock to make sure the students got in safely. In this excerpt from her memoir, *Warriors Don't Cry*, Beals describes how the soldiers escorted them

"Groups of soldiers on guard were lined at intervals several feet apart."

Copyright © BookheadEd Learning, LLC

1   The next morning, Wednesday, September 25, at 8 A.M., as we turned the corner near the Bateses' home, I saw them, about fifty uniformed soldiers of the 101st. Some stood still with their rifles at their sides, while others manned the jeeps parked at the curb. Still other troops walked about holding walkie-talkies to their ears. As I drew nearer to them I was fascinated by their well-shined boots. Grandma had always said that well-kept shoes were the mark of a disciplined individual. Their guns were also glistening as though they had been polished, and the creases were sharp in the pant legs of their uniforms.

2   I had heard all those newsmen say "Screaming Eagle Division of the 101st," but those were just words. I was seeing human beings, flesh-and-blood men with eyes that looked back at me. They resembled the men I'd seen in army pictures on TV and on the movie screen. Their faces were white, their expressions blank.

3   There were lots of people of both races standing around, talking to one another in whispers. I recognized some of the ministers from our churches. Several of them nodded or smiled at me. I was a little concerned because many people, even those who knew me well, were staring as though I were different from them.

4   Thelma and Minnijean stood together inspecting the soldiers close up while the other students milled about. I wondered what we were waiting for. I was told there was an assembly at Central with the military briefing the students.

5   Reporters hung from trees, perched on fences, stood on cars and darted about with their usual urgency. Cameras were flashing on all sides. There was an **eerie** hush over the crowd, not unlike the way I'd seen folks behave outside the home of the deceased just before a funeral.

6   There were tears in Mother's eyes as she whispered good-bye. "Make this day the best you can," she said.

7   "Let's bow our heads for a word of prayer." One of our ministers stepped from among the others and began to say some comforting words. I noticed tears

NOTES

Skill:
Informational
Text Structure

The signal words "the next morning" as well as the day, date, and time are all clues that the author is presenting events in sequential order. This shows me that this is the beginning of a real-life account being told in the text.

NOTES

were streaming down the faces of many of the adults. I wondered why they were crying and just at that moment when I had more hope of staying alive and keeping safe than I had since the **integration** began.

8   "Protect those youngsters and bring them home. Flood the Holy Spirit[1] into the hearts and minds of those who would attack our children."

9   "Yes, Lord," several voices echoed.

10 One of the soldiers stepped forward and beckoned the driver of a station wagon to move it closer to the driveway. Two jeeps moved forward, one in front of the station wagon, one behind. Guns were mounted on the hoods of the jeeps.

11 We were already a half hour late for school when we heard the order "Move out" and the leader motioned us to get into the station wagon. As we collected ourselves and walked toward the caravan, many of the adults were crying openly. When I turned to wave to Mother Lois, I saw tears streaming down her cheeks. I couldn't go back to comfort her.

12 Sarge, our driver, was friendly and pleasant. He had a Southern accent, different from ours, different even from the one Arkansas whites had. We rolled away from the curb lined with people waving at us. Mama looked even more **distraught**. I remembered I hadn't kissed her good-bye.

13 Our convoy moved through streets lined with people on both sides, who stood as though they were waiting for a parade. A few friendly folks from our community waved as we passed by. Some of the white people looked totally horrified, while others raised their fists to us. Others shouted ugly words.

14 We pulled up to the front of the school. Groups of soldiers on guard were lined at intervals several feet apart. A group of twenty or more was running at breakneck speed up and down the street in front of Central High School, their rifles with **bayonets** pointed straight ahead. Sarge said they were doing crowd control—keeping the mob away from us.

15 About twenty soldiers moved toward us, forming an olive-drab square with one end open. I glanced at the faces of my friends. Like me, they appeared to be impressed by the **imposing** sight of military power. There was so much to see, and everything was happening so quickly. We walked through the open end of the square. Erect, rifles at their sides, their faces stern, the soldiers did not make eye contact as they surrounded us in a protective cocoon. After a long moment, the leader motioned us to move forward.

Skill:
Word Patterns and Relationships

I haven't seen the word breakneck used before, but it must be an adjective because it describes the speed of the soldiers.

I can see that the intensity of the crowd is causing the soldiers to rush. I can infer that the word breakneck means "extremely fast."

---

1. **Holy Spirit** In Christianity, the Holy Spirit is the third figure of the Trinity.

16 I felt proud and sad at the same time. Proud that I lived in a country that would go this far to bring justice to a Little Rock girl like me, but sad that they had to go to such great lengths. Yes, this is the United States, I thought to myself. There is a reason that I salute the flag. If these guys just go with us this first time, everything's going to be okay.

17 We began moving forward. The eerie silence of that moment would be forever etched into my memory. All I could hear was my own heartbeat and the sound of boots clicking on the stone.

18 Everyone seemed to be moving in slow motion as I peered past the raised bayonets of the 101st soldiers. I walked on the concrete path toward the front door of the school, the same path the Arkansas National Guard had blocked us from days before. We approached the stairs, our feet moving in unison to the rhythm of the marching click-clack sound of the Screaming Eagles. Step by step we climbed upward—where none of my people had ever before walked as a student. We stepped up the front door of Central High School and crossed the threshold into that place where angry segregationist[2] mobs had forbidden us to go.

Excerpted from *Warriors Don't Cry* by Melba Pattillo Beals, published by Washington Square Press.

2. **segregationist** a person who believes in enforced separation of people belonging to different racial groups

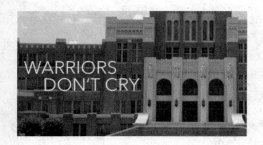

First Read

Read *Warriors Don't Cry*. After you read, complete the Think Questions below.

☁ THINK QUESTIONS

1. Refer to one or more details from the text to support your understanding of why soldiers are escorting Beals and other students—both from ideas that are directly stated and ideas that you have inferred from clues in the text.

2. Write two or three sentences exploring how the presence of the students affects different individuals in the crowd in different ways. Cite evidence from the text in your sentences.

3. Cite textual evidence to show how Beals feels about being escorted through the crowds.

4. Use context clues to determine the meaning of the word **distraught** as it is used in *Warriors Don't Cry*. Write your definition of *distraught* here and tell how you found it. Then, use a dictionary to confirm the precise pronunciation of *distraught*.

5. The Latin root *integrat-* most closely means "made whole" or "renewed." Using this information, what do you think the word **integration** means as it is used in paragraph 7? Write your best definition here and explain how you figured it out.

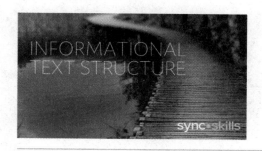

Skill:
Informational Text Structure

Use the Checklist to analyze Informational Text Structure in *Warriors Don't Cry*. Refer to the sample student annotations about Informational Text Structure in the text.

••• CHECKLIST FOR INFORMATIONAL TEXT STRUCTURE

In order to determine the overall structure of a text, note the following:

✓ the topic(s) and how the author organizes information about the topic(s)

✓ patterns in a paragraph or section of text that reveal the text structure, such as:

- sequences, including the order of events or steps in a process
- problems and their solutions
- cause-and-effect relationships
- comparisons

✓ the overall structure of the text and how each section contributes to the development of ideas

To analyze how a particular sentence, paragraph, chapter, or section fits into the overall structure of a text and contributes to the development of the ideas, use the following questions as a guide:

✓ What organizational patterns reveal the text structure the author uses to present information?

✓ How does a particular sentence, paragraph, chapter, or section fit into the overall structure of the text? How does it affect the development of the author's ideas?

✓ In what ways does the text structure contribute to the development of ideas in the text?

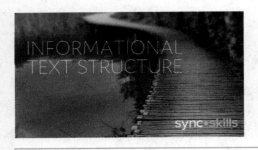

Skill:
Informational Text Structure

Reread paragraphs 17–18 of *Warriors Don't Cry.* Then, using the Checklist on the previous page, answer the multiple-choice questions below.

⟳ YOUR TURN

1. This question has two parts. First, answer Part A. Then, answer Part B.

   Part A: How does the text structure the author uses in the excerpt make one moment particularly effective?

   ○ A. The author uses vivid, sensory details to describe the scene in sequential order.

   ○ B. The author defines the essential qualities of her own heartbeat.

   ○ C. The author discusses the details of moving forward in order of importance.

   ○ D. The author explains how the problem of moving forward was solved.

   Part B: Which of the following details does NOT support your answer to Part A?

   ○ A. "Everyone seemed to be moving in slow motion as I peered past the raised bayonets of the 101st soldiers."

   ○ B. "I walked on the concrete path toward the front door of the school . . ."

   ○ C. ". . . where none of my people had ever before walked as a student."

   ○ D. "We stepped up the front door of Central High School and crossed the threshold . . ."

Skill: Word Patterns and Relationships

Use the Checklist to analyze Word Patterns and Relationships in *Warriors Don't Cry*. Refer to the sample student annotations about Word Patterns and Relationships in the text.

••• CHECKLIST FOR WORD PATTERNS AND RELATIONSHIPS

In order to determine the relationship between particular words to better understand each of the words, note the following:

- ✓ any unfamiliar words in the text

- ✓ the surrounding words and phrases in order to better understand the meanings or possible relationships between words

- ✓ examples of part/whole, item/category, or other relationships between words, such as cause/effect, where what happens as a result of something

- ✓ the meaning of a word

To use the relationship between particular words to better understand each of the words, consider the following questions:

- ✓ Are these words related to each other in some way? How?

- ✓ What kind of relationship do these words have?

- ✓ Can any of these words be defined by using a part/whole, item/category, or cause/effect relationship?

WORD PATTERNS AND RELATIONSHIPS

sync skills

Skill: Word Patterns and Relationships

Reread paragraphs 17–18 from *Warriors Don't Cry*. Then, using the Checklist on the previous page, answer the multiple-choice questions below.

⟳ YOUR TURN

1. In paragraph 17, the author explains the silence as *eerie*. Then, the author goes on to describe the *eerie* nature of the event in paragraph 18. This is an example of what kind of word relationship?

   ○ A. Cause/effect relationship

   ○ B. Word patterns

   ○ C. Item/category relationship

   ○ D. Part/whole relationship

2. The word *threshold* in paragraph 18 is related to another word or phrase in that sentence through a part/whole relationship. Which word or phrase helps you understand what *threshold* means?

   ○ A. crossed

   ○ B. forbidden

   ○ C. mob

   ○ D. front door

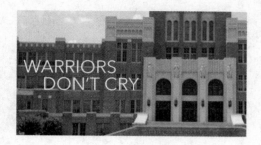

Close Read

Reread *Warriors Don't Cry*. As you reread, complete the Skills Focus questions below. Then use your answers and annotations from the questions to help you complete the Write activity.

◎ SKILLS FOCUS

1. Identify how Beals uses a sequential text structure to set the scene at the beginning of the excerpt. Explain how details and signal words reveal the text structure.

2. Identify how Beals's description of the order of events on September 25, 1957 contributes to the development of ideas in the text. Explain how details and signal words reveal the text structure.

3. Identify two unknown words in the text and explain how you used word relationships in order to determine their meanings.

4. Highlight evidence in the excerpt that provides details about Beals's personal reaction to events. Explain what Beals wants readers to understand after reading this text.

5. Identify evidence that helps you determine what event Beals is describing in this excerpt from *Warriors Don't Cry* and explain what the event is.

✎ WRITE

INFORMATIVE: Identify the author's message in the excerpt and describe how the use of a sequential text structure helps her develop that message effectively. Then choose two or three paragraphs from the text and explain the essential role that each one plays in the development of ideas in the text. What information does each paragraph contribute to the order of events that Beals describes in her story? Be sure to support your ideas with textual evidence.

Damon and Pythias

DRAMA
Fan Kissen
1964

Introduction

The Greek legend of Damon and Pythias follows the lives of two friends on the island of Sicily. When Pythias is sentenced to death for questioning the cruel laws of their tyrant king, Damon strikes a bargain with the king that puts his life and friendship with Pythias at risk. How much are people really willing to risk for the people they care about? Read the following dramatization of the Greek legend, adapted as a one-act play by author Fan Kissen in 1964.

"There's no telling what a man will do when it's a question of his own life against another's."

CAST OF CHARACTERS

Damon	**Mother**
Pythias	**Narrator**
King	**First Voice**
Soldier	**Second Voice**
First Robber	**Third Voice**
Second Robber	

1 *(Sound: Iron door opens and shuts. Key in lock.)*

2 *(Music: Up full and out.)*

3 **Narrator.** Long, long ago there lived on the island of Sicily[1] two young men named Damon and Pythias. They were known far and wide for the strong friendship each had for the other. Their names have come down to our own times to mean true friendship. You may hear it said of two persons:

Skill:
Plot

The play is about two close friends. As I read, I will examine what the characters do and say, and if they change as the plot moves forward.

4 **First Voice.** Those two? Why, they're like Damon and Pythias!

5 **Narrator.** The king of that country was a cruel tyrant. He made cruel laws, and he showed no **mercy** toward anyone who broke his laws. Now, you might very well wonder:

6 **Second Voice.** Why didn't the people rebel?

7 **Narrator.** Well, the people didn't dare rebel because they feared the king's great and powerful army. No one dared say a word against the king or his laws—except Damon and Pythias. One day a soldier overheard Pythias speaking against a new law the king had proclaimed.

8 **Soldier.** Ho, there! Who are you that dares to speak so about our king?

9 **Pythias** *(unafraid)*. I am called Pythias.

---

1. **Sicily** one of the 20 regions of Italy and the largest island in the Mediterranean Sea

NOTES

10 **Soldier.** Don't you know it is a crime to speak against the king or his laws? You are under arrest! Come and tell this opinion of yours to the king's face!

11 *(Music: A few short bars in and out.)*

12 **Narrator.** When Pythias was brought before the king, he showed no fear. He stood straight and quiet before the throne.

13 **King** *(hard, cruel)*. So, Pythias! They tell me you do not approve of the laws I make.

14 **Pythias.** I am not alone, Your Majesty, in thinking your laws are cruel. But you rule the people with such an iron hand[2] that they dare not complain.

15 **King** *(angry)*. But you have the daring to complain for them! Have they **appointed** you their champion?

16 **Pythias.** No, Your Majesty. I speak for myself alone. I have no wish to make trouble for anyone. But I am not afraid to tell you that the people are suffering under your rule. They want to have a voice in making the laws for themselves. You do not allow them to speak up for themselves.

17 **King.** In other words, you are calling me a tyrant! Well, you shall learn for yourself how a tyrant treats a rebel! Soldier! Throw this man into prison!

18 **Soldier.** At once, Your Majesty! Don't try to resist, Pythias!

19 **Pythias.** I know better than to try to resist a soldier of the king! And for how long am I to remain in prison, Your Majesty, merely for speaking out for the people?

20 **King** *(cruel)*. Not for very long, Pythias. Two weeks from today, at noon, you shall be put to death in the public square as an example to anyone else who may dare to question my laws or acts. Off to prison with him, soldier!

21 *(Music: In briefly and out.)*

22 **Narrator.** When Damon heard that his friend Pythias had been thrown into prison and the **severe** punishment that was to follow, he was heartbroken. He rushed to the prison and persuaded the guard to let him speak to his friend.

23 **Damon.** Oh, Pythias! How terrible to find you here! I wish I could do something to save you!

Skill: Greek and Latin Affixes and Roots

I see the word persuaded and I know that it is a verb because Damon is taking action to see his friend Pythias. The root word suade means "to urge." I can infer that Damon is trying his hardest to access the jail.

---

2. **iron hand** referring to the exercise of power in a severe or ruthless manner

Pythias. Nothing can save me, Damon, my dear friend. I am prepared to die. But there is one thought that troubles me greatly.

Damon. What is it? I will do anything to help you.

Pythias. I'm worried about what will happen to my mother and my sister when I'm gone.

Damon. I'll take care of them, Pythias, as if they were my own mother and sister.

Pythias. Thank you, Damon. I have money to leave them. But there are other things I must arrange. If only I could go to see them before I die! But they live two days' journey from here, you know.

Damon. I'll go to the king and beg him to give you your freedom for a few days. You'll give your word to return at the end of that time. Everyone in Sicily knows you for a man who has never broken his word.

Pythias. Do you believe for one moment that the king would let me leave this prison, no matter how good my word may have been all my life?

Damon. I'll tell him that I shall take your place in this prison cell. I'll tell him that if you do not return by the appointed day, he may kill me in your place!

Pythias. No, no, Damon! You must not do such a foolish thing! I cannot—I will not—let you do this! Damon! Damon! Don't go! (*to himself*) Damon, my friend! You may find yourself in a cell beside me!

(*Music: In briefly and out.*)

Damon (*begging*). Your Majesty! I beg of you! Let Pythias go home for a few days to bid farewell to his mother and sister. He gives his word that he will return at your appointed time. Everyone knows that his word can be trusted.

King. In ordinary business affairs—perhaps. But he is now a man under sentence of death. To free him even for a few days would strain his honesty—any man's honesty—too far. Pythias would never return here! I consider him a traitor, but I'm certain he's no fool.

Damon. Your Majesty! I will take his place in the prison until he comes back. If he does not return, then you may take my life in his place.

King (*astonished*). What did you say, Damon?

Copyright © BookheadEd Learning, LLC

NOTES

Skill:
Plot

Even in conflict, their friendship is strong. Damon will risk his life for Pythias. This is the inciting incident that sets the series of events in motion.

Reading & Writing Companion **609**

38 **Damon.** I'm so certain of Pythias that I am offering to die in his place if he fails to return on time.

39 **King.** I can't believe you mean it!

40 **Damon.** I do mean it, Your Majesty.

41 **King.** You make me very curious, Damon, so curious that I'm willing to put you and Pythias to the test. This exchange of prisoners will be made. But Pythias must be back two weeks from today, at noon.

42 **Damon.** Thank you, Your Majesty!

43 **King.** The order with my official seal³ shall go by your own hand, Damon. But I warn you, if your friend does not return on time, you shall surely die in his place! I shall show no mercy!

44 *(Music: In briefly and out.)*

45 **Narrator.** Pythias did not like the king's bargain with Damon. He did not like to leave his friend in prison with the chance that he might lose his life if something went wrong. But at last Damon persuaded him to leave, and Pythias set out for his home. More than a week went by. The day set for the death sentence drew near. Pythias did not return. Everyone in the city knew of the **condition** on which the king had permitted Pythias to go home. Everywhere people met, the talk was sure to turn to the two friends.

46 **First Voice.** Do you suppose Pythias will come back?

47 **Second Voice.** Why would he stick his head under the king's axe once he's escaped?

48 **Third Voice.** Still, would an honorable man like Pythias let such a good friend die for him?

49 **First Voice.** There's no telling what a man will do when it's a question of his own life against another's.

50 **Second Voice.** But if Pythias doesn't come back before the time is up, he will be killing his friend.

51 **Third Voice.** Well, there's still a few days' time. I, for one, am certain that Pythias will return in time.

3. **seal** wax, lead, or other material with an individual design stamped into it to show that it has come from the person who claims to have issued it

52 **Second Voice.** And I am just as certain that he will not. Friendship is friendship, but a man's own life is something stronger, I say!

53 **Narrator.** Two days before the time was up, the king himself visited Damon in his prison cell.

54 *(Sound: Iron door unlocked and opened.)*

55 **King** *(mocking).* You see now, Damon, that you were a fool to make this bargain. Your friend has tricked you! He will not come back here to be killed! He has deserted you!

56 **Damon** *(calm and firm).* I have faith in my friend. I know he will return.

57 **King** *(mocking).* We shall see!

58 *(Sound: Iron door shut and locked.)*

59 **Narrator.** Meanwhile, when Pythias reached the home of his family, he arranged his business affairs so that his mother and sister would be able to live comfortably for the rest of their years. Then he said a last farewell to them before starting back to the city.

60 **Mother** *(in tears).* Pythias, it will take you only two days to get back. Stay another day, I beg you!

61 **Pythias.** I dare not stay longer, Mother. Remember, Damon is locked up in my prison cell while I'm gone. Please don't make it harder for me! Farewell! Don't weep for me. My death may help to bring better days for all our people.

62 **Narrator.** So Pythias began his return journey in plenty of time. But bad luck struck him on the very first day. At twilight, as he walked along a lonely stretch of woodland, a rough voice called:

63 **First Robber.** Not so fast there, young man! Stop!

64 **Pythias** *(startled).* Oh! What is it? What do you want?

65 **Second Robber.** Your money bags.

66 **Pythias.** My money bags? I have only this small bag of coins. I shall need them for some last favors, perhaps, before I die.

67 **First Robber.** What do you mean, before you die? We don't mean to kill you, only to take your money.

68 **Pythias.** I'll give you my money, only don't delay me any longer. I am to die by the king's order three days from now. If I don't return to prison on time, my friend must die in my place.

69 **First Robber.** A likely story! What man would be fool enough to go back to prison ready to die?

70 **Second Robber.** And what man would be fool enough to die for you?

71 **First Robber.** We'll take your money, all right. And we'll tie you up while we get away.

72 **Pythias** *(begging).* No! No! I must get back to free my friend! *(fade)* I must go back!

73 **Narrator.** But the two robbers took Pythias's money, tied him to a tree and went off as fast as they could. Pythias struggled to free himself. He cried out for help as loud as he could for a long time. But no one traveled through that lonesome woodland after dark. The sun had been up for many hours before he finally managed to free himself from the ropes that had tied him to the tree. He lay on the ground, hardly able to breathe.

74 *(Music: In briefly and out.)*

75 **Narrator.** After a while Pythias got to his feet. Weak and dizzy from hunger and thirst and his struggle to free himself, he set off again. Day and night he traveled without stopping, **desperately** trying to reach the city in time to save Damon's life.

76 *(Music: Up and out.)*

77 **Narrator.** On the last day, half an hour before noon, Damon's hands were tied behind his back, and he was taken into the public square. The people muttered angrily as Damon was led in by the jailer. Then the king entered and seated himself on a high platform.

78 *(Sound: Crowd voices in and hold under single voices.)*

79 **Soldier** *(loud).* Long live the king!

80 **First Voice** *(low).* The longer he lives, the more miserable our lives will be!

81 **King** *(loud, mocking).* Well, Damon, your lifetime is nearly up. Where is your good friend Pythias now?

82 **Damon** *(firm)*. I have faith in my friend. If he has not returned, I'm certain it is through no fault of his own.

83 **King** *(mocking)*. The sun is almost overhead. The shadow is almost at the noon mark. And still your friend has not returned to give you back your life!

84 **Damon** *(quiet)*. I am ready, and happy, to die in his place.

85 **King** *(harsh)*. And you shall, Damon! Jailer, lead the prisoner to the—

86 *(Sound: Crowd voices up to a roar, then under.)*

87 **First Voice** *(over noise)*. Look! It's Pythias!

88 **Second Voice** *(over noise)*. Pythias has come back!

89 **Pythias** *(breathless)*. Let me through! Damon!

90 **Damon.** Pythias!

91 **Pythias.** Thank the gods I'm not too late!

92 **Damon** *(quiet, sincere)* I would have died for you gladly, my friend.

93 **Crowd Voices** *(loud, demanding)*. Set them free! Set them both free!

94 **King** (loud). People of the city! *(crowd voices out)* Never in all my life have I seen such faith and friendship, such loyalty between men. There are many among you who call me harsh and cruel. But I cannot kill any man who proves such strong and true friendship for another. Damon and Pythias, I set you both free. *(roar of approval from crowd)* I am king. I command a great army. I have stores of gold and precious jewels. But I would give all my money and my power for one friend like Damon and Pythias!

95 *(Sound: Roar of approval from crowd up briefly and out.)*

96 *(Music: Up and out.)*

"Damon and Pythias" by Fan Kissen, Student Edition. Copyright ©1964, 1949 by Houghton Mifflin Harcourt Publishing Company. All rights reserved. Reproduced by permission of the publisher, Houghton Mifflin Harcourt Publishing Company.

First Read

Read "Damon and Pythias." After you read, complete the Think Questions below.

☁ THINK QUESTIONS

1. Why does Damon decide to take Pythias's place in jail? Cite specific evidence from the text to support your answer.

2. Why does Pythias not immediately return to Damon? Cite specific evidence from the text to support your answer.

3. What does the king decide to do in the end and why? Cite specific evidence from the text to support your answer.

4. Read the following dictionary entry:

   severe

   se•vere \sə'vir\

   adjective

   1. (of something bad) intense
   2. (of punishment of a person) strict or harsh

   Which definition most closely matches the meaning of **severe** as it is used in the excerpt? Write the correct definition of *severe* here and explain how you figured it out.

5. Use context clues to determine the definition of **desperately** as it used in the text. Then check a print or online dictionary to verify your inferred definition of *desperately*.

PLOT

Skill:
Plot

Use the Checklist to analyze Plot in "Damon and Pythias." Refer to the sample student annotations about Plot in the text.

••• CHECKLIST FOR PLOT

In order to determine the plot and how a particular story's or drama's plot unfolds, note the following:

- ✓ specific plot events as they occur in the story

- ✓ the series of episodes as they occur

- ✓ ways characters respond or change as the plot moves toward a resolution

- ✓ dialogue between or among characters or actions that reveal their growth or change

To describe how a particular story's or drama's plot unfolds in a series of episodes as well as how the characters respond or change as the plot moves toward a resolution, consider the following questions:

- ✓ What is the plot? What are the key events in the plot?

- ✓ How does the series of episodes in the drama help the plot unfold ?

- ✓ How do the characters respond or change as the plot moves through the conflict and toward a resolution?

PLOT

Skill:
Plot

Reread lines 79–92 from "Damon and Pythias." Then, using the Checklist on the previous page, answer the multiple-choice questions below.

⟳ YOUR TURN

1. In lines 79–83, the king —

   ○ A. prevents Pythias from returning.
   ○ B. frightens Damon by calling the jailer.
   ○ C. is unable to convince Damon that his friend has abandoned him.
   ○ D. convinces Damon his friendship was not as strong as he thought.

2. Which statement best describes the characters Damon and Pythias at the drama's resolution?

   ○ A. They are loyal and have a true friendship.
   ○ B. Their friendship is hard work, but worth it in the end.
   ○ C. Damon and Pythias can't teach the king about friendship.
   ○ D. Damon is affected by wealth and power while Pythias is not.

Reread lines 79–92 of "Damon and Pythias." Then, answer the multiple-choice questions below.

↻ YOUR TURN

1. This question has two parts. First, answer Part A. Then, answer Part B.

   Part A: Based on his last speech, how has the king been changed by the events in the plot?

   ○ A. He realizes the people think he is harsh and cruel.
   ○ B. The king is ready to give up his wealth to the people.
   ○ C. He has moved from cruelty to understanding.
   ○ D. The king admits he is lonely.

   Part B: Which of the following details BEST supports your answer to Part A?

   ○ A. "There are many among you who call me harsh and cruel."
   ○ B. "Never in all my life have I seen such faith and friendship, such loyalty between men."
   ○ C. "I am king. I command a great army."
   ○ D. "But I cannot kill any man who proves such strong and true friendship for another."

Please note that excerpts and passages in the StudySync® library and this workbook are intended as touchstones to generate interest in an author's work. The excerpts and passages do not substitute for the reading of entire texts, and StudySync® strongly recommends that students seek out and purchase the whole literary or informational work in order to experience it as the author intended. Links to online resellers are available in our digital library. In addition, complete works may be ordered through an authorized reseller by filling out and returning to StudySync® the order form enclosed in this workbook.

Reading & Writing Companion   **617**

Skill: Greek and Latin Affixes and Roots

Use the Checklist to analyze Greek and Latin Affixes and Roots in "Damon and Pythias." Refer to the sample student annotations about Greek and Latin Affixes and Roots in the text.

••• CHECKLIST FOR GREEK AND LATIN AFFIXES AND ROOTS

In order to identify Greek and Latin affixes and roots, note the following:

✓ the root

✓ the prefix and/or suffix

To use common, grade-appropriate Greek or Latin affixes and roots as clues to the meaning of a word, use the following questions as a guide:

✓ Can I identify the root of this word? Should I look in a dictionary or other resource?

✓ What is the meaning of the root?

✓ Can I identify the prefix and/or suffix of this word? Should I look in a dictionary or other resource?

✓ What is the meaning of the prefix and/or suffix?

✓ Does this suffix change the word's part of speech?

✓ How do the word parts work together to define the word's meaning and part of speech?

Skill: Greek and Latin Affixes and Roots

Reread lines 75–80 from "Damon and Pythias." Then, using the Checklist on the previous page, answer the multiple-choice questions below.

🔄 YOUR TURN

1. The word *platform* in line 77 is the combination of two words with Greek or Latin roots. *Form* is from the Greek for "shape." Based on context, which of the following do you think is the meaning of *plat*?

   ○ A. small
   ○ B. large
   ○ C. flat
   ○ D. round

2. The Latin word *miserabilis* means "pitiable and wretched." Therefore, the most likely meaning of *miserable* in line 80 is—

   ○ A. unpleasant
   ○ B. majestic
   ○ C. repetitive
   ○ D. uninteresting

Close Read

Reread "Damon and Pythias." As you reread, complete the Skills Focus questions below. Then use your answers and annotations from the questions to help you complete the Write activity.

◎ SKILLS FOCUS

1. Identify a scene that reveals important details about the plot and explain what they are.

2. Highlight evidence in the dialogue that helps you understand who Damon, Pythias, and the king are, and what they want. Explain what you learn about each character.

3. Identify two unknown words in the text that have common Greek or Latin roots or affixes. Explain how you used the roots or affixes to understand the words' meanings.

4. Highlight evidence that shows how the king changes over the course of the play.

5. Think about the storyline and what it is trying to convey. Then identify evidence in the play that helps you answer the following question: What does the resolution suggest about life in general? Provide an answer based on the evidence.

✏ WRITE

LITERARY ANALYSIS: How do Damon and Pythias respond to conflict as the drama unfolds? Does their friendship ever waver? What do their responses to conflict reveal about their characters? Use evidence and relevant examples of dialogue from the text to support your answer.

Amigo Brothers

FICTION
Piri Thomas
1978

Introduction

Piri Thomas (1928–2011) grew up in New York City's rough Spanish Harlem neighborhood and began writing his acclaimed autobiography *Down These Mean Streets* while serving a prison term for attempted robbery. Known for the tough reality portrayed in his works, Thomas's literary output includes memoirs, short stories, essays, and poems. In his story "Amigo Brothers," amateur boxers and best friends Antonio and Felix must fight against each other to determine which one will advance to the Golden Gloves Championship.

"Let's stop a while, bro. I think we both got something to say to each other."

1   Antonio Cruz and Felix Varga were both seventeen years old. They were so together in friendship that they felt themselves to be brothers. They had known each other since childhood, growing up on the lower east side of Manhattan in the same tenement[1] building on Fifth Street between Avenue A and Avenue B.

2   Antonio was fair, lean, and lanky, while Felix was dark, short, and husky. Antonio's hair was always falling over his eyes, while Felix wore his black hair in a natural Afro style.

3   Each youngster had a dream of someday becoming lightweight champion of the world. Every chance they had the boys worked out, sometimes at the Boys Club on 10th Street and Avenue A and sometimes at the pro's gym on 14th Street. Early morning sunrises would find them running along the East River Drive, wrapped in sweat shirts, short towels around their necks, and handkerchiefs Apache style around their foreheads.

4   While some youngsters were into street negatives, Antonio and Felix slept, ate, rapped, and dreamt positive. Between them, they had a collection of *Fight* magazines second to none, plus a scrapbook filled with torn tickets to every boxing match they had ever attended, and some clippings of their own. If asked a question about any given fighter, they would immediately zip out from their memory banks divisions, weights, records of fights, knock-outs, technical knock-outs, and draws or losses.

5   Each had fought many **bouts** representing their community and had won two gold-plated medals plus a silver and bronze medallion. The difference was in their style. Antonio's lean form and long reach made him the better boxer, while Felix's short and muscular frame made him the better slugger. Whenever they had met in the ring for sparring sessions, it had always been hot and heavy.

Skill:
Character

The friends are different physically and in boxing styles, but both are competitive.

---

1. **tenement** a large building with apartments or rooms for rent, often in a poor urban area

6   Now, after a series of elimination bouts, they had been informed that they were to meet each other in the division finals that were scheduled for the seventh of August, two weeks away—the winner to represent the Boys Club in the Golden Gloves Championship Tournament.

7   The two boys continued to run together along the East River Drive. But even when joking with each other, they both sensed a wall rising between them.

8   One morning less than a week before their bout, they met as usual for their daily work-out. They fooled around with a few jabs at the air, slapped skin, and then took off, running lightly along the dirty East River's edge.

9   Antonio glanced at Felix who kept his eyes purposely straight ahead, pausing from time to time to do some fancy leg work while throwing one-twos followed by upper cuts to an imaginary jaw. Antonio then beat the air with a barrage of body blows and short devastating lefts with an overhand jaw-breaking right.

10 After a mile or so, Felix puffed and said, "Let's stop a while, bro. I think we both got something to say to each other."

11 Antonio nodded. It was not natural to be acting as though nothing unusual was happening when two ace-boon[2] buddies were going to be blasting each other within a few short days.

12 They rested their elbows on the railing separating them from the river. Antonio wiped his face with his short towel. The sunrise was now creating day.

13 Felix leaned heavily on the river's railing and stared across to the shores of Brooklyn. Finally, he broke the silence.

14 "Man, I don't know how to come out with it."

15 Antonio helped. "It's about our fight, right?"

16 "Yeah, right." Felix's eyes squinted at the rising orange sun.

17 "I've been thinking about it too, *panin*[3]. In fact, since we found out it was going to be me and you, I've been awake at night, pulling punches on you, trying not to hurt you."

 Skill:
Character

*These close friends are going to compete against each other. They will both want to win. This will **definitely** be a conflict.*

---

2. **ace-boon** (slang) really close, as in friendship
3. *panin* (Spanish) "buddy" or "pal"

18   "Same here. It ain't natural not to think about the fight. I mean, we both are *cheverote*[4] fighters and we both want to win. But only one of us can win. There ain't no draws in the eliminations."

19   Felix tapped Antonio gently on the shoulder. "I don't mean to sound like I'm bragging, bro. But I wanna win, fair and square."

20   Antonio nodded quietly. "Yeah. We both know that in the ring the better man wins. Friend or no friend, brother or no . . ."

21   Felix finished it for him. "Brother. Tony, let's promise something right here. Okay?"

22   "If it's fair, *hermano*[5], I'm for it." Antonio admired the courage of a tug boat pulling a barge five times its welterweight[6] size.

23   "It's fair, Tony. When we get into the ring, it's gotta be like we never met. We gotta be like two heavy strangers that want the same thing and only one can have it. You understand, don'tcha?"

24   "*Si,* I know." Tony smiled. "No pulling punches. We go all the way."

25   "Yeah, that's right. Listen, Tony. Don't you think it's a good idea if we don't see each other until the day of the fight? I'm going to stay with my Aunt Lucy in the Bronx. I can use Gleason's Gym for working out. My manager says he got some sparring partners with more or less your style."

26   Tony scratched his nose **pensively**. "Yeah, it would be better for our heads." He held out his hand, palm upward. "Deal?"

27   "Deal." Felix lightly slapped open skin.

28   "Ready for some more running?" Tony asked lamely.

29   "Naw, bro. Let's cut it here. You go on. I kinda like to get things together in my head."

30   "You ain't worried, are you?" Tony asked.

31   "No way, man." Felix laughed out loud. "I got too much smarts for that. I just think it's cooler if we split right here. After the fight, we can get it together again like nothing ever happened."

---

4. ***cheverote*** (Spanish) the greatest
5. ***hermano*** (Spanish) brother
6. **welterweight** a weight in boxing and other sports ranging from 140 to 147 pounds

Copyright © BookheadEd Learning, LLC

32   The amigo brothers were not ashamed to hug each other tightly.

33   "Guess you're right. Watch yourself, Felix. I hear there's some pretty heavy dudes up in the Bronx. *Suavecito*[7], okay?"

34   "Okay. You watch yourself too, *sabe*[8]?"

35   Tony jogged away. Felix watched his friend disappear from view, throwing rights and lefts. Both fighters had a lot of psyching up to do before the big fight.

36   The days in training passed much too slowly. Although they kept out of each other's way, they were aware of each other's progress via the ghetto grapevine.

37   The evening before the big fight, Tony made his way to the roof of his tenement. In the quiet early dark, he peered over the ledge. Six stories below the lights of the city blinked and the sounds of cars mingled with the curses and the laughter of children in the street. He tried not to think of Felix, feeling he had succeeded in psyching his mind. But only in the ring would he really know. To spare Felix hurt, he would have to knock him out, early and quick.

38   Up in the South Bronx, Felix decided to take in a movie in an effort to keep Antonio's face away from his fists. The flick was *The Champion* with Kirk Douglas, the third time Felix was seeing it.

39   The champion was getting the daylights beat out of him. He was saved only by the sound of the bell.

40   Felix became the champ and Tony the challenger.

41   The movie audience was going out of its head. The champ hunched his shoulders grunting and sniffing red blood back into his broken nose. The challenger, confident that he had the championship in the bag, threw a left. The champ countered with a dynamite right.

42   Felix's right arm felt the shock, Antonio's face, superimposed on the screen, was hit by the awesome force of the blow. Felix saw himself in the ring, blasting Antonio against the ropes. The champ had to be forcibly restrained. The challenger fell slowly to the canvas.

43   When Felix finally left the theatre, he had figured out how to psyche himself for tomorrow's fight. It was Felix the Champion vs. Antonio the Challenger.

---

7. **suavecito** (Spanish) nice and smooth
8. **sabe** (Spanish) "you know?"

44 He walked up some dark streets, deserted except for small pockets of wary-looking kids wearing gang colors.

45 Despite the fact that he was Puerto Rican like them, they eyed him as a stranger to their turf. Felix did a fast shuffle, bobbing and weaving, while letting loose a torrent of blows that would demolish whatever got in its way. It seemed to impress the brothers, who went about their own business.

46 Finding no takers, Felix decided to split to his aunt's. Walking the streets had not relaxed him, neither had the fight flick. All it had done was to stir him up. He let himself quietly into his Aunt Lucy's apartment and went straight to bed, falling into a fitful sleep with sounds of the gong for Round One.

Skill: Character

Antonio's thoughts show that he has a conflict between wanting to win and valuing his friendship with Felix. Both friends start to change and distance themselves from each other as the story continues.

47 Antonio was passing some heavy time on his rooftop. How would the fight tomorrow **affect** his relationship with Felix? After all, fighting was like any other profession. Friendship had nothing to do with it. A gnawing doubt crept in. He cut negative thinking real quick by doing some speedy fancy dance steps, bobbing and weaving like mercury. The night air was blurred with perpetual motions of left hooks and right crosses. Felix, his *amigo* brother, was not going to be Felix at all in the ring. Just an opponent with another face. Antonio went to sleep, hearing the opening bell for the first round. Like his friend in the South Bronx, he prayed for victory, via a quick clean knock-out in the first round.

48 Large posters plastered all over the walls of local shops announced the fight between Antonio Cruz and Felix Vargas as the main bout.

49 The fight had created great interest in the neighborhood. Antonio and Felix were well liked and respected. Each had his own loyal following.

50 Antonio's fans had unbridled faith in his boxing skills. On the other side, Felix's admirers trusted in his dynamite-packed fists.

51 Felix had returned to his apartment early in the morning of August 7th and stayed there, hoping to avoid seeing Antonio. He turned the radio on to *salsa* music sounds and then tried to read while waiting for word from his manager.

52 The fight was scheduled to take place in Tompkins Square Park. It had been decided that the gymnasium of the Boys Club was not large enough to hold all the people who were sure to attend. In Tompkins Square Park, everyone who wanted could view the fight, whether from ringside or window fire escapes or tenement rooftops.

53 The morning of the fight Tompkins Square was a beehive of activity with numerous workers setting up the ring, the seats, and the guest speakers' stand. The scheduled bouts began shortly after noon and the park had begun filling up even earlier.

Tompkins Square Park in New York City

54 The local junior high school across from Tompkins Square Park served as the dressing room for all the fighters. Each was given a separate classroom with desk tops, covered with mats, serving as resting tables. Antonio thought he caught a glimpse of Felix waving to him from a room at the end of the corridor. He waved back just in case it had been him.

55 The fighters changed from their street clothes into fighting gear. Antonio wore white trunks, black socks, and black shoes. Felix wore sky blue trunks, red socks, and white boxing shoes. Each had dressing gowns to match their fighting trunks with their names neatly stitched on the back.

56 The loudspeakers blared into the open windows of the school. There were speeches by dignitaries, community leaders, and great boxers of yesteryear. Some were well prepared, some **improvised** on the spot. They all carried the same message of great pleasure and honor at being part of such a historic event. This great day was in the tradition of champions **emerging** from the streets of the lower east side.

57 Interwoven with the speeches were the sounds of the other boxing events. After the sixth bout, Felix was much relieved when his trainer Charlie said, "Time change. Quick knock-out. This is it. We're on."

58 Waiting time was over. Felix was escorted from the classroom by a dozen fans in white T-shirts with the word FELIX across their fronts.

59 Antonio was escorted down a different stairwell and guided through a roped-off path.

60 As the two climbed into the ring, the crowd exploded with a roar. Antonio and Felix both bowed gracefully and then raised their arms in acknowledgment.

61 Antonio tried to be cool, but even as the roar was in its first birth, he turned slowly to meet Felix's eyes looking directly into his. Felix nodded his head and Antonio responded. And both as one, just as quickly, turned away to face his own corner.

Please note that excerpts and passages in the StudySync® library and this workbook are intended as touchstones to generate interest in an author's work. The excerpts and passages do not substitute for the reading of entire texts, and StudySync® strongly recommends that students seek out and purchase the whole literary or informational work in order to experience it as the author intended. Links to online resellers are available in our digital library. In addition, complete works may be ordered through an authorized reseller by filling out and returning to StudySync® the order form enclosed in this workbook.

Reading & Writing Companion **627**

62   Bong—bong—bong. The roar turned to stillness.

63   "Ladies and Gentlemen, *Señores y Señoras.*"

64   The announcer spoke slowly, pleased at his bilingual efforts.

65   "Now the moment we have all been waiting for—the main event between two fine young Puerto Rican fighters, products of our lower east side.

66   "In this corner, weighing 134 pounds, Felix Vargas. And in this corner, weighing 133 pounds, Antonio Cruz. The winner will represent the Boys Club in the tournament of champions, the Golden Gloves. There will be no draw. May the best man win."

67   The cheering of the crowd shook the window panes of the old buildings surrounding Tompkins Square Park. At the center of the ring, the referee was giving instructions to the youngsters.

68   "Keep your punches up. No low blows. No punching on the back of the head. Keep your heads up. Understand. Let's have a clean fight. Now shake hands and come out fighting."

69   Both youngsters touched gloves and nodded. They turned and danced quickly to their corners. Their head towels and dressing gowns were lifted neatly from their shoulders by their trainers' nimble fingers. Antonio crossed himself. Felix did the same.

70   BONG! BONG! ROUND ONE. Felix and Antonio turned and faced each other squarely in a fighting pose. Felix wasted no time. He came in fast, head low, half hunched toward his right shoulder, and lashed out with a straight left. He missed a right cross as Antonio slipped the punch and countered with one-two-three lefts that snapped Felix's head back, sending a mild shock coursing through him. If Felix had any small doubt about their friendship affecting their fight, it was being neatly dispelled.

71   Antonio danced, a joy to behold. His left hand was like a piston pumping jabs one right after another with seeming ease. Felix bobbed and weaved and never stopped boring in. He knew that at long range he was at a disadvantage. Antonio had too much reach on him. Only by coming in close could Felix hope to achieve the dreamed-of knockout.

72   Antonio knew the dynamite that was stored in his *amigo* brother's fist. He ducked a short right and missed a left hook. Felix trapped him against the ropes just long enough to pour some punishing rights and lefts to Antonio's

NOTES

hard midsection. Antonio slipped away from Felix, crashing two lefts to his head, which set Felix's right ear to ringing.

73 Bong! Both *amigos* froze a punch well on its way, sending up a roar of approval for good sportsmanship.

74 Felix walked briskly back to his corner. His right ear had not stopped ringing. Antonio gracefully danced his way toward his stool none the worse, except for glowing glove burns, showing angry red against the whiteness of his midribs.

75 "Watch that right, Tony." His trainer talked into his ear. "Remember Felix always goes to the body. He'll want you to drop your hands for his overhand left or right. Got it?"

76 Antonio nodded, spraying water out between his teeth. He felt better as his sore midsection was being firmly rubbed.

77 Felix's corner was also busy.

78 "You gotta get in there, fella." Felix's trainer poured water over his curly Afro locks. "Get in there or he's gonna chop you up from way back."

79 *Bong! Bong!* Round two. Felix was off his stool and rushed Antonio like a bull, sending a hard right to his head. Beads of water exploded from Antonio's long hair.

80 Antonio, hurt, sent back a blurring barrage of lefts and rights that only meant pain to Felix, who returned with a short left to the head followed by a looping right to the body. Antonio countered with his own flurry, forcing Felix to give ground. But not for long.

81 Felix bobbed and weaved, bobbed and weaved, occasionally punching his two gloves together.

82 Antonio waited for the rush that was sure to come. Felix closed in and feinted with his left shoulder and threw his right instead. Lights suddenly exploded inside Felix's head as Antonio slipped the blow and hit him with a pistonlike left, catching him flush on the point of his chin.

83 Bedlam broke loose as Felix's legs momentarily buckled. He fought off a series of rights and lefts and came back with a strong right that taught Antonio respect.

84 Antonio danced in carefully. He knew Felix had the habit of playing possum when hurt, to sucker an opponent within reach of the powerful bombs he carried in each fist.

85 A right to the head slowed Antonio's pretty dancing. He answered with his own left at Felix's right eye that began puffing up within three seconds.

86 Antonio, a bit too eager, moved in too close and Felix had him entangled into a rip-roaring, punching toe-to-toe slugfest that brought the whole Tompkins Square Park screaming to its feet.

87 Rights to the body. Lefts to the head. Neither fighter was giving an inch. Suddenly a short right caught Antonio squarely on the chin. His long legs turned to jelly and his arms flailed out desperately. Felix, grunting like a bull, threw wild punches from every direction. Antonio, groggy, bobbed and weaved, evading most of the blows. Suddenly his head cleared. His left flashed out hard and straight catching Felix on the bridge of his nose.

88 Felix lashed back with a haymaker, right off the ghetto streets. At the same instant, his eye caught another left hook from Antonio. Felix swung out trying to clear the pain. Only the frenzied screaming of those along the ringside let him know that he had dropped Antonio. Fighting off the growing haze, Antonio struggled to his feet, got up, ducked, and threw a smashing right that dropped Felix flat on his back.

89 Felix got up as fast as he could in his own corner, groggy but still game. He didn't even hear the count. In a fog, he heard the roaring of the crowd, who seemed to have gone insane. His head cleared to hear the bell sound at the end of the round. He was very glad. His trainer sat him down on the stool.

90 In his corner, Antonio was doing what all fighters do when they are hurt. They sit and smile at everyone.

91 The referee signaled the ring doctor to check the fighters outs. He did so and then gave his okay. The cold water sponges brought **clarity** to both *amigo* brothers. They were rubbed until their circulation ran free.

92 *Bong!* Round three—the final round. Up to now it had been tic-tac-toe, pretty much even. But everyone knew there could be no draw and that this round would decide the winner.

93 This time, to Felix's surprise, it was Antonio who came out fast, charging across the ring. Felix braced himself but couldn't ward off the barrage of punches. Antonio drove Felix hard against the ropes.

94   The crowd ate it up. Thus far the two had fought with *mucho corazón*. Felix tapped his gloves and commenced his attack anew. Antonio, throwing boxer's caution to the winds, jumped in to meet him.

95   Both pounded away. Neither gave an inch and neither fell to the canvas. Felix's left eye was tightly closed. Claret red blood poured from Antonio's nose. They fought toe-to-toe.

96   The sounds of their blows were loud in contrast to the silence of a crowd gone completely mute.

97   *Bong! Bong! Bong!* The bell sounded over and over again. Felix and Antonio were past hearing. Their blows continued to pound on each other like hailstones.

98   Finally the referee and the two trainers pried Felix and Antonio apart. Cold water was poured over them to bring them back to their senses.

99   They looked around and then rushed toward each other. A cry of alarm surged through Tompkins Square Park. Was this a fight to the death instead of a boxing match?

100 The fear soon gave way to wave upon wave of cheering as the two *amigos* embraced.

101 No matter what the decision, they knew they would always be champions to each other.

102 *BONG! BONG! BONG!* "Ladies and Gentlemen. *Señores* and *Señoras*. The winner and representative to the Golden Gloves Tournament of Champions is . . ."

103 The announcer turned to point to the winner and found himself alone. Arm in arm the champions had already left the ring.

©1978 by Piri Thomas, STORIES FROM EL BARRIO. Reproduced by permission of the Trust of Piri J. Thomas and Suzanne Dod Thomas.

First Read

Read "Amigo Brothers." After you read, complete the Think Questions below.

1. Why does the narrator refer to Antonio Cruz and Felix Varga as the "amigo brothers"? How are the boys alike? How are they different? Cite specific evidence from paragraphs 1–3 to support your answer.

2. How does the reader know that boxing is important to Antonio and Felix? Cite specific evidence from paragraphs 3 and 4 to support your response.

3. Why is the upcoming division match a challenge for Antonio and Felix's friendship? Explain how the boys share a similar point of view about the match. Cite specific evidence from paragraphs 11–25 to support your response.

4. Use context clues to determine the meaning of the word **pensively** as it is used in paragraph 26.

5. The Latin word *imprōvīsus* means "unforeseen" or "unexpected." Use this information to infer the meaning of the word **improvised** as it appears in paragraph 56 of the text. Write your best definition here and explain how you figured it out.

Skill:
Character

Use the Checklist to analyze Character in "Amigo Brothers." Refer to the sample student annotations about Character in the text.

••• CHECKLIST FOR CHARACTER

In order to determine how the characters respond or change as the plot moves toward a resolution, note the following:

- ✓ the characters in the story, including the protagonist and antagonist

- ✓ key events in the series of episodes in the plot, especially events that cause characters to react, respond, or change in some way

- ✓ characters' responses as the plot reaches a climax, and moves toward a resolution of the problem facing the protagonist

- ✓ the resolution of the conflict in the plot and the ways it affects each character

To describe how the plot of a particular story or drama unfolds in a series of episodes as well as how the characters respond or change as the plot moves toward a resolution, consider the following questions:

- ✓ How do the characters' responses change or develop from the beginning to the end of the story?

- ✓ Do the characters in the story change? Which event or events in the story cause a character to change?

- ✓ Is there an event in the story that provokes, or causes, a character to make a decision?

- ✓ Do the characters' problems reach a resolution? How?

- ✓ How does the resolution affect the characters?

Skill:
Character

Reread paragraphs 97–103 from "Amigo Brothers." Then, using the Checklist on the previous page, answer the multiple-choice questions below.

⟳ YOUR TURN

1. Based on how Felix and Antonio act in paragraphs 97 through 99 after the bell sounds, the reader can conclude that —

   ○ A. the audience wants them to keep fighting.
   ○ B. each boy is overtaken by the desire to win.
   ○ C. the boys hate each other.
   ○ D. they are both sweaty.

2. The author's description of the event and what it means in paragraphs 99 and 100 reveals that the boys —

   ○ A. choose their friendship over winning.
   ○ B. are ready to hear the announcer name the winner.
   ○ C. realize they are endangering each other.
   ○ D. are badly injured and about to collapse.

3. The boys' final act in the last paragraph show that they —

   ○ A. need medical help.
   ○ B. have given up boxing.
   ○ C. think they are both winners.
   ○ D. do not want to be champions.

Close Read

Reread "Amigo Brothers." As you reread, complete the Skills Focus questions below. Then use your answers and annotations from the questions to help you complete the Write activity.

SKILLS FOCUS

1. Think about the responses that Antonio and Felix have to events in the story. How do these responses both slowly reveal their individual characters and also help to develop the plot? Write a response to this question, citing evidence from the text to support your claim.

2. Highlight evidence that reveals how Antonio and Felix are similar and different. Explain how these similarities and differences affect the story's plot.

3. Identify details in the text that show how Antonio and Felix's relationship changes over the course of the story. Explain how these details help you infer a theme.

4. Identify and summarize the events of the story in a way that maintains meaning and logical order.

5. Identify evidence in "Amigo Brothers" that reveals the central conflict the two characters face. Explain what the conflict is.

WRITE

LITERARY ANALYSIS: What efforts do Antonio and Felix make to achieve their dreams? What do their efforts reveal about them? In what ways are Antonio and Felix similar to and different from each other? How do they change as the plot moves toward a resolution? Write a response to these questions, citing evidence from the text to support your answers.

Please note that excerpts and passages in the StudySync® library and this workbook are intended as touchstones to generate interest in an author's work. The excerpts and passages do not substitute for the reading of entire texts, and StudySync® strongly recommends that students seek out and purchase the whole literary or informational work in order to experience it as the author intended. Links to online resellers are available in our digital library. In addition, complete works may be ordered through an authorized reseller by filling out and returning to StudySync® the order form enclosed in this workbook.

Reading & Writing Companion   **635**

Introduction

The second book by author Thanhhà Lai (b. 1965) introduces readers to an American-born Vietnamese family. Twelve-year-old Mai—who wants nothing more than to vacation with friends in Laguna Beach over the summer—is asked to accompany her grandmother, Bà, to Vietnam to figure out if her grandfather is still alive. In this excerpt, Mai is still adjusting to life in the Vietnamese village when Bà begins to open up about her past.

"Bà understands; she always has."

1   We're under the mosquito net again, getting ready for a nap. After being force-fed at breakfast and lunch today, we're tired. I was made to eat so much sticky rice and mung beans, my belly feels like it's packed with bricks. I'm still burping, trying to digest it all.

2   The net is supposed to be used only at night but I wouldn't let Bà roll ours up. Mosquitoes hunt from dusk to dawn, but I bet there are some who stretch the hours. I feel safer inside the net, lying here and scratching like I have fleas. Bà has already told me scratching only makes it worse. If I ignore the itches, according to her, soon my blood will no longer **react** to the poison. This mind-over-matter thing has never worked for me.

3   I've thought about playing up the mosquito angle, maybe scratch myself bloody, moan a lot, shake like I have malaria[1]. That might get me airlifted to Laguna. But doctors back home would run tests and figure out I faked the whole thing and Mom would ship me right back, probably for the entire summer. So I've got to suck it up and wait for the detective to bring the guard. Then Bà can ask all her questions. Tears. Acceptance. Incense. Home. Not much else can happen.

4   Bà pulls out her Tiger Balm. Bad, bad sign. How could I have forgotten about her cure-all weapon? I stop scratching and forbid myself to touch even one pink bump, but it's too late. Bà is twisting open the shiny metal lid and reaching out for me. Why did I have to call attention to myself? She holds up my right arm and **meticulously** rubs the ointment on each pink dot. You know what a minty, burning, menthol-y goo does to mosquito bites? It makes them itch even more! But I can't reason with Bà about Tiger Balm, which she has **anointed** with the power to blast away headaches, backaches, joint aches, stomachaches, nausea, seasickness, carsickness, burns, bites, gas, congestions . . . just to name a few.

NOTES

Skill:
Language, Style
and Audience

I can tell from the author's word choice that the narrator is not happy to be with her grandmother. She would rather scratch herself, bleed, and pretend to have a disease! The tone sounds sarcastic, and she seems selfish.

---

1. **malaria** an illness that causes fever and is transmitted by mosquitoes in many tropical and subtropical regions

5 Now Bà wants my other arm. Noooo. I quickly stick my finger into the jar, scoop out a **pungent** gob and pretend to rub it on my bites. I'm actually massaging it on the flat skin surrounding the bumps. Even so, it burns. Bà waits for me to assault my calves and ankles and feet and neck and face. My eyes have turned into waterfalls. Tiger Balm is no joke. Finally, Bà closes the lid.

6 *"Guess what once floated on that wall?"* Bà asks. I always understand whatever Bà says because she uses only the words she has taught me.

7 Through stinging eyes, I kinda see that on the wall used to be a mural, made of blue tiles. Most have fallen off, leaving pockmarks on the dingy wall. Everything in the house is cracked and gray. Outside, the year *1929* is carved into the wood above the doorway. Bà said Ông was born that year and, to celebrate, his father designed a house inspired by his travels: one story, tile roof, brick walls, windows facing every direction, rooms that extend out instead of up, and a garden that claimed much more land than the house itself.

8 I suddenly remember the word for blue, *"Xanh."*

9 *"Yes. Remember our stories about the goddess in a blue robe that drifts like tea vapors? Remnants of her gown still remain."*

10 I do remember, smiling big to show Bà. Twice a day I used to hear long stories, one at nap time and one before bed. Then I went to kindergarten and stopped listening.

11 *"I have known Ông since the beginning of memories, matched as one from his seventh year, my fifth. Marriage to be delayed until he had studied in France, I in Japan. Yet war reached us. We were joined at eighteen, sixteen. Too soon. The day of our wedding people arrived at our door. They bore drums and flags and silver gift trays covered in red velvet. The first two days proved simple to hide from him, so many relatives, so many ceremonies. But the third day, four men with muscles like twisted laundry carried me in a palanquin[2] to his parents' door. As taught, I took steps light as a crane's into the house, bowed before the ancestral altar. While everyone prayed, I retreated inside the first room with a door.*

12 *"This one. The bridal chamber. In pink silk a bed floated, from above a blue goddess gazed. I pushed an armoire[3] against the door and sat on the floor counting the thumps from my heart. Out there they pleaded, then threatened,*

---

2. **palanquin** in India and the East, a covered vehicle for one passenger, made of a large box carried on two horizontal poles by four or six servants
3. **armoire** a wardrobe, typically ornate and antique

then my father thundered. Yet, I sat. The season was spring. Peach petals drifted outside the open window. I jumped up. Too late. Ông was perched on the windowsill, having climbed the peach tree. I pushed him back and slammed the bamboo shutters. His shape showed through, even the hint of curls by his ears. His voice seeped through too. Ah, that voice. In such a voice, sharp tones shattered and landed in drops of bells. He talked until the sun shriveled to an orange-yellow seed. He talked until I released the shutters.

Skill:
Language, Style and Audience

13 "For years now, I've counted the hours I had lost, that day and days after, when I was reading or visiting relatives or daydreaming, hours I could have been beside him. For years, I've counted the hours ever after as I wait for some part of him to return to me. I'm no dreamer. Raising seven children during war has a way of slapping reality into one's fate. And yet, against reason, I continue to wait."

14 "Ông sống?" Ông alive? I suck in a huge breath, willing this to be the right moment to ask. I softly squeeze Bà's hand to mean I've been thinking about this for some time.

Bà's tone seems melancholy; she misses her husband. She regrets the time they had apart and wishes she could be with him now. I feel bad for her when I read this, but also hopeful that she's still waiting for him.

15 Bà understands; she always has. I don't know how, but Bà has always known how I feel at any given moment, especially when I'm sad, especially when I'm in need of a quartered lemon drop.

16 "I do not live on butterfly wings, my child. His chances of remaining among us rank as likely as finding an ebony orchid. Yet I hold on to hope because I have been unable to imagine his ending. If intact, he would have returned to this room. We promised should life separate us, we would rejoin under the blue goddess. He never returned to us, but he never truly departed. I came here knowing I will unlikely be granted him in person, but perhaps I will be allowed to reclaim something of his, anything at all. The guard knows how Ông spent his days, what he ate, what he wore, what he said, the weight in his eyes, the shade of his skin, the whistle of his breaths. I need to absorb every morsel deemed knowable, then I have **vowed** to release the heaviness of longing."

17 Bà lets go of my hand and turns from me. Time to let her rest.

18 My body loosens and expands, remembering how it used to make room for her words to wiggle deep into the tiny crevices along my bones, muscles, and joints. Becoming a part of me. I've always been able to imagine her as a rich girl who grew up in wartime and ended up raising seven children alone. She always says, "Cờ đến tay, phải phất." Flag in hand, you must wave it. It wasn't about being brave or extraordinary so much as inhaling all the way to her core and accepting her responsibilities.

19   But I have never understood how she got through her loss. How do you know someone almost since birth, then one day you know absolutely nothing more about him at all? Ông made plans, she told me, plans of how to educate their children, how to care for their parents, how to wait for peace, how to behave in old age. They did not plan on being apart after he was thirty-seven and she thirty-five. I used to think that was old, but that was much younger than Mom and Dad now.

20   Bà has fallen asleep. Her snores will deepen. I roll toward her and inhale Tiger Balm mixed with BenGay, all the way down to my toes. The most tingly, comforting scent there is.

Excerpted from *Listen, Slowly* by Thanhhà Lai, published by HarperCollins.

First Read

Read *Listen, Slowly*. After you read, complete the Think Questions below.

☁ THINK QUESTIONS

1. What inferences can you make about Mai's character from the first four paragraphs? Cite evidence from the text to support your response.

2. What is the significance to Bà of the blue tiles on the wall? Use evidence from the text to support your response.

3. How has Mai's perspective changed by the end of the excerpt? Cite evidence from the text to support your response.

4. The Latin word *pungens* means "to sting." Use this information to help infer the meaning of the word **pungent** as it appears in paragraph 5. Write your best definition of *pungent* here and explain how you figured it out.

5. Use context clues to determine the meaning of the word **vowed** as it is used in paragraph 16. Write your best definition of *vowed* here and explain how you figured out its meaning.

Skill:
Language, Style, and Audience

Use the Checklist to analyze Language, Style, and Audience in *Listen, Slowly*. Refer to the sample student annotations about Language, Style, and Audience in the text.

••• CHECKLIST FOR LANGUAGE, STYLE, AND AUDIENCE

In order to determine an author's style, do the following:

- ✓ identify and define any unfamiliar words or phrases

- ✓ use context, including the meaning of surrounding words and phrases

- ✓ note specific words and phrases that the author uses to create a response in the reader

- ✓ note possible reactions to the author's word choice

- ✓ note the tone that the author is communicating through the choices of words

To analyze the impact of specific word choice on meaning and tone, ask the following questions:

- ✓ How did the language impact your understanding of the text's meaning?

- ✓ What stylistic choices can you identify in the text? How does the style influence your understanding of the language?

- ✓ How could various audiences interpret this language? What possible different emotional responses can you list?

- ✓ How does the writer's choice of words impact or create a specific tone in the text?

Skill:
Language, Style, and Audience

Reread paragraphs 19–20 from *Listen, Slowly*. Then, using the Checklist on the previous page, answer the multiple-choice questions below.

⟳ YOUR TURN

1. What does the author's tone and word choice in paragraph 19 reveal about how Mai feels about her grandmother?

   ○ A. She is angry with her grandmother.
   ○ B. She has empathy for her and admires her strength.
   ○ C. She misses her grandfather as well.
   ○ D. She is upset her grandmother made her come to Vietnam.

2. Which of the following words best describes the tone created by Mai's description of her grandmother's ointments (paragraph 20)?

   ○ A. dislike
   ○ B. fear
   ○ C. calm
   ○ D. excitement

LISTEN, SLOWLY

Close Read

Reread *Listen, Slowly*. As you reread, complete the Skills Focus questions below. Then use your answers and annotations from the questions to help you complete the Write activity.

◎ SKILLS FOCUS

1. Identify evidence of how the author uses figurative language such as metaphors and personification to develop the personalities of Mai and Bà. Explain what the figurative language tells you about the characters.

2. Identify places where the author uses specific word choice or tone to create Mai's voice. Explain how this language helps you understand Mai's feelings.

3. Identify places in the text where the author uses words or phrases to express Bà's personality. Explain what these words or phrases tell you about Bà as a character.

4. Highlight evidence that suggests that Mai is interested in Bà's story and is brought closer to her by their conversation. Explain your reasoning.

✏ WRITE

LITERARY ANALYSIS: How does the author use language to develop the audience's understanding of Mai and Bà? What does their conversation in the excerpt say about them as individuals and as family members? Cite evidence from the text to support your response.

Charles

FICTION
Shirley Jackson
1948

Introduction

Shirley Jackson (1916–1965) was a popular and prolific writer in her short life. Before her death at age 48, she published six novels, two memoirs, four children's books, and a collection of short stories. Her two best known works are "The Lottery" and *The Haunting of Hill House*, which was nominated for the National Book Award and has been described by bestselling horror writer Stephen King as one of the "two great novels of the supernatural in the last hundred years." "Charles" follows in the suspense-and-twist tradition of the controversial and often-anthologized short story, "The Lottery," whose haunting incident takes place on June 27th—a day forever named Shirley Jackson Day in the author's

"Well, Charles was bad again today."

Skill:
Point of View

The phrase "my son" says that the narrator is Laurie's mother. She uses the pronouns my, I, and me, so the story is told in the first person. The reader knows and sees only what the narrator describes.

1   The day my son Laurie started kindergarten he **renounced** corduroy overalls with bibs and began wearing blue jeans with a belt; I watched him go off the first morning with the older girl next door, seeing clearly that an era of my life was ended, my sweet-voiced nursery-school tot replaced by a long-trousered, swaggering character who forgot to stop at the corner and wave good-bye to me.

2   He came running home the same way, the front door slamming open, his cap on the floor, and the voice suddenly become raucous shouting, "Isn't anybody *here*?"

3   At lunch he spoke insolently to his father, spilled his baby sister's milk, and remarked that his teacher said we were not to take the name of the Lord in vain.

4   "How *was* school today?" I asked, **elaborately** casual.

5   "All right," he said.

6   "Did you learn anything?" his father asked.

7   Laurie regarded his father coldly. "I didn't learn nothing," he said.

8   "Anything," I said. "Didn't learn anything."

9   "The teacher spanked a boy, though," Laurie said, **addressing** his bread and butter.

10   "For being fresh[1]," he added, with his mouth full.

11   "What did he do?" I asked. "Who was it?"

---

1. **fresh** showing overconfidence or disrespect

12 Laurie thought. "It was Charles," he said. "He was fresh. The teacher spanked him and made him stand in the corner. He was awfully fresh."

13 "What did he do?" I asked again, but Laurie slid off his chair, took a cookie, and left, while his father was still saying, "See here, young man."

14 The next day Laurie remarked at lunch, as soon as he sat down, "Well, Charles was bad again today." He grinned enormously and said, "Today Charles hit the teacher."

15 "Good heavens," I said, mindful of the Lord's name, "I suppose he got spanked again?"

16 "He sure did," Laurie said. "Look up," he said to his father.

17 "What?" his father said, looking up.

18 "Look down," Laurie said. "Look at my thumb. Gee, you're dumb." He began to laugh insanely.

19 "Why did Charles hit the teacher?" I asked quickly.

20 "Because she tried to make him color with red crayons," Laurie said. "Charles wanted to color with green crayons so he hit the teacher and she spanked him and said nobody play with Charles but everybody did."

21 The third day—it was a Wednesday of the first week—Charles bounced a see-saw on to the head of a little girl and made her bleed, and the teacher made him stay inside all during recess. Thursday Charles had to stand in a corner during story-time because he kept pounding his feet on the floor. Friday Charles was **deprived** of black-board privileges because he threw chalk.

22 On Saturday I remarked to my husband, "Do you think kindergarten is too unsettling for Laurie? All this toughness and bad grammar, and this Charles boy sounds like such a bad influence."

23 "It'll be alright," my husband said reassuringly. "Bound to be people like Charles in the world. Might as well meet them now as later."

24 On Monday Laurie came home late, full of news. "Charles," he shouted as he came up the hill; I was waiting **anxiously** on the front steps. "Charles," Laurie yelled all the way up the hill, "Charles was bad again."

25 "Come right in," I said, as soon as he came close enough. "Lunch is waiting."

Skill:
Point of View

The narrator reveals that she feels anxious, or nervous, waiting for Laurie. She only knows what has happened from what Laurie says. This limits the point of view.

Please note that excerpts and passages in the StudySync® library and this workbook are intended as touchstones to generate interest in an author's work. The excerpts and passages do not substitute for the reading of entire texts, and StudySync® strongly recommends that students seek out and purchase the whole literary or informational work in order to experience it as the author intended. Links to online resellers are available in our digital library. In addition, complete works may be ordered through an authorized reseller by filling out and returning to StudySync® the order form enclosed in this workbook.

Reading & Writing
Companion

647

26　"You know what Charles did?" he demanded, following me through the door. "Charles yelled so in school they sent a boy in from first grade to tell the teacher she had to make Charles keep quiet, and so Charles had to stay after school. And so all the children stayed to watch him."

27　"What did he do?" I asked.

28　"He just sat there," Laurie said, climbing into his chair at the table. "Hi, Pop, y'old dust mop."

29　"Charles had to stay after school today," I told my husband. "Everyone stayed with him."

30　"What does this Charles look like?" my husband asked Laurie. "What's his other name?"

31　"He's bigger than me," Laurie said. "And he doesn't have any rubbers² and he doesn't wear a jacket."

32　Monday night was the first Parent-Teachers meeting, and only the fact that the baby had a cold kept me from going; I wanted passionately to meet Charles's mother. On Tuesday Laurie remarked suddenly, "Our teacher had a friend come to see her in school today."

33　"Charles's mother?" my husband and I asked simultaneously.

34　"Naaah," Laurie said scornfully. "It was a man who came and made us do exercises, we had to touch our toes. Look." He climbed down from his chair and squatted down and touched his toes. "Like this," he said. He got solemnly back into his chair and said, picking up his fork, "Charles didn't even *do* exercises."

35　"That's fine," I said heartily. "Didn't Charles want to do exercises?"

36　"Naaah," Laurie said. "Charles was so fresh to the teacher's friend he wasn't *let* do exercises."

37　"Fresh again?" I said.

38　"He kicked the teacher's friend," Laurie said. "The teacher's friend just told Charles to touch his toes like I just did and Charles kicked him."

39　"What are they going to do about Charles, do you suppose?" Laurie's father asked him.

---

2. **rubbers** rubber overshoes that people wear to protect their shoes

40   Laurie shrugged elaborately. "Throw him out of school, I guess," he said.

41   Wednesday and Thursday were routine; Charles yelled during story hour and hit a boy in the stomach and made him cry. On Friday Charles stayed after school again and so did all the other children.

42   With the third week of kindergarten Charles was an institution in our family; the baby was being a Charles when she cried all afternoon; Laurie did a Charles when he filled his wagon full of mud and pulled it through the kitchen; even my husband, when he caught his elbow in the telephone cord and pulled the telephone and a bowl of flowers off the table, said, after the first minute, "Looks like Charles."

43   During the third and fourth weeks it looked like a reformation in Charles; Laurie reported grimly at lunch on Thursday of the third week, "Charles was so good today the teacher gave him an apple."

44   "What?" I said, and my husband added warily, "You mean Charles?"

45   "Charles," Laurie said. "He gave the crayons around and he picked up the books afterward and the teacher said he was her helper."

46   "What happened?" I asked incredulously.

47   "He was her helper, that's all," Laurie said, and shrugged.

48   "Can this be true about Charles?" I asked my husband that night. "Can something like this happen?"

49   "Wait and see," my husband said cynically. "When you've got a Charles to deal with, this may mean he's only plotting." He seemed to be wrong. For over a week Charles was the teacher's helper; each day he handed things out and he picked things up; no one had to stay after school.

50   "The PTA meeting's next week again," I told my husband one evening. "I'm going to find Charles's mother there."

51   "Ask her what happened to Charles," my husband said. "I'd like to know."

52   "I'd like to know myself," I said.

53   On Friday of that week things were back to normal. "You know what Charles did today?" Laurie demanded at the lunch table, in a voice slightly awed. "He told a little girl to say a word and she said it and the teacher washed her mouth out with soap and Charles laughed."

54   "What word?" his father asked unwisely, and Laurie said, "I'll have to whisper it to you, it's so bad." He got down off his chair and went around to his father. His father bent his head down and Laurie whispered joyfully. His father's eyes widened.

55   "Did Charles tell the little girl to say *that*?" he asked respectfully.

56   "She said it *twice*," Laurie said. "Charles told her to say it *twice*."

57   "What happened to Charles?" my husband asked.

58   "Nothing," Laurie said. "He was passing out the crayons."

59   Monday morning Charles abandoned the little girl and said the evil word himself three or four times, getting his mouth washed out with soap each time. He also threw chalk.

60   My husband came to the door with me that evening as I set out for the PTA meeting. "Invite her over for a cup of tea after the meeting," he said. "I want to get a look at her."

61   "If only she's there." I said prayerfully.

62   "She'll be there," my husband said. "I don't see how they could hold a PTA meeting without Charles's mother."

63   At the meeting I sat restlessly, scanning each comfortable matronly face, trying to determine which one hid the secret of Charles. None of them looked to me haggard enough. No one stood up in the meeting and apologized for the way her son had been acting. No one mentioned Charles.

64   After the meeting I identified and sought out Laurie's kindergarten teacher. She had a plate with a cup of tea and a piece of chocolate cake; I had a plate with a cup of tea and a piece of marshmallow cake. We maneuvered up to one another cautiously, and smiled.

65   "I've been so anxious to meet you," I said. "I'm Laurie's mother."

66   "We're all so interested in Laurie," she said.

67   "Well, he certainly likes kindergarten," I said. "He talks about it all the time."

68   "We had a little trouble **adjusting**, the first week or so," she said primly, "but now he's a fine helper. With occasional lapses, of course."

69 "Laurie usually adjusts very quickly," I said. "I suppose this time it's Charles's influence."

70 "Charles?"

71 "Yes," I said, laughing, "you must have your hands full in that kindergarten, with Charles."

72 "Charles?" she said. "We don't have any Charles in the kindergarten."

"Charles" from THE LOTTERY by Shirley Jackson. Copyright ©1948, 1949 by Shirley Jackson. Copyright renewed 1976, 1977 by Laurence Hyman, Barry Hyman, Mrs. Sarah Webster and Mrs. Joanne Schnurer. Reprinted by permission of Farrar, Straus and Giroux.

CHARLES

First Read

Read "Charles." After you read, complete the Think Questions below.

☁ THINK QUESTIONS

1. How does Laurie's behavior suddenly change when he leaves for his first day of kindergarten? Cite textual evidence from the selection to support your answer.

2. Write two or three sentences describing how Charles, as Laurie tells it, disrupts the kindergarten classroom during the first week of school.

3. Why is the narrator scanning each "comfortable matronly face" at the PTA meeting? Be sure to use textual evidence in your response.

4. Read the following dictionary entry:

   address ad•dress \ə'dres\
   noun

   1. the number and street of a residence or business
   2. a speech delivered before an audience or crowd

   verb

   1. to deal with or direct efforts toward
   2. to speak to an audience

   Addressing is the present participle form of the verb *address*. Which definition of *address* most closely matches the meaning of *addressing* as it is used in paragraph 9? Write the correct definition of *addressing* here and explain how you figured out the correct meaning.

5. Which context clues help you determine the meaning of **deprived** as it is used in paragraph 21 of "Charles"? Write your own definition of *deprived* and explain which words or phrases helped you understand its meaning.

Skill:
Point of View

Use the Checklist to analyze Point of View in "Charles." Refer to the sample student annotations about Point of View in the text.

••• CHECKLIST FOR POINT OF VIEW

In order to identify the point of view of the narrator or speaker in a text, note the following:

✓ the speaker(s) or narrator(s)

✓ how much the narrator(s) or speaker(s) knows and reveals

✓ what the narrator(s) or speaker(s) says or does that reveals how he or she feels about other characters and events in the poem or story

To explain how an author develops the point of view of the narrator or speaker in a text, consider the following questions:

✓ Is the narrator or speaker objective and honest? Or does he or she mislead the reader? How?

✓ What is the narrator's or the speaker's point of view?

- Is the narrator or speaker "all-knowing," or omniscient?

- Is the narrator or speaker limited to revealing the thoughts and feelings of just one character?

- Are there multiple narrators or speakers telling the story?

- Is the narrator a character within the story or telling the story from the "outside"?

✓ How does the narrator or speaker reveal his or her thoughts about the events or the other characters in the story or poem? How does the narrator's or speaker's experiences and cultural background affect his or her thoughts?

Please note that excerpts and passages in the StudySync® library and this workbook are intended as touchstones to generate interest in an author's work. The excerpts and passages do not substitute for the reading of entire texts, and StudySync® strongly recommends that students seek out and purchase the whole literary or informational work in order to experience it as the author intended. Links to online resellers are available in our digital library. In addition, complete works may be ordered through an authorized reseller by filling out and returning to StudySync® the order form enclosed in this workbook.

Reading & Writing Companion

653

Skill:
Point of View

Reread paragraphs 63–72 of "Charles." Then, using the Checklist on the previous page, answer the multiple-choice questions below.

↻ YOUR TURN

1. What does the story's ending reveal about the first-person point of view of the narrator?
   - ○ A. The narrator is confused by the teacher's final statement.
   - ○ B. The narrator knew that Laurie was misbehaving.
   - ○ C. The narrator didn't know that Charles wasn't real or that it was her child who was misbehaving.
   - ○ D. The narrator knew that Charles wasn't real the whole time.

2. How would the story be different if told from a third-person omniscient point of view?
   - ○ A. Readers would have known all along that Charles was Laurie since they would know all the characters' thoughts and feelings.
   - ○ B. Readers would be observers who experience the story through one character, so they would find out that Charles was Laurie at the same time as the narrator.
   - ○ C. The author would address readers directly to explain that Charles wasn't real.
   - ○ D. Readers would be able to identify closely with the teacher's viewpoint.

CHARLES

Close Read

Reread "Charles." As you reread, complete the Skills Focus questions below. Then use your answers and annotations from the questions to help you complete the Write activity.

◎ SKILLS FOCUS

1. Highlight evidence that indicates from which point of view "Charles" is told. Explain what the point of view is and why you think the author selected it.

2. Identify specific evidence in the story that shows how the narrator's limited point of view affects her description of characters or events.

3. A character's personality consists of the traits that make the character different from others, such as whether the character is honest or devious. Highlight examples of Laurie's words and actions that reveal his personality. Explain how these words or actions help develop the plot.

4. When you summarize a text, you state the main ideas or events and the most important details in your own words. Highlight events in the story that are central to the plot. Then summarize the most important events in your own words.

5. Laurie's tales about Charles are central to the story. Highlight evidence that shows how Laurie's feelings about Charles change over the course of the story. Explain what this tells you about Laurie.

✎ WRITE

ARGUMENTATIVE: At the end of "Charles," the reader and the narrator both learn that the title character is a person who is unknown to the teacher. This suggests that Laurie's mother, the narrator, has a limited point of view. Therefore, what exactly has been going on throughout Laurie's first weeks of kindergarten? What clues, if any, are presented that the narrator overlooks? Develop an argument in which you state what you think has actually happened in the story and whether you think that the narrator should have known all along that Laurie was lying to her.

Please note that excerpts and passages in the StudySync® library and this workbook are intended as touchstones to generate interest in an author's work. The excerpts and passages do not substitute for the reading of entire texts, and StudySync® strongly recommends that students seek out and purchase the whole literary or informational work in order to experience it as the author intended. Links to online resellers are available in our digital library. In addition, complete works may be ordered through an authorized reseller by filling out and returning to StudySync® the order form enclosed in this workbook.

Reading & Writing Companion   **655**

Saying
Yes

POETRY
Diana Chang
1974

Introduction

Author of nine books, Diana Chang (1924–2009) is considered to be the first Chinese American to publish a novel in the United States. She was a trailblazing writer and New Yorker who also lived in Nanjing, Shanghai, and Beijing. Her poem "Saying Yes" most likely emerged from autobiographical roots.

"Are you Chinese?"
"Yes."
"American?"
"Yes."

1   "Are you Chinese?"
2   "Yes."

3   "American?"
4   "Yes."

5   "Really Chinese?"
6   "No . . . not **quite**."

7   "Really American?"
8   "Well, actually, you see . . ."

9   But I would **rather** say
10   yes
11   Not neither-nor,
12   not maybe,
13   but both, and not only

14   The homes I've had,
15   the ways I am

16   I'd rather say it twice,
17   yes

©1974 by Diana Chang. Reproduced by permission of Kacie Chang.

WRITE

POETRY: Have you ever been asked a question about yourself that was impossible to give a yes or no answer to? Use Chang's poem as a model for inspiration and write a lyrical conversation in Chang's style. It can be autobiographical or entirely imagined. As in Chang's poem, be sure to include lines of dialogue at the beginning and a concluding stance at the end that makes it clear what your poem's speaker really wants to say. Title your poem either "Saying Yes" or "Saying No."

The All-American Slurp

FICTION
Lensey Namioka
1987

Introduction

Prolific young-adult author Lensey Namioka (b. 1929) emigrated from China to the United States when she was nine years old. She often writes with levity about Chinese and Japanese families and themes of Americanization. Her short story "The All-American Slurp" follows a family that finds the true gauntlet for assimilation at the dinner table.

"The Gleasons' dinner party wasn't so different from a Chinese meal after all."

NOTES

**Skill:
Setting**

From the details in this paragraph, I can tell that the story takes place in America and that the characters are new to the country. Being new to a place might create a conflict in the story.

1 The first time our family was invited out to dinner in America, we disgraced ourselves while eating celery. We had emigrated to this country from China, and during our early days here we had a hard time with American table manners.

2 In China we never ate celery raw, or any other kind of vegetable raw. We always had to disinfect the vegetables in boiling water first. When we were presented with our first relish tray, the raw celery caught us unprepared.

3 We had been invited to dinner by our neighbors, the Gleasons. After arriving at the house, we shook hands with our hosts and packed ourselves into a sofa. As our family of four sat stiffly in a row, my younger brother and I stole glances at our parents for a clue as to what to do next.

4 Mrs. Gleason offered the relish tray to Mother. The tray looked pretty, with its tiny red radishes, curly sticks of carrots, and long, slender stalks of pale green celery. "Do try some of the celery, Mrs. Lin," she said. "It's from a local farmer, and it's sweet."

5 Mother picked up one of the green stalks, and Father followed suit. Then I picked up a stalk, and my brother did too. So there we sat, each with a stalk of celery in our right hand.

6 Mrs. Gleason kept smiling. "Would you like to try some of the dip, Mrs. Lin? It's my own recipe: sour cream and onion flakes, with a dash of Tabasco sauce."

7 Most Chinese don't care for dairy products, and in those days I wasn't even ready to drink fresh milk. Sour cream sounded perfectly revolting. Our family shook our heads in unison.

8 Mrs. Gleason went off with the relish tray to the other guests, and we carefully watched to see what they did. Everyone seemed to eat the raw vegetables quite happily.

9 Mother took a bite of her celery. *Crunch.* "It's not bad!" she whispered.

10 Father took a bite of his celery. *Crunch*. "Yes, it *is* good," he said, looking surprised.

11 I took a bite, and then my brother. *Crunch, crunch*. It was more than good; it was delicious. Raw celery has a slight sparkle, a zingy taste that you don't get in cooked celery. When Mrs. Gleason came around with the relish tray, we each took another stalk of celery, except my brother. He took two.

12 There was only one problem: long strings ran through the length of the stalk, and they got caught in my teeth. When I help my mother in the kitchen, I always pull the strings out before slicing celery.

13 I pulled the strings out of my stalk. *Z-z-zip, z-z-zip*. My brother followed suit. *Z-z-zip, z-z-zip*. To my left, my parents were taking care of their own stalks. *Z-z-zip, z-z-zip, z-z-zip*.

14 Suddenly I realized that there was dead silence except for our zipping. Looking up, I saw that the eyes of everyone in the room were on our family. Mr. and Mrs. Gleason, their daughter Meg, who was my friend, and their neighbors the Badels—they were all staring at us as we busily pulled the strings off our celery.

15 That wasn't the end of it. Mrs. Gleason announced that dinner was served and invited us to the dining table. It was **lavishly** covered with platters of food, but we couldn't see any chairs around the table. So we helpfully carried over some dining chairs and sat down. All the other guests just stood there. Mrs. Gleason bent down and whispered to us, "This is a buffet dinner. You help yourselves to some food and eat it in the living room."

16 Our family beat a retreat back to the sofa as if chased by enemy soldiers. For the rest of the evening, too **mortified** to go back to the dining table, I nursed[1] a bit of potato salad on my plate.

17 Next day Meg and I got on the school bus together. I wasn't sure how she would feel about me after the spectacle our family made at the party. But she was just the same as usual, and the only reference she made to the party was, "Hope you and your folks got enough to eat last night. You certainly didn't take very much. Mom never tries to figure out how much food to prepare. She just puts everything on the table and hopes for the best."

18 I began to relax. The Gleasons' dinner party wasn't so different from a Chinese meal after all. My mother also puts everything on the table and hopes for the best.

• • •

---

1. **nursed** drank or ate slowly

NOTES

19   Meg was the first friend I had made after we came to America. I eventually got acquainted with a few other kids in school, but Meg was still the only real friend I had.

20   My brother didn't have any problems making friends. He spent all his time with some boys who were teaching him baseball, and in no time he could speak English much faster than I could—not better, but faster.

21   I worried more about making mistakes, and I spoke carefully, making sure I could say everything right before opening my mouth. At least I had a better accent than my parents, who never really got rid of their Chinese accent, even years later. My parents had both studied English in school before coming to America, but what they had studied was mostly written English, not spoken.

22   Father's approach to English was a scientific one. Since Chinese verbs have no tense, he was fascinated by the way English verbs changed form according to whether they were in the present, past imperfect, perfect, pluperfect, future, or future perfect tense. He was always making diagrams of verbs and their inflections, and he looked for opportunities to show off his mastery of the pluperfect and future perfect tenses, his two favorites. "I shall have finished my project by Monday," he would say smugly.

23   Mother's approach was to memorize lists of polite phrases that would cover all possible social situations. She was constantly muttering things like "I'm fine, thank you. And you?" Once she accidentally stepped on someone's foot and hurriedly blurted, "Oh that's quite all right!" Embarrassed by her slip, she **resolved** to do better next time. So when someone stepped on *her* foot, she cried, "You're welcome!"

24   In our own different ways, we made progress in learning English. But I had another worry, and that was my appearance. My brother didn't have to worry, since Mother bought him blue jeans for school, and he dressed like all the other boys. But she insisted that girls had to wear skirts. By the time she saw that Meg and the other girls were wearing jeans, it was too late. My school clothes were bought already, and we didn't have money left to buy new outfits for me. We had too many other things to buy first, like furniture, pots, and pans.

25   The first time I visited Meg's house, she took me upstairs to her room, and I wound up trying on her clothes. We were pretty much the same size, since Meg was shorter and thinner than average. Maybe that's how we became friends in the first place. Wearing Meg's jeans and T-shirt, I looked at myself in the mirror. I could almost pass for an American—from the back, anyway. At

least the kids in school wouldn't stop and stare at me in the hallways, which was what they did when they saw me in my white blouse and navy blue skirt that went a couple of inches below the knees.

26   When Meg came to my house, I invited her to try on my Chinese dresses, the ones with a high collar and slits up the sides. Meg's eyes were bright as she looked at herself in the mirror. She struck several sultry poses, and we nearly fell over laughing.

. . .

27   The dinner party at the Gleasons' didn't stop my growing friendship with Meg. Things were getting better for me in other ways too. Mother finally bought me some jeans at the end of the month, when father got his paycheck. She wasn't in any hurry about buying them at first, until I worked on her. This is what I did. Since we didn't have a car in those days, I often ran down to the neighborhood store to pick up things for her. The groceries cost less at a big supermarket, but the closest one was many blocks away. One day, when she ran out of flour, I offered to borrow a bike from our neighbor's son and buy a ten-pound bag of flour at the big supermarket. I mounted the boy's bike and waved to my Mother. "I'll be back in five minutes!"

28   Before I started pedaling, I heard her voice behind me. "You can't go out in public like that! People can see all the way up your thighs!"

29   "I'm sorry," I said innocently. "I thought you were in a hurry to get the flour." For dinner we were going to have pot-stickers (fried Chinese dumplings), and we needed a lot of flour.

pot-stickers (fried Chinese dumplings)

30   "Couldn't you borrow a girl's bicycle?" complained Mother. "That way your skirt won't be pushed up."

31   "There aren't too many of those around," I said. "Almost all the girls wear jeans while riding a bike, so they don't see any point in buying a girl's bike."

32   We didn't eat pot-stickers that evening, and Mother was thoughtful. Next day we took the bus downtown and she bought me a pair of jeans. In the same week, my brother made the baseball team of his junior high school, Father started taking driving lessons, and Mother discovered rummage sales. We soon got all the furniture we needed, plus a dartboard and a 1,000-piece jigsaw puzzle (fourteen hours later, we discovered that it was a 999-piece

Skill:
Setting

These details tell me
that the Lakeview
restaurant is a very
formal place. I think the
Lin family might feel
nervous or unsure
about what to do in
this setting.

jigsaw puzzle). There was hope that the Lins might become a normal American family after all.

. . .

33   Then came our dinner at the Lakeview restaurant.

34   The Lakeview was an expensive restaurant, one of those places where a head waiter dressed in tails **conducted** you to your seat, and the only light came from candles and flaming desserts. In one corner of the room a lady harpist played tinkling melodies.

35   Father wanted to celebrate, because he had just been promoted. He worked for an electronics company, and after his English started improving, his superiors decided to appoint him to a position more suited to his training. The promotion not only brought a higher salary but was also a tremendous boost to his pride.

36   Up to then we had eaten only in Chinese restaurants. Although my brother and I were becoming fond of hamburgers, my parents didn't care much for western food, other than chow mein.

37   But this was a special occasion, and father asked his coworkers to recommend a really elegant restaurant. So there we were at the Lakeview, stumbling after the headwaiter in the murky dining room.

38   At our table we were handed our menus, and they were so big that to read mine I almost had to stand up again. But why bother? It was mostly in French, anyway.

39   Father, being an engineer, was always systematic. He took out a pocket French dictionary. "They told me that most of the items would be in French, so I came prepared." He even had a pocket flashlight, the size of a marking pen. While mother held the flashlight over the menu, he looked up the items that were in French.

40   "*Paté en croute*," he muttered. "Let's see . . . *paté* is paste . . . *croute* is crust . . . hmm . . . a paste in crust."

41   The waiter stood looking patient. I squirmed and died at least fifty times.

42   At long last Father gave up. "Why don't we just order four complete dinners at random?" he suggested.

43   "Isn't that risky?" asked Mother. "The French eat some rather peculiar things, I've heard."

44   "A Chinese can eat anything a Frenchman can eat," Father declared.

45   The soup arrived in a plate. How do you get soup up from a plate? I glanced at the other diners, but the ones at the nearby tables were not on their soup course, while the more distant ones were invisible in the darkness.

46   Fortunately my parents had studied books on western etiquette before they came to America. "Tilt your plate," whispered my mother. "It's easier to spoon the soup up that way."

47   She was right. Tilting the plate did the trick. But the etiquette book didn't say anything about what you did after the soup reached your lips. As any respectable Chinese knows, the correct way to eat your soup is to slurp. This helps to cool the liquid and prevent you from burning your lips. It also shows your appreciation.

48   We showed our appreciation. *Shloop*, went my father. *Shloop*, went my mother. *Shloop, shloop*, went my brother, who was the hungriest.

49   The lady harpist stopped playing to take a rest. And in the silence, our family's consumption of soup suddenly seemed unnaturally loud. You know how it sounds on a rocky beach when the tide goes out and the water drains from all those little pools? They go *shloop, shloop, shloop*. That was the Lin family, eating soup.

50   At the next table a waiter was pouring wine. When a large *shloop* reached him, he froze. The bottle continued to pour, and red wine flooded the tabletop and into the lap of a customer. Even the customer didn't notice anything at first, being also hypnotized by the *shloop, shloop, shloop*.

51   It was too much. "I need to go to the toilet," I mumbled, jumping to my feet. A waiter, sensing my urgency, quickly directed me to the ladies' room.

52   I splashed cold water on my burning face, and as I dried myself with a paper towel, I stared into the mirror. In this perfumed ladies' room, with its pink and silver wallpaper and marbled sinks, I looked completely out of place. What was I doing here? What was our family doing in the Lakeview restaurant? In America?

53   The door to the ladies' room opened. A woman came in and glanced **curiously** at me. I retreated into one of the toilet cubicles and latched the door.

54   Time passed—maybe half an hour, maybe an hour. Then I heard the door open again, and my mother's voice. "Are you in there? You're not sick, are you?"

55 There was real concern in her voice. A girl can't leave her family just because they slurp their soup. Besides, the toilet cubicle had a few drawbacks as a permanent residence. "I'm all right," I said, undoing the latch.

56 Mother didn't tell me how the rest of the dinner went, and I didn't want to know. In the weeks following, I managed to push the whole thing into the back of my mind, where it jumped out at me only a few times a day. Even now, I turn hot all over when I think of the Lakeview restaurant.

• • •

57 But by the time we had been in this country for three months, our family was definitely making progress toward becoming Americanized. I remember my parents' first PTA meeting. Father wore a neat suit and tie, and Mother put on her first pair of high heels. She stumbled only once. They met my homeroom teacher and beamed as she told them that I would make honor roll soon at the rate I was going. Of course Chinese etiquette forced Father to say that I was a very stupid girl and Mother to protest that the teacher was showing favoritism toward me. But I could tell they were both very proud.

• • •

58 The day came when my parents announced that they wanted to give a dinner party. We had invited Chinese friends to eat with us before, but this dinner was going to be different. In addition to a Chinese-American family, we were going to invite the Gleasons.

59 "Gee, I can hardly wait to have dinner at your house," Meg said to me. "I just *love* Chinese food."

60 That was a relief. Mother was a good cook, but I wasn't sure if people who ate sour cream would also eat chicken gizzards stewed in soy sauce.

61 Mother decided not to take a chance with the chicken gizzards. Since we had western guests, she set the table with large dinner plates, which we never used in Chinese meals. In fact we didn't use individual plates at all, but picked up food from the platters in the middle of the table and brought it directly to our rice bowls. Following the practice of Chinese-American restaurants, Mother also placed large serving spoons on the platters.

62 The dinner started well. Mrs. Gleason exclaimed at the beautifully arranged dishes of food: the colorful candied fruit in the sweet-and-sour pork dish, the noodle-thin shreds of chicken meat stir-fried with tiny peas, and the glistening pink prawns in a ginger sauce.

63   At first I was too busy enjoying my food to notice how the guests were doing. But soon I remembered my duties. Sometimes guests were too polite to help themselves and you had to serve them with more food.

64   I glanced at Meg, to see if she needed more food, and my eyes nearly popped out at the sight of her plate. It was piled with food: the sweet-and-sour meat pushed right against the chicken shreds, and the chicken sauce ran into the prawns. She had been taking food from a second dish before she finished eating her helping from the first!

65   Horrified, I turned to look at Mrs. Gleason. She was dumping rice out of her bowl and putting it on her dinner plate. Then she ladled prawns and gravy on top of the rice and mixed everything together, the way you mix sand, gravel, and cement to make concrete.

66   I couldn't bear to look any longer, and I turned to Mr. Gleason. He was chasing a pea around his plate. Several times he got it to the edge, but when he tried to pick it up with his chopsticks, it rolled back to the center of the plate again. Finally, he put down his chopsticks and picked up the pea with his fingers. He really did! A grown man!

67   All of us, our family and the Chinese guests, stopped eating to watch the activities of the Gleasons. I wanted to giggle. Then I caught my mother's eyes on me. She frowned and shook her head slightly, and I understood the message: the Gleasons were not used to Chinese ways, and they were just coping the best they could. For some reason I thought of celery strings.

68   When the main courses were finished, mother brought out a platter of fruit. " I hope you weren't expecting a sweet dessert," she said. " Since the Chinese don't eat dessert, I didn't think to prepare any."

69   "Oh, I couldn't possibly eat dessert!" cried Mrs. Gleason. "I'm simply stuffed!"

70   Meg had different ideas. When the table was cleared, she announced that she and I were going for a walk. "I don't know about you, but I feel like dessert," she told me, when we were outside. "Come on, there's a Dairy Queen down the street. I could use a big chocolate milkshake!"

71   Although I didn't really want anything more to eat, I insisted on paying for the milkshakes. After all, I was still hostess.

72   Meg got her large chocolate milkshake and I had a small one. Even so, she was finishing hers while I was only half done. Toward the end she pulled hard on her straw and went *shloop, shloop*.

NOTES

73 "Do you always slurp when you eat a milkshake?" I asked before I could stop myself.

74 Meg grinned. "Sure. All Americans slurp."

©1987 by Lensey Namioka. Reproduced by permission of Lensey Namioka.

First Read

Read "The All-American Slurp." After you read, complete the Think Questions below.

☁ THINK QUESTIONS

1. What problems does the narrator's family have when they go to dinner at their neighbors, the Gleasons? Cite textual evidence to support your answer.

2. How do the members of the narrator's family each tackle the problems that come from trying to learn English in their own way? Cite specific evidence from the text to support your answer.

3. At the Chinese dinner the narrator's family prepares for their neighbors, what happens that surprises the narrator? Cite specific evidence from the text to support your answer.

4. Read the following dictionary entry:

   mortify
   mor•ti•fy \môrdə,fī\

   verb

   1. to make someone feel shame or embarrassment
   2. to control or suppress by will

   Which definition most closely matches the meaning of **mortified** in paragraph 16? Write the correct definition of *mortified* here and explain how you figured it out.

5. Use context clues to determine the meaning of the word **conducted** as it is used in paragraph 34. Write your best definition of *conducted* here and explain how you inferred its meaning.

Skill: Setting

Use the Checklist to analyze Setting in "The All-American Slurp." Refer to the sample student annotations about Setting in the text.

••• CHECKLIST FOR SETTING

In order to identify how the plot of a particular story or drama unfolds in a series of episodes, note the following:

- ✓ key elements in the plot

- ✓ the setting(s) in the story

- ✓ how the plot unfolds in a series of episodes

- ✓ how the setting shapes the plot

To describe how the plot of a particular story or drama unfolds in a series of episodes, consider the following questions:

- ✓ When and where does this story take place?

- ✓ How does the plot unfold in a series of episodes?

- ✓ How does the setting affect the plot? How does it affect the characters and their responses to events? How does the setting help move the plot to a resolution?

Skill: Setting

Reread paragraphs 14–18 from "The All-American Slurp." Then, using the Checklist on the previous page, answer the multiple-choice questions below.

⟳ YOUR TURN

1. Based on paragraph 16, the reader can conclude that —

   ○ A. the Lin family feels out of place in the Gleasons' house.
   ○ B. the Lin family feels comfortable in the Gleasons' house.
   ○ C. the Lin family enjoys buffet-style dining.
   ○ D. the Lin family hates dinner parties.

2. How does the setting influence the Lin family's behavior in the excerpt?

   ○ A. The Lins are overly excited to eat dinner at the Gleasons' house, which is why they behave strangely.
   ○ B. The Lins are glad to finally become friends with an American family.
   ○ C. The Lins are unsure how to behave at the Gleasons' dinner party, which is why they make a few embarrassing mistakes.
   ○ D. The Lins are disgusted by American food.

3. Which paragraph shows the similarities between the narrator's family and Meg's family?

   ○ A. 14
   ○ B. 15
   ○ C. 16
   ○ D. 18

THE ALL-AMERICAN SLURP

Close Read

Reread "The All-American Slurp." As you reread, complete the Skills Focus questions below. Then use your answers and annotations from the questions to help you complete the Write activity.

◎ SKILLS FOCUS

1. Identify how the immigrant experience of learning English affects each character as the story's plot unfolds.

2. Identify how the two dinner parties in the story shape the plot, using specific examples from these events in your response.

3. Identify evidence that suggests what the narrator learns about culture when she catches Meg slurping her milkshake. What theme about the blending of cultures does this suggest?

4. In "Saying Yes," the speaker claims to be a part of two cultures. Identify ways in which the narrator in "The All-American Slurp" is also part of two cultures.

5. In "Saying Yes," the speaker tells the story of her identity. She describes how others often ask her to define herself. In "The All-American Slurp," identify evidence that suggests how the narrator would answer the same questions about Chinese and American identity.

✎ WRITE

DISCUSSION: "Saying Yes" and "The All-American Slurp" both feature distinct cultural settings. How does each text make use of Chinese and American cultures to influence the development of plot and character? Compare and contrast the relationships between setting, plot, and character in the two texts. Remember to support your ideas with evidence from the texts. In a discussion with your peers, use evidence from both texts as well as personal experience to respond to these questions.

Helen Keller

POETRY
Langston Hughes
1931

Introduction

The fiction and poetry of Missouri-born Langston Hughes (1902–1967) has resonated with readers for generations. As one of the leading figures of a literary movement known as the Harlem Renaissance, Hughes typically wrote about African American experiences and struggles. In this poem, however, he turns his attention to a Southern white woman who also faced a great struggle—Helen Keller. Deaf and blind from a young age, Keller overcame her physical limitations to become a beloved author and activist.

"She,
Within herself,
Found loveliness . . ."

1   She,
2   In the dark,
3   Found light
4   Brighter than many ever see.
5   She,
6   Within herself,
7   Found loveliness,
8   Through the soul's own **mastery.**
9   And now the world receives
10 From her **dower:**
11 The message of the strength
12 Of inner power.

WRITE

PERSONAL RESPONSE: The speaker of the poem says of Helen Keller that "She,/ Within herself,/ Found loveliness,/ Through the soul's own mastery." What does it mean to find something "within" yourself? When a person faces a challenge, why might it be necessary to turn inward rather than look for answers from other people or the outside world? In a personal response, record your conclusions. Include examples from the poem and your own prior experience to support your conclusions.

Please note that excerpts and passages in the StudySync® library and this workbook are intended as touchstones to generate interest in an author's work. The excerpts and passages do not substitute for the reading of entire texts, and StudySync® strongly recommends that students seek out and purchase the whole literary or informational work in order to experience it as the author intended. Links to online resellers are available in our digital library. In addition, complete works may be ordered through an authorized reseller by filling out and returning to StudySync® the order form enclosed in this workbook.

Reading & Writing
Companion

675

The Story of My Life
(Chapter IV)

INFORMATIONAL TEXT
Helen Keller
1903

Introduction

Serious illness at the age of 19 months left Helen Keller both blind and deaf. Serving as an inspiration to millions, Keller overcame those handicaps and went on to become a renowned author and social activist. In this passage from her autobiography, six-year-old Helen meets the person who will change her life forever, her private teacher Anne Sullivan.

"I did not know what the future held of marvel or surprise for me."

Excerpt from Chapter IV

1   The most important day I remember in all my life is the one on which my teacher, Anne Mansfield Sullivan, came to me. I am filled with wonder when I consider the immeasurable contrasts between the two lives which it connects. It was the third of March, 1887, three months before I was seven years old.

Helen Keller with her teacher, Anne Mansfield Sullivan

2   On the afternoon of that eventful day, I stood on the porch, dumb, expectant. I guessed vaguely from my mother's signs and from the hurrying to and fro in the house that something unusual was about to happen, so I went to the door and waited on the steps. The afternoon sun penetrated the mass of honeysuckle that covered the porch, and fell on my upturned face. My fingers lingered almost unconsciously on the familiar leaves and blossoms which had just come forth to greet the sweet southern spring. I did not know what the future held of marvel or surprise for me. Anger and bitterness had preyed upon me continually for weeks and a deep languor had succeeded this passionate struggle.

3   Have you ever been at sea in a dense fog, when it seemed as if a tangible white darkness shut you in, and the great ship, tense and anxious, **groped** her way toward the shore with plummet[1] and sounding-line, and you waited with beating heart for something to happen? I was like that ship before my education began, only I was without compass or sounding-line, and had no way of knowing how near the harbour was. "Light! give me light!" was the wordless cry of my soul, and the light of love shone on me in that very hour.

---

1. **plummet** a weighed tool used to measure depth in water

4   I felt approaching footsteps. I stretched out my hand as I supposed to my mother. Some one took it, and I was caught up and held close in the arms of her who had come to **reveal** all things to me, and, more than all things else, to love me.

5   The morning after my teacher came she led me into her room and gave me a doll. The little blind children at the Perkins **Institution** had sent it and Laura Bridgman had dressed it; but I did not know this until afterward. When I had played with it a little while, Miss Sullivan slowly spelled into my hand the word "d-o-l-l." I was at once interested in this finger play and tried to imitate it. When I finally succeeded in making the letters correctly I was flushed with childish pleasure and pride. Running downstairs to my mother I held up my hand and made the letters for doll. I did not know that I was spelling a word or even that words existed; I was simply making my fingers go in monkey-like imitation. In the days that followed I learned to spell in this uncomprehending way a great many words, among them pin, hat, cup and a few verbs like sit, stand and walk. But my teacher had been with me several weeks before I understood that everything has a name.

6   One day, while I was playing with my new doll, Miss Sullivan put my big rag doll into my lap also, spelled "d-o-l-l" and tried to make me understand that "d-o-l-l" applied to both. Earlier in the day we had had a tussle over the words "m-u-g" and "w-a-t-e-r." Miss Sullivan had tried to impress it upon me that "m-u-g" is mug and that "w-a-t-e-r" is water, but I persisted in **confounding** the two. In despair she had dropped the subject for the time, only to renew it at the first opportunity. I became impatient at her repeated attempts and, seizing the new doll, I dashed it upon the floor. I was keenly delighted when I felt the fragments of the broken doll at my feet. Neither sorrow nor regret followed my passionate outburst. I had not loved the doll. In the still, dark world in which I lived there was no strong **sentiment** or tenderness. I felt my teacher sweep the fragments to one side of the hearth[2], and I had a sense of satisfaction that the cause of my discomfort was removed. She brought me my hat, and I knew I was going out into the warm sunshine. This thought, if a wordless sensation may be called a thought, made me hop and skip with pleasure.

7   We walked down the path to the well-house, attracted by the fragrance of the honeysuckle with which it was covered. Some one was drawing water and my teacher placed my hand under the spout. As the cool stream gushed over one hand she spelled into the other the word water, first slowly, then rapidly. I stood still, my whole attention fixed upon the motions of her fingers. Suddenly I felt a misty consciousness as of something forgotten--a thrill of returning thought; and somehow the mystery of language was **revealed** to me. I knew

2. **hearth** the stone, brick, or concrete fireplace floor and area in front of the fireplace

NOTES

then that "w-a-t-e-r" meant the wonderful cool something that was flowing over my hand. That living word awakened my soul, gave it light, hope, joy, set it free! There were barriers still, it is true, but barriers that could in time be swept away.

8 I left the well-house eager to learn. Everything had a name, and each name gave birth to a new thought. As we returned to the house every object which I touched seemed to quiver with life. That was because I saw everything with the strange, new sight that had come to me. On entering the door I remembered the doll I had broken. I felt my way to the hearth and picked up the pieces. I tried vainly to put them together. Then my eyes filled with tears; for I realized what I had done, and for the first time I felt repentance and sorrow.

9 I learned a great many new words that day. I do not remember what they all were; but I do know that mother, father, sister, teacher were among them—words that were to make the world blossom for me, "like Aaron's rod, with flowers." It would have been difficult to find a happier child than I was as I lay in my crib at the close of that eventful day and lived over the joys it had brought me, and for the first time longed for a new day to come.

✏ WRITE

PERSONAL RESPONSE: When Keller realizes that the "finger play" in her palm actually signifies the water she's feeling, she experiences an epiphany: everything has a name. Think about an important discovery you made as a child. Perhaps you learned the correct meaning of a word you misunderstood or found out that a growling dog may bite. In a personal response, compare and contrast your experience with Keller's and draw conclusions about how learning can affect children.

The Miracle Worker

DRAMA
William Gibson
1956

Introduction

*T*he Miracle Worker by William Gibson (1914–2008) was not only an award-winning Broadway play, but also an Academy Award-winning film. Based on the autobiography of Helen Keller, *The Story of My Life*, *The Miracle Worker* presents an emotional account of Keller's early life, after an illness caused her to lose her sight and hearing. The excerpt here comes from Act III of the play and illustrates the unflagging efforts of teacher Annie Sullivan to break through Helen's walls of darkness and silence. In sharing the story of Helen Keller, who went on to become a world-famous author and political activist, Gibson provides a powerful portrait of two strong-willed women guided by the spirit of determination.

"She's testing you. You realize?"

CHARACTERS:

ANNIE SULLIVAN: young teacher trained to work with the blind and deaf; in her early twenties
HELEN KELLER: child who has been blind and deaf since infancy; now seven years old
KATE KELLER: Helen's mother; in her early thirties
CAPTAIN KELLER: Helen's father; middle-aged
JAMES KELLER: Captain Keller's grown son by a previous marriage; in his early twenties
AUNT EV: Captain Keller's sister; middle-aged
VINEY: Keller family servant

TIME: The 1880s
PLACE: In and around the Keller homestead in Tuscumbia, Alabama

1   [Now in the family room the rear door opens, and HELEN steps in. She stands a moment, then sniffs in one deep grateful breath, and her hands go out **vigorously** to familiar things, over the door panels, and to the chairs around the table, and over the silverware on the table, until she meets VINEY; she pats her flank approvingly.]

2   VINEY: Oh, we glad to have you back too, prob'ly.

3   [HELEN hurries groping to the front door, opens and closes it, removes its key, opens and closes it again to be sure it is unlocked, gropes back to the rear door and repeats the procedure, removing its key and hugging herself gleefully. AUNT EV is next in by the rear door, with a relish tray; she bends to kiss HELEN'S cheek. HELEN finds KATE behind her, and thrusts the keys at her.]

4   KATE: What? Oh.

5   [To EV]

6   Keys.

Skill: Dramatic Elements and Structure

The setting gives useful information. I can imagine how the characters looked in 1880s Alabama and how the room is set up. I can get a good sense of Helen from the stage directions, even though she can't say anything. She's grateful to be home and she knows the location of all the familiar things in the house. She touches them.

NOTES

7 [She pockets them, lets HELEN feel them.]

8 Yes, I'll keep the keys. I think we've had enough of locked doors, too.

9 [JAMES, having earlier put ANNIE'S suitcase inside her door upstairs and taken himself out of view around the corner, now reappears and comes down the stairs as ANNIE and KELLER mount the porch steps. Following them into the family room, he pats ANNIE'S hair in passing, rather to her surprise.]

10 JAMES: Evening, general.

11 [He takes his own chair opposite. VINEY bears the empty water pitcher out to the porch. The remaining suggestion of garden house is gone now, and the water pump is unobstructed; VINEY pumps water into the pitcher. KATE surveying the table breaks the silence.]

12 KATE: Will you say grace, Jimmie?

13 [They bow their heads, except for HELEN, who palms her empty plate and then reaches to be sure her mother is there. JAMES considers a moment, glances across at ANNIE, lowers his head again, and obliges.]

14 JAMES [Lightly]: And Jacob was left alone, and wrestled with an angel until the breaking of the day; and the hollow of Jacob's thigh was out of joint, as he wrestled with him; and the angel said, Let me go, for the day breaketh. And Jacob said, I will not let thee go, except thou bless me. Amen.

15 [ANNIE has lifted her eyes suspiciously at JAMES, who winks expressionlessly and **inclines** his head to HELEN.]

16 Oh, you angel.

17 [The others lift their faces; VINEY returns with the pitcher, setting it down near KATE, then goes out the rear door; and ANNIE puts a napkin around HELEN.]

18 AUNT EV: That's a very strange grace, James.

19 KELLER: Will you start the muffins, Ev?

20 JAMES: It's from the Good Book, isn't it?

21 AUNT EV [Passing a plate]: Well, of course it is. Didn't you know?

22 JAMES: Yes, I knew.

23 KELLER [Serving]: Ham, Miss Annie?

24   ANNIE: Please.

25   AUNT EV: Then why ask?

26   JAMES: I meant it is from the Good Book, and therefore a fitting grace.

27   AUNT EV: Well, I don't know about that.

28   KATE [With the pitcher]: Miss Annie?

29   ANNIE: Thank you.

30   AUNT EV: There's an awful lot of things in the Good Book that I wouldn't care to hear just before eating.

31   [When ANNIE reaches for the pitcher, HELEN removes her napkin and drops it to the floor. ANNIE is filling HELEN'S glass when she notices it; she considers HELEN'S bland expression a moment, then bends, **retrieves** it, and tucks it around HELEN'S neck again.]

32   JAMES: Well, fitting in the sense that Jacob's thigh was out of joint, and so is this piggie's.

33   AUNT EV: I declare, James—

34   KATE: Pickles, Aunt Ev?

35   AUNT EV: Oh, I should say so, you know my opinion of your pickles—

36   KATE: This is the end of them, I'm afraid. I didn't put up nearly enough last summer, this year I intend to— [She interrupts herself, seeing HELEN **deliberately** lift off her napkin and drop it again to the floor. She bends to retrieve it, but ANNIE stops her arm.]

37   KELLER [Not noticing]: Reverend looked in at the office today to complain his hens have stopped laying. Poor fellow, he was out of joint, all he could— [He stops too, to frown down the table at KATE, HELEN, and ANNIE in turn, all suspended in mid-motion.]

38   JAMES [Not noticing]: I've always suspected those hens.

39   AUNT EV: Of what?

40   JAMES: I think they're Papist. Has he tried— [He stops, too, following KELLER'S eyes. ANNIE now stops to pick the napkin up.]

NOTES

41 AUNT EV: James, now you're pulling my—lower extremity, the first thing you know we'll be—

42 [She stops, too, hearing herself in the silence. ANNIE, with everyone now watching, for the third time puts the napkin on HELEN. HELEN yanks it off, and throws it down. ANNIE rises, lifts HELEN'S plate, and bears it away. HELEN, feeling it gone, slides down and commences to kick up under the table; the dishes jump. ANNIE **contemplates** this for a moment, then coming back takes HELEN'S wrists firmly and swings her off the chair. HELEN struggling gets one hand free, and catches at her mother's skirt; when KATE takes her by the shoulders, HELEN hangs quiet.]

43 KATE: Miss Annie.

44 ANNIE: No.

45 KATE [A pause]: It's a very special day.

46 ANNIE [Grimly]: It will be, when I give in to that.

47 [She tries to disengage HELEN'S hand; KATE lays hers on ANNIE'S.]

48 ANNIE: Captain Keller.

49 KELLER [Embarrassed]: Oh, Katie, we—had a little talk, Miss Annie feels that if we indulge Helen in these—

Skill: Dramatic Elements and Structure

Annie and Aunt Ev's disagreement tells me about their characters. Annie thinks Helen should experience the consequences when she breaks rules, but Aunt Ev doesn't want to punish her. She thinks that Helen should be able to do what she wants. I wonder if this is the main conflict that drives the plot.

50 AUNT EV: But what's the child done?

51 ANNIE: She's learned not to throw things on the floor and kick. It took us the best part of two weeks and—

52 AUNT EV: But only a napkin, it's not as if it were breakable!

53 ANNIE: And everything she's learned is? Mrs. Keller, I don't think we should—play tug-of-war for her, either give her to me or you keep her from kicking.

54 KATE: What do you wish to do?

55 ANNIE: Let me take her from the table.

56 AUNT EV: Oh, let her stay, my goodness, she's only a child, she doesn't have to wear a napkin if she doesn't want to her first evening—

57 ANNIE [Level]: And ask outsiders not to interfere.

NOTES

58   AUNT EV [Astonished]: Out—outsi—I'm the child's aunt!

59   KATE [Distressed]: Will once hurt so much, Miss Annie? I've—made all Helen's favorite foods, tonight.

60   [A pause.]

61   KELLER [Gently]: It's a homecoming party, Miss Annie.

62   [ANNIE after a moment releases HELEN. But she cannot accept it, at her own chair she shakes her head and turns back, intent on KATE.]

63   ANNIE: She's testing you. You realize?

64   JAMES [To ANNIE]: She's testing you.

65   KELLER: Jimmie, be quiet.

66   [JAMES sits, tense.]

67   Now she's home, naturally she—

68   ANNIE: And wants to see what will happen. At your hands. I said it was my main worry, is this what you promised me not half an hour ago?

69   KELLER [Reasonably]: But she's not kicking, now—

70   ANNIE: And not learning not to. Mrs. Keller, teaching her is **bound** to be painful, to everyone. I know it hurts to watch, but she'll live up to just what you demand of her, and no more.

71   JAMES [Palely]: She's testing you.

72   KELLER [Testily]: Jimmie.

73   JAMES: I have an opinion, I think I should—

74   KELLER: No one's interested in hearing your opinion.

75   ANNIE: I'm interested, of course she's testing me. Let me keep her to what she's learned and she'll go on learning from me. Take her out of my hands and it all comes apart.

Excerpted from *The Miracle Worker* by William Gibson, published by Simon & Schuster.

Copyright © BookheadEd Learning, LLC

First Read

Read *The Miracle Worker*. After you read, complete the Think Questions below.

THINK QUESTIONS

1. Who is Annie Sullivan, and why is she at the Keller homestead in Tuscumbia, Alabama? Cite evidence from information and ideas that are directly stated and from ideas you have inferred from clues in the text.

2. How would you describe Annie's emotions? Why is she feeling this way? Cite evidence from the text to support your answer.

3. What do you think Annie means when she says, "Take her out of my hands and it all comes apart"? Cite evidence from the text to support your answer.

4. Use context clues to determine the meaning of **retrieves** as it is used in line 31. Write your definition of *retrieves* and explain how you figured out its meaning.

5. Read the following dictionary entry:

bound \bound\
noun

1. a limitation or restriction
2. a leap or jump

verb

1. to walk in leaping or jumping strides

adjective

1. certain or likely to do something

Which definition most closely matches the meaning of **bound** as it is used in line 70? Write the appropriate definition of *bound* here and explain how you figured out the correct meaning.

Skill: Dramatic Elements and Structure

Use the Checklist to analyze Dramatic Elements and Structure in *The Miracle Worker*. Refer to the sample student annotations about Dramatic Elements and Structure in the text.

••• CHECKLIST FOR DRAMATIC ELEMENTS AND STRUCTURE

In order to identify the dramatic elements and structure of a play, note the following:

- ✓ the order of acts and scenes in the play

- ✓ what happens in each act and scene

- ✓ how the acts and scenes work together to develop the plot

- ✓ the setting of the play and how it changes by act and scene

- ✓ the information in stage directions, including lighting, sound, and set, as well as details about characters, including exits and entrances

To analyze how a particular scene fits into the overall structure of a text and contributes to the development of the theme, setting, or plot, consider the following questions:

- ✓ When does this particular scene appear?

- ✓ How does this scene fit into the overall structure of the text?

- ✓ How do setting, characters, and other elements in the scene contribute to the development of the setting and plot?

- ✓ What does the scene contribute to the theme or message of the drama?

Skill: Dramatic Elements and Structure

Reread lines 68–75 from *The Miracle Worker*. Then, using the Checklist on the previous page, answer the multiple-choice questions below.

↻ YOUR TURN

1. What does the dialogue between Captain Keller and Annie in lines 68–70 tell the reader about the drama's theme?

    ○ A. Annie is interested in having Captain Keller discontinue his service.
    ○ B. Annie is going to continue to fight to help Helen learn, even if it's hard.
    ○ C. Annie is afraid that Helen will lose the will to learn as time passes.
    ○ D. Annie is irritated that James is not willing to do what it takes for Helen to learn.

2. What does the stage direction in line 72 reveal about Captain Keller's attitude toward his son James?

    ○ A. Captain Keller values James's opinions.
    ○ B. Captain Keller thinks James is being too hard on Annie.
    ○ C. Captain Keller does not value James's opinions.
    ○ D. Captain Keller encourages James to speak during family meetings.

3. In what way is Annie's dialogue in line 75 likely to affect the plot?

    ○ A. It is likely Helen will be taken from the table.
    ○ B. It is likely Helen will be allowed to stay at the table.
    ○ C. It is likely Annie will resign her teaching post.
    ○ D. It is likely Annie and James will begin to date.

Close Read

Reread *The Miracle Worker*. As you reread, complete the Skills Focus questions below. Then use your answers and annotations from the questions to help you complete the Write activity.

◎ SKILLS FOCUS

1. One of the purposes of stage directions is to describe the actions of the characters. Highlight evidence in the stage directions for *The Miracle Worker* that helps you understand the conflicts among various characters. Explain how the evidence helps you understand the conflict that drives the plot.

2. Identify evidence in the dialogue of conflict between the characters in *The Miracle Worker*. Explain what the dialogue reveals about the plot.

3. One of the themes in *The Miracle Worker* is the ability of a teacher to transform a student's life. Identify evidence in the drama that develops this theme and explain your reasoning.

4. Highlight examples of dialogue where Helen is discussed. What do the characters' words reveal about what they want for Helen?

5. In Chapter IV of *The Story of My Life,* Helen Keller tells the story of meeting Annie Sullivan, the teacher who changed her life. Langston Hughes tells Helen's story of overcoming her physical challenges in his poem "Helen Keller." Identify evidence that helps you determine what story William Gibson tells in *The Miracle Worker*. Explain what the story is.

✏ WRITE

COMPARE AND CONTRAST: What is the conflict in the play and how is it resolved? Compare the conflict and resolution of the conflict in the play with those that are presented in "Helen Keller" by Langston Hughes and Keller's autobiography, *The Story of My Life*. Cite specific scenes or dialogue that contribute to the play's conflict and resolution to support your response.

Extended
Oral
Project and
Grammar

EXTENDED
ORAL
PROJECT

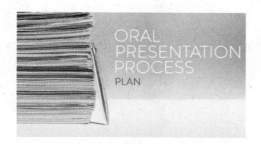

Oral Presentation Process: Plan

PLAN	DRAFT	REVISE	EDIT AND PRESENT

Stories are powerful. It's easy to get lost in a great fiction story like "Damon and Pythias," or a true account, like that of Melba Pattillo Beals in *Warriors Don't Cry*. All stories, including those from the *Making Your Mark* unit, have the ability to influence your perspective, or how you see the world. Your own stories are powerful, too. Maybe you've lived through something that shaped one of your core beliefs. Is there an event in your life that contributed to a strong opinion you hold? What is it?

WRITING PROMPT

What is something you believe in?

Think about something for which you hold a position or take a stance. How did you come to adopt this position? What experience, event, person, or story shaped your belief? Give an organized presentation with a specific stance and position. Tell a story from your life that explains how you adopted your position. Your story should focus on a singular moment or experience from your life and clearly relate to your position or stance. As you prepare your presentation, consider the following:

- A position or stance is a belief or opinion that you hold.

- A story that supports your position should have a clear beginning, middle, and end.

- Your presentation should be about yourself.

In your presentation, be sure to employ the following in order to communicate your ideas effectively:

- a specific stance and position

- eye contact

- speaking rate

- volume

- enunciation

- natural gestures

- media components or visual displays

- conventions of language

Introduction to Oral Presentation

Argumentative oral presentations that are based on personal experiences use anecdotes, or short stories about people and events, to support a specific position or stance held by the speaker. They are organized in a classic story structure and use effective speaking techniques to communicate ideas. The characteristics of this type of argumentative oral presentation include:

- a specific position or stance

- anecdotes, or stories, that support the position or stance

- a classic story structure with a beginning, middle, and end

- consistent eye contact and natural gestures

- clear oral communication

- integration of multimedia and visual displays

- a works cited page

As you continue with this Extended Oral Project, you'll receive more instruction and practice at crafting each of the characteristics of argumentative writing to create your own oral presentation.

Before you get started on your own argumentative oral presentation, read this oral presentation that one student, Lorenzo, wrote in response to the writing prompt. As you read the Model, highlight and annotate the features of argumentative writing that Lorenzo included in his oral presentation.

STUDENT MODEL

NOTES

Dress for Success

Introduction:

I choose to wear comfortable clothes. Some people scoff at my jorts (jean shorts), but these faded beauties are as soft as a blanket. Others have questioned my sock choices. But it makes no difference to me whether one sock is green and ankle-length and the other is knee-high and ornamented with Halloween pumpkins. My t-shirt is two sizes too large for the tallest kid in school, and definitely too big for me.

Dress for Success

Author: Lorenzo

Claim:

But I find both utility and pride in the clothing I wear. I believe that your clothes should make it possible for you to do the thing you love the most.

Clothing should...

- Create pride in the wearer
- Be useful and beneficial to the wearer
- Make it possible to do what you love

NOTES

Narrative Context:

The thing I love the most is drumming. You may not be familiar with just how physically intense drumming can be, but some drummers really go wild when they play.

What I wear when I play is important—hence my unstylish uniform; but I didn't always know that.

Narrative Beginning:

Last year, I was going for a spot at the prestigious Summer Music Academy. SMA is a music camp. However, this camp is neither crafts nor kayaking. This camp is ten hours a day of musical boot camp, where young hopefuls like myself learn to hone their technique from the best teachers. Some of whom are even famous!

I drum daily. So, I was pumped to audition. Let me revise that statement: I was both pumped and terrified! Still, I knew that if I drummed my heart out, I would be fine. I might even get in.

Summer Music Academy Info

- Musical boot camp for young musicians admitted through audition only
- Ten hours of instrumental practice and theory per day
- World famous teachers

Narrative Middle:

Ariana, who is my older sister, is the smartest and coolest person I know. I look up to her, and I know she cares about me. So, when she took me shopping for my audition and outfitted me in a suit, I tried to quiet the voice in my head that said: *this ridiculous suit isn't you.*

And so, at the suggestion (more like demand) of my sister Ariana (who gets scary when she makes demands), I wore a tight, uncomfortable suit to the biggest audition of my life.

Narrative Climax:

I walked into my audition with my head held high (because my collar was so stiff) and my arms calmly at my sides (because I could barely move them). I sat down behind the drum set, picked up my sticks, and created a beat.

Well, I tried to. When I wanted to tappa-tappa-tappa-kish, I tappa-tappa-tappa-missed. The sounds I produced had neither beat nor rhythm. My arms were stuck so tightly in my sleeves that I kept missing the surface of the drum. It was like *Titanic, Part 2*. I went full speed ahead and—bam—I ran right into the iceberg.

I failed, and the judges unanimously agreed.

Narrative Falling Action:

I slunk out of the audition room, totally embarrassed. I felt that I had made a fool of myself. As I waited for my ride, this girl sat down next to me. She was carrying an instrument in a big case. She said, "Hey, I'm Jules. Sorry it didn't work out in there."

I shook my head. I was too upset to talk.

Jules said, "You know, I bombed my first big performance because I insisted on wearing these crazy, white, studded high heels during my solo. Right in the middle of everything, I not only fell over but also knocked three other saxophonists out of their chairs!" She laughed at herself. "It's not about what you wear, it's about how you play."

Gems of Advice from Jules

- "I bombed my first big performance because I insisted on wearing these crazy white, studded high heels during my solo."
- "It's not about what you wear, it's about how you play."

Narrative Falling Action Detail:

I looked at Jules, who was dressed plainly in jeans and flannel. She had braces and messy long brown hair, but there was something about her that was truly cool. I thought about the drummers I had seen in photos and videos. Like Jules, they were truly cool and wore clothes that made drumming easy.

NOTES

Narrative End:

That night when I got home, I took off my suit and immediately put back on my uniform of jorts and t-shirt. I set up my selfie stick and turned my phone on video mode. I pressed record and played the set I intended to play earlier. I moved like electricity. More importantly, I felt like myself.

That night I sent the SMA my video, hoping the judges might recognize my skills and passion for drumming. A week later, the message I had been waiting for arrived in my inbox.

Be True to Yourself

- I put on my jorts and felt like myself.
- The judges saw the real me in my video: a passionate, skilled drummer.

Conclusion:

According to scientists at Northwestern University, ". . . new research shows that wearing certain items of clothing identified with certain qualities could help improve performance…" (McGregor). Whether it's a three-piece suit or a pair of jorts and a too-big t-shirt, wear the clothes that help you do the things you love. My name is Lorenzo and I am a proud, jorts-wearing student at the Summer Music Academy.

Works Cited

McGregor, Jena. "New Study: What You Wear Could Affect How Well You Work."
  The Washington Post, 10 Mar. 2012,
  www.washingtonpost.com/blogs/post-leadership/post/new-study-what-you-wear-
  could-affect-how-well-you-work/2011/04/01/gIQAssHomR_blog.html.

✏ WRITE

Writers often take notes about ideas before they sit down to prepare their presentation. Think about what you've learned so far about oral presentations and organizing argumentative writing to help you begin prewriting.

- **Purpose:** What are some things that you believe in?

- **Audience:** What message do you want your audience to take away from your presentation?

- **Position/Claim:** Which of these could you tell a story about to illustrate your position?

- **Relevant Evidence/Anecdote:** What happened to help you adopt this position? What challenge or conflict did you have to deal with? Did you learn something or change in some way?

- **Engaging the Audience/Oral Presentation Skills:** How do you want to tell your story? Will you be humorous, serious, inspirational? How can you use technology and visuals to engage your audience?

Response Instructions

Use the questions in the bulleted list to write a one-paragraph summary. Your summary should describe what will happen in your argumentative oral presentation.

Don't worry about including all of the details now; focus only on the most essential and important elements. You will refer back to this short summary as you continue through the steps of the writing process.

Skill: Evaluating Sources

First, reread the sources you gathered and identify the following:

- what kind of source it is, including video, audio, or text, and where the source comes from
- where information seems inaccurate, biased, or outdated
- where information seems irrelevant or incomplete

In order to use advanced searches to gather relevant, credible, and accurate print and digital sources, use the following questions as a guide:

- Is the source material written by a recognized expert on the topic?
- Is the source material published by a well-respected author or organization?
- Is the material up-to-date or based on the most current information?
- Is the material factual, and can it be verified by another source?
- Is the source material connected to persons or organizations that are objective and unbiased?
- Does the source contain omissions of important information?

Please note that excerpts and passages in the StudySync® library and this workbook are intended as touchstones to generate interest in an author's work. The excerpts and passages do not substitute for the reading of entire texts, and StudySync® strongly recommends that students seek out and purchase the whole literary or informational work in order to experience it as the author intended. Links to online resellers are available in our digital library. In addition, complete works may be ordered through an authorized reseller by filling out and returning to StudySync® the order form enclosed in this workbook.

Reading & Writing Companion   701

YOUR TURN

Read the factors below. Then, complete the chart by sorting them into those that show that a source is credible and reliable and those that do not.

Factors	
A	The text is based on the opinions of one person.
B	The author is a reporter for an internationally recognized newspaper.
C	The article is from the 1950s.
D	The text is informational and includes research from a well-recognized university.
E	The website is for a personal podcast.
F	The article includes clear arguments based on facts.

Credible and Reliable	Not Credible or Reliable

YOUR TURN

Complete the chart by filling in the title and author of a source you are considering using for your own oral presentation and answering the questions about it.

Question	My Source
Source Title and Author: Are the title and author clearly identified? What are they?	
Reliability: Is the material up-to-date or based on the most current information?	
Credibility: Is the source material written by a recognized expert on the topic? Is the source material published by a well-respected author or organization?	
Accuracy: Is the material factual, and can it be verified by another source?	

Skill: Organizing an Oral Presentation

••• CHECKLIST FOR ORGANIZING AN ORAL PRESENTATION

In order to present claims and findings using appropriate eye contact, adequate volume, and clear pronunciation, do the following:

- decide whether your presentation will be delivered to entertain, critique, inform, or persuade

- identify your audience in order to create your content

- choose a style for your oral presentation, either formal or informal

- present claims and any information you have found, sequencing your ideas and information logically

- make sure your descriptions, facts, and details accentuate and support the main idea of your presentation

- include multimedia components such as graphics, images, music or sound effects, and visual displays in your presentation to clarify information

- use appropriate eye contact, adequate volume, and clear pronunciation

To present claims and findings using appropriate eye contact, adequate volume, and clear pronunciation, consider the following questions:

- Have I decided on the purpose of my presentation and identified my audience?

- Have I put my facts and ideas in a logical sequence?

- Did I make sure the descriptions, facts, and details accentuate and support the main idea of my presentation?

- Do my facts and details accentuate and support the main idea?

- Did I include multimedia components to clarify information?

- Have I practiced using appropriate eye contact, adequate volume, and clear pronunciation?

⟳ YOUR TURN

Read each idea below. Then, complete the chart by matching each idea with its correct place in the presentation sequence.

	Ideas
A	I kept clipping a little more here and there, trying to even up the poor dog's coat.
B	Believe me, there is nothing cute about a bald golden retriever.
C	Never assume that anyone can do something just because the process looks easy.
D	photo of a golden retriever
E	Unfortunately for my dog, you can't glue hair back on.
F	Now I know that there are some things an amateur shouldn't tackle—like clipping a dog.
G	I woke up one morning and thought, "How hard could it be to clip my golden retriever?"

Presentation Sequence	Idea
Hook	
Position	
Story beginning	
Story middle	
Story end	
How experience shaped position	
Media or visual component	

YOUR TURN

Complete the chart below by writing a short summary of your ideas for each section of your presentation.

Outline	Summary
Hook	
Position	
Story beginning	
Story middle	
Story end	
How experience shaped position	
Media or visual component	

Skill: Considering Audience and Purpose

••• CHECKLIST FOR CONSIDERING AUDIENCE AND PURPOSE

In order to present claims and findings using appropriate eye contact, adequate volume, and clear pronunciation, note the following:

- when writing your presentation, sequence your ideas, facts, or explanations in a logical order, such as the order in which events occurred

- use pertinent, or valid, and important facts and details to support and accentuate, or highlight, the main ideas or themes in your presentation

- use appropriate eye contact

- speak at an adequate volume, so you can be heard by everyone

- use correct pronunciation

- remember to adapt, or change, your speech according to your task, and if it is appropriate, use formal English and not language you would use in ordinary conversation

To better understand how to present claims and findings and use appropriate eye contact, adequate volume, and clear pronunciation, consider the following questions:

- Have I used appropriate eye contact when giving my presentation?

- Did I speak at an adequate volume and use correct pronunciation?

- Did I sequence ideas in a logical order, such as the order in which events occurred?

- Have I used valid and important facts and details? Have I accentuated, or highlighted, these details?

- If necessary, have I used formal English in my presentation?

YOUR TURN

Read the excerpts from Nik and Dakota's presentation on characters below. Then, complete the chart by identifying whether the register is formal or informal.

	Excerpts
A	Because he's a troublemaker!
B	And the way characters are designed is called characterization.
C	And, like with all those characters, their traits are revealed through their own words, thoughts, and actions.
D	Like Elmer Fudd for Bugs Bunny.
E	I know! There are so many good ones!
F	The main character is called the protagonist.

Formal	Informal

WRITE

Take turns reading your presentation aloud to a partner. When you finish, write a reflection about how well your register, vocabulary, tone, and voice suited your audience and purpose. What aspects did you apply well? What aspects did you struggle with? How can you improve in the future?

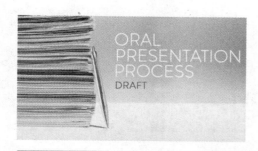

Oral Presentation Process: Draft

PLAN	DRAFT	REVISE	EDIT AND PRESENT

You have already made progress toward writing your oral presentation. Now it is time to draft your oral presentation.

✏ WRITE

Use your plan and other responses in your Binder to draft your oral presentation. You may also have new ideas as you begin drafting. Feel free to explore those new ideas as you have them. You can also ask yourself these questions:

- Have I taken a specific position or stance?

- Have I included anecdotes, or stories, that support my position or stance?

- Have I employed a classic story structure with a clear beginning, middle, and end?

Before you submit your draft, read it over carefully. You want to be sure you've responded to all aspects of the prompt.

Here is Lorenzo's oral presentation draft. As you read, identify details that help Lorenzo grab his audience's attention and understand his position. As he continues to revise and edit his narrative, he will find and improve weak spots in his writing, as well as correct any language or punctuation mistakes.

NOTES

Skill:
Communicating
Ideas

Lorenzo revises sentences to add information or to clarify meaning for the audience.

STUDENT MODEL: FIRST DRAFT

Dress for Success

~~I choose to wear comfortable clothes. Some people scoff at my jorts, but these faded beauties are as soft as a blanket.~~ I choose to wear comfortable clothes. Some people scoff at my jorts (jean shorts), but these faded beauties are as soft as a blanket. Others have questioned my sock choices. But it makes no difference to me whether one sock is green and ankle-length and the other is knee-high and ornamented with Halloween pumpkins. My t-shirt is two sizes too large for the tallest kid in school, and definitely too big for me. But I find both utility and pride in the clothing I wear. I believe that your clothes should make it possible for you to do the thing you love the most.

The thing I love the most is drumming. You may not be familiar with just how physically intense drumming can be, but some drummers really go wild when they play.

What I wear when I play is important. This explains my unstylish uniform.

I wore a tight, uncomfortable suit to the biggest audition of my life. I was going for a spot at the prestigious Summer Music Academy. SMA is a music camp. However, this camp is neither crafts or kayaking. This camp is ten hours a day of musical boot camp, where young hopefuls like me learn to hone their technique from the best teachers. Some of who are even famous!

I drum daily, so, I was pumped to audition, let me revise that statement, I was like woah man! Still, I knew that if I drummed my heart out, I would be fine. I might even get in.

Ariana, who is my older sister, is not only the scariest and smartest and coolest person I know. I look up to her, and I know she cares about me. So, when she took me shopping for my audition and outfitted me in a suit, I tried to quit the voice in my head that said: *this rediculous suit isn't you.*

And so, at the suggestion (more like demand) of my sister Ariana (who gets scary when she makes demands), I wore a tight, uncomfortable suit to the biggest audition of my life.

I walked into my audition with my head held high and my arms calmly at my sides. I sat down behind the drum set, picked up my sticks, and created a beat.

Please note that excerpts and passages in the StudySync® library and this workbook are intended as touchstones to generate interest in an author's work. The excerpts and passages do not substitute for the reading of entire texts, and StudySync® strongly recommends that students seek out and purchase the whole literary or informational work in order to experience it as the author intended. Links to online resellers are available in our digital library. In addition, complete works may be ordered through an authorized reseller by filling out and returning to StudySync® the order form enclosed in this workbook.

Reading & Writing Companion   711

Well, I tried to. The sounds I produced had neither beat nor rhythm. My arms were stuck so tightly in my sleeves that I kept missing the surface of the drum. It was like *Titanic, Part 2*. I went full speed ahead and—bam—I ran right into the iceberg.

I failed, and the judges unanimusly agreed.

I walked out of the audition room, totally embarrassed. I felt that I had made a fool of myself. As I waited for my ride, this girl sat down next to me. She was carrying an instrument in a big case. She said, "Hey, I'm Jules. Sorry it didn't work out in there."

I shook my head. I was too upset to talk.

Jules said, "You know, I bombed my first big performance because I insisted on wearing these crazy, white, studded high heels during my solo. Right in the middle of everything, I fell over but also knocked three other saxophonists out of their chairs!" She laughed at her. "It's not about what you wear, it's about how you play."

I looked at Jules, which was dressed plainly in jeans and flannel. She had braces and messy long brown hair, but there was something about her that was so totally awesome dude. I thought about the drummers I had seen in photos and videos. Like Jules, they were truly cool and wore clothes that made drumming easy.

~~That night when I got home, I took off my suit. I immediately put back on my uniform of jorts and t-shirt. I set up my selfie stick. Then I turned my phone on video mode. I pressed record and played the set I intended to play earlier. I moved like electricity, and I felt like me.~~

That night when I got home, I took off my suit and immediately put back on my uniform of jorts and t-shirt. I set up my selfie stick and turned my phone on video mode. I pressed record and played the set I intended to play earlier. I moved like electricity. More importantly, I felt like myself.

That night I sent the SMA my video, hoping the judges might recognize my skills and passion for drumming. A week later, the message I had been waiting for arrived in my inbox.

Scientists at Northwestern University, have done studies that prove that the clothes we wear affect how we think and what we feel. Our clothes give us confidence. Whether it's a three-piece suit or a pair of jorts and a too-big t-shirt, wear the clothes that help you do the things you love. My name is Lorenzo and I am a proud, jorts-wearing student at the Summer Music Academy.

Works Cited

McGregor, Jena. "New Study: What You Wear Could Affect How Well You Work." *The Washington Post*, 10 Mar. 2012, www.washingtonpost.com/blogs/post-leadership/post/new-study-what-you-wear-could-affect-how-well-you-work/2011/04/01/gIQAssHomR_blog.html.

Skill: Reasons and Relevant Evidence

Lorenzo wants to include evidence to explain how comfy clothes helped him achieve his goal. He examines his argumentative oral presentation—he clearly states his claim, and he adds reasons and relevant evidence to support his position.

Skill: Sources and Citations

Lorenzo realizes that he should have a Works Cited list. He makes sure to include the author, title, publisher, publication day, and the web address. By including all the required information, Lorenzo gives proper credit to the sources he used. It also lets readers find these sources on their own.

Skill: Communicating Ideas

••• CHECKLIST FOR COMMUNICATING IDEAS

In order to present claims and findings using appropriate eye contact, adequate volume, and clear pronunciation, note the following:

- when writing your presentation, sequence your ideas, facts, or explanations in a logical order, such as the order in which events occurred

- use pertinent, or valid, and important facts and details to support and accentuate, or highlight, the main ideas or themes in your presentation

- remember to use appropriate eye contact

- speak at an adequate volume, so you can be heard by everyone

- use correct pronunciation

To better understand how to present claims and findings and use appropriate eye contact, adequate volume, and clear pronunciation, consider the following questions:

- Have I used appropriate eye contact when giving my presentation?

- Did I speak at an adequate volume and use correct pronunciation?

- Did I sequence ideas in a logical order, such as the order in which events occurred?

- Have I used valid and important facts and details? Have I accentuated these details?

YOUR TURN

Read the examples of students using different presentation strategies to communicate their ideas. Then, complete the chart by identifying the correct strategy to match each example.

Strategies	
A	make eye contact
B	use gestures
C	pay attention to posture
D	speak clearly

Example	Strategy
A student moves her arm in a quick downward motion when talking about a tree crashing to the ground.	
A student slows his rate of speech and clearly enunciates his position.	
A student looks directly at one audience member and then another while speaking.	
A student stands front and center with her shoulders squared.	

✏ WRITE

Take turns reading your presentation aloud to a partner.

When you are presenting:

- Employ steady eye contact to help keep your listeners' attention.

- Use appropriate speaking rate, volume, and enunciation to clearly communicate with your listeners.

- Use natural gestures to add meaning and interest as you speak.

- Keep in mind conventions of language, and avoid informal or slang speech.

When you finish, write a reflection about your experience of using presentation strategies to effectively communicate your ideas. Which strategies did you implement well? Which strategies did you struggle with? Which strategies did you find most helpful? How can you improve in the future?

Skill: Reasons and Relevant Evidence

Copyright © BookheadEd Learning, LLC

••• CHECKLIST FOR REASONS AND RELEVANT EVIDENCE

As you begin to determine what reasons and relevant evidence will support your claim(s), use the following questions as a guide:

- What is the claim (or claims) that I am making in my argument?

- Are the reasons I have included clear and easy to understand?

- What relevant evidence am I using to support this claim?

- Have I selected evidence from credible sources, and are they relevant to my claim?

- Am I quoting the source evidence accurately?

Use the following steps as a guide to help you determine how you will support your claim(s) with clear reasons and relevant evidence, using credible sources:

- identify the claim(s) you will make in your argument

- establish clear reasons for making your claim(s)

- select evidence from credible sources that will convince others to accept your claim(s)

  > look for reliable and relevant sources of information online, such as government or educational websites

  > search print resources such as books written by an expert or authority on a topic

- explain the connection between your claim(s) and the evidence selected

YOUR TURN

Choose the best answer for each question.

1. Which sentence, added to the end of the paragraph in the box, would best support Lorenzo's claim?

> Jules said, "You know, I bombed my first big performance because I insisted on wearing these crazy, white, studded high heels during my solo. Right in the middle of everything, I fell over but also knocked three other saxophonists out of their chairs!" She laughed at herself.

- ○ A. "Man, I was uncomfortable!"
- ○ B. "It's not about what you wear, it's about how you play."
- ○ C. "I was so upset."
- ○ D. "So, wear whatever you want, whenever you want to!"

2. Which reason should Lorenzo add to clarify the end of his oral presentation, in the box below?

> My name is Lorenzo and I am a proud, jorts-wearing student at the Summer Music Academy.

- ○ A. So, in conclusion, wear what you like.
- ○ B. You can wear a three-piece suit or a too-big t-shirt.
- ○ C. I'm so happy my dream came true—Summer Music Academy is the place for me!
- ○ D. Whether it's a three-piece suit or a pair of jorts and an oversized t-shirt, wear the clothes that help you do the things you love.

 WRITE

Use the questions in the checklist to revise your oral presentation.

Skill:
Sources and Citations

••• CHECKLIST FOR SOURCES AND CITATIONS

In order to cite and gather sources of information, do the following:

- select and gather information from a variety of print and digital sources relevant to a topic

- check that sources are credible, or reliable and trustworthy, and avoid relying on or overusing one source

- be sure that facts, details, and other information support the central idea or claim and demonstrate your understanding of the topic or text

- use parenthetical citations or footnotes or endnotes to credit sources

- include all sources in a bibliography or Works Cited list, following a standard format:

  > Halall, Ahmed. *The Pyramids of Ancient Egypt*. New York: Central Publishing, 2016.

  > for a citation or footnote, include the author, title, and page number

To check that sources are gathered and cited correctly, consider the following questions:

- Did I give credit to sources for all of my information to avoid plagiarism?

- Have I relied on one source, instead of looking for different points of view on my topic in other sources?

- Did I include all my sources in my bibliography or Works Cited list?

- Are my citations formatted correctly using a standard, accepted format?

⟳ YOUR TURN

Choose the best answer to each question.

1. Lorenzo did not reference any print sources in his presentation; however, if he had found a book on drumming that included a chapter on what drummers should wear, what information should he have included at the end of a sentence referencing this material?

   ○ A. Add the author's last name in parentheses after the quotation.
   ○ B. Add the page number in parentheses after the quotation.
   ○ C. Add the author's last name and the page number in parentheses after the quotation.
   ○ D. He wouldn't need a citation.

2. Below is a citation for another article that Lorenzo found but did not use in his presentation. What information is he missing?

> Hutson, Matthew and Tori Rodriguez. "Dress for Success: How Clothes Influence Our Performance." *Scientific American*. www.scientificamerican.com/article/dress-for-success-how-clothes-influence-our-performance/.

   ○ A. None. All the information is there.
   ○ B. The title of the article is missing.
   ○ C. The name(s) of the author(s) is missing.
   ○ D. The date of publication is missing.

✎ WRITE

Use the questions in the checklist to write and revise your Works Cited list. Refer to the *MLA Handbook* as needed.

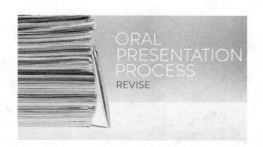

Oral Presentation Process: Revise

PLAN	DRAFT	REVISE	EDIT AND PRESENT

You have written a draft of your oral presentation. You have also received input from your peers about how to improve it. Now you are going to revise your draft.

◀◀ REVISION GUIDE

Examine your draft to find areas for revision. Keep in mind your purpose and audience as you revise for clarity, development, organization, and style. Use the guide below to help you review:

Review	Revise	Example
Clarity		
Highlight any places in your presentation where your position or ideas are unclear because of a lack of information or vague wording.	Revise sentences to add information or to clarify meaning for the audience.	I choose to wear comfortable clothes. Some people scoff at my jorts (jean shorts), but these faded beauties are as soft as a blanket.
Development		
Identify places where you can add interesting details or use humor to make your point and keep your audience engaged.	Insert descriptive details or use hyperbole or other forms of humor to enliven your discussion.	I walked into my audition with my head held high (because my collar was so stiff) and my arms calmly at my sides (because I could barely move them). I sat down behind the drum set, picked up my sticks, and created a beat.

Review	Revise	Example
Organization		
Annotate the places in your presentation where you begin your story or transition from the beginning to the middle or from the middle to the end.	Add a transition that makes it clear that you are beginning your story or moving from the beginning to the middle or from the middle to the end.	• What I wear is important—hence my unstylish uniform. But I didn't always know that. • Last year, I was going for a spot at the prestigious Summer Music Academy. SMA is a music camp.
Style: Word Choice		
Identify simple action verbs.	Select sentences to rewrite using more expressive action verbs.	I ~~walked~~ slunk out of the audition room, totally embarrassed.
Style: Sentence Variety		
Look for strings of sentences that have similar lengths. Annotate any place where a conjunction or transition could vary the length of the sentences you use.	Use conjunctions to join together short, choppy sentences or separate long sentence by adding a transition.	That night when I got home, I took off my ~~suit. I~~ suit and immediately put back on my uniform of jorts and t-shirt. I set up my ~~selfie stick. Then I~~ selfie stick and turned my phone on video mode. I pressed record and played the set I intended to play earlier. I moved like ~~electricity, and~~ electricity. More importantly, I felt like myself.

✏ WRITE

Use the guide above, as well as your peer reviews, to help you evaluate your oral presentation to determine areas that should be revised.

Grammar: Reflexive and Intensive Pronouns

A reflexive pronoun refers to a noun or another pronoun and indicates that the same person or thing is involved. A reflexive pronoun is formed by adding *-self* or *-selves* to certain personal and possessive pronouns. Reflexive and intensive pronouns take the following forms:

Singular: *myself, yourself, himself, herself, itself*   Plural: *ourselves, yourselves, themselves*

Text	Explanation
Those were all the things **he** had, but **he** also had **himself**. *Hatchet*	The reflexive pronoun *himself* is singular and refers to the pronoun *he*.

An intensive pronoun adds emphasis to a noun or pronoun that has already been named.

Text	Explanation
Jammed into this small space were tools, books, journals, mechanical projects, aircraft parts—and **Feng himself**, who rarely finished work before 3 a.m. *The Father of Chinese Aviation*	The intensive pronoun *himself* is singular and adds emphasis to the noun *Feng*.

Observe these rules when using reflexive and intensive pronouns.

Rule	Correct	Incorrect
When a personal pronoun refers to the subject of a sentence, always use a reflexive pronoun.	Marjorie treated **herself** to an ice cream cone.	Marjorie treated her to an ice cream cone. (*Her* is meant to refer to *Marjorie*.)
A reflexive pronoun refers to the subject; it does not take the place of the subject.	Mae and **you** will be team captains.	Mae and yourself will be team captains.

⟳ YOUR TURN

1. How should this sentence be changed?

> The students painted the mural themselves.

- ○ A. Change **themselves** to **itself**.
- ○ B. Change **themselves** to **themself**.
- ○ C. Change **themselves** to **theirselves**.
- ○ D. No change needs to be made to this sentence.

2. How should this sentence be changed?

> Helmets are needed for extra weight when divers theirselves do not need to move around much.

- ○ A. Change **theirselves** to **themselves**.
- ○ B. Change **theirselves** to **himself**.
- ○ C. Change **theirselves** to **themself**.
- ○ D. No change needs to be made to this sentence.

3. How should this sentence be changed?

> Jamie and myself are thinking of joining a band.

- ○ A. Change **Jamie** to **Herself**.
- ○ B. Change **myself** to **himself**.
- ○ C. Change **myself** to **I**.
- ○ D. No change needs to be made to this sentence.

4. How should this sentence be changed?

> Author Rachel Carson didn't see the ocean for ourselves until after college.

- ○ A. Change **ourselves** to **himself**.
- ○ B. Change **ourselves** to **herself**.
- ○ C. Change **ourselves** to **themself**.
- ○ D. No change needs to be made to this sentence.

Grammar: Sentence Variety

A sentence is a group of words that expresses a complete thought. All sentences begin with a capital letter and end with a punctuation mark. Different kinds of sentences have different purposes. You can vary your use of different kinds of sentences for style, to enhance meaning, or interest your reader or listener.

A **declarative sentence** makes a statement. It ends with a period. Declarative sentences give information to the reader in a clear way.

> They would tear the world apart to find him.
>
> *Hatchet*

An **interrogative sentence** asks a question. It ends with a question mark. Questions can be used to engage the reader or listener.

> Was it the first day or the second day?
>
> *Hatchet*

An **exclamatory sentence** expresses a strong emotion. It ends with an exclamation point. Writers often use exclamatory sentences with a more informal style of writing that portrays emotion.

> That's beautiful!
>
> *Master Harold . . . and the boys*

An **imperative sentence** gives a command or makes a request. It ends with a period. It can end with an exclamation point if the command expresses a strong emotion. Imperative sentences often begin with a verb, and the subject of imperative sentences is often an understood *you*. Imperative sentences can be used when a writer wants to convince or persuade the reader of his or her point of view, or to show how a character commands something in a story.

> **(You)** Come! Dine with us to-morrow.
>
> *A Christmas Carol*

⟳ YOUR TURN

1. How should these sentences be changed?

> Large amounts of "black gold" were discovered in Alaska in 1968 "Black gold" is another name for oil

- ○ A. Capitalize the **b** in the first **"black gold."**
- ○ B. Insert a period after **1968** and the word **oil**.
- ○ C. Insert a period after the word **oil**.
- ○ D. No change needs to be made to these sentences.

2. How should these sentences be changed?

> Who were the first white settlers in Alaska? Russians built a settlement on Kodiak Island in 1984. Why did the Russians want to settle in Alaska They went there to look for furs.

- ○ A. Insert a question mark after the word **furs**.
- ○ B. Delete the period after **1984** and insert a question mark.
- ○ C. Insert a question mark between **Alaska** and **They**.
- ○ D. No change needs to be made.

3. How should this sentence be changed?

> I heard my sister yell from the bathroom, "I dropped my ring down the sink!"

- ○ A. Delete the exclamation point and add a period.
- ○ B. Change the **I** to **You**.
- ○ C. Add another exclamation point to the end.
- ○ D. No change needs to be made to this sentence.

4. Choose the correct punctuation mark that completes the sentence below.

> The sign in the cafeteria said, "Throw away your trash before you leave?"

- ○ A. Delete the question mark and add an exclamation point at the end.
- ○ B. Delete the question mark and add a period at the end.
- ○ C. Add the word **you** to the beginning of the sentence and leave the question mark.
- ○ D. No change needs to be made to this sentence.

Grammar: Style

When presenting to an audience of peers, the speaker should use conventional grammar and punctuation, and maintain a semi-formal style.

Rule	Text
Maintain a semi-formal style.	Ariana, who is my older sister, is the smartest and coolest person I know.
When writing and speaking in semi-formal style, use the correct form of pronouns.	I felt that I had made a fool of **myself**.
When writing and speaking in semi-formal style, use correct punctuation.	The day was so beautiful; it seemed like anything could happen.
Use a consistent tone throughout your presentation.	I choose to wear comfortable clothes. (beginning) My name is Lorenzo and I am a proud, jorts-wearing student at the Summer Music Academy. (end)

Do not use slang terms, or informal style.

Correct	Incorrect
I drum daily. So, I was pumped to audition. Let me revise that statement: I was both pumped and terrified! Still, I knew that if I drummed my heart out, I would be fine. I might even get in.	I was like, so pumped to audition, but I knew I could do it. I was also way scared too.
I was upset, and yelled, "Stop that!"	I was like, hey man, don't do that!

Please note that excerpts and passages in the StudySync® library and this workbook are intended as touchstones to generate interest in an author's work. The excerpts and passages do not substitute for the reading of entire texts, and StudySync® strongly recommends that students seek out and purchase the whole literary or informational work in order to experience it as the author intended. Links to online resellers are available in our digital library. In addition, complete works may be ordered through an authorized reseller by filling out and returning to StudySync® the order form enclosed in this workbook.

Reading & Writing Companion

727

⟳ YOUR TURN

1. Which sentence is an example of the correct style for an oral presentation at school?

   ○ A. They knew he had been busy, all by him.
   ○ B. I was so super upset.
   ○ C. Even though I was exhausted, I knew I had to complete the job myself.
   ○ D. How much farther is there to go!

2. Which sentence is an example of the correct style for an oral presentation at school?

   ○ A. There are many lessons to be learned, even from people and places you might not expect.
   ○ B. He learned him lesson.
   ○ C. There are many lessons to be learned, even from themselves?
   ○ D. We learned like so many cool lessons.

3. How should the style of these sentences be changed?

What I wear when I play is important. I wear an unstylish uniform. I didn't always know that.

   ○ A. Drumming is the best! I wear what I want!
   ○ B. What I wear when I play is important—hence my unstylish uniform; but I didn't always know that.
   ○ C. What I wear is important because of drumming—I wear what is best for myself.
   ○ D. Do you wear stylish clothes? What I wear is important.

4. How should the style of this sentence be changed?

I moved like electricity, and I felt like me.

   ○ A. I felt like me when I played.
   ○ B. I moved like electricity. More importantly, I felt like myself.
   ○ C. Have you ever moved like electricity. I did, myself.
   ○ D. There was electricity in the air.

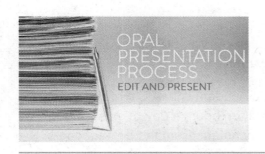

Oral Presentation Process: Edit and Present

PLAN	DRAFT	REVISE	EDIT AND PRESENT

You have revised your argumentative oral presentation based on your peer feedback and your own examination.

Now, it is time to edit your oral presentation. When you revised, you focused on the content of your presentation. You probably looked at the clarity of your position and argument, the development of your story structure, and whether your word choices and anecdotes were engaging and supportive of your position. When you edit, you focus on the mechanics of your oral presentation, paying close attention to things like grammar and punctuation.

Use the checklist below to guide you as you edit:

☐ Have I ensured that all pronouns are in the correct form?

☐ Have I varied my sentence patterns for meaning and listener interest?

☐ Have I maintained a consistent style and tone?

☐ Do I have any sentence fragments or run-on sentences?

☐ Have I spelled everything correctly?

Notice some edits Lorenzo has made:

- Created sentence variety by changing two choppy sentences into one longer, more varied sentence and adding a new, short sentence.

- Changed the incorrect usage of *or* to *nor*.

- Changed an incorrect intensive pronoun.

- Maintained consistency in style by changing slang dialogue to more descriptive words.

~~What I wear when I play is important. This explains my unstylish uniform.~~ What I wear when I play is important—hence my unstylish uniform. But I didn't always know that.

Last year, I was going for a spot at the prestigious Summer Music Academy. SMA is a music camp. However, this camp is neither crafts ~~or~~ nor kayaking. This camp is ten hours a day of musical boot camp, where young hopefuls like ~~me~~ myself learn to hone their technique from the best teachers. Some of who are even famous!

I drum daily. So, I was pumped to audition. Let me revise that statement~~,~~ : ~~was like woah man!~~ I was both pumped and terrified! Still, I knew that if I drummed my heart out, I would be fine. I might even get in.

✏ WRITE

Use the questions above, as well as your peer reviews, to help you evaluate your argumentative oral presentation to determine areas that need editing. Then edit your oral presentation to correct those errors.

Once you have made all your corrections, you are ready to present your work. You may present it to your class or to a group of your peers. You can record your presentation to share with family and friends, or to post on your blog. If you publish online, share the link with your family, friends, and classmates.

Stage Sets Through History

INFORMATIONAL TEXT

Introduction

How has the experience of viewing a play changed over time? Even when the dialogue is the same as it was hundreds of years ago, the look of the play is different, thanks to the scenery that surrounds it.

V VOCABULARY

transported

carried away to

symmetrical

describing something with two halves that are identical

derives

originates from

aligned

to agree with or be in the correct or matching position

perspective

drawing something in two dimensions to add length, height, and depth

NOTES

☰ READ

1   Suppose you go to a Broadway musical. The curtain rises. You see the dramatic scenery. You may be **transported** to a jungle. You may find yourself on a 1960s city block. The stage set, or scenery, tells you when and where the action will take place.

2   Theater has entertained people for nearly 3,000 years. It took a long time for stage sets to become an important part of that entertainment.

EARLY STAGES

3   In the time of the ancient Greeks, heroes and villains performed on a bare stage.

Amphitheater at Acropolis, Athens

4   The first scenery was a small tent on the stage. Actors changed their clothes there. The tent was called a *skene*. The word *scenery* **derives** from that word.

5   Sophocles wrote plays in ancient Greece. He may have been the first person to use painted scenery. A painted cloth hung on the skene. It showed a place or set a mood. We call such a painting a *backdrop*.

ADDING SCENERY

6   In 1600s Italy, scenery became a key part of plays. Two inventions led to this change. One was the understanding of **perspective** in art. In stage sets, perspective could make things look far away. The other invention was a new kind of stage. This type of stage had a proscenium arch, which helped to frame the performers. The architect Giovanni Battista Aleotti perfected this design in 1618. It is still used today.

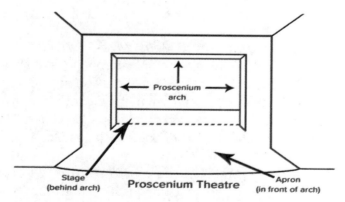

Proscenium arch

Stage (behind arch)   **Proscenium Theatre**   Apron (in front of arch)

7   During the 1600s, stage sets were grand, but they were not realistic. Aleotti painted scenes on canvas. These scenes lined the back of the stage. They were fancy and **symmetrical**. The same set stayed up for the whole play.

REALISTIC SETTINGS

8   The 1800s saw big changes in stage sets. Plays became more realistic, and the setting was now very important. Designers made the stage look like a boxed room. They used furniture and props that matched the set. The set fit the historical period of the play. A so-called "box set" might even have a ceiling. The whole set fit onto the stage. The idea was that the audience formed the invisible "fourth wall" of the set. Audience members felt as though they were peering into a real home. They could watch the action from their seats behind the fourth wall.

9   Today, set designs are sometimes realistic. Sometimes, though, they have just a few objects on the stage. The objects give hints to the setting. A ladder might stand in for a fire escape. A piano on the apron might indicate a jazz club. A bale of hay or a painted silo might let an audience imagine the calves and chickens on a farm in Oklahoma.

THEN AND NOW

10   Suppose you saw Shakespeare's *The Merry Wives of Windsor* in the 1600s. The stage set would have been a painted backdrop. It might show the town of Windsor. If you saw the play in the 1800s, the stage set would change for every scene and act. It might show a room at the Garter Inn. It might change to show Windsor Park. Each canvas backdrop would look as real as possible. Each would be **aligned** to the time when the play takes place.

11   If you saw the play today, you might see a bare set. The set might use the apron as well as the stage. It might include just tiny hints about the scenery. A sign might tell you that you are in the Garter Inn. A tree in a pot might stand for Windsor Park. The play has not changed, but the use of stage sets has changed a great deal.

First Read

Read the story. After you read, answer the Think Questions below.

☁ THINK QUESTIONS

1. What is the main topic of the text?

   _____

   _____

2. What information does this text give?

   _____

   _____

3. What is one way plays and stage sets have changed in the present day?

   _____

   _____

4. Use context to confirm the meaning of the word *aligned* as it is used in "Stage Sets Through History." Write your definition of *aligned* here.

   _____

   _____

5. What is another way to say that the word "scenery" *derives* from the word "skene"?

   _____

   _____

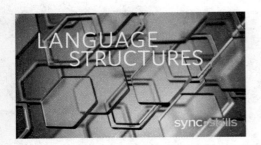

Skill:
Language Structures

★ DEFINE

In every language, there are rules that tell how to **structure** sentences. These rules define the correct order of words. In the English language, for example, a **basic** structure for sentences is subject, verb, and object. Some sentences have more **complicated** structures.

You will encounter both basic and complicated **language structures** in the classroom materials you read. Being familiar with language structures will help you better understand the text.

••• CHECKLIST FOR LANGUAGE STRUCTURES

To improve your comprehension of language structures, do the following:

✓ Monitor your understanding.

- Ask yourself: Why do I not understand this sentence? Is it because I do not understand some of the words? Or is it because I do not understand the way the words are ordered in the sentence?

- Pay attention to coordinating conjunctions.

  > **Coordinating conjunctions** are used to join words or groups of words that have equal grammatical importance.

  > The coordinating conjunction *and* shows that two or more things are true of a person, object, or event.

    Example: Josefina is a good athlete **and** student.

  > The coordinating conjunction *or* shows a choice between different possibilities.

    Example: Josefina can either do her homework **or** go for a run.

  > The coordinating conjunction *but* shows a contrast between people, objects, or events.

    Example: Josefina wants to run **but** should finish her homework first.

- Break down the sentence into its parts.

  > Ask yourself: What ideas are expressed in this sentence? Are there conjunctions that join ideas or show contrast?

✓ Confirm your understanding with a peer or teacher.

YOUR TURN

Read the sentence from the text. Write the letter of the correct function of the underlined conjunction in the sentence.

Function	
A	connecting choices
B	connecting contrasting ideas
C	connecting similar or related ideas
D	connecting similar or related words

Sentence	Function
They used furniture <u>and</u> props that matched the set.	
Plays became more realistic, <u>and</u> the setting was now very important.	
A bale of hay <u>or</u> a painted silo might let an audience imagine the calves and chickens on a farm in Oklahoma.	
During the 1600s, stage sets were grand, <u>but</u> they were not realistic.	

Skill:
Visual and Contextual Support

★ DEFINE

Visual support is an image or an object that helps you understand a text. **Contextual support** is a **feature** that helps you understand a text. By using visual and contextual supports, you can develop your vocabulary so you can better understand a variety of texts.

First, preview the text to identify any visual supports. These might include illustrations, graphics, charts, or other objects in a text. Then, identify any contextual supports. Examples of contextual supports are titles, heads, captions, and boldface terms. Write down your **observations**.

Then, write down what those visual and contextual supports tell you about the meaning of the text. Note any new vocabulary that you see in those supports. Ask your peers and your teacher to **confirm** your understanding of the text.

••• CHECKLIST FOR VISUAL AND CONTEXTUAL SUPPORT

To use visual and contextual support to understand texts, do the following:

- ✓ Preview the text. Read the title, headers, and other features. Look at any images and graphics.

- ✓ Write down the visual and contextual supports in the text.

- ✓ Write down what those supports tell you about the text.

- ✓ Note any new vocabulary that you see in those supports.

- ✓ Create an illustration for the reading and write a descriptive caption.

- ✓ Confirm your observations with your peers and teacher.

YOUR TURN

Read the following excerpt from the text. Then, complete the multiple-choice questions below.

from "Stage Sets Through History"

ADDING SCENERY

In 1600s Italy, scenery became a key part of plays. Two inventions led to this change. One was the understanding of perspective in art. In stage sets, perspective could make things look far away. The other invention was a new kind of stage. This type of stage had a proscenium arch, which helped to frame the performers. The architect Giovanni Battista Aleotti perfected this design in 1618. It is still used today.

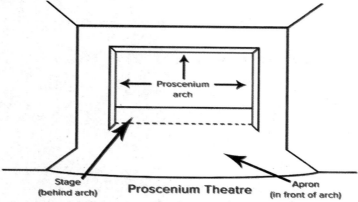

1. The heading tells you that in the period of history described in this section

    ○ A. people did not yet use scenery in plays
    ○ B. plot was more important than scenery
    ○ C. scenery became a part of stage sets
    ○ D. actors had to build their own scenery

2. According to the diagram, the "new kind of stage" was known as a(n)

    ○ A. apron
    ○ B. proscenium
    ○ C. arch
    ○ D. stage

STAGE SETS
THROUGH
HISTORY

Close Read

✏ WRITE

INFORMATIVE: Choose one section of "Stage Sets Through History" to summarize in a short report. Begin with a topic sentence. Then tell the main ideas and details of the section in your own words. Pay attention to the spelling of plural nouns as you write.

Use the checklist below to guide you as you write.

☐ Which section did you choose to summarize?

☐ What was the topic of that section?

☐ What are some key ideas you learned from that section?

Use the sentence frames to organize and write your informative paragraph.

In the section of text called "_____,"

the author tells about _____.

At the time being discussed, _____

_____.

For example, _____

_____.

One feature of scenery in these times might have been _____

_____.

Six Too Many

DRAMA

Introduction

In Nonno's Italian childhood, the holidays featured a special feast. His grandchildren are used to more modern traditions. Lydia is willing to be open-minded, but Ben is miserable as the meal begins. Can his grandfather win him over?

VOCABULARY

distinctive
characteristic of or special to one person or thing

vigil
a period of watching and waiting, as in preparation for a holy day

delectable
highly delicious or pleasing

tureen
a deep, covered serving dish

succession
a group of things or people following one after another

NOTES

≡ READ

1 [*SCENE 1: A modern-day dining room. MOTHER, BEN, and LYDIA are seated at a long table with a holiday centerpiece and candles. A Christmas tree is visible through an archway.*]

2 MOTHER (*turning to her children*): Now, remember, kids—we are skipping the usual turkey and stuffing. Nonno asked to share something **distinctive** from his childhood.

3 BEN (*sulking*): We know, Mom. The Feast of the Seven Dumb Fishes. Like fish are what people eat on Christmas Eve!

4 LYDIA: Well, I like fish—some kinds, anyway. And it's Nonno's house.

5 BEN (*crossly*): I could see one fish, maybe, as an appetizer. But seven? That's at least six too many.

NOTES

6 MOTHER: Shh. Here comes Nonno with the first course!

7 [*NONNO (Grandfather) enters proudly, bearing a platter.*]

8 MOTHER (*helping to serve*): Tell us about the dish, Papa! Salt cod, **delectable**! (BEN *groans.*)

9 NONNO: Well, it's not everyone's cup of tea, but it is traditional to start the meal this way. We'll be having a **succession** of small plates, like that tapas restaurant that is Lydia's favorite. Just a few bites until the final dish . . . (BEN *groans again.*)

10 LYDIA: Ignore Ben, Nonno. He's been driving us up the wall complaining about traditions.

11 NONNO (*winking*): Well, there are traditions and traditions, you know. My family's Christmas Eve tradition is probably just a bit older than yours, Ben! We have served this kind of food for generations.

12 MOTHER: Originally, the idea was that we Italians were waiting for Christmas, holding a kind of **vigil**, and eating meat was not allowed.

13 NONNO: That's right, and just as we always had eaten fish on Fridays, we ate fish on Christmas Eve. (*He sits, takes his fork, and starts to eat the salt cod. BLACKOUT.*)

14 [*SCENE 2: Later, that same evening. The family is still at the table, which is littered with dishes. NONNO enters, bearing a* **tureen**.]

15 LYDIA (*groaning*): Oh, Nonno, I honestly don't think I could eat another bite! Those clams were wonderful, but the gross little octopus bodies on skewers nearly killed me!

16 NONNO: Nonsense! I spent all day making this from scratch; it's Ben's favorite! (*He lifts the lid, and steam rises.*)

17 BEN (*amazed*): Nonno! You made a cioppino? We haven't had fish stew since Nonna died! I actually forgot it existed!

18 NONNO: Your grandmother would never forgive me if I didn't include a cioppino. I remember when you were small, you would call her on the phone and tell her to make it for you the next time you visited.

19 BEN: It was such an important part of our trips to see you! I would help Nonna in the kitchen, and she always called on you to chop the heads off the fish.

20 MOTHER (*a bit tearfully*): I'm surprised you remember, Ben—you were so little!

21 LYDIA: I barely remember, but that glorious smell is reminding me!

22 NONNO (*serving the stew into bowls*): This, in a nutshell, is why we take our ancestors' traditions and pass them down. Smelling this wonderful stew reminds me of your grandmother, but it also reminds me of my own grandmother in Salerno. One day, perhaps, Ben or Lydia will make the Feast of the Seven Fishes for their children, and the smells and tastes will take them back to today.

23 BEN (*rising to help* NONNO *hand around the bowls*): We will come early next year so you can show me how to make cioppino. I definitely will need you to chop off the heads, though. (MOTHER *and* LYDIA *look at each other in surprise, shrug, and laugh.*)

24 LYDIA: What happened to "six too many"?

25 BEN (*shrugging*): Seven was just right. Although I must say salt cod is not my favorite.

26 NONNO (*raising his glass*): To traditions! (*The others toast and drink. CURTAIN.*)

First Read

Read the play. After you read, answer the Think Questions below.

☁ THINK QUESTIONS

1. Who are the main characters in the play? What is their relationship?

   _____

   _____

2. Where and when do the two scenes in the play take place?

   _____

   _____

3. At the end of the play, who changes his or her mind? Explain.

   _____

   _____

4. Use context to confirm the meaning of the word *succession* as it is used in "Six Too Many." Write your definition of *succession* here.

   _____

   _____

5. What is another way to say that a meal is *distinctive*?

   _____

   _____

Please note that excerpts and passages in the StudySync® library and this workbook are intended as touchstones to generate interest in an author's work. The excerpts and passages do not substitute for the reading of entire texts, and StudySync® strongly recommends that students seek out and purchase the whole literary or informational work in order to experience it as the author intended. Links to online resellers are available in our digital library. In addition, complete works may be ordered through an authorized reseller by filling out and returning to StudySync® the order form enclosed in this workbook.

Reading & Writing
Companion   **745**

Skill:
Analyzing Expressions

★ DEFINE

When you read, you may find English expressions that you do not know. An **expression** is a group of words that communicates an idea. Three types of expressions are idioms, sayings, and figurative language. They can be difficult to understand because the meanings of the words are different from their **literal**, or usual, meanings.

An **idiom** is an expression that is commonly known among a group of people. For example, "It's raining cats and dogs" means it is raining heavily. **Sayings** are short expressions that contain advice or wisdom. For instance, "Don't count your chickens before they hatch" means do not plan on something good happening before it happens. Figurative language is when you describe something by comparing it with something else, either directly (using the words *like* or *as*) or indirectly. For example, "I'm as hungry as a horse" means I'm very hungry. None of the expressions are about actual animals.

••• CHECKLIST FOR ANALYZING EXPRESSIONS

To determine the meaning of an expression, remember the following:

✓ If you find a confusing group of words, it may be an expression. The meaning of words in expressions may not be their literal meaning.

  • Ask yourself: Is this confusing because the words are new? Or because the words do not make sense together?

✓ Determining the overall meaning may require that you use one or more of the following:

  • context clues

  • a dictionary or other resource

  • teacher or peer support

✓ Highlight important information before and after the expression to look for clues.

♻ YOUR TURN

Read the following excerpt from the text. Then, complete the multiple-choice questions below.

---

from "Six Too Many"

LYDIA [*groaning*]: Oh, Nonno, I honestly don't think I could eat another bite! Those clams were wonderful, but the gross little octopus bodies on skewers nearly killed me!

NONNO: Nonsense! I spent all day making this from scratch; it's Ben's favorite! [*He lifts the lid, and steam rises.*]

---

1. When Lydia says the octopus "nearly killed" her, she means that

   ○ A. she choked on the skewers
   ○ B. octopi can be dangerous
   ○ C. she prefers clams
   ○ D. the dish was too much for her

2. The context clue that best supports this is:

   ○ A. "Oh, Nonno"
   ○ B. "don't think I could eat another bite"
   ○ C. "clams were wonderful"
   ○ D. "on skewers"

3. Which word or words from Nonno's speech are an expression?

   ○ A. Nonsense
   ○ B. all day
   ○ C. from scratch
   ○ D. Ben's favorite

4. What does Nonno's expression probably mean?

   ○ A. "from start to finish"
   ○ B. "with itchy components"
   ○ C. "with a pointed object"
   ○ D. "scraped together with fingernails"

Please note that excerpts and passages in the StudySync® library and this workbook are intended as touchstones to generate interest in an author's work. The excerpts and passages do not substitute for the reading of entire texts, and StudySync® strongly recommends that students seek out and purchase the whole literary or informational work in order to experience it as the author intended. Links to online resellers are available in our digital library. In addition, complete works may be ordered through an authorized reseller by filling out and returning to StudySync® the order form enclosed in this workbook.

Reading & Writing
Companion   **747**

Skill:
Analyzing and Evaluating Text

 ★ **DEFINE**

Analyzing and **evaluating** a text means reading carefully to understand the author's **purpose** and **message**. In informational texts, authors may provide information or opinions on a topic. They may be writing to inform or persuade a reader. In fictional texts, the author may be **communicating** a message or lesson through their story. They may write to entertain or to teach the reader something about life.

Sometimes authors are clear about their message and purpose. When the message or purpose is not stated directly, readers will need to look closer at the text. Readers can use textual evidence to make inferences about what the author is trying to communicate. By analyzing and evaluating the text, you can form your own thoughts and opinions about what you read.

••• **CHECKLIST FOR ANALYZING AND EVALUATING TEXT**

In order to analyze and evaluate a text, do the following:

✓ Look for details that show why the author is writing.

- Ask yourself: Is the author trying to inform, persuade, or entertain? What are the main ideas of this text?

✓ Look for details that show what the author is trying to say.

- Ask yourself: What is the author's opinion about this topic? Is there a lesson I can learn from this story?

✓ Form your own thoughts and opinions about the text.

- Ask yourself: Do I agree with the author? Does this message apply to my life?

⟳ YOUR TURN

Student Instructions: Read the following excerpt from the text. Then, complete the multiple choice questions below.

---

from "Six Too Many"

NONNO (*serving the stew into bowls*): This, in a nutshell, is why we take our ancestors' traditions and pass them down. Smelling this wonderful stew reminds me of your grandmother, but it also reminds me of my own grandmother in Salerno. One day, perhaps, Ben or Lydia will make the Feast of the Seven Fishes for their children, and the smells and tastes will take them back to today.

---

1. Nonno hopes to persuade his grandchildren to

   ○ A. eat the stew he has made
   ○ B. reflect on their past
   ○ C. remember their grandmother
   ○ D. pass on a nice tradition

2. What happens to Nonno when he smells the fish stew?

   ○ A. He pretends that he is at home in Italy.
   ○ B. He realizes how much he loves his grandchildren.
   ○ C. He recalls important people from his past.
   ○ D. He imagines a future time with Lydia and Ben.

3. What does the author probably believe about traditions?

   ○ A. They should change with the times.
   ○ B. They are important to protect and to pass on.
   ○ C. They are mostly meaningful to older people.
   ○ D. They have little to do with modern life.

4. What is Nonno's lesson for Ben?

   ○ A. Family traditions can connect the present to the past.
   ○ B. Grandparents are a valuable part of your life.
   ○ C. Not everyone is lucky enough to have a grand feast.
   ○ D. A life of service is a good and happy life.

Please note that excerpts and passages in the StudySync® library and this workbook are intended as touchstones to generate interest in an author's work. The excerpts and passages do not substitute for the reading of entire texts, and StudySync® strongly recommends that students seek out and purchase the whole literary or informational work in order to experience it as the author intended. Links to online resellers are available in our digital library. In addition, complete works may be ordered through an authorized reseller by filling out and returning to StudySync® the order form enclosed in this workbook.

Reading & Writing
Companion   **749**

SIX TOO MANY

Close Read

✏ WRITE

PERSONAL NARRATIVE: In "Six Too Many," Ben changes his mind about some traditions. Think of a tradition that your family has. It may have to do with holidays, or it may be completely unrelated. Describe the tradition using specific details, and tell your feelings about it. Give reasons for your feelings. Have they changed over time? Pay attention to main and helping verbs as you write.

Use the checklist below to guide you as you write.

☐ What is one tradition that your family has?

☐ How did you feel about this tradition in the past? Why?

☐ How do you feel about this tradition now? Why?

Use the sentence frames to organize and write your personal narrative.

One tradition my family has is _____

_____.

We always _____

_____.

When I was younger, I felt _____

_____.

More recently, I feel _____

_____.

studysync®

ASSIGNMENTS   BINDER   LIBRARY

True to Yourself

UNIT 6

True to Yourself

Who are you meant to be?

Genre Focus: REALISTIC FICTION

Texts

 Paired Readings

Extended Writing Project and Grammar

English Language Learner Resources

Who are you meant to be?

SVETLANA CHMAKOVA

Svetlana Chmakova (b. 1979) was born and raised in Russia, where she lived until the age of sixteen. Her family then moved to Canada, and Chmakova began to make stories in the form of manga, the Japanese style of narrative comics and graphic novels. She spends her time in both Canada and California, and publishes books about middle schoolers in the throes of everything from daily drama to epic battles against dark forces. Chmakova likes to draw ideas for characters from people-watching on the subway.

RITA DOVE

In 1993, the Library of Congress appointed Rita Dove (b. 1952) United States Poet Laureate, making Dove not only the youngest poet to ever be presented with the title, but also the first woman and first African American to hold the position. Dove, who lives and works in Virginia, has authored short stories, a novel, a play, essays, and many books of poetry. Her Pulitzer Prize-winning collection *Thomas and Beulah* (1986) is a sequence of poems based on the lives of her grandparents.

W.E.B. DUBOIS

"Either the United States will destroy ignorance or ignorance will destroy the United States," stated W. E. B. Du Bois (1868–1963) in a speech. The words and writings of this prolific activist, writer, historian, and professor continue to influence the fields of sociology and political science today. Du Bois was the first African American to earn a doctorate at Harvard University, and was a co-founder of the National Association for the Advancement of Colored People (NAACP) in 1909.

RUSSELL FREEDMAN

Russell Freedman (1929–2018) was born into a literary family—his father worked in a publishing house and his mother worked in a bookstore. After returning from service in the Korean War, Freedman became a reporter and editor for the Associated Press. His first book was *Teenagers Who Made History* (1961), a collection of stories of notable teenagers, and thereafter he wrote many historically focused books and biographies about individuals who created significant inventions or showed courage through difficult circumstances.

HENRY FORD

Before becoming one of the foremost pioneers of the industrial world, Henry Ford (1863–1947) was a rebellious child. At the age of sixteen, Ford left home to apprentice as a machinist in Detroit. This early passion for industry eventually led him to develop his first automobile, which he termed the "Quadricycle," in 1896. The rest, as they say, is history. Ford's Model T car and the assembly line that made its mass production possible in 1908 became the basis for personal transportation and industrial manufacturing ever since.

NIKKI GRIMES

Born and raised in New York City, Nikki Grimes (b. 1950) began writing poems at the age of six and has been a writer ever since. "Books were my survival tools," she said of her childhood. "They were how I got by, and how I coped with things. Books carried me away." An author of poetry and fiction for both children and adults, Grimes has taught at schools in Sweden, Tanzania, Russia, and China. Her artistic talents are not limited to writing, Grimes has also performed as a singer and dancer, exhibited photographs, and crafted jewelry.

REBECCA HARRINGTON

Since her undergraduate years at the University of Minnesota—Twin Cities, Rebecca Harrington has pursued her joint interests of science and journalism. Beginning her career writing for *The Minnesota Daily*, Harrington went on to receive her Master's degree in the Science, Health and Environmental Reporting Program at New York University. Since then, she has covered topics such as rocket launches, solar energy, and the Zika virus for various magazines and newspapers.

ROSA PARKS

Called "the first lady of civil rights" by the United States Congress, activist Rosa Parks (1913–2005) is best known for refusing to give up her seat on a Montgomery, Alabama, bus in 1955. Parks, the secretary of the Montgomery chapter of the NAACP at the time, was ordered by the bus driver to surrender her seat in the "colored" section to a white passenger. When her act of civil disobedience resulted in arrest, she inspired the black community in Montgomery to boycott the buses for over a year.

JACKIE ROBINSON

Brooklyn Dodgers baseball player Jackie Robinson (1919–1972) made history in 1947 when he walked onto the field as the first African American player in the MLB in the 20th century. His ten-year career saw a World Series Championship win for the Dodgers and earned Robinson a place in the National Baseball Hall of Fame in 1962. Martin Luther King Jr. called Robinson "a legend and symbol in his own time," as his accomplishments reached far beyond the baseball diamond, calling attention to the value and urgency of integration.

AMANDA SPERBER

Amanda Sperber (b. 1986) is an American journalist from Mamaroneck, New York, who splits time between Kenya, Somalia, and the United States. Sperber primarily covers stories that focus on conflict, crises, and developments in East African countries. Early in her career as a reporter, Sperber traveled and volunteered around the world, opening herself to new perspectives and ways of communicating in such places as Ghana, the West Indies, and the United Kingdom.

BEN MIKAELSEN

Many photographs of the Bolivian American author Ben Mikaelsen (b. 1952) also include a 750-pound black bear named Buffy. Mikaelsen rescued Buffy when he was a cub, and they shared a home in Montana—inside and outside—as family for twenty-six years. Growing up in Bolivia, Mikaelsen, who has always loved caring for animals, had many pets: dogs and cats, a sloth, and even a pet kudamundi. His novels often focus on the relationship between humankind and nature.

Bronx Masquerade

FICTION
Nikki Grimes
2002

Introduction

The teenage narrators of this highly acclaimed novel by American author and poet Nikki Grimes (b. 1950) have no outlet for expression until they come together in Mr. Ward's high school English class. Provided an opportunity to read their poems and lyrics to the class on popular "open mike" Fridays, the voices of the students intertwine to produce a powerful message of identity and awareness. Two of them, Devon and Janelle, are featured in this excerpt.

"But what about the rest of me? Forget who I really am, who I really want to be."

Devon Hope

1   Jump Shot. What kind of name is that? Not mine, but try telling that to the brothers at school. That's all they ever call me.

2   You'd think it was written somewhere. Tall guys must be jocks[1]. No. Make that tall *people*, 'cause Diondra's got the same problem. Everybody expects her to shoot hoops. The difference is, she's got no talent in that direction. Ask me, she's got no business playing b-ball. That's my game.

3   I've got good height and good hands, and that's a fact. But what about the rest of me? Forget who I really am, who I really want to be. The law is be cool, be tough, play ball, and use books for weight training—not reading. Otherwise, everybody gives you grief. Don't ask me why I care, especially when the grief is coming from a punk like Wesley. Judging from the company he keeps, he's a gangsta in sheep's clothing[2]. I don't even know why he and Tyrone **bother** coming to school. It's clear they don't take it seriously, although maybe they're starting to. That's according to Sterling, who believes in praying for everybody and giving them the **benefit** of the doubt. I love the preacher-man, but I think he may be giving these brothers too much credit. Anyway, when I hang around after school and any of the guys ask me, "Yo, Devon, where are you going?" I tell them I'm heading for the gym to meet Coach and work on my layup. Then once they're out the door, I cut upstairs to the library to sneak a read.

4   It's not much better at home. My older brother's always after me to hit the streets with him, calls me a girly man for loving books and jazz[3].

5   Don't get me wrong. B-ball is all right. Girls like you, for one thing. But it's not *you* they like. It's Mr. Basketball. And if that's not who you are inside, then it's not you they're liking. So what's the point? Still, I don't mind playing, just not all the time.

Skill:
Summarizing

Overall, it seems like Devon's peers are not seeing his true self. I would summarize these paragraphs by saying: Although Devon likes basketball, he has other interests that define his character.

I wonder if these details will contribute to the overarching summary.

---

1. **jock** a person whose primary interests involve athletics or sports
2. **gangsta in sheep's clothing** a play on the idiom "wolf in sheep's clothing," referring to someone (or something) who hides their true intentions
3. **jazz** a type of music of African American origin characterized by improvisation, emerging at the beginning of the 20th century

6 This year is looking better. My English teacher has got us studying the Harlem Renaissance, which means we have to read a lot of poetry. That suits me just fine, gives me a reason to drag around my beat-up **volumes** of Langston Hughes and Claude McKay. Whenever anybody bugs me about it, all I have to say is "Homework." Even so, I'd rather the brothers not catch me with my head in a book.

7 The other day, I duck into the library, **snare** a corner table, and hunker down with *3000 Years of Black Poetry*. Raynard sees me, but it's not like he's going to tell anybody. He hardly speaks, and he never hangs with any of the brothers I know. So I breathe easy. I'm sure no one else has spotted me until a head pops up from behind the stacks. It's Janelle Battle from my English class. I freeze and wait for the **snickers** I'm used to. Wait for her to say something like: "What? Coach got you *reading* now? Afraid you're gonna flunk out and drop off the team?" But all she does is smile and wave. Like it's no big deal for me to be in a library reading. Like I have a right to be there if I want. Then she pads over, slips a copy of *The Panther & the Lash* on my table, and walks away without saying a word. It's one of my favorite books by Langston Hughes. How could she know? Seems like she's noticed me in the library more often than I thought.

8 Janelle is all right. So what if she's a little plump? At least when you turn the light on upstairs, somebody's home. She's smart, and she doesn't try hiding it. Which gets me thinking. Maybe it's time I quit sneaking in and out of the library like some thief. Maybe it's time I just started being who I am.

9 Open Mike
Bronx Masquerade
By Devon Hope

I woke up this morning
exhausted from hiding
the me of me
so I stand here **confiding**
there's more to Devon
than jump shot and rim.
I'm more than tall
and lengthy of limb.
I dare you to peep
behind these eyes,
discover the poet
in tough-guy disguise.
Don't call me Jump Shot.
My name is Surprise.

Skill:
Summarizing

In this section, Janelle seems to inspire Devon to be true to himself. Here is how I would summarize this paragraph: Janelle's independence motivates Devon to begin thinking differently about how he acts; he wants to start being himself.

NOTES

Janelle Battle

10 "Janelle Hope. Mrs. Janelle Hope. Mrs. Devon Hope." Dream on, fool. You can stand here in the girls' room and practice saying that name 'til your tongue falls out, or the change bell rings, whichever comes first, and it still won't ever be true. Face it. Devon is Denzel Washington, and you are Thighs "R" Us.

11 I can hear Lupe now. "Stop putting yourself down. You have a very pretty face. Besides, you have a lot more going for you." Yeah, well, I guess that's true. I mean, I am smart and funny, and I know I'm a good person. But this is high school, and nobody seems to care about that. Why couldn't I be tall and elegant like Diondra, or have Judianne's perfect **complexion**, all smooth, super-rich fudge? Better yet, why couldn't I look like Tanisha, or Gloria? Then I might have a chance with somebody like Devon. But I don't, so forget it.

12 Devon is different from the other jocks, though. How many guys you know read Claude McKay for fun? Seems like every time I go to the library, I catch him squeezed into a corner like he's got something to hide. He smiled at me last time I saw him there. That's something, isn't it? He didn't have to smile, even if I did smile and wave first. And he seemed to like the poem I read at the last Open Mike Friday.

13 I can't believe I'm getting up in front of people and talking about personal stuff, and liking it. I'm saying things that I would never tell anybody, usually. But, I don't know. There's something about reading poetry. It's almost like acting. The room is kind of set up like a stage, anyway. Mr. Ward turns most of the lights out, and we stand in a spot in front of the video camera. Once he switches it on, it's like you become somebody else, and you can say anything, as long as it's in a poem. Then, when you're finished, you just disappear into the dark and sit down, and you're back to being your own self. Gloria says it's the same for her.

14 "Hey, Janelle."

15 Oh, no. It's Miss Big Mouth Fifth Avenue in another one of her original getups. Where'd she come from?

16 "Hey, Judianne." I thought the bathroom was empty. How long was she there? I hope she didn't hear me talking to the mirror. That's all I need, to have the whole school laughing about me having a crush on Devon. Lord, please don't let that happen. It's bad enough they call me Battle of the Bulge behind my back.

17 I wish, I wish, I wish. God, I wish people could see me on the inside. I know I'm beautiful there.

NOTES

18   Open Mike
Inside
By Janelle Battle

Daily
I notice you frown
at my thick casing,
feel you poke me
with the sharp tip
of your booted words.
You laugh,
rap my woody shell
with wicked whispers shaped
like knuckles,
then toss me aside.
Lucky for me,
I don't bruise easily.
Besides,
your loss
is someone else's gain
for I am coconut,
and the heart of me
is sweeter
than you know.

Excerpted from *Bronx Masquerade* by Nikki Grimes, published by Dial Books.

First Read

Read *Bronx Masquerade*. After you read, complete the Think Questions below.

 THINK QUESTIONS

1. How does Devon feel about his nickname? Respond with evidence from the text.

2. Why does Devon hide his true interests? Cite evidence from the text to support your response.

3. What social pressures does Janelle face? Be sure to refer back to the text in your response.

4. Use context to determine the meaning of the word **volumes** as it is used in paragraph 6. Write your definition of *volumes* here and explain how you arrived at it.

5. Use context to determine the meaning of the word **snickers** as it is used in paragraph 7. Write your definition here and identify clues that helped you figure out its meaning. Then check the meaning in a dictionary.

Skill:
Summarizing

Use the Checklist to analyze Summarizing in *Bronx Masquerade*. Refer to the sample student annotations about Summarizing in the text.

Copyright © BookheadEd Learning, LLC

••• CHECKLIST FOR SUMMARIZING

In order to determine how to write an objective summary of a text, note the following:

✓ in a nonfiction text, examine details to identify the main idea, making notations in a notebook or graphic organizer

✓ in literature, note the setting, characters, and events in the plot, including the problem the characters face and how it is resolved

✓ answers to the basic questions *who, what, where, when, why,* and *how*

✓ stay objective, and do not add your own personal thoughts, judgments, or opinions to the summary

To provide an objective summary of a text free from personal opinions or judgments, consider the following questions:

✓ What are the answers to basic *who, what, where, when, why,* and *how* questions in literature and works of nonfiction?

✓ Are all of the details I have summarized in a work of literature relevant and important to the plot?

✓ In what order should I put the main ideas and most important details in a work of nonfiction to make my summary logical?

✓ Is my summary objective, or have I added my own thoughts, judgments, or personal opinions?

Skill:
Summarizing

Reread paragraphs 16–19 of *Bronx Masquerade*. Then, using the Checklist on the previous page, answer the multiple-choice questions below.

↻ YOUR TURN

1. Which sentence provides the BEST objective summary of paragraph 16?

   ○ A. Janelle sees Judianne in the bathroom in the library. She is surprised to see her and wishes she would leave.

   ○ B. Judianne enters the bathroom while Janelle is talking in the mirror. Janelle is embarrassed as she thinks she may be bullied.

   ○ C. Janelle is in the bathroom in the library when Judianne walks in. Earlier that day, Janelle has been ruthlessly bullied by her peers.

   ○ D. Judianne hears Janelle talking to herself in the bathroom about wanting to date Devon. She makes fun of Janelle.

2. Which of the following answers provides the BEST objective summary of Janelle's poem in paragraph 18?

   ○ A. Janelle is bullied by her peers at school, but she doesn't let it get to her because she believes she has more to offer than just looks.

   ○ B. Janelle pretends not to hear her peers' unkind words. She thinks there is more to life than appearance.

   ○ C. Janelle's life at school is rough. She wishes people could see the real her.

   ○ D. Janelle's peers are aggressive toward her at school. Her poetry is a way to cope with their bullying.

BRONX MASQUERADE

Close Read

Reread *Bronx Masquerade*. As you reread, complete the Skills Focus questions below. Then use your answers and annotations from the questions to help you complete the Write activity.

◎ SKILLS FOCUS

1. Create an objective summary of Devon's "Open Mike" poem. Include textual evidence to support your summary.

2. Read the following dictionary entry:

   direction
   di•rec•tion \də-ˈrek-shən\

   Noun

   1. a course along which something moves
   2. general aim or purpose
   3. an authoritative command
   4. instructions on how to accomplish a task or goal

   Which definition most closely matches the meaning of **direction** as it is used in paragraph 2? Write the appropriate definition of *direction* here and explain how you figured out the correct meaning.

3. Using evidence from the text, explain how the author develops the points of view of Devon and Janelle, and note how their points of view differ in their poems.

4. Explain how Devon and Janelle are true to themselves, despite feeling pressure from their peers. Use textual evidence to support your explanation.

✏ WRITE

DISCUSSION: In *Bronx Masquerade*, Devon and Janelle are ready for their classmates to know who they truly are. Do you think that Devon and Janelle can be accepted for who they really are by their peers? Do you think they can help each other? Why or why not? Summarize Devon and Janelle's experiences with each other and with their peers to plan for a debate. Use evidence from the text to support your position.

A BEACON of Hope:

The Story of Hannah Herbst

INFORMATIONAL TEXT
Rebecca Harrington
2015

Introduction

The Discovery Education 3M Young Scientist Challenge has a simple mission: "to foster a new generation of American scientists at an age when interest in science generally declines." To enter, students from around the country (grades 5–8) are encouraged to submit a solution to a problem facing either them, their community, or the world at large. Each finalist gets the opportunity to work directly with a scientist in the hopes of bringing their idea to fruition. The 2015 winner was then-eighth-grader Hannah Herbst from Boca Raton, Florida. The problem she wanted to solve: the global energy crisis. Her solution: BEACON.

"I could use the skills I acquired to take action in an attempt to mitigate the global energy crisis."

1   In 2015, an eighth grader named Hannah Herbst from Boca Raton, Florida won the Discovery Education 3M Young Scientist Challenge.

2   At just 14 years old, she designed and built a small **turbine** called BEACON, for Bringing Electricity Access to Countries Through Ocean Energy Collection.

3   "Shortly after school began," Herbst wrote in a blog post for the contest, "I received a letter from my nine-year-old pen pal[1] in Ethiopia. She wrote about how she has no access to lights, a steady flow of fresh water to drink, and other basic necessities. I recognized that her situation was not unique and believed that I could use the skills I **acquired** to take action in an attempt to **mitigate** the global energy crisis."

4   So Hannah got to work on her ocean energy probe[2]. She spent four months researching her idea, she wrote in another blog post, before she designed the turbine as a computer model, and then produced 3D-printed **prototypes.** Herbst even got approval from the city of Boca Raton to test her design in the intercoastal waterway[3].

5   There, she explains in her contest entry video, the ocean tidal energy drives the propeller at the bottom of the probe, which then powers the hydroelectric generator[4] at the top of the probe via a pulley system inside, turning ocean tides into usable power.

6   Herbst's calculations show that if she scaled up BEACON, it could charge three car batteries **simultaneously** in less than an hour. She suggests the turbine could be used in developing countries to renewably power pumps to **desalinate** water, run centrifuges that help test blood for diseases, and power electric buoys for **maritime** navigation.

---

1. **pen pal** someone with whom correspondence is regularly exchanged
2. **probe** a mechanical instrument sent to explore unfamiliar terrain
3. **intercoastal waterway** a 3,000-mile inland waterway along the Atlantic and Gulf of Mexico coasts of the United States
4. **generator** a machine that converts the energy of motion into electricity

7 Herbst became interested in science at an engineering camp during the summer before seventh grade. When she got there, she realized she was the only girl.

8 "I knew that I was the minority," she wrote, "but after successfully programming and constructing robots that day, my love and passion for science and engineering was discovered."

9 And she hopes other young scientists will find their passion, too. "If you're reading this blog post and are in middle school, I hope that you will apply for the Discovery Education and 3M Young Scientist Challenge," Herbst wrote. "It is such an amazing opportunity to explore, **innovate**, and work with a scientist from 3M to develop your prototype. I hope to see YOU posting blogs next year!"

✏️ WRITE

PERSONAL RESPONSE: "A BEACON of Hope: The Story of Hannah Herbst" describes a teen's invention that could help power an entire nation. If you were to create an invention to help a nation in need, what would it be? Why? Support your response with evidence from the article as well as personal experience. As you make connections between Hannah's life and your own, include anything that may have impacted your ideas about your potential invention.

Please note that excerpts and passages in the StudySync® library and this workbook are intended as touchstones to generate interest in an author's work. The excerpts and passages do not substitute for the reading of entire texts, and StudySync® strongly recommends that students seek out and purchase the whole literary or informational work in order to experience it as the author intended. Links to online resellers are available in our digital library. In addition, complete works may be ordered through an authorized reseller by filling out and returning to StudySync® the order form enclosed in this workbook.

Reading & Writing Companion 767

Shree Bose:
Never Too Young to Change the World

INFORMATIONAL TEXT
Amanda Sperber
2017

Introduction

Amanda Sperber is a freelance journalist who has lived and worked all over the world. In this article, she writes about Shree Bose, a cancer researcher who won the Grand Prize in the 2011 Google Science Fair. Bose was victorious out of 10,000 participants, ages 17 or 18, from 91 different countries around the world. Since receiving the honor, Bose has used her platform to encourage interest in STEM education and has continued her own education as well, graduating from Harvard University and beginning a MD/PhD program at Duke University School of Medicine.

"They all told her she was too young."

Turning Tragedy into Inspiration

NOTES

1　When she was 15, Shree Bose traveled from her home in Fort Worth, Texas, to visit her grandfather in India. He was dying of cancer. Shree had been close to her grandfather even though she lived far away. "While I think the barrier of living on the other side of the world definitely **posed** a challenge to being able to talk as often as we would have liked, my grandfather was close to both my brother and me," Shree says. "He would visit when we were younger, and when we got a bit older and would travel to India, he would sit and talk with us for hours."

Skill:
Media

The section heading suggests an important event in Shree's life. The map emphasizes how far it was to visit her grandfather. From these details I conclude that her grandfather's illness was both a tragedy and an inspiration for Shree.

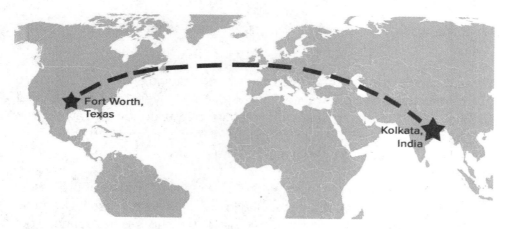

Fort Worth, Texas

Kolkata, India

2　In Kolkata, a city in eastern India, Shree sat with her grandfather, and, seeing his discomfort, realized her purpose in life: she wanted to fight vicious diseases like cancer. She wanted to play a role in **relieving** people's pain. "When my grandfather passed away," Shree says, "it was the first time where I said, 'This is what I want to do with my life. This is what I want to make an impact in.'"

Please note that excerpts and passages in the StudySync® library and this workbook are intended as touchstones to generate interest in an author's work. The excerpts and passages do not substitute for the reading of entire texts, and StudySync® strongly recommends that students seek out and purchase the whole literary or informational work in order to experience it as the author intended. Links to online resellers are available in our digital library. In addition, complete works may be ordered through an authorized reseller by filling out and returning to StudySync® the order form enclosed in this workbook.

Reading & Writing Companion　**769**

NOTES

3 Shree had always been creative. She enjoyed building things that solved problems or addressed issues she saw in her daily life. For example, in fifth grade she made a remote controlled garbage can that she thought might be helpful to disabled students struggling to take the garbage out to the curb.

4 Now, she wanted to take on cancer. It was time to take things to the next level.

5 Shree returned to the United States and started reading everything she could get her hands on about cancer. She looked at everything from cancer survivors' blog posts to research journals published by scientists. She watched hours of YouTube videos. "I found myself really loving being able to imagine what was going on within cells," she recalls.

6 Shree had never studied cancer before. She emailed dozens of professors around Fort Worth to ask about studying in one of their labs. She just wanted a chance to experiment and learn. They all told her she was too young. "I got **rejected** by a lot of professors before I found one person who was willing to take me on," she says.

7 That person was Dr. Alakananda Basu, a professor at the University of North Texas Health Science Center in Fort Worth. Although she was young and inexperienced, Shree won over Dr. Basu with her energy and passion for learning. "What I find most exciting is your enthusiasm," Shree says Dr. Basu told her. "And if you keep that while working in my lab, I'll take you."

8   Under Dr. Basu's **supervision**, Shree started research on counteracting resistance to the chemotherapy[1] drug cisplatin, which is given to women with ovarian cancer[2]. She also discovered a **unique** platform to share her research in 2011, the first year of the Google Science Fair. "They actually had a little banner ad [on the Google homepage]," she recalls. "And I remember I didn't think too much about it until my Dad mentioned it to me again."

9   The Google Science Fair is entirely online. Participants demonstrate their projects on websites they make themselves. Shree had never made a website, but she went for it and entered one. So did a lot of other students. In fact, 10,000 students from 91 countries submitted projects to the competition its first year.

Skill: Media

The website screenshot with this text shows how Shree's research results were displayed online. Without both features, Shree's work might be hard to understand.

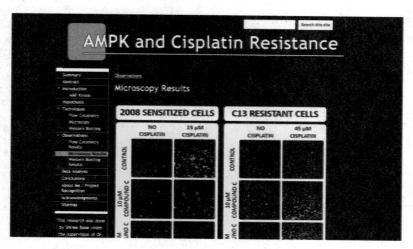

10   Shree won.

1. **chemotherapy** a widely used treatment to prevent cancer cells from dividing and growing
2. **ovarian cancer** cancer that begins in one or more ovum

11 "I remember the entire experience as very much of a whirlwind that didn't feel real in a lot of ways. Even so many years later, that experience shaped the excitement with how I approach science and how I approach telling others about my work, and that's a blessing I'll take forward into my life," she says.

Starting Young

12 Shree was only six years old when she conducted her first experiment. Her first goal was to change vegetables into more interesting colors. She wanted to know if she would eat foods like spinach more often if they were more exciting colors. "It was very much like, 'I am very bored by the color, so if you make it bright and shiny I will put it in my mouth,'" she says of her first-grade project.

13 Her parents took her seriously. They bought her a spinach plant, blue food coloring, and a syringe to inject into the plant. "They had a big role in how I ended up thinking of science as something I could do," she says.

14 The spinach plant was successfully dyed blue. Shree forgot to water it, though, and it died in two weeks. "That was my first science project," she says. She took the dead plant to her first science fair in second grade. "I actually think I got laughed at," she recalls.

15 Despite the setback, she continued to allow her interests to lead her. Her technique improved with time. She completed projects like the electronic garbage can, for which Shree won a regional award. She also developed a traction pad to help cars get out of the mud when she was in sixth grade.

16 And, of course, she later became a Google Science Fair champion. Winning that competition changed Shree's life. She met President Barack Obama. *Glamour* magazine named her one of its '21 Amazing Young Women of the Year'. She received emails from all around the country from cancer patients and their family members.

17   The most important change, though, was in how Shree saw herself. "Before, the judges seemed practically superhuman, like nothing a regular kid from Texas could aspire to be," she wrote in a 2012 article in the Huffington Post titled, "How the Google Science Fair Changed My Life." "When I met them in person, I realized that they were just really intelligent and really hard-working — the kind of person everyone has the potential to become. Those are the people who are out there changing the world."

Inspiring the Next Shree Bose

18   Shree's youthful involvement in science isn't just important because of her incredible achievements. It is important because participation in science is not as common in young women as it is in young men. Fewer young women engaging in science, technology, engineering, and math (otherwise known as STEM) as youths means fewer girls will become women with jobs in STEM. Statistics support this: according to the National Girls Collaborative Project, women make up just 29% of the science and engineering workforce.

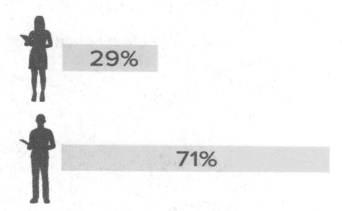

19 There are currently more jobs in STEM fields than in any other industry. For example, the National Council for Women and Information Technology (NCWIT) estimates that there will be around 1.4 million computer specialist job openings expected in the U.S. by 2018. Americans need to fill those jobs, and the best bet to make the best products is to fill at least half of these jobs with women.

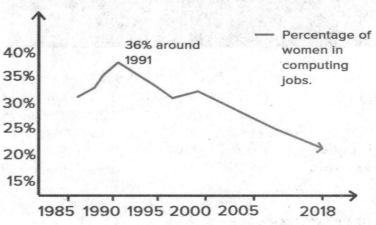

Percentage of women in computing occupations

**Skill:
Word Meaning**

I can tell equality is a noun because it is a thing that is good for society. The text is talking about how there aren't as many women as men in STEM. So I think equality means there would be the same number, like equal.

The first definition matches my guess when I replace equality with it in the sentence, and the other two don't make sense!

20 Science, engineering, and technology jobs impact our everyday lives. "I think any societal barriers to that pioneering spirit, whether gender or otherwise, puts the world at a disadvantage, since there are so many more discoveries waiting to be made," Shree says.

21 Shree believes STEM fields would benefit from having more women involved. As she says, "I think it's absolutely essential for women to be in STEM, not just because of the obvious reasons that we can be and equality is good for society, but also because women have unique perspectives and experiences that can inform new ways of approaching scientific problems."

22 Shree sees the larger culture around STEM to be very focused on boys and men. "I think there's a very ingrained sense that science is a male profession. That hearkens back to an earlier era, and the remnants of that still influence us. I think as more and more trailblazing women pave the way, we're going to see a broad shift in that thinking, but it's going to take work," she says.

23 Because there are fewer women in STEM now, there are fewer female mentors for girls and young women interested in STEM. When girls don't see women in the field, they may assume STEM is not for them, either. "I have

been fortunate to have some incredible female mentors and role models, and I think that their examples have taught me to think in innovative ways and push the boundaries of scientific inquiry," Shree says.

24 After winning the Google Science Fair in 2011, Shree enrolled at Harvard University. At Harvard, she mentored young people. They often asked how she got started in STEM. She would tell them about doing research, finding Dr. Basu, and getting involved in a lab for hands-on experience. However, she didn't have suggestions about how to get started with the "E" in STEM: engineering. Shree knew engineering could be interesting and fun, but she didn't have a way to show that to the students she mentored. So, once again, after defining a problem, Shree Bose came up with a solution.

25 She and two colleagues built Piper, a toolkit that allows users to build electronics and gadgets while they play Minecraft. Piper comes in a box as a completely unassembled computer. Young people put it together themselves and then link their own computer using a small microchip. With that, they can upgrade the unit with physical wires and switches so they can handle each piece and understand how the parts make up a whole. The goal is to engage young people in the nuts and bolts, so to speak, of the engineering process.

26 Shree earned her undergraduate degree from Harvard in 2016. She's continuing her education, at Duke University School of Medicine in Durham, North Carolina. In medical school she rotates quickly through different specialities. "I'm learning a lot really quickly," she says of the experience.

27   When she finishes at Duke, Shree hopes to work as a pediatric oncologist, taking care of kids with blood diseases and cancer. For now, though, she's open to all possibilities and to whatever opportunities come her way. "We'll see," she says. "Check back in with me in seven years!"

AMANDA SPERBER is an East Africa-based foreign correspondent. She files for Al Jazeera, The Daily Beast, New Foreign Policy, Glamour, The Guardian, Harper's, News Deeply, The Times of London, VICE Magazine and related publications.

First Read

Read "Shree Bose: Never Too Young to Change the World." After you read, complete the Think Questions below.

☁ THINK QUESTIONS

1. What was Shree Bose's first experiment? Explain how the same qualities she showed in conducting this first experiment have continued throughout her scientific career, citing textual evidence to support your answer.

2. Who was one of the most important people to help Shree Bose discover her understanding of science? Explain this mentor's role, citing specific textual evidence in your response.

3. How did the Google Science Fair change Shree Bose's life? How did it change her perspective on the world? Be sure to include textual evidence or inferences in your response.

4. Read the following dictionary entry:

relieve
re•lieve /rə'lēv/

verb

1. to cause pain or difficulty to become less serious
2. to release someone from duty by taking their place
3. to take a burden from someone

Which definition most closely matches the meaning of the word **relieving** as it is used in the text? Write the correct definition, and describe how you know which meaning of *relieving* fits in the text.

5. Which neighboring words and phrases help you determine the meaning of **unique** as it is used in the text? Write your own definition of *unique,* and explain how you were able to determine the meaning through context. Then use a dictionary to confirm your conclusion.

Please note that excerpts and passages in the StudySync® library and this workbook are intended as touchstones to generate interest in an author's work. The excerpts and passages do not substitute for the reading of entire texts, and StudySync® strongly recommends that students seek out and purchase the whole literary or informational work in order to experience it as the author intended. Links to online resellers are available in our digital library. In addition, complete works may be ordered through an authorized reseller by filling out and returning to StudySync® the order form enclosed in this workbook.

Reading & Writing Companion

777

Skill:
Media

Use the Checklist to analyze Media in "Shree Bose: Never Too Young to Change the World." Refer to the sample student annotations about Media in the text.

••• CHECKLIST FOR MEDIA

In order to determine how information is presented in different media or formats, note the following:

- ✓ how the same topic can be treated, or presented, in more than one medium, including visually, quantitatively, or orally

- ✓ how treatments of a topic through different kinds of sources can give you more information about the topic

- ✓ details that are emphasized or missing in each medium and the reasons behind these choices

- ✓ how, if different details are stressed, a reader or viewer may begin to think about the subject in a new way

To integrate information presented in different media or formats, consider the following questions:

- ✓ Which details are missing or emphasized in each medium? What do you think are the reasons behind these choices, and what effect do they have?

- ✓ What information can you learn by analyzing and comparing these two sources of information?

- ✓ How does integrating information from different media help you to develop a more coherent, or logical, understanding of a topic?

- ✓ How does interpreting information from diverse media and formats contribute to a topic, text, or issue under study?

Copyright © BookheadEd Learning, LLC

Skill:
Media

Reread paragraphs 18–19 from "Shree Bose: Never Too Young to Change the World." Then, using the Checklist on the previous page, answer the multiple-choice questions below.

⟳ YOUR TURN

1. The heading suggests that this section will be about —

   ○ A. finding a researcher to replace Shree Bose.
   ○ B. how to interest other young women in science.
   ○ C. ways to teach science in schools.
   ○ D. finding young women to compete in science fairs.

2. The purpose of the first visual in the excerpt is to —

   ○ A. show that the number of women in STEM jobs is increasing.
   ○ B. illustrate the future projected number of men and women in STEM jobs.
   ○ C. illustrate the difference in the number of women and men in STEM jobs.
   ○ D. show the employment opportunities available for women in STEM jobs.

3. The second chart illustrates the author's ideas in paragraph 19 by showing that —

   ○ A. at least 50% of the computing jobs available in 2018 will be filled by women because of the NCWIT.
   ○ B. there will be no women in computing jobs by 2018 unless something is done to stop the decline.
   ○ C. there will not be enough women in computing to fill half the number of computing jobs available by 2018.
   ○ D. many of the computing jobs available in 2018 will go unfilled because fewer women are entering computing.

Skill:
Word Meaning

Use the Checklist to analyze Word Meaning in "Shree Bose: Never Too Young to Change the World." Refer to the sample student annotations about Word Meaning in the text.

••• CHECKLIST FOR WORD MEANING

In order to find the pronunciation of a word or determine or clarify its precise meaning or its part of speech, do the following:

- ✓ determine the word's part of speech

- ✓ consult reference materials, both print and digital, to find the pronunciation of a word, determine its precise meaning and ascertain its part of speech

In order to verify the preliminary determination of the meaning of a word or phrase, do the following:

- ✓ use context clues to make an inference about the word's meaning

- ✓ consult a dictionary to verify your preliminary determination of the meaning

- ✓ be sure to read all of the definitions, and then decide which definition makes sense in its context

To determine a word's precise meaning or part of speech, ask the following questions:

- ✓ What is the word describing?

- ✓ How is the word being used in the phrase or sentence?

- ✓ Have I consulted my reference materials?

Skill:
Word Meaning

Reread paragraphs 11–15 from "Shree Bose: Never Too Young to Change the World." Then, using the Checklist on the previous page, answer the multiple-choice questions below.

↻ YOUR TURN

1. Which definition best matches the way the word *whirlwind* is used in paragraph 11? Remember to pay attention to the word's part of speech as you make your decision.

   ○ A. Definition 1
   ○ B. Definition 2
   ○ C. Definition 3
   ○ D. Definition 4

2. Which definition best matches the way the word *setback* is used in paragraph 15?

   ○ A. Definition 1
   ○ B. Definition 2
   ○ C. Definition 3
   ○ D. Definition 4

Please note that excerpts and passages in the StudySync® library and this workbook are intended as touchstones to generate interest in an author's work. The excerpts and passages do not substitute for the reading of entire texts, and StudySync® strongly recommends that students seek out and purchase the whole literary or informational work in order to experience it as the author intended. Links to online resellers are available in our digital library. In addition, complete works may be ordered through an authorized reseller by filling out and returning to StudySync® the order form enclosed in this workbook.

Reading & Writing Companion

781

Close Read

Reread "Shree Bose: Never Too Young to Change the World." As you reread, complete the Skills Focus questions below. Then use your answers and annotations from the questions to help you complete the Write activity.

◎ SKILLS FOCUS

1. Identify examples of the author's use of different media formats to present information about Shree's scientific approach to problem-solving, in addition to the text. Explain how the use of media helps you understand Shree's approach.

2. Identify evidence that supports the author's central idea that Shree Bose is a problem-solver. Explain how the evidence helps further explain the central idea.

3. Highlight examples in the text where the author uses different media or formats as well as words to help readers understand the author's concern about the number of women in STEM fields.

Explain how the information helps illustrate the problem.

4. Use context clues to make your best guess at the definition of *equality* as it is used in paragraph 21. After you've guessed, look *equality* up in the dictionary and determine the correct definition in this context.

5. Highlight evidence in the text that explains how Shree Bose answered the unit's essential question: Who are you meant to be? Find evidence in the text to support your answer.

✏ WRITE

INFORMATIVE: What qualities make a great problem-solver? You read that Hannah Herbst set out to solve the global energy crisis to help her pen pal in Ethiopia. How does Shree Bose find solutions to scientific and everyday problems encountered throughout her life? How does the author's use of information presented in different media or formats as well as in words help illustrate Shree's scientific approach to finding solutions? Use evidence from both the text and charts, visuals, or other quantitative information to support your ideas.

Letter to His Daughter

INFORMATIONAL TEXT
W.E.B. Du Bois
1914

Introduction

W.E.B. Du Bois (1868–1963) was one of the cofounders of the National Association for the Advancement of Colored People (NAACP), a writer, a civil rights activist, and the first African American man to earn a PhD from Harvard. The letter here is of a personal nature: when she was 14, Du Bois's daughter, Yolande, crossed the ocean to study at Bedales School in England. In this letter to her, Du Bois cautions her of the strange and wonderful things she might encounter in this new place, and imparts his own practical advice about how to meet the challenges ahead.

"Remember that most folk laugh at anything unusual, whether it is beautiful, fine or not."

NOTES

Skill:
Context Clues

What does "gradually" mean? in paragraph 2 I see that this word is an adverb because it ends in -ly. It must describe something. Maybe time?

This explains that Du Bois thinks his daughter will love the old world over time. Does "gradually" mean happening slowly over a period of time?

Skill: Figurative Language

Du Bois compares new experiences with a cold bath and a big bedroom. The comparisons connect something new with something familiar. The author wants to express that bravery is required in her situation.

New York, October 29, 1914

Dear Little Daughter:

1 I have waited for you to get well settled before writing. By this time I hope some of the strangeness has worn off and that my little girl is working hard and regularly.

2 Of course, everything is new and unusual. You miss the newness and smartness of America. Gradually, however, you are going to sense the beauty of the old world: its calm and eternity and you will grow to love it.

3 Above all remember, dear, that you have a great opportunity. You are in one of the world's best schools, in one of the world's greatest modern empires. Millions of boys and girls all over this world would give almost anything they possess to be where you are. You are there by no **desert** or **merit** of yours, but only by lucky chance.

4 Deserve it, then. Study, do your work. Be honest, frank and fearless and get some grasp of the real values of life. You will meet, of course, curious little annoyances. People will wonder at your dear brown and the sweet **crinkley** hair. But that simply is of no importance and will soon be forgotten. Remember that most folk laugh at anything unusual, whether it is beautiful, fine or not. You, however, must not laugh at yourself. You must know that brown is as pretty as white or prettier and crinkley hair as straight even though it is harder to comb. The main thing is the YOU beneath the clothes and skin—the ability to do, the will to **conquer**, the determination to understand and know this great, wonderful, curious world. Don't shrink from new experiences and custom. Take the cold bath bravely. Enter into the spirit of your big bed-room. Enjoy what is and not **pine** for what is not. Read some good, heavy, serious books just for discipline: Take yourself in hand and **master** yourself. Make yourself do unpleasant things, so as to gain the upper hand of your soul.

NOTES

5   Above all remember: your father loves you and believes in you and expects
    you to be a wonderful woman.

6   I shall write each week and expect a weekly letter from you.

    Lovingly yours,
    Papa

Reprinted from The Correspondence of W.E.B. Du Bois, Volume I. Copyright
© 1973 by the University of Massachusetts Press.

Please note that excerpts and passages in the StudySync® library and this workbook are intended as touchstones to generate
interest in an author's work. The excerpts and passages do not substitute for the reading of entire texts, and StudySync®
strongly recommends that students seek out and purchase the whole literary or informational work in order to experience it as
the author intended. Links to online resellers are available in our digital library. In addition, complete works may be ordered
through an authorized reseller by filling out and returning to StudySync® the order form enclosed in this workbook.

Reading & Writing
Companion

785

First Read

Read "Letter to His Daughter." After you read, complete the Think Questions below.

 THINK QUESTIONS

1. Why do you think W.E.B. Du Bois decided to write this letter to his daughter? Cite evidence from the letter in your response.

2. In paragraph 4, Du Bois offers his daughter some words of encouragement as she begins a new chapter of her life. Citing examples from the text, explain what he thinks is most important for his daughter to remember.

3. What does W.E.B. Du Bois's letter to his daughter tell you about him as a father? Cite specific examples from the text to support your analysis.

4. In paragraph 4, which context clues help you determine the definition of the word **pine**? Write your best definition of the word *pine* and explain how you inferred its meaning.

5. Read the following dictionary entry:

master

mas•ter \mastər\

noun

1. a person who holds an advanced college degree
2. a person skilled in a particular art or profession

verb

1. to gain control of or overcome
2. to learn a skill or trade thoroughly

adjective

1. having great skill or proficiency

Which definition most closely matches the meaning of **master** in paragraph 4? Write the correct definition of *master* here and explain how you figured it out.

Skill:
Figurative Language

Use the Checklist to analyze Figurative Language in "Letter to His Daughter." Refer to the sample student annotations about Figurative Language in the text.

••• CHECKLIST FOR FIGURATIVE LANGUAGE

To determine the meaning of figures of speech in a text, note the following:

- ✓ words that mean one thing literally and suggest something else

- ✓ similes, such as "strong as an ox"

- ✓ metaphors, such as "her eyes were stars"

- ✓ personification, such as "the daisies danced in the wind"

- ✓ idioms, or expressions whose meanings cannot be understood from the meanings of the individual words that make it up, such as "this test will be a piece of cake"

In order to interpret the meaning of a figure of speech in context, ask the following questions:

- ✓ Does any of the descriptive language in the text compare two seemingly unlike things?

- ✓ Do any descriptions include "like" or "as" that indicate a simile?

- ✓ Is there a direct comparison that suggests a metaphor?

- ✓ Is a human quality used to describe an animal, object, force of nature or idea that suggests personification?

- ✓ Does the author use idioms, or phrases that mean something different from their literal meaning?

- ✓ How does the use of this figure of speech change your understanding of the thing or person being described?

Skill:
Figurative Language

Reread paragraph 4 from "Letter to His Daughter." Then, using the Checklist on the previous page, answer the multiple-choice questions below.

↻ YOUR TURN

1. What does the idiom "gain the upper hand" mean?

○ A. to take control

○ B. to beat someone in a fight

○ C. to wrestle with someone

○ D. to raise one's hand

2. For what purpose does Du Bois use figures of speech in this passage?

○ A. They show Du Bois will punish his daughter if she doesn't succeed.

○ B. They show Du Bois does not have faith in his daughter's skills.

○ C. They show Du Bois thinks his daughter has the power to take control over her own life.

○ D. They show Du Bois fears for his daughter's soul.

Skill:
Context Clues

Use the Checklist to analyze Context Clues in "Letter to His Daughter." Refer to the sample student annotations about Context Clues in the text.

••• CHECKLIST FOR CONTEXT CLUES

In order to use context as a clue to infer the meaning of a word or phrase, note the following:

✓ clues about the word's part of speech

✓ clues in the surrounding text about the word's meaning

✓ signal words that cue a type of context clue, such as:

- *for example* or *for instance* to signal an example context clue
- *like, similarly,* or *just as* to signal a comparison clue
- *but*, *however*, or *unlike* to signal a contrast context clue

To determine the meaning of a word or phrase as it is used in a text, consider the following questions:

✓ What is the overall sentence, paragraph, or text about?

✓ How does the word function in the sentence?

✓ What clues can help me determine the word's part of speech?

✓ What text clues can help me figure out the word's definition?

✓ Are there any examples that show what the word means?

✓ What do I think the word means?

To verify the preliminary determination of the meaning of the word or phrase based on context, consider the following questions:

✓ Does the definition I inferred make sense in the context of the sentence?

✓ Which of the dictionary's definitions makes sense in the context of the sentence?

Skill:
Context Clues

Reread paragraph 4 of "Letter to His Daughter." Then, using the Checklist on the previous page, answer the multiple-choice questions below.

YOUR TURN

1. This question has two parts. First, answer Part A. Then, answer Part B.

   Part A: What does the word **frank** at the beginning of the passage mean based on the context provided in paragraph 4?

   ○ A. humble

   ○ B. careful

   ○ C. irritated

   ○ D. open

   Part B: Which piece of evidence BEST supports your answer to Part A?

   ○ A. "You will meet, of course, curious little annoyances."

   ○ B. "But that simply is of no importance and will soon be forgotten."

   ○ C. ". . . the ability to do, the will to **conquer**, the determination to understand and know. . . "

   ○ D. "Make yourself do unpleasant things, so as to gain the upper hand of your soul."

Close Read

Reread "Letter to His Daughter." As you reread, complete the Skills Focus questions below. Then use your answers and annotations from the questions to help you complete the Write activity.

◎ SKILLS FOCUS

1. In paragraph 4, W.E.B. Du Bois says to his daughter, "Take the cold bath bravely. Enter into the spirit of your big bed-room." Highlight the figurative language and the surrounding sentences that provide context. Explain what you think Du Bois means based on the context.

2. At the end of paragraph 4, Du Bois tells Yolande, "Take yourself in hand and master yourself. Make yourself do unpleasant things, so as to gain the upper hand of your soul." Highlight the figurative language and explain what you think he is asking Yolande to do.

3. Read the following dictionary entry:

   smartness
   smart•ness \'smɑːtnəs\

   noun

   1. the quality of being intelligent
   2. the quality of being quick
   3. the quality of being new and attractive

   Which definition most closely matches the meaning of **smartness** as it is used in paragraph 2? Write the appropriate definition of smartness here and explain how you figured out the correct meaning.

4. Use context clues to determine what the author means when he writes "curious little annoyances."

5. Think about the unit's Essential Question: "Who are you meant to be?" Although Du Bois does not ask Yolande this question, the idea that he wants her to think about her future is implicit in what he says to her. Highlight evidence of this in the letter and explain your reasoning.

✎ WRITE

LITERARY ANALYSIS: In his letter to his daughter, W.E.B. Du Bois often uses figurative language, which allows readers to know more about him. What do his metaphors tell us about who he is and how he thinks people should live? Which of his values or beliefs are evident in his letter? Be sure to include evidence from the text in your response.

The Story Behind the Bus

INFORMATIONAL TEXT
The Henry Ford® Museum
2002

Introduction

The Henry Ford® museum houses a large collection of items of historical significance, including John F. Kennedy's presidential limousine, Abraham Lincoln's seat from Ford's Theatre, and the bus on which civil rights activist Rosa Parks took her famous stand against segregation. This excerpt from the museum's website offers background information on Rosa Parks and the circumstances surrounding her December 1955 arrest in Montgomery, Alabama.

"When I made that decision," she said later, "I knew that I had the strength of my ancestors with me."

1   On December 1, 1955, Rosa Parks, a 42-year-old African American woman who worked as a seamstress, boarded this Montgomery City bus to go home from work. On this bus on that day, Rosa Parks initiated a new era in the American quest for freedom and equality.

2   She sat near the middle of the bus, just behind the 10 seats reserved for whites. Soon all of the seats in the bus were filled. When a white man entered the bus, the driver (following the standard practice of **segregation**) insisted that all four blacks sitting just behind the white section give up their seats so that the man could sit there. Mrs. Parks, who was an active member of the local NAACP[1], quietly refused to give up her seat.

3   Her action was spontaneous and not premeditated, although her previous civil rights involvement and strong sense of justice were obvious influences. "When I made that decision," she said later, "I knew that I had the strength of my ancestors with me."

4   She was arrested and convicted of violating the laws of segregation, known as "Jim Crow laws." Mrs. Parks appealed her conviction and thus formally challenged the legality of segregation.

5   At the same time, local civil rights activists initiated a boycott of the Montgomery bus system. In cities across the South, segregated bus companies were daily reminders of the **inequities** of American society. Since African Americans made up about 75 percent of the riders in Montgomery, the boycott posed a serious economic threat to the company and a social threat to white rule in the city.

6   A group named the Montgomery Improvement Association, composed of local activists and ministers, organized the boycott. As their leader, they chose a young Baptist minister who was new to Montgomery: Martin Luther King, Jr. Sparked by Mrs. Parks's action, the boycott lasted 381 days, into December 1956 when the U.S. Supreme Court ruled that the segregation law

---

1. **NAACP** an acronym for the National Association for the Advancement of Colored Persons, a United States civil rights organization dedicated to advancing justice for African Americans

was **unconstitutional** and the Montgomery buses were **integrated**. The Montgomery Bus Boycott was the beginning of a revolutionary era of non-violent mass protests in support of civil rights in the United States.

7   It was not just an accident that the civil rights movement began on a city bus. In a famous 1896 case involving a black man on a train, *Plessy v. Ferguson*, the U.S. Supreme Court enunciated the "separate but equal" rationale for Jim Crow. Of course, facilities and treatment were never equal.

8   Under Jim Crow customs and laws, it was relatively easy to separate the races in every area of life except transportation. Bus and train companies couldn't afford separate cars and so blacks and whites had to occupy the same space.

9   Thus, transportation was one the most **volatile** arenas for race relations in the South. Mrs. Parks remembers going to elementary school in Pine Level, Alabama, where buses took white kids to the new school but black kids had to walk to their school.

10 "I'd see the bus pass every day," she said. "But to me, that was a way of life; we had no choice but to accept what was the custom. *The bus was among the first ways I realized there was a black world and a white world*" (emphasis added).

11 Montgomery's Jim Crow customs were particularly harsh and gave bus drivers great latitude in making decisions on where people could sit. The law even gave bus drivers the authority to carry guns to enforce their edicts. Mrs. Parks' attorney Fred Gray remembered, "Virtually every African-American person in Montgomery had some negative experience with the buses. But we had no choice. We had to use the buses for transportation."

12 Civil rights advocates had outlawed Jim Crow in interstate train travel, and blacks in several Southern cities attacked the practice of segregated bus systems. There had been a bus boycott in Baton Rouge, Louisiana, in 1953, but black leaders compromised before making real gains. Joann Robinson, a black university professor and activist in Montgomery, had suggested the idea of a bus boycott months before the Parks arrest.

13 Two other women had been arrested on buses in Montgomery before Parks and were considered by black leaders as potential clients for challenging the law. However, both were rejected because black leaders felt they would not gain white support. When she heard that the well-respected Rosa Parks had been arrested, one Montgomery African American woman exclaimed, "They've messed with the wrong one now."

14 In the South, city buses were lightning rods for civil rights activists. It took someone with the courage and character of Rosa Parks to strike with lightning. And it required the commitment of the entire African American community to fan the flames ignited by that lightning into the fires of the civil rights revolution.

✏ WRITE

PERSONAL RESPONSE: When have you calmly or peacefully stood up for something that is important to you or that you believe in? Write about this experience after reflecting on the information in "The Story Behind the Bus." Before you begin, ask yourself, "How did Rosa Parks demonstrate her belief?" Support your response with evidence from the text.

Please note that excerpts and passages in the StudySync® library and this workbook are intended as touchstones to generate interest in an author's work. The excerpts and passages do not substitute for the reading of entire texts, and StudySync® strongly recommends that students seek out and purchase the whole literary or informational work in order to experience it as the author intended. Links to online resellers are available in our digital library. In addition, complete works may be ordered through an authorized reseller by filling out and returning to StudySync® the order form enclosed in this workbook.

Reading & Writing Companion   **795**

Rosa

POETRY
Rita Dove
1986

Introduction

studysync ᵗᵛ

Rita Dove (b. 1952) is a highly regarded African American poet and author who won the 1987 Pulitzer Prize for Poetry. Dove's poetic works explore a variety of topics, including historical and political events, and she is known for capturing complex emotions succinctly. Her poem "Rosa" is a tribute to Rosa Parks, the activist who helped end segregation by quietly refusing to leave her seat on

"Doing nothing was the doing"

NOTES

1 How she sat there,
2 the time right inside a place
3 so wrong it was ready.

4 That **trim** name with
5 its dream of a bench
6 to rest on. Her **sensible** coat.

7 Doing nothing was the doing:
8 the clean flame of her gaze
9 **carved** by a camera flash.

10 How she stood up
11 when they bent down to **retrieve**
12 her purse. That **courtesy**.

"Rosa", from ON THE BUS WITH ROSA PARKS by Rita Dove. Copyright ©
1999 by Rita Dove. Used by permission of W. W. Norton & Company, Inc.

✏ WRITE

PERSONAL RESPONSE: Who is someone you admire? Write a poem about this person imitating Rita Dove's approach in "Rosa." Before you begin, consider how the speaker in the poem shows admiration for Rosa Parks. Include details to make your reasons for admiring this person clear.

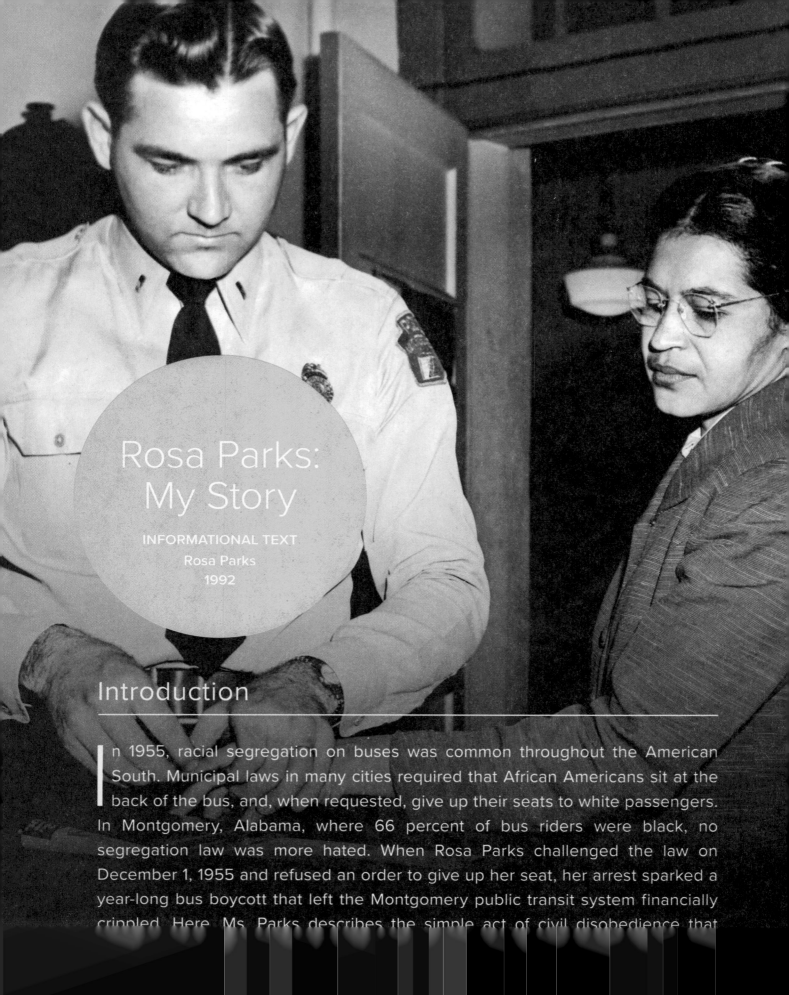

Rosa Parks: My Story

INFORMATIONAL TEXT
Rosa Parks
1992

Introduction

In 1955, racial segregation on buses was common throughout the American South. Municipal laws in many cities required that African Americans sit at the back of the bus, and, when requested, give up their seats to white passengers. In Montgomery, Alabama, where 66 percent of bus riders were black, no segregation law was more hated. When Rosa Parks challenged the law on December 1, 1955 and refused an order to give up her seat, her arrest sparked a year-long bus boycott that left the Montgomery public transit system financially crippled. Here, Ms. Parks describes the simple act of civil disobedience that

"No, the only tired I was, was tired of giving in."

Excerpt from Chapter 8: "You're Under Arrest"

1   When I got off from work that evening of December 1, I went to Court Square as usual to catch the Cleveland Avenue bus home. I didn't look to see who was driving when I got on, and by the time I recognized him, I had already paid my fare[1]. It was the same driver who had put me off the bus back in 1943, twelve years earlier. He was still tall and heavy, with red, rough-looking skin. And he was still mean-looking. I didn't know if he had been on that route before—they switched the drivers around sometimes. I do know that most of the time if I saw him on a bus, I wouldn't get on it.

2   I saw a vacant seat in the middle section of the bus and took it. I didn't even question why there was a vacant seat even though there were quite a few people standing in the back. If I had thought about it at all, I would probably have figured maybe someone saw me get on and did not take the seat but left it vacant for me. There was a man sitting next to the window and two women across the aisle.

3   The next stop was the Empire Theater, and some whites got on. They filled up the white seats, and one man was left standing. The driver looked back and noticed the man standing. Then he looked back at us. He said, "Let me have those front seats," because they were the front seats of the black section. Didn't anybody move. We just sat right where we were, the four of us. Then he spoke a second time: "Y'all better make it light on yourselves and let me have those seats."

4   The man in the window seat next to me stood up, and I moved to let him pass by me, and then I looked across the aisle and saw that the two women were also standing. I moved over to the window seat. I could not see how standing up was going to "make it light" for me. The more we gave in and **complied**, the worse they treated us.

---

1. **fare** money paid to use public transportation

> Skill:
> Informational
> Text Elements

Parks begins this section of text with the specific date and location where this important event took place. Then, she identifies a key individual and provides some details about him.

> Skill: Connotation
> and Denotation

The denotation of "complied" is "did what was requested"; however, the word is often associated negatively. Here Parks associates "complied" with giving in, and with "the worse they treated us." The connotations suggest that Parks views compliance as a bad choice.

Skill:
Informational
Text Elements

Here Parks shares a
personal anecdote
about her grandfather.
Then she sets the
record straight and
explains that she was
not tired or old, just fed
up. She is trying to
explain the true
motivation behind her
action.

Skill: Connotation
and Denotation

Again, Parks has
chosen a word with
strong negative
connotations to
emphasize the danger of
her situation. The use
of the term manhandled
adds a sinister or
dangerous tone: she is
saying that the police
could treat her roughly
or even beat her.

5 I thought back to the time when I used to sit up all night and didn't sleep, and my grandfather would have his gun right by the fireplace, or if he had his one-horse wagon going anywhere, he always had his gun in the back of the wagon. People always say that I didn't give up my seat because I was tired, but that isn't true. I was not tired physically, or no more tired than I usually was at the end of a working day. I was not old, although some people have an image of me as being old then. I was forty-two. No, the only tired I was, was tired of giving in.

6 The driver of the bus saw me still sitting there, and he asked was I going to stand up. I said, "No." He said, "Well, I'm going to have you arrested." Then I said, "You may do that." These were the only words we said to each other. I didn't even know his name, which was James Blake, until we were in court together. He got out of the bus and stayed outside for a few minutes, waiting for the police.

7 As I sat there, I tried not to think about what might happen. I knew that anything was possible. I could be manhandled or beaten. I could be arrested. People have asked me if it **occurred** to me then that I could be the test case the NAACP had been looking for. I did not think about that at all. In fact if I had let myself think too deeply about what might happen to me, I might have gotten off the bus. But I chose to remain.

8 Meanwhile there were people getting off the bus and asking for transfers, so that began to loosen up the crowd, especially in the back of the bus. Not everyone got off, but everybody was very quiet. What conversation there was, was in low tones; no one was talking out loud. It would have been quite interesting to have seen the whole bus empty out. Or if the other three had stayed where they were, because if they'd had to arrest four of us instead of one, then that would have given me a little support. But it didn't matter. I never thought hard of them at all and never even **bothered** to criticize them.

9 Eventually two policemen came. They got on the bus, and one of them asked me why I didn't stand up. I asked him, "Why do you all push us around?" He said to me, and I quote him exactly, "I don't know, but the law is the law and you're under arrest." One policeman picked up my purse, and the second one picked up my shopping bag and escorted me to the squad car. In the squad car they returned my personal belongings to me. They did not put their hands on me or force me into the car. After I was seated in the car, they went back to the driver and asked him if he wanted to swear out a warrant. He answered that he would finish his route and then come straight back to swear out the warrant. I was only in custody, not legally arrested, until the warrant was signed.

10 As they were driving me to the city desk, at City Hall, near Court Street, one of them asked me again, "Why didn't you stand up when the driver spoke to you?" I did not answer. I remained silent all the way to City Hall.

11 As we entered the building, I asked if I could have a drink of water, because my throat was real dry. There was a fountain, and I was standing right next to it. One of the policemen said yes, but by the time I bent down to drink, another policeman said, "No, you can't drink no water. You have to wait until you get to the jail." So I was **denied** the chance to drink a sip of water. I was not going to do anything but wet my throat. I wasn't going to drink a whole lot of water, even though I was quite thirsty. That made me angry, but I did not respond.

12 At the city desk they filled out the necessary forms as I answered questions such as what my name was and where I lived. I asked if I could make a telephone call and they said, "No." Since that was my first arrest, I didn't know if that was more **discrimination** because I was black or if it was standard practice. But it seemed to me to be more discrimination. Then they escorted me back to the squad car, and we went to the city jail on North Ripley Street.

13 I wasn't frightened at the jail. I was more resigned than anything else. I don't recall being real angry, not enough to have an argument. I was just prepared to accept whatever I had to face. I asked again if I could make a telephone call. I was ignored.

14 They told me to put my purse on the counter and to empty my pockets of personal items. The only thing I had in my pocket was a tissue. I took that out. They didn't search me or handcuff me.

15 I was then taken to an area where I was fingerprinted and where mug shots were taken. A white matron[2] came to escort me to my jail cell, and I asked again if I might use the telephone. She told me that she would find out.

16 She took me up a flight of stairs (the cells were on the second level), through a door covered with iron mesh, and along a dimly lighted corridor. She placed me in an empty dark cell and slammed the door closed. She walked a few steps away, but then she turned around and came back. She said, "There are two girls around the other side, and if you want to go over there with them instead of being in a cell by yourself, I will take you over there."

Excerpted from *Rosa Parks: My Story* by Rosa Parks, published by Puffin Books.

---

2. **matron** a woman whose job is to be in charge of other women usually serving as a guard, warden, or attendant

First Read

Read *Rosa Parks: My Story*. After you read, complete the Think Questions below.

☁ THINK QUESTIONS

1. Refer to one or more details in the text to explain how Rosa's previous interaction with the bus driver might have contributed to her actions on December 1.

2. Use details from the text to explain other factors Parks believes contributed to her actions on December 1, 1955. What do other people seem to think contributed? Does Parks agree?

3. How do the law enforcement officials behave in expected and unexpected ways during Rosa's arrest? Support your answer with textual evidence.

4. Use context to determine the meaning of the word **manhandled** as it is used in *Rosa Parks: My Story*. Write your definition of *manhandled* here and tell how you got it.

5. The Latin word *discriminare* means "to separate." Use this knowledge, along with the context clues provided in the passage, to determine the meaning of **discrimination**. Write your definition of *discrimination* here and explain how you figured it out.

Skill:
Informational Text Elements

Use the Checklist to analyze Informational Text Elements in *Rosa Parks: My Story*. Refer to the sample student annotations about Informational Text Elements in the text.

••• CHECKLIST FOR INFORMATIONAL TEXT ELEMENTS

In order to identify a key individual, event, or idea in a text, note the following:

- ✓ examples that describe or explain important ideas, events, or individuals in the text

- ✓ anecdotes in the text. An anecdote is a personal story an author passes on to readers

- ✓ how a key individual, event, or idea is introduced or illustrated

- ✓ other features, such as charts, maps, sidebars, and photos that might provide additional information outside of the main text

To analyze in detail how a key individual, event, or idea is introduced, illustrated, or elaborated in a text, consider the following questions:

- ✓ How does the author introduce or illustrate a key individual, event, or idea?

- ✓ What key details does the author include to describe or elaborate on important information in the text?

- ✓ Does the author include any anecdotes? What do they add to the text?

- ✓ What other features, if any, help readers to analyze the events, ideas, or individuals in the text?

Skill:
Informational Text Elements

sync•skills

Reread paragraphs 3 and 4 from *Rosa Parks: My Story*. Then, using the Checklist on the previous page, answer the multiple-choice questions below.

↻ YOUR TURN

1. Which sentence from paragraph 3 is an example of supporting evidence from Parks's autobiography?

   ○ A. Then he spoke a second time: "Y'all better make it light on yourselves and let me have those seats."

   ○ B. The driver looked back and noticed the man standing.

   ○ C. Then he looked back at us.

   ○ D. Didn't anybody move.

2. Which sentence from paragraph 4 is a pertinent example from Parks's autobiography?

   ○ A. The man in the window seat next to me stood up, and I moved to let him pass by me, and then I looked across the aisle and saw that the two women were also standing.

   ○ B. I moved over to the window seat.

   ○ C. I could not see how standing up was going to "make it light" for me.

   ○ D. The more we gave in and **complied,** the worse they treated us.

Skill: Compare and Contrast

Use the Checklist to analyze Compare and Contrast in *Rosa Parks: My Story*. Refer to the sample student annotations about Compare and Contrast in the text.

••• CHECKLIST FOR COMPARE AND CONTRAST

In order to determine how to compare and contrast one author's presentation of events with that of another, use the following steps:

- ✓ first, choose two texts with similar subjects or topics, such as an autobiography and a biography of the same person, or a news report of an event and a narrative nonfiction account of the same event

- ✓ next, identify the author's approach to the subject in each genre

- ✓ after, explain how the point of view is different in each text

- ✓ finally, analyze ways in which the texts are similar and different in their presentation of specific events and information

  - whether the nonfiction narrative account contains dialogue that may not have been spoken, or may have been altered in some way

  - what the author of an autobiography might know that a biographer might never be able to uncover or research

To compare and contrast one author's presentation of events with that of another, consider the following questions:

- ✓ How does the author approach each topic or subject?

- ✓ What are the similarities and differences in the presentation of events in each text?

Skill:
Compare and Contrast

Reread paragraphs 9 and 10 from "The Story Behind the Bus" and paragraph 5 from *Rosa Parks: My Story*. Then, using the Checklist on the previous page, answer the multiple-choice questions below.

⟳ YOUR TURN

1. Which of the following do both passages have in common?

    ○ A. They are both written from Parks' perspective.

    ○ B. Both discuss common misconceptions about Parks' actions on December 1, 1955.

    ○ C. They both describe experiences Parks' had as a child growing up in a segregated community.

    ○ D. Both texts discuss the consequences of the Montgomery Bus Boycott.

2. Match the textual evidence that contrasts the author's presentation of information regarding why Rosa Parks refused to give up her seat to the correct text.

    ○ A. "People always say that I didn't give up my seat because I was tired, but that isn't true . . . No, the only tired I was, was tired of giving in."

    ○ B. Her action was spontaneous and not premeditated, although her previous civil rights involvement and strong sense of justice were obvious influences.

    _____ "The Story Behind the Bus"

    _____ *Rosa Parks: My Story*

Skill:
Connotation and Denotation

Use the Checklist to analyze Connotation and Denotation in *Rosa Parks: My Story*. Refer to the sample student annotations about Connotation and Denotation in the text.

••• CHECKLIST FOR CONNOTATION AND DENOTATION

In order to identify the denotative meanings of words and phrases, use the following steps:

✓ first, note unfamiliar words and phrases; key words used to describe important individuals, events, or ideas; or words that inspire an emotional reaction

✓ next, verify the denotative meaning of words by consulting a reference work such as a dictionary, glossary, or thesaurus

To better understand the meaning of words and phrases as they are used in a text, including connotative meanings, ask the following questions:

✓ What is the genre or subject of the text? How does that affect the possible meaning of a word or phrase?

✓ Does the word create a positive, negative, or neutral emotion?

✓ What synonyms or alternative phrasing help you describe the connotative meaning of the word?

To determine the meaning of words and phrases as they are used in a text, including connotative meanings, ask the following questions:

✓ What is the meaning of the word or phrase? What is the connotation as well as the denotation?

✓ If I substitute a synonym based on denotation, is the meaning the same? How does it change the meaning of the text?

Please note that excerpts and passages in the StudySync® library and this workbook are intended as touchstones to generate interest in an author's work. The excerpts and passages do not substitute for the reading of entire texts, and StudySync® strongly recommends that students seek out and purchase the whole literary or informational work in order to experience it as the author intended. Links to online resellers are available in our digital library. In addition, complete works may be ordered through an authorized reseller by filling out and returning to StudySync® the order form enclosed in this workbook.

Reading & Writing Companion

807

Skill:
Connotation and Denotation

Reread paragraph 12 of *Rosa Parks: My Story*. Then, using the Checklist on the previous page, answer the multiple-choice questions below.

↻ YOUR TURN

1. This question has two parts. First, answer Part A. Then, answer Part B.

   Part A Which of the following is most likely the intended connotation of *discrimination?*

   ○ A. negative—the word suggests confusion and lack of information

   ○ B. neither positive nor negative—the word suggests a separate kind of treatment that is no worse or better.

   ○ C. negative—the word suggests racism and unfair treatment.

   ○ D. positive—the word suggests that Parks was being treated better than others

   Part B Which phrase from the passage best supports your answer in Part A?

   ○ A. "was my first arrest"

   ○ B. "because I was black"

   ○ C. "it was standard practice"

   ○ D. "filled out the necessary forms"

Close Read

Reread *Rosa Parks: My Story*. As you reread, complete the Skills Focus questions below. Then use your answers and annotations from the questions to help you complete the Write activity.

◎ SKILLS FOCUS

1. The primary purpose of an autobiography is to detail the events of an individual's life, and these events must be supported with evidence and pertinent examples. Analyze how Parks uses supporting evidence and pertinent examples to support her purpose for writing by illuminating information about key individuals, ideas, or events.

2. In *Rosa Parks: My Story*, the author uses several words whose connotations are specific to her story. Select a word from the text, identify its denotation, and then explain its connotation as used in the context.

3. In the poem "Rosa," Rita Dove expresses the idea that "Doing nothing was the doing." Identify evidence in the autobiography that supports this claim and explain your reasoning.

4. Identify evidence in *Rosa Parks: My Story* that illustrates how Parks was true to herself and how her actions shaped who she was meant to be.

✏ WRITE

COMPARE AND CONTRAST: Rosa Parks, Rita Dove, and the author of "The Story Behind the Bus" all have a story to share about upsetting the balance of power. How does each author introduce, illustrate, or elaborate this idea of power? How are their arguments about power similar and different? In your response, remember to make connections to ideas in the previous texts that you've read.

Please note that excerpts and passages in the StudySync® library and this workbook are intended as touchstones to generate interest in an author's work. The excerpts and passages do not substitute for the reading of entire texts, and StudySync® strongly recommends that students seek out and purchase the whole literary or informational work in order to experience it as the author intended. Links to online resellers are available in our digital library. In addition, complete works may be ordered through an authorized reseller by filling out and returning to StudySync® the order form enclosed in this workbook.

Reading & Writing Companion   **809**

Eleanor Roosevelt:
A Life of Discovery

INFORMATIONAL TEXT
Russell Freedman
1993

Introduction

nitially reluctant to be a president's wife, "poor little rich girl" Eleanor Roosevelt (1884–1962) rose to the challenge of being in the national spotlight. Bright, energetic, and courageous, she became the most celebrated and admired first lady the White House had ever known. As an invaluable researcher for her husband during the years of the Great Depression, and later a representative of the United Nations, Eleanor raised the bar of possibilities for all first ladies who followed her.

"Americans had never seen a First Lady like her. . ."

Excerpt from Chapter One: First Lady

1   Eleanor Roosevelt never wanted to be a president's wife. When her husband Franklin won his **campaign** for the presidency in 1932, she felt deeply troubled. She dreaded the prospect of living in the White House.

2   Proud of her accomplishments as a teacher, a writer, and a political power in her own right, she feared that she would have to give up her hard-won independence in Washington. As First Lady, she would have no life of her own. Like other presidential wives before her, she would be assigned the traditional role of official White House hostess, with little to do but greet guests at receptions and preside over formal state dinners.

3   "From the personal standpoint, I did not want my husband to be president," she later confessed. "It was pure selfishness on my part, and I never mentioned my feelings on the subject to him."

4   Mrs. Roosevelt did her duty. During her years in the White House, the executive mansion[1] bustled with visitors at teas, receptions, and dinners. At the same time, however, she cast her fears aside and seized the opportunity to transform the role of America's First Lady. Encouraged by her friends, she became the first wife of a president to have a public life and career.

5   Americans had never seen a First Lady like her. She was the first to open the White House door to reporters and hold on-the-record[2] press conferences[3], the first to drive her own car, to travel by plane, and to make many official trips by herself. "My missus goes where she wants to!" the president boasted.

---

1. **executive mansion** the White House is considered the "executive" branch of the U.S. government
2. **on-the-record** making one's statements official or public
3. **press conference** an interview granted to journalists by a prominent person in order to communicate information and answer questions

NOTES

6   She was the first president's wife to earn her own money by writing, lecturing, and broadcasting. Her earnings usually topped the president's salary. She gave most of the money to charity.

7   When she insisted on her right to take drives by herself, without a chauffeur or a police escort, the Secret Service, worried about her safety, gave her a pistol and begged her to carry it with her. "I [took] it and learned how to use it," she told readers of her popular newspaper column. "I do not mean by this that I am an expert shot. I only wish I were . . . . My opportunities for shooting have been far and few between, but if the necessity arose, I do know how to use a pistol."

8   She had come a long way since her days as an obedient society matron[4], and, before then, a **timid** child who was "always afraid of something." By her own account, she had been an "ugly duckling" whose mother told her, "You have no looks, so see to it that you have manners." Before she was ten, both of her unhappy parents were dead. She grew up in a time and place where a woman's life was ruled by her husband's interests and needs, and dominated by the domestic duties of wife and mother. "It was not until I reached middle age," she wrote, "that I had the courage to develop interests of my own, outside of my duties to my family."

9   Eleanor Roosevelt lived in the White House during the Great Depression and the Second World War. In her endless travels through America, she served as a fact-finder and trouble-shooter for her husband and an impassioned publicist for her own views about social justice and world peace. She wanted people to feel that their government cared about them. After Franklin Roosevelt's death, she became a major force at the United Nations, where her efforts on behalf of human rights earned her the title, First Lady of the World.

10 People meeting her for the first time often were startled by how "unjustly" the camera treated her. Photographs had not prepared them for her warmth and dignity and **poise**. An unusually tall woman, she moved with the grace of an athlete, and when she walked into a room, the air seemed charged with her **vibrancy**. "No one seeing her could fail to be moved," said her friend Martha Gellhorn. "She gave off light, I cannot explain it better."

11 For thirty years from the time she entered the White House until her death in 1962, Eleanor Roosevelt was the most famous and at times the most **influential** woman in the world. And yet those who knew her best were most impressed by her simplicity, by her total lack of self-importance.

---

4. **matron** a dignified married woman

12   "About the only value the story of my life may have," she wrote, "is to show that one can, even without any particular gifts, overcome obstacles that seem insurmountable if one is willing to face the fact that they must be overcome; that, in spite of timidity and fear, in spite of a lack of special talents, one can find a way to live widely and fully."

Excerpted from *Eleanor Roosevelt: A Life of Discovery* by Russell Freedman, published by Clarion Books.

 WRITE

PERSONAL RESPONSE: Eleanor Roosevelt did not wish to become First Lady of the United States. Yet she was able to overcome her fear to become one of the most beloved First Ladies in history. Consider how Eleanor's life might relate to your own. Is there a task or dream you would like to achieve? How can you, like Eleanor, overcome any fears you might have in order to achieve success? In your response, write about the goal or dream you have been afraid to achieve. Then, explain what strategy you can use, like Eleanor, to overcome that fear.

Please note that excerpts and passages in the StudySync® library and this workbook are intended as touchstones to generate interest in an author's work. The excerpts and passages do not substitute for the reading of entire texts, and StudySync® strongly recommends that students seek out and purchase the whole literary or informational work in order to experience it as the author intended. Links to online resellers are available in our digital library. In addition, complete works may be ordered through an authorized reseller by filling out and returning to StudySync® the order form enclosed in this workbook.

Reading & Writing Companion   **813**

Brave

FICTION
Svetlana Chmakova
2017

Introduction

Svetlana Chmakova (b. 1979), a Russian and Canadian comic artist, published *Brave* as a sequel to her graphic novel, *Awkward*. Brave follows Jensen, a middle school boy who dreams of saving the world. Jensen soon finds that saving the world and following his dreams aren't as easy as they sound, and he must learn to be brave as he faces challenges along the way.

"I may be just a regular kid at regular Berrybrook Middle School . . . but I am going to save the world."

Please note that excerpts and passages in the StudySync® library and this workbook are intended as touchstones to generate interest in an author's work. The excerpts and passages do not substitute for the reading of entire texts, and StudySync® strongly recommends that students seek out and purchase the whole literary or informational work in order to experience it as the author intended. Links to online resellers are available in our digital library. In addition, complete works may be ordered through an authorized reseller by filling out and returning to StudySync® the order form enclosed in this workbook.

Reading & Writing Companion   **815**

NOTES

6

---

1. **sunspot** dark spot or patch appearing from time to time on the sun's surface, known to cause magnetic disturbances on Earth

7

Skill: Language, Style and Audience

In Jensen's daydream he says "I can't wait to be." This language choice shows that he's excited for the future. In the next panel, Jensen's name is in capital letters with multiple exclamation points. His daydream gets interrupted, and his attitude changes.

9

Skill: Language, Style and Audience

I can see that the other students and the teacher are frustrated because the author included angry and sarcastic words and phrases directed at Jensen. The tone seems very tense.

Reading & Writing Companion

11

Please note that excerpts and passages in the StudySync® library and this workbook are intended as touchstones to generate interest in an author's work. The excerpts and passages do not substitute for the reading of entire texts, and StudySync® strongly recommends that students seek out and purchase the whole literary or informational work in order to experience it as the author intended. Links to online resellers are available in our digital library. In addition, complete works may be ordered through an authorized reseller by filling out and returning to StudySync® the order form enclosed in this workbook.

Reading & Writing Companion

821

12

14

2. **running the gauntlet** enduring an intimidating or dangerous task

NOTES

17

From *Brave* by Svetlana Chmakova. Copyright © 2017 by Svetlana Chmakova. Used by permission of Yen Press, an imprint of the Hachette Book Group USA Inc.

First Read

Read the excerpt from the graphic novel *Brave*. After you read, complete the Think Questions below.

 THINK QUESTIONS

1. Why does Jensen carry around a book titled "Zombie Survival Guide"? Cite evidence from page 6 to support your response.

2. According to pages 14–16, how does Jensen deal with challenges?

3. Why do the other kids leave Jensen alone when Jenny, Akilah, and Felipe arrive? Cite evidence from the text to support your response.

4. Based on context clues from page 6, determine the meaning of **apocalypse** as it is used in the text. Then confirm your inferred meaning by checking an online or print dictionary.

5. Read the following dictionary entry:

   lurk
   \lərk\

   verb

   1. to remain hidden while waiting to pounce (said of a person or animal)
   2. to be difficult to detect, but still threatening
   3. to read internet message boards without writing on them

   Which definition most closely matches the meaning of *lurk* on page 6 and again on page 14? Write the correct definition of *lurk* here and explain how you figured it out.

Skill: Language, Style, and Audience

Use the Checklist to analyze Language, Style, and Audience in *Brave*. Refer to the sample student annotations about Language, Style, and Audience in the text.

••• CHECKLIST FOR LANGUAGE, STYLE, AND AUDIENCE

In order to determine an author's style, do the following:

- ✓ identify and define any unfamiliar words or phrases

- ✓ use context, including the meaning of surrounding words and phrases

- ✓ note specific words and phrases that the author uses to create a response in the reader

- ✓ note possible reactions to the author's word choice

To analyze the impact of specific word choice on meaning and tone, ask the following questions:

- ✓ How did the language impact your understanding of the meaning of the text?

- ✓ What stylistic choices can you identify in the text? How does the style influence your understanding of the language?

- ✓ How could different audiences interpret this language? What different possible emotional responses can you list?

- ✓ How does the writer's choice of words create a specific tone in the text?

Skill: Language, Style, and Audience

Reread pages 10 and 11 of *Brave*. Then, using the Checklist on the previous page, answer the multiple-choice questions below.

⟳ YOUR TURN

1. This question has two parts. First, answer Part A. Then, answer Part B.

   Part A What does the word choice on these pages tell you about Jensen's character and the tone of the story?

   ○ A. They show that Jensen is always sad and thinks the worst will happen.

   ○ B. They show that Jensen doesn't have many challenges.

   ○ C. They show that even though Jensen is often bullied, he remains optimistic.

   ○ D. They show that Jensen doesn't care what other students think of him and that bullies don't bother him.

   Part B Which of the following details DOES NOT support your response to Part A?

   ○ A. "We're in the art club together."

   ○ B. "It's okay. Next class will be better."

   ○ C. "I just need to get there without—"

   ○ D. "Later! But hopefully never!"

Please note that excerpts and passages in the StudySync® library and this workbook are intended as touchstones to generate interest in an author's work. The excerpts and passages do not substitute for the reading of entire texts, and StudySync® strongly recommends that students seek out and purchase the whole literary or informational work in order to experience it as the author intended. Links to online resellers are available in our digital library. In addition, complete works may be ordered through an authorized reseller by filling out and returning to StudySync® the order form enclosed in this workbook.

Reading & Writing Companion

831

Close Read

Reread *Brave*. As you reread, complete the Skills Focus questions below. Then use your answers and annotations from the questions to help you complete the Write activity.

⊙ SKILLS FOCUS

1. Identify panels in *Brave* where the illustrations and speech bubbles work together to help you understand how Jensen views life. Explain how these visuals enhance your understanding of Jensen.

2. Identify panels in *Brave* where the style of the speech bubbles, used for characters other than Jensen, allows the audience to interpret the text's meaning. Explain what the style of the speech bubbles adds to your understanding.

3. Eleanor Roosevelt described herself as a shy 'ugly duckling' who only later in life got the courage to be herself. Highlight evidence that suggests how Jensen might relate to Roosevelt's childhood. Explain your reasoning.

4. Identify two unknown words from the passage and explain how to use word patterns and relationships to determine their meanings.

5. Identify panels in *Brave* that help you predict how Jensen might answer the Essential Question: "Who are you meant to be?" Explain how you think he might answer based on the evidence.

✏ WRITE

DISCUSSION: What does it mean to be true to yourself? In a discussion with your peers, imagine how Jensen and Eleanor Roosevelt would respond to this question. What would they say? What advice would they offer? How might they agree or disagree? Cite examples of specific word choices and tone that express how they are true to themselves.

I Never Had It Made:

An Autobiography of Jackie Robinson

INFORMATIONAL TEXT
Jackie Robinson
1972

Introduction

In 1947, Jackie Robinson (1919–1972), a talented baseball player and man of great character, made history as the first African American baseball player to "break the color barrier" and play in modern Major League Baseball. In this excerpt from his autobiography, Robinson reflects back on his experience and its impact on American society.

". . . a sport can`t be called national if blacks are barred from it."

From the Preface: Today
Jackie Robinson

Skill: Author's Purpose and Point of View

I think Robinson's purpose must be to inform the reader because he gives details about the time, place, and the importance he gives to a special day in his life.

Skill: Central or Main Idea

I can see that Jackie Robinson endured hard times in baseball because of his race. I think this is the central idea of the paragraph.

These details directly support the idea that Robinson dealt with hate and went through hard times.

1 I guess if I could choose one of the most important moments in my life, I would go back to 1947, in the Yankee Stadium in New York City. **It** was the opening day of the world series and I was for the first time playing in the series as a member of the Brooklyn Dodgers team. It was a history-making day. It would be the first time that a black man would be allowed to **participate** in a world series. I had become the first black player in the major leagues.

2 I was proud of that and yet I was uneasy. I was proud to be in the hurricane eye[1] of a significant breakthrough and to be used to prove that a sport can't be called national if blacks are barred from it. Branch Rickey, the president of the Brooklyn Dodgers, had rudely awakened America. He was a man with high ideals, and he was also a shrewd businessman. Mr. Rickey had shocked some of his fellow baseball tycoons and angered others by deciding to smash the unwritten law that kept blacks out of the big leagues. He had chosen me as the person to lead the way.

3 It hadn't been easy. Some of my own teammates refused to accept me because I was black. I had been forced to live with snubs and rebuffs and rejections. Within the club, Mr. Rickey had put down rebellion by letting my teammates know that anyone who didn't want to accept me could leave. But the problems within the Dodgers club had been minor compared to the opposition outside. It hadn't been that easy to fight the resentment expressed by players on other teams, by the team owners, or by **bigoted** fans screaming "n-----." The hate mail piled up. There were threats against me and my family and even out-and-out attempts at physical harm to me.

4 Some things counterbalanced this ugliness. Black people supported me with total loyalty. They supported me morally: they came to sit in a **hostile** audience in unprecedented numbers to make the turnstiles[2] hum as they never had

1. **hurricane eye** the center of a storm
2. **turnstile** a mechanical gate of revolving horizontal arms allowing only one person at a time to pass through

before at ballparks all over the nation. Money is America's God, and business people can dig black power if it **coincides** with green power, so these fans were important to the success of Mr. Rickey's "Noble Experiment."

5   Some of the Dodgers who swore they would never play with a black man had a change of mind, when they realized I was a good ballplayer who could be I in their earning a few thousand more dollars in world series money. After the initial resistance to me had been crushed, my teammates started to give me tips in how to improve my game. They hadn't changed because they liked me any better; they had changed because I could help fill their wallets.

6   My fellow Dodgers were not decent out of self-interest alone. There were heartwarming experiences with some teammates; there was Southern-born Pee Wee Reese, who turned into a staunch friend. And there were others.

7   Mr. Rickey stands out as the man who inspired me the most. He will always have my admiration and respect. Critics had said, "Don't you know that your precious Mr. Rickey didn't bring you up out of the black leagues because he loved you? Are you stupid enough not to understand that the Brooklyn club profited hugely because of what your Mr. Rickey did?"

8   Yes, I know that. But I also know what a big gamble he took. A **bond** developed between us that lasted long after I had left the game. In a way I feel I was the son he had lost and he was the father I had lost.

9   There was more than just making money at stake in Mr. Rickey's decision. I learned that his family was afraid that his health was being undermined by the resulting pressures and that they pleaded with him to abandon the plan. His peers and fellow baseball moguls exerted all kinds of influence to get him to change his mind. Some of the press condemned him as a fool and a demagogue[3]. But he didn't give in.

10   In a very real sense, black people helped make the experiment succeed. Many who came to the ball park had not been baseball fans before I began to play in the big leagues. Suppressed and repressed for so many years, they needed a victorious black man as a symbol. It would help them believe in themselves. But black support of the first black man in the majors was a complicated matter. The breakthrough created as much danger as it did hope. It was one thing for me out there on the playing field to be able to keep my cool in the face of insults. But it was another for all those black people sitting in the stands to keep from overreacting when they sensed a racial slur or an unjust decision. . . . I learned from Rachel, who had spent hours in the

---

3. **demagogue** a leader who appeals to ignorance and prejudice rather than using rational argument

Copyright © BookheadEd Learning, LLC

Skill: Central or Main Idea

I think Jackie is trying to say that he was accepted by his team after they realized he could help earn them money.

The fact that his teammates were using him further supports the idea that he was mistreated because of his race.

stands, that clergymen and laymen had held meetings in the black community to spread the word. We all knew about the help of the black press. Mr. Rickey and I owed them a great deal.

11 Children from all races came to the stands. The very young seemed to have no hangup at all about my being black. They just wanted me to be good, to deliver, to win. The inspiration of their innocence is amazing. I don't think I'll ever forget the small, shrill voice of a tiny white kid who, in the midst of a racially tense atmosphere during an early game in a Dixie town, cried out, "Attaboy, Jackie." It broke the tension and it made me feel I had to succeed.

12 The black and the young were my cheering squads. But also there were people—neither black nor young—people of all races and faiths and in all parts of the country, people who couldn't care less about my race.

13 Rachel was even more important to my success. I know that every successful man is supposed to say that without his wife he could never have accomplished success. It is gospel in my case. Rachel shared those difficult years that led to this moment and helped me through all the days thereafter. She has been strong, loving, gentle, and brave, never afraid to either criticize or comfort me.

Excerpted from *I Never Had It Made* by Jackie Robinson, published by HarperCollins Publishers

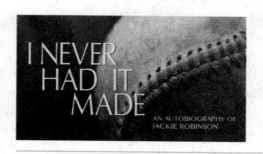

First Read

Read *I Never Had It Made: An Autobiography of Jackie Robinson*. After you read, complete the Think Questions below.

 THINK QUESTIONS

1. Why does Jackie Robinson feel uneasy about the opening day of the World Series? Refer to direct evidence as well as to clues you infer from the text.

2. Use details from the text to write two or three sentences describing the different ways people treated Jackie Robinson.

3. Write two or three sentences exploring who Jackie Robinson credits with contributing to his success and why. Support your answer with textual evidence.

4. Use context to determine the meaning of the word **bigoted** as it is used in paragraph 3 of *I Never Had It Made: An Autobiography of Jackie Robinson*. Write your definition here and identify clues that helped you figure out its meaning.

5. Use the context clues provided in the passage to determine the meaning of the word **coincides** as it is used in paragraph 4 of *I Never Had It Made*. Write your definition here and identify clues that helped you figure out its meaning. Then check the meaning in a dictionary.

Please note that excerpts and passages in the StudySync® library and this workbook are intended as touchstones to generate interest in an author's work. The excerpts and passages do not substitute for the reading of entire texts, and StudySync® strongly recommends that students seek out and purchase the whole literary or informational work in order to experience it as the author intended. Links to online resellers are available in our digital library. In addition, complete works may be ordered through an authorized reseller by filling out and returning to StudySync® the order form enclosed in this workbook.

Reading & Writing Companion   **837**

Skill: Author's Purpose and Point of View

Use the Checklist to analyze Author's Purpose and Point of View in *I Never Had It Made: An Autobiography of Jackie Robinson*. Refer to the sample student annotations about Author's Purpose and Point of View in the text.

••• CHECKLIST FOR AUTHOR'S PURPOSE AND POINT OF VIEW

In order to identify author's purpose and point of view, note the following:

✓ facts, statistics, and graphic aids as these indicate that the author is writing to inform

✓ the author's use of emotional or figurative language, which may indicate that the author is trying to persuade readers or stress an opinion

✓ descriptions that present a complicated process in plain language, which may indicate that the author is writing to explain

✓ the language the author uses, as figurative and emotional language can be clues to the author's point of view on a subject or topic

To determine the author's purpose and point of view in a text, consider the following questions:

✓ How does the author convey, or communicate, information in the text?

✓ Does the author use figurative or emotional language? For what purpose?

✓ Does the author make use of charts, graphs, maps and other graphic aids?

Skill: Author's Purpose and Point of View

Reread paragraphs 9–12 from *I Never Had It Made: An Autobiography of Jackie Robinson*. Then, using the Checklist on the previous page, answer the multiple-choice questions below.

⟳ YOUR TURN

1. The author's purpose for including the information about Mr. Rickey in paragraph 9 may have been to explain that —

   - ○ A. Mr. Rickey was not well when he put his plan into action.
   - ○ B. Mr. Rickey stuck with his decisions for many reasons.
   - ○ C. the press easily influenced Mr. Rickey.
   - ○ D. other baseball moguls supported Mr. Rickey's plan.

2. What is one idea the author wants readers to understand from the information in paragraph 10?

   - ○ A. The black press held meetings to support Jackie Robinson.
   - ○ B. Black baseball fans filled the stands when Jackie Robinson played.
   - ○ C. Black people were willing to face possible danger to support Jackie Robinson.
   - ○ D. Black baseball fans helped Jackie Robinson keep his cool on the field.

3. What do the details in paragraphs 11 and 12 suggest about Robinson's point of view regarding his fans?

   - ○ A. Robinson believed that children were the primary reason for his success.
   - ○ B. Robinson believed that adults were the most racially prejudiced against him.
   - ○ C. Jackie Robinson believed that race was not an issue for many people who supported him.
   - ○ D. Robinson believed that only black people and young children showed support for him.

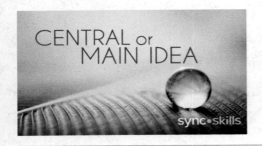

Skill:
Central or Main Idea

Use the Checklist to analyze Central or Main Idea in *I Never Had It Made: An Autobiography of Jackie Robinson*. Refer to the sample student annotations about Central or Main Idea in the text.

••• CHECKLIST FOR CENTRAL OR MAIN IDEA

In order to identify a central idea of a text, note the following:

✓ the topic or subject of the text

✓ the central or main idea, if it is explicitly stated

✓ details in the text that convey the theme

To determine a central idea of a text and how it is conveyed through particular details, consider the following questions:

✓ What main idea do the details in one or more paragraphs explain or describe?

✓ What bigger idea do all the paragraphs support?

✓ What is the best way to state the central idea? How might you summarize the text and message?

✓ How do particular details in the text convey the central idea?

Skill:
Central or Main Idea

Reread paragraphs 9–11 of *I Never Had It Made: An Autobiography of Jackie Robinson*. Then, using the Checklist on the previous page, answer the multiple-choice questions below.

↻ YOUR TURN

1. Which statement best expresses the central idea of paragraph 9?

   ○ A. Mr. Rickey's choice to draft Jackie was risky for both the team and for his own success.
   ○ B. Jackie trusted Mr. Rickey and hoped that his health would not decline because of baseball.
   ○ C. Mr. Rickey wished his peers would understand and support his decision to sign Jackie.
   ○ D. The press and Mr. Rickey's colleagues bashed his decision and ultimately changed his mind.

2. Which statement best expresses the central idea of the whole passage (paragraphs 9–11)?

   ○ A. Jackie Robinson was a talented baseball player who was supported by Mr. Rickey.
   ○ B. Jackie Robinson greatly appreciated the encouragement of his peers while with the Dodgers.
   ○ C. Jackie Robinson relied on Mr. Rickey, his fans, and the black community to flourish.
   ○ D. Jackie Robinson wished that he had more assistance from the white community.

Please note that excerpts and passages in the StudySync® library and this workbook are intended as touchstones to generate interest in an author's work. The excerpts and passages do not substitute for the reading of entire texts, and StudySync® strongly recommends that students seek out and purchase the whole literary or informational work in order to experience it as the author intended. Links to online resellers are available in our digital library. In addition, complete works may be ordered through an authorized reseller by filling out and returning to StudySync® the order form enclosed in this workbook.

Reading & Writing
Companion

841

Close Read

Reread *I Never Had It Made: An Autobiography of Jackie Robinson*. As you reread, complete the Skills Focus questions below. Then use your answers and annotations from the questions to help you complete the Write activity.

◎ SKILLS FOCUS

1. Several people and groups affected Jackie Robinson's life in a positive way as he broke the color barrier in baseball. Identify evidence of the effect these people and groups had on Robinson and explain what he wants the reader to understand about their effect on him.

2. How does the cause/effect relationship between the word *counterbalanced* and the examples in paragraph 4 that follow help you determine the meaning of the word? Cite evidence from the paragraph to support your answer.

3. Robinson credits the black community with helping make his entry into the major leagues a success. Identify evidence of the black community's contributions and explain how you would restate the main ideas and the most important details in your own words.

4. What is the central or main idea of paragraph 2 of the text? Cite textual evidence to support your response.

5. Identify evidence that supports the idea that many factors helped Jackie Robinson become who he was meant to be. Explain your reasoning.

✏ WRITE

ARGUMENTATIVE: Jackie Robinson once said, "A life is not important except in the impact it has on other lives." How does the excerpt from his autobiography, *I Never Had It Made: An Autobiography of Jackie Robinson* support this statement? Thinking of this quote, why do you think Robinson chose to write an autobiography? Include evidence from the text as you form your response.

Touching Spirit Bear

FICTION
Ben Mikaelsen
2001

Introduction

Cole Matthews is an angry teenager with a talent for getting into trouble. This time, however, he's facing jail time for brutally beating up a fellow classmate, Peter Driscal. When Cole's parole officer, Garvey, offers him an alternative to prison in a Native American program called Circle Justice, Cole jumps at the opportunity—even though he's skeptical of just about anything and anyone. As part of his rehabilitation, Cole is sent by a Tlingit elder to a remote island in the Alaskan wilderness to think about his mistakes and discover his place in the order of things. Winner of the Nautilus Book Award, *Touching Spirit Bear* is Bolivian-American children's author Ben Mikaelsen's gripping tale about how Cole faces his demons

"You're part of a much bigger circle. Learn your place or you'll have a rough time."

NOTES

Chapter 2

1   The heavy load of supplies caused the skiff to wallow through the waves. Cole examined the boxes filled with canned foods, clothes, bedroll, ax, cooking gear, heavy rain gear, rubber boots, and even school work he was supposed to complete. He chuckled. Fat chance he'd ever do any schoolwork.

2   Several weeks earlier, Edwin, the Tlingit[1] elder from Drake, had built a **sparse** one-room wood shelter for Cole on the island. He described the interior as bare except for a small wood stove and a bed—a good place for a soul to think and heal.

3   Cole resented the cabin and all this gear. When his father had agreed to pay all the expenses of banishment, it was just another one of his buyouts. Cole had news for him. This was just a sorry game. He twisted harder at the handcuffs and winced at the pain. He wasn't afraid of pain. He wasn't afraid of anyone or anything. He was only playing along until he could escape. He glanced back at Garvey. The whole Circle Justice thing had been such a joke. Back in Minneapolis, he had been forced to plead guilty and ask the Circle for help changing his life.

4   Asking for help was a simple con job, but he hadn't liked the idea of pleading guilty. "That's like hanging myself," he had complained to Garvey.

5   "You can **withdraw** your guilty plea and go through standard justice any time you want," Garvey said. "But once you go to trial, it's too late for Circle Justice." When Cole hesitated, Garvey added, "I thought you liked being in control, Champ."

6   Cole didn't trust anyone, but what choice did he have? "Okay," he answered **reluctantly.** "But if you're lying, you'll be sorry."

7   Garvey feigned surprise. "Let me get this straight, Champ. You figure if I'm scared of you, you can trust me?" He smiled thinly. "You sure have a lot to learn about trust."

———————————————

1. **Tlingit** indigenous peoples of the Pacific Northwest

NOTES

8   "Quit calling me Champ," Cole mumbled. "That's not my name." Then grudgingly he held his tongue. Nobody was going to make him lose his cool. This was a game he planned to win. "So," he asked, "how soon do I start this Circle Justice stuff?"

9   "You can apply, but that doesn't mean you're automatically accepted. First the Circle committee will visit with you. They'll talk to Peter Driscal and his family, your parents, and others to decide if you're serious about wanting change. It might take weeks." Garvey hesitated. "Remember something else. You're wasting everybody's time if you don't truly want to change."

10   Cole nodded obediently, like a little puppy that would follow every rule and jump through any hoop. When he reached the island, that would all come to a screeching stop. Then he would prove to the whole world he was nobody's fool.

11   Cole heard the motor slow and realized that Edwin was guiding the skiff toward a protected bay on the large island ahead. The distant green-black forests were **shrouded** in gray mist. Cole spotted the tiny shelter that had been built for him near the trees, above the shoreline. Black tar paper covered the small wooden structure. Cole spit again at the waves. If these fossils really thought he was going to live in that shack for a whole year, they were nuts.

12   As the skiff[2] scraped the rocks, Garvey jumped out and pulled the boat ashore. Still handcuffed, Cole crawled awkwardly over the bow onto the slippery rocks. Edwin began immediately to unload the supplies.

13   "Why don't you take my handcuffs off and let me help?" Cole asked.

14   Garvey and Edwin ignored his question. One at a time they carried the heavy cardboard boxes up to the shelter and stacked them inside the door. When they finished, Edwin motioned for Cole to follow him up to the mossy bench of ground above the tide line. Cole **moseyed** along slowly, not catching up to Edwin until they reached the trees.

15   Edwin turned to Cole. "Nobody's going to baby-sit you here. If you eat you'll live. If not, you'll die. This land can provide for you or kill you." He pointed into the forest. "Winters are long. Cut plenty of wood or you'll freeze. Keep things dry, because wet kills."

16   "I'm not afraid of dying," Cole boasted.

17   Edwin smiled slightly. "If death stares you straight in the face, believe me, son, you'll get scared." He pointed to a tall plant with snake-like branches. "This

---

2. **skiff** a shallow open boat with sharp bow and square stern

Skill:
Setting

The setting is clearly the forest and the way Edwin describes it, it seems that it is potentially deadly. Cole could get really hurt if he isn't careful. I wonder how this will affect Cole in the story

island is covered with Devil's Club. Don't grab it or hundreds of tiny thistles will infect your hands and make them swell up like sausages." Edwin motioned toward the head of the bay, a quarter mile away. "The stream over there is where you get fresh water."

18   "Why didn't you put my camp closer to the stream?"

19   "Other animals come here for water, too," Edwin said. "How would you feel if a bear made its den beside the stream?"

20   Cole shrugged. "I'd kill it."

21   The potbellied[3] elder nodded with a knowing smile. "Animals feel the same way. Don't forget that." He turned to Cole and placed a hand on his shoulder. Cole tried to pull away, but Edwin gripped him like a clamp. "You aren't the only creature here. You're part of a much bigger circle. Learn your place or you'll have a rough time."

22   "What is there to learn?"

23   "Patience, gentleness, strength, honesty," Edwin said. He looked up into the trees. "Animals can teach us more about ourselves than any teacher." He stared away toward the south. "Off the coast of British Columbia, there is a special black bear called the Spirit Bear. It's pure white and has pride, dignity, and honor. More than most people."

24   "If I saw a Spirit Bear, I'd kill it," Cole said.

25   Edwin tightened his grip as if in warning. "Whatever you do to the animals, you do to yourself. Remember that."

26   "You're crazy, old man," Cole said, twisting free of Edwin's grip. Edwin continued speaking calmly as if nothing had happened. "Don't eat anything unless you know what it is. Plants, berries, and mushrooms can kill you. There's a book in with the supplies to study if you want to learn what is safe to eat. I suggest you read every word. Life is up to you now. I don't know how it was for you in the big city, but up here you live and die by your actions. We'll be out to check on you in a couple of days. After that, Garvey will head home and I'll drop off supplies every few weeks. Any questions?"

27   Cole smirked. He didn't plan on eating any shrubs or berries. "Why did you bring me out so far?" he asked mockingly. "Were you afraid I'd escape?"

**Skill:
Setting**

Edwin is setting up Cole's camp near the stream, and trying to give Cole advice about how to function in the wild.

Edwin seems to be humble. His experiences in this setting have shaped him and he has gained wisdom. It seems like he hopes the same for Cole.

---

3. **potbellied** having a large stomach

28   Edwin looked out across the bay and drew in a deep breath. "Years ago, I was brought here myself when my spirit got lost. This is a good place to find yourself."

29   "This place sucks!" Cole mumbled.

30   Edwin pulled out a key and turned Cole roughly around to remove his handcuffs. "Anger keeps you lost," he said, as he started back toward the shelter. "You can find yourself here, but only if you search."

31   Rubbing at the raw skin on his wrists, Cole followed.

Excerpted from *Touching Spirit Bear* by Ben Mikaelsen, published by HarperCollins.

First Read

Read *Touching Spirit Bear*. Then complete the Think Questions below.

 THINK QUESTIONS

1. What, if anything, is Garvey's "angle" in the excerpt from Chapter 1? What is he trying to accomplish in his visits with Cole? Use evidence from the text to support your response.

2. Why did Cole agree to live on a secluded island? What does he hope to do once he arrives on the island? Explain, with reference to the text.

3. In the final passage of the excerpt, Edwin tells Cole, "Whatever you do to the animals, you do to yourself. Remember that." What is the meaning of this statement? Why might it be important for young Cole to remember? Cite textual evidence to support your response.

4. Read the following dictionary entry:

   withdraw
   with·draw

   verb

   1. to remove money from a bank account
   2. to no longer participate in a group activity
   3. to leave or exit
   4. to recall or take back a statement

   Decide which definition best matches the word **withdraw** as it is used in *Touching Spirit Bear*. Write that definition of *withdraw* here and indicate which clues found in the text helped you determine the meaning.

5. Describing the Alaskan coastline in paragraph 11, the narrator observes that "distant green-black forests were **shrouded** in gray mist." Using context clues, write your best definition of the word *shrouded* and explain how you figured it out.

Skill:
Setting

Use the Checklist to analyze Setting in *Touching Spirit Bear*. Refer to the sample student annotations about Setting in the text.

••• CHECKLIST FOR SETTING

In order to identify how the plot of a particular story or drama unfolds in a series of episodes, note the following:

✓ key elements in the plot

✓ the setting(s) in the story

✓ how the plot unfolds in a series of episodes

✓ how the setting shapes the plot and the characters

To describe how the plot of a particular story or drama unfolds in a series of episodes, consider the following questions:

✓ When and where does this story take place?

✓ How does the plot unfold in a series of episodes?

✓ How does the setting affect the plot? How does it affect the characters and their responses to events? How does the setting help move the plot to a resolution?

Please note that excerpts and passages in the StudySync® library and this workbook are intended as touchstones to generate interest in an author's work. The excerpts and passages do not substitute for the reading of entire texts, and StudySync® strongly recommends that students seek out and purchase the whole literary or informational work in order to experience it as the author intended. Links to online resellers are available in our digital library. In addition, complete works may be ordered through an authorized reseller by filling out and returning to StudySync® the order form enclosed in this workbook.

Reading & Writing Companion   **849**

SETTING

sync

Skill:
Setting

Reread paragraphs 23–29 of *Touching Spirit Bear*. Then, using the Checklist on the previous page, answer the multiple-choice questions below.

♻ YOUR TURN

1. This question has two parts. First, answer Part A. Then, answer Part B.

   Part A: In the excerpt, how does the setting influence Cole's character?

   ○ A. Cole is irritated. He wishes that he could be in another rehabilitation program.

   ○ B. Cole doesn't take Edwin's advice about being one with nature seriously; therefore, Cole is overconfident.

   ○ C. Cole is respectful in his interactions with Edwin as he understands that he must conquer the setting to survive.

   ○ D. Cole does not grasp the idea that he must be one with nature, so he hastily plans an epic escape.

   Part B: Which piece of evidence BEST supports your answer to Part A?

   ○ A. "'Patience, gentleness, strength, honesty,' Edwin said."

   ○ B. "'If I saw a Spirit Bear, I'd kill it,'" Cole said.

   ○ C. "'He didn't plan on eating any shrubs or berries.'"

   ○ D. "'This is a good place to find yourself.'"

Close Read

Reread *Touching Spirit Bear*. As you reread, complete the Skills Focus questions below. Then use your answers and annotations from the questions to help you complete the Write activity.

◎ SKILLS FOCUS

1. Highlight examples of Cole's responses to his surroundings, to other characters, and to their actions. Explain how Cole's responses influence events in the plot.

2. Identify major events of the plot and summarize what happens in a way that maintains meaning and logical order.

3. Identify evidence of how the setting influences the conflict in *Touching Spirit Bear*. Explain the impact of the setting on the conflict.

4. Highlight evidence that indicates the point of view from which the story is told. Identify the point of view and explain why you think the author chose it.

5. Identify evidence that supports the idea that Edwin hopes the island will help Cole become who he is meant to be. Explain your reasoning.

✎ WRITE

NARRATIVE: The excerpt explains that Cole's father "agreed to pay all the expenses of banishment, [as] it was just another one of his buyouts." Pretend that you are Cole's father, and you are writing a letter to your son. Explain your reasons for paying for the Circle Justice program and how you hope it will help Cole change. How do you think this setting will affect Cole's life? Use descriptive details from the text in your letter.

Please note that excerpts and passages in the StudySync® library and this workbook are intended as touchstones to generate interest in an author's work. The excerpts and passages do not substitute for the reading of entire texts, and StudySync® strongly recommends that students seek out and purchase the whole literary or informational work in order to experience it as the author intended. Links to online resellers are available in our digital library. In addition, complete works may be ordered through an authorized reseller by filling out and returning to StudySync® the order form enclosed in this workbook.

Reading & Writing Companion

851

Extended
Writing
Project and
Grammar

EXTENDED
WRITING
PROJECT
RESEARCH WRITING

Research Writing Process: Plan

PLAN	DRAFT	REVISE	EDIT AND PUBLISH

Many things you read contain references to people, places, things, and events from different time periods or cultures. *Rosa Parks: My Story*, for instance, takes the reader back in time to the civil rights movement of the 1960s. *Bronx Masquerade* transports readers to a high school in New York City. A reader's curiosity could lead him or her to explore a variety of topics after reading such rich texts.

WRITING PROMPT

Where did Shree Bose draw inspiration for her cancer research? For kids in the 1960s, what were some of the differences between growing up in the North or in the South? Are Spirit Bears real?

Consider the texts included in the *True to Yourself* unit, identify a topic you would like to know more about, and write a research report about that topic. In the process, you will learn how to select a research question, develop a research plan, gather and evaluate source materials, and synthesize and present your research findings. Regardless of which topic you choose, be sure your research paper includes the following:

- an introduction
- supporting details from credible sources
- a clear text structure
- a conclusion
- multimedia components such as charts, images, or video
- a works cited page

Writing to Sources

As you gather ideas and information from the texts in the unit, be sure to:

- use evidence from multiple sources; and
- avoid overly relying on one source.

Please note that excerpts and passages in the StudySync® library and this workbook are intended as touchstones to generate interest in an author's work. The excerpts and passages do not substitute for the reading of entire texts, and StudySync® strongly recommends that students seek out and purchase the whole literary or informational work in order to experience it as the author intended. Links to online resellers are available in our digital library. In addition, complete works may be ordered through an authorized reseller by filling out and returning to StudySync® the order form enclosed in this workbook.

Reading & Writing Companion

853

Introduction to Research Writing

Research writing examines a topic and presents ideas by citing and analyzing information from credible, or trustworthy, sources. Good research papers use textual evidence—including facts, statistics, examples, and details from reliable sources—to supply information about a topic and to support analysis of complex ideas. Research helps writers not only discover and confirm facts, but also draw new conclusions about a topic. The characteristics of research writing include:

- an introduction with a clear thesis statement

- supporting details, relevant facts, and quotations from credible sources

- analysis of the details to explain how they support the thesis

- a clear and logical text structure

- parenthetical citations

- a conclusion that wraps up your ideas

- a works cited page

As you continue with this Extended Writing Project, you'll receive more instruction and practice at crafting each of the characteristics of research writing to create your own research paper.

Before you get started on your own research paper, read a research paper that one student, Kelaiah, wrote in response to the writing prompt. As you read the Model, highlight and annotate the features of research writing that Kelaiah included in her research paper.

☰ STUDENT MODEL

Do Spirit Bears Exist?

1 In *Touching Spirit Bear*, a Tlingit elder named Edwin prepares Cole for living alone on a remote island. He explains, "Off the coast of British Columbia, there is a special black bear called the Spirit Bear. It's pure white, and has pride, dignity, and honor" (Mikaelsen 18). When Cole threatens to kill any Spirit Bear he meets, Edwin warns, "Whatever you do to the animals, you do to yourself" (Mikaelsen 18). Edwin and Cole are fictional characters, but are Spirit Bears real? Spirit Bears do exist. They are considered special not only by the people of the First Nations communities—who have lived near them for thousands of years—but also by researchers and environmentalists. A look at the Spirit Bear's habitat, as well as its cultural and environmental significance, reveals this unique animal's role in the world.

Habitat and Characteristics of Spirit Bears

2 Spirit Bears are a rare subspecies of the American Black Bear. The Spirit Bear is known by different names, including the White Bear, Ghost Bear, *Moskgm'ol*, Kermode Bear, and its scientific name *Ursus americanus kermodei* (Shoumatoff). The animal lives only in the Great Bear Rainforest, a 21-million-acre wilderness along British Columbia's central coast that has been called "the Amazon of the North" (Kennedy).

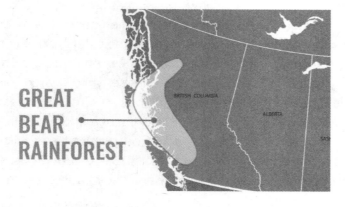

GREAT BEAR RAINFOREST

3　Unlike the hot, steamy jungles of the Amazon, the Great Bear Rainforest is a cold, rocky island habitat. According to writer Bruce Barcott, the Spirit Bear is "a walking contradiction—a white black bear." Despite having white fur, the Spirit Bear is not a polar bear or an albino. Its cream-colored fur is the result of a rare recessive gene. A white bear cub is produced when both parents, which may be black or white, carry the rare gene (Groc 78–79, Barcott, Shoumatoff).

Spirit Bear Population

4　Only 20 percent of the bears in the Great Bear Rainforest are white (N. Amer. Bear Ctr.). The bears survive on a diet of salmon, berries, and seaweed (Shoumatoff). There may be as many as 400 or as few as 100 Spirit Bears alive today (Langlois, Groc 79, N. Amer. Bear Ctr.). As geography professor Chris Darimont explains, "no one really knows how many bears there are in the Great Bear Rainforest" (Shoumatoff). This is because the Spirit Bear has a deep cultural significance to the First Nations people.

Spirit Bears and Indigenous Communities

5　The First Nations communities call the bear "*moskgm'ol*, which means 'white bear,' and view the animal as sacred" (Groc 79). In traditional stories, the bear is "a giver of good luck and power" (Shoumatoff). However, Doug Neasloss, the chief of one First Nations tribe, says that many people didn't know about Spirit Bears until recently because "the stories about these white-coated relatives of black bears were kept secret" (Langlois). The reason was practical: "Elders feared that if word of their existence spread, spirit bears— like black and grizzly bears—would be pursued and killed by fur trappers or trophy hunters" (Langlois). Since the 1980s, the First Nations people have worked to preserve their traditions by protecting the forest and its wildlife. They "believed the forest was worth more intact, and the bears it sheltered—grizzly, black, and Kermode—were worth more to the [First Nations] alive than killed by trophy hunters" (Langlois). Today, people come from all over the world to see the Spirit Bear, not to hunt it.

Protecting Spirit Bears

6 Protecting the Spirit Bear is not just important to the First Nations people; it's also important for the environment. The Spirit Bears play an important role in keeping the rainforest healthy. Spirit Bears take the salmon they catch in the rivers into the forest to eat (Shoumatoff, Groc 79). As the carcasses decay and their nutrients "are absorbed by the forest floor, the nutrients from the ocean are effectively transferred to the trees" (Groc 79). The health of the bears and the forest are connected (Shoumatoff). If the Spirit Bear suffers a decline, so will the rainforest.

Threats to Spirit Bears

7 Today there are many threats to the Spirit Bear, including overfishing, logging, and hunting. Overfishing means there is less food for all the bears in the rainforest. When there are fewer salmon, aggressive grizzlies wander into the Spirit Bears' territory looking for food, and they drive the white bears away (Groc 80, Shoumatoff). In addition, loggers are removing the old cedar trees that Spirit Bears need for hibernating (Groc 82). Hunting is another issue. While it is illegal to kill a Spirit Bear, until 2017 it was legal to hunt black bears, many of which are carriers of the gene needed to produce Spirit Bears (Groc 83, Langlois). Killing a black bear is like killing a Spirit Bear's chances of being born.

8   In *Touching Spirit Bear*, Cole threatens to kill a Spirit Bear. Edwin reminds him to "learn your place or you'll have a rough time" (Mikaelsen 17). Unlike Cole, the First Nations communities and many scientists and environmentalists recognize the value of the Spirit Bear. While not everyone might believe that the bear has special powers, they, like Edwin, should recognize and respect this animal's important role in the Great Bear Rainforest and its deep connections to the First Nations people.

Works Cited

Barcott, Bruce. "Spirit Bear." *National Geographic,* Aug. 2011, www. nationalgeographic.com/magazine/2011/08/kermode-bear.html.

Groc, Isabelle. "Spirits of the Forest." *BBC Wildlife Magazine,* vol. 33, no. 10, Sept. 2015, pp. 76–83.

Kennedy, Taylor. "Great Bear Rainforest." *NationalGeographic.com,* www.nationalgeographic.com/travel/canada/great-bear-rainforest-british-columbia/.

Langlois, Krista. "First Nations Fight to Protect the Rare Spirit Bear from Hunters." *National Geographic,* 26 Oct. 2017, news. nationalgeographic.com/2017/10/wildlife-watch-hunting-great-bear-rainforest-spirit-bear/.

Mikaelsen, Ben. *Touching Spirit Bear.* HarperCollins Publishers, 2001.

North American Bear Center. "What is a Spirit Bear?" *Bear.org,* 2018, www.bear.org/website/bear-pages/black-bear/basic-bear-facts/101-what-is-a-spirit-bear.html

Shoumatoff, Alex. "This Rare, White Bear May Be the Key to Saving a Canadian Rainforest." *Smithsonian Magazine,* Sept. 2015, www. smithsonianmag.com/science-nature/rare-white-bear-key-saving-canadian-rainforest-180956330/.

WRITE

Writers often take notes about ideas before they sit down to write. Think about what you've learned so far about organizing research writing to help you begin prewriting.

- **Purpose:** What topic from the unit do you find most interesting? What do you want to learn about that topic?

- **Audience:** Who is your audience and what message do you want to express to your audience?

- **Focus:** How can you use a research question to focus your research?

- **Sources:** What kind of sources will help you answer that question?

- **Organization:** What text structure should you use to share the information with readers?

Response Instructions

Use the questions in the bulleted list to write a one-paragraph research summary. Your summary should describe what you plan to research and discuss in your research paper.

Don't worry about including all of the details now; focus only on the most essential and important elements. You will refer back to this short summary as you continue through the steps of the writing process.

Skill:
Planning Research

••• CHECKLIST FOR PLANNING RESEARCH

In order to develop a research plan drawing on several sources, do the following:

- make a list of research tasks

  > if it is not assigned to you, decide on a major research question

  > develop a research plan, a series of steps you can follow to find information to answer your question

- search for information

  > look for information on your topic in a variety of sources, both online and in books and other reference sources

  > if you don't find the information that you need to answer your research question, you may need to modify it

  > refocus and revise your research plan

To develop and revise a research plan, consider the following questions:

- Is the source reliable and credible? How do I know?
- How does the source address themes, concepts, or other areas related to my research?
- Does information in one source contradict, or disprove, information in another source? How might I resolve these differences?
- Do I need to change my major research question?

To write a research plan, follow these steps:

- Write down the steps you will follow in order to find information that will help you answer your research question. These steps may include looking up your topic in an encyclopedia to gather general information, using online search engines, and checking out books from your school or local library.

- If you don't find the information you need following your initial research plan, think of other steps you can follow and revise your research plan accordingly.

⟳ YOUR TURN

Read the research questions below. Then, complete the chart by matching each question to the correct category.

Research Questions	
A	What sports and teams did Jackie Robinson play for?
B	What kinds of things inspire poets?
C	How did Jackie Robinson succeed?
D	What accomplishments made Eleanor Roosevelt one of the most influential women of her time?
E	How did Jackie Robinson overcome adversity to become a successful baseball player in the all-white league?
F	Why do some First Ladies become famous?
G	Where did Rita Dove draw inspiration for her poetry?
H	Why was Eleanor Roosevelt called *First Lady of the World*?
I	What inspired Rita Dove to write "Rosa"?

Too Narrow	Just Right	Too Broad

Please note that excerpts and passages in the StudySync® library and this workbook are intended as touchstones to generate interest in an author's work. The excerpts and passages do not substitute for the reading of entire texts, and StudySync® strongly recommends that students seek out and purchase the whole literary or informational work in order to experience it as the author intended. Links to online resellers are available in our digital library. In addition, complete works may be ordered through an authorized reseller by filling out and returning to StudySync® the order form enclosed in this workbook.

Reading & Writing Companion   **861**

YOUR TURN

Brainstorm questions for formal research. Then evaluate each question to determine whether it is too narrow, too broad, or just right using the secondary set of questions listed in the checklist. Select a question that is just right. Then complete the chart below by writing a short research plan for your report.

Question	Plan
Possible Research Questions:	
Selected Research Question:	
Step 1:	
Step 2:	
Step 3:	
Revise My Research Plan:	

Skill:
Evaluating Sources

••• CHECKLIST FOR EVALUATING SOURCES

First, reread the sources you gathered and identify the following:

- what kind of source it is, including video, audio, or text, and where the source comes from
- where information seems inaccurate, biased, or outdated
- where information seems irrelevant or incomplete

In order to use advanced searches to gather relevant, credible, and accurate print and digital sources, use the following questions as a guide:

- Is the source material written by a recognized expert on the topic?
- Is the source material published by a well-respected author or organization?
- Is the material up-to-date or based on the most current information?
- Is the material factual, and can it be verified by another source?
- Is the source material connected to persons or organizations that are objective and unbiased?
- Does the source contain omissions of important information?

After evaluating sources, revise your research plan as needed:

- Eliminate sources that are not reliable or credible and that contain bias and faulty reasoning.
- Search for other trustworthy sources that you can use instead.

⟳ YOUR TURN

Read the sentences below. Then, complete the chart by sorting them into sources that are credible and reliable and sources that are not.

	Sources
A	The article has no information about the author other than her name.
B	The author supports arguments with current information and statistics.
C	The text uses clear and strong logic.
D	The author is an environmental scientist.
E	The article leaves out any information that could contradict its main ideas.
F	The text relies on emotional appeals to persuade readers.

Credible and Reliable	Not Credible and Reliable

↻ YOUR TURN

Complete the chart by filling in the title and author of a source and answering the questions about it.

Question	My Source
Source Title and Author	
Reliability: Has the source material been published in a well-established book, periodical, or website?	
Reliability: Is the source material up-to-date or based on the most current information?	
Credibility: Is the source material written by a recognized expert on the topic?	
Credibility: Is the source material published by a well-respected author or organization?	
Bias: Is the source material objective and unbiased?	
Bias: Does the source contain omissions of important information that supports other viewpoints?	
Faulty Reasoning: Does the source contain faulty reasoning?	
Evaluation: Should I use this source in my research report?	

Skill:
Research and Note-Taking

In order to conduct short research projects, drawing on several sources and refocusing the inquiry when appropriate, note the following:

- think of a question you would like to have answered

- look up your topic in an encyclopedia to find general information

- find specific, up-to-date information in books and periodicals, on the Internet, and, if appropriate, from interviews with experts

- use the library's computerized catalog to locate books on your topic, and if you need help finding or using any of these resources, ask a librarian

- make sure that each source you use is closely related to your topic

- if necessary, refocus, or change, your topic if you have difficulty finding information about it

To introduce a topic and organize ideas, concepts, and information using an organizational strategy, consider the following questions:

- Is the information relevant and related to my topic?

- Where could I look to find additional information?

- Is the information I have found current and up-to-date?

To synthesize information from sources while taking research notes, follow these steps:

- Read a source and take notes to gather relevant information about your research topic.

- Read another source.

- Identify any new, relevant information that you find in this source.

- Ask yourself: How does this new information change or refine what I have learned from other sources?

- Write down notes about how your understanding of your topic has changed or improved through your reading of a variety of sources.

⟳ YOUR TURN

Read each bullet point from Kelaiah's note cards below. Then, complete the chart by sorting them into those that are culturally important and those that are environmentally important.

	Bullet Points
A	Source 1: Spirit Bears are important to the Great Bear Rainforest ecosystem and forest growth because they take the salmon they catch back to the forest to eat. As the carcasses decay and their nutrients "are absorbed by the forest floor, the nutrients from the ocean are effectively transferred to the trees" (79).
B	Source 7: Salmon is essential to the ecosystem. Bears carry the salmon into the forest, where the carcasses rot and release nitrogen into the soil. Trees, flowering plants, and even snails and slugs soak up this rich fertilizer. Everything is connected: "the sea feeds the forest, and the bears are the bearers of these nutritious infusions" (Shoumatoff).
C	Source 7: The bear is traditionally seen as "a giver of good luck and power" (Shoumatoff).
D	Source 2: According to First Nations chief Doug Neasloss, until recently many people didn't know Spirit Bears existed because "the stories about these white-coated relatives of black bears were kept secret" (Langlois).
E	Source 1: First Nations communities call the bear "*moskgm'ol,* which simply means 'white bear,' and view the animal as sacred" (79).
F	Source 1: Loggers are removing the old cedar trees that Spirit Bears need for hibernating (82).

Cultural Importance	Environmental Importance

✎ WRITE

Use the steps from the checklist as well as the Skill Model to identify and gather relevant information from a variety of sources. Write note cards for your sources. When you have finished, write a short paragraph that details how you plan to synthesize the information from at least two sources.

Research Writing Process: Draft

| PLAN | DRAFT | REVISE | EDIT AND PUBLISH |

You have already made progress toward writing your research paper. Now it is time to draft your research paper.

✏ WRITE

Use your plan, other responses in your Binder, and your source notes to draft your research paper. You may also have new ideas as you begin drafting. Feel free to explore those new ideas as you have them. You can also ask yourself these questions:

- Have I fully supported my thesis statement?
- Have I analyzed information from a variety of sources, including features to gain background information on my topic?
- Have I synthesized information from a variety of sources?
- Have I included supporting evidence from my sources?
- Does the text structure help me to communicate my ideas?

Before you submit your draft, read it over carefully. You want to be sure that you've responded to all aspects of the prompt.

Here is Kelaiah's research paper draft. As you read, identify Kelaiah's main ideas. As she continues to revise and edit her paper, she will find and improve weak spots in her writing, as well as correct any language or punctuation mistakes.

NOTES

Do Spirit Bears Exist?

In *Touching Spirit Bear*, Edwin prepares Cole for living alone on a remote island. He explains, Off the coast of British Columbia, there is a special black bear called the Spirit Bear. It's pure white, and has pride, dignity, and honor (Mikaelsen 18). When Cole threatens to kill any Spirit Bear he meets, Edwin warns, "Whatever you do to the animals, you do to yourself (Mikaelsen 18). Edwin and Cole are fictional characters, but are Spirit Bears real? Spirit Bears do exist. They are considered special not only by the people of the first nations communities, who have lived near them for thousands of years, but also by researchers and environmentalists. A look at the Spirit Bear's habitat, as well as its cultural and environmental significance reveals this unique animal's roll in the world.

Spirit Bears are a rare subspecies of the American Black Bear. The Spirit Bear is known by different names, including the White Bear, Ghost Bear, Moksgm'ol, Kermode Bear, and its scientific name *Ursus americanus kermodei* (Shoumatoff). The animal lives only in the Great Bear Rainforest, which has been called "the Amazon of the North" (Kennedy). Unlike the jungles of the Amazon, the Great Bear Rainforest is a cold, rocky island place. According to writer Bruce Barcott, the Spirit Bear is a contradiction. Despite having white fur, the Spirit bear is not a polar bear or an albino. Its cream colored fur is the result of a rare recessive gene (Groc 78, Barcott, Shoumatoff). Only 20 percent of the bears in the Great Bear Rainforest are white (NABC). The bears survive on a diet of salmon, berries, and seaweed (Shoumatoff). There may be as many as 400 or as few as 100 Spirit Bears alive today (Langlois, Groc 79, NABC). No one really knows how many bears there are in the Great Bear Rainforest (Shoumatoff).

NOTES

**Skill:
Critiquing Research**

Kelaiah used her new note cards as well as information from the sources she had already read to add another section to her informative research paper.

**Skill:
Print and Graphic Features**

Kelaiah added a heading to be more specific and organized and to better preview the section's content. She also italicized an important word. The image of the Spirit Bear helped convey key ideas to her readers in an interesting way.

Spirit Bears and Indigenous Communities

The First Nations communities call the bear "*moskgm'ol*, which means 'white bear,' and view the animal as sacred" (Groc 79). In traditional stories, the bear is "a giver of good luck and power" (Shoumatoff). However, Doug Neasloss, the chief of one First Nations tribe, says that many people didn't know about Spirit Bears until recently because "the stories about these white-coated relatives of black bears were kept secret" (Langlois). The reason was practical: "Elders feared that if word of their existence spread, spirit bears—like black and grizzly bears—would be pursued and killed by fur trappers or trophy hunters" (Langlois). Since the 1980s, the First Nations people have worked to preserve their traditions by protecting the forest and its wildlife. They "believed the forest was worth more intact, and the bears it sheltered—grizzly, black, and Kermode—were worth more to the [First Nations] alive than killed by trophy hunters" (Langlois). Today, people come from all over the world to see the Spirit Bear, not to hunt it.

Protecting the Spirit Bear is not just important to the First Nations people; it's also important for the environment. The Spirit Bears play an important role in keeping the rainforest healthy. Spirit Bears take the salmon they catch in the rivers into the forest to eat (shoumatoff, Groc). As the carcasses decay, their nutrients are absorbed by the forest floor, the nutrients from the ocean are effectively transferred to the trees (Groc). The health of the bears and the forest, are connected (Shoumatoff). If the Spirit Bear suffers a decline, so will the rainforest.

NOTES

Protecting the Spirit Bear is not just important to the First Nations people; it's also important for the environment. The Spirit Bears play an important role in keeping the rainforest healthy. Spirit Bears take the salmon they catch in the rivers into the forest to eat (Shoumatoff, Groc 79). As the carcasses decay and their nutrients "are absorbed by the forest floor, the nutrients from the ocean are effectively transferred to the trees" (Groc 79). The health of the bears and the forest are connected (Shoumatoff). If the Spirit Bear suffers a decline, so will the rainforest.

Today there are many threats to the Spirit Bear, including overfishing logging and hunting. Overfishing means there is less food for all the bears in the rainforest. When there are fewer salmon, agresive grizzlies encroach on the Spirit Bears' territory looking for food, and they drive the white bears away (Groc 80, Shoumatoff). In addition, loggers are removing the old cedar trees that Spirit Bears need for hibernating (Groc 82). Hunting is yet another issue. While it is illegal to kill a Spirit Bear, until 2017 it was legal to hunt black bears, many of which are carriers of the gene needed to produce Spirit Bears (Groc 83, Langlois). Killing a black bear is like killing a Spirit Bear's chances of being born.

In Touching Spirit Bear, Cole threatens to kill a Spirit Bear. Edwin reminds him to Learn your place or you'll have a rough time (Mikaelsen 18). Unlike Cole, the first nations communities, and many scientists, and environmentalists recognize the value of the Spirit Bear. While not everyone might believe that the bear has special powers, they, like Edwin, should recognize and respect this animal's important roll in the Great Bear Rainforest and its deep connections to the first Nations people.

Works Cited

Barcott, Bruce. "Spirit Bear." ~~*National Geographic*, Aug. 2011.~~

Groc, Isabelle. "Spirits of the Forest." ~~*BBC Wildlife Magazine*, vol. 33, no. 10, pp. 76–83.~~

Barcott, Bruce. "Spirit Bear." *National Geographic*, Aug. 2011, www.nationalgeographic.com/magazine/2011/08/kermode-bear.html.

Groc, Isabelle. "Spirits of the Forest." *BBC Wildlife Magazine*, vol. 33, no. 10, Sept. 2015, pp. 76– 83.

Skill: Paraphrasing

Kelaiah realized she had plagiarized from "Spirits of the Forest" by Isabelle Groc. She reviewed her notes and the original article to see how she could paraphrase. After highlighting keywords and phrases, Kelaiah also decided to include a quote from the author.

Skill: Sources and Citations

Kelaiah adds the website address to the end of the Barcott citation. She adds the publication date to the Groc citation, and she adds the webpage name to the Langlois citation. By including all the required information, Kelaiah gives proper credit to the sources she used. It also lets her readers find these sources.

Kennedy, Taylor. "Great Bear Rainforest." *NationalGeographic.com*, https://www.nationalgeographic.com/travel/canada/great-bear-rainforest-british-columbia/.

~~Langlois, Krista. "First Nations Fight to Protect the Rare Spirit Bear from Hunters." 26 Oct. 2017, https://news.nationalgeographic.com/2017/10/wildlife-watch-hunting-great-bear-rainforest-spirit-bear/.~~

Langlois, Krista. "First Nations Fight to Protect the Rare Spirit Bear from Hunters." *National Geographic*, 26 Oct. 2017, news.nationalgeographic.com/2017/10/wildlife-watch-hunting-great-bear-rainforest-spirit-bear/.

Mikaelsen, Ben. *Touching Spirit Bear*. HarperCollins Publishers, 2001.

North American Bear Center. "What is a Spirit Bear?" *Bear.org*, 2018, https://www.bear.org/website/bear-pages/black-bear/basic-bear-facts/101-what-is-a-spirit-bear.html.

Shoumatoff, Alex. "This Rare, White Bear May Be the Key to Saving a Canadian Rainforest." *Smithsonian Magazine*, Sept. 2015, https://www.smithsonianmag.com/science-nature/rare-white-bear-key-saving-canadian-rainforest-180956330/.

Skill:
Critiquing Research

In order to conduct short research projects to answer a question, drawing on several sources, do the following:

- gather relevant, or important, information from different print and digital sources
- evaluate your research
- if necessary, refocus or change your question
- assess or evaluate your sources and decide whether they are trustworthy

To evaluate and use relevant information while conducting short research projects, consider the following questions:

- Does my research come from multiple print and digital sources?
- Am I able to evaluate my sources and determine which ones are trustworthy?
- Are there specific terms or phrases in my research question that I can use to adjust my search?
- Can I use *and*, *or*, or *not* to expand or limit my search?
- Can I use quotation marks to search for exact phrases?

Please note that excerpts and passages in the StudySync® library and this workbook are intended as touchstones to generate interest in an author's work. The excerpts and passages do not substitute for the reading of entire texts, and StudySync® strongly recommends that students seek out and purchase the whole literary or informational work in order to experience it as the author intended. Links to online resellers are available in our digital library. In addition, complete works may be ordered through an authorized reseller by filling out and returning to StudySync® the order form enclosed in this workbook.

Reading & Writing
Companion

873

♻ YOUR TURN

Kelaiah's friend Hope shared her research plan with Kelaiah. In the first column, they listed some critiques of Hope's research. Complete the chart by matching Hope's next steps to each critique.

	Next Steps
A	She should make her search terms more specific by using keywords, phrases, and unique terms with quotation marks and terms like *and*, *or*, and *not*.
B	After doing some research and taking notes, she should think about additional, focused research questions about her topic that will help her modify her research plan.
C	Hope should check that the sources are well-known and respected. She should make sure her sources are from experts in their field, university websites, or well-respected publications. When in doubt, she should ask a teacher.
D	Hope should go to a library and ask the librarian to help find her encyclopedias and nonfiction texts to use in her research paper.

Critiques	Next Steps
Kelaiah is unsure about the accuracy, reliability, and credibility of Hope's sources.	
Hope did a general online search for information and got over a million results.	
Hope only has two sources and both of them are online resources.	
Hope has one general research question, and she is not sure if she will have enough information for a complete informative research paper.	

↻ YOUR TURN

Complete the chart by answering the questions and writing a short summary of what you will do to make changes to your research plan.

Common Questions or Critiques	My Answers and Next Steps
Do you have enough relevant information from a mix of both digital and print sources?	
Did you use search terms effectively when conducting online searches?	
Are your sources and research accurate, reliable, and credible?	
Did you generate additional, focused questions to further and improve your research?	

Please note that excerpts and passages in the StudySync® library and this workbook are intended as touchstones to generate interest in an author's work. The excerpts and passages do not substitute for the reading of entire texts, and StudySync® strongly recommends that students seek out and purchase the whole literary or informational work in order to experience it as the author intended. Links to online resellers are available in our digital library. In addition, complete works may be ordered through an authorized reseller by filling out and returning to StudySync® the order form enclosed in this workbook.

Reading & Writing Companion **875**

Skill:
Paraphrasing

••• CHECKLIST FOR PARAPHRASING

In order to paraphrase, note the following:

- make sure you understand what the author is saying after reading the text carefully
- words and phrases that are important to include in a paraphrase to maintain the meaning of the text
- any words or expressions that are unfamiliar
- avoid plagiarism by acknowledging all sources for both paraphrased and quoted material

To paraphrase texts, consider the following questions:

- Do I understand the meaning of the text?
- Does my paraphrase of the text maintain its original meaning? Have I missed any key points or details?
- Have I determined the meanings of any words from the text that are unfamiliar to me?
- Have I avoided plagiarism by acknowledging all my sources for both paraphrased and quoted material?

↻ YOUR TURN

Read the original text excerpt about Langston Hughes in the first column. Complete the chart by matching the keywords to the text excerpt by writing them in the second column. Then, in the third column, paraphrase the original text excerpt using the keywords. Remember to cite the author and page number in parentheses. Part of the first row is done for you as an example.

Keywords				
Paris	jobs	Mexico	reflect	west coast
experience	busboy	Columbia	black	café
Busboys and Poets	1924	Hughes	music	culture
Africa	suffering	travel	America	Midwest
Lincoln	Washington, D.C.	laughter	poet	personal

Original Text Excerpt	Keywords	Paraphrased Text
Hughes had had an incredibly varied life before he became the literary lion of Harlem. He was raised in the Midwest, spent time with his estranged father in Mexico, and studied at Columbia and Lincoln University. He held many jobs, most famously as a busboy—an employment that gives the title to the well-known Washington, D.C. literary café, Busboys and Poets. "Why Langston Hughes Still Reigns as a Poet for the Unchampioned," David C. Ward		To paraphrase: Before settling in Harlem, Hughes had many life experiences. He lived in the Midwest and Mexico, and attended Columbia and Lincoln Universities. He was employed many places, most notably as a busboy at the famous café Busboys and Poets in Washington, D.C. (Ward)

Original Text Excerpt	Keywords	Paraphrased Text
Hughes refused to differentiate between his personal experience and the common experience of black America. He wanted to tell the stories of his people in ways that reflected their actual culture, including both their suffering and their love of music, laughter, and language itself. "Langston Hughes," American Academy of Poets		
Leaving Columbia in 1922, Hughes spent the next three years in a succession of menial jobs. But he also traveled abroad. He worked on a freighter down the west coast of Africa and lived for several months in Paris before returning to the United States late in 1924. By this time, he was well known in African American literary circles as a gifted young poet. "Hughes Life and Career," Arnold Rampersad		

✏ WRITE

Choose one or two parts of your research paper where information is still in the author's words without quotations or citations or where you can better paraphrase. Revise those sections using the questions in the checklist. When you have finished revising this section of your research paper, write out your revision as well as the original excerpt underneath.

Skill:
Sources and Citations

••• CHECKLIST FOR SOURCES AND CITATIONS

In order to cite and gather sources of information, do the following:

- select and gather information from a variety of print and digital sources relevant to a topic
- check that sources are credible, or reliable and trustworthy, and avoid relying on or overusing one source
- be sure that facts, details, and other information support the central idea or claim and demonstrate your understanding of the topic or text
- use parenthetical citations or footnotes or endnotes to credit sources
- include all sources in a bibliography or works cited list, following a standard format:

  > Halall, Ahmed. *The Pyramids of Ancient Egypt.* New York: Central Publishing, 2016.

  > for a citation or footnote, include the author, title, and page number

To check that sources are gathered and cited correctly, consider the following questions:

- Did I give credit to sources for all of my information to avoid plagiarism?
- Have I relied on one source, instead of looking for different points of view on my topic in other sources?
- Did I include all my sources in my bibliography or works cited list?
- Are my citations formatted correctly using a standard, accepted format?

↻ YOUR TURN

Choose the best answer to each question.

1. Below is a section from a previous draft of Kelaiah's research paper. What change should Kelaiah make to improve the clarity of her citations?

> In *Touching Spirit Bear*, Cole threatens to kill a Spirit Bear. Edwin reminds him to "learn your place or you'll have a rough time." Unlike Cole, the First Nations communities and many scientists and environmentalists recognize the value of the Spirit Bear. While not everyone might believe that the bear has special powers, they, like Edwin, should recognize and respect this animal's important role in the Great Bear Rainforest and its deep connections to the First Nations people.

- ○ A. Add the author's last name in parentheses after the quotation.
- ○ B. Add the page number in parentheses after the quotation.
- ○ C. Add the author's last name and the page number in parentheses after the quotation.
- ○ D. No change needs to be made.

2. Below is a section from a previous draft of Kelaiah's works cited page. Which revision best corrects her style errors?

> *The Salmon Bears: Giants of the Great Bear Rainforest*. Read, Nicholas, and Ian McAllister. 2010, Orca Book Publishers.

- ○ A. Read, Nicholas, and Ian McAllister. *The Salmon Bears: Giants of the Great Bear Rainforest*. Orca Book Publishers.
- ○ B. *The Salmon Bears: Giants of the Great Bear Rainforest*. Read, Nicholas, and Ian McAllister. 2010, Orca Book Publishers.
- ○ C. Read, Nicholas, and Ian McAllister, 2010. *The Salmon Bears: Giants of the Great Bear Rainforest*. Orca Book Publishers.
- ○ D. Read, Nicholas, and Ian McAllister. *The Salmon Bears: Giants of the Great Bear Rainforest*. Orca Book Publishers, 2010.

✎ WRITE

Use the questions in the checklist to revise your works cited list. When you have finished revising your citations, write your list. Refer to the *MLA Handbook* as needed.

Skill:
Print and Graphic Features

••• CHECKLIST FOR PRINT AND GRAPHIC FEATURES

First, reread your draft and ask yourself the following questions:

- To what extent would including formatting, graphics, or multimedia be effective in achieving my purpose?

- Which formatting, graphics, or multimedia seem most important for conveying information to the reader?

- How is the addition of the formatting, graphics, or multimedia useful to aiding comprehension?

To include formatting, graphics, and multimedia, use the following questions as a guide:

- How can I use formatting to better organize information? Consider adding:

  > titles   > subheadings   > boldface and italicized terms

  > headings   > bullets

- How can I use graphics to better convey information? Consider adding:

  > charts   > tables   > diagrams

  > graphs   > timelines   > figures and statistics

- How can I use multimedia to add interest and variety? Consider adding a combination of:

  > photographs

  > art

  > audio

  > video

YOUR TURN

Choose the best answer to each question.

1. Kelaiah has decided to include a map image with a body paragraph titled "Habitat and Characteristics of Spirit Bears." Read the section below. How does including a map make this section of her paper more effective?

Habitat and Characteristics of Spirit Bears

Spirit Bears are a rare subspecies of the American Black Bear. The Spirit Bear is known by different names, including the White Bear, Ghost Bear, *Moskgm'ol*, Kermode Bear, and its scientific name *Ursus americanus kermodei* (Shoumatoff). The animal lives only in the Great Bear Rainforest, a 21-million-acre wilderness along British Columbia's central coast that has been called "the Amazon of the North" (Kennedy).

GREAT BEAR RAINFOREST

○ A. The image helps readers see where Spirit Bears live.

○ B. The image helps Kelaiah organize her information more effectively.

○ C. The image is an example of multimedia used to add variety and interest to her research paper.

○ D. The image is a print feature that will highlight a specific section of the text.

2. Kelaiah needs a heading that best reflects the content of this body paragraph in her draft. Reread the first few sentences of the section and then select the best option.

Only 20 percent of the bears in the Great Bear Rainforest are white (N. Amer. Bear Ctr.). The bears survive on a diet of salmon, berries, and seaweed (Shoumatoff). There may be as many as 400 or as few as 100 Spirit Bears alive today (Langlois, Groc 79, N. Amer. Bear Ctr.). As geography professor Chris Darimont explains, "no one really knows how many bears there are in the Great Bear Rainforest" (Shoumatoff). This is because the Spirit Bear has a deep cultural significance to the First Nations people.

○ A. Number of Spirit Bears

○ B. Spirit Bear Population

○ C. Diet of Spirit Bears

○ D. Cultural Significance

⟳ YOUR TURN

Complete the chart below by brainstorming ideas of how you can use print and graphic features to improve your research paper.

Print and Graphic Feature or Multimedia	My Ideas and Changes
How can I use formatting to better organize information?	
How can I use graphics to better convey information?	
How can I use multimedia to add interest and variety?	

Research Writing Process: Revise

PLAN	DRAFT	REVISE	EDIT AND PUBLISH

You have written a draft of your research paper. You have also received input from your peers about how to improve it. Now you are going to revise your draft.

◀◀ REVISION GUIDE

Examine your draft to find areas for revision. Keep in mind your purpose and audience as you revise for clarity, development, organization, and style. Use the guide below to help you review:

Review	Revise	Example
Clarity		
Label details that are important to understanding your topic, such as people, places, or characteristics. Annotate any details where the meaning is unclear.	Add description to clarify the meaning or enhance understanding.	The animal lives only in the Great Bear Rainforest, a 21-million-acre wilderness along British Columbia's central coast that ~~which~~ has been called "the Amazon of the North" (Kennedy).
Development		
Identify key ideas in your research paper. Annotate places where additional description or information could help develop your ideas.	Make sure you have a strong main idea in each paragraph, and add description or information to develop your ideas.	Despite having white fur, the Spirit Bear is not a polar bear or an albino. Its cream-colored fur is the result of a rare recessive gene. A white bear cub is produced when both parents, which may be black or white, carry the rare gene (Groc 78–79, Barcott, Shoumatoff).

Review	Revise	Example
Organization		
Review your body paragraphs. Identify and annotate any sentences that don't flow in a clear and logical way.	Rewrite the sentences so they appear in a clear and logical order, starting with a strong transition or topic sentence. Make sure to include a transition between body paragraphs.	As geography professor Chris Darimont explains, "no one really knows how many bears there are in the Great Bear Rainforest" (Shoumatoff). This is because the Spirit Bear has a deep cultural significance to the First Nations people. The First Nations communities call the bear "*moskgm'ol*, which means 'white bear' and view the animal as sacred" (Groc 79).
Style: Word Choice		
Identify weak or repetitive words or phrases that do not clearly express your ideas to the reader.	Replace weak or repetitive words and phrases with more descriptive ones that better convey your ideas	Unlike the hot, ~~wet~~ steamy jungles of the Amazon, the Great Bear Rainforest is a cold, rocky island ~~place~~ habitat.
Style: Sentence Variety		
Read your informative essay aloud. Annotate places where introducing quotations from your sources could enhance the academic tone of your paper.	Revise some sentences or paragraphs to include relevant quotations.	According to writer Bruce Barcott, the Spirit Bear is ~~a contradiction.~~ "a walking contradiction—a white black bear."

✏ WRITE

Use the guide above, as well as your peer reviews, to help you evaluate your research paper to determine areas that should be revised. Also be sure to assess how well your print features, graphics, images, videos, or other media help to communicate and support your ideas.

DASHES
AND
HYPHENS

sync•skills

Grammar:
Dashes and Hyphens

The hyphen [-] is a punctuation mark used to show a division of a word between syllables. It is also used in compound nouns and number words.

Follow these rules and examples when using hyphens:

Rule	Text
Use a hyphen or hyphens in compound nouns. Check a dictionary to see if a word is written with a hyphen.	Still other troops walked about holding **walkie-talkies** to their ears. *Warriors Don't Cry*
Some compound nouns, such as *father-in-law*, are always hyphenated.	So Moses gave heed to the voice of his **father-in-law** and did all that he had said. *The Book of Exodus*
Use a hyphen in compound numbers from twenty-one through ninety-nine.	Not mine, not mine, not mine, but Mrs. Price is already turning to page **thirty-two**, and math problem number four. *Eleven*

A dash [—] looks like a long hyphen. When you are writing a sentence, use a dash or dashes to show a sudden break or a change of thought or speech. Using a dash or dashes is also an effective way of emphasizing a thought or giving new information.

Rule	Text
Use a pair of dashes if the new thought or emphasized information is in the middle of a sentence.	She will be gone for one year—**less, with luck**—or she will bring her children to be with her. *Enrique's Journey*
Use one dash if the new thought or emphasized information is at the end of a sentence.	He walked the bike into the backyard, which was lush with plants—**roses in their last bloom, geraniums, hydrangeas, pansies with their skirts of bright colors.** *Born Worker*

YOUR TURN

1. How should this sentence be changed?

   > The music style I like least—it's also my best friend's favorite is pop.

   ○ A. Put a dash after **favorite**.
   ○ B. Remove the dash after **least**.
   ○ C. Put a dash after **style**.
   ○ D. No change needs to be made to this sentence.

2. How should this sentence be changed?

   > My dad, a high-ranking officer in the United States Army, is an *aide-de-camp* to a general.

   ○ A. Delete the hyphen in **high-ranking**.
   ○ B. Add a hyphen between **United** and **States**.
   ○ C. Delete the hyphens in ***aide-de-camp***.
   ○ D. No change needs to be made to this sentence.

3. How should this sentence be changed?

   > My mother—she's struggling with her eyesight—has to use eyedrops four times a day.

   ○ A. Remove both dashes.
   ○ B. Remove the dash after **eyesight**.
   ○ C. Put a dash after **eyedrops**.
   ○ D. No change needs to be made to this sentence.

4. How should this sentence be changed?

   > In the historical novel set in China in the eighteenth century, the young bride moved into the house of her in laws.

   ○ A. Add a hyphen between the words **historical** and **novel**.
   ○ B. Add a hyphen between the words **eighteenth** and **century**.
   ○ C. Add a hyphen between the words **in** and **laws**.
   ○ D. No change needs to be made to this sentence.

quotation
marks
and italics

Grammar:
Quotation Marks and Italics

Use either italics or quotation marks to identify titles of works, such as pieces of writing or films. Titles of longer works, including books, plays, and magazines, should be italicized. Titles of shorter works, such as poems, short stories, essays, and magazine or newspaper articles, should be put in quotation marks.

In addition to titles of longer works, also use italics for the name of a plane, train, or ship.

Correct	Incorrect
Have you read the novel *The Wind in the Willows*?	Have you read the novel "The Wind in the Willows"?
I am writing an essay on the poem "Jabberwocky."	I am writing an essay on the poem *Jabberwocky*.
They took a train called the *Empire Builder* across seven states.	They took a train called the Empire Builder across seven states.

Follow these rules for how to use quotation marks or italics when identifying titles.

Rule	Text
Use italics to identify the title of a book, play, film, television series, magazine, or newspaper. In handwritten materials, underlining takes the place of italics.	Today, according to the **Asbury Park Press**, each New Jersey school district spends more than thirty thousand dollars a year on supplies, software, additional personnel, and staff and teacher training devoted to anti-bullying measures. *Bullying in Schools*
Use quotation marks for the title of a short story, essay, poem, song, magazine or newspaper article, or book chapter.	The California Invasive Plant Inventory updates the 1999 **"Exotic Pest Plants of Greatest Ecological Concern in California."** California Invasive Plant Inventory

↻ YOUR TURN

1. How should this sentence be changed?

> The article titled "Guide Dogs" in yesterday's Pittsburgh Post-Gazette was really heartwarming.

- ○ A. Delete the quotation marks around **Guide Dogs**.
- ○ B. Insert quotation marks around **Pittsburgh Post-Gazette**.
- ○ C. Italicize **Pittsburgh Post-Gazette**.
- ○ D. No change needs to be made to this sentence.

2. How should this sentence be changed?

> I read an article titled *Penguins* in this month's *National Geographic*.

- ○ A. Remove the italics from **Penguins**.
- ○ B. Remove the italics from **Penguins** and insert quotation marks around **Penguins**.
- ○ C. Remove the italics from **National Geographic** and insert quotation marks around **National Geographic**.
- ○ D. No change needs to be made to this sentence.

3. How should this sentence be changed?

> The cast gave an encore of the song "Do-Re-Mi" after their performance of The Sound of Music.

- ○ A. Remove the quotation marks from **Do-Re-Mi** and italicize **Do-Re-Mi**.
- ○ B. Insert quotation marks around **The Sound of Music**.
- ○ C. Italicize **The Sound of Music**.
- ○ D. No change needs to be made to this sentence.

4. How should this sentence be changed?

> I just finished reading the book *A Night to Remember*, about the sinking of the RMS Titanic.

- ○ A. Remove the italics from **A Night to Remember** and insert quotation marks around **A Night to Remember**.
- ○ B. Insert quotation marks around **Titanic**.
- ○ C. Italicize **Titanic**.
- ○ D. No change needs to be made to this sentence.

Grammar:
Run-on Sentences

A run-on sentence is two or more sentences incorrectly written as one sentence. Run-on sentences can confuse readers, and correcting them adds variety to the writing, clarifies ideas, and keeps readers interested. In order to correct a run-on sentence, do one of the following:

- Change the independent clauses into two separate sentences with a period.
- Separate the independent clauses with a semicolon (;).
- Separate the independent clauses with a comma and a coordinating conjunction: *and, or, but.*
- Separate the independent clauses with a subordinating conjunction (*because, although,* etc.).

Run-on Sentence	Correction	Example
Our living quarters are in a warehouse area, the mess hall is really good and it even has a coffee shop.	Replace the comma with a semicolon.	Our living quarters are in a warehouse area; the mess hall is really good and it even has a coffee shop. *Sunrise Over Fallujah*
He was about ten paces from me so I could see him clearly, I was sure that he was dead, but I lifted the spear and took good aim at him.	Add a period to separate the independent clauses into two separate sentences.	He was about ten paces from me so I could see him clearly. I was sure that he was dead, but I lifted the spear and took good aim at him. *Island of the Blue Dolphins*

↻ YOUR TURN

1. How should this sentence be changed?

> The actors are sewing their own costumes it is quite a challenge.

- ○ A. Insert a comma after **costumes**.
- ○ B. Insert a semicolon after the word **costumes**.
- ○ C. Capitalize the word **it**.
- ○ D. No change needs to be made to this sentence.

2. How should this sentence be changed?

> George and Hernando are walking to the park, I am riding my bicycle.

- ○ A. Remove the comma.
- ○ B. Replace the comma with a period.
- ○ C. Add a semicolon after **walking**.
- ○ D. No change needs to be made to this sentence.

3. How should this sentence be changed?

> Mike is reading *The Adventures of Tom Sawyer*, but Jamie is reading *The Prince and the Pauper*.

- ○ A. Replace the comma with a period.
- ○ B. Capitalize the word **but**.
- ○ C. Replace the period with a question mark at the end.
- ○ D. No change needs to be made to this sentence.

4. How should this sentence be changed?

> The train was stalled on the track I was unable to get home until well after 7 PM.

- ○ A. Insert a comma between **track** and **I**.
- ○ B. Place a comma and the word *and* between **track** and **I**.
- ○ C. Place a period after **stalled**.
- ○ D. No change needs to be made to this sentence.

Research Writing Process: Edit and Publish

PLAN	DRAFT	REVISE	EDIT AND PUBLISH

You have revised your research paper based on your peer feedback and your own examination.

Now, it is time to edit your research paper. When you revised, you focused on the content of your research paper. You probably critiqued your research, paraphrased, and looked at your sources, citations, and print and graphic features. When you edit, you focus on the mechanics of your research paper, paying close attention to things like grammar and punctuation.

Use the checklist below to guide you as you edit:

☐ Have I used quotation marks and italics correctly?

☐ Have I used dashes and hyphens correctly?

☐ Have I capitalized the names and titles of people correctly?

☐ Do I have any sentence fragments or run-on sentences?

☐ Have I spelled everything correctly?

Notice some edits Kelaiah has made:

- Italicize a book title.

- Add a quotation mark to a quotation.

- Capitalize the name of a people.

- Add dashes.

- Correct a spelling error.

In ~~Touching Spirit Bear,~~ *Touching Spirit Bear,* Edwin prepares Cole for living alone on a remote island. He explains, "Off the coast of British Columbia, there is a special black bear called the Spirit Bear. It's pure white, and has pride, dignity, and ~~honor~~ honor" (Mikaelsen 18). When Cole threatens to kill any Spirit Bear he meets, Edwin warns, "Whatever you do to the animals, you do to ~~yourself~~ yourself" (Mikaelsen 18). Edwin and Cole are fictional characters, but Spirit Bears do exist. They are considered special not only by the people of the ~~first nations~~ First Nations ~~communities,~~ communities—who have lived near them for thousands of years—but also by researchers and environmentalists. A look at the Spirit Bear's habitat, as well as its cultural and environmental significance, reveals this unique animal's ~~roll~~ role in the world.

✏ WRITE

Use the questions above, as well as your peer reviews, to help you evaluate your research paper to determine areas that need editing. Then edit your research paper to correct those errors.

Finally, read over your research paper one more time, making sure that you have cited all your sources of quoted, paraphrased, or summarized material. Recall that within the body of your paper, you should put the author's last name and page number, if applicable, in parentheses at the end of the sentence that contains borrowed material. In addition, make sure that all sources cited are listed in your works cited list at the end of your research paper. It is very important to cite all your sources so that you can avoid plagiarism.

Once you have made all your corrections, you are ready to publish your work. You can distribute your writing to family and friends, present it to your class, hang it on a bulletin board, or post it on your blog. If you publish online, share the link with your family, friends, and classmates.

Middle School Loneliness

FICTION

Introduction

A Hispanic boy is well-liked at his middle school. He is captain of the basketball team. Then his family moves to a new city. He must attend a new school. The problems begin the very first day. How will he make friends? He must

V VOCABULARY

accurate

free from mistakes; correct

enthusiastic

excited and interested in what is going on

isolated

being alone and apart from others

succeeded

achieved a desired result

≡ READ

 NOTES

1   I used to think I had it made. I was the captain of the basketball team and president of the math club.

2   One summer, my dad accepted a job in a different city and we moved. Worry rained down and soaked into my life as I left my best friends. Like me, they spoke Spanish at home, ate the same foods, and loved basketball. I would be among strangers who might not understand my background. My first day in the new school proved my fears were **accurate**.

3   I was the only Hispanic student. The first week of classes was terrible. I was completely **isolated**. No one spoke to me, and no one sat with me at lunch.

4   Then I saw a notice from Coach Wilson about basketball tryouts. I felt at home as I raced up and down the court trying to impress Coach. He wanted me on the team but warned me things might be difficult. The team members were close friends and did not like strangers. I was new. I liked being on a team again, but Coach's words made me feel uncomfortable.

5   The first practice was disappointing, like other experiences at that school. Jeremy was team captain. His best friend, Nathan, was a great player. Jeremy shouted out orders to others but never to me. Finally, Coach blew the whistle and called for a meeting. He described new plays and said Jeremy was

expected to pass the ball to me. I was supposed to make some baskets. I knew Jeremy and Nathan didn't think I could be a valuable team member. But Coach had spoken, and his word was law on the court.

6   I had no friends on the team. One day, Jeremy and Nathan talked about a hard problem in math class. They said that if they didn't pass Friday's test, they would be off the team. I thought about their problem. They treated me badly, but we couldn't lose great players, and I wanted to win the championship game. I offered to help them, and they accepted.

7   We worked together on the court and off. The team started winning, and **enthusiastic** students came to cheer us on. Jeremy's and Nathan's math grades went up like skyrockets. I didn't sit alone at lunch anymore because my teammates sat with me. Going to a new school is not easy, but I coped with the challenges and **succeeded**.

Middle School
Loneliness

First Read

Read the story. After you read, answer the Think Questions below.

1. What is the main character's problem?

   _____

   _____

2. Who ends up needing the narrator's help?

   _____

   _____

3. At the end of the story, what has changed in the narrator's life?

   _____

   _____

4. Use context to confirm the meaning of the word *enthusiastic* as it is used in "Middle School Loneliness." Write your definition of *enthusiastic* here.

   _____

   _____

5. What is another way to say that a person feels *isolated*?

   _____

   _____

Please note that excerpts and passages in the StudySync® library and this workbook are intended as touchstones to generate interest in an author's work. The excerpts and passages do not substitute for the reading of entire texts, and StudySync® strongly recommends that students seek out and purchase the whole literary or informational work in order to experience it as the author intended. Links to online resellers are available in our digital library. In addition, complete works may be ordered through an authorized reseller by filling out and returning to StudySync® the order form enclosed in this workbook.

Reading & Writing
Companion   **897**

Skill:
Analyzing Expressions

Copyright © BookheadEd Learning, LLC

★ DEFINE

When you read, you may find English expressions that you do not know. An **expression** is a group of words that communicates an idea. Three types of expressions are idioms, sayings, and figurative language. They can be difficult to understand because the meanings of the words are different from their **literal**, or usual, meanings.

An **idiom** is an expression that is commonly known among a group of people. For example, "It's raining cats and dogs" means it is raining heavily. **Sayings** are short expressions that contain advice or wisdom. For instance, "Don't count your chickens before they hatch" means do not plan on something good happening before it happens. Figurative language is when you describe something by comparing it with something else, either directly (using the words *like* or *as*) or indirectly. None of the expressions are about actual animals.

••• CHECKLIST FOR ANALYZING EXPRESSIONS

To determine the meaning of an expression, remember the following:

✓ If you find a confusing group of words, it may be an expression. The meaning of words in expressions may not be their literal meaning.

- Ask yourself: Is this confusing because the words are new? Or because the words do not make sense together?

✓ Determining the overall meaning may require that you use one or more of the following:

- context clues

- a dictionary or other resource

- teacher or peer support

✓ Highlight important information before and after the expression to look for clues.

⟳ YOUR TURN

Student Instructions: Read the following excerpt from the text. Then, complete the multiple-choice questions below.

From "Middle School Loneliness"

I heard them say if they didn't pass Friday's test, they'd get kicked off the team. I thought seriously about their problem. We couldn't afford to lose great players.

---

1. Based on the excerpt, what could happen to get the boys kicked off the team?

   ○ A. They do their best.
   ○ B. They are mean to the narrator.
   ○ C. They are not great players.
   ○ D. They do not pass a test.

2. If you are "kicked off" a team, what happens?

   ○ A. You become a starting player for the team.
   ○ B. You may no longer play for the team.
   ○ C. You play a certain position on the team.
   ○ D. You get angry at the team members.

3. In this excerpt, why is the narrator worried?

   ○ A. He does not want good players to leave his team.
   ○ B. He thinks that the boys will blame him.
   ○ C. He fears that his problem will affect the team.
   ○ D. He believes that his friends need money.

4. If a team can't "afford to lose great players," what does that mean?

   ○ A. The team needs to spend more to pay the players.
   ○ B. The players need to work hard to be great.
   ○ C. Losing great players would harm the team.
   ○ D. Great players are expensive to find and keep.

Skill:
Visual and Contextual Support

★ DEFINE

Visual support is an image or an object that helps you understand a text. **Contextual support** is a **feature** that helps you understand a text. By using visual and contextual supports, you can develop your vocabulary so you can better understand a variety of texts.

First, preview the text to identify any visual supports. These might include illustrations, graphics, charts, or other objects in a text. Then, identify any contextual supports. Examples of contextual supports are titles, heads, captions, and boldface terms. Write down your **observations**.

Then, write down what those visual and contextual supports tell you about the meaning of the text. Note any new vocabulary that you see in those supports. Ask your peers and your teacher to **confirm** your understanding of the text.

••• CHECKLIST FOR VISUAL AND CONTEXTUAL SUPPORT

To use visual and contextual support to understand texts, do the following:

✓ Preview the text. Read the title, headers, and other features. Look at any images and graphics.

✓ Write down the visual and contextual supports in the text.

✓ Write down what those supports tell you about the text.

✓ Note any new vocabulary that you see in those supports.

✓ Create an illustration for the reading and write a descriptive caption.

✓ Confirm your observations with your peers and teacher.

⟳ YOUR TURN

Suppose that your class created visual supports for some of the sports phrases in "Middle School Loneliness." Match the pictures to the phrases they illustrate.

Phrase Options	
A	make some baskets
B	describe new plays
C	shout out orders
D	pass the ball

1.

2.

3.

4.

Visual Support	Phrase

Reading & Writing Companion

Close Read

✏ WRITE

NARRATIVE: The narrator's experience at his new school changes by the end of the story. Reread the last paragraph of the text, and look for examples of how his life is different. Then, write a longer version of the paragraph, and include additional details to explain what school is like for him now. Make sure to include specific words and phrases that help readers understand the narrator's middle school experience. Pay attention to irregularly spelled words as you write.

Use the checklist below to guide you as you write.

☐ How has the narrator's life changed?

☐ What are some important people or places to the narrator?

☐ What words can you include to show middle school life?

Use the sentence frames to organize and write your narrative.

We started to work together. On the court, _____

_____.

Jeremy's and Nathan's math grades improved. I continued to help _____

_____.

I didn't sit alone at lunch anymore. Instead, _____.

Going to a new school is not easy, _____.

Shakespeare in Harlem

INFORMATIONAL TEXT

Introduction

The Harlem Renaissance produced music, art, and writing that changed America. Right in the middle of the action was Langston Hughes, a young man from the Midwest who became a key voice in Harlem—and the world

VOCABULARY

influenced

had an effect on; guided

deferred

put off to a later time

evokes

recalls to mind

anthologies

published collections of poems or other writings

prolific

very productive

NOTES

☰ READ

1 **Shakespeare in Harlem**

2 He was raised in the Midwest and spent time with his father in Mexico. However, we tend to think of Langston Hughes as a New Yorker. His was one of the strongest voices of the Harlem Renaissance, a time when that neighborhood in New York City became the center of African-American culture. A poet, playwright, novelist, and autobiographer, Hughes earned the nickname "Shakespeare in Harlem."

3 Back in grade school, James Mercer Langston Hughes was already writing. He was named class poet in middle school. His English teachers introduced him to poetry by Carl Sandburg and Walt Whitman. Walt Whitman's poetry had **influenced** Carl Sandburg's work. In turn, both poets influenced Hughes's writing from an early age. His best work **evokes** their interest in ordinary people's everyday lives.

4   Hughes was only 24 when he published his first collection of poetry, *The Weary Blues*. Like much of Hughes's poetry, this book reflects the rhythms and themes of African-American music. This earliest work contains many of Hughes's most famous poems, including "The Negro Speaks of Rivers" and "Dream Variations."

5   Hughes did not just live in Harlem at the liveliest time in its history. He took part in the cultural revolution that was happening there. Drama, painting, music, and writing were part of that revolution. Hughes made friends with many of Harlem's most talented singers, writers, and thinkers.

6   As the Harlem Renaissance ended in the 1930s, Hughes turned his attention to the theater world. Theater was more profitable than poetry. He wrote a play about race in the South. It ran on Broadway for a year. Later, he even wrote words for an opera.

7   By the 1940s, Hughes was writing a newspaper column about racial issues. He continued to write poems. He wrote lyrics for a Broadway musical. He was as **prolific** as Shakespeare. Like Shakespeare, too, he gave us dozens of beautiful lines and phrases that have showed up in other writers' works. Examples include "a raisin in the sun," "a dream **deferred**," "hold fast to dreams," "I am the darker brother," and "black like me."

8   Hughes wrote of the joy and suffering of ordinary people. As he got older, his writing became more political. He protested unfair social conditions. He fought against racism. He tried to give readers pride in their culture. He told his own story in a two-volume autobiography. He won literary prizes. He shared his knowledge with younger writers. Even today, 50 years after his death, his poems continue to appear in **anthologies**. His poem "Harlem" is one of our most popular American poems. Surely, his old nickname was no exaggeration.

SHAKESPEARE
IN HARLEM

First Read

Read the story. After you read, answer the Think Questions below.

☁ THINK QUESTIONS

1. Who is the subject of the biography? Why is he well-known?

_____

_____

2. What was happening in Harlem when Hughes arrived there?

_____

_____

3. What did Hughes write besides poetry?

_____

_____

4. Use context to confirm the meaning of the word *influenced* as it is used in "Shakespeare in Harlem." Write your definition of *influenced* here.

_____

_____

5. What is another way to say that an author is *prolific*?

_____

_____

Skill:
Language Structures

★ DEFINE

In every language, there are rules that tell how to **structure** sentences. These rules define the correct order of words. In the English language, for example, a **basic** structure for sentences is subject, verb, and object. Some sentences have more **complicated** structures.

You will encounter both basic and complicated **language structures** in the classroom materials you read. Being familiar with language structures will help you better understand the text.

••• CHECKLIST FOR LANGUAGE STRUCTURES

To improve your comprehension of language structures, do the following:

✓ Monitor your understanding.

- Ask yourself: Why do I not understand this sentence? Is it because I do not understand some of the words? Or is it because I do not understand the way the words are ordered in the sentence?

✓ Break down the sentence into its parts.

- Pay attention to comparatives and superlatives. The **comparative** form compares things. The **superlative** form compares more than two things.

- Ask yourself: Are there comparatives or superlatives in this sentence? What are they comparing?

- Form a **comparative** by adding -er to the end of the word or by adding *more* before the word.

✓ Confirm your understanding with a peer or teacher.

Please note that excerpts and passages in the StudySync® library and this workbook are intended as touchstones to generate interest in an author's work. The excerpts and passages do not substitute for the reading of entire texts, and StudySync® strongly recommends that students seek out and purchase the whole literary or informational work in order to experience it as the author intended. Links to online resellers are available in our digital library. In addition, complete works may be ordered through an authorized reseller by filling out and returning to StudySync® the order form enclosed in this workbook.

Reading & Writing
Companion

907

YOUR TURN

Read the following excerpt from the text. Then, write the correct adjective to the chart that follows.

---

from "Shakespeare in Harlem"

Hughes wrote of the joy and suffering of ordinary people. As he got older, his writing became more political. He protested unfair social conditions. He fought against racism. He tried to give readers pride in their culture. He told his own story in a two-volume autobiography. He won literary prizes. He shared his knowledge with younger writers. Even today, 50 years after his death, his poems continue to appear in anthologies. His poem "Harlem" is one of our most popular American poems. Surely, his old nickname was no exaggeration.

	Adjectives from the Text
A	more political
B	younger
C	older
D	most popular

Description	Adjective from the Text
Comparative adjective that compares the age of other writers to Hughes's age	
Superlative adjective that compares one of Hughes's poems to all American poems	
Comparative adjective that compares Hughes's later writing to his earlier writing	
Comparative adjective that compares Hughes's age to his age before	

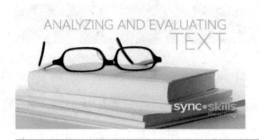

Skill:
Analyzing and Evaluating Text

★ DEFINE

Analyzing and **evaluating** a text means reading carefully to understand the author's **purpose** and **message**. In informational texts, authors may provide information or opinions on a topic. They may be writing to inform or persuade a reader. In fictional texts, the author may be **communicating** a message or lesson through their story. They may write to entertain, or to teach the reader something about life.

Sometimes authors are clear about their message and purpose. When the message or purpose is not stated directly, readers will need to look closer at the text. Readers can use text evidence to make inferences about what the author is trying to communicate. By analyzing and evaluating the text, you can form your own thoughts and opinions about what you read.

••• CHECKLIST FOR ANALYZING AND EVALUATING TEXT

In order to analyze and evaluate a text, do the following:

✓ Look for details that show *why* the author is writing.

  • Ask yourself: Is the author trying to inform, persuade, or entertain? What are the main ideas of this text?

✓ Look for details that show *what* the author is trying to say.

  • Ask yourself: What is the author's opinion about this topic? Is there a lesson I can learn from this story?

✓ Form your own thoughts and opinions about the text.

  • Ask yourself: Do I agree with the author? Does this message apply to my life?

YOUR TURN

Read the following excerpt from the text. Then, complete the multiple-choice questions below.

---

from "Shakespeare in Harlem"

6 By the 1940s, Hughes was writing a newspaper column about racial issues. He continued to write poems. He wrote lyrics for a Broadway musical. He was as prolific as Shakespeare. Like Shakespeare, too, he gave us dozens of beautiful lines and phrases that have showed up in other writers' works. Examples include "a raisin in the sun," "a dream deferred," "hold fast to dreams," "I am the darker brother," and "black like me."

7 Hughes wrote of the joy and suffering of ordinary people. As he got older, his writing became more political. He protested unfair social conditions. He fought against racism. He tried to give readers pride in their culture. He told his own story in a two-volume autobiography. He won literary prizes. He shared his knowledge with younger writers. Even today, 50 years after his death, his poems continue to appear in anthologies. His poem "Harlem" is one of our most popular American poems. Surely, his old nickname was no exaggeration.

---

1. **What is one way in which the author compares Hughes to Shakespeare?**

    ○ A. The author points out that both wrote a great deal.
    ○ B. The author connects both to a revolutionary time.
    ○ C. The author demonstrates how their cities shaped them.
    ○ D. The author suggests that Hughes borrowed words from Shakespeare.

2. **What is a second way in which the author compares Hughes to Shakespeare?**

    ○ A. The author indicates that both wrote political tracts.
    ○ B. The author states that others have used both men's words.
    ○ C. The author notes that both shared their knowledge with young writers.
    ○ D. The author suggests that both wrote about ordinary people.

3. **What message does the author hope that readers take from this passage?**

    ○ A. A true artist gives readers pride.
    ○ B. Most poets do other things as well.
    ○ C. Poets may or may not be remembered.
    ○ D. Hughes was truly a great talent.

Close Read

SHAKESPEARE
IN HARLEM

✏ WRITE

LITERARY ANALYSIS: Does the author of "Shakespeare in Harlem" make you believe that Langston Hughes was a great and important writer? Does reading "Shakespeare in Harlem" make you want to read poetry and prose by Langston Hughes? State your feelings about Hughes after having read "Shakespeare in Harlem." Use evidence from the text to support your opinion. Pay attention to possessive case as you write.

Use the checklist below to guide you as you write.

☐ How does the author feel about Langston Hughes?

☐ What evidence supports that opinion?

☐ Is the opinion convincing? Why or why not?

☐ What is your reaction to what you read?

Use the sentence frames to organize and write your literary analysis.

The author of "Shakespeare in Harlem" believes that Langston Hughes _____

_____.

The author includes evidence such as _____ and _____.

Based on what I read in "Shakespeare in Harlem," I now think that _____

_____.

PHOTO/IMAGE CREDITS:

p. 751, iStock.com/borchee
p. 753, iStock.com/XiXinXing
p. 754, Svetlana Chmakova - Vince Talotta/Contributor/Toronto Star/Getty
p. 754, Rita Dove - Getty Images Europe: Barbara Zanon/Contributor
p. 754, W.E.B. Dubouis - nsf/Alamy Stock Photo
p. 754, Russell Freedman
p. 754, Henry Ford-Interim Archives/Getty Images
p. 755, Nikki Grimes - Photo credit: Aaron Lemen
p. 755, Rebecca Harrington - New York Daily News/Contributor/New York Daily News/Getty
p. 755, Rosa Parks - PictureLux/The Hollywood Archive/Alamy Stock Photo
p. 755, Jackie Robinson - Everett Collection Inc/Alamy Stock Photo
p. 756, iStock.com
p. 761, iStock.com
p. 762, iStock.com/Smithore
p. 764, iStock.com
p. 766, iStock.com/ai_yoshi
p. 768, iStock.com/RomoloTavani
p. 769, StudySync
p. 770, Shree Bose
p. 771, Shree Bose
p. 771, Photo by Andrew Federman
p. 773, Official White House Photo by Pete Souza
p. 773, StudySync
p. 774, StudySync
p. 775, Piper
p. 777, iStock.com/RomoloTavani
p. 778, iStock.com/Hohenhaus
p. 779, iStock.com/Hohenhaus
p. 780, iStock.com/janrysavy
p. 781, iStock.com/janrysavy
p. 782, iStock.com/RomoloTavani
p. 783, iStock.com/
p. 786, iStock.com/
p. 787, iStock.com/fotogaby
p. 788, iStock.com/fotogaby
p. 789, iStock.com/donatas1205
p. 790, iStock.com/donatas1205
p. 791, iStock.com/
p. 792, iStock.com/ErikaMitchell
p. 796, Underwood Archives/Contributor
p. 798, Underwood Archives/Archive Photos/Getty Images
p. 802, Underwood Archives/Archive Photos/Getty Images
p. 803, iStock.com/eskaylim
p. 804, iStock.com/eskaylim
p. 805, iStock.com/Martin Barraud
p. 806, iStock.com/Martin Barraud
p. 807, iStock.com/Orla
p. 808, iStock.com/Orla
p. 809, Underwood Archives/Archive Photos/Getty Images
p. 810, Public Domain
p. 814, ©iStock.com/baona
p. 815, From Brave by Svetlana Chmakova. Copyright © 2017 by Svetlana Chmakova. Used by permission of Yen Press, an imprint of the Hachette Book Group USA Inc.
p. 816, From Brave by Svetlana Chmakova. Copyright © 2017 by Svetlana Chmakova. Used by permission of Yen Press, an imprint of the Hachette Book Group USA Inc.
p. 817, From Brave by Svetlana Chmakova. Copyright © 2017 by Svetlana Chmakova. Used by permission of Yen Press, an imprint of the Hachette Book Group USA Inc.
p. 818, From Brave by Svetlana Chmakova. Copyright © 2017 by Svetlana Chmakova. Used by permission of Yen Press, an imprint of the Hachette Book Group USA Inc.
p. 819, From Brave by Svetlana Chmakova. Copyright © 2017 by Svetlana Chmakova. Used by permission of Yen Press, an imprint of the Hachette Book Group USA Inc.
p. 820, From Brave by Svetlana Chmakova. Copyright © 2017 by Svetlana Chmakova. Used by permission of Yen Press, an imprint of the Hachette Book Group USA Inc.
p. 821, From Brave by Svetlana Chmakova. Copyright © 2017 by Svetlana Chmakova. Used by permission of Yen Press, an imprint of the Hachette Book Group USA Inc.
p. 822, From Brave by Svetlana Chmakova. Copyright © 2017 by Svetlana Chmakova. Used by permission of Yen Press, an imprint of the Hachette Book Group USA Inc.
p. 823, From Brave by Svetlana Chmakova. Copyright © 2017 by Svetlana Chmakova. Used by permission of Yen Press, an imprint of the Hachette Book Group USA Inc.

p. 824, From Brave by Svetlana Chmakova. Copyright © 2017 by Svetlana Chmakova. Used by permission of Yen Press, an imprint of the Hachette Book Group USA Inc.
p. 825, From Brave by Svetlana Chmakova. Copyright © 2017 by Svetlana Chmakova. Used by permission of Yen Press, an imprint of the Hachette Book Group USA Inc.
p. 826, From Brave by Svetlana Chmakova. Copyright © 2017 by Svetlana Chmakova. Used by permission of Yen Press, an imprint of the Hachette Book Group USA Inc.
p. 827, From Brave by Svetlana Chmakova. Copyright © 2017 by Svetlana Chmakova. Used by permission of Yen Press, an imprint of the Hachette Book Group USA Inc.
p. 828, From Brave by Svetlana Chmakova. Copyright © 2017 by Svetlana Chmakova. Used by permission of Yen Press, an imprint of the Hachette Book Group USA Inc.
p. 829, ©iStock.com/baona
p. 830, iStock.com/antoni_halim
p. 831, iStock.com/antoni_halim
p. 832, ©iStock.com/baona
p. 833, iStock.com
p. 837, PaulTessier/iStock.com
p. 839, iStock.com/Brostock
p. 840, iStock.com/Brostock
p. 840, iStock.com/ThomasVogel
p. 841, iStock.com/ThomasVogel
p. 842, iStock.com
p. 843, ©iStock.com/Lynn_Bystrom
p. 848, ©iStock.com/Lynn_Bystrom
p. 849, iStock.com/Max_Xie
p. 850, iStock.com/Max_Xie
p. 851, ©iStock.com/Lynn_Bystrom
p. 851, iStock.com/borchee
p. 852, iStock.com/hanibaram, iStock.com/seb_ra, iStock.com/Martin Barraud
p. 853, iStock.com/Martin Barraud
p. 855, StudySync
p. 856, jonmccormackphoto/iStock.com
p. 857, Paul Nicklen/National Geographic Image Collection/Getty Images
p. 860, iStock.com/koya79
p. 863, iStock.com/Mutlu Kurtbas
p. 866, iStock.com/DNY59
p. 868, iStock.com/Martin Barraud
p. 870, Paul Nicklen/National Geographic Image Collection/Getty Images
p. 873, iStock.com
p. 876, iStock.com/horiyan
p. 879, iStock.com/tofumax
p. 881, iStock.com/me4o
p. 882, StudySync
p. 884, iStock.com/Martin Barraud
p. 886, ©iStock.com/Thomas Shanahan
p. 888, ©iStock.com/kyoshino
p. 890, ©iStock.com/wildpixel
p. 892, iStock.com/Martin Barraud
p. 894, iStock.com/robertiez
p. 895, iStock.com
p. 895, stevecoleimages/iStock
p. 895, iStock.com/Jewelsy
p. 895, petesaloutos/iStock
p. 897, iStock.com/robertiez
p. 898, iStock.com/Ales_Utovko
p. 900, iStock.com/AlexandrBognat
p. 901, iStock.com/RapidEye
p. 901, iStock.com/Slobo
p. 901, iStock.com
p. 901, iStock.com
p. 902, iStock.com/robertiez
p. 903, iStock.com/alexkich
p. 904, mangostock/iStock
p. 904, iStock.com
p. 904, iStock.com/Milenko Bokan
p. 904, iStock.com
p. 904, iStock.com/hanohiki
p. 906, iStock.com/alexkich
p. 907, iStock.com/BlackJack3D
p. 909, iStock.com/kyoshino
p. 911, MBPROJEKT_Maciej_Bledowski/iStock.com

Text Fulfillment
Through StudySync

If you are interested in specific titles, please fill out the form below and we will check availability through our partners.

ORDER DETAILS

Date:

TITLE	AUTHOR	Paperback/ Hardcover	Specific Edition *If Applicable*	Quantity

SHIPPING INFORMATION

Contact:

Title:

School/District:

Address Line 1:

Address Line 2:

Zip or Postal Code:

Phone:

Mobile:

Email:

BILLING INFORMATION   ☐ *SAME AS SHIPPING*

Contact:

Title:

School/District:

Address Line 1:

Address Line 2:

Zip or Postal Code:

Phone:

Mobile:

Email:

PAYMENT INFORMATION

☐ CREDIT CARD   Name on Card:

Card Number: Expiration Date: Security Code:

☐ PO   Purchase Order Number:

StudySync Text Fulfillment, BookheadEd Learning, LLC
610 Daniel Young Drive | Sonoma, CA 95476